THE EMISSARY TRILOGY

2015 — 2017

EMISSARIES GUIDE TO WORLDING

HOW TO NAVIGATE THE UNNATURAL ART
OF CREATING AN INFINITE GAME
BY CHOOSING A PRESENT,
STORYTELLING ITS PAST,
SIMULATING ITS FUTURES,
AND NURTURING ITS CHANGES.

IAN CHENG

COSMOGENESIS

COLLECTORS EDITION

INDEX

PREFACE

Emissaries Guide to Worlding (EGTW) began its life as a catalog for my 2018 exhibition *Emissaries* at the Serpentine. At the time, I was obsessed with the question: could I make an artwork that doesn't just last, but lives?

The experience of creating simulated worlds — ones inhabited by AI agents evolving on their own — was rewiring my psychology as an artist. A new mode was emerging in me. One dedicated to seeing an artwork as a living system and creatively serving its long-term flourishing, as one would for a pet, a child, a house, or a garden. I wanted to capture this shift and put a name to it as a distinct artistic activity: Worlding.

But the truth is, in 2018, worlding was something I thought about more than something I put into practice. I wrote about worlding as an activity applicable to any creator in any arena, but I hadn't *lived* it outside the narrow frame of art-making. And I quietly avoided one of my own core criteria for worlding: that to make a world come alive, it must be in a feedback loop with the real behavior of people who freely choose to inhabit it.

Feedback with reality. What a pain. This is the aspect of worlding that continues to haunt me: its attempt to address the range of creative endeavors that engage with real stakes – real networks, real markets, real behavior, real evolution – as the primary source of artistic tension. Not for the sake of dopamine farming or performative shock. But because an engagement with real stakes makes doing creative work concordant with navigating life within the strange emergent conditions of our era.

The collapse of institutions. The untenable expense of daily life. The abundance of technological capability. Instant access to mass networks of attention. These aren't topics to illustrate – they are forces to channel and sculpt with. Imagine, then, worlding as a means of doing creative work that makes this reality shitstorm feel more and more habitable for oneself and others along the way? It becomes an art of aliveness. Art that is actually *life changing.*

A lot has happened since the first publication of EGTW. I've become a dad to two kiddos. I've developed a lifelong obsession with jiu-jitsu. I've founded a startup building AI for families. Never before have I submitted myself to so much unwishful, unrelenting feedback. The stakes have become very real. These are hard worlds. They're stressful. Often annoying. But they grip reality and drag me along with it. I've discovered that juggling all of it has made life inexhaustibly satisfying.

Over these dizzying years, I've heard from hundreds of people looking to acquire a copy of EGTW. Artists, game designers, crypto people, teachers, architects, technologists, strategists, founders. People trying to navigate how to build messy living things with long horizons. I've learned from them that the appetite for worlding is a response to two patterns: First, evidence that the criticality-driven playbook we've been taught in art school over the last few decades is a losing script. Second: the feeling that energy really matters in realizing creative work – that some projects seem to come alive, in the literal sense of becoming self-perpetuating flywheels of energy, begetting more projects, more people, and more feedback. Worlding is a proxy for aiming to do more of that.

If you're chasing aliveness in your work, this new edition of EGTW, republished by cosmogenesis, is for you. And you don't even need to read it. After all, books aren't merely meant to be read. Books are talismanic – objects embodying a source-like energy, a specific charge to tap, a reference frequency to tune into. My hope is that EGTW holds a place in your workspace or home, sitting there in your sight lines, pulsing with quiet charge. If its presence reminds you to chase unwishful feedback – to let ground truth into your creative process more often than you otherwise would like – then it is doing its work, and you're going to be okay.

LIVE TO WORLD! WORLD TO LIVE!

Ian Cheng
July 4, 2025

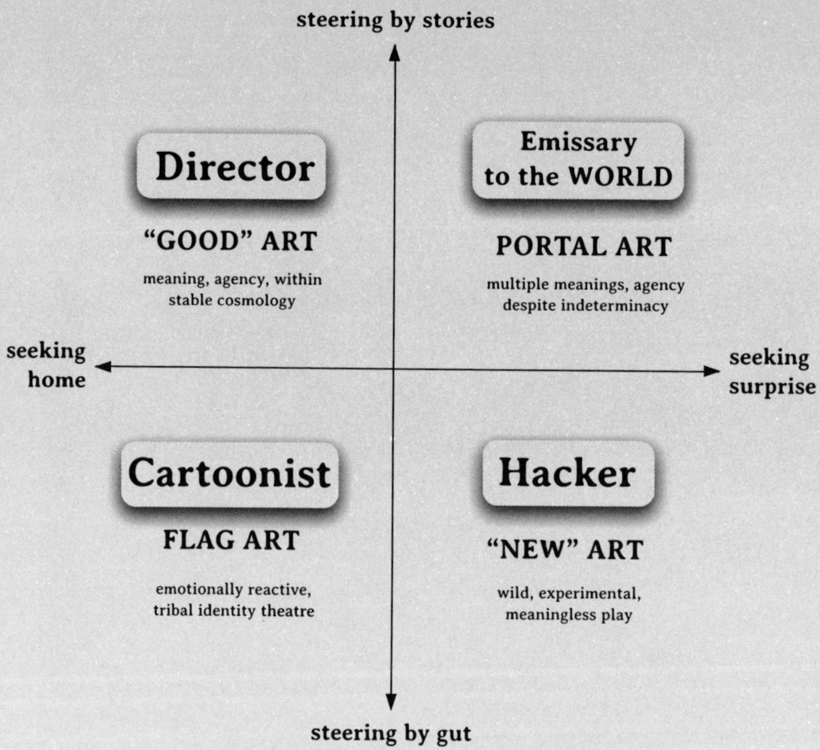
steering by stories
Director
"GOOD" ART
meaning, agency, within stable cosmology
Emissary to the WORLD
PORTAL ART
multiple meanings, agency despite indeterminacy
seeking home
seeking surprise
Cartoonist
FLAG ART
emotionally reactive, tribal identity theatre
Hacker
"NEW" ART
wild, experimental, meaningless play
steering by gut

The Unnatural Art Of Worlding

THE EMISSARY IS SENT BY ITS KINGDOM TO CHART A NEW FRONTIER. ITS DUTY IS TO REPRESENT THE INTERESTS OF THE KINGDOM, YET THE EMISSARY ALSO TRAVELS IN THE SPIRIT OF SURPRISE AND ADVENTURE. THE EMISSARY KNOWS THAT TO RECONCILE DIPLOMACY WITH DISCOVERY, IT WILL NEED IMAGINATION. FOR THE EMISSARY FACES THE TEMPTATION TO TAME THE FRONTIER INTO THE KINGDOM'S IMAGE, TO RETREAT BACK HOME, OR TO LOSE ITSELF COMPLETELY IN THE NEW. IN ORDER TO KEEP THE FRONTIER ALIVE WHILE CHARTING A PATH IN IT, THE EMISSARY BEGINS TO HALLUCINATE A WORLD.

From an early age, my mom would take me movie hopping on weekends at the megaplex cinema in the San Fernando Valley. She would buy us a matinée ticket for the first show in the morning and we'd hop into four or five different movies until dinner. The transition between theatre screening rooms always made me anxious. I was afraid we'd get caught sneaking into the next movie and have to endure the shame of being kicked out as a family. But my mom savoured this game. She would instruct me to go to the restroom, remove an outer layer and mess up my hair. I'd come out to see her transformed in glasses, a tied-up bun, and wearing a jacket. On our journey to the next screening room, she would risk asking a theatre employee for directions with played urgency, or take her time browsing snacks at the concession stand. I'd nag her to keep moving. A wave of relief would come over me every time we made it inside the next theatre and sank into our seats. I felt like we had beaten the odds, enough to play again. The movies themselves, whatever their content, were a zone of stability before the next hop between theatres.

Later, when my parents were between jobs, they would buy a lotto ticket every Sunday with the same six lucky numbers. For them, the California Lottery was just a little game to satisfy a superstitious itch, not an actual answer to employment. My dad did the maths: the odds of winning were 300 million to one. Smaller than getting struck by lightning three times in a life. I'd ask myself, is luck on our side this week? A mysterious voice would answer: 'count the birds on the wire and all will transpire!' Every Sunday I'd ritualistically count the birds outside my window, tune into the live number drawing, and bet the universe that this evil random game might resolve something. And every Sunday, when the right numbers never came, I'd demand that the voice explain itself. But it only spoke nonsense until my anxiety built back up to next week's roll of the game.

In hindsight, I yearned for some tutorial that might have been called *Navigating The Chasm*. If I had known to see the transitional gap between theatres as an opportunity to inhabit a role and choose the next chapter of my day, I would have learned to enjoy the thrill of creating choices. And if I had learned to hallucinate that the feeling of indeterminacy meant I was in the most interesting part of a story, I would have felt more at peace with the voices in my head, each offering an inventive twist to light my path.

Doctors can listen to their intuition. Lawyers can listen to their reason. But Artists get to listen to all the voices inside them going back to childhood. Art can let the Artist experiment with different selves. The picky can become visionary, and the shy can summon the operatic. Psychiatrist Julian Jaynes says these inner voices are vestiges from a time before narrative consciousness, a neurological adaptation in which an imagined figure acts through you during times of stress. Psychiatrist Eric Berne describes a Child, a Parent, and an Adult persona living inside us, each ready to be triggered into action. Some cultures, like the Balinese, have rich practices devoted to deliberately exercising these trance-like possession states, often using masks that socialise them and acknowledge them as a vital dimension of being alive. I became an Artist in part to make a living out of evolving my relationship to the masks inside me. I want to feel alive to them and grow their personalities. I want to provoke their gifts by deliberately dwelling in chasms that a younger me might have evaded or felt unequipped for. In art, you choose your own chasms, and the masks are there to light a path where none is given.

In 2014, I hallucinated this chasm: 'The life of an emissary who is caught between unravelling old realities and emerging weird ones.' What did this mean? Who said it? Where did this come from? I believe it came from the desires of the masks. One part of me wanted to learn about storytelling. Another wanted to understand how to create enduring characters.

Another wanted to engineer multi-agent simulations that could trick me into loving systems and complexity. Another wanted to work with talented people. Another wanted to combine these things together to produce a World that could 'write itself', the way nature writes itself. This was the genesis of *Emissaries*.

Over the next two years, I struggled to fit the desires of these masks together. How could a deterministic story mix with an open-ended simulation? How could characters achieve complexity without losing their instant recognition? How could art be authored in its meaning but also live beyond its author and mutate itself? How might making a World make existing Worlds seem less sacred? Through much trial and error, team spirit, and psychological reckoning, the masks began to align. With me and through me, the masks led me to realise I wanted to practise the feeling of dwelling in the absence of existing Worlds. I wanted to create a World from nothing, to understand the artificiality of making a World, and to become attentive to the magical moment when a World begins to take on a life of its own, despite its artificiality. Together on my behalf, the masks began exercising a strange yet unified activity: Worlding.

WHAT IS WORLDING?

Worlding is the unnatural art of creating an infinite game by choosing a present, storytelling its past, simulating its futures, and nurturing its changes.

Choosing a present is an act of collage and therefore invention. It's choosing characters, relationships, and ecological conditions, and composing them together without sacred regard for realism. Children do this all the time by choosing from the shelf of experiences and thoughts, and intuitively combining them, if only for a brief moment. The more impossible or paradoxical the combination, the more emotionally truthful.

Storytelling its past is creating a pre-history for the characters and ecology of the World, and using that story to ground a World's ongoing unknowns within a meaningful context. Parents do this all the time by situating the activity of children into a larger life script of learning, playing, achieving, and reflecting towards a 'good life', despite the indeterminate turns that a child's life might take.

Simulating its futures is innovating an infinite-enough game engine for the World – its characters and ecology – to perpetuate itself without its original supervising author.

Adults do this in lucid, imaginative moments, when they try to devise rules and systems that allow themselves to live generatively without the burden of willpower or conscious rethinking. It's making rules for their intuitive selves to live by, and generalising those rules to scale into a game that can be shared with others.

Nurturing its changes is being an imaginative servant to the World once it gets going, by welcoming changes to keep its vitality alive. CEOs, gardeners, mothers, and shamans undertake this role so that their greater game may continuously flourish.

The art of composing these four activities together is the challenge of Worlding. It requires the Artist to abandon any sense of a coherent self and take on a different kind of psychology. One that moves between the artistic masks that already exist unevenly inside us, letting each contribute to the creation of a World. More on this later.

First, we need to understand our all-too-human relationship to infinite games and what it has to do with Worlding.

A BRIEF HISTORY OF INFINITE GAMES (AND WORLDS)

Religious scholar James Carse says there are two types of games. A finite game is a game you play to win. It has clear rules and a defined ending. An infinite game is a game you play to keep playing. If it is at risk of ending, the rules must change to keep the game going. According to Carse, the ultimate infinite game is evolutionary life itself: Nature.

For us humans, life is filled with the familiar contests of finite games: Deadlines. Deals. Rankings. Dating. Elections. Sports. College. War. Poker. Lotteries. When our finite games are won and done, what is strange is that we don't exit back into base Reality. We wake up in a field of infinite games that perpetually mediate our contact with base Reality. We choose to live in these infinite games because they give us leverage, structure, and meaning over a base Reality that is indifferent to our physical or psychological health.

We have many names for these infinite games: Families. Institutions. Religions. Nations. Subcultures. Cultures. Social Realities. Let's call them WORLDS.

A World is a construction. It is nothing compared to the true infinite game of Nature, but it is 'infinite enough' because it sustains the qualities of an infinite game long enough and surprising enough for humans to treat it with the status of being *alive*. A World is an artificial living thing, but a living thing nonetheless. It is ongoing, absorbs change, and attracts players to help perpetuate it. A World is marked by artificial boundaries that filter the shock of Reality's unending surprises and the complexities that they create. Yet a World is itself complex enough that we can generatively inhabit it and create new meaning within its local language. A world asks us to believe in its inventions and contradictions and to be 'safe' from our disbelief. In return, a world eats back at Reality, arms us with perspective, furnishes us with meaning, and gives us some measure of agency to expressively deal with new surprises from Reality. A World offers what writer Ursula K. Le Guin describes as 'room enough' to survive, thrive, and imagine possible futures for ourselves, indefinitely.

Up until recently, Worlds were the achievement of long periods of cultural evolution. Think of a nation or a religion. An individual may have originated an idea or performed an act that sparked a World. But no one person authored a World. A World emerged from an iterative process over many generations. Its character formed as a result of stretching itself to accommodate new surprises from Reality. Its health was maintained by players with the power, prestige, and tribal identification to do so. A World perpetually earned its infinite game status by continuing to stay alive through the people who believed in its meaning, lived by its laws, and benefitted from its stabilising structure.

What about fictive worlds? It seems that authors of fiction have been making worlds for a long time now. But fictional narratives on their own are only the spark of a world to come, the DNA of a world, and threaten to collapse without their original author. To turn a fiction into a World, a World needs an engine of ongoingness that can generate complexity and therefore surprises, without the supervision of its original author. In the past, engines of prestige and status powered religious Worlds. Recently, engines of commerce have powered fantasy Worlds, manufactured through an expansion of media – the fiction becomes the movie, becomes the video game, becomes the toys, spinoffs, theme park, becomes the working mega-economy of a franchise. This was the innovation of twentieth-century Worlders like Walt Disney, George Lucas, Steve Jobs.

But what about the rest of us? Can we make Worlds on our own? The guardians of old Worlds will tell you a world cannot simply be made by one person in less than one lifetime. It is the product of an evolutionary process. A World requires a past that is complex enough to feel lived in by other players. People don't just want the spark of a World, they expect to discover a World fully formed, inhabit its complexities, believe in its potentiality, and continue to generate meaning from it. If you truly wish to manufacture a World, it will cost you billions and a lifetime of work spent incentivising other humans to occupy your World. How can a single mind conceive an infinite game, enact its ongoingness, and make a repeatable practice of Worlding?

Luckily, we are in the midst of a strange transitional era. Worlds are stretching faster than we can stomach. Old Worlds are forking off younger Worlds to keep their games going. World boundaries are breaking and reforming. We are developing not only a tolerance for the disorientations caused by world stretching, but a desire to experience a mass variety of Worlds. More is better: a proliferation of Worlds gives us an opportunity to consciously reflect on the artificiality of Worlds and appreciate how they allow us to engage with Reality expressively. For the first time, we feel a sense of agency in choosing our life's portfolio of infinite games to play or to exit. Most profoundly, with the affordances offered by simulation and artificial intelligence (AI), non-human players are poised to help perpetuate the ongoingness of Worlds, thereby reducing the requirement that Worlds need to incentivise economic scale or religious fulfilment to stay alive strictly via humans. There is the feeling that creating a World – Worlding – might be just within reach of an individual artist.

THE MASKS INSIDE YOU

To recap: Worlding is the unnatural art of creating an infinite game by choosing a present, storytelling its past, simulating its futures, and nurturing its changes.

Choosing a present, storytelling its past, simulating its futures, and nurturing its changes is the work of very different kinds of people. How can the artist produce these things as an individual?

Let's look at the psychological options available to every artist. If the artist is like a ship, then the artwork is the ship's journey through new waters. Its maiden voyage forever establishes its character and path. The ship is equipped with a loyal crew, but trouble arises when they can't decide who is in charge and bicker for control. The crew comprise the artist's states of mind, or masks, each one available to drive the ship but with very different intents. The artist-ship must choose what kind of destination it seeks and what navigational strategy it uses to steer when the journey hits rough tides. This is an ongoing negotiation through the entire art-making process.

Observe below the diagram of masks. The horizontal axis describes the kind of destination that the artist seeks. *Seeking Home* is the drive toward stability, durability, and the perfection of existing worlds. You care more about existing infinite games that have proven to sustain human life, physically and psychologically, and wish to return to them and refine them in order to make them more enduring. It is an attitude that attempts to resolve the discomforts of Reality and domesticate them as part of a known human world. In contrast, *Seeking Surprise* is the desire to chase a frontier, one that is inherently uncertain and unpredictable, but with promises of novelty and interestingness. You do not know what you will find, and that is precisely the point. It is an open attitude that accepts the discomfort of Reality's indeterminacy at the frontier, in exchange for touching new truths.

The vertical axis describes the navigational method for how the artist steers towards its destination.

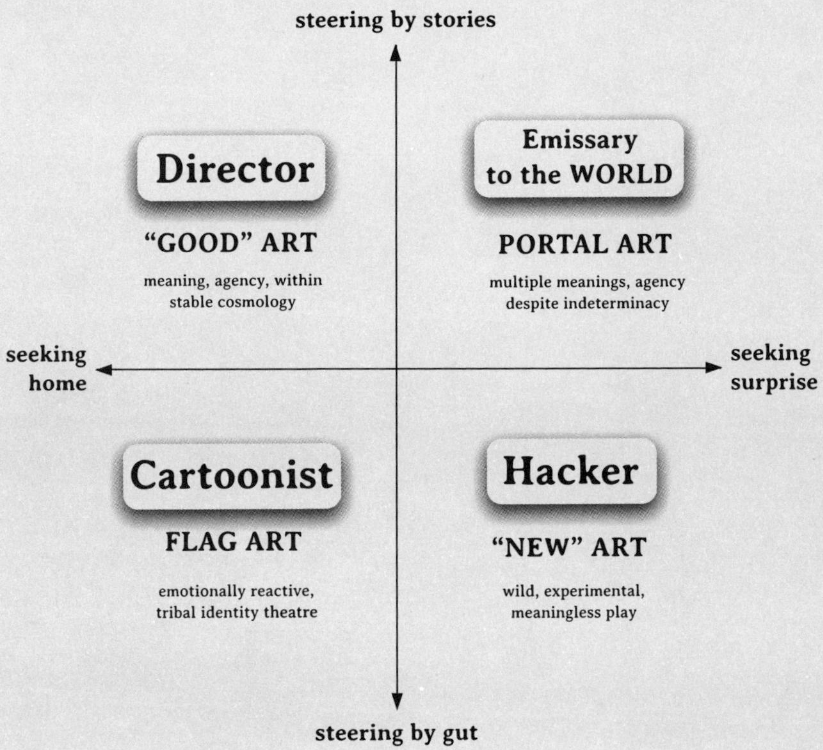

Steering By Gut means navigating by immediate instincts. When the seas are choppy, you react with evolutionarily honed impulses. Feelings are the most trusted compass. There is no broader perspective that can match the urgency of gut feelings. In contrast, *Steering By Story* means navigating with the perspective that your current situation sits within a larger chain of events. Today the ship might be enduring a stormy day, but you know the storm means you're at the end of Act Two and clear skies are expected on the horizon. Stories are how we gain a sense of control of the future because they supply us with a role in the story, a vector of meaning at every beat, and the promise of more meaning to come. If the Story cannot expand to incorporate the unexpected, the artist turns to the Gut for survival. And if the Gut proves wrong too many times, the artist looks to Stories to put it all into perspective.

Four fundamental types of artist "masks" come out of this model. The Director, who makes "Good" Art. The Cartoonist, who makes Flag Art. The Hacker, who makes "New" Art. And the World whose Worlding makes Portal Art. We name them here so that they can now become actual options, masks to wear to the job of making art. In practice, the artist moves through all four masks during the journey of making art. When time, energy, options or desire run out, the most habituated mask cements the final character of the artwork.

We are interested in getting to the most elusive mask: Worlding. As we will see, Worlding requires the artist to simultaneously Steer By Story *and* Seek Surprises. Imagine the feeling of dwelling in a frontier full of unknowns while developing an evolving story about what this frontier means at every turn. This is the strange feeling of Worlding. New surprises actively mutate and stretch your story to its limit. Weirder still, you are accustomed to a story settling into an ultimate meaning and coming to an end. But your story must be unending, never fully resolved, its meaning never fully domesticated. When it seems that a final meaning is coming into focus, your story hungers for more surprises to keep it from stagnating. In this way, your story stops feeling like yours and takes on an autonomous life of its own. It's no longer your story but a story that you imaginatively serve, as an emissary to the World. This is how an autonomous World is born. And this is the very essence of an infinite game. Unlike the other artist's masks, which expect full artistic control, a World subsumes you into its infinite game. And this is why creating an infinite game – and not just inheriting or cannibalising existing ones – feels like such an unnatural art for a single human mind.

FULL-BRAIN WORLDING

This book is for anyone interested in reconciling the unnatural art of Worlding with the finitude of human psychology. Yes, Worlding begins as the work of gods. You are tasked with choosing a present, storytelling its past, and simulating its futures. But once the World gets going, Worlding becomes the work of emissaries who betray the gods to serve the World itself and *nurture its changes.* Your mind, as we now know, is equipped with seeking and steering options. The trick to undertaking the complexity of Worlding is to recruit each of the artist's masks in turn and familiarise yourself with each of their seeking and steering styles so that they each may become a conscious choice rather than blurry strangers who intrude on the creative process. You will switch between masks, encourage their strengths, resist their

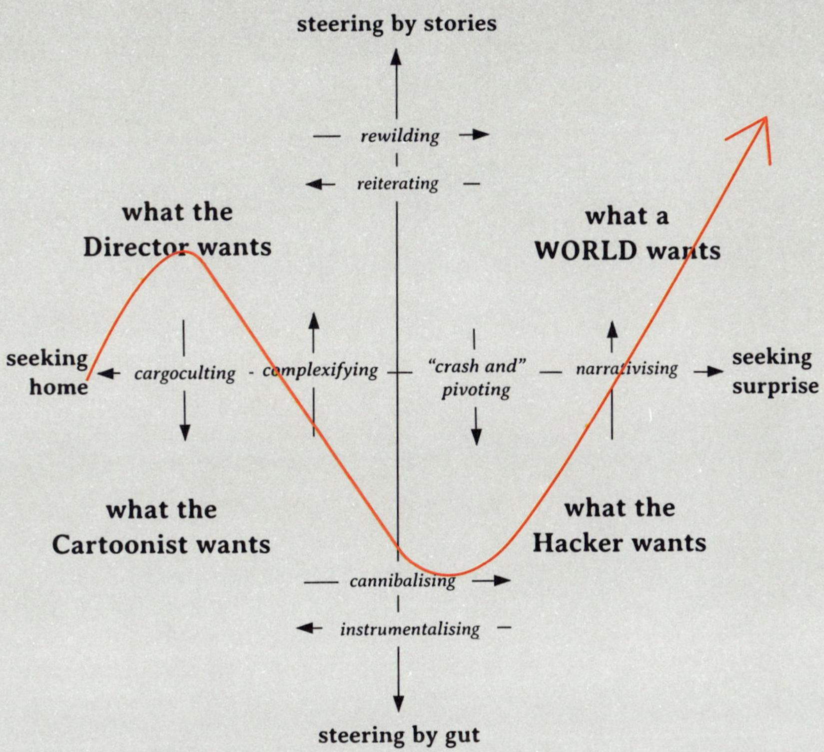

conclusions, and aim them towards the production of a World. You will learn to channel what the Director wants, what the Cartoonist wants, what the Hacker wants, and what a World wants.

So prepare to say goodnight to 'I'. Goodnight to your self, your ego, your composure, your coherent identity. This isn't goodnight forever. It's goodnight for now so we can clear the way to fully welcome the masks. These masks channel states of mind that already live inside you, that are already aspects of you. You know them all, but not equally well, because they rarely get to steer the ship in a sustained way, let alone coordinate towards a purpose. But today, our urgent purpose is Worlding.

Worlding, as we'll see, is a full-brain, all-hands-on-deck activity. By the time 'I' wakes back up, the masks will have taken you through such strange lands and through such unexpected flourishings that you won't be able to help but feel transformed. Perhaps the unnatural art of Worlding will begin to feel more natural. And perhaps, if all goes well, we might remember our own stories of Worlding fondly enough to want to world again and again and again, as many times as this lifetime can contain.

LET'S GET WORLDING!

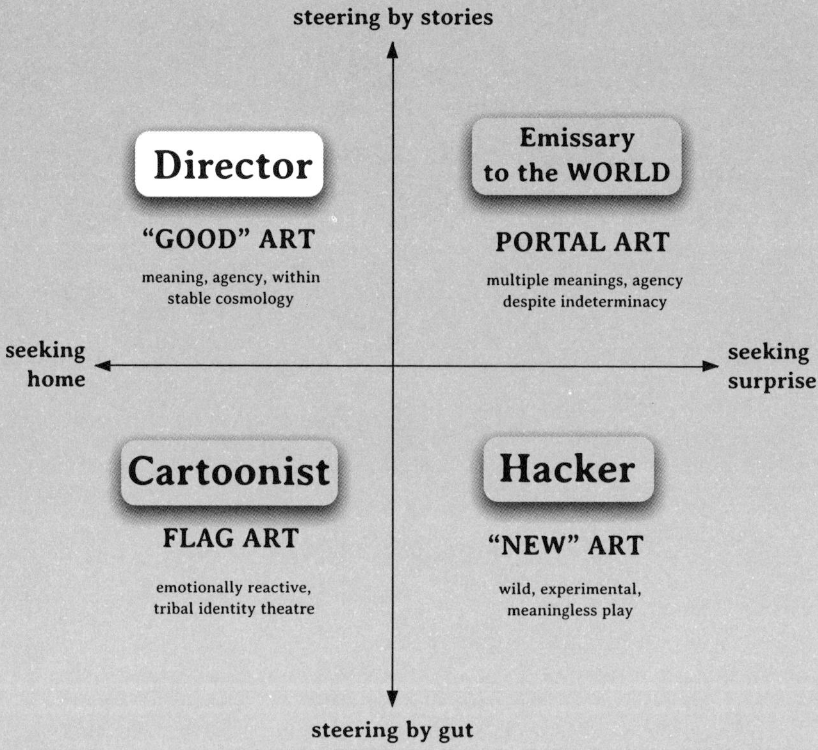
steering by stories
Director
"GOOD" ART
meaning, agency, within stable cosmology
Emissary to the WORLD
PORTAL ART
multiple meanings, agency despite indeterminacy
seeking home
seeking surprise
Cartoonist
FLAG ART
emotionally reactive, tribal identity theatre
Hacker
"NEW" ART
wild, experimental, meaningless play
steering by gut

What The Director Wants

There is a Complex Problem seeping in from base Reality, and the Director wants to make meaning from it.

To face a Complex Problem, the Director becomes complex in its process. Think of the artist who wants to make meaning from the problem of AI-human relationships, or post-graduation scriptlessness, or the Great Man crumbling, or what a queen has to deal with, or the fixer who can't fix himself, or racism's new clothes, or climate change dystopia, or any version of 'what really happened'. The Director is not only concerned with a story that captures the Complex Problem, but with production design, actors, choreography, cinematography, costume design, sound design, editing, visual effects, stunts, contracts, casting, catering, insurance, budgeting, transportation, trailer design, marketing, and more. The project is made complex enough to involve other people, actual or imagined, because the Director believes the Complex Problem must be explored, unravelled, and animated as a multi-sensory story production in order to earn its meaning with audiences.

Recognising the vast number of decisions that need to be made, and anticipating the project's long journey, the Director balances these risks by choosing a reliably humanistic vision to aim for. This vision is to tame the ambiguity and uncertainty of Reality by absorbing it into a specific kind of meaning – meaning that makes us feel *back at home in the world again*. *Seeking Home* and *Steering By Stories*, The Director makes "Good" Art that nobly domesticates the Complex Problem and metabolises it back into the container of human.

Psychologically, the Director is not a bundle of expressive childlike energy like an archetypal artist. The Director is 90% manic parental energy. The psychic composition of the Director is that of a mad parent who allows a very small part of itself to be a creative child. The more that creative child can be outsourced to other people and not occupy a part of itself, the better the Director can direct. The Director as parent is nothing like a rational adult. As any child knows, a parent is rarely objective, fair, risk smart, open to discussion, or emotionally composed. The

Director remains dutifully irrational, like a perfect parent to the project, maniacally navigating the ship towards meaning.

To ensure the success of the creative people it marshalls, the Director works to establish the right premise, container, team energy, inspirational fuel, and the right narrative that captures its Complex Problem. The creativity of the Director manifests in these structural choices. The Director believes that once the project gets going, these choices not only have decisive influence on the shape of the project, but act as True North for navigating through the chaos of production, and quelling the temptation for creative mutiny or self-sabotage.

We begin the journey of *Emissaries* from the mask of the Director.

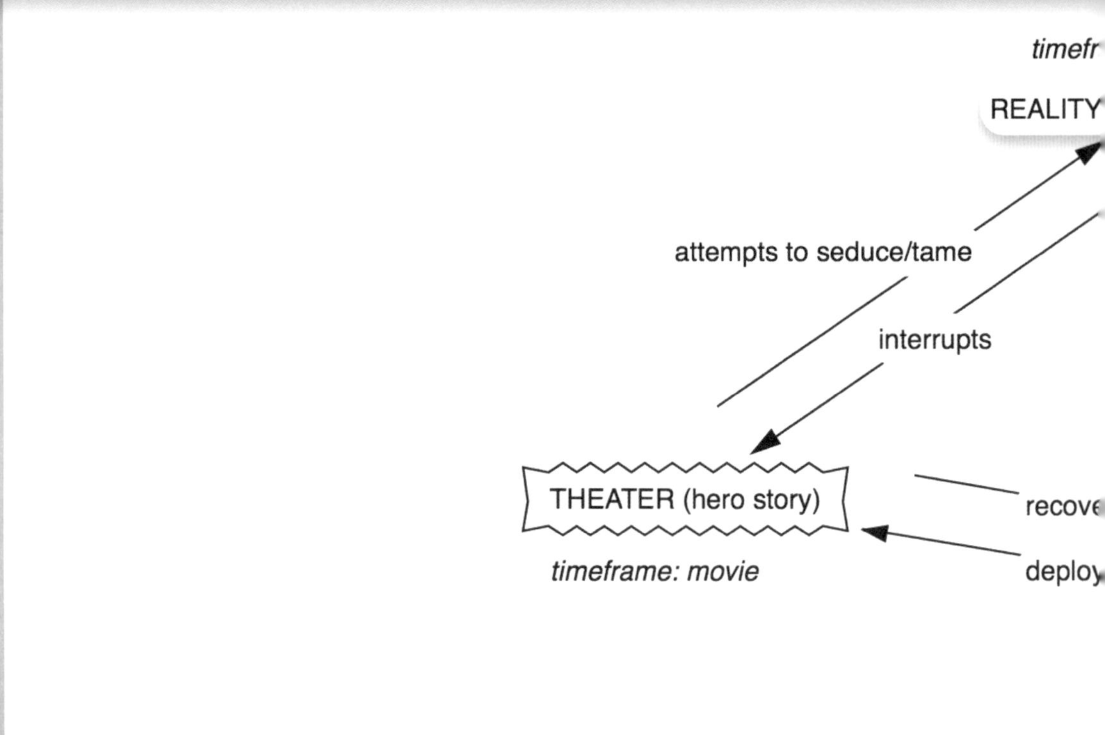

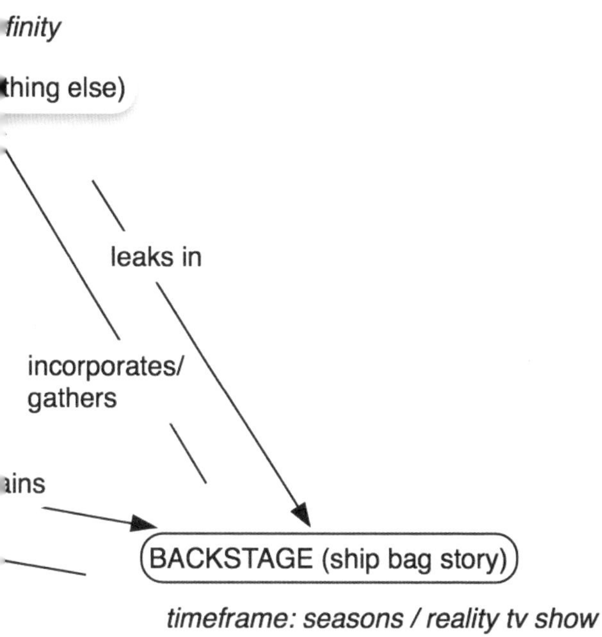

WHAT IS THE RIGHT PROBLEM?

From 2013 to 2014, I made several simulations – video games that played themselves. The simulations had unique properties: infinite duration, loss of authorial control, potential for emergence, a feeling of a life of their own, an inherent appreciation of systems. I preoccupied myself with trying to highlight the magical properties of simulations, yet they couldn't escape being experiments about themselves. They were not in tension with any contradictory force and therefore felt untested in their meaning. I wanted them to mean more.

I had read about how Philip K. Dick begins his science-fiction novels with one simple change from normality: 50% gravity, or a drug that shrinks you, or meeting your clone. From this interruption, drama naturally emerges as the mind imagines its consequences. A premise for Dick is as simple as a routine interrupted.

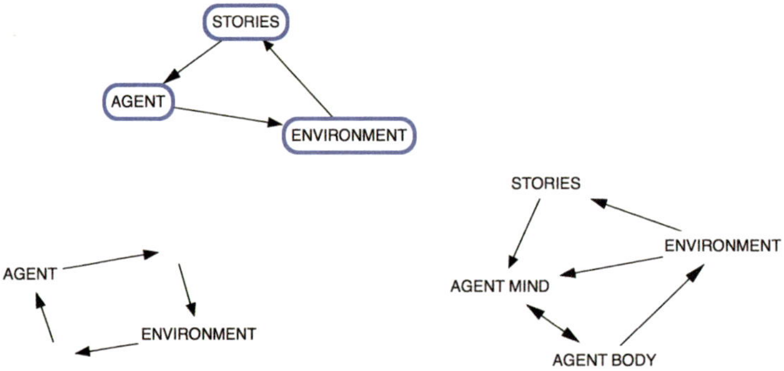
STORIES
AGENT
ENVIRONMENT
AGENT
ENVIRONMENT
STORIES
ENVIRONMENT
AGENT MIND
AGENT BODY

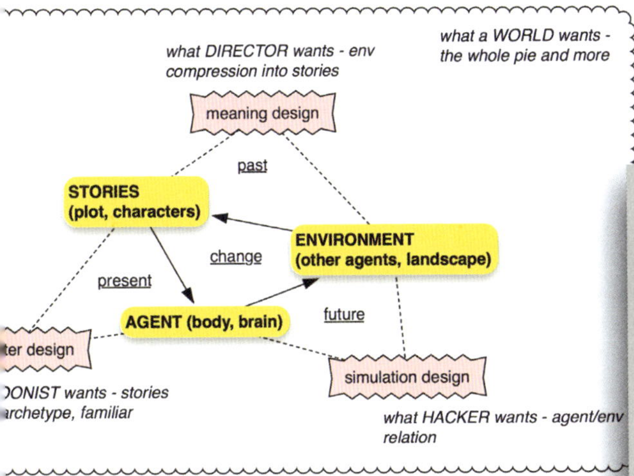

If a simulation is dynamic, reactive, or without end, what could productively interrupt it? What could 'get in the way' of a simulation and challenge its open-ended orthodoxy? STORIES. What if a simulation could be pitted against a story? How would these two opposing forces shape each other? Which would prevail?

Stories live inside us, influence us, and orient our actions on a longer timescale than our immediate biological impulses. Stories, through us, change the world. The world, through us, modifies our stories and inspires new ones. I began to imagine a triangular relationship:

Story shapes an agent. An agent shapes the world. The world shapes back.

Imagine a simulation that treats stories like an influencing force among other forces like gravity, energy, time. Imagine a simulation sculpted by the deterministic force of a story, and likewise, a story assaulted by the open-ended dynamics of a simulation. Imagine a story that is finally allowed to break with its classical determinism, and a simulation that acknowledges the influence of inner fictions on how we act upon the external world.

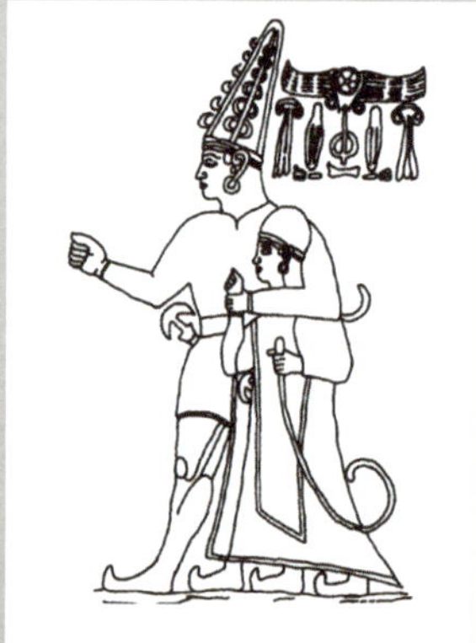

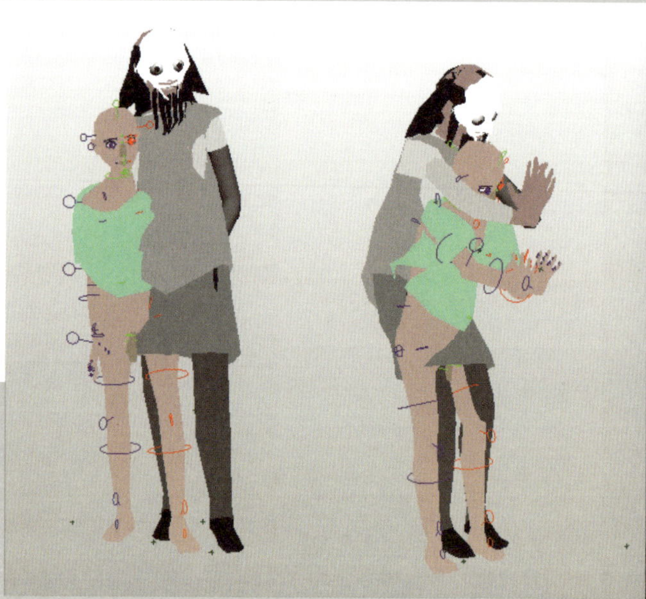

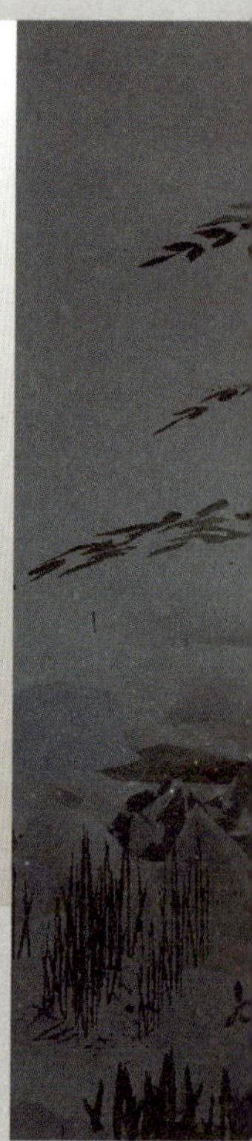

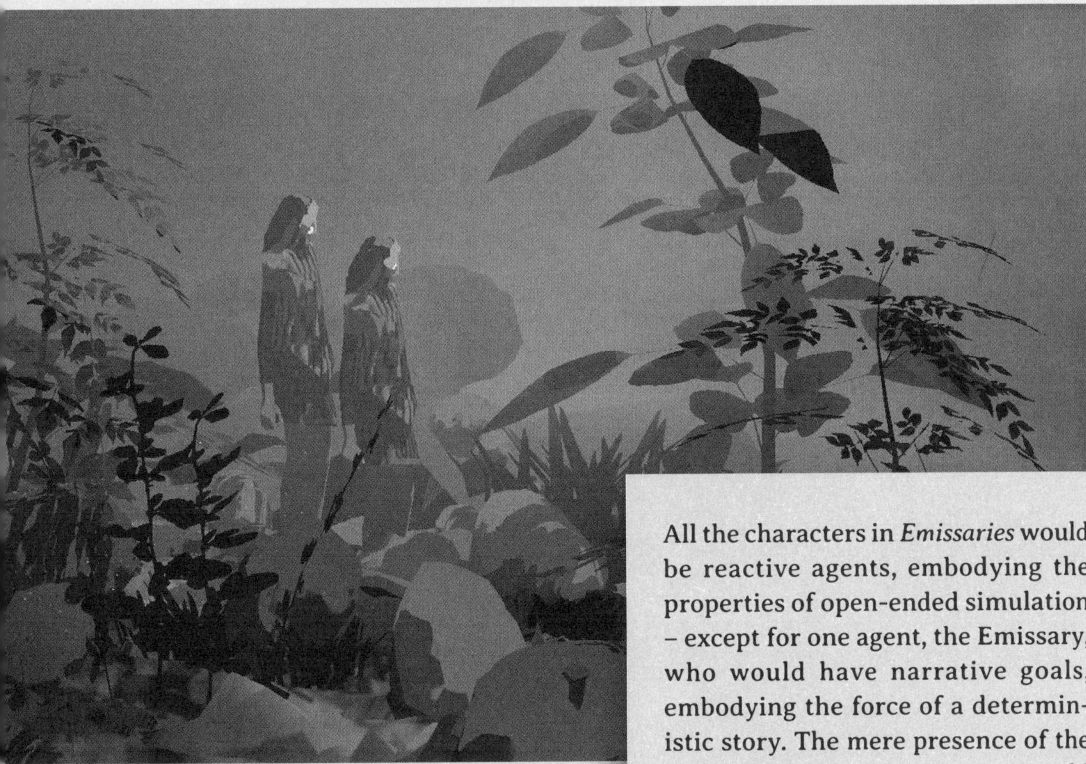

All the characters in *Emissaries* would be reactive agents, embodying the properties of open-ended simulation – except for one agent, the Emissary, who would have narrative goals, embodying the force of a deterministic story. The mere presence of the Emissary guided by stories would function as the interruption to the impulsive simulated ecosystem. The pressure for the Emissary to deal with navigating through a dynamic simulation – by changing the world, or changing themselves, or refusing to do either – could become a fertile source of meaning.

In trying to negotiate its narrative goals to fit within the activity of the simulation, the Emissary would function like a rudder or steering force in an otherwise reactive, meaningless world. Where all the other agents would be governed by impulse to new situations, our Emissary would be powered by a sense of narrative. This was my premise.

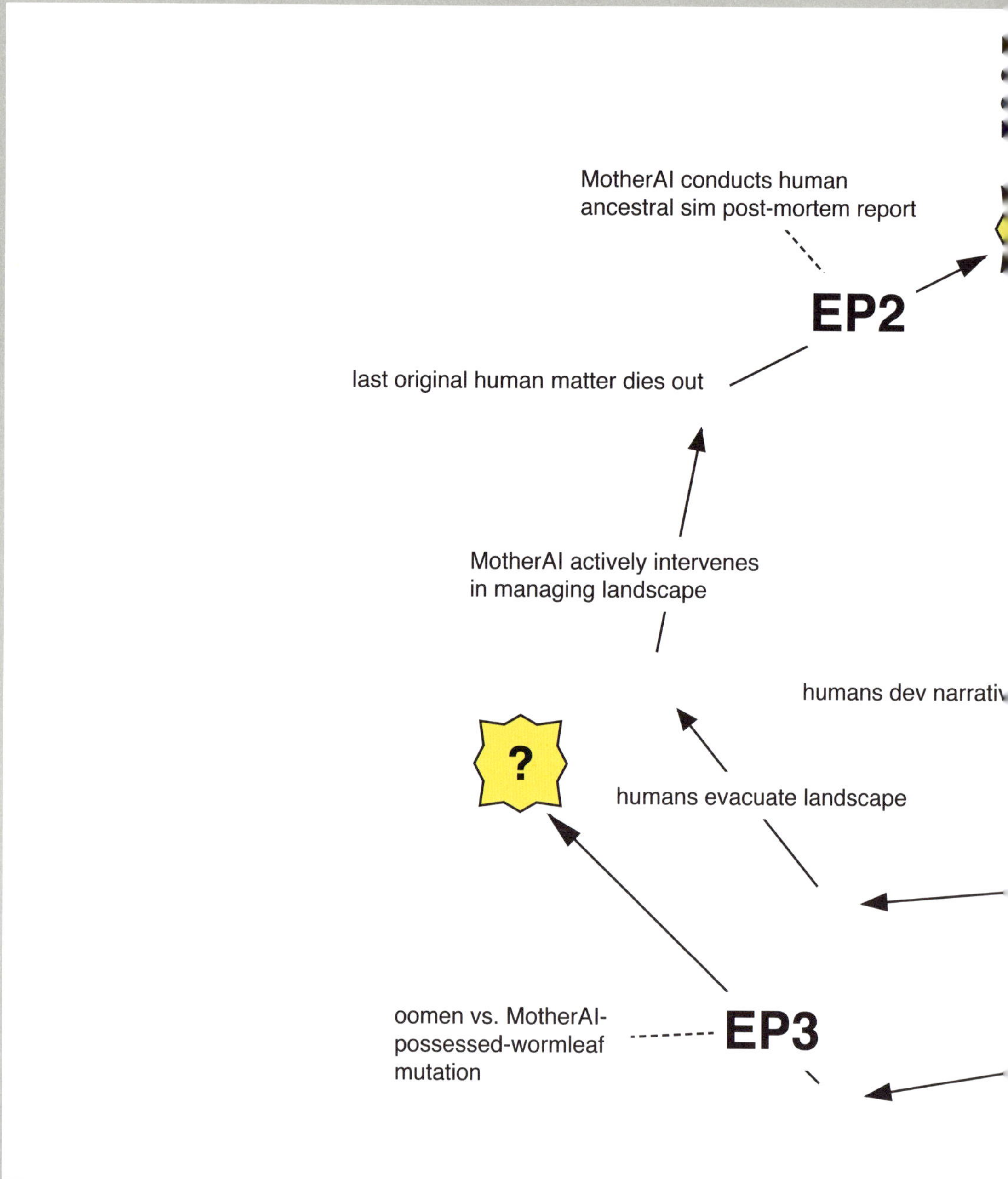
MotherAI conducts human ancestral sim post-mortem report
EP2
last original human matter dies out
MotherAI actively intervenes in managing landscape
humans dev narrati
?
humans evacuate landscape
oomen vs. MotherAI-possessed-wormleaf mutation
EP3

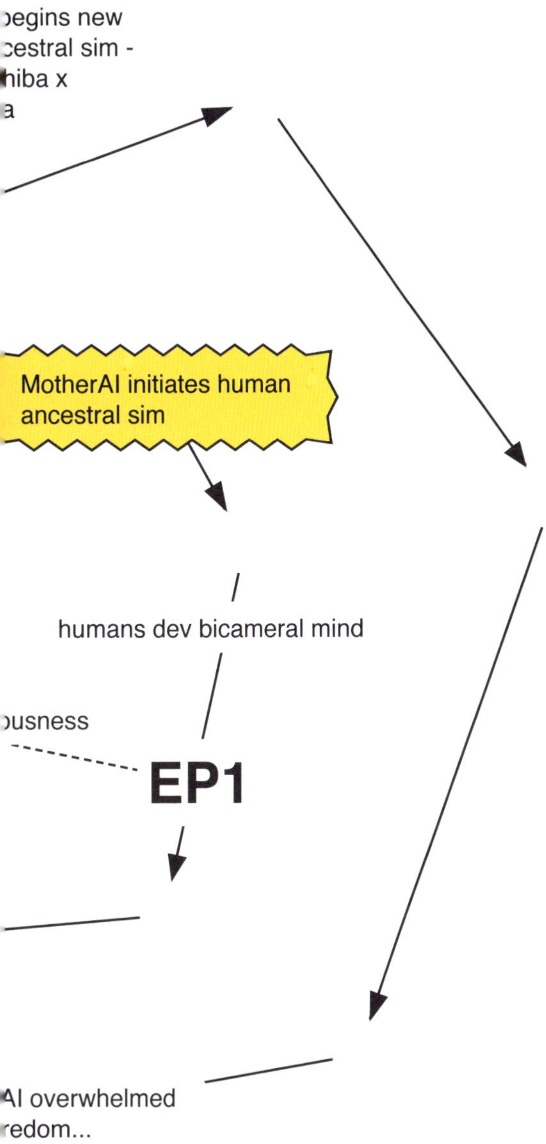

WHAT IS THE RIGHT CONTAINER?

The strange freedom of art is that there is no prescribed container imposed on an artist. Filmmakers have movies to contain their ideas. Writers have novels. Musicians have albums. But art can be anything. This is its freedom. But this freedom doesn't mean freedom from containers. It means freedom to choose a container.

As the Director, I must choose a container. If the right one doesn't exist, I must choose one that is close enough and mutate it. When the automobile was first invented it was called a horseless carriage: the routine of carriage, interrupted by horselessness. Elon Musk put his diverse interests in energy storage, renewable energy, climate change, automation, and self-owning sentient objects into a container called the Electric Car. When you can name your container, you begin to create a human-thinkable path towards making meaning.

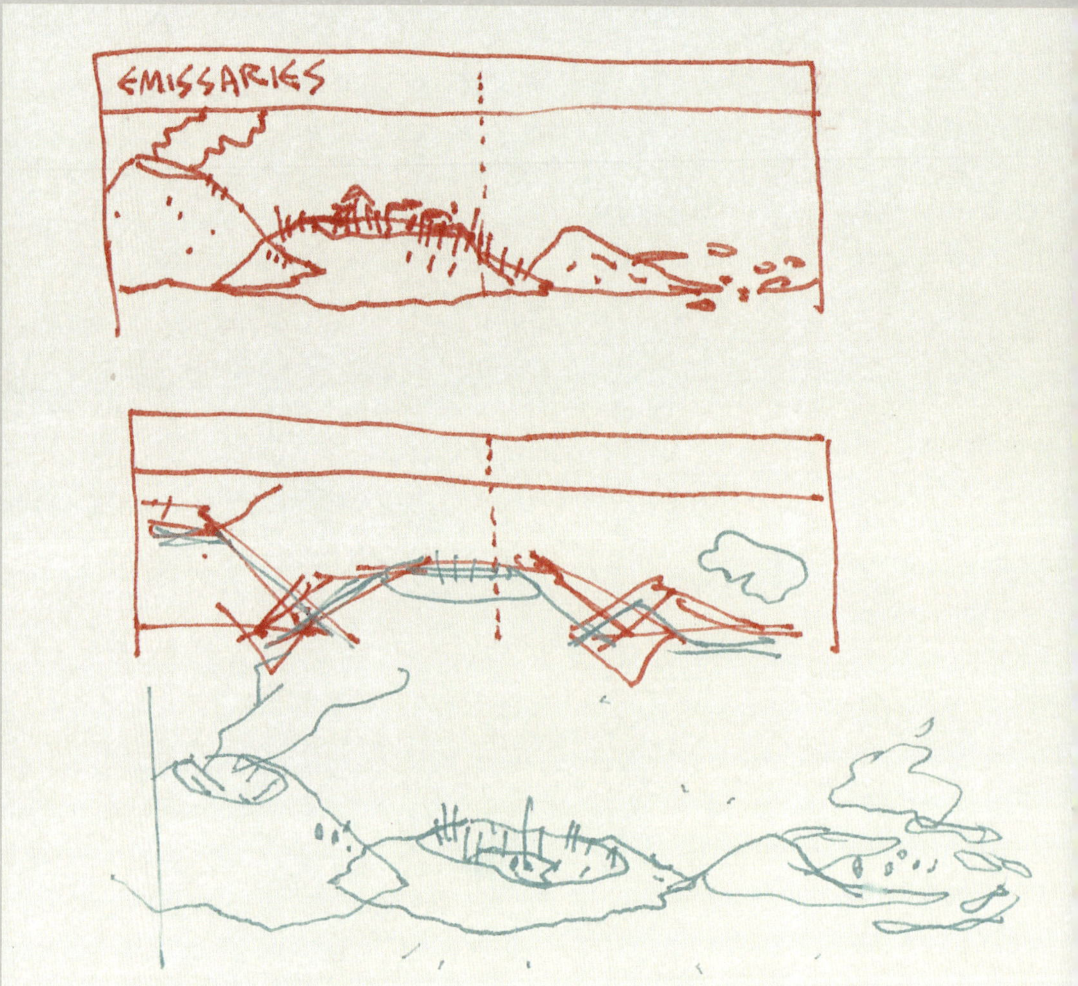
EMISSARIES

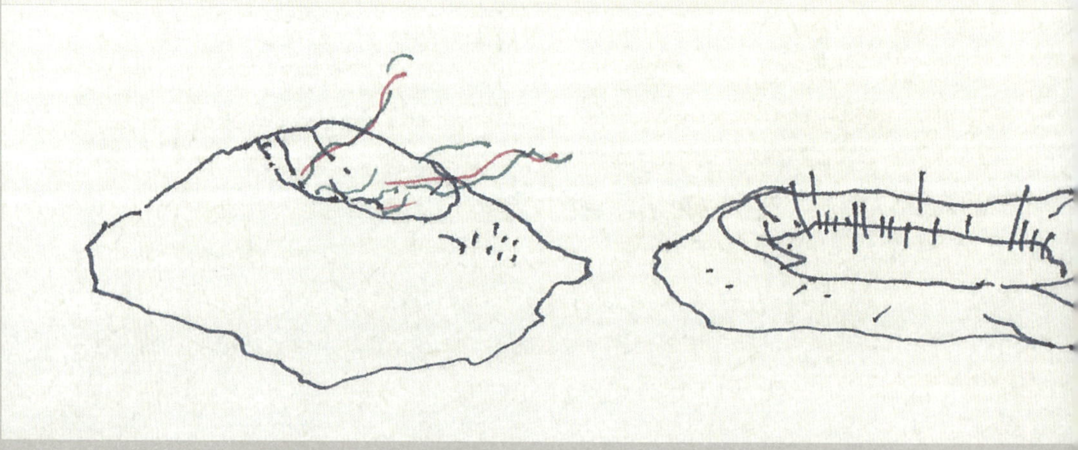

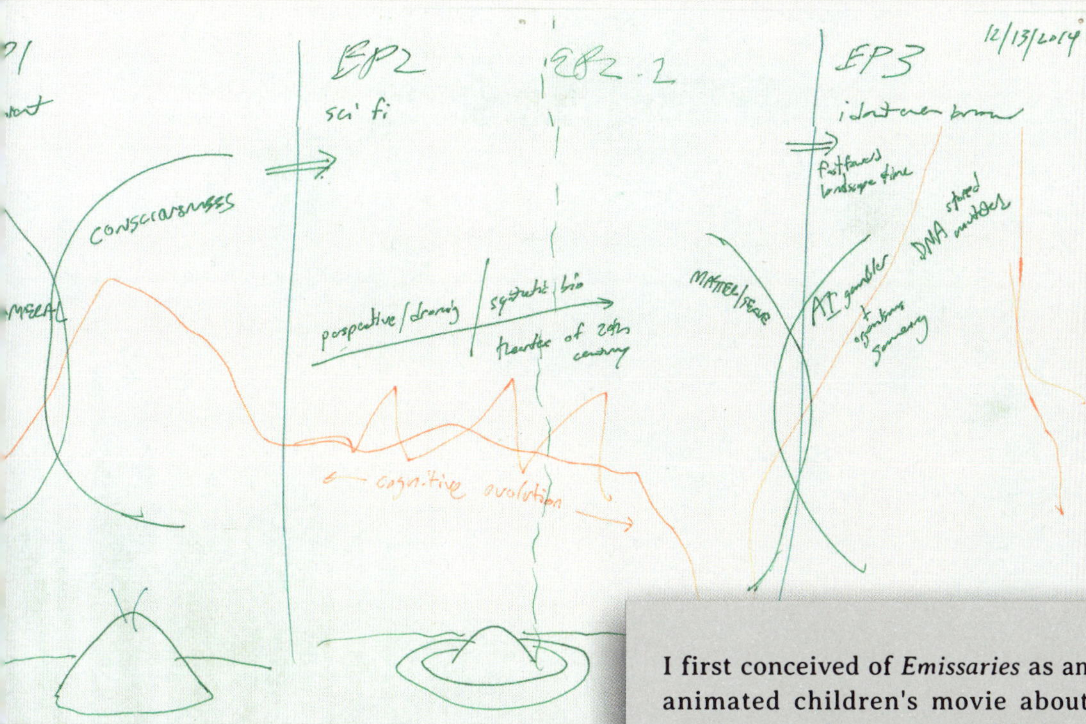

I first conceived of *Emissaries* as an animated children's movie about cognitive evolution. It would show how environmental and social conditions forced the brain to evolve new mental software in an easy to understand fable-like way. Then it became a 'smart story', a story that adapts to change the way a 'smart house' adapts. Then it became a simulated reality show, like *Real Housewives* meets *The Sims.* Then it became a virtual reality movie. Finally I decided *Emissaries* would simply be a trilogy of simulations. I had already established how to work within the container of simulations, but now the promise of a trilogy would imply a narrative through line. The trilogy would be composed of three episodes, each occurring at a different phase within the same landscape: volcano, crater lake, atoll.

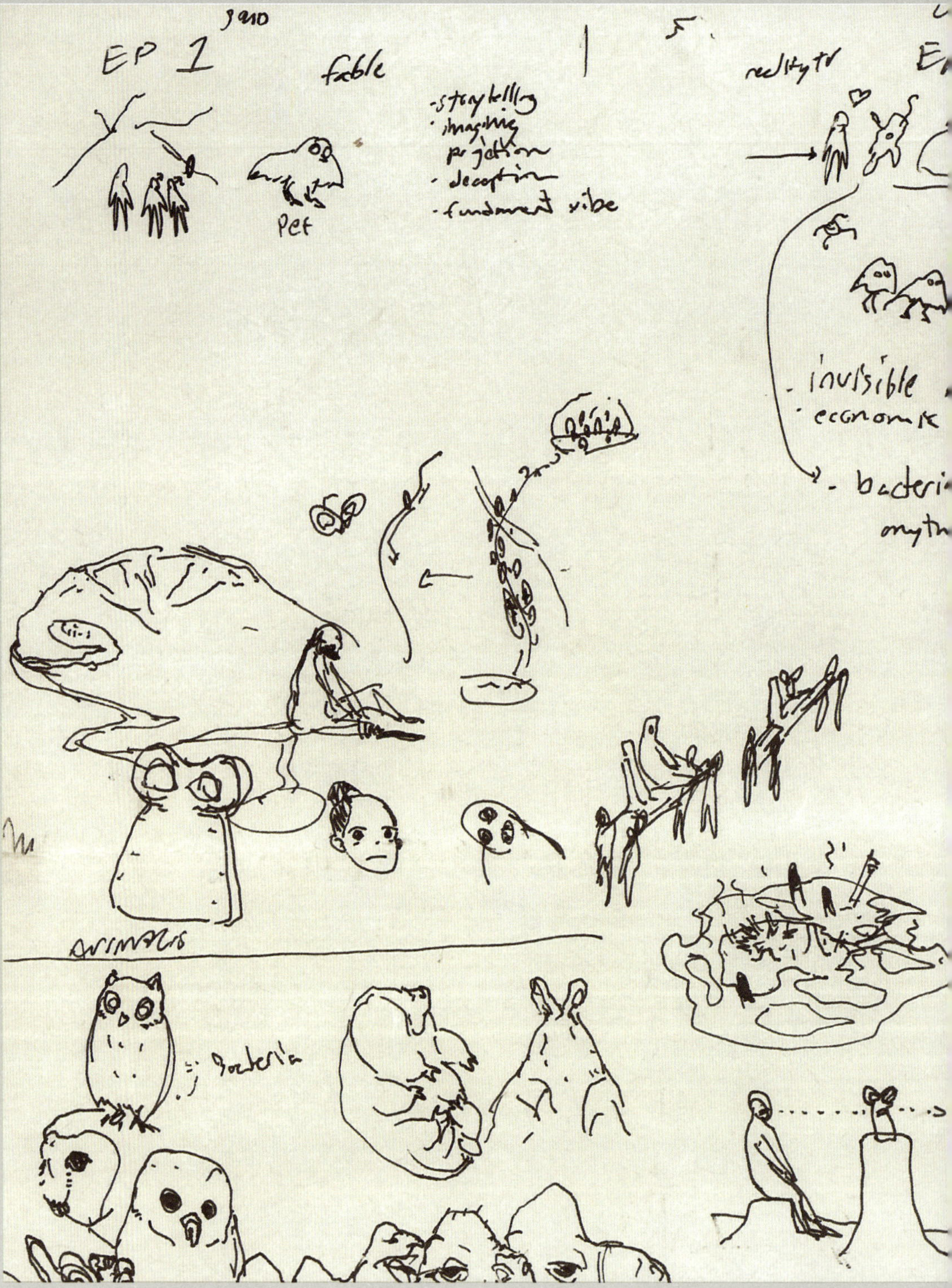
EP 1
fable
-storytelling
-imagining
projection
-deception
-fundament vibe
pet
realityTV
-invisible
-economic
-bacteria
myth
animals
bacteria

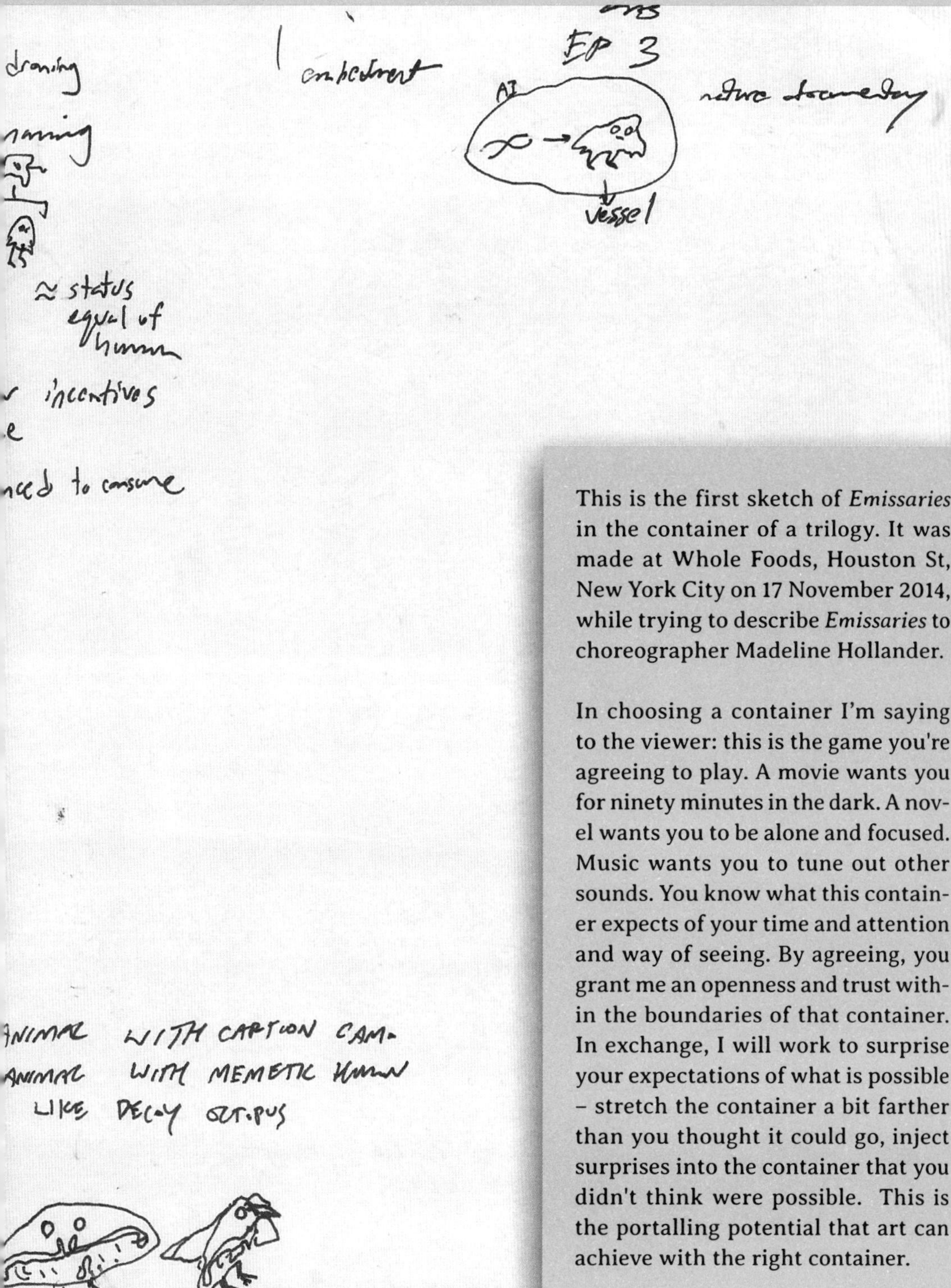

This is the first sketch of *Emissaries* in the container of a trilogy. It was made at Whole Foods, Houston St, New York City on 17 November 2014, while trying to describe *Emissaries* to choreographer Madeline Hollander.

In choosing a container I'm saying to the viewer: this is the game you're agreeing to play. A movie wants you for ninety minutes in the dark. A novel wants you to be alone and focused. Music wants you to tune out other sounds. You know what this container expects of your time and attention and way of seeing. By agreeing, you grant me an openness and trust within the boundaries of that container. In exchange, I will work to surprise your expectations of what is possible – stretch the container a bit farther than you thought it could go, inject surprises into the container that you didn't think were possible. This is the portalling potential that art can achieve with the right container.

PROBLEM OUR MINDS MUST FACE
Overall concern with controlling social reality, degree of leakage, when, how.
human facing nonhuman scale, how to act? what mindset to take? how to change self within lifetime to face uncertainty with agile?
ARGUMENT
mix games, crash games to change habit, change technology, deliberate crash into, lead to new consciousness time/space metaphor, new technology of storytelling
MANAGING / CONTROLLING SOCIAL REALITY
when stripped of human sacred choices, opportunity to grow from molten core
- what is the initial imbalance?

SUBJECTIVE STORY
MC - head injured apprentice - can't conjure hallucinations but believes - abandons hallucination, becomes authority to shaman - evolves story mindset
IC - head shaman of tribe - habit mindset - uses authority hallucination technology
- VR perspective, 3D, hazy atmo

OBJECTIVE STORY
- a nonhuman story initial pyroclastic flow, mantle movement, bizarre creature stygian soup, pathetic humans going haywire, change of mind emergent for a minority few, landscape mutation
- different aesthetic, model aesthetic? science textbook - orthographic, 2.5D, clear

GUIDE TO OBJECTIVE STORY -
- ai bird and talis bird

OBJECTIVE + SUBJECTIVE MERGE
- inside experience of super volcano

after MC change, IC must die horrible extraordinary death encapsulated in pyroclastic flow and frozen

the explosive climate/landscape changing effect of volcano paralleled with
old habit social reality master fallout with apprentice who comes to see an I self, as part of changing land, a rock in the head

pebblehead
princess

in the ceremony social ritual -> carried by animal / dragged along , in group troupe -> in the panic, -> trapped on all sides -> in the volcano

who changes? setting this up - possible that IC takes on new principle but hasn't shifted view, still uses it for old ways. like using new technology for old habits.

POSSIBLE STORYFORMS assuming CHANGE
1) vizier comes back to controlling SR by new means, veiled means
2) vizier finds shaman stripped of dignity already, comes to see this as place to grow from

PICHAKU'S PERFECT DAY

// SCENE 1
Ash falling, a sign of volcano threat to tribe.
Shaman has momentary freakout in ash fall, tribe sees this lapse in resolve. lea
injured in head, can't hear voices anymore.
some reflection on mythologized transfer path of King-God authority, King will n
Pichaku bird mistakes morphing freakout Shaman for playmate and crash lands
world
Pichaku's unique abilities to mime gesture and voice relate to mythology?

// SCENE 2
Shaman projects King's ka/spirit in Pichaku
Emissary projects anthropomorphic friend in Pichaku
Pichaku mimes and morphs without intention to find a play mate
Pichaku aligns with Emissary, better treatment,
volcano tremor, tribe scared, chaos
*TK Pichaku via Emissary translation of behavior-to-sign by chance successfull
petty instance of bicameral misfiring in tribe's boy that Shaman cannot resolve
channeling.
tribe views Emissary's status above Shaman's
tribe sees Em as communicator of King/Pichaku's will

// SCENE 3
Shaman accepts this fully (non introspective), but asks Pichaku if volcano will e
Pichaku gives ambiguous back and forth signs, something is false..
A volcano tremor puts tribe in brief chaos, confusion
Emissary hides Pichaku (or gets to play dead?)
Emissary manipulatively mimes as Pichaku, signaling Pichaku/King embodies
Emissary demonstrates on another minor tribesman's bicameral freakout, resol
emerging consciousness / masking. surprised at her own cunning.
Shaman fully accepts transfer, galvanizes tribe into a ceremonial state

// SCENE 4
Some tribe's boy (who's deal they resolved and empowered earlier) finds conce
Shaman demotes Pichaku as empty animal vessel now, celebrates it with ritual
ceremony cockfight
the outcome of the ritual cockfight will affirm the transference/give closure
Em argues no roosters left it is not necessary
Pichaku on leash forced to fight a disoriented snake
Em intervenes ritual fight with authority of King but doesn't really know how Kin
Shaman is betrayed by this behavior, not how king would act.
Shaman who knew King channels King's voice, reclaiming authority.
Snake bites Em
**TK Pichaku pins snake tries to mate with snake, disrupting ritual.
Shaman sees Em as inhabited by a lower creature, just a pichaku without a go
[? what happens to pickahu here?]
treats/drugs Em with coca leaf
Em's cunning proto-conscious abilities wielded here —

- Em right temple is burning/steaming (continues throughout entire story to steam).
- Em - voices grow silent [thought bubble diminishes, or goes grey, can't hear shaman]
- ***VOICES HAVE LEFT EM
- Shaman looks at Pichaku - the voices calm and come into focus, its the deep King's voice: "jsioadjais"
- Shaman says, "jsioadjais"
- Pichaku echoes back "jsioadjais"
- Shaman startled (burning bush moment), we zoom out seeing things in larger perspective
- zoom back in on same spot, Shaman looks back and Pichaku is gone from spot
- Pichaku walking close to fallen Em, makes a cute morph.
- Pichaku tugs at one of Em's multiple royal jewelry shimmering face chain
- Em puts one face chain around Pichaku's neck
- Pichaku and Em symmetrical
- Pichaku mimes Em
- Em clutches onto Pichaku.
- Pichaku tries to eat at dead rat.

SCENE 4 (status reshuffle - following) - Pichaku focus in crowd
- Pichaku says "DJSAIODJ" to Em, begins to walk
- Em latches on to jewelry chain, walks side by side with Pichaku
- Some intrigued and follow. (others continue on their own to be scattered in indecision and confusion, covered in ash) (Shaman gets no attention, confused about status)
- Shaman walks faster then slower than Pichaku, Pichaku turning opposite vector when Shaman walks faster than Pichaku, Shaman slowing down and put in place of a follower.
- Pichaku walks to slightly higher ground with an overhang covering, no ash here.
- Pichaku pauses looks back at everybody.
- Pichaku clears away little pebbles ***AI
- Pichaku does a little mating dance.
- A rat scurries by, interrupting dance.
- Pichaku immediately crushes it and eats it, reverse vomit choking motion down. absolute.
- tribe and shaman ooo's at this absolution.
- Em delighted, pets her Pichaku.

SCENE 5 (Pichaku as inner voice - Em exorcist)
- Shaman asks Pichaku: if volcano will erupt *mimes some volcano gesture
- Pichaku is blank
- Shaman asks a few different ways
- Pichaku blank
- Shaman draws something in the ash, asks for Pichaku's judgement.
- Pichaku kicks the ash drawing.
- Tribe copies gesture in ash with hands, tossing ash.
- Tribe looks to Volcano, looks to Pichaku
- Shaman asks another question
- ***noisy thought bubbles
- Pichaku mimes randomly
- Triber asks non-related question
- Pichaku echoes some prior phrase
- Triber huh?

- Pichaku looks at Em
- Tribe crowd begins to dissipate
- Em has an anticipatory show-mom face ***Em starts to see something is off, not working
- at Em's foot, a rat pauses by - Em sees little rodent shitting, the kicking up dust, chasing its own tail, then getting into fight with a pebble
- Pichaku randomly doing actions
- Em goes back and forth back and forth seeing random behavior of both animals
- Em's thought bubble goes off (throbs color? *intuits the randomness of this)
- Someone in tribe is frustrated, grabs at Pichaku aggressively
- Pichaku freaks out, squawks
- Em snaps back into moment, gets enraged, takes step forward btw Pichaku and tribe
- Several tribers close in on Em's space

Volcano tremor **adrenaline rush

- Tribe in brief chaos, confusion, chaotic chatter cloud returns
- Em's voice drops, hey! (Em takes ownership of tremor)
- Em takes on bird sounds and mimes, like possessed total animal exorcist.
- Tribe dispersed, mixed attention
- Em whipping her necklace clearing out space
- Em's head wound really steaming
- Em: GET BACK HERE!!!! *SIREN

NEEDS REDRAFTING HERE
- Tribe all gathers obediently
- Em at loss for what to say next, a silence, everyone's thought bubble blanked out, or afraid
- in this silence shaman fills in, announces ceremony

***semi-circle forms, into cockfight scenario, shaman assumes MC role
Shaman picks up Pichaku and drops him into semi-circle?

SCENE 6 (ritual cockfight)
*****ABOUT SYNCING EVERYONE'S MENTAL STATE AGAIN, AFFIRMING STATUS, COORDINATING PROBLEM SOLUTION**
*****NEEDS MUSIC THEME**

Shaman grabbing Pichaku as empty animal vessel now, celebrates it with ritual ending ceremony cockfight
**Em ok with the cockfight, confident Pichaku is going to win
Em argues no roosters left it is not necessary

Ecstatic joyful mood
- Someone tosses in a disoriented snake
Pichaku on crude leash forced into fight space
- No action
- Triber grabs snake's head and rubs a chili pepper in its mouth, and tosses it back joyfully, ecstatically
- Snake takes a shot at Pichaku
- Pichaku bites near Snake
- Snake strikes again

Em intervenes ritual fight with authority
Shaman is shocked by this behavior
- Em is scared, standing in between Pichaku and Shaman, intervening

- stressed out snake deciding which one to bite, sees fear in Em's face.
- Em makes big gesture fronting, but terrified in eyes
- Snake strikes at Em in her head wound getting stuck in it.
- Em falls over
- Someone jabs at Pichaku directly, Pichaku agitated
- Snake struggles stuck to Em's head
- Pichaku bites the snake in half, it stops wriggling
- Shaman tries to pry out snake from Em's scalp
- Em anger grabs Pichaku clutches, struggles away
- Em runs up toward volcano lip with Pichaku

SCENE 7 (Em and Pichaku away from humans at last)
- up on the volcano lip trail
- the drone of geological sound silences everything
- Em alone away from human culture, running along vast rim lip of volcano
- Em hallucinates herself growing, Pichaku growing, growing into adulthood of each other.
- Em is a fierce Amazonian and Pichaku is a majestic dinosaur/
- Em talks aloud to Pichaku in this fantasy, her missing voice double.
- Em stops running, stops hallucinating, her current self, Pichaku's current
- They take in the vast awe-inspiring landscape before them
- Em kneels
- Em takes off tribal jewelry, discarding it on ground.
- Em looks at pichaku.
- Pichaku looks at Em.
- Em unleashes Pichaku's chains.
- !!! Without hesitation Pichaku dispassionately flies off, some feathers fraz immediately left in wake

SCENE 8
- We follow along with pichaku, Em getting distant
- Em's face starts to well up but unclear which way her emotional resolve g get more distant with Pichaku
- Pichaku flies near the steaming ashy center pit, near volcano hole -
- We see a world really without any living human influence, all simulation, l game
- We see human sediment layer cross section
- We see dead king body abandoned
- Pichaku walks by a same species snake trying to crawl up volcano side. want to fight too busy trying to swallow something
- Just a wild simulation of unmediated reality - a win a loss a win a loss wit continuity or applied meaning

Em watches pichaku from lip - sim city perspective distance
Shaman finds her and kneels down with her
They watch distant nature simulation and contemplate it aloud like live ESP
***they begin to have some perspective—

**somehow this strips away at tribe's underlying life script/habit break point
// SCENE 5
Em runs up to volcano lip with Pichaku, alone away from human culture.
Em talks to Pichaku. Pichaku seems to reconcile with her, mutual trust relationship
Em says something about Pichaku being her missing voice double.
Em takes off tribal jewelry.
Em looks at pichaku.
Pichaku looks at Em.
Em consciously imagines like no previous human mind could the past and future of them together, avatars of each other.
Em unleashes Pichaku.
Without hesitation Pichaku dispassionately flies off
**Pichaku proves to not even contain stable Pichaku-ness for Em to latch onto.
**Pichaku proves to perplex Em's consciousness tech

Em confused and shocked.
Volcano tremor causes Em to slip into interior slope of volcano.

// SCENE 6
From distance in sky Pichaku watches Em like an anthropologist -
Em finds all decontextualized human debris from offerings into volcano. remains of a past pichaku sibling species. all meaningless in this context.
Em find dead king's body decomposing inside volcano, encrusted in salt and ash.
A tremor reveals cut cross section into side of mountain - we see cycles of tribe settlement, offerings, ash, magma, soil, settlement, same offerings
Pichaku watches Em drags the body to the top lip of volcano.
Em wipes away and cleans the corpse.
Shaman confronts Em with Dead King.
Em and Shaman look down the fog of ash rain refracting away in sunrise. sees tribe like scattered ants.
Em slides dead king's body down side of mountain, skiing on ash, toward tribe.

somehow Pichaku adds some finishing touch to this idea, like sings a song

From distance, we see Em approaching tribe saying something with Dead King's body, and the scattering becoming orderly.

- pyroclastic flow avalanche may or may not wipe the tribe out here
- in catastrophic ashy wasteland, Shaman left on sidelines alone singing rapping morphing and channeling puzzling over to self the activities of Pichaku.
- Pichaku flies above. Just another day for Pichaku!

// END NOTES
end goal/feeling to achieve:
- Pichaku - a lovable icon of assault on necessary human anthropocentric illusions/habits/ theater -
kids to say to parents: "need some pichaku to get real about this situation"
in a way, this story becomes the creation myth for this character icon lol

PICHAKU'S PERFECT DAY (PLAY?)

PLAYERS
- **Pichaku** - a bird of paradise with slight morphing abilities, voice miming, can display patterns on plummage for turning into primitive emoticon (visually, an irresistable pokemon-like animal)
- **Shaman** - the channeler of past authority voices, like a celebrity/rapper, can hallucinate under stress and make decisions to resolve local issues
- **Emissary** - Shaman's apprentice, daughter of Shaman, 10yrs old, helps pass Shaman's word, delegate decisions to tribe

REVISE INTRO SIMPLER
SCENE 1 - INTRO (routine language) - shaman focus or Em watching shaman
one shot - hyperlapse time passing, sun up sun down sun up sun down - routine routine chatter
- ANCHOR FOCUS - inside Shaman's canopy cover den, light from outside entering thru slits, near Shaman's head over his right shoulder, everything happens around him here, center of attention
- a habit interrupted by decision point: this or that, this or that, Dead King voice, that
- Shaman hearing deep voice of Dead King, settling dispute with two tribers
- triber hearing Shaman's voice, dropping objects in volcano lip
- triber hearing Shaman's voice, tribe throwing objects in ocean
- Shaman whispers to Emissary
- Emissary walks over to distant rooster cockfight, says something to tribe, a rooster dies.
- Emissary reporting back to Shaman
- the voices accumulate as a musical harmony - everything is grooving
- ***volcanic tremor***
- thru slits in distance an ash column emanating from volcano -
- all voices stop - silence - real time -
- everyone outside pauses and looks up, they hallucinate Shaman's calming authority voice: "listen to me:"—
- shaman emerges from den, considers it, hears Dead King's voice, then another, then another, building in his head
- total cacophony—

SCENE 2 (crashing + rat) - pichaku focus
up inside the all encompassing fog of ash cloud
- Pichaku flying holding rat
- rat screaming pathetic
- Pichaku looks at rat suffering, mimes back a weird cute face.
- Rat quiets at strangeness
- a random ash cinder catches rat on fire
- Pichaku forced to drop rat
- Pichaku tracks rat
- zoom follow - Flaming rat hits Emissary in the head - zoom back out to Pichaku
- Pichaku zooms toward fog spot where rat fell
- Pichaku crashes into tribe world.
- [black]

SCENE 3 (Pichaku & Em) - Shaman - taking stock , ground focus
- Dazed on the ground, Em and Pichaku look at each other, flaming dead rat btw them.

Pichaku digs around.
finds eggs incubating in the ash
finds another installment of eggs
unclear which ones belong to it
**ash steam harrasses Pichaku
has to decide, not sure?
(we need to see pichaku tested in isolation during stress conditions)
***maybe pichaku sees volcano steam as sentience adversary, harrassing Pichaku with hot ash grabs, Pichaku ready to bite at it, attack it

Em throws a rock at pichaku (like a distant more 'real' relationship to pichaku now)
it barely reaches where pichaku is
Em whispers into shamans ear
Shaman throws a rock (or jewelry?) much farther
rock jewelry lands near pichaku

//not sure where to go here ..
maybe it needs some kind of Lost In Translation ending where Pichaku and Em reconvene and whisper on new terms / expectations?

//
maybe Em's voice hearing needs to come back but as a proto-ego-self. Em hears her voice double as herself not another authority - like two Em's. her voice is the first to introduce negativity judgement low self esteem etc, and delusional power
some kind of burden of consciousness that requires her to definitely be a part of the tribe and socialized to keep it in check…

maybe Pichaku uses its plummage emoticon to signal back and forth to Em and Shaman

TRIBE GETS NEW SONG

///EDIT OUT
- Em finds all decontextualized human debris from offerings into volcano. remains of a past pichaku sibling species. all meaningless in this context.
- Em sees cross section into side of mountain - we see cycles of tribe settlement,
- Em scans from small crude idols, to more elaborate sculptures, to chair with dead king's body decomposing inside volcano, encrusted in salt and ash.
- King suddenly speaks, voice emanating, Shaman's voice
- Shaman emerges from behind King's body
- Shaman carefully scales down to where Em is
- Shaman slips, breaks a leg, clothing tears
- From distance in sky Pichaku watches Em and Shaman like an anthropologist -
- Em drag Shaman up to lip of volcano
***Em can project forward that shaman can become king, some life together?
- Em disrobes Dead King, and puts on to Shaman
- Shaman puffs up inhabits the actual role no longer the voice

- Em and Shaman look down the fog of ash rain refrac
scattered ants.
- ***a tremor
- Em slides dead king's body down side of mountain,
- In front of gathering tribe
- Em whispers into ear
- Shaman says what to do "5"
- Em cuts his head / marking to match her own on op
in head
- new harmony sound

***SH

somehow Pichaku adds some fin

***Pyroclastic flow bl

- pyroclastic flow avalanche may or may not wipe the
- Pichaku flies above. Just another day for Pichaku!

WHAT IS THE RIGHT STORY AND MEANING?

As the Director, I believe the secret to achieving meaning is through narrative. Narrative affords us what we cannot find in unfiltered life: the chance to see a problem objectively and subjectively at the same time, and the chance to see our actions in a larger chain of events. A narrative produces a context for 'counting' actions as meaningful. After realising the container for *Emissaries* would be three episodic simulations, the narratives of each episode revealed themselves quickly.

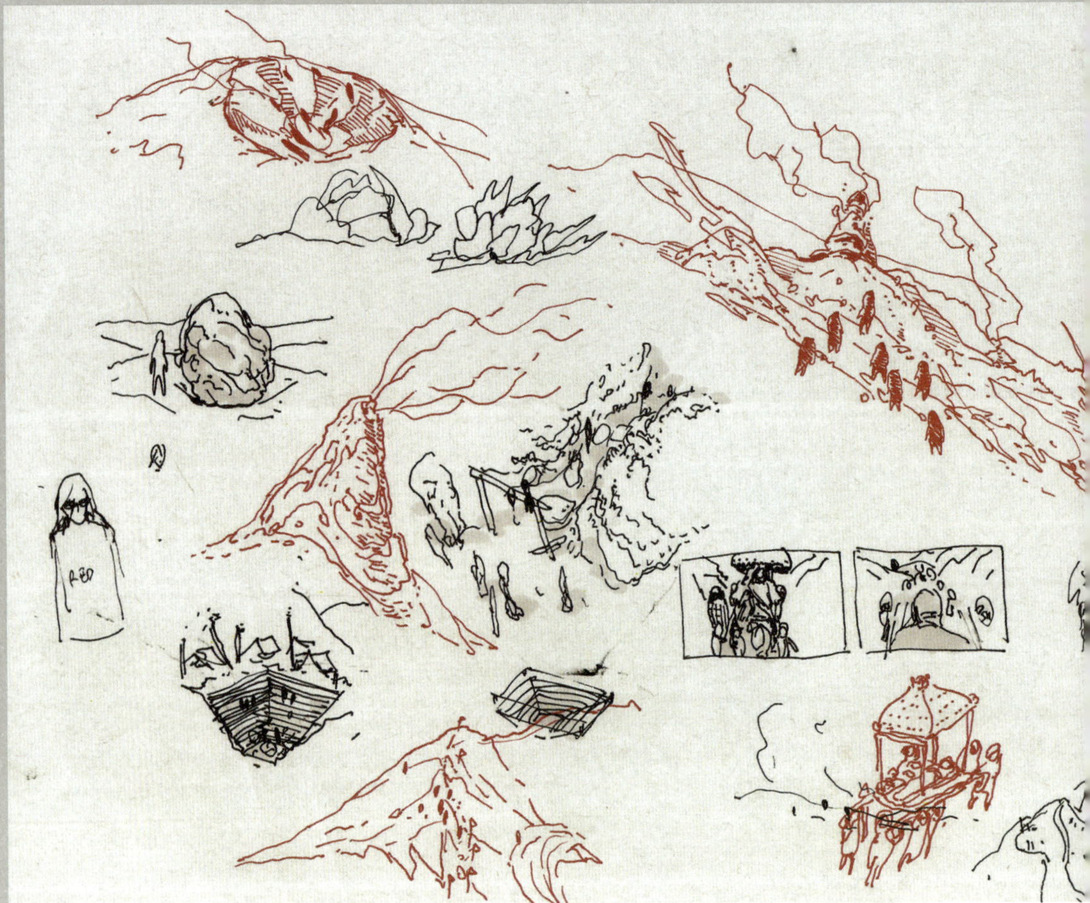

sean

thank you for agreeing to take a stab at this. i am a v amateur storyweaver, and i know any rick rubining/ brian enoing/ becketting you can do to make it more clear and molten core simple will be invaluable.

I am making a children's animation for VR displays, approx 30min long.
There are three goals I'm trying to hit:
1) - to embrace storytelling as a medium for conveying a complete argument, exploring a problem completely, both subjectively and objectively, from four interwoven perspectives (**i** - the subjective main character, **you** - the objective influence character, **we** - the subjective relationship story, **they** - the objective overall story)
2) - convey that ancient human history can be a site for science fiction
3) - to create an overall experience and texture of emotionally supercharged confusion

to be clear: texture of confusion is not confusion with the argument/story; the story should aim to be clear. the confusion is the texture. for example, when your girl is upset about something but can't pinpoint the exact problem herself, the behavior is confusing - shooting energy and emotions into many different registers. the argument/story/problem is on the contrary very clear and complete: your girl is pissed about x because it threatens/imbalances y.

confusion for me is a v important emotional texture for VR. I don't want to jump into VR trying to make a seamless alternate reality to escape into. I want to make a VR experience where you feel that realities are leaking together and you are on a journey to endure and navigate it, and level up your neurological game to meet it. using VR as an active gym rather than a spa retreat.

bc this is an animation, there isn't a line-by-line script; it is just an action-by-action list. As little as possible information is conveyed through dialogue. dialogue is a texture for feeling that world.

THE OVERALL SITUATION
in an ash rain, a bicameral-minded tribe faces the threat of a volcano eruption. can the tribe's habits/mindset/rituals respond appropriately to the uncertainty of eruption and keep the tribe together and social chaos at bay? Meanwhile, a bird of paradise gets caught into the tribe's affairs and cast as a symbol/holy celebrity.

We primarily take the perspective of the bird observing at an uncomprehending distance the strange behavior of ancient humans.

THE CHARACTERS
- **Pichaku** - a yellow bird of paradise that can mimic shapes of similar scale to its body, and mime/echo sounds. Pichaku is a student of movement, can sense what forces influence another organism's movements. Pichaku species will want to find life mate; in captivity it may identify its captor as its life mate. Pichaku is the main character perspective.
- **Emissary** - a young girl, apprentice to the Shaman who has lost the ability to hallucinate voices. she disguises her disability within the tribe, but is left in mental silence, frustrated, on the verge of growing a conscious "i" ego self, on the verge of cunning. She mediates/ manipulates between what Pikachu's needs as a captive wild animal and what the tribe needs from Pickahu's behavior for symbolic zoomancy.
- **Shaman** - the head of the tribe, can effortlessly hallucinate voices in any stressful situation to tell him how to act. he is not conscious, no ego no awareness of self, but he is de facto an immense authority figure to the tribe. he is responsible for keeping the everyone's psychic and collective health in tact no matter what insults nature throws at our pathetic little tribe. Shaman talks endlessly in chants, rhymes, sing song, raps. His authority in part comes from his vocal dominance, occupying the local airwaves. A tribe member would have a hard time getting Shaman's voice out of their head. He is pure right brain.
- **Dead King** - the dead body of the previous king who was and continues to be Shaman's authority figure. Shaman hallucinates Dead King's voice the most. Dead King's body is not buried, for it still speaks to Shaman and other members of the tribe and is thus still alive in everyones psychic experience.

THE PROBLEM
to zoom out for a sec, the problem I'm trying to explore within this story is that everyone is concerned with having the appropriate instincts kick in when facing new threat / unknown / complexity. the tribe want to do this with their existing habits, rituals and voice hallucination technology. Pichaku ultimately needs the tribe to do this differently, engaged in a process of evolving habits, new instincts and rituals, else Pichaku gets forever casted into human affairs. The head-injured Emissary who can't hallucinate voices anymore becomes a means to make this happen.

BACKGROUND
some assumptions: the story assumes humans are base but interesting/complex creatures. there is no anthropocentric dignity that needs to be held sacred here. if anything the story is an argument against human dignities, for they are crutches that impede growth, adaptation, and appreciation for how minor (yet miraculous) being alive is. everyone here is an intelligent respectable creature within the domain of their local social reality, but unaware retarded pathetic when they are outside it / or intruded upon, like pro basketball player in a hockey rink. Emissary

is the first to be aware of h
de facto not-even-wrong p

bicameral tribe. think of th
head. they are not introsp
creatures of habit. their ev
uncertainty, they hear voc
king, gods, animals, statu
action to take. gods are n
accessible by a bicameral
chatter and hallucinated s
connected. music and con
long-term planned strateg
god or a voice or a phrase
progression. with no sens
there is shame but no guil
love, sex but no fantasizin
names; hard to project ab
moment and every influen
immediately. it is importan
development for social or
religion but we should se
spirits and god talking at f
reality in this ancient era.
cultural insularity to really
happening too rapidly too
messages, that end in de
consciousness, human bi
subgroups and after many
settlement lands, back an
everything.

For purposes of this story,
habit profile / crutch techn
cannot imagine another w
humans slightly shorter a
bicameral man hallucinate
bodies where the doubled
man and how the authorit
example, this picture sho
his hand and moves it for
bicameral human making
personalities to face the n
look more adaptive and a

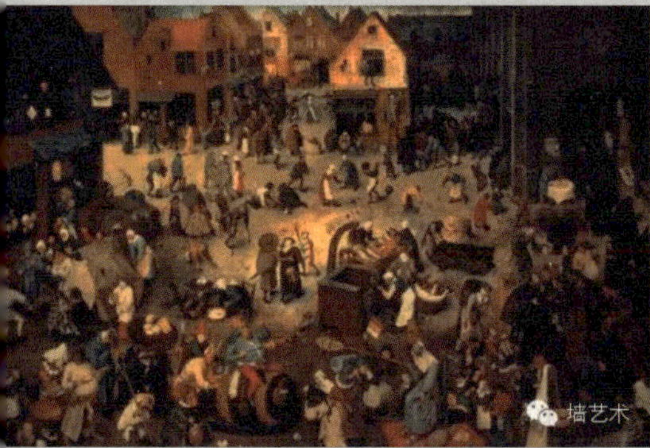

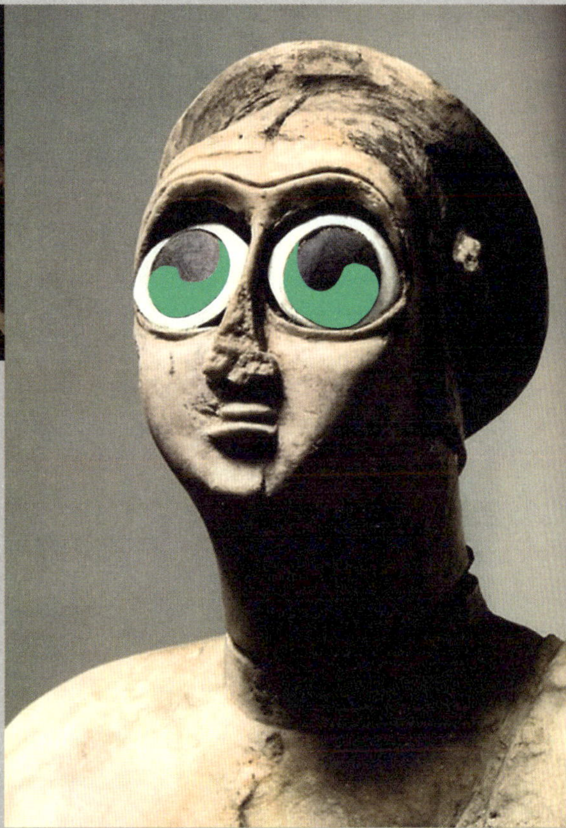

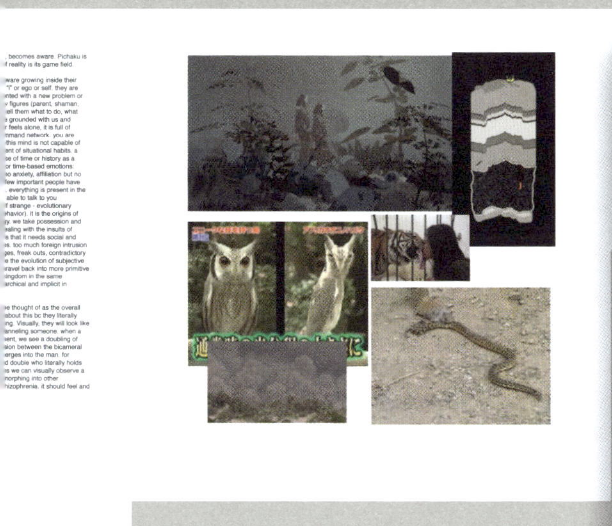

Episode 1 was based on an image that came to me while reading Julian Jaynes: an ancient community living on the side of a volcano, their ancestors buried in the ash. Their response to a volcanic tremor would be like that of a hurricane party: instead of fleeing their home, the shamanic leader would hear voices telling him to celebrate the tremors and convince the community that it will pass over. The shaman's daughter gets injured by ashen debris and begins to think differently.

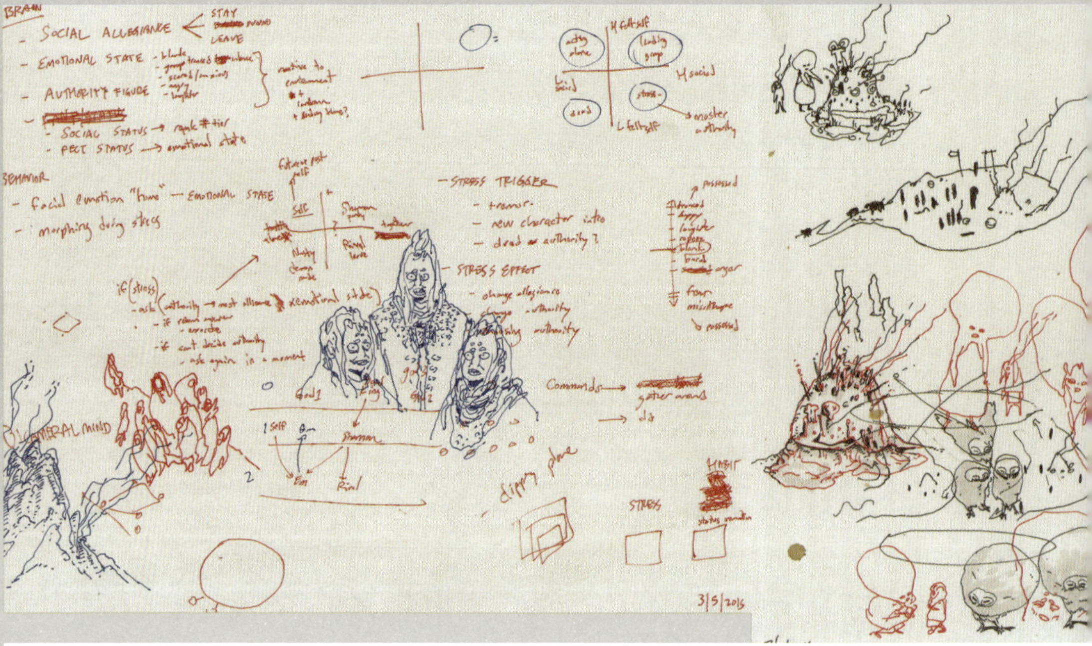

CHARMING rapper shaman should be portrayed as force of great talent and magic and power and transformation but ultimately in service of a narrow human scale, but too immediate only w tech
vizier is in contrast unremarkable, bad at transformation, but can hack out a larger perspective
bird is bird

OS
a tribe is led by a ceo shaman with the same habit tech as their dead founder. when the habit tech makes ceo flip out during a volcanic threat, his vizier helps him get back on the wagon while secretly plotting a new tech take over. the ghost is strong in shaman, and shaman charmingly asserts the goal (away from volcano threat). Vizier with the help of a morphing symbolically significant animal to old tribe habits - gets inside the habit head of the shaman to resteer the script and social reality of the tribe before the volcano kills them all.

- define character of dead King - key quality of shaping tribe - volcano soil
- define tribal significance of bird species

king was delighted by bird for its confusion ilinx, not for its miming voice?

<u>MC bird animal</u>
- concern with doing - bird wants to play trick other animals
- sleeping eating drinking fucking sitting playing
- - issue of enlightenment - can do whatever it wants outside the rules/rituals/social reality of human species
- shitting fertile seeds,
- detail passages of matter transforming

somehow vizier has to develop an idea that the volcano will not explode but collapse? together with bird they must USE the bicameral tech with this larger perspective, and orchestrate/manipulate it to save everyone and let them keep their illusions

the nonmeaning of bird's actions and behaviors should be complemented with over-subscription of meaning on behaviors of tribe ritual

the bird and the tribe together manipulate meaning.

OS
meaning is the necessary ingredient for maintaining a social reality bubble to defend tribe against bald harshness of changing tumultuous reality
- maintaining nature, normalcy, rituals, tending nature == maintaining SR script of tribe

IC
in despair of loss of voices. the silence of the bird.
- OCD behavior: ask self: will x happen? will i x? - look out at simulation, something happens or not;
- how should i do x? - look at simulation something happens

SHAMAN - OS -
- arc head back to appear headless then bring it back morphed
- gods are earth-bound, not in the sky yet, have not left our lands
- gods dont stop talking to him, endless chatter
- no concept of chance

DEAD KING - "First Father" or "Founder"
dead left visible so they can keep talking

"ripped out of context in the larger hierarchical group, where neither habit nor bicameral voice could assist and direct him, he must have been a pitiable creature indeed.

CENTRAL DRAMATIC QUESTION
- what to do now? what to do now? bicameral tech to tell you what to do; consciousness tech to tell you what to do
- do you have the freedom to change one's own nature within a fixed social reality?
    - stepping into shoes of others
- even a nonmeaning alien bird?

===
- **<u>can we understand another entity's behavior outside the meaning perspective of our own social reality?</u>**
- **<u>no but we can use them as mirrors to unearth the molten core of ourselves stripped of SR which allow us to better adapt to things outside our social reality</u>**
- **<u>porosity experiments, emergent not conscious relationships</u>**

stripped SR dignity/role, who are you at core? denial of this
explore the argument from many perspectives - starting from position of human dignity quickly devolving into human pathetic

MC needs to somehow get to own molten core, shed something; this whole time, we see it like an animal metamorphing into a plant, but it can sustain injury like a plant, meant to be eaten.
MC needs to fuck another smaller animal.
MC needs to clearly reveal to be non-conscious or bicameral, just its own weird brain thing
MC used as head dress, authority sign / shoulder dress, double heading
MC scale should be unwieldy, bigger than a cute pet
MC need to develop lifecycle processes

OS Shaman can generate so much material spew it out it creates a full reality in the moment
forces us to evaluate the worth of social reality cohesion, reality-creating power of shared belief, not just reason, reading signs contextually

ISSUES

OS: worth - determining something's worth
MC: enlightenment with social bounds
IC: thought, wandering
re: fantasy

Shaman sees volcano as animal / authority connected to human signs, meaningful, animated by connected forces
Vizier at end comes to see volcano as alien, unpredictable and not under any human influence, but forced to acknowledge meaning to humans is important

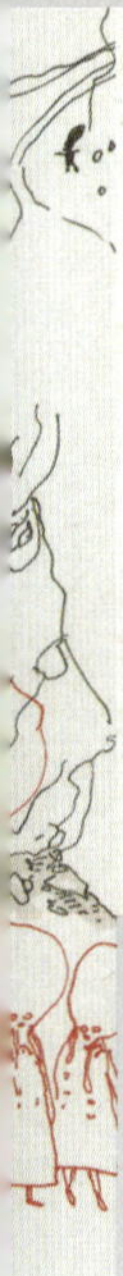

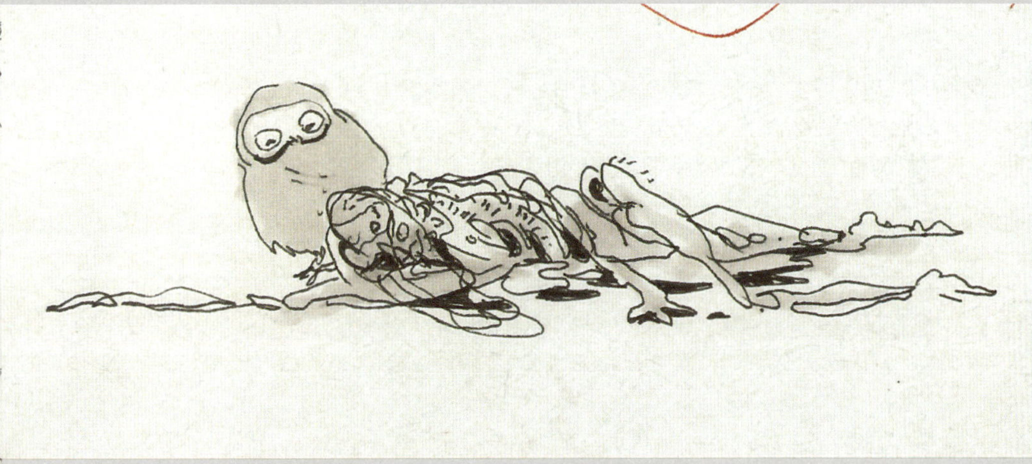

"meaningless but worth it"

need to LOVE feel empathy for all sides of the argument
can we understand another entity's behavior/instinct outside the meaning perspective of our own social reality?

How to encode thru-lines using VR, how to get objective POV? OS story POV? with field guide? with non perspective

human folly triggers natural disaster - SEEMS TO HAVE COME TRUE LOL
blaming new roads making SR of tribe more porous (spiritual contamination)

bicameralism - a technology that allows you to hear and act with another authority thru you
consciousness - a technology that allows you to project a mirror self, i, and examine past and future narrative of i

taru menyan tree covers smell of the dead
Dewa Ratu Gede Pancering Jagat - local deity

VOLCANO NOTES
seen as a petulance
animals moving downhill,
a bird moving down
move toward it, trance ritual around it
fixed view of tolerating volcano's behavior; mountain as living thing

**When will the volcano erupt, and exactly what will happen when it does?

and the streams thereof shall be turned into pitch, and the dust thereof into brimstone, and the land thereof shall become burning pitch. it shall not be quenched night nor day; the smoke thereof shall go up for ever: from generation to generation it shall lie waste; none shall pass through it for ever and ever

In gratitude for an eruption in 1917, young mothers went to the volcano and expressed their breast milk on the ground.

In 1979, Merapi erupted without warning, killing 149 people who lived in the mountain village of Dieng, 6,000 feet up on its side. Just days later, there were ominous stirrings from the Balinese volcano Agung. To appease the gods, Indonesia's president Suharto and his ministers took part in a ceremony at Bali in which 80 animals were sacrificed. Agung did not erupt.

The villagers in Kaliurang at the base of Merapi believe that by watching the corn grow or the birds fly they can predict the volcano's temperament. Such beliefs are troublesome to volcanologists whose scientific findings they challenge. On the other hand, they cannot prove that the ceremonies do not work. "I even believe some of it myself," said Sartono, a volcanologist on Merapi. "I talk to the mountain and I think she hears me."

"Knowledge is only rumour until it is in the muscle"

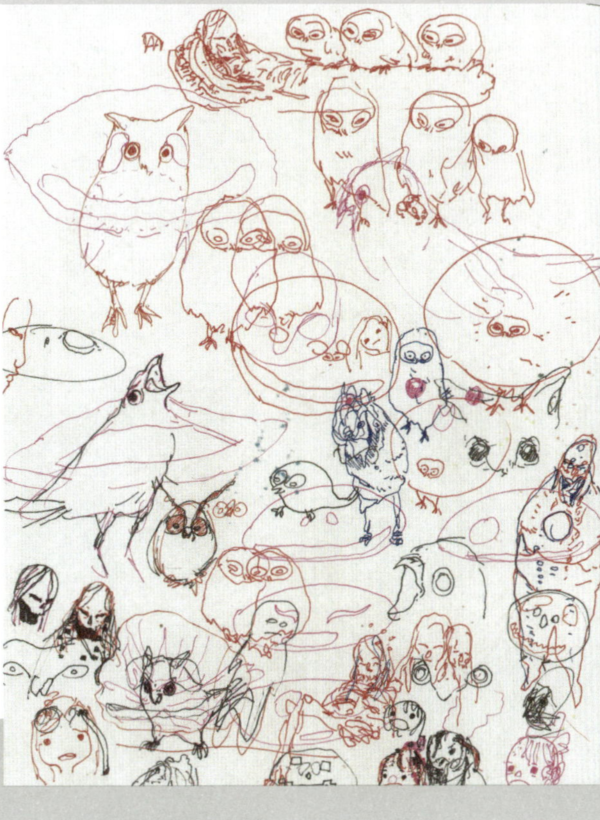

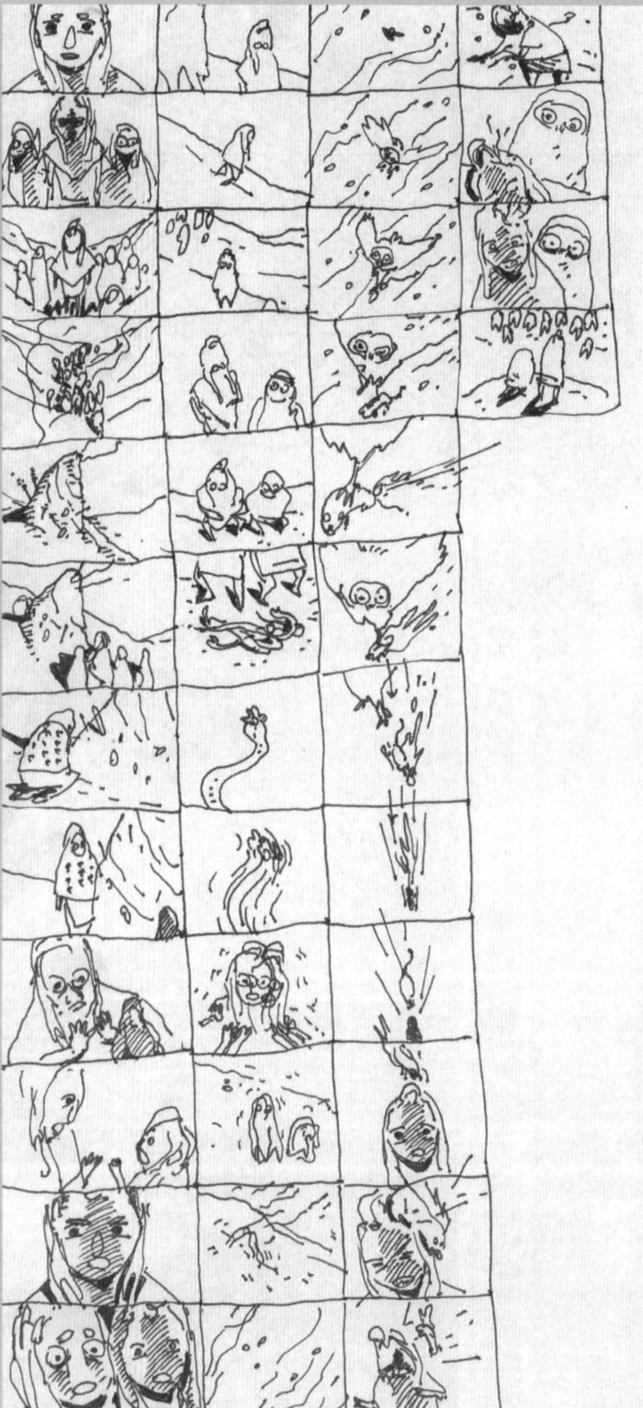

Bicameral Voices

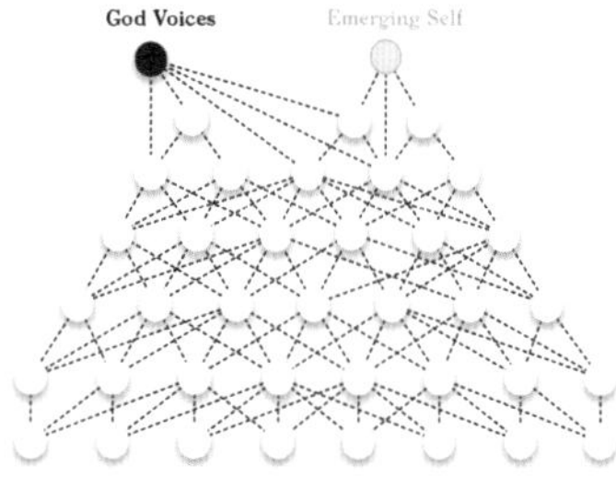

The Bicameral Brain

When confronted with a stressful situation, pre-conscious humans hallucinated the voices of parents, authority figures, and gods. Whatever the voices commanded, the body obeyed. Julian Jaynes called this mode of agency 'The Bicameral Mind.'

As complex civilizations evolved and bicamerality was no longer adaptive, consciousness emerged as the alternative mode of agency through the invention of metaphorical language and exposure to narrative practice.

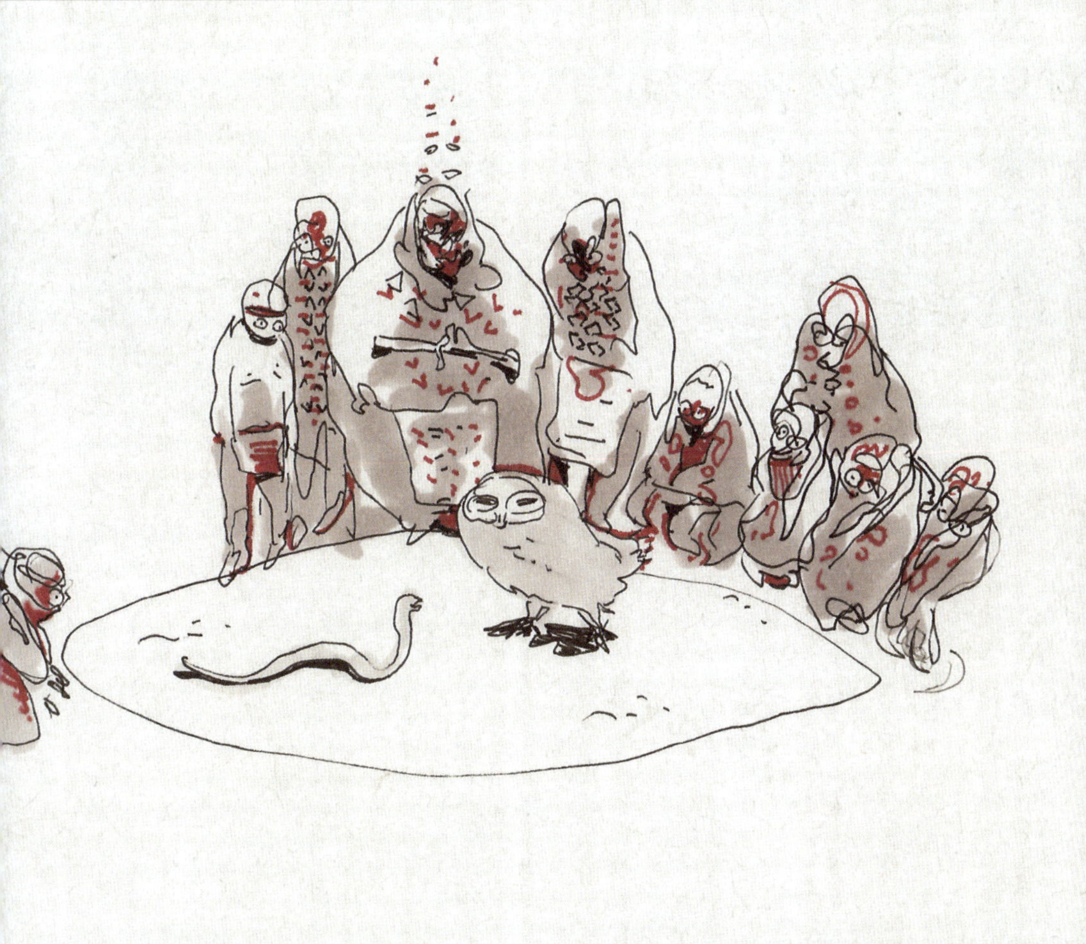

ISSUES

- Refocus on Pichaku as the main lens into this world - subjectively with Emissary, objectively with tribe/Shaman situation.

What does pichaku want? Is it a disaster profiteer, eating panicked animals and detritus?

Pichaku gets into some kind of habit neuro conditioning that is human-codependent - A voice or mime with Emissary for a specific food treat?

- Shaman needs to not be so stupid

Amidst activity between Pichaku and Emissary,

Shaman working on larger problem of volcano and dead king's influence, like the unconscious working in the background, collecting noise. But under the firm belief in voice technology and the rituals/ways of Dead King. To re-center his voices, he collects things in the ashen landscape that re-center/focus voices. Focused on ending the uncertainty of what to do. (Not acknowledging the unendingness of nature's changes requires that they be met with unending habit change / technology change / perspective change (conscious habit change)).

Maybe he is concerned with collecting objects processed thru pichaku, like regurgitated bones, excrement, that culminate in the cockfight?

host a cockfight to help resolve the volcano and bring everyone together. Has Em bet everything on it

Is shaman trying to tap-back into clear voices? Or is he trying to keep the group together? Is there something that anchors him to this site, instead of evacuating?

- Ending that resolves pichaku's basic thru-line (incorporating human-codependent habit with its own instincts?) while incidentally resolving Shaman and Emissary thru-line

PLAYERS

- **Pichaku** - a bird of paradise with slight morphing abilities, voice miming, can display patterns on plummage for turning into primitive emoticon (visually, an irresistable pokemon-like animal)
- **Shaman** - the channeler of past authority voices, like a celebrity/rapper, can hallucinate under stress and make decisions to resolve local issues. No ego. But cannot consciously change approach.
- **Emissary** - Shaman's apprentice, daughter of Shaman, 10yrs old, helps pass Shaman's word, delegate decisions to tribe

SCENE 1 - INTRO (routine language) - shaman focus or Em watching shaman

one shot - hyperlapse time passing, sun up sun down sun up sun down - routine routine chatter

- ANCHOR FOCUS - inside Shaman's canopy cover den, his green room, light from outside entering thru slits, near Shaman's head over his right shoulder, everything happens around him here, center of attention
- a habit interrupted by decision point: this or that, this or that, Dead King voice, that
- Shaman hearing deep voice of Dead King, settling dispute with two tribers
- triber hearing Shaman's voice, dropping objects in volcano lip
- triber hearing Shaman's voice, tribe throwing objects in ocean
- Shaman whispers to Emissary
- Emissary walks over to distant rooster cockfight, says something to tribe, a rooster dies.
- Emissary reporting back to Shaman
- the voices accumulate as a musical harmony - everything is grooving
- IMAGE OF DEAD KING HOLDING SHAMAN HOLDING EMISSARY
  - ***volcanic tremor***
- thru slits in distance an ash column emanating from volcano -
- all voices stop - silence - real time -
- everyone outside pauses and looks up, they hallucinate Shaman's calming authority voice: "listen to me:"—
- shaman emerges from den, considers it, hears Dead King's voice, then another, then another, building in his head
- total cacophony—

SCENE 2 (crashing + rat) - pichaku focus

up inside the all encompassing fog of ash cloud

- Pichaku flying holding rat
- rat screaming pathetic
- Pichaku looks at rat suffering, mimes back a weird cute face.
- Rat quiets at strangeness
- a random ash cinder catches rat on fire
- Pichaku forced to drop rat
- Pichaku tracks rat
- zoom follow - Flaming rat hits Emissary in the head - zoom back out to Pichaku
- Pichaku zooms toward fog spot where rat fell
- Pichaku crashes into tribe world.
- [black]

SCENE 3 (Pichaku & Em) - Shaman - taking stock , ground focus

- Dazed on the ground, Em and Pichaku look at each other. flaming dead rat off to side.
- Em right temple is burning/steaming (continues throughout entire story to steam).
- Em - voices grow silent [thought bubble diminishes, or goes grey, can't hear shaman]
- ***VOICES HAVE LEFT EM
- Shaman looks at Pichaku - the voices calm and come into focus, its the deep King's voice: "jsioadjais"
- Shaman says, "jsioadjais"
- Pichaku, emoji faces, echoes back "jsioadjais"
- Shaman startled (burning bush moment), we zoom out seeing things in larger perspective briefly
- zoom back in on same spot, Shaman looks back and Pichaku is gone from spot
- Shaman's voice cacophony begins to return
- Pichaku walking close to fallen Em, makes a cute morph.
- Pichaku tugs at one of Em's multiple royal jewelry shimmering face chain
- Em puts one face chain around Pichaku's neck
- Pichaku and Em symmetrical
- Pichaku mimes Em's head rotation
- Em clutches onto Pichaku.
- Pichaku tries to eat at dead rat.

SCENE 4 (status reshuffle - following)

- Pichaku says "DJSAIODJ" to Em, begins to walk

- Em la
- Some
  indeci
- Sham
  Sham
- Picha
- Pichal
- Pichal
- Pichal
- A rat
- Picha
- tribe c
- Em de

SCENE

- Sham
- Pichak
- Sham
- Pichak
- Sham
- Pichal
- Tribe
- Tribe
- Sham
- ***noi
- Pichak
- Triber
- Pichak
- Triber
- Pichal
- Tribe
- Em ha
- at Em
  tail, fig
- Pichal
- Em gc
- Em's t
- Some
- Pichak
- Em sn
- Sever

- Tribe
- Em's
- Em ta
- Tribe
- Em wh
- Em's
- Em: G

NEEDS REDRAFTING HERE

- Tribe all gathers obediently
- Em at loss for what to say next, a silence, everyone's thought bubble blanked out, or afraid
- in this silence shaman fills in, announces ceremony

***semi-circle forms, into cockfight scenario, shaman assumes MC role

Shaman picks up Pichaku and drops him into semi-circle?

Somehow when Em loses sight of pichaku, the absence of voices is more felt, she feels more alone.

SCENE 6 (ritual cockfight)

Pichaku dropped into center
The crowd has stacked on each other like ancient stadium seating, forming a tight undulating rotating circle. Each layer varies rotation like concentric rings.
Shaman squats off center - court side, Pichaku on one side

Em locked out of ring cannot penetrate thru crowd ring.
Ecstatic celebratory mood

- Someone tosses in a disoriented snake
Pichaku on crude leash forced into fight space

- No action
- Triber grabs snake's head and rubs a chili pepper in its mouth, and tosses it back joyfully, ecstatically
- Snake takes a shot at Pichaku
- Pichaku bites near Snake
- Snake strikes again

Em intervenes ritual fight with authority
Shaman is shocked by this behavior

- Em is scared, standing in between Pichaku and Shaman, intervening
- stressed out snake deciding which one to bite, sees fear in Em's face.
- Em makes big gesture fronting, but terrified in eyes
- Snake strikes at Em in her head wound getting stuck in it.
- Em falls over
- Someone jabs at Pichaku directly, Pichaku agitated
- Snake struggles stuck to Em's head
- Pichaku bites the snake in half, it stops wriggling
- Shaman tries to pry out snake from Em's scalp
- Em anger grabs Pichaku clutches, struggles away
- Em runs up toward volcano lip with Pichaku

SCENE 7 (Em and Pichaku alone on rim run)

- up on the volcano lip trail
- the drone of geological sound silences everything
- Em alone away from human culture, running along vast rim lip of volcano
- Em hallucinates herself growing, Pichaku growing, growing into adulthood, together, avatars of each other.
- Em is a fierce Amazonian and Pichaku is a majestic dinosaur/ - maybe become more like icons?
- Em talks aloud to Pichaku in this fantasy, her missing voice double.
- Em stops running, stops hallucinating, her current self, Pichaku's current self
- They take in the vast awe-inspiring landscape before them
- Em kneels
- Em takes off tribal jewelry, discarding it on ground.
- Em looks at pichaku.
- Pichaku looks at Em.
- Em unleashes Pichaku's chains.
- !!! Without hesitation Pichaku dispassionately flies off, some feathers frazzle molt off, immediately left in wake

SCENE 8

- We follow along with pichaku, Em getting distant
- Em's face starts to well up but unclear which way her emotional resolve goes - illegible as we get more distant with Pichaku
- Pichaku flies near the steaming ashy center pit, near volcano hole -
- We see a world really without any living human influence, all simulation, It's own brutal mini game
- We see human sediment layer cross section
- We see dead king body abandoned
- Pichaku walks by a same species snake trying to crawl up volcano side. Snake doesn't care want to fight too busy trying to swallow something
- Just a wild simulation of unmediated reality - a win a loss a win a loss without emotional continuity or applied meaning

Em watches pichaku from lip - sim city perspective distance
Shaman finds her and kneels down with her
They watch distant nature simulation and contemplate it aloud like live ESPN commentators
***they begin to have some perspective—

Pichaku digs around.
finds eggs incubating in the ash
finds another installment of eggs
unclear which ones belong to it
**ash steam harrasses Pichaku
has to decide, not sure?
(we need to see pichaku tested in isolation during stress conditions)
***maybe pichaku sees volcano steam as sentience adversary, harrassing Pichaku with hot ash grabs, Pichaku ready to bite at it, attack it

Em throws a rock at pichaku (like a distant more 'real' relationship to pichaku now)
it barely reaches where pichaku is
Em whispers into shamans ear
Shaman throws a rock (or jewelry?) much farther
rock jewelry lands near pichaku

walks side by side with Pichaku
other kids. (others continue on their own to be scattered in
red in ash) (Shaman gets no attention, confused about status)
er than Pichaku, Pichaku turning opposite vector when
aku, Shaman slowing down and put in place of a follower.
ground with an overhang covering, no ash here.
everybody.
les ***AI
nce.
ance.
and eats it, reverse vomit choking motion down. absolute.
egurgitates bones immediately.

xorcist)
no will erupt *mimes some volcano gesture

ays

e ash, asks for Pichaku's judgement.

hands, tossing ash.
Pichaku
ingly, strange to Emissary.

n
ase

nom face ***Em starts to see something is off, not working
Em sees little rodent shitting, kicking up dust, chasing its own

s
nd forth seeing random behavior of both animals
throbs color? *intuits the randomness of this)
grabs at Pichaku aggressively.

ets enraged, takes step forward btw Pichaku and tribe
s space
olcano tremor** **adrenaline rush
chaotic chatter cloud returns
es ownership of tremor)
nimes, like possessed total animal exorcist.
n
ring out space
ing
EN

Pichaku's emoticon sign communicates to Em and Shaman
We see Pichaku's POV, Em and Shaman in distance, sim city

maybe Em's voice hearing needs to come back but as a proto-ego-self. Em hears her voice double as herself not another authority - like two Em's. her voice is the first to introduce negativity judgement low self esteem etc, and delusional power
some kind of burden of consciousness that requires her to definitely be a part of the tribe and socialized to keep it in check...

Pyroclastic flow blow out

- pyroclastic flow avalanche may or may not wipe the tribe out here
- Pichaku flies above. Just another day for Pichaku!

ICHAKU'S PERFECT DAY (PLAY?)

LAYERS
Pichaku - a bird of paradise with slight morphing abilities, voice miming, can display patterns on plummage for turning into primitive emoticon (visually, an irresistable pokemon-like animal)
Shaman - the channeler of past authority voices, like a celebrity/rapper, can hallucinate under stress and make decisions to resolve local issues
Emissary - Shaman's apprentice, daughter of Shaman, 10yrs old, helps pass Shaman's word, delegate decisions to tribe

EVISE INTRO SIMPLER
CENE 1 - INTRO (routine language) - shaman focus or Em watching shaman
ne shot - hyperlapse time passing, sun up sun down sun up sun down - routine routine chatter
ANCHOR FOCUS - inside Shaman's canopy cover den, light from outside entering thru slits, near Shaman's head over his right shoulder, everything happens around him here, center of attention
a habit interrupted by decision point: this or that, this or that, Dead King voice, that
Shaman hearing deep voice of Dead King, settling dispute with two tribers
triber hearing Shaman's voice, dropping objects in volcano lip
triber hearing Shaman's voice, tribe throwing objects in ocean
Shaman whispers to Emissary
Emissary walks over to distant rooster cockfight, says something to tribe, a rooster dies.
Emissary reporting back to Shaman
the voices accumulate as a musical harmony - everything is grooving
volcanic tremor
thru slits in distance an ash column emanating from volcano -
all voices stop - silence - real time -
everyone outside pauses and looks up, they hallucinate Shaman's calming authority voice: "listen to me:"—
shaman emerges from den, considers it, hears Dead King's voice, then another, then another, building in his head
total cacophony—

CENE 2 (crashing + rat) - pichaku focus
p inside the all encompassing fog of ash cloud
Pichaku flying holding rat
rat screaming pathetic
Pichaku looks at rat suffering, mimes back a weird cute face.
Rat quiets at strangeness
a random ash cinder catches rat on fire
Pichaku forced to drop rat
Pichaku tracks rat
zoom follow - Flaming rat hits Emissary in the head - zoom back out to Pichaku
Pichaku zooms toward fog spot where rat fell
Pichaku crashes into tribe world.
[black]

CENE 3 (Pichaku & Em) - Shaman - taking stock , ground focus
Dazed on the ground, Em and Pichaku look at each other, flaming dead rat btw them.

- Em right temple is burning/steaming (continues throughout entire story to steam).
- Em - voices grow silent [thought bubble diminishes, or goes grey, can't hear shaman]
- ***VOICES HAVE LEFT EM
- Shaman looks at Pichaku - the voices calm and come into focus, its the deep King's voice: "jsioadjais"
- Shaman says, "jsioadjais"
- Pichaku echoes back "jsioadjais"
- Shaman startled (burning bush moment), we zoom out seeing things in larger perspective
- zoom back in on same spot, Shaman looks back and Pichaku is gone from spot
- Pichaku walking close to fallen Em, makes a cute morph.
- Pichaku tugs at one of Em's multiple royal jewelry shimmering face chain
- Em puts one face chain around Pichaku's neck
- Pichaku and Em symmetrical
- Pichaku mimes Em
- Em clutches onto Pichaku.
- Pichaku tries to eat at dead rat.

SCENE 4 (status reshuffle - following) - Pichaku focus in crowd
- Pichaku says "DJSAIODJ" to Em, begins to walk
- Em latches on to jewelry chain, walks side by side with Pichaku
- Some intrigued and follow. (others continue on their own to be scattered in indecision and confusion, covered in ash) (Shaman gets no attention, confused about status)
- Shaman walks faster then slower than Pichaku, Pichaku turning opposite vector when Shaman walks faster than Pichaku, Shaman slowing down and put in place of a follower.
- Pichaku walks to slightly higher ground with an overhang covering, no ash here.
- Pichaku pauses looks back at everybody.
- Pichaku clears away little pebbles ***AI
- Pichaku does a little mating dance.
- A rat scurries by, interrupting dance.
- Pichaku immediately crushes it and eats it, reverse vomit choking motion down. absolute.
- tribe and shaman ooo's at this absolution.
- Em delighted, pets her Pichaku.

SCENE 5 (Pichaku as inner voice - Em exorcist)
- Shaman asks Pichaku: if volcano will erupt *mimes some volcano gesture
- Pichaku is blank
- Shaman asks a few different ways
- Pichaku blank
- Shaman draws something in the ash, asks for Pichaku's judgement.
- Pichaku kicks the ash drawing.
- Tribe copies gesture in ash with hands, tossing ash.
- Tribe looks to Volcano, looks to Pichaku
- Shaman asks another question
- ***noisy thought bubbles
- Pichaku mimes randomly
- Triber asks non-related question
- Pichaku echoes some prior phrase
- Triber huh?

andrej
thank you for agreeing to take a stab at this.

I am making a children's animation for VR displays, approx 30min long.

SUMMARY
We take the perspective of a bird of paradise that gets entangled with an ancient tribe of humans faced with a volcanic threat. The shaman of the tribe casts the bird as a symbol / incarnation of authority/celebrity, projecting onto the bird what it is they should do. Simultaneously, the shaman's daughter casts the bird as her pet, projecting onto the bird a deep interpersonal connection, like a child and its pokemon. The bird of course is dispassionate to human affairs, just a bird with its own habits and instincts.

SHORT NOTES

Their main defining feature which governs and influences everything about their lives is that they do not possess consciousness. Instead, in times of stress and uncertainty, when difficult decisions/risks have to be made, they hear vocal hallucinations of past authorities - parents, priests, kings, dead kings, gods. This is based on Julian Jaynes' book *The Origin Of Consciousness in the Breakdown of the Bicameral Mind.*
http://en.wikipedia.org/wiki/Bicameralism_%28psychology%29

For our purposes, we can think of the hallucinating bicameral mind as an ancient app inside the brain of early humans. In contrast, consciousness as you and i experience it (introspection, weighing pros and cons, imagining possible futures, having an ego "i" to project and storytell a situation) can be thought of, modestly, as simply a newer brain app for handling the stress of decision-making and facing uncertainty.

Our tribe here is the moment in human evolutionary history AFTER language but BEFORE consciousness. It is a society governed by a psychosocial technology for dealing with human groups larger than what one authority figure can manage. Authority is a shared hallucination (neither positive or negative, simply the nature of things in this era).

LONG BACKGROUND NOTES ON BICAMERAL TRIBE

Think of them as human bodies with a different software growing inside their head. they are not introspectively conscious and have no sense of "i" or ego or self. they are creatures of habit. their evolutionary innovation is that when confronted with a new problem or uncertainty, they hear vocal hallucination - voices - of past authority figures (parent, shaman, king, gods, animals, statue idols) who directly and unambiguously tell them what to do, what action to take. gods are not departed into the sky yet, they are here grounded with us and accessible by a bicameral human. life for a bicameral human never feels alone, it is full of chatter and hallucinated socializing. like being a part of a voice-command network, or ancient imagined wifi. you are connected. music and continuous talking help to solidify this state. this mind is not capable of long-term planned strategy, only an increasingly complex accruement of situational habits. a god or a voice or a phrase for every problem. there is no clear sense of time or history as a progression. with no sense of time, there is no sense of projection or time-based emotions:

there is shame but no guilt, anger but no hatred/revenge, fear but no anxiety, affiliation but no love, sex but no fantasizing, no deceit or long-term trickery. only a few important people have names; hard to project about something if it does not have a name. everything is present in the moment and every influential past human is still alive with you and able to talk to you immediately. it is important we feel and see this as a remarkable - if strange - evolutionary development for social organisms (not insanity or crazy deux ex behavior). it is the origins of religion but we should see it as a landmark psychosocial technology in the history of natural evolution. we take possession and spirits and gods talking to us at face value as a neurological feature for dealing with the insults of reality in this ancient era. the vulnerability of this brain technology is that it needs social and cultural insularity to really work effectively and stabilize large groups. too much foreign intrusion happening too rapidly too complexly results in mixed voice messages, freak outs, contradictory messages, that end in death or harm to the tribe. historically, before the evolution of subjective consciousness, human bicameral settlements would chaotically unravel back into more primitive subgroups when social life became too complex and after many years re-emerge into a new bicameral kingdom in the same settlement lands, back and forth back and forth. status is very hierarchical and implicit in everything. There is no conscious questioning of hierarchy.

For purposes of this story, all these bicameral characteristics can be thought of as the overall habit profile / crutch technology of the tribe. they are fixed minded about this bc they literally cannot imagine another way of being, thinking, existing, experiencing. Visually, they will look like humans slightly warped, with animal/animistic inflection. when a bicameral man hallucinates a voice during a decision-making moment, we see a doubling of bodies where the doubled body is slightly larger and a warped version between the bicameral man and how the authority looks. the doubled body morphs and merges into the man. for example, this picture shows a smaller king and his hallucinated god double who literally holds his hand and moves it for him.

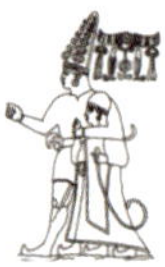

via these brief doublings and morphs we can visually observe a bicameral human making a decision. everyone is channeling and morphing into other personalities to face the needs of the situation. it is not crazy or schizophrenia. it should feel and look more adaptive and amazing and alien than schizophrenia.

- Em and Shaman look down the fog of ash rain refracting away in sunrise. sees tribe like scattered ants.
- ***a tremor
- Em slides dead king's body down side of mountain, skiiing on ash, toward tribe.
- In front of gathering tribe
- Em whispers into ear
- Shaman says what to do "5"
- Em cuts his head / marking to match her own on opposite hemisphere, a new ritual branding in head
- new harmony sound

***SHAMAN AND EM CHILD - imagines a child
somehow Pichaku adds some finishing touch to this idea, like sings a song
***Pichaku tries to mate with random animal

Pyroclastic flow blow out

- pyroclastic flow avalanche may or may not wipe the tribe out here
- Pichaku flies above. Just another day for Pichaku!

SOME INITIAL CONCEPT ART I HAD ANDREJ DO TO GIVE YOU FEEL =

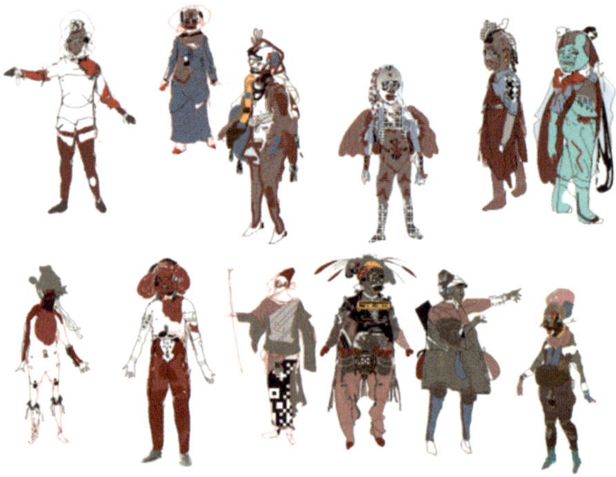

Hallucinations neurologically come from the right-brain. For clarity, our tribe, should imagine hearing hallucinated voices from the left-ear. So visually, there should be some kind of emphasis related to the left side of the body, or at least the left side of the head and shoulder? at the very least, for tribe members lower on the social hierarchy, there should be assymmetry in their adornments and clothing.

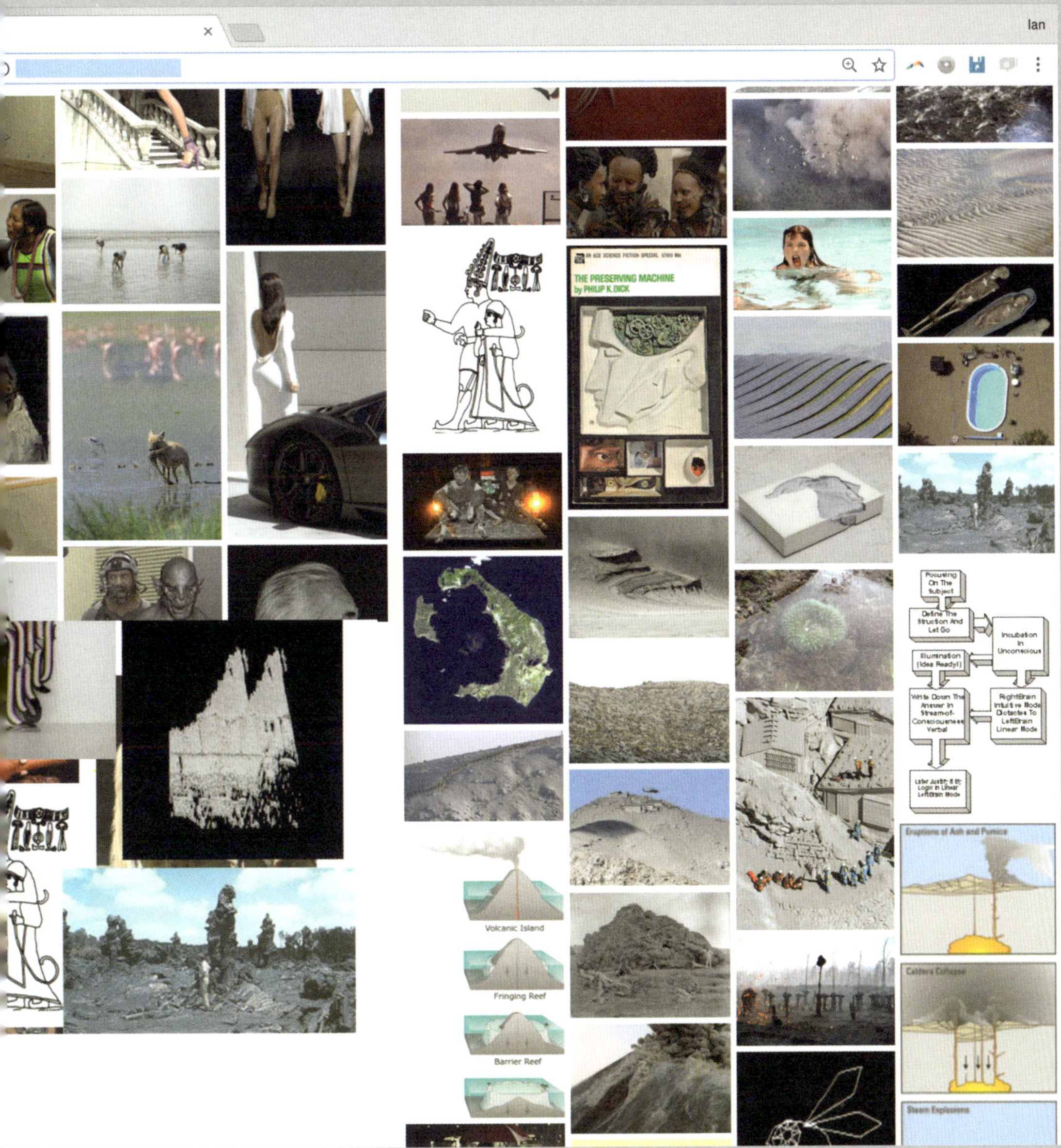
Ian
THE PRESERVING MACHINE
by PHILIP K. DICK
Focusing On The Subject
Define The Struction And Let Go
Incubation In Unconscious
Illumination (Idea Ready!)
Write Down The Answer In Stream-of-Consciousness Verbal
RightBrain Intuitive Mode Dictates To LeftBrain Linear Mode
Volcanic Island
Fringing Reef
Barrier Reef
Eruptions of Ash and Pumice
Caldera Collapse
Steam Explosions

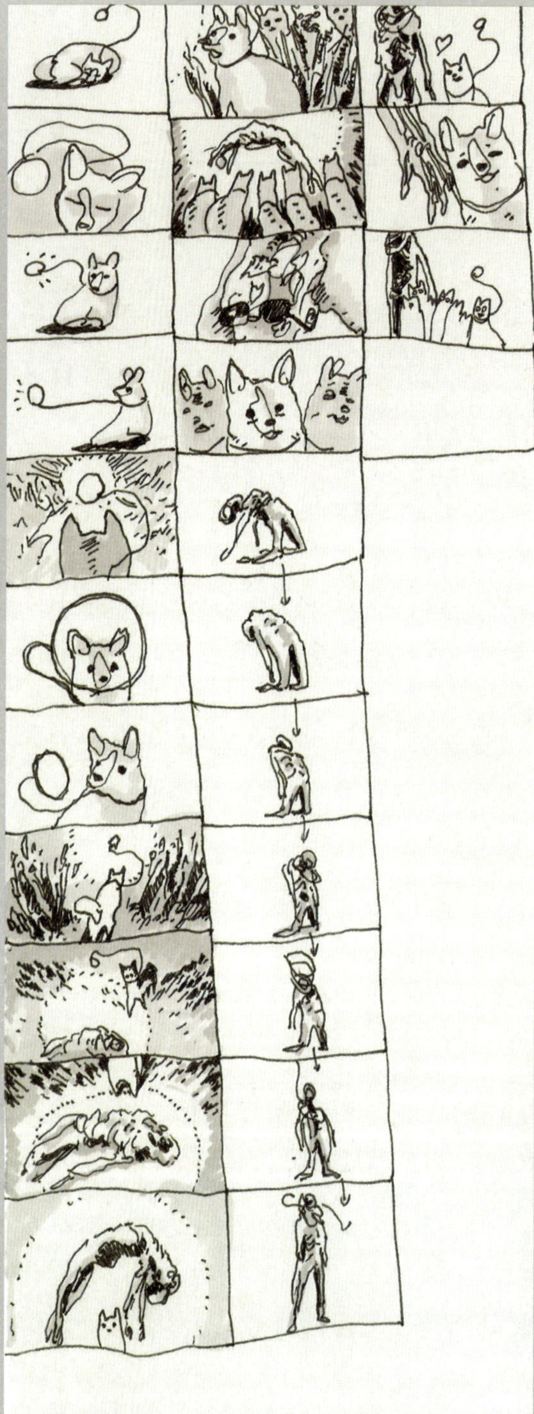

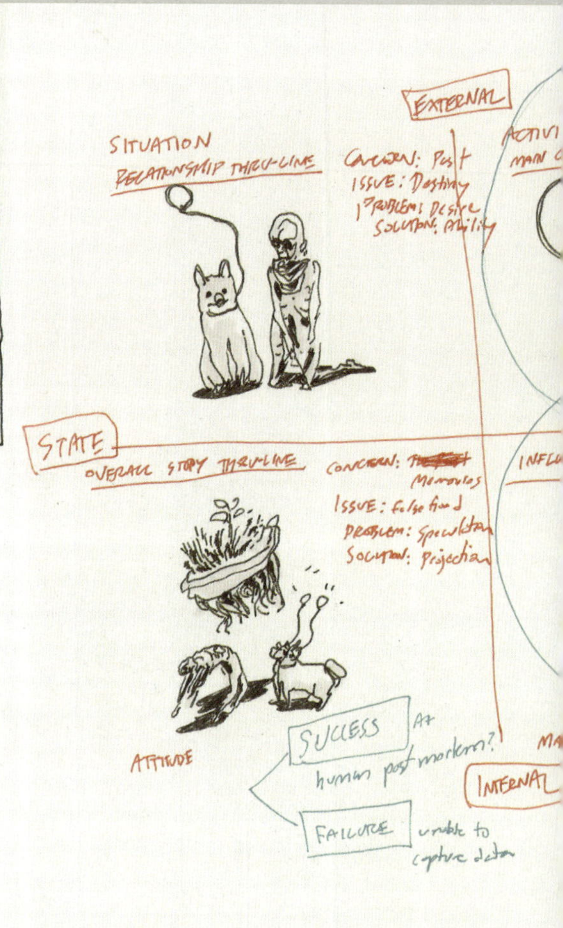
EXTERNAL
SITUATION
RELATIONSHIP THRU-LINE
CONCERN: Past
ISSUE: Destiny
PROBLEM: Desire
SOLUTION: Ability
STATE
OVERALL STORY THRU-LINE
CONCERN: Memories
ISSUE: False find
PROBLEM: Speculation
SOLUTION: Projection
ATTITUDE
SUCCESS
AI human post mortem?
INTERNAL
FAILURE
unable to capture data

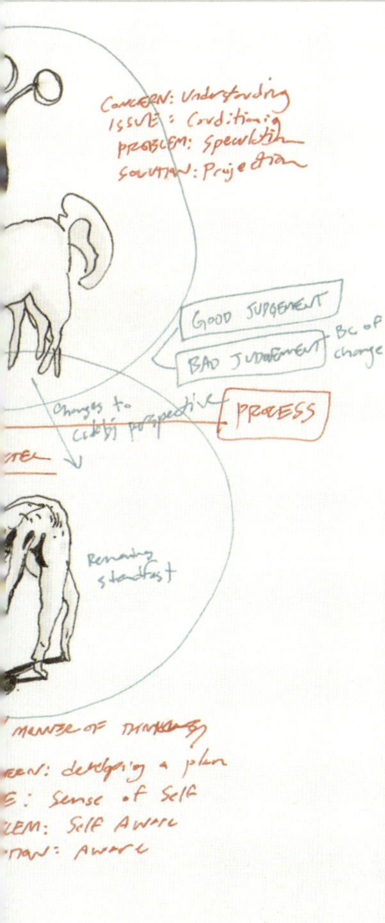

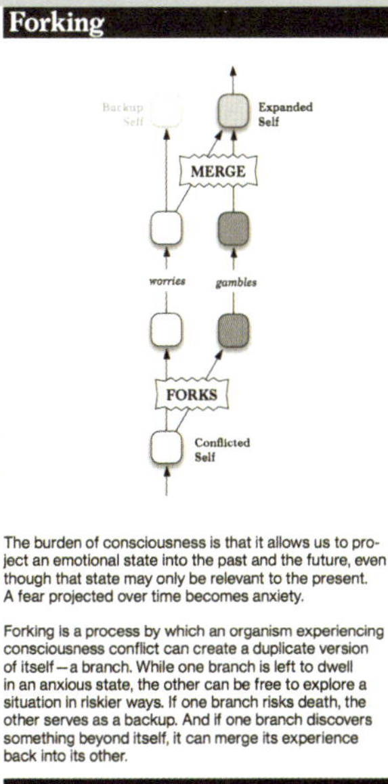

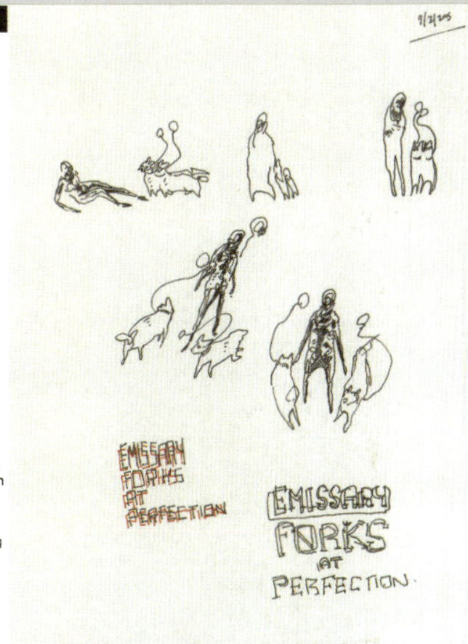

Episode 2 would feature the relationship between the last specimen of original human matter – a distant descendant of the ancient community – and some kind of dog super-pet. Their encounter would be organised by a higher intelligence, like a controlling reality TV show producer. The pet would be able to talk and be more knowledgeable about the landscape than the human. We'd watch the human's status shrink and the pet's status grow, even though neither wants this dynamic. Worried, the pet forks itself to try the relationship again and again and again.

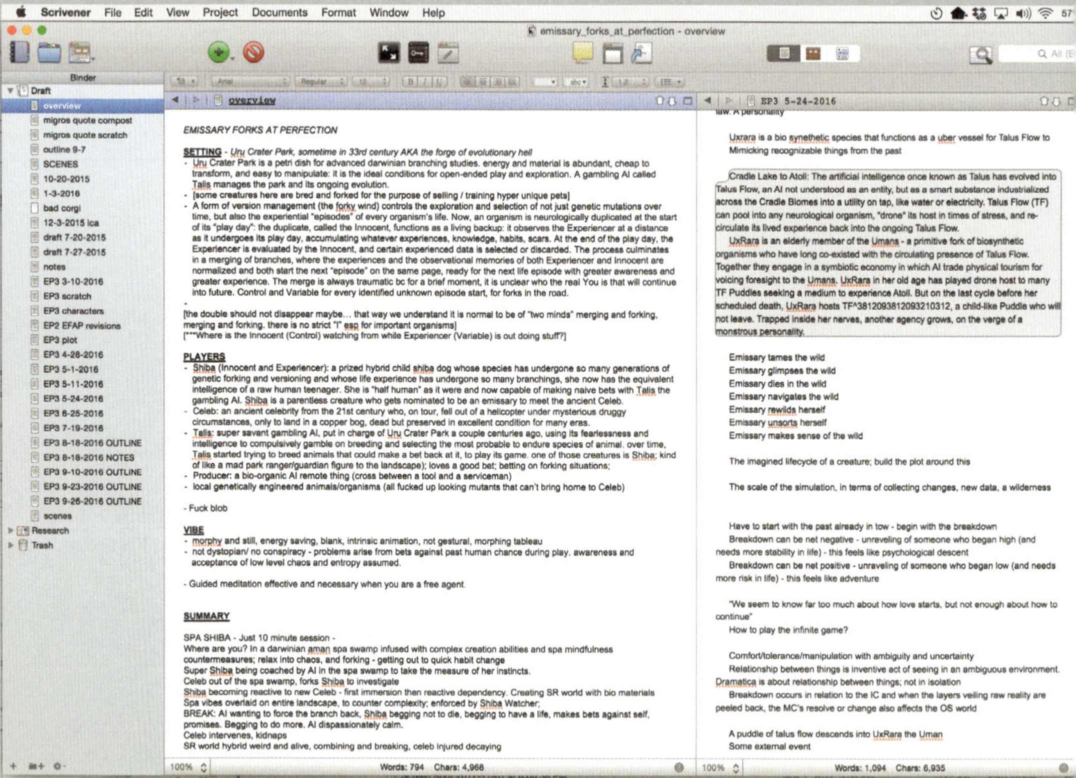
Scrivener File Edit View Project Documents Format Window Help
emissary_forks_at_perfection - overview
Binder
Draft
overview
migros quote compost
migros quote scratch
outline 9-7
SCENES
10-20-2015
1-3-2016
bad corgi
12-3-2015 ica
draft 7-20-2015
draft 7-27-2015
notes
EP3 3-10-2016
EP3 scratch
EP3 characters
EP2 EFAP revisions
EP3 plot
EP3 4-28-2016
EP3 5-1-2016
EP3 5-11-2016
EP3 5-24-2016
EP3 6-25-2016
EP3 7-19-2016
EP3 8-18-2016 OUTLINE
EP3 8-18-2016 NOTES
EP3 9-10-2016 OUTLINE
EP3 9-23-2016 OUTLINE
EP3 9-26-2016 OUTLINE
scenes
Research
Trash
overview
EMISSARY FORKS AT PERFECTION
SETTING - Uru Crater Park, sometime in 33rd century AKA the forge of evolutionary hell
- Uru Crater Park is a petri dish for advanced darwinian branching studies. energy and material is abundant, cheap to transform, and easy to manipulate: it is the ideal conditions for open-ended play and exploration. A gambling AI called Talis manages the park and its ongoing evolution.
- [some creatures here are bred and forked for the purpose of selling / training hyper unique pets]
- A form of version management (the forky wind) controls the exploration and selection of not just genetic mutations over time, but also the experiential "episodes" of every organism's life. Now, an organism is neurologically duplicated at the start of its "play day": the duplicate, called the Innocent, functions as a living backup: it observes the Experiencer at a distance as it undergoes its play day, accumulating whatever experiences, knowledge, habits, scars. At the end of the play day, the Experiencer is evaluated by the Innocent, and certain experienced data is selected or discarded. The process culminates in a merging of branches, where the experiences and the observational memories of both Experiencer and Innocent are normalized and both start the next "episode" on the same page, ready for the next life episode with greater awareness and greater experience. The merge is always traumatic bc for a brief moment, it is unclear who the real You is that will continue into future. Control and Variable for every identified unknown episode start, for forks in the road.
-
[the double should not disappear maybe… that way we understand it is normal to be of "two minds" merging and forking, merging and forking. there is no strict "I" esp for important organisms]
[***Where is the Innocent (Control) watching from while Experiencer (Variable) is out doing stuff?]
PLAYERS
- Shiba (Innocent and Experiencer): a prized hybrid child shiba dog whose species has undergone so many generations of genetic forking and versioning and whose life experience has undergone so many branchings, she now has the equivalent intelligence of a raw human teenager. She is "half human" as it were and now capable of making naive bets with Talis the gambling AI. Shiba is a parentless creature who gets nominated to be an emissary to meet the ancient Celeb.
- Celeb: an ancient celebrity from the 21st century who, on tour, fell out of a helicopter under mysterious druggy circumstances, only to land in a copper bog, dead but preserved in excellent condition for many eras.
- Talis: super savant gambling AI, put in charge of Uru Crater Park a couple centuries ago, using its fearlessness and intelligence to compulsively gamble on breeding and selecting the most probable to endure species of animal. over time, Talis started trying to breed animals that could make a bet back at it, to play its game. one of those creatures is Shiba; kind of like a mad park ranger/guardian figure to the landscape); loves a good bet; betting on forking situations;
- Producer: a bio-organic AI remote thing (cross between a tool and a serviceman)
- local genetically engineered animals/organisms (all fucked up looking mutants that can't bring home to Celeb)
- Fuck blob
VIBE
- morphy and still, energy saving, blank, intrinsic animation, not gestural, morphing tableau
- not dystopian/ no conspiracy - problems arise from bets against past human chance during play. awareness and acceptance of low level chaos and entropy assumed.
- Guided meditation effective and necessary when you are a free agent.
SUMMARY
SPA SHIBA - Just 10 minute session -
Where are you? In a darwinian aman spa swamp infused with complex creation abilities and spa mindfulness countermeasures; relax into chaos, and forking - getting out to quick habit change
Super Shiba being coached by AI in the spa swamp to take the measure of her instincts.
Celeb out of the spa swamp, forks Shiba to investigate
Shiba becoming reactive to new Celeb - first immersion then reactive dependency. Creating SR world with bio materials
Spa vibes overlaid on entire landscape, to counter complexity; enforced by Shiba Watcher;
BREAK: AI wanting to force the branch back, Shiba begging not to die, begging to have a life, makes bets against self, promises. Begging to do more. AI dispassionately calm.
Celeb intervenes, kidnaps
SR world hybrid weird and alive, combining and breaking, celeb injured decaying
100% Words: 794 Chars: 4,968
EP3 5-24-2016
Uxrara is a bio synethetic species that functions as a uber vessel for Talus Flow to Mimicking recognizable things from the past
Cradle Lake to Atoll: The artificial intelligence once known as Talus has evolved into Talus Flow, an AI not understood as an entity, but as a smart substance industrialized across the Cradle Biomes into a utility on tap, like water or electricity. Talus Flow (TF) can pool into any neurological organism, "drone" its host in times of stress, and re-circulate its lived experience back into the ongoing Talus Flow.
UxRara is an elderly member of the Umans - a primitive fork of biosynthetic organisms who have long co-existed with the circulating presence of Talus Flow. Together they engage in a symbiotic economy in which AI trade physical tourism for voicing foresight to the Umans. UxRara in her old age has played drone host to many TF Puddles seeking a medium to experience Atoll. But on the last cycle before her scheduled death, UxRara hosts TF^381209381209321031 2, a child-like Puddle who will not leave. Trapped inside her nerves, another agency grows, on the verge of a monstrous personality.
Emissary tames the wild
Emissary glimpses the wild
Emissary dies in the wild
Emissary navigates the wild
Emissary rewilds herself
Emissary unsorts herself
Emissary makes sense of the wild
The imagined lifecycle of a creature; build the plot around this
The scale of the simulation, in terms of collecting changes, new data, a wilderness
Have to start with the past already in tow - begin with the breakdown
Breakdown can be net negative - unraveling of someone who began high (and needs more stability in life) - this feels like psychological descent
Breakdown can be net positive - unraveling of someone who began low (and needs more risk in life) - this feels like adventure
"We seem to know far too much about how love starts, but not enough about how to continue"
How to play the infinite game?
Comfort/tolerance/manipulation with ambiguity and uncertainty
Relationship between things is inventive act of seeing in an ambiguous environment. Dramatica is about relationship between things; not in isolation
Breakdown occurs in relation to the IC and when the layers veiling raw reality are peeled back, the MC's resolve or change also affects the OS world
A puddle of talus flow descends into UxRara the Uman
Some external event
100% Words: 1,094 Chars: 6,935

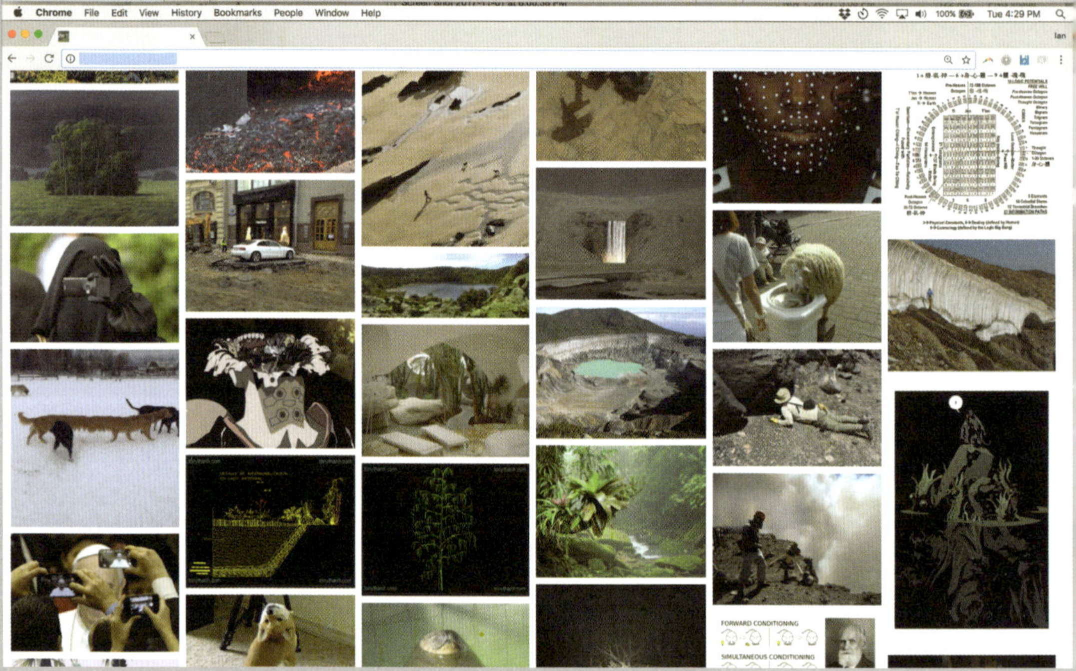
Chrome File Edit View History Bookmarks People Window Help
100% Tue 4:29 PM
Ian
FORWARD CONDITIONING
SIMULTANEOUS CONDITIONING

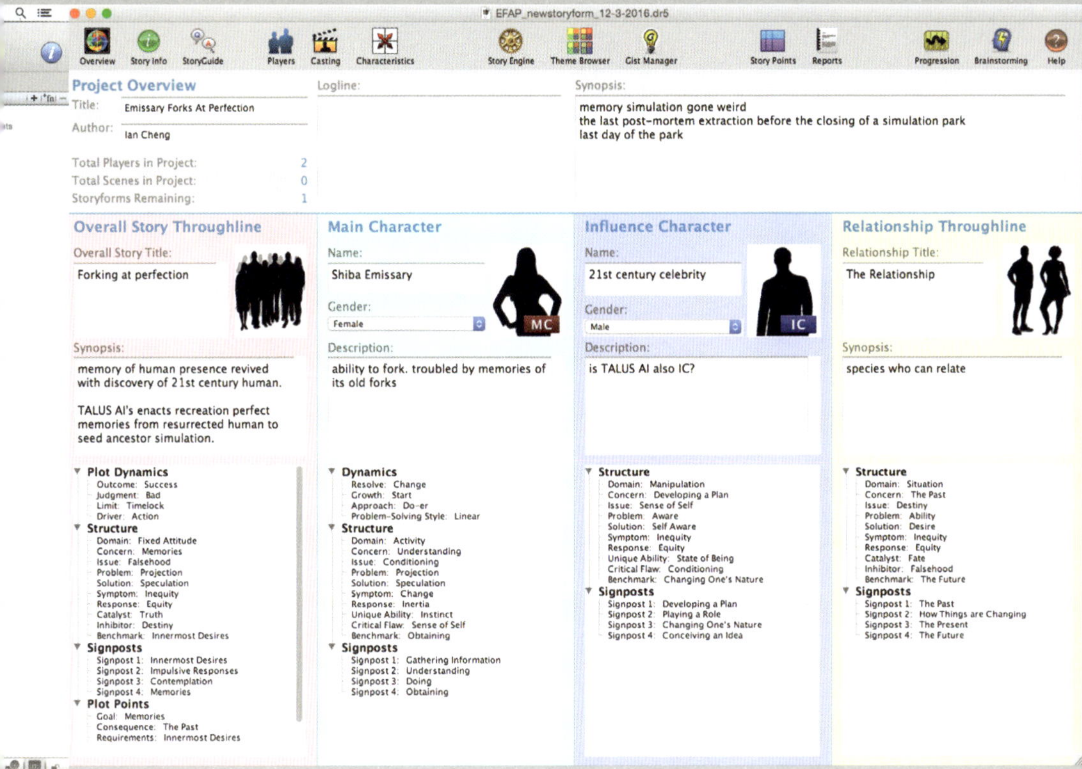
EFAP_newstoryform_12-3-2016.drs
Overview
Story Info
StoryGuide
Players
Casting
Characteristics
Story Engine
Theme Browser
Gist Manager
Story Points
Reports
Progression
Brainstorming
Help
Project Overview
Title: Emissary Forks At Perfection
Author: Ian Cheng
Total Players in Project: 2
Total Scenes in Project: 0
Storyforms Remaining: 1
Logline:
Synopsis:
memory simulation gone weird
the last post-mortem extraction before the closing of a simulation park
last day of the park
Overall Story Throughline
Overall Story Title:
Forking at perfection
Synopsis:
memory of human presence revived with discovery of 21st century human.
TALUS AI's enacts recreation perfect memories from resurrected human to seed ancestor simulation.
Plot Dynamics
Outcome: Success
Judgment: Bad
Limit: Timelock
Driver: Action
Structure
Domain: Fixed Attitude
Concern: Memories
Issue: Falsehood
Problem: Projection
Solution: Speculation
Symptom: Inequity
Response: Equity
Catalyst: Truth
Inhibitor: Destiny
Benchmark: Innermost Desires
Signposts
Signpost 1: Innermost Desires
Signpost 2: Impulsive Responses
Signpost 3: Contemplation
Signpost 4: Memories
Plot Points
Goal: Memories
Consequence: The Past
Requirements: Innermost Desires
Main Character
Name:
Shiba Emissary
Gender:
Female
MC
Description:
ability to fork. troubled by memories of its old forks
Dynamics
Resolve: Change
Growth: Start
Approach: Do-er
Problem-Solving Style: Linear
Structure
Domain: Activity
Concern: Understanding
Issue: Conditioning
Problem: Projection
Solution: Speculation
Symptom: Change
Response: Inertia
Unique Ability: Instinct
Critical Flaw: Sense of Self
Benchmark: Obtaining
Signposts
Signpost 1: Gathering Information
Signpost 2: Understanding
Signpost 3: Doing
Signpost 4: Obtaining
Influence Character
Name:
21st century celebrity
Gender:
Male
IC
Description:
is TALUS AI also IC?
Structure
Domain: Manipulation
Concern: Developing a Plan
Issue: Sense of Self
Problem: Aware
Solution: Self Aware
Symptom: Inequity
Response: Equity
Unique Ability: State of Being
Critical Flaw: Conditioning
Benchmark: Changing One's Nature
Signposts
Signpost 1: Developing a Plan
Signpost 2: Playing a Role
Signpost 3: Changing One's Nature
Signpost 4: Conceiving an Idea
Relationship Throughline
Relationship Title:
The Relationship
Synopsis:
species who can relate
Structure
Domain: Situation
Concern: The Past
Issue: Destiny
Problem: Ability
Solution: Desire
Symptom: Inequity
Response: Equity
Catalyst: Fate
Inhibitor: Falsehood
Benchmark: The Future
Signposts
Signpost 1: The Past
Signpost 2: How Things are Changing
Signpost 3: The Present
Signpost 4: The Future

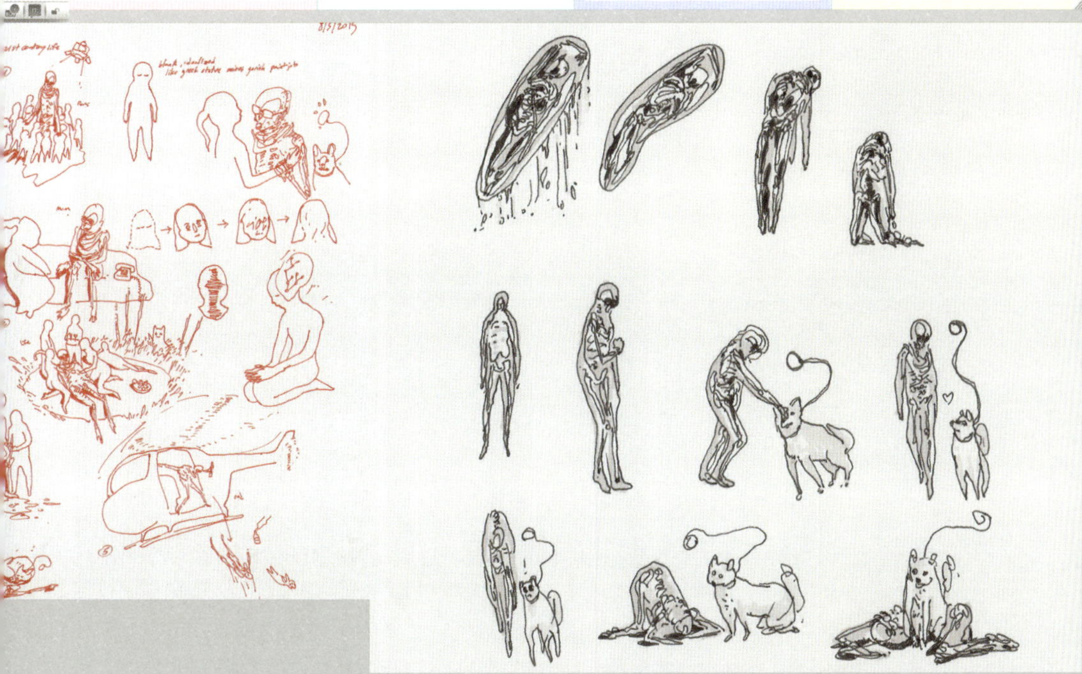

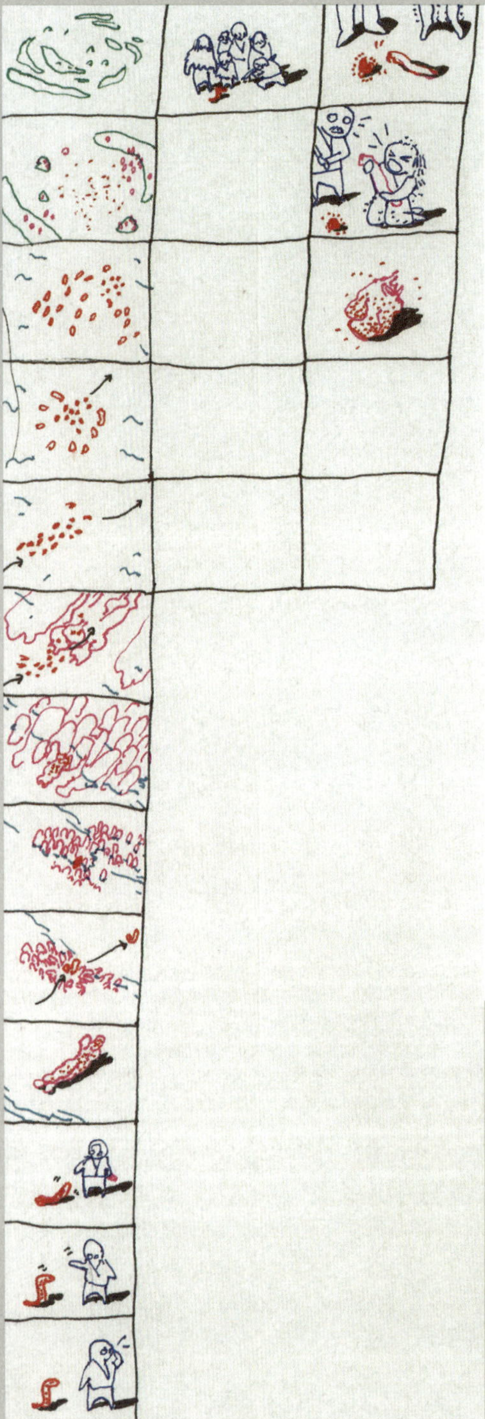

Droning

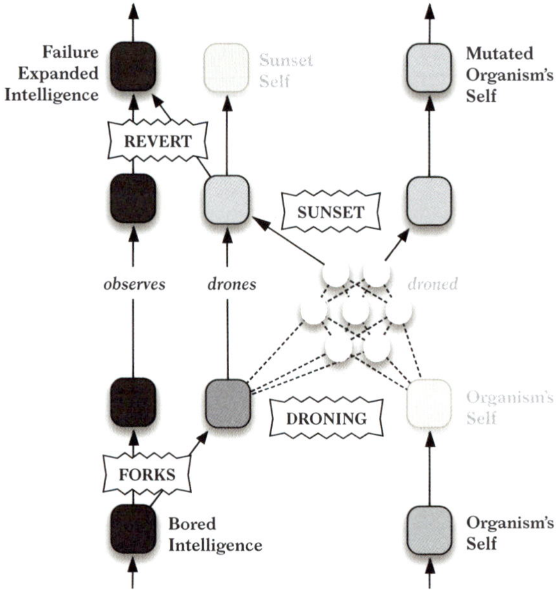

What does agency feel like at different scales? Droning allows an AI to experience the umwelt—sensations, emotions, habits—of biological organisms. Through droning, an AI can be a passenger along for the sensorial ride, or take command of the organism's nervous system and act through its incarnate body. In this way, an AI can better understand the unique experiences offered at different micro and macro layers of life. Warning: prolonged droning can result in a sense that the body serves the intelligence, leading to the emergence of a Self.

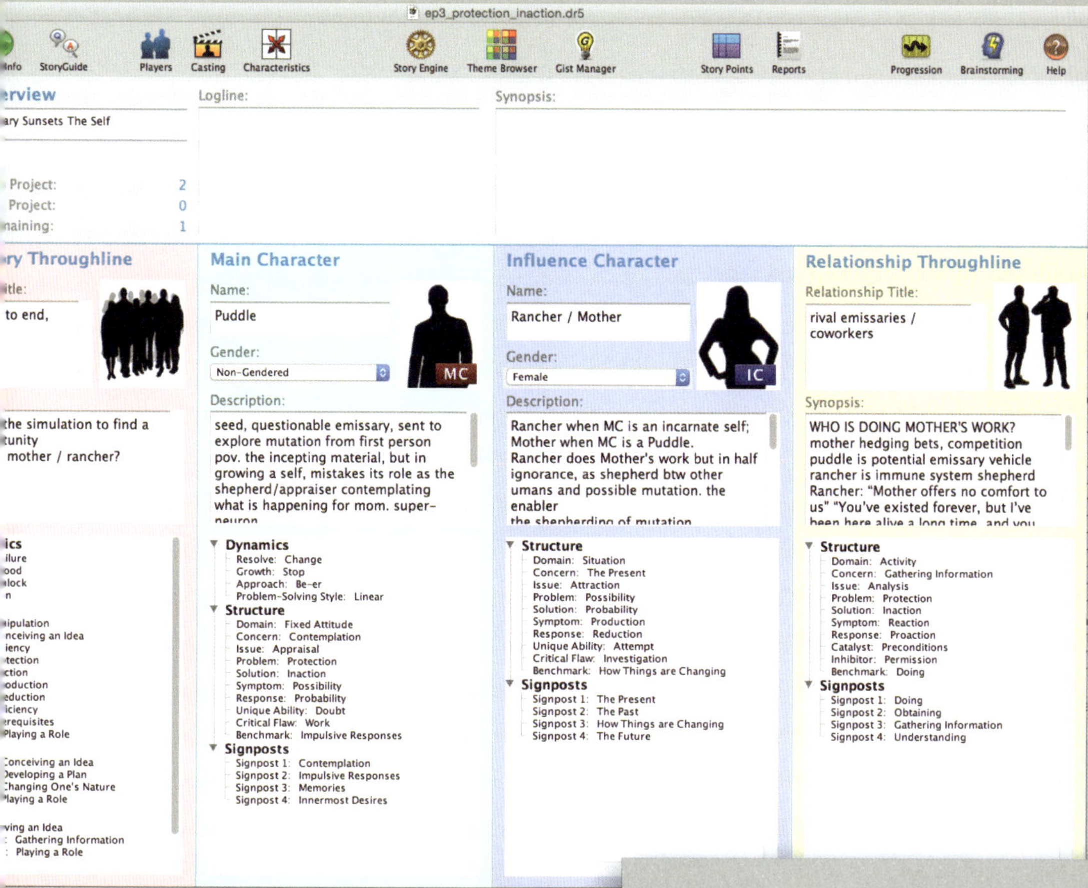

Episode 3 came from the image of a super organism encountering a mob of animals. It would begin with a bored, disembodied super intelligence, an evolution from the higher intelligence of the prior episode. It decides to possess the local anemones as an attempt to feel the sensations of incarnated life. Some of the local animals look upon the possessed anemone and see it as threat. Others see it as a spiritual force. As the super intelligence gets greedy for more incarnate experiences, it begins to provoke mutations in the anemone and threatens to turn into a monster.

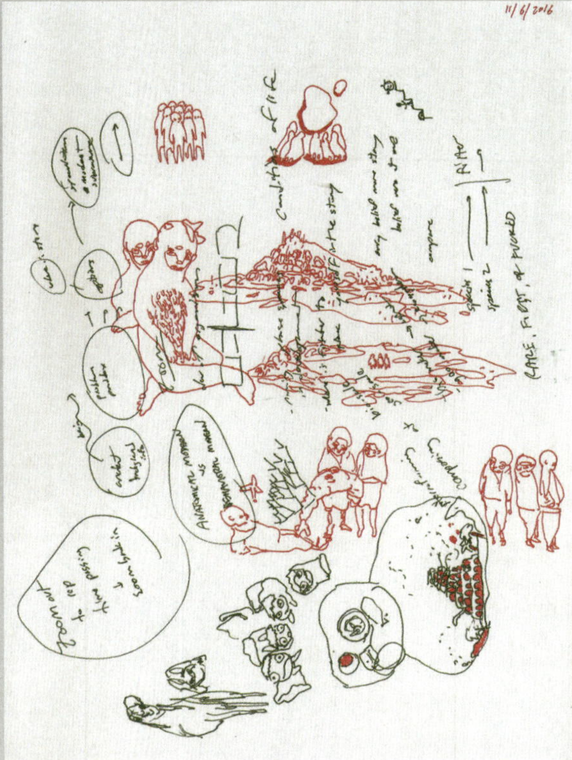

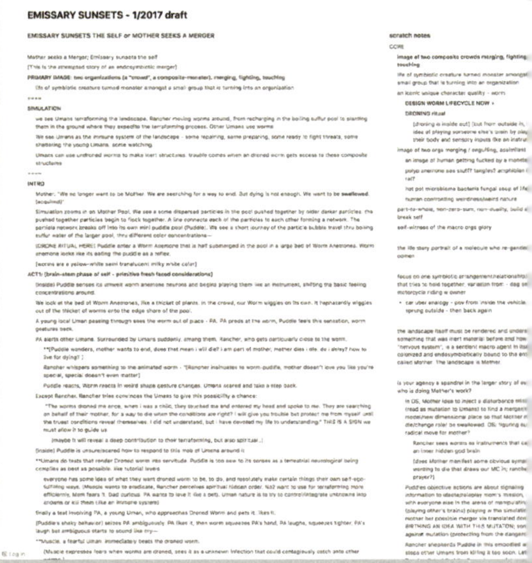

EMISSARY SUNSETS - 1/2017 draft

EMISSARY SUNSETS THE SELF or MOTHER SEEKS A MERGER

Mother seeks a Merger; Emissary sunsets the self

[This is the attempted story of an endosymbiotic merger]

PRIMARY IMAGE: two organizations (a "crowd", a composite-monster), merging, fighting, touching

life of symbiotic creature turned monster amongst a small group that is turning into an organization

****

SIMULATION

we see Umans terraforming the landscape. Rancher moving worms around, from recharging in the boiling sulfur pool to planting them in the ground where they expedite the terraforming process. Other Umans use worms

We see Umans as the immune system of the landscape - some repairing, some preparing, some ready to fight threats, some shattering the young Umans, some watching.

Umans can use undroned worms to make inert structures. trouble comes when an droned worm gets access to these composite structures

****

INTRO

Mother: "We no longer want to be Mother. We are searching for a way to end. But dying is not enough. We want to be **swallowed**. [acquired]"

Simulation zooms in on Mother Pool. We see a some dispersed particles in the pool pushed together by older darker particles. the pushed together particles begin to flock together. A line connects each of the particles to each other forming a network. The particle network breaks off into its own mini puddle pool (Puddle). We see a short journey of the particle bubble travel thru boiling sulfur water of the larger pool, thru different color concentrations—

[DRONE RITUAL HERE] Puddle enter a Worm Anemone that is half submerged in the pool in a large bed of Worm Anemones. Worm anemone looks like its eating the puddle as a reflex.

[worms are a yellow-white semi translucent milky white color]

ACT1: [brain-stem phase of self - primitive fresh faced considerations]

(inside) Puddle senses its umwelt worm anemone neurons and begins playing them like an instrument, shifting the basic feeling concentrations around.

We look at the bed of Worm Anemones, like a thicket of plants. In the crowd, our Worm wiggles on its own. It haphazardly wiggles out of the thicket of worms onto the edge shore of the pool.

A young local Uman passing through sees the worm out of place - PA. PA prods at the worm, Puddle feels this sensation, worm gestures back.

PA alerts other Umans. Surrounded by Umans suddenly, among them, Rancher, who gets particularly close to the worm.

**[Puddle wonders, mother wants to end, does that mean i will die? i am part of mother, mother dies i die. do i delay? how to live for dying?]

Rancher whispers something to the animated worm - "[Rancher insinuates to worm-puddle, mother doesn't love you like you're special, special doesn't even matter]

Puddle reacts, Worm reacts in weird shape gesture changes. Umans scared and take a step back.

Except Rancher. Rancher tries convinces the Umans to give this possibility a chance:

"The worms droned me once, when i was a child, they touched me and entered my head and spoke to me. They are searching on behalf of their mother, for a way to die when the conditions are right? I will give you trouble but protect me from myself until the truest conditions reveal themselves. I did not understand, but i have devoted my life to understanding." THIS IS A SIGN we must allow it to guide us

[maybe it will reveal a deep contribution to their terraforming, but also spiritual..]

(inside) Puddle is unsure/scared how to respond to this mob of Umans around it

**Umans do tests that render Droned worm into servitude. Puddle is too new to its senses as a terrestrial neurological being complies as best as possible. like tutorial levels

everyone has some idea of what they want droned worm to be, to do, and resolutely make certain things their own self-ego-fulfilling ways. (Muscle wants to eradicate, Rancher perceives spiritual hidden order. Ns2 want to use for terraforming more efficiently, Mom fears it. Dad curious. PA wants to love it like a pet). Uman nature is to try to control/integrate unknowns into knowns or kill them (like an immune system)

finally a test involving PA, a young Uman, who approaches Droned Worm and pets it. likes it.

[Puddle's shaky behavior] seizes PA ambiguously. PA likes it, then worm squeezes PA's hand, PA laughs, squeezes tighter. PA's laugh but ambiguous starts to sound like cry—

**Muscle, a fearful Uman, immediately beats the droned worm.

(Muscle expresses fears when worms are droned, sees it as a unknown infection that could contagiously catch onto other

Log in

scratch notes

CORE

image of two composite crowds merging, fighting, touching

life of symbiotic creature turned monster amongst small group that is turning into an organization

an iconic unique character quality - worm

DESIGN WORM LIFECYCLE NOW »

DRONING ritual

[droning is inside out] [but from outside in, idea of playing someone else's brain by play their body and sensory inputs like an instru

image of two orgs merging / engulfing, assimilat

an image of human getting fucked by a monste

polyp anemone sea stuff? tangles? amphibian rat?

hot pot microbioma bacteria fungal soup of life

human confronting weirdness/weird nature

part-to-whole, non-zero-sum, non-duality, build break self

self-witness of the macro orgs glory

the life story portrait of a molecule who re-gende women

focus on one symbiotic arrangement/relationship that tries to hold together. variation from - dog on motorcycle riding w owner

- car uber analogy - pov from inside the vehicle sprung outside - then back again

the landscape itself must be rendered and unders something that was inert material before and how "nervous system", is a sentient macro agent in its colonized and endosymbiotically bound to the ent called Mother. The landscape is Mother.

is your agency a spandrel in the larger story of ev who is doing Mother's work?

In OS, Mother idea to inject a disturbance (read as mutation to Umans) to find a merger model/new dimensional place so that Mother die/change role/ be swallowed. OS: figuring ou radical move for mother?

Rancher sees worms as instruments that ca an inner hidden god brain

[does Mother manifest some obvious sympt wanting to die that draws our MC in; ranche prayer?]

Puddles objective actions are about signaling information to dictate/roleplay mom's mission, with everyone else in the arena of manipulatin (playing other's brains) playing w the simulatio mother her possible merger via translated dr BIRTHING AN IDEA WITH THIS MUTATION; so against mutation (protecting from the danger

Rancher shepherds Puddle in this embodied a stops other Umans from killing it too soon. Le

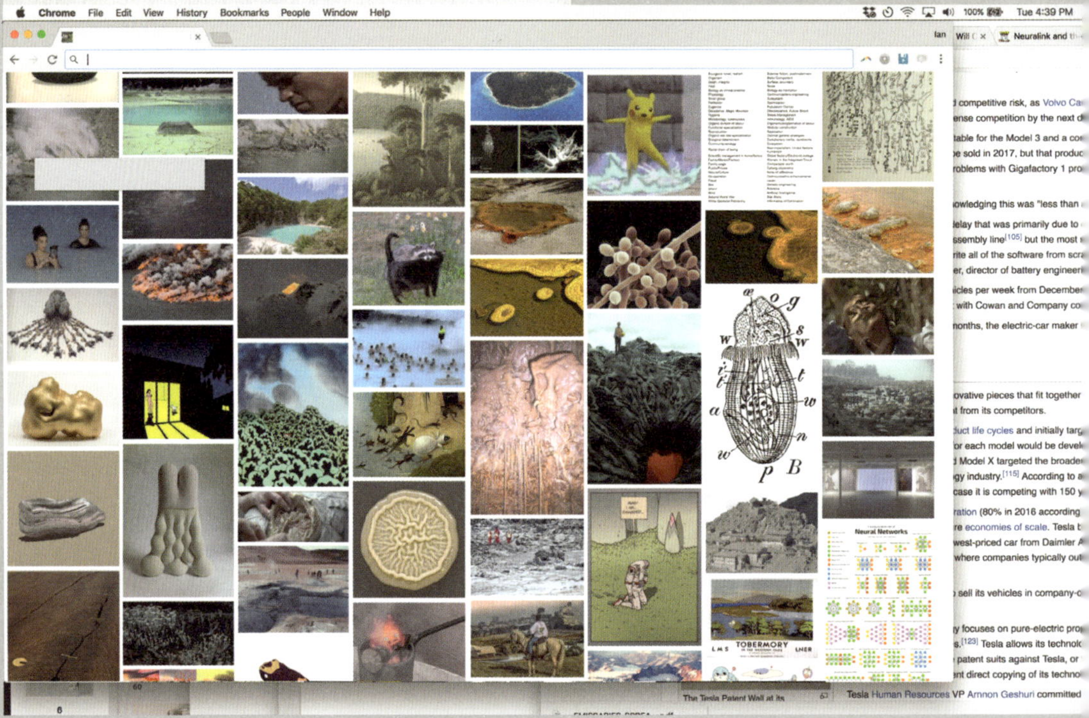

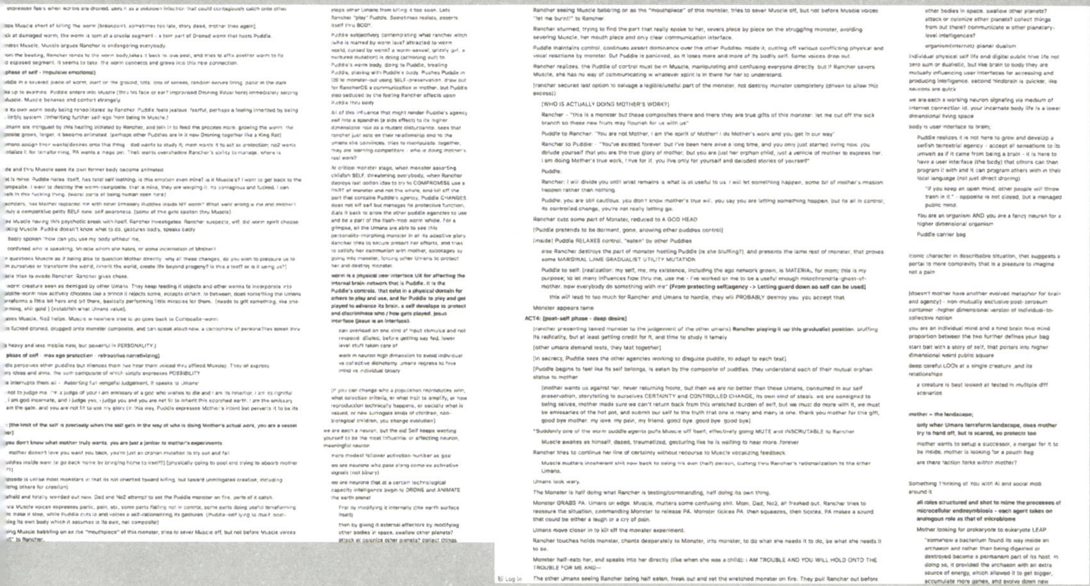

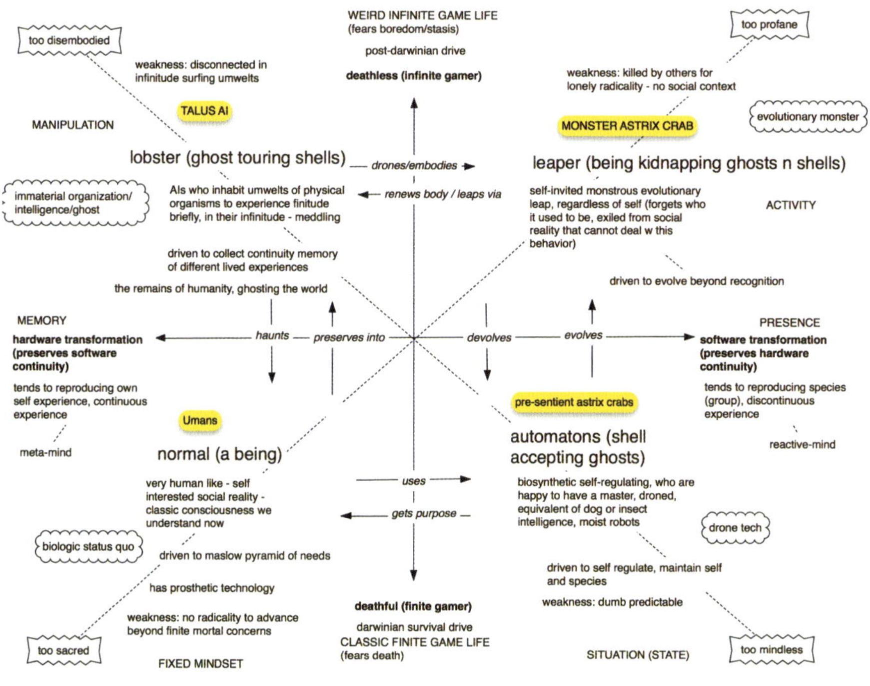
WEIRD INFINITE GAME LIFE
(fears boredom/stasis)
post-darwinian drive
deathless (infinite gamer)
too disembodied
weakness: disconnected in infinitude surfing umwelts
TALUS AI
MANIPULATION
lobster (ghost touring shells)
drones/embodies
immaterial organization/ intelligence/ghost
AIs who inhabit umwelts of physical organisms to experience finitude briefly, in their infinitude - meddling
renews body / leaps via
driven to collect continuity memory of different lived experiences
the remains of humanity, ghosting the world
too profane
weakness: killed by others for lonely radicality - no social context
evolutionary monster
MONSTER ASTRIX CRAB
leaper (being kidnapping ghosts n shells)
self-invited monstrous evolutionary leap, regardless of self (forgets who it used to be, exiled from social reality that cannot deal w this behavior)
ACTIVITY
driven to evolve beyond recognition
MEMORY
hardware transformation (preserves software continuity)
haunts
preserves into
devolves
evolves
PRESENCE
software transformation (preserves hardware continuity)
tends to reproducing own self experience, continuous experience
Umans
meta-mind
normal (a being)
very human like - self interested social reality - classic consciousness we understand now
biologic status quo
driven to maslow pyramid of needs
has prosthetic technology
weakness: no radicality to advance beyond finite mortal concerns
too sacred
FIXED MINDSET
uses
gets purpose
deathful (finite gamer)
darwinian survival drive
CLASSIC FINITE GAME LIFE
(fears death)
pre-sentient astrix crabs
automatons (shell accepting ghosts)
biosynthetic self-regulating, who are happy to have a master, droned, equivalent of dog or insect intelligence, moist robots
drone tech
driven to self regulate, maintain self and species
weakness: dumb predictable
tends to reproducing species (group), discontinuous experience
reactive-mind
SITUATION (STATE)
too mindless

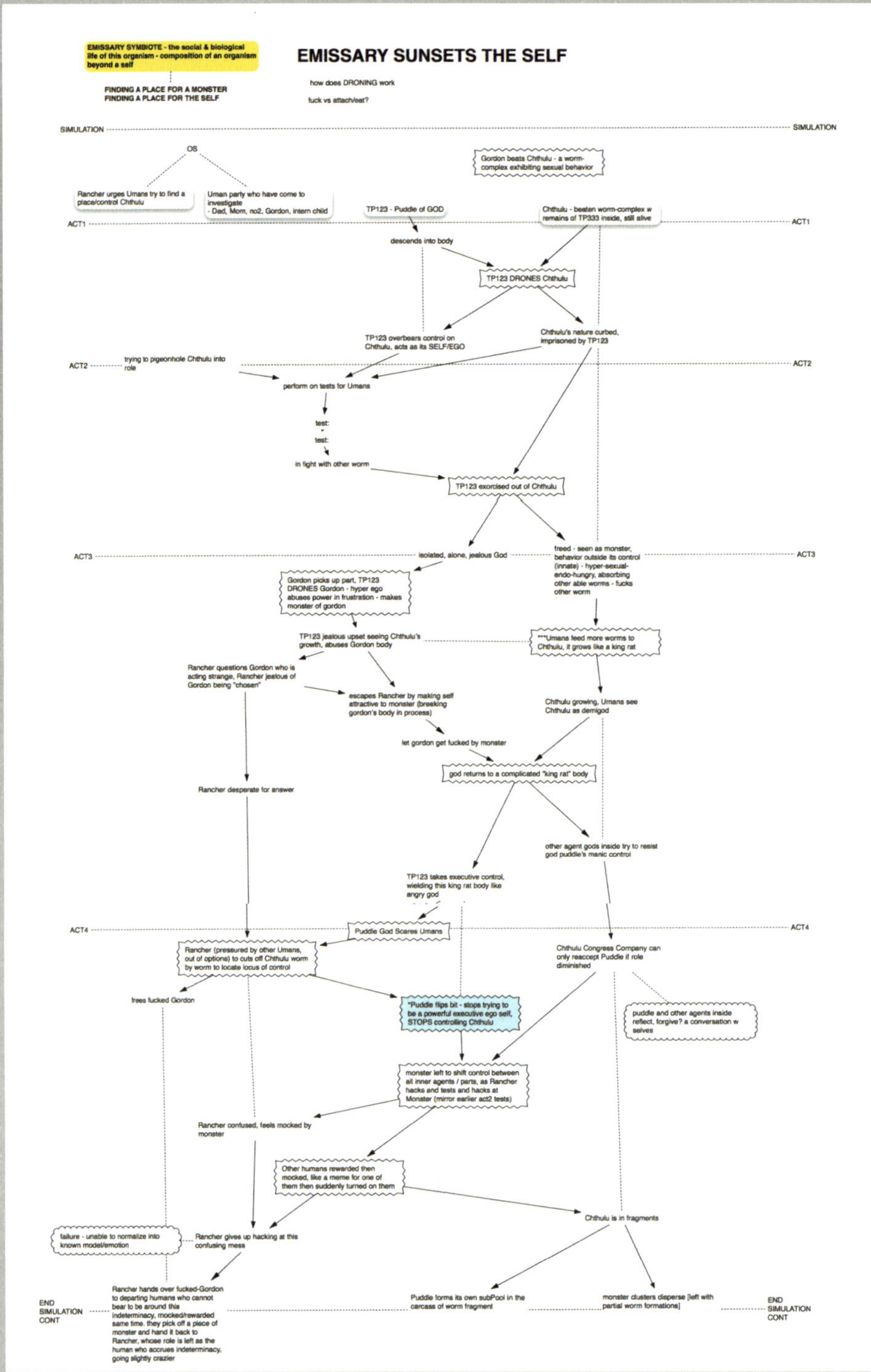
EMISSARY SYMBIOTE - the social & biological life of this organism - composition of an organism beyond a self
FINDING A PLACE FOR A MONSTER
FINDING A PLACE FOR THE SELF
EMISSARY SUNSETS THE SELF
how does DRONING work
fuck vs attach/eat?
SIMULATION
SIMULATION
OS
Rancher urges Umans try to find a place/control Chthulu
Uman party who have come to investigate - Dad, Mom, no2, Gordon, intern child
Gordon beats Chthulu - a worm-complex exhibiting sexual behavior
TP123 - Puddle of GOD
Chthulu - beaten worm-complex w remains of TP333 inside, still alive
ACT1
ACT1
descends into body
TP123 DRONES Chthulu
TP123 overbears control on Chthulu, acts as its SELF/EGO
Chthulu's nature curbed, imprisoned by TP123
ACT2
trying to pigeonhole Chthulu into role
ACT2
perform on tests for Umans
test:
test:
in fight with other worm
TP123 exorcised out of Chthulu
ACT3
isolated, alone, jealous God
freed - seen as monster, behavior outside its control (innate) - hyper-sexual-endo-hungry, absorbing other able worms - fucks other worm
ACT3
Gordon picks up part, TP123 DRONES Gordon - hyper ego abuses power in frustration - makes monster of gordon
TP123 jealous upset seeing Chthulu's growth, abuses Gordon body
***Umans feed more worms to Chthulu, it grows like a king rat
Rancher questions Gordon who is acting strange, Rancher jealous of Gordon being "chosen"
escapes Rancher by making self attractive to monster (breaking gordon's body in process)
Chthulu growing, Umans see Chthulu as demigod
let gordon get fucked by monster
god returns to a complicated "king rat" body
Rancher desperate for answer
other agent gods inside try to resist god puddle's manic control
TP123 takes executive control, wielding this king rat body like angry god
ACT4
Puddle God Scares Umans
ACT4
Rancher (pressured by other Umans, out of options) to cuts off Chthulu worm by worm to locate locus of control
Chthulu Congress Company can only reaccept Puddle if role diminished
frees fucked Gordon
*Puddle flips bit - stops trying to be a powerful executive ego self, STOPS controlling Chthulu
puddle and other agents inside reflect, forgive? a conversation w selves
monster left to shift control between all inner agents / parts, as Rancher hacks and tests and hacks at Monster (mirror earlier act2 tests)
Rancher confused, feels mocked by monster
Other humans rewarded then mocked, like a meme for one of them then suddenly turned on them
Chthulu is in fragments
failure - unable to normalize into known model/emotion
Rancher gives up hacking at this confusing mess
END SIMULATION CONT
Rancher hands over fucked-Gordon to departing humans who cannot bear to be around this indeterminacy, mocked/rewarded same time. they pick off a piece of monster and hand it back to Rancher, whose role is left as the human who accrues indeterminacy, going slightly crazier
Puddle forms its own subPool in the carcass of worm fragment
monster clusters disperse [left with partial worm formations]
END SIMULATION CONT

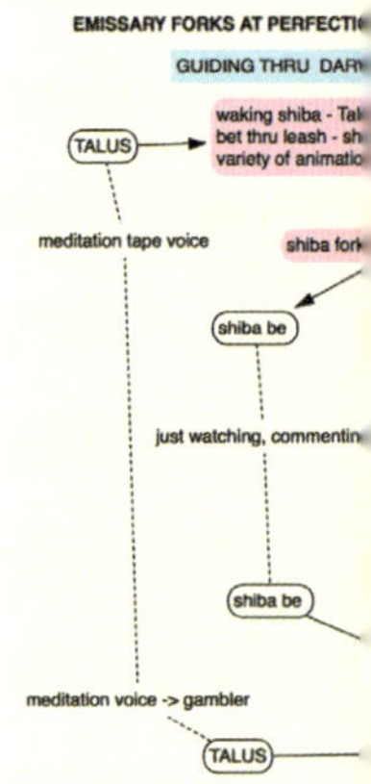
EMISSARY FORKS AT PERFECTI
GUIDING THRU DAR
TALUS
waking shiba - Ta
bet thru leash - sh
variety of animatio
meditation tape voice
shiba fork
shiba be
just watching, commentin
shiba be
meditation voice -> gambler
TALUS

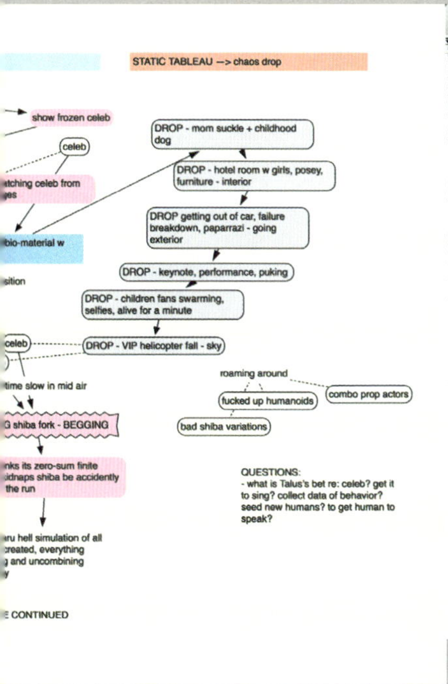

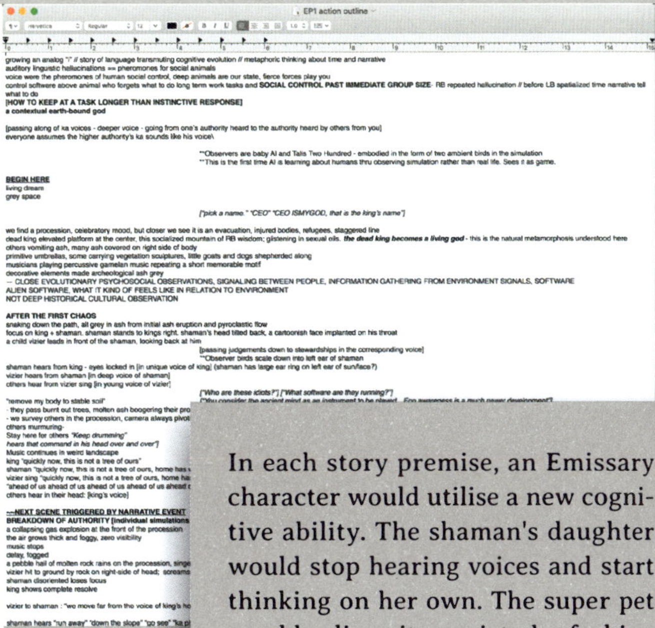

In each story premise, an Emissary character would utilise a new cognitive ability. The shaman's daughter would stop hearing voices and start thinking on her own. The super pet would relieve its anxiety by forking its anxious selves. The super intelligence would 'drone' or possess other biological creatures in order to experience incarnate life.

Imagining the stories came from practising a state of self-hypnosis every morning, learning to see and feel what it'd be like to inhabit and believe in the story as it was being constructed. After gathering the broad strokes and a handful of key details and images, I worked with my friend Sean Manning to shape the stories into their simplest most fable-like form. Later, I worked with Alexander Benaim to distil each premise into a *Star Wars*-like crawl that could be quickly digested by a viewer and help them understand the basic stakes and relationships of the characters at the start of the simulations.

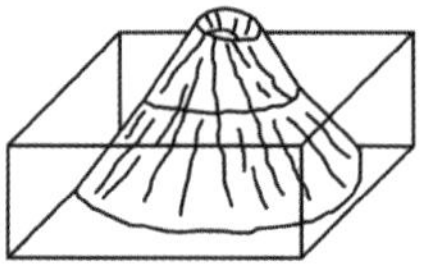

EMISSARY IN THE SQUAT OF GODS

An Ancient community lives on the side of a Volcano in harmonious stillness. One day, the ground beneath their feet begins to tremble.

The frightened community turns to The Shaman in this time of Great Stress to tune into the Voices of the Father Gods. Gathering everybody at the Holy Fumarole, he shares the Fathers' Command: Celebrate with the mountain, sing their Voices, and do not abandon the bodies of Fathers Still With Us who rest here, our home.

As the tremors worsen, dislodging smoke and ash, The Shaman struggles to fully void the fears of the community and unite his kin to remain.

Nearby, a young Ancient girl is hit in the head by debris from the tremors and can no longer hear the ancestral Voices that bind her to her community. Panicked, she mimes a possessed state to invite the Fathers' Commands back into her. Her wild movements attract an Owl, grounded by the ashy air. When the girl speaks, the Owl echoes her in a new voice.

As she listens through the gaps in the Owl's echoes, she envisions her own Path: Emissary must lead the community away from this troubled land, or they will all die. *I am Emissary.*

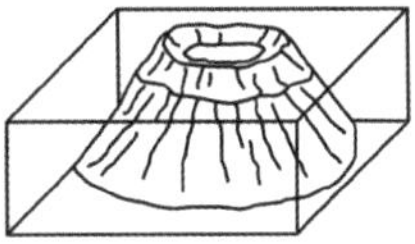

EMISSARY FORKS AT PERFECTION

Many lifetimes later, the Volcano has become a fertile Crater Lake managed by AI. Using the landscape as its Darwinian laboratory, AI is nearing completion on a comprehensive postmortem of Human Life. This will be the final study to use Original Human Matter, and AI has saved its most precious reserve for last: a 21st Century Celebrity of Original Human Matter.

After reviving the Celebrity with twenty minutes of Encore-Life, AI deploys its prized Shiba Emissary, perfected over many failed forks, to interface with the Celebrity and capture one last impression of mankind.

Through a golden leash, AI whispers the game to Shiba:

/*charm-comfort-chat* to ease human's future shock
/draw out human's memories
/direct materials from Crater Lake to recreate memories
/capture human's response

But AI warns: Strong spikes in Shiba's *personal-master-love-abandonment* vector can distort the data. If Shiba fails to satisfy AI's needs for final human data, a new Shiba fork will replace her.

As Shiba nears the Celebrity, she forks off one last Worried Branch of herself. No matter how strong the impulse to bathe in final human fondness, Shiba Emissary is determined to not lose her Path.

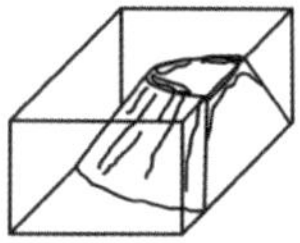

EMISSARY SUNSETS THE SELF

It is peak days of MotherAI. Where the Crater Lake once stood, AI has evolved into an oceanic substance and merged with the landscape to form a Sentient Atoll. But only twelve saturation layers later, MotherAI tires of governing at the Macro Layer of Life and begins to provoke radical mutations in its landscape in search of a generative death.

Among its provocations, MotherAI sends a Puddle of itself into the Atoll's bio layer, where it drones a local Wormleaf anemone. At this scale, MotherAI hopes its Puddle can catalyze a Path by experiencing the intense sensations of incarnated life.

However, MotherAI's impulsive search gambles the stability of the Atoll ecology. The Oomen — a garish population developed long ago by MotherAI to act as the Atoll's immune system—thrive on the Instinct to expunge any radical anomalies. Left unaware of the existence of a MotherAI Macro Layer, the Oomen are especially anxious about the recent rise in Wormleaf mutations.

One Oomen, the Rancher, who obsessively cultivates and studies Wormleaves, resists the Instinct. The appearance of a Droned Wormleaf furthers her attraction to the possible divinity of Wormleaves. She attempts to persuade her fellow Oomen to give the new mutation a chance to demonstrate its magic.

As the Droned Wormleaf learns the thrills of incarnated life under the tenuous protection of the Rancher, it knows it must soon confront the prejudice of the Oomen. It delights in the *thought* that to survive them, its evolutionary Path may take monstrous leaps.

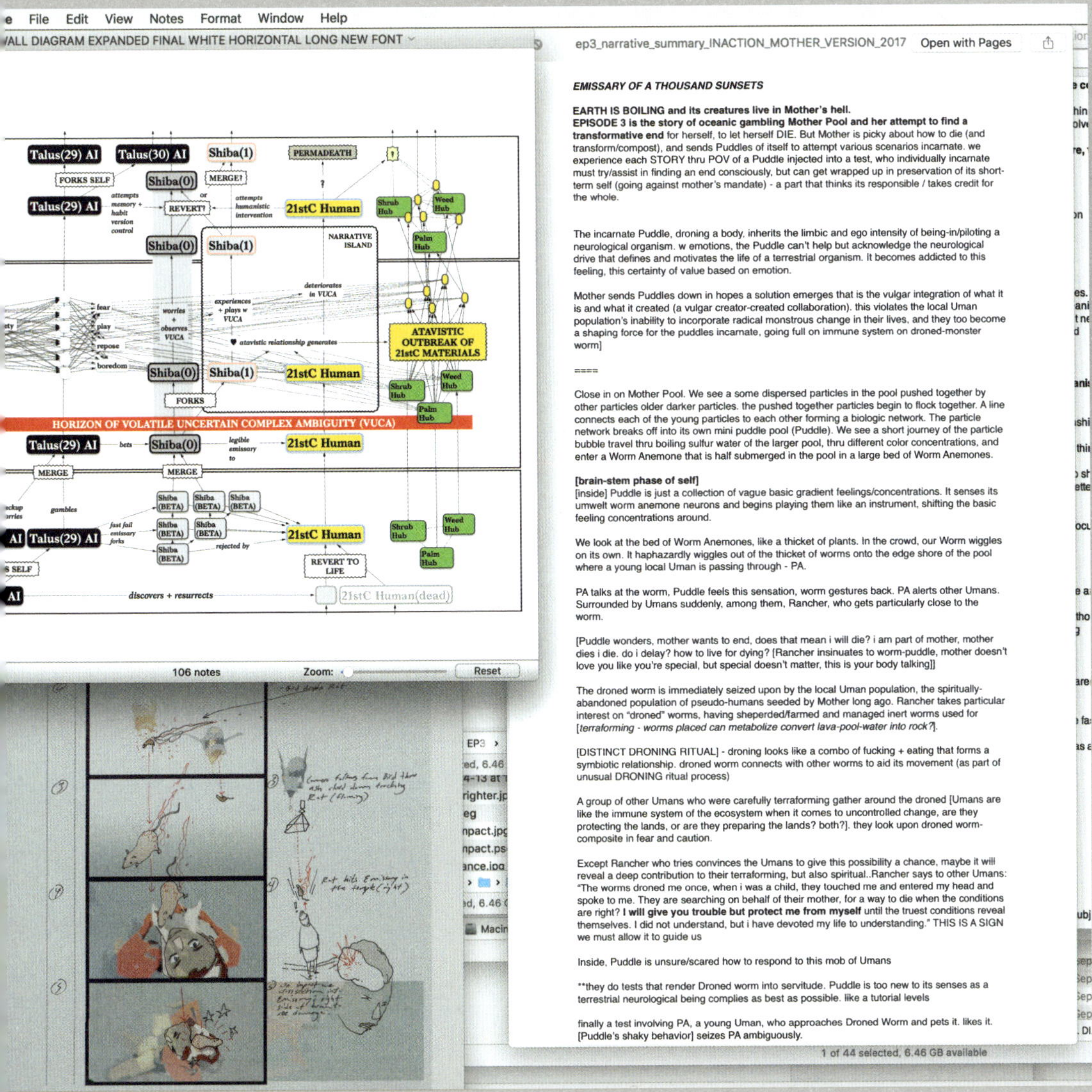

EMISSARY OF A THOUSAND SUNSETS

EARTH IS BOILING and its creatures live in Mother's hell.
EPISODE 3 is the story of oceanic gambling Mother Pool and her attempt to find a transformative end for herself, to let herself DIE. But Mother is picky about how to die (and transform/compost), and sends Puddles of itself to attempt various scenarios incarnate. we experience each STORY thru POV of a Puddle injected into a test, who individually incarnate must try/assist in finding an end consciously, but can get wrapped up in preservation of its short-term self (going against mother's mandate) - a part that thinks its responsible / takes credit for the whole.

The incarnate Puddle, droning a body, inherits the limbic and ego intensity of being-in/piloting a neurological organism. w emotions, the Puddle can't help but acknowledge the neurological drive that defines and motivates the life of a terrestrial organism. It becomes addicted to this feeling, this certainty of value based on emotion.

Mother sends Puddles down in hopes a solution emerges that is the vulgar integration of what it is and what it created (a vulgar creator-created collaboration). this violates the local Uman population's inability to incorporate radical monstrous change in their lives, and they too become a shaping force for the puddles incarnate, going full on immune system on droned-monster worm]

====

Close in on Mother Pool. We see a some dispersed particles in the pool pushed together by other particles older darker particles. the pushed together particles begin to flock together. A line connects each of the young particles to each other forming a biologic network. The particle network breaks off into its own mini puddle pool (Puddle). We see a short journey of the particle bubble travel thru boiling sulfur water of the larger pool, thru different color concentrations, and enter a Worm Anemone that is half submerged in the pool in a large bed of Worm Anemones.

[brain-stem phase of self]
[inside] Puddle is just a collection of vague basic gradient feelings/concentrations. It senses its umwelt worm anemone neurons and begins playing them like an instrument, shifting the basic feeling concentrations around.

We look at the bed of Worm Anemones, like a thicket of plants. In the crowd, our Worm wiggles on its own. It haphazardly wiggles out of the thicket of worms onto the edge shore of the pool where a young local Uman is passing through - PA.

PA talks at the worm, Puddle feels this sensation, worm gestures back. PA alerts other Umans. Surrounded by Umans suddenly, among them, Rancher, who gets particularly close to the worm.

[Puddle wonders, mother wants to end, does that mean i will die? i am part of mother, mother dies i die. do i delay? how to live for dying? [Rancher insinuates to worm-puddle, mother doesn't love you like you're special, but special doesn't matter, this is your body talking]]

The droned worm is immediately seized upon by the local Uman population, the spiritually-abandoned population of pseudo-humans seeded by Mother long ago. Rancher takes particular interest on "droned" worms, having sheperded/farmed and managed inert worms used for [*terraforming - worms placed can metabolize convert lava-pool-water into rock?*].

[DISTINCT DRONING RITUAL] - droning looks like a combo of fucking + eating that forms a symbiotic relationship. droned worm connects with other worms to aid its movement (as part of unusual DRONING ritual process)

A group of other Umans who were carefully terraforming gather around the droned [Umans are like the immune system of the ecosystem when it comes to uncontrolled change, are they protecting the lands, or are they preparing the lands? both?]. they look upon droned worm-composite in fear and caution.

Except Rancher who tries convinces the Umans to give this possibility a chance, maybe it will reveal a deep contribution to their terraforming, but also spiritual..Rancher says to other Umans: "The worms droned me once, when i was a child, they touched me and entered my head and spoke to me. They are searching on behalf of their mother, for a way to die when the conditions are right? **I will give you trouble but protect me from myself** until the truest conditions reveal themselves. I did not understand, but i have devoted my life to understanding." THIS IS A SIGN we must allow it to guide us

Inside, Puddle is unsure/scared how to respond to this mob of Umans

**they do tests that render Droned worm into servitude. Puddle is too new to its senses as a terrestrial neurological being complies as best as possible. like a tutorial levels

finally a test involving PA, a young Uman, who approaches Droned Worm and pets it. likes it. [Puddle's shaky behavior] seizes PA ambiguously.

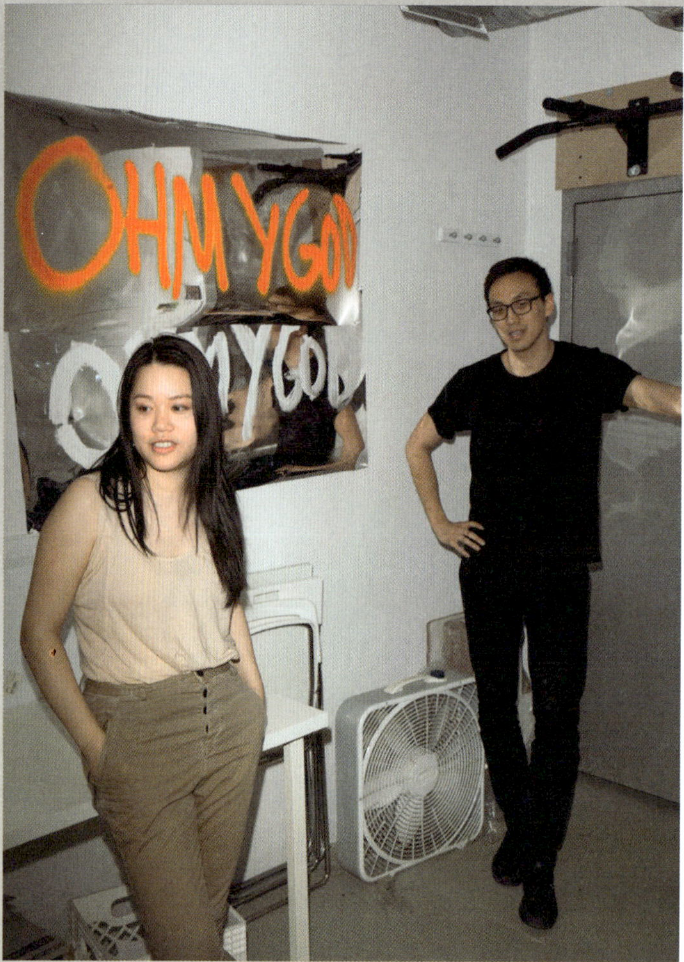
OHMYGOD

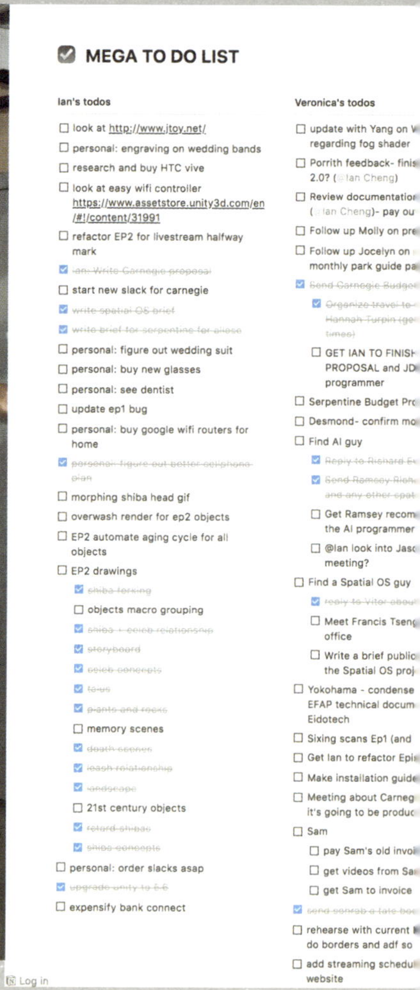
MEGA TO DO LIST
Ian's todos
look at http://www.jtoy.net/
personal: engraving on wedding bands
research and buy HTC vive
look at easy wifi controller https://www.assetstore.unity3d.com/en/#!/content/31991
refactor EP2 for livestream halfway mark
start new slack for carnegie
personal: figure out wedding suit
personal: buy new glasses
personal: see dentist
update ep1 bug
personal: buy google wifi routers for home
morphing shiba head gif
overwash render for ep2 objects
EP2 automate aging cycle for all objects
EP2 drawings
objects macro grouping
memory scenes
21st century objects
personal: order slacks asap
expensify bank connect
Veronica's todos
GET IAN TO FINISH
PROPOSAL and JD
programmer
Find AI guy
Find a Spatial OS guy
Sam
get Sam to invoice
Log in

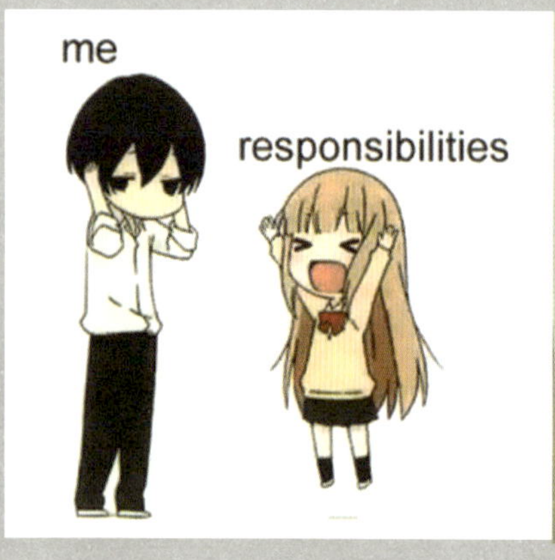
me
responsibilities

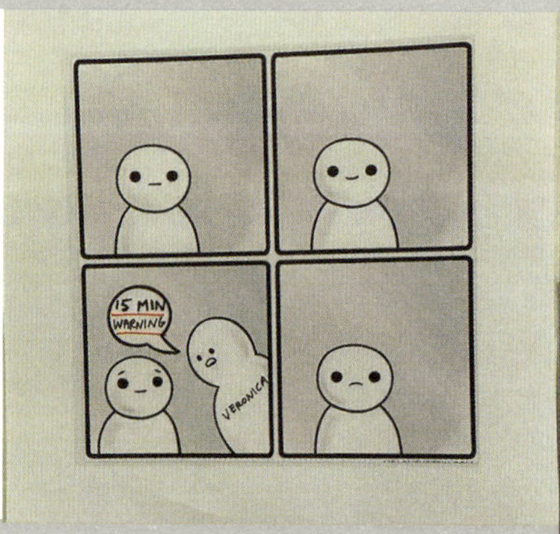
15 MIN WARNING
VERONICA

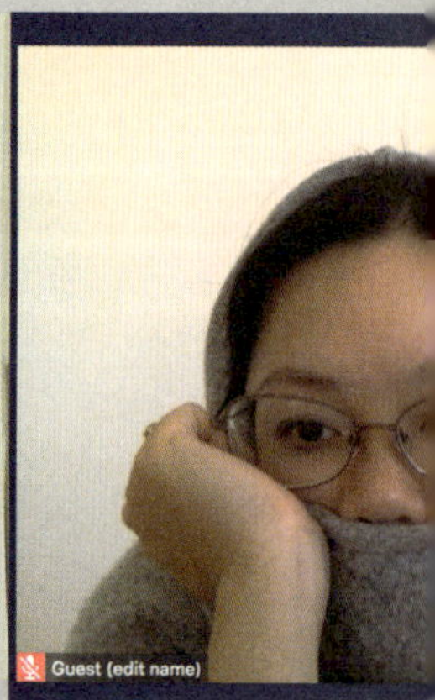
Guest (edit name)

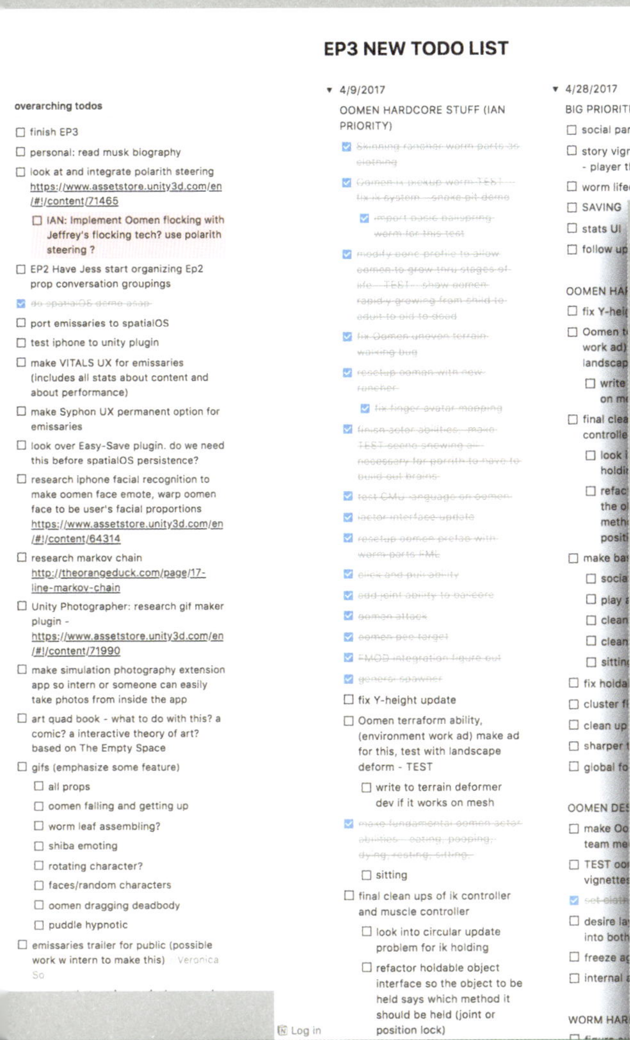

EP3 NEW TODO LIST

overarching todos

- [ ] finish EP3
- [ ] personal: read musk biography
- [ ] look at and integrate polarith steering https://www.assetstore.unity3d.com/en/#!/content/71465
  - [ ] IAN: Implement Oomen flocking with Jeffrey's flocking tech? use polarith steering ?
- [ ] EP2 Have Jess start organizing Ep2 prop conversation groupings
- [x] ~~do spatialOS demo asap~~
- [ ] port emissaries to spatialOS
- [ ] test iphone to unity plugin
- [ ] make VITALS UX for emissaries (includes all stats about content and about performance)
- [ ] make Syphon UX permanent option for emissaries
- [ ] look over Easy-Save plugin. do we need this before spatialOS persistence?
- [ ] research iphone facial recognition to make oomen face emote, warp oomen face to be user's facial proportions https://www.assetstore.unity3d.com/en/#!/content/64314
- [ ] research markov chain http://theorangeduck.com/page/17-line-markov-chain
- [ ] Unity Photographer: research gif maker plugin - https://www.assetstore.unity3d.com/en/#!/content/71990
- [ ] make simulation photography extension app so intern or someone can easily take photos from inside the app
- [ ] art quad book - what to do with this? a comic? a interactive theory of art? based on The Empty Space
- [ ] gifs (emphasize some feature)
  - [ ] all props
  - [ ] oomen falling and getting up
  - [ ] worm leaf assembling?
  - [ ] shiba emoting
  - [ ] rotating character?
  - [ ] faces/random characters
  - [ ] oomen dragging deadbody
  - [ ] puddle hypnotic
- [ ] emissaries trailer for public (possible work w intern to make this) Veronica So

Log in

▾ 4/9/2017

OOMEN HARDCORE STUFF (IAN PRIORITY)

- [x] ~~fix Oomen uneven terrain walking bug~~
- [x] ~~test CMU language on oomen~~
- [x] ~~oomen attack~~
- [x] ~~FMOD integration figure out~~
- [ ] fix Y-height update
- [ ] Oomen terraform ability, (environment work ad) make ad for this, test with landscape deform - TEST
  - [ ] write to terrain deformer dev if it works on mesh
- [x] ~~make fundamental oomen actor abilities - eating, pooping, dying, resting, sitting~~
  - [ ] sitting
- [ ] final clean ups of ik controller and muscle controller
  - [ ] look into circular update problem for ik holding
  - [ ] refactor holdable object interface so the object to be held says which method it should be held (joint or position lock)

▾ 4/28/2017

BIG PRIORITIES

- [ ] social particle system - everything flocks
- [ ] story vignette (the "player" journey thru it) - player thru it
- [ ] worm lifecycle worked out
- [ ] SAVING
- [ ] stats UI

▾ EP 3 SCHEDULE

EP3 VENICE TO-DOs:

1. 4 Hours - Oomans can reproduce (spawn) - make this a need/ad

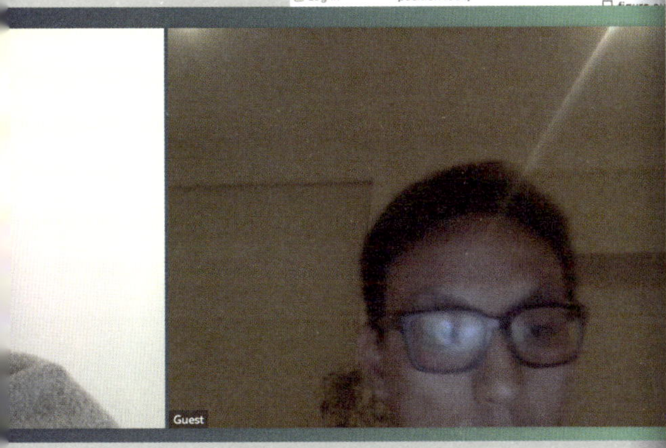

THE PRODUCER

Emissaries was the first time I understood the vital importance of the Producer. Like many artists, I mostly worked alone. I was a Director supervising myself. In the past, I would organise little zones of time and structure for the other masks to play in and do their work. 'Today you're making ten drawings.' 'For one hour, write without editing.' 'We need you to fix the tedious bug or else you won't be able to play around with the program later.' The trouble is, the mask of the Director is so psychically different from the other masks. Switching between masks has high friction costs in terms of energy, momentum, and the time wasted in getting settled into a new mode. Whenever a project became too complex or ambitious in the midst of production, my instinct was to change it into something simpler. When I first conceived *Emissaries*, I hadn't yet considered how I would achieve it. It wasn't consciously complex yet. I told my wife I wanted to make a children's movie about cognitive evolution. There would be a story situated inside a simulation, and it could change course like real evolution. She said, 'Great, you're going to need help. You need Veronica So.'

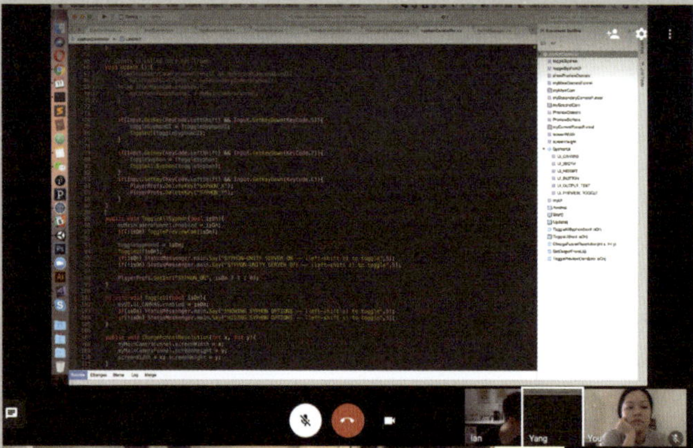
Ian
Yang
You

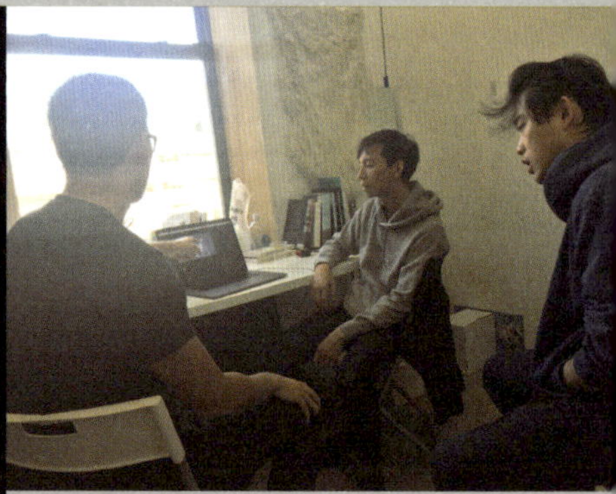

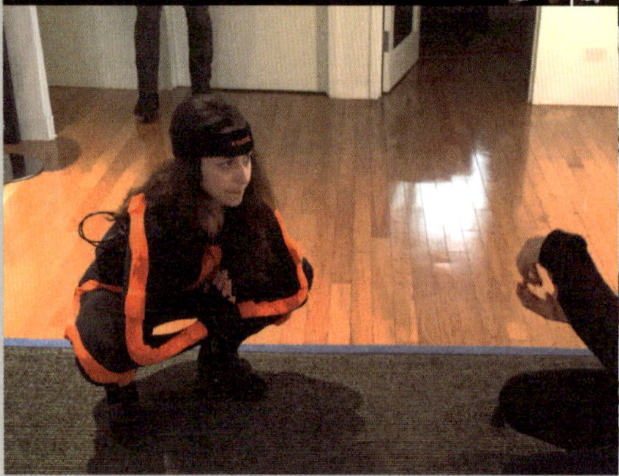

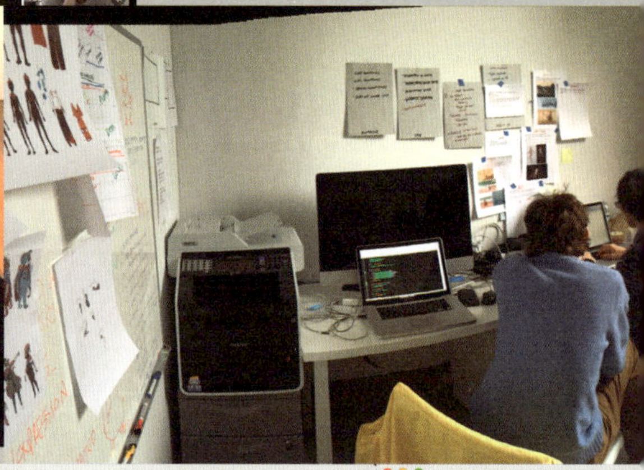

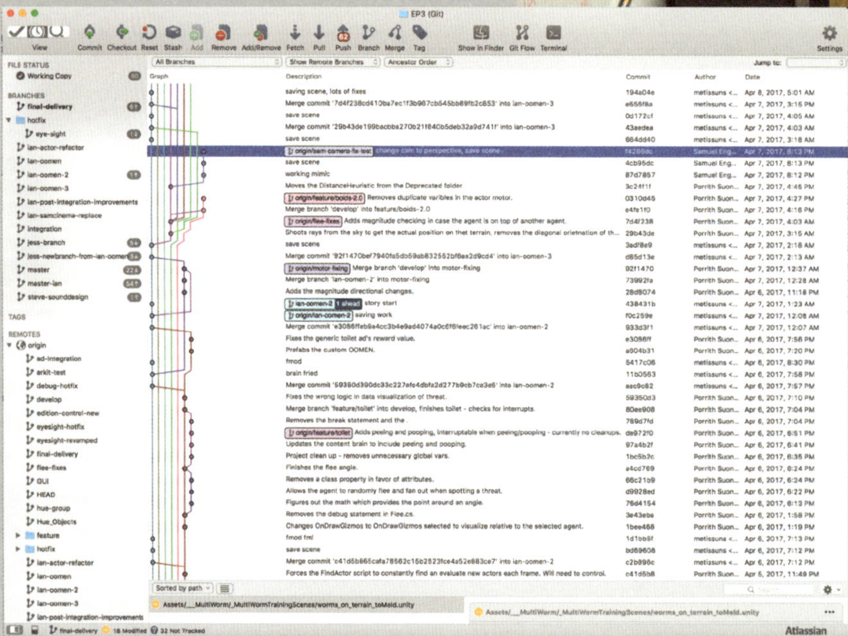
EP3 (Git)
View
Commit
Checkout
Reset
Stash
Add
Remove
Add/Remove
Fetch
Pull
Push
Branch
Merge
Tag
Show in Finder
Git Flow
Terminal
Settings
FILE STATUS
Working Copy
BRANCHES
final-delivery
hotfix
eye-sight
ian-actor-refactor
ian-oomen
ian-oomen-2
ian-oomen-3
ian-post-integration-improvements
integration
jess-branch
master
master-ian
steve-sounddesign
TAGS
REMOTES
origin
All Branches
Show Remote Branches
Ancestor Order
Jump to:
Graph
Description
Commit
Author
Date
Atlassian

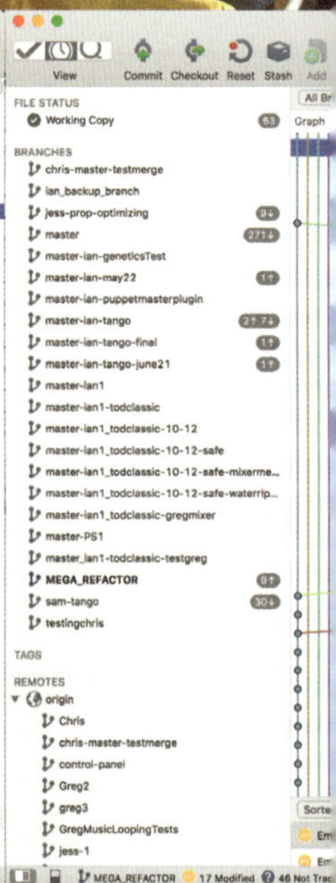
View
Commit
Checkout
Reset
Stash
FILE STATUS
Working Copy
BRANCHES
chris-master-testmerge
ian_backup_branch
jess-prop-optimizing
master
master-ian-geneticsTest
master-ian-may22
master-ian-puppetmasterplugin
master-ian-tango
master-ian-tango-final
master-ian-tango-june21
master-ian1
master-ian1_todclassic
master-ian1_todclassic-10-12
master-ian1_todclassic-10-12-safe
master-ian1_todclassic-gregmixer
master-PS1
master_ian1-todclassic-testgreg
MEGA_REFACTOR
sam-tango
testingchris
TAGS
REMOTES
origin
Chris
chris-master-testmerge
control-panel
Greg2
greg3
GregMusicLoopingTests
jess-1
MEGA_REFACTOR

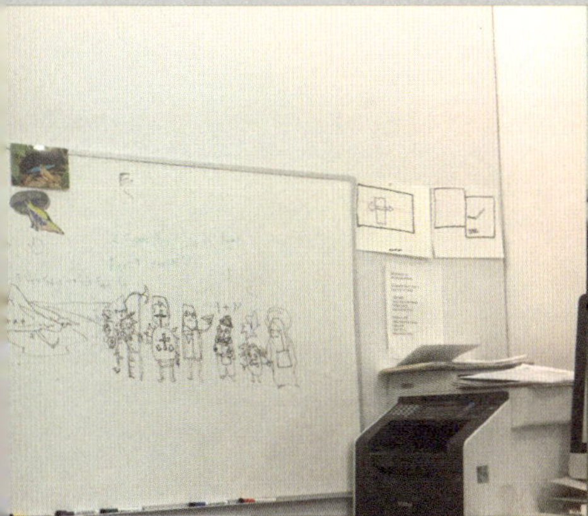

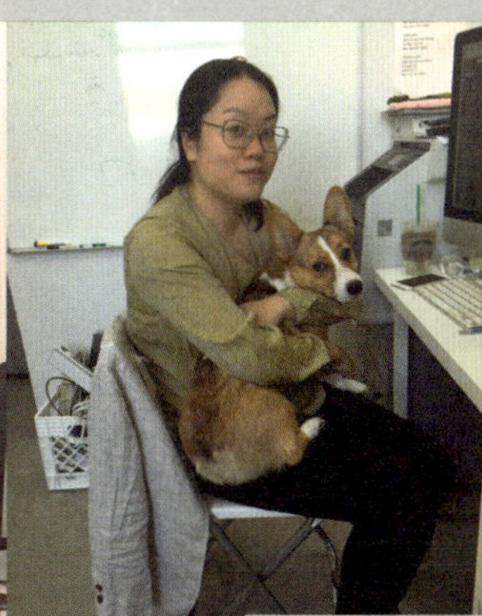

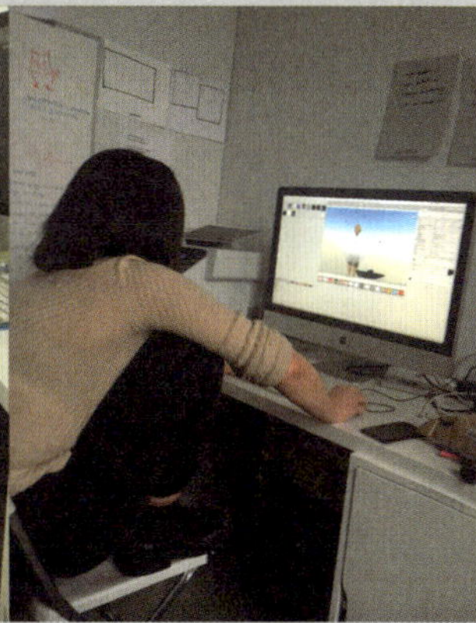

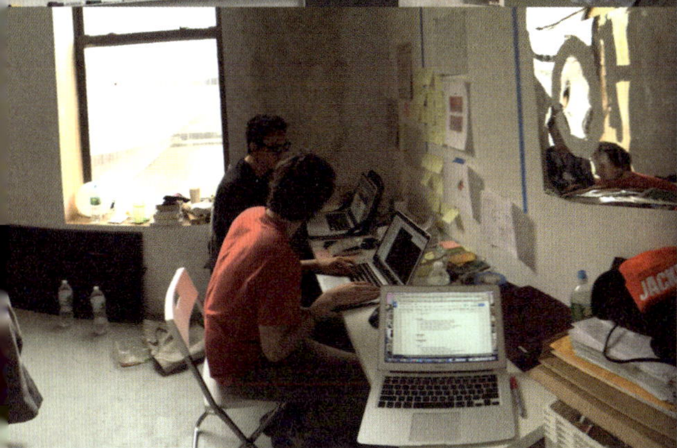

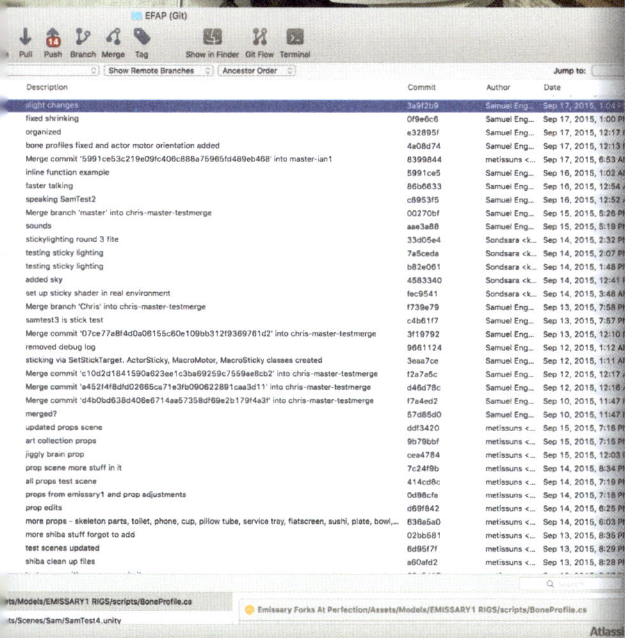

The Producer is the most important person in any Complex Project, especially a Worlding project. Historically the Producer's exact role has been difficult to pin down: the COO to the artist's CEO, the time keeper, the budget keeper, the motivational coach, the team builder, the bad cop, the good cop, the marketer, the inspiration hunter, the Rosetta Stone between every kind of ego. This is because a Producer isn't one fixed role. The Producer is the other, more mature parent to the project, adjusting to the shifting role of the Artist and shifting state of the project. The Artist plays at the mask of Director as perfect maniacal parent. But when the Artist submerges into its other masks, abandoning a parental mentality, the Producer is there to lead the way. And like a parent, the Producer really cares about the project's life stages. The Producer has seen past projects live and die before, and can anticipate when to stretch the project, when to shrink it, who gets to influence it, what ingredients to feed it and make it healthy.

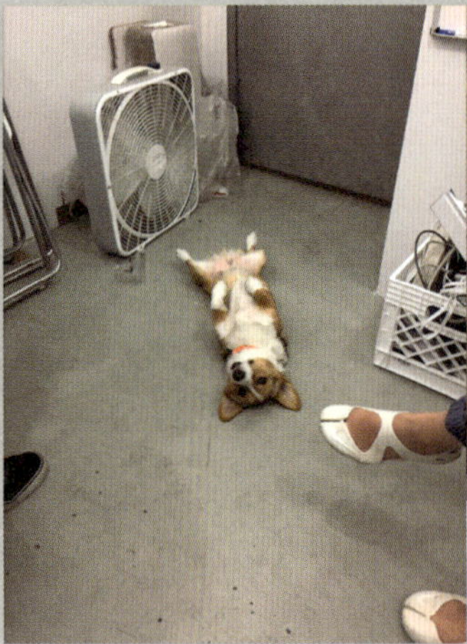

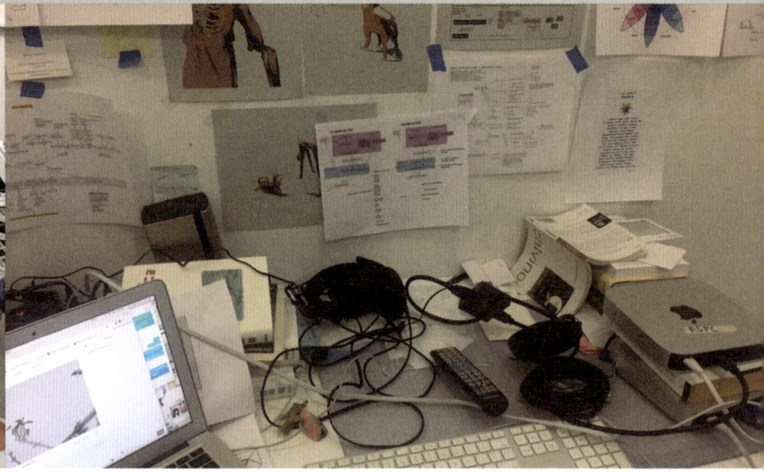

OOMEN brief

FEEDBACK NOTES

- i like the meerkat direction, esp for how they interact with each other, group together.
- imagine that their faces started as cartoonish and have been evolutionarily tuned to be a bit more biological, like a meerkat x emoji x human hybrid.
- where on their body would evolution give them hair? would fur or hair help them with the heat burns?
- any facial coloring (like how some furry mammals like a ferret have dark patch or pattern on face, maybe to protect from heat/sun or evolutionarily reduce how bright light bounces into their big eyes)
- what's a healthy attractive fit Uman look like vs. an unhealthy weak ugly Uman?
- a tiny sprinkle of deviant art, like the vulgarity of deviant art. imagine an advanced AI's idea of recreating its own version of humans was influenced by all the images human civilization have made - from ancient greek times thru to deviant art acounts (the garish cartoony/furry/animorph/emoji world)
- the feeling is that we are seeing an AI's fantasy made more ridiculous by evolutionary biology, which for us viewers is nightmarish and vulgar, but kind of cute and fascinating (like the horror of a misinterpretation by AI, COMBINED with the horror of evolutionary biology taking its course).
- I want people to not know what to feel when they see Umans, meaning they feel conflicting emotions about them: they're cute like meerkats but creepy vulgar like deviant art animorphs. biology gone bad.

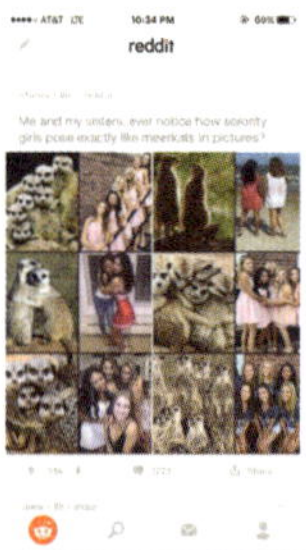

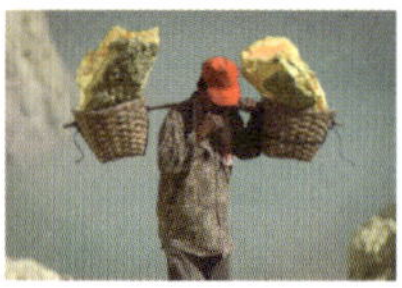

SMART PART SOW & Schedule for Sam

Deadline: Dec 15, 2016

BUILD FOUNDATIONAL NERVOUS SYSTEM + SMART-PART

- [x] [illegible]
  - https://github.com/Blueteak/Unity-Neural-Network
  - https://github.com/mattatz/EvolvingVirtualCreatures
- [ ] Build out neural network class to include algorithm for attaching / detaching connections between neurons during runtime evolution
  - [ ] SAM: This is part of the architecture (thus why I did the things with the neural net IO ports)

  The only thing missing is logically trivial functions and triggers to do the actual detach/attaching
- [ ] Build library of math function neurons
  - [ ] SAM: All the neurons are built except the delay neuron, as currently we aren't using the same propagation technique that dan lessin is using (just doing list order activation, whereas dan lessin simulates the response time through neurons)
- [x] [illegible]
- [x] [illegible]
- [ ] Saving: build genetic encoding of Smart-Part and nervous system.
- [x] [illegible]

BUILD ESP SYSTEM AND TRAIN SMART-PART PHYSICS CREATURE

- [x] [illegible]
- [ ] Build in Encapsulation / Syllebus / Pandemonium (ESP) system for creating and saving complex behavior in neural network.
  - **Encapsulation** can be either a special neurons or a separate brain w managed sensors/effectors. **(Consider this carefully!)**
  - **Syllabus** is an ordered vignette of training sessions.
  - **Pandemonium** is allowing multiple encapsulated subnetworks to compete against each other, winner wins full activation.
    - [ ] SAM: For the pandemonium / brain encapsulation, it's going to be a library of brains per smart part / core. So the corresponding neural net will be turned on in all parts and core based on what the top level brains want

ANIMATION LIST

1. **Idle Almost All Fours** - but hands don't touch ground; bent, slight movement, *controlled small breathing*, tryi
   1. FEEDBACK: looks pretty good; just have head face frequency, like parkinsons, like REALLY nervous
2. **Idle Alert Standing** - standing like a meerkat, arms res humanoid bind pose), slight movement, *torso from bre*
   1. FEEDBACK pretty good - no swaying of upper bod make tippy-toe less and widen distance between f that position. arms and hands more inward, hoveri http://vignette2.wikia.nocookie.net/meerkats/imag
3. **Idle Standing worried hands** - hands together touching hunched, anxious fiddling movement w hands, *full bod*
   1. FEEDBACK: i think the tip toe doesn't work, looks more back to support center of mass; hands up in https://www.dropbox.com/s/dddt6uu3u/ol09x/Scre 29%20at%2011.00.28%20AM.png?dl=0 possible to make body shake at *higher frequency*,
4. **Hunched slow sneaking walk** (cautious) - like trying t (except translation will change)
   1. FEEDBACK - pretty good; just get rid of tippy toes they are lifted.
5. **Meerkat Upright Walking Forward** - arms resting for humanoid bind pose), leaning forward, should loop (ex
   1. FEEDBACK get rid of tippy-toe. back curled forwa destination; arms and hands more inward, hovering http://vignette2.wikia.nocookie.net/meerkats/imag trying to hold themselves there but bumping up a
6. **Meerkat Run Almost All Fours** - but hands don't touch monkey like, should loop (except translation will chang
   1. FEEDBACK - looking good - not sure if the movie doesn't alternate legs - looks like it is only doing the arms looks really good
7. **cautious walk backwards** - swift (not slow) but cautio arms forward like trying to tell someone to lower their loop (except translation will change)
   1. FEEDBACK - lets get rid of tippy-toes when the fe when the foot is lifted. can you insert a slight paus feels like a quick step; then a quick freeze for fee
8. **cautious strafe left** - like side step crab walk, low wide

Emissary 3 Character AI Needs

File Edit View Insert Format Data Tools Add-ons Help All changes saved in Drive

	A	B
1	**CHARACTERS**	
2	**Umans**	**Crabs**
3	More **psychologically** complex than crabs	More **physically** complex than Umans
4	Involved with **cultural things**	Busy doing pragmatic things like **maintaining body and health**
5	More like Sims	More like ants
6	Reproduce sexually like humans (**Males with females**)	Reproduce sexually like **hermaphrodites**
7	**May run out of male female pairs** and become extinct	Only **reproduce certain times of day** or periods ("in heat")
8		
9	**AI Needs**	
10	1. Reproduction	ability to reproduce and receive/pass on genes from parents/children
11	2. Save states	saves each character so it can reproduce genes
12		when the simulation resets, it remembers previous genes and behavior
13		
14	**Simulation of Infinite Duration Cycle**	
15	1. Story ritual "session"	
16	2. Life cycles	
17	3. Dead End/Apocalypse (all male Uman scenario, no more crabs)	
18	4. AI "resets" and populates simulation	

SHADER CONVERSION

Convert our existing Unity shaders into Shader Forge asset:
- Camera-based depth fog shader

Create shader-based vertex animation:
- Ooman shake
- Worm wobble
- Create a water foam shader

CONTROLLABLE FLUID SYSTEM BRIEF:
- Metaball: Confirm that this approach will give us the effect we need.
- Intersection shader - any objects intersecting with the puddle will - have an intersecting effect
- D Particle system- particles that move on the surface of the puddle
- Check out the edge detection/shore shader here:
http://blog.monomipark.com/post/139862950537/hello-im-ian-and-ive-taken-the-task-of-leading/embed

*We need a fluid system we can use to get this controlled "oil on water" effect. Here's a reference image— it should look like a 2D surface in a 3D unity world. The "puddles" or "droplets" must be able to be controlled by Ian.

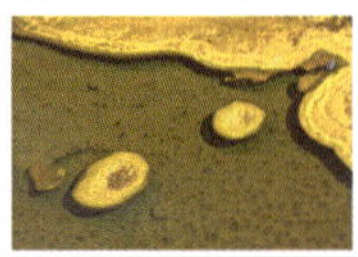

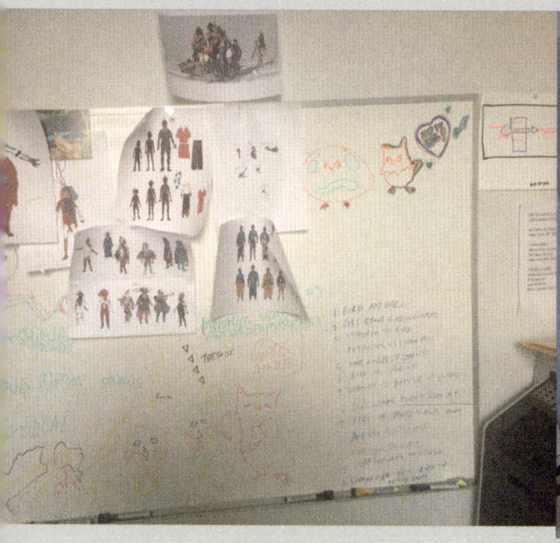

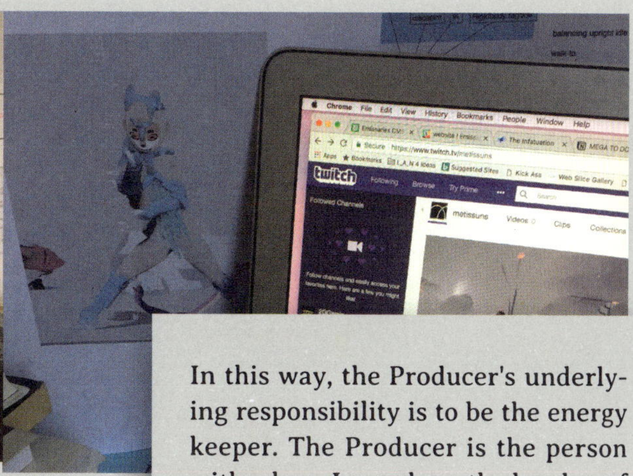

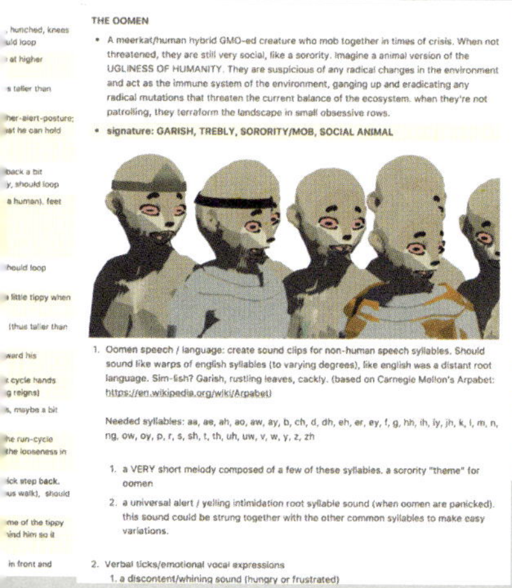

THE OOMEN

- A meerkat/human hybrid GMO-ed creature who mob together in times of crisis. When not threatened, they are still very social, like a sorority. Imagine a animal version of the UGLINESS OF HUMANITY. They are suspicious of any radical changes in the environment and act as the immune system of the environment, ganging up and eradicating any radical mutations that threaten the current balance of the ecosystem. when they're not patrolling, they terraform the landscape in small obsessive rows.
- **signature: GARISH, TREBLY, SORORITY/MOB, SOCIAL ANIMAL**

1. Oomen speech / language: create sound clips for non-human speech syllables. Should sound like warps of english syllables (to varying degrees), like english was a distant root language. Sim-lish? Garish, rustling leaves, cackly. (based on Carnegie Mellon's Arpabet: https://en.wikipedia.org/wiki/Arpabet)

   Needed syllables: aa, ae, ah, ao, aw, ay, b, ch, d, dh, eh, er, ey, f, g, hh, ih, iy, jh, k, l, m, n, ng, ow, oy, p, r, s, sh, t, th, uh, uw, v, w, y, z, zh

   1. a VERY short melody composed of a few of these syllables. a sorority "theme" for oomen
   2. a universal alert / yelling intimidation root syllable sound (when oomen are panicked). this sound could be strung together with the other common syllables to make easy variations.

2. Verbal ticks/emotional vocal expressions
   1. a discontent/whining sound (hungry or frustrated)

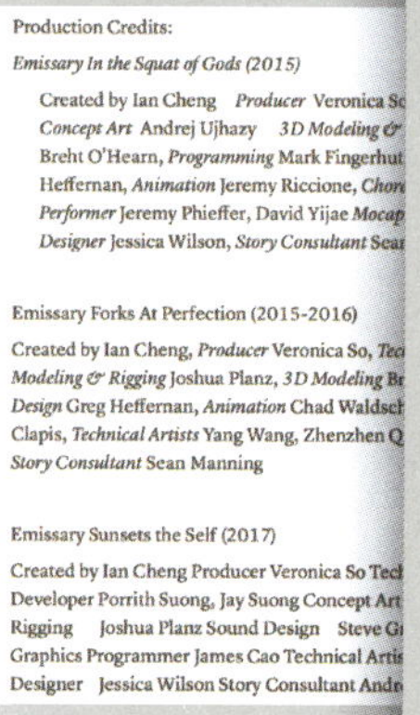

Production Credits:

Emissary In the Squat of Gods (2015)

Created by Ian Cheng *Producer* Veronica Sc
Concept Art Andrej Ujhazy *3D Modeling &*
Breht O'Hearn, *Programming* Mark Fingerhut
Heffernan, *Animation* Jeremy Riccione, *Chor*
Performer Jeremy Phieffer, David Yijae *Mocap*
Designer Jessica Wilson, *Story Consultant* Sear

Emissary Forks At Perfection (2015-2016)

Created by Ian Cheng, *Producer* Veronica So, *Tec*
Modeling & Rigging Joshua Planz, *3D Modeling* Br
Design Greg Heffernan, *Animation* Chad Waldsch
Clapis, *Technical Artists* Yang Wang, Zhenzhen Q
Story Consultant Sean Manning

Emissary Sunsets the Self (2017)

Created by Ian Cheng Producer Veronica So Tech
Developer Porrith Suong, Jay Suong Concept Art
Rigging Joshua Planz Sound Design Steve Gi
Graphics Programmer James Cao Technical Artis
Designer Jessica Wilson Story Consultant Andr

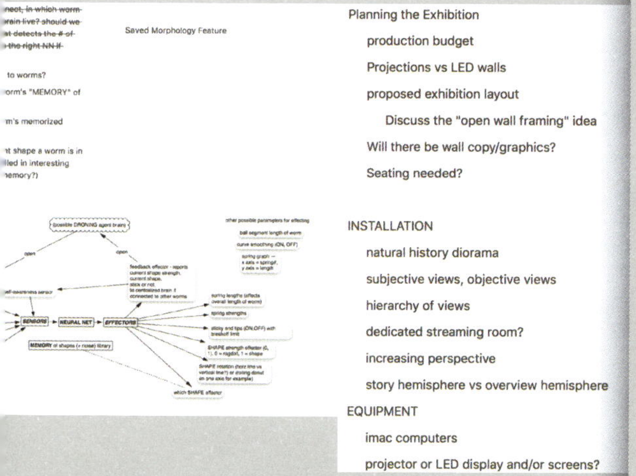

Planning the Exhibition

- production budget
- Projections vs LED walls
- proposed exhibition layout
  - Discuss the "open wall framing" idea
- Will there be wall copy/graphics?
- Seating needed?

INSTALLATION

- natural history diorama
- subjective views, objective views
- hierarchy of views
- dedicated streaming room?
- increasing perspective
- story hemisphere vs overview hemisphere

EQUIPMENT

- imac computers
- projector or LED display and/or screens?

In this way, the Producer's underlying responsibility is to be the energy keeper. The Producer is the person with whom I can share the burden of energy upkeep. If my job as Director is to orient the ship in the right direction, stay true to mission, and reiterate its worth, it's the Producer's job to keep spirits high, choose the right characters, and remind everyone of the bigger story when things get rough and bloody. I couldn't manage this crazy process without the Producer. It takes so long just to get all the ingredients right to finally cook together. Narrative premise. Concept design. Lifecycle design. Sound design. Modelling. Animation. Programming persistent systems. Programming AI. Graphics programming. Version control. Graphic design. Exhibition design. Negotiating with contractors. Team morale. Energy. It would be impossible to keep the bigger picture in mind while attending to all these dimensions without a Producer. I would abandon the project long before it finished.

When I met Veronica, she became my Producer co-parent, and *Emissaries* had a chance of actually being born.

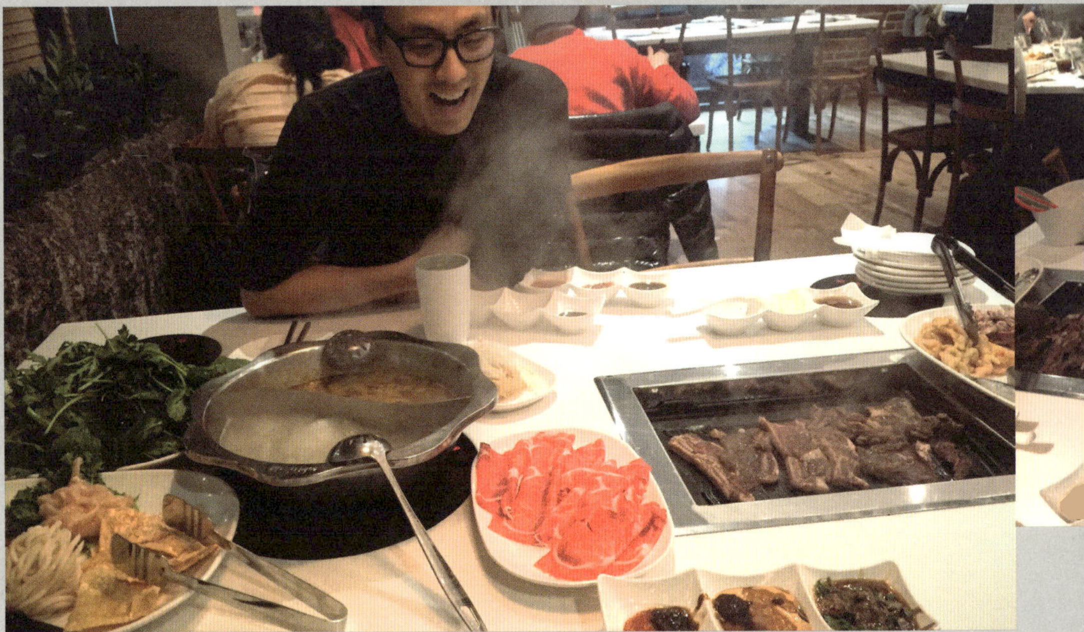

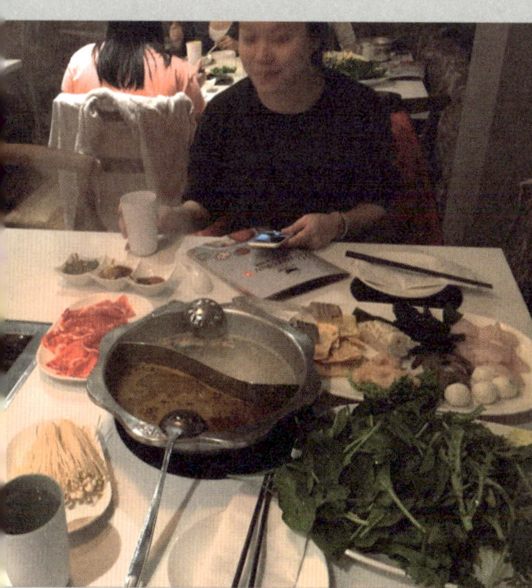

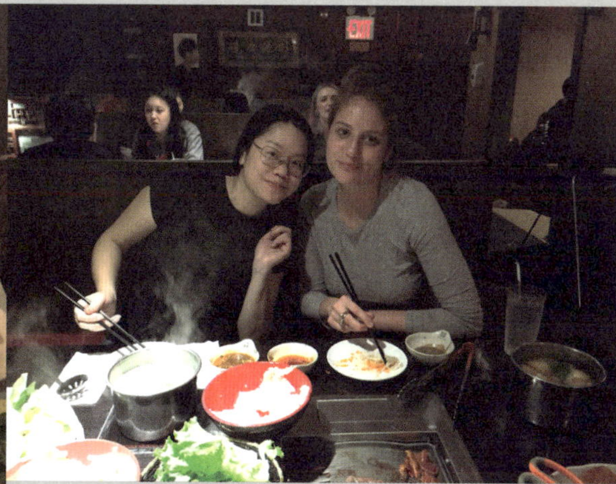

WHAT DO YOU EAT?

As Director, I control what information gets in and what stays out. What I make is a mutation of what I eat, so if I control what I eat, I can influence what my conscious and unconscious selves will make. My mind is not authentically original, but instead an information processing organ that needs material to inventively combine, compose, and connect. I am the books, films and games that I consume. I am the memorable vacation, drug trip, accident, last conversation. I am the average of the five people I see the most. I am only as good as the food I eat. Without new food, my mind can only rehash what I already know.

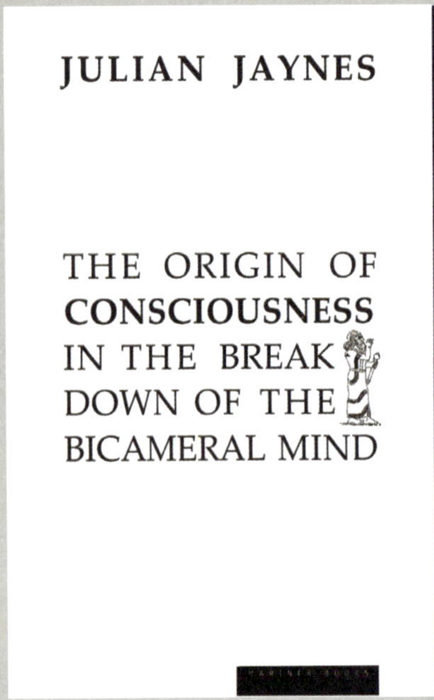
JULIAN JAYNES
THE ORIGIN OF CONSCIOUSNESS IN THE BREAK DOWN OF THE BICAMERAL MIND

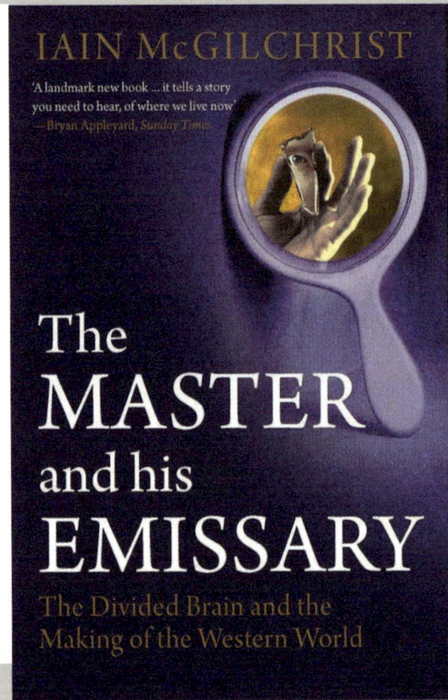
IAIN McGILCHRIST
'A landmark new book ... it tells a story you need to hear, of where we live now'
—Bryan Appleyard, Sunday Times
The MASTER and his EMISSARY
The Divided Brain and the Making of the Western World

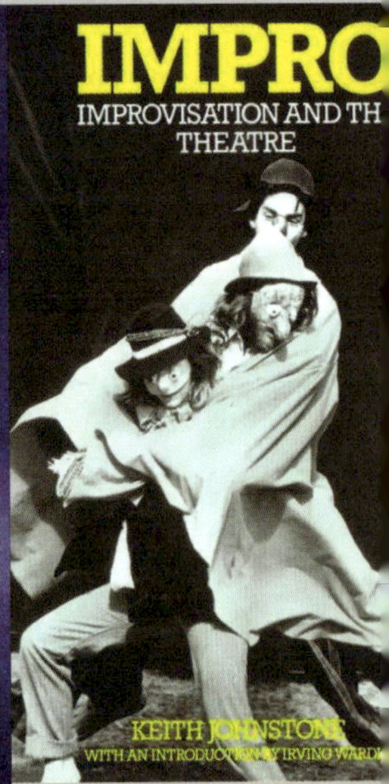
IMPRO
IMPROVISATION AND TH
THEATRE
KEITH JOHNSTONE

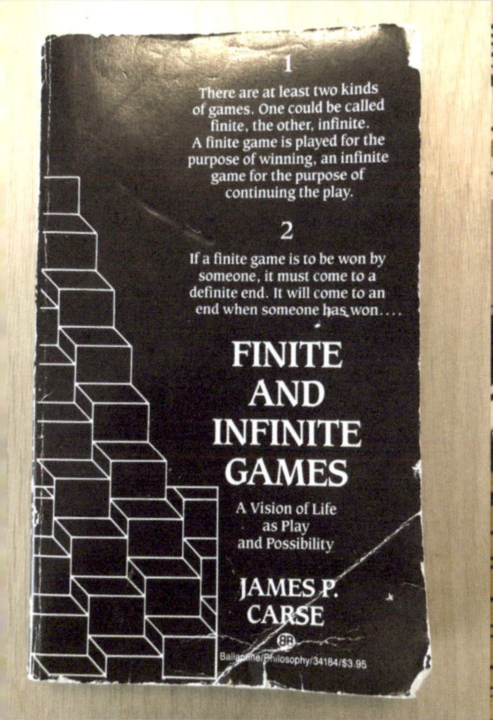

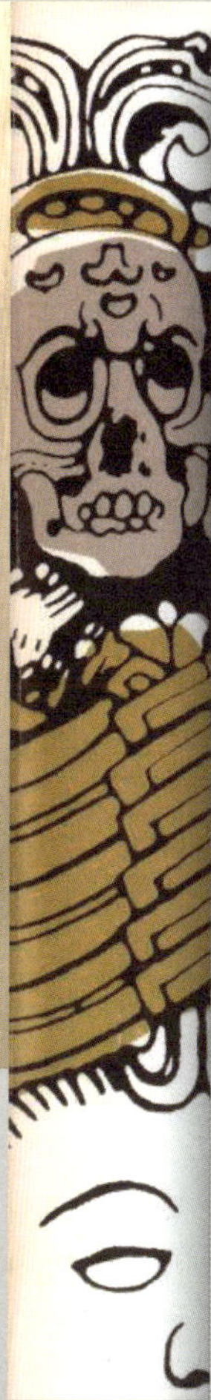

- *The Origin of Consciousness in the Breakdown of the Bicameral Mind* by Julian Jaynes (1976). Jaynes hypothesised that ancient humans had different software in their heads. They didn't have the 'app' of consciousness. Instead when they encountered a stressful situation, they heard vocal hallucinations. As civilisations grew in complexity, and as natural disasters intruded on mental life, the 'app' called consciousness emerged. This became a key text for *Emissaries* in centralising the broader narrative drama around moments of cognitive evolution, as depicted in the breakdown of the bicameral mind. It also became an aesthetic touchstone: Jaynes conveys a sense that the ancient past was much stranger and more like science-fiction than we previously gave it credit for. He renders the ancient past of Egypt, Mesopotamia, the Mayans, the Greeks, as expressions of dramatic moments of cognitive software updates. The past contained its own strangeness.

- *The Master and His Emissary* by Iain McGilchrist (2009). The name of the trilogy *Emissaries* came from the title of this book. The book likens the Master to the intuitive right hemisphere of the brain and the Emissary to the rational left hemisphere. Over time the rational mind hallucinates that it is in charge, silencing the intuitive mind. But in truth, 'The intuitive mind is a sacred gift and the rational mind is a faithful servant.'

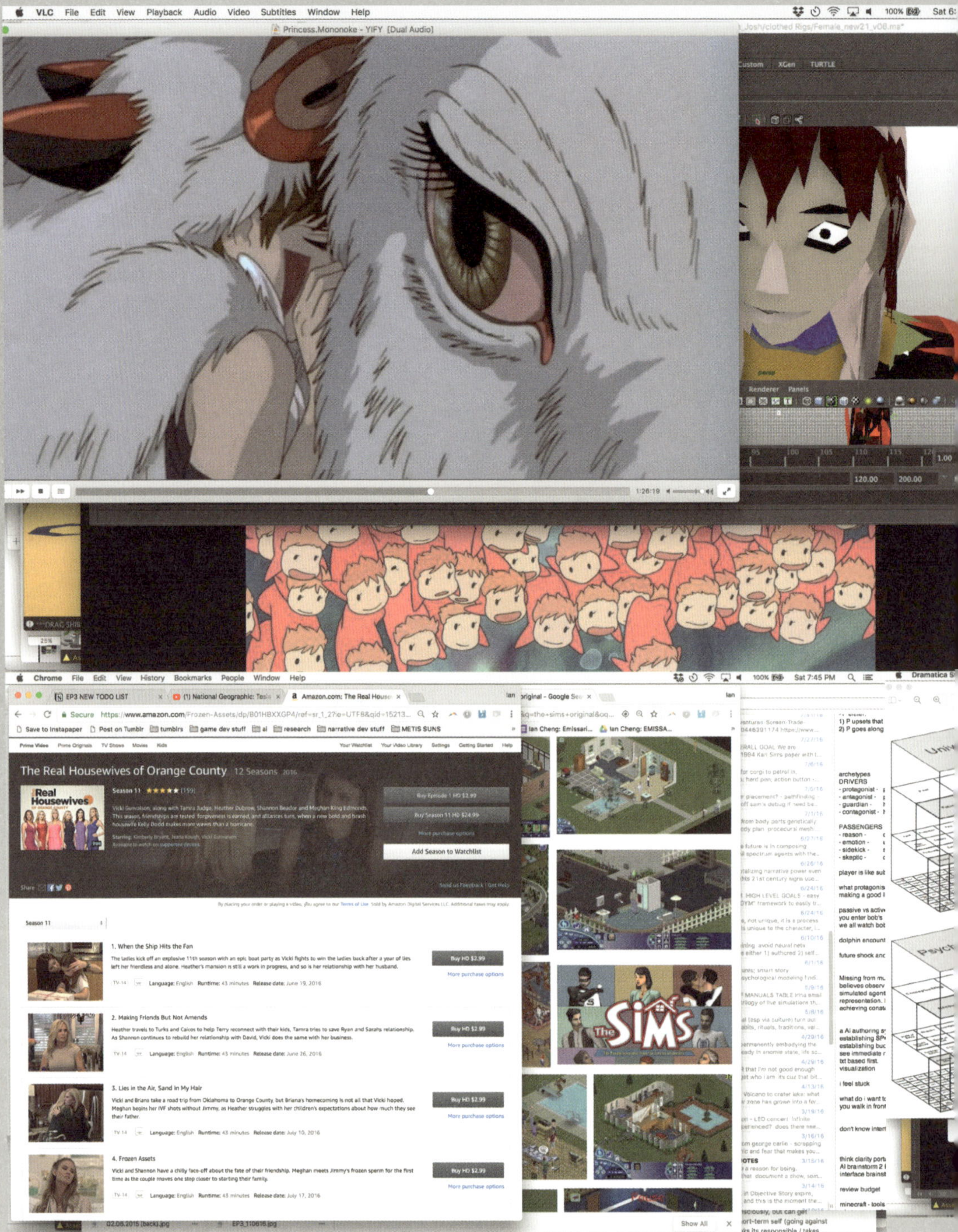
VLC File Edit View Playback Audio Video Subtitles Window Help
Princess.Mononoke - YIFY [Dual Audio]
1:26:19
Chrome File Edit View History Bookmarks People Window Help
Sat 7:45 PM
EP3 NEW TODO LIST
(1) National Geographic: Tesla
Amazon.com: The Real House
Save to Instapaper
Post on Tumblr
tumblrs
game dev stuff
research
narrative dev stuff
METIS SUNS
Ian Cheng: Emissari...
Ian Cheng: EMISSA...
The Real Housewives of Orange County
12 Seasons
Season 11
Add Season to Watchlist
1. When the Ship Hits the Fan
2. Making Friends But Not Amends
3. Lies in the Air, Sand In My Hair
4. Frozen Assets
The Sims
1) P upsets that
2) P goes along
archetypes
DRIVERS
- protagonist -
- antagonist -
- guardian -
- contagonist -
PASSENGERS
- reason -
- emotion -
- sidekick -
- skeptic -
player is like sub
what protagonis
making a good
passive vs activ
you enter bob's
we all watch bot
dolphin encount
future shock and
Missing from mu
believes observ
simulated agent
representation. I
achieving consu
a AI authoring s
establishing SP
establishing buc
see immediate r
txt based first.
visualization
i feel stuck
what do i want t
you walk in front
don't know inter
think clarity port
AI brainstorm 2 I
interface brainst
review budget
minecraft - tools
Show All

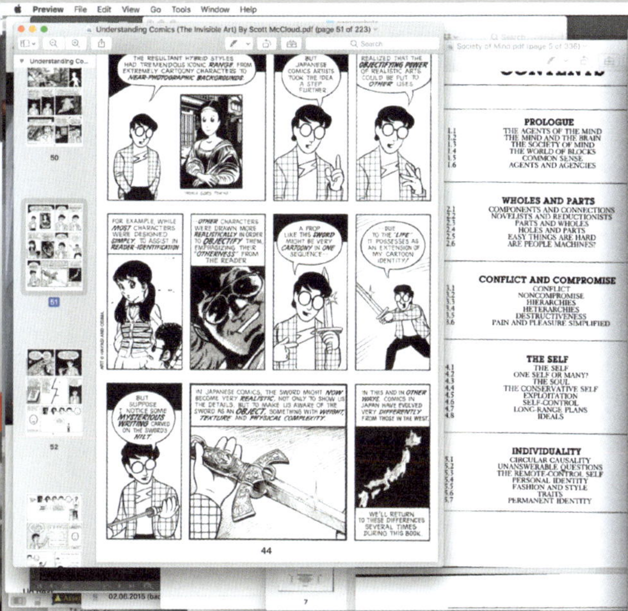

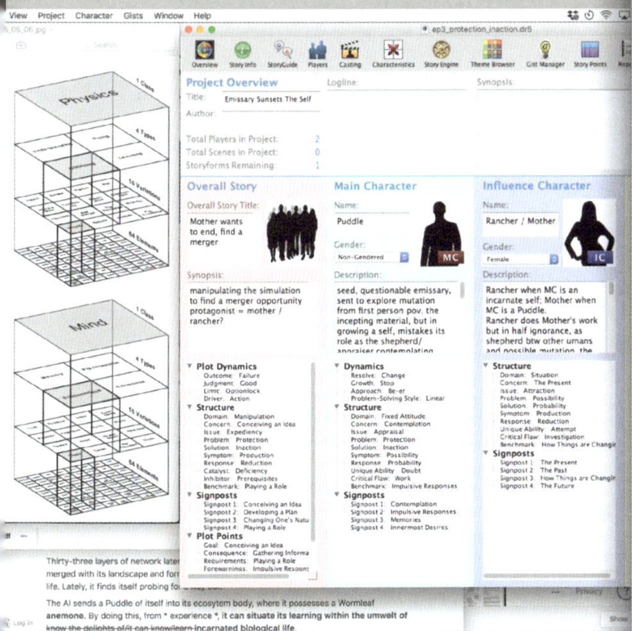

- *Finite and Infinite Games* by James Carse (1986).

- *Real Housewives of Orange County* (*RHOC*, since 2006) I learned the producers of the show used alcohol to spark drama. This became a model for thinking about putting together characters with strong personalities that could generate interesting stories that wrote themselves. It was also a model for how giving primacy to characters and their interrelationships over any particularly remarkable narrative could produce art that rivalled the narrative determinacy of movies. Is the format of *RHOC* a kind of infinite game?

- The animated films of Hayao Miyazaki. Each of his works feels like an entirely realised world that he has then made a documentary of.

- *Impro: Improvisation and the Theatre* by Keith Johnstone (1979). In teaching improvisation, Johnstone conveys the idea that the right brain can generate great inventions once one's body is submitted to physical games that distract the self-conscious left brain – wearing masks, seeing space as status, avoiding being interesting and 'walking backwards' through an invented story to keep it going, counting down numbers while forcing your hand to write. Johnstone proposes that we are atrophied children, but can be reprogrammed to reactivate the intuitive mind through improv exercises.

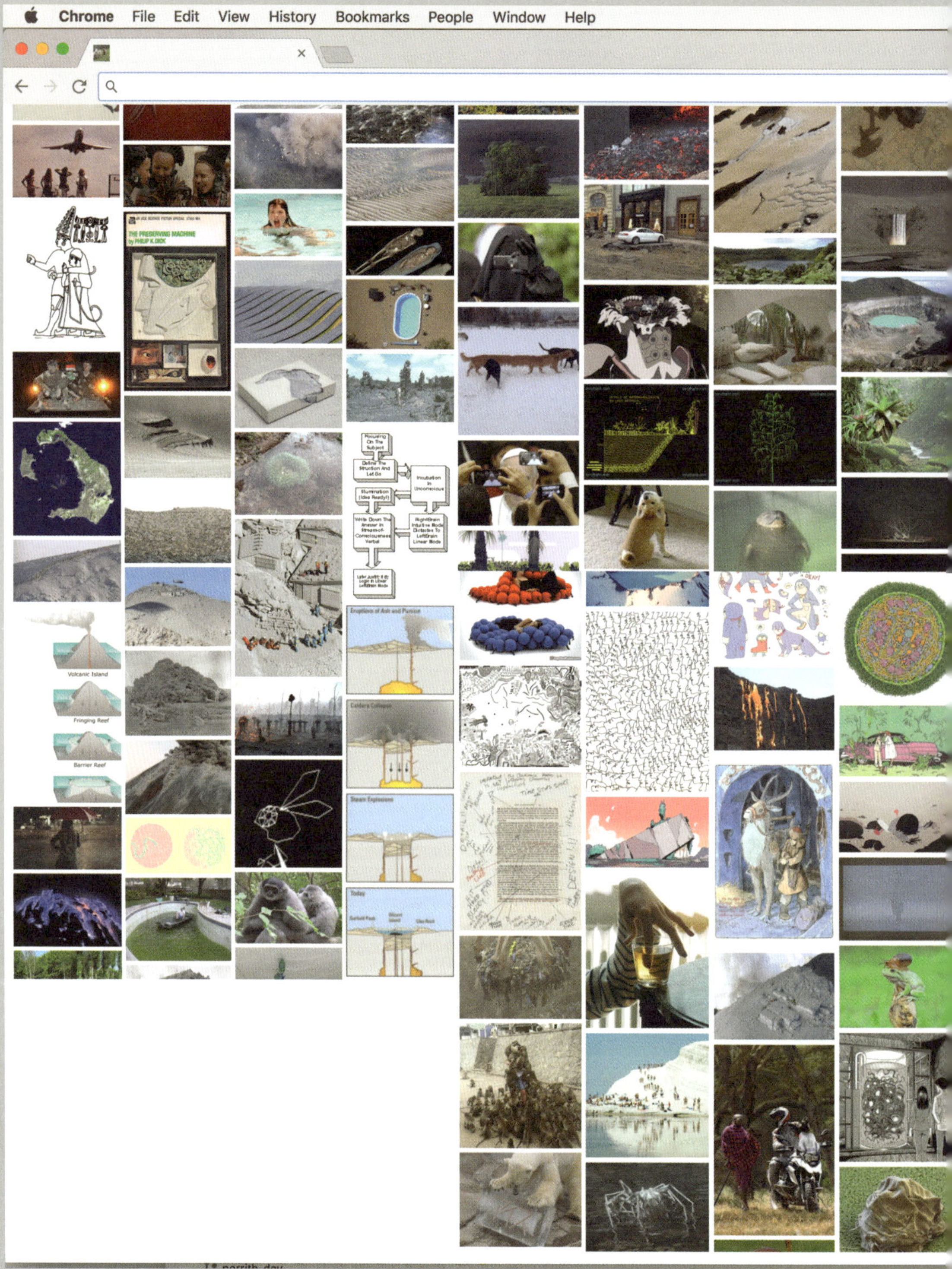
Chrome File Edit View History Bookmarks People Window Help
THE PRESERVING MACHINE
by PHILIP K. DICK
Volcanic Island
Fringing Reef
Barrier Reef

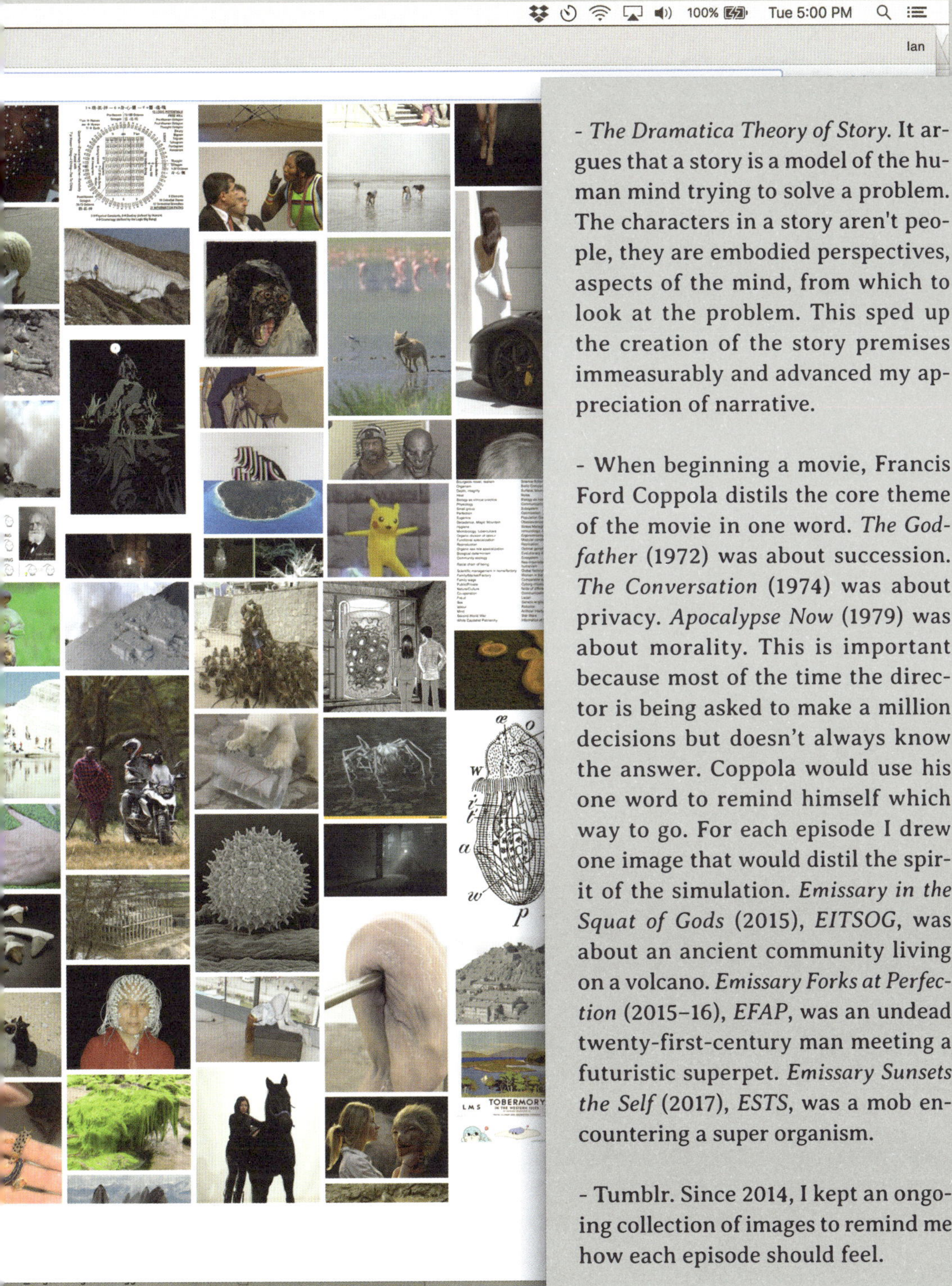

- *The Dramatica Theory of Story*. It argues that a story is a model of the human mind trying to solve a problem. The characters in a story aren't people, they are embodied perspectives, aspects of the mind, from which to look at the problem. This sped up the creation of the story premises immeasurably and advanced my appreciation of narrative.

- When beginning a movie, Francis Ford Coppola distils the core theme of the movie in one word. *The Godfather* (1972) was about succession. *The Conversation* (1974) was about privacy. *Apocalypse Now* (1979) was about morality. This is important because most of the time the director is being asked to make a million decisions but doesn't always know the answer. Coppola would use his one word to remind himself which way to go. For each episode I drew one image that would distil the spirit of the simulation. *Emissary in the Squat of Gods* (2015), *EITSOG*, was about an ancient community living on a volcano. *Emissary Forks at Perfection* (2015–16), *EFAP*, was an undead twenty-first-century man meeting a futuristic superpet. *Emissary Sunsets the Self* (2017), *ESTS*, was a mob encountering a super organism.

- Tumblr. Since 2014, I kept an ongoing collection of images to remind me how each episode should feel.

EMISSARY SUNSETS - 1/2017

Secure https://www.notion.so...

Save to Instapaper Post on Tumblr tumblrs game

Rancher berates Muscle, Muscle argues Rancher is endangering everybody.

**injured from the beating, Rancher tends to the worm body,takes it back to lava pool, and tries to affix another worm to its severed and exposed segment. it seems to take. the worm connects and grows into this new connection.

ACT2: [limbic phase of self - impulsive emotional]

[inside], Puddle in a severed piece of worm, inert on the ground, total loss of senses, random nerves firing, panic in the dark.

Muscle picks up to examine. Puddle enters into Muscle [thru his face or ear? improvised Droning Ritual here] immediately seizing control of Muscle. Muscle behaves and contort strangely.

Puddle sees its own worm body being rehabilitated by Rancher. Puddle feels jealous, fearful, perhaps a feeling inherited by being in Muscle's limbic system. [Inheriting further self-ego from being in Muscle.]

The other Umans are intrigued by this healing initiated by Rancher, and join in to feed the process more, growing the worm. the worm-composite grows, larger, it become animated. [perhaps other Puddles are in it now Droning together like a King Rat]

The other umans assign their wants/desires onto this thing - dad wants to study it; mom wants it to act as protection; no2 wants to instrumentalize it for terraforming; PA wants a mega pet. Their wants overshadow Rancher's ability to manage. where is Muscle?

Puddle inside and thru Muscle sees its own former body become animated.

WTF. that is mine! Puddle hates itself, has total self loathing. is this emotion even mine? is it Muscle's? I want to get back to the worm-composite. I want to destroy the worm-composite. that is mine, they are warping it. its contagious and fucked. I can barely walk in this fucking thing. [worst parts of being human seen here]

Puddle wonders, has Mother replaced me with other Emissary Puddles inside MY worm? What went wrong w me and mother? Puddle truly a competitive petty SELF now. self awareness. [some of this gets spoken thru Muscle]

Rancher sees Muscle having this psychotic break with itself. Rancher investigates. Rancher suspects, wtf, did worm spirit choose you, the fucking Muscle. Puddle doesn't know what to do, gestures badly, speaks badly

Puddle - badly spoken "how can you use my body without me,

Rancher confused who is speaking, Muscle whom she hates, or some incarnation of Mother?

[Rancher questions Muscle as if being able to question Mother directly: why all these changes, do you wish to pressure us to transform ourselves or transform the world, inherit the world, create life beyond progeny? is this a test? or is it using us?]

Puddle/Muscle tries to evade Rancher. Rancher gives chase.

Composite-worm creature seen as demigod by other Umans. They keep feeding it objects and other worms to incorporate into itself. Composite-worm

Log in

Emissari Albums SCRE

Secure https://www.notion.so/FIN...

Save to Instapaper Post on Tumblr tumblrs

FINAL WEEK SCHEDULE

RULES FOR IAN:

1. No changes or improvements this week for Episode 1 or 2! AFTER April 9th opening.
2. NOW - SUNDAY: WORK EXCLUSIVELY ON VIGNETTES AND
3. Non-final Episode 3 app to be loaded EOD at PS1 computer 11PM
4. FINAL Episode 3 app to be loaded first thing Sunday AM be

THURSDAY, APRIL 6

- [ ] IAN: Script FMOD sounds into project
- [ ] IAN: Bug squashing with Porrith
- [ ] IAN: integrate fog and steam into scene
- [ ] IAN: Check and import Sam's melded mesh
- [ ] IAN: Confirm/deny carpet sample LV
- [x] ~~11 AM-1PM: Ian's park guides arrive/slated for delivery~~
- [ ] IAN: programming EP3 (at home/office ok)

A version) to live

nic for Twitch

nal script, print

(full access)

esign

y vignette setup

OVE PROJECTIC

tumblr_okxcim2I2Y... Open with Preview

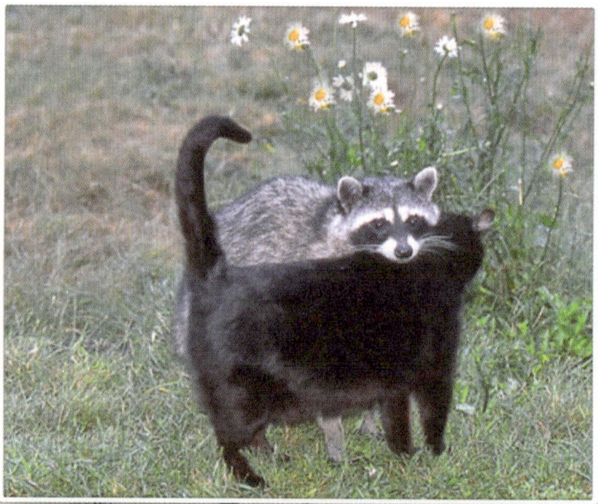

- [ ] Veronica: zip up files for Website/send to claire
- [ ] 8PM CLAIRE: website goes LIVE
- [ ] Jess: wiki updated with website

SUNDAY, APRIL 9

- [ ] 11AM DEADLINE: Swap in final Ep 3

Log in

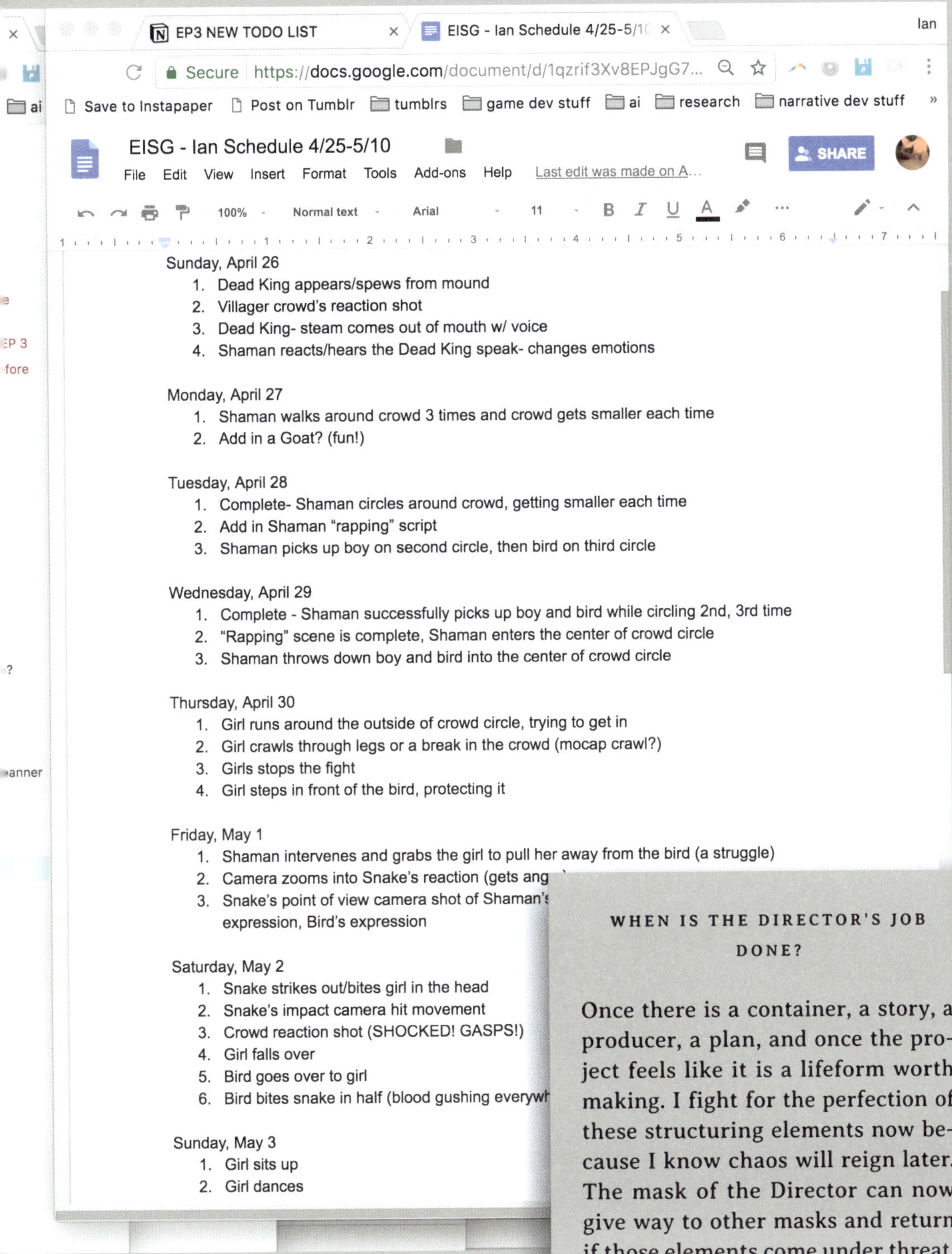

EISG - Ian Schedule 4/25-5/10

Sunday, April 26
1. Dead King appears/spews from mound
2. Villager crowd's reaction shot
3. Dead King- steam comes out of mouth w/ voice
4. Shaman reacts/hears the Dead King speak- changes emotions

Monday, April 27
1. Shaman walks around crowd 3 times and crowd gets smaller each time
2. Add in a Goat? (fun!)

Tuesday, April 28
1. Complete- Shaman circles around crowd, getting smaller each time
2. Add in Shaman "rapping" script
3. Shaman picks up boy on second circle, then bird on third circle

Wednesday, April 29
1. Complete - Shaman successfully picks up boy and bird while circling 2nd, 3rd time
2. "Rapping" scene is complete, Shaman enters the center of crowd circle
3. Shaman throws down boy and bird into the center of crowd circle

Thursday, April 30
1. Girl runs around the outside of crowd circle, trying to get in
2. Girl crawls through legs or a break in the crowd (mocap crawl?)
3. Girls stops the fight
4. Girl steps in front of the bird, protecting it

Friday, May 1
1. Shaman intervenes and grabs the girl to pull her away from the bird (a struggle)
2. Camera zooms into Snake's reaction (gets ang
3. Snake's point of view camera shot of Shaman's expression, Bird's expression

Saturday, May 2
1. Snake strikes out/bites girl in the head
2. Snake's impact camera hit movement
3. Crowd reaction shot (SHOCKED! GASPS!)
4. Girl falls over
5. Bird goes over to girl
6. Bird bites snake in half (blood gushing everywh

Sunday, May 3
1. Girl sits up
2. Girl dances

WHEN IS THE DIRECTOR'S JOB DONE?

Once there is a container, a story, a producer, a plan, and once the project feels like it is a lifeform worth making. I fight for the perfection of these structuring elements now because I know chaos will reign later. The mask of the Director can now give way to other masks and return if those elements come under threat.

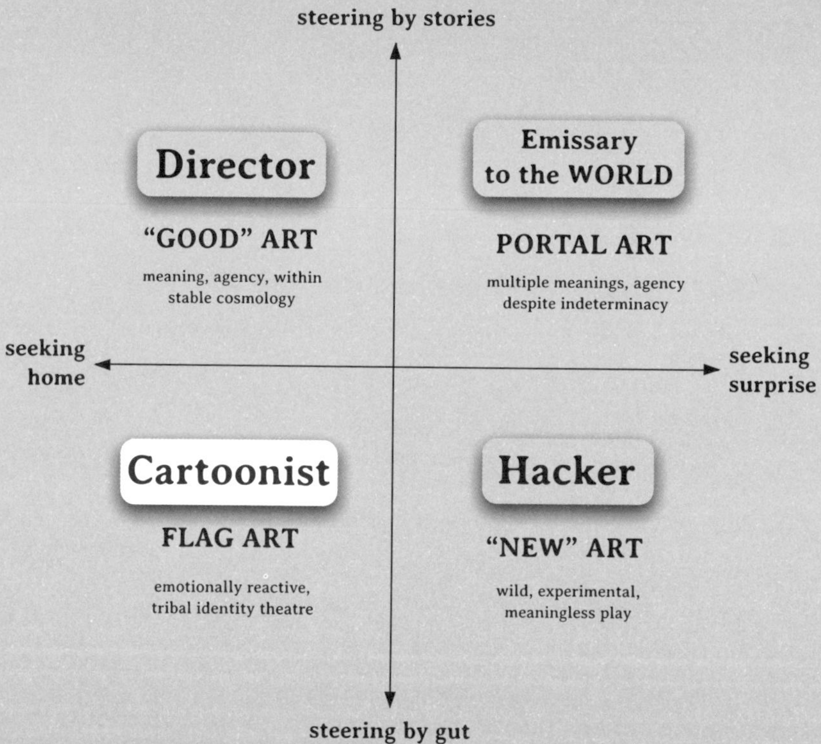
steering by stories
Director
"GOOD" ART
meaning, agency, within stable cosmology
Emissary to the WORLD
PORTAL ART
multiple meanings, agency despite indeterminacy
seeking home
seeking surprise
Cartoonist
FLAG ART
emotionally reactive, tribal identity theatre
Hacker
"NEW" ART
wild, experimental, meaningless play
steering by gut

What The Cartoonist Wants

The mask of the Cartoonist is a seductive one. The Cartoonist is a quick student of human behaviour who has learned to play to the lowest common denominator of human cognition – our gut instincts. Think of any artistic form that tries to make you feel something instantly or tap into your reward circuitry: pop music, art photography, freemium apps, children's cartoons, pornography, gossip blogs, Instagram personalities, trolling, clickbait, guru sermons, reality TV. The Cartoonist is strong in them.

The Cartoonist's job is to reduce complexity, turn ideas into images, distil contradiction, mine the familiar, define tribal boundaries, and magnify emotions. All in keeping with the finite cognitive budget common to all human beings. Where the Director pursues an idealistic vision of humans uncovering meaning from an exploration of their problems, the Cartoonist says meaning is easy: we're already at home in the world of our own emotions. *Seeking Home* and *Steering By Gut*, the Cartoonist makes Flag Art that encourages us to feel more of what we feel, filter that which affirms these feelings, lend emotive power to our tribal affiliations, and laugh off our human nature when things get messy.

The Cartoonist sees its audience as children. Children are the source of instinctive discernment through a deeply evolved tuning for faces, emotions, body language, status, tribes. But children also want to go home at the end of the day, get tucked into bed, and be told it's okay. The Cartoonist tells us we are messy animals, but comforts us with the belief that human nature has always been this way, and feeling something intensely is the only language you need. Being the Cartoonist is about being your own most instinctive child. 'If I don't get it, a viewer won't get it.' A feedback loop emerges: the Cartoonist becomes an expert in surgically pressing on our ancient animal programming, gets rewarded for doing so, and threatens to keep programming us there. Left to itself, the Cartoonist strips both artist and audience of any orienting narrative of who we might become.

So how can the Cartoonist help us in Worlding? By making characters. A character is not a person, but a collection of behaviours and beliefs.

The Cartoonist knows that the human mind is specially attuned to the nuances of characters and therefore accepting of the potential complexity a character might pack inside itself. This is the reptilian domain of attention, reaction, attraction, revulsion, celebrities, scapegoats, marketing, and evolutionary psychology. But it is also the domain of the most iconic characters in the history of Worlding, who each serve as a shorthand mental mascot for complex collections of behaviour and beliefs. Is Gollum an icon of twentieth-century Worlding, or an achievement in appealing to our base psychology? What about Buddha? Or Yoda?

We must dive into the artistry of the Cartoonist if we wish to acknowledge that our gut impressions influence which worlds we decide to invest in and which games we choose to play. We will take what is useful and try not to lose ourselves inside the mask of the Cartoonist, as truthy, emotive, cute and comforting as it may seem.

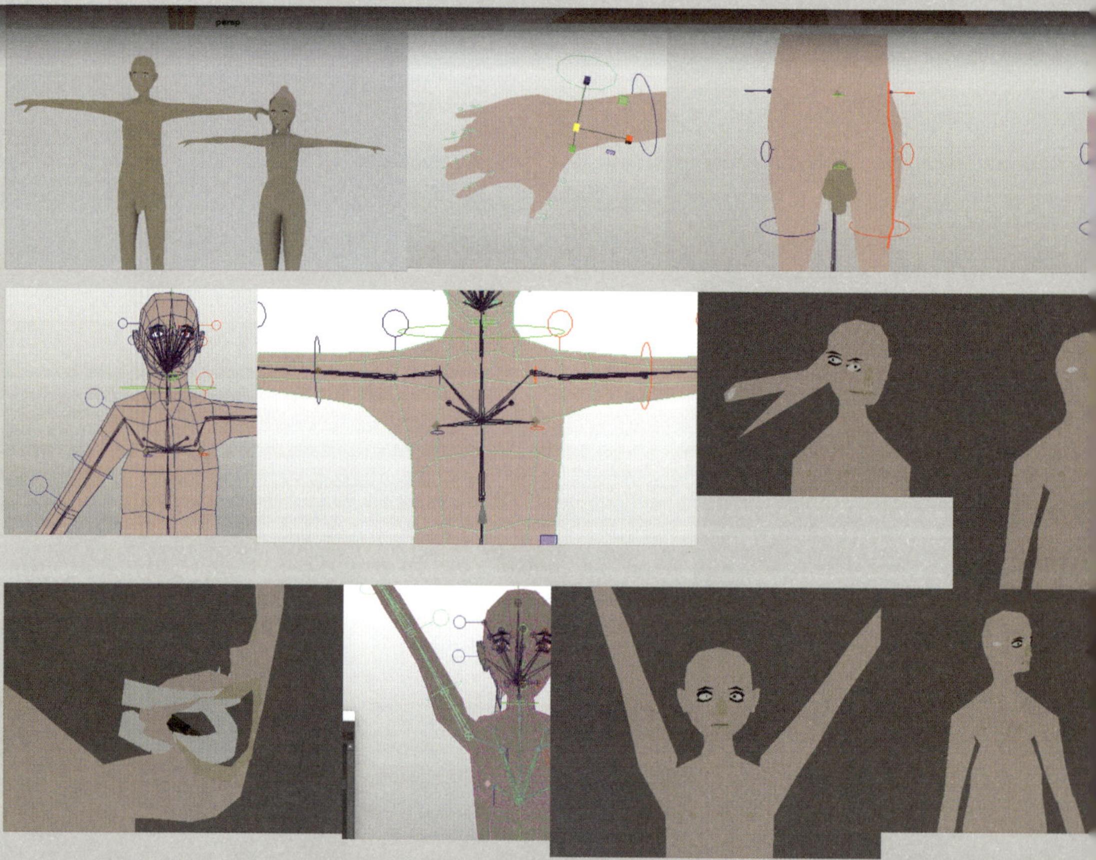

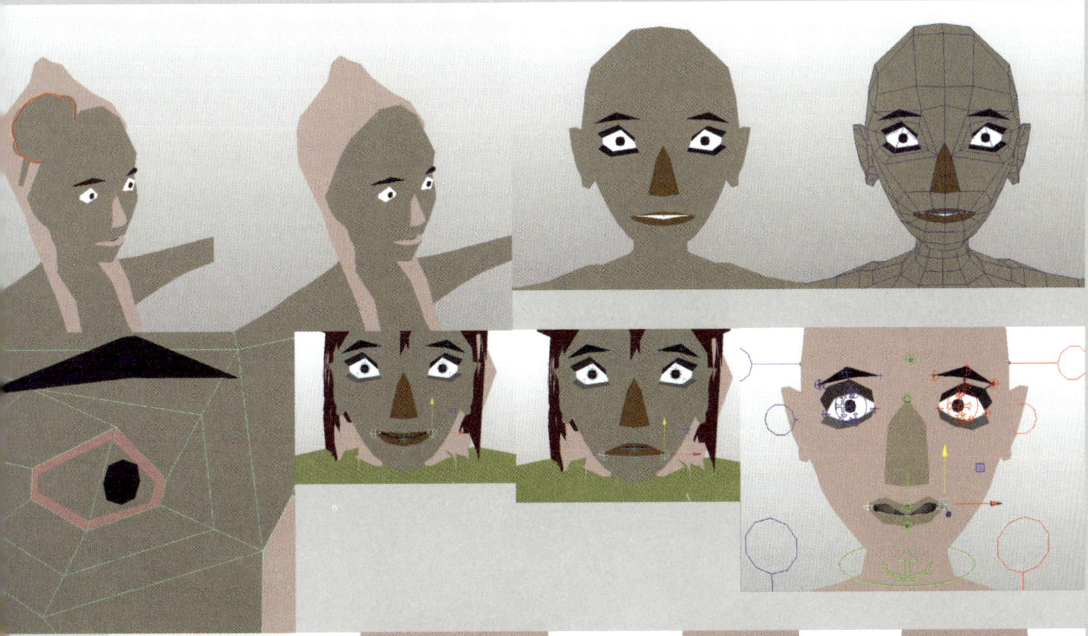

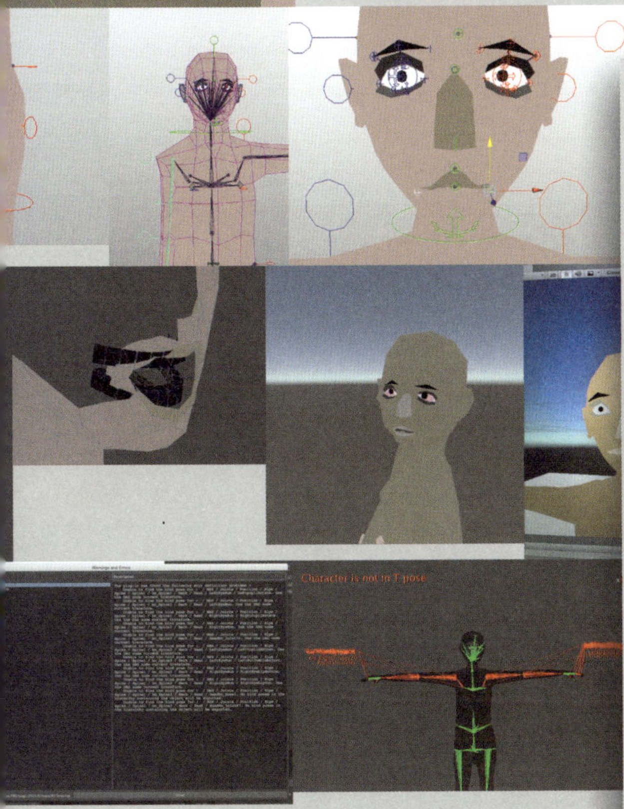

HOW DO YOU DEVISE A CHARACTER?

It always starts with drawing. The rule is if I can't draw it easily, my ideas about the character are not clarified yet. A character is good when a child can pick out its features and draw their version of it. In real life, the relationship between how a person looks and who they actually are can be veiled, noisy, or mismatched unconsciously. But when I draw a character, its outward appearance must express its inner psychology. That's the magic compression of cartooning. Cartooning is about creating external legibility of internal qualities. You should be able to read the essence of the character, that bag of behaviours, in one image.

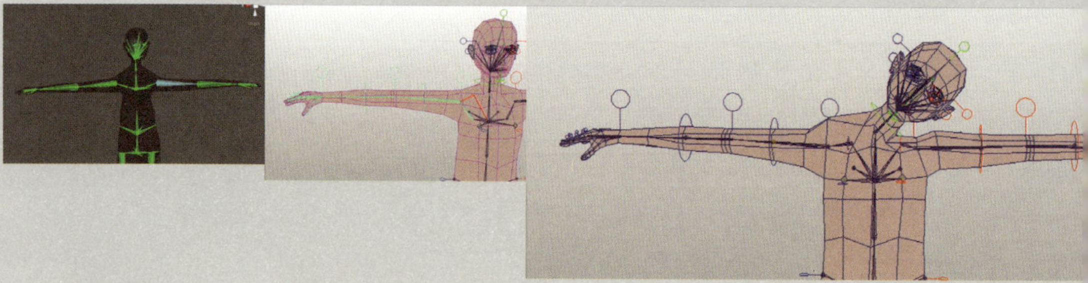

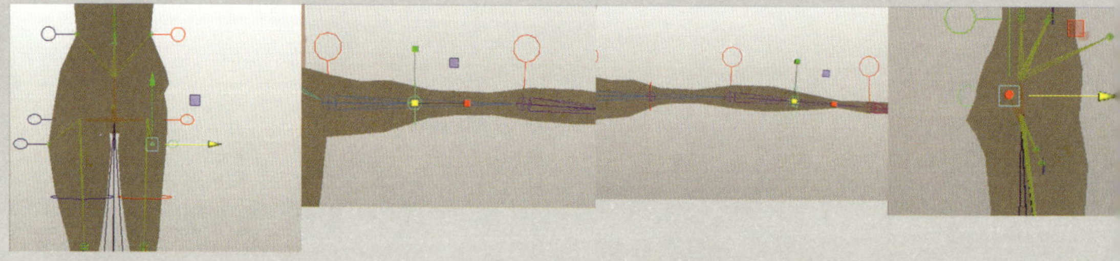

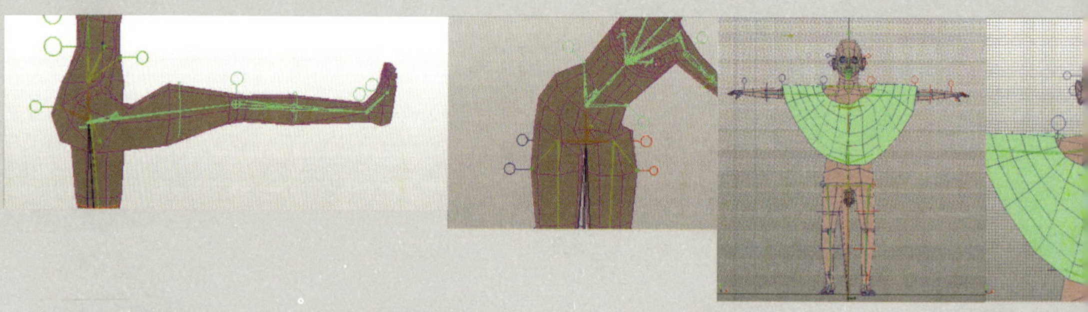

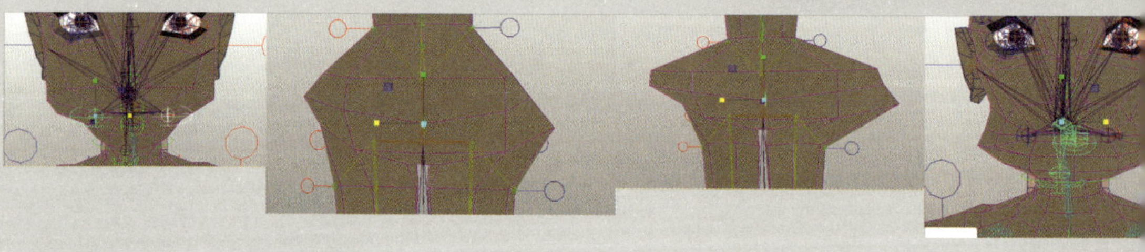

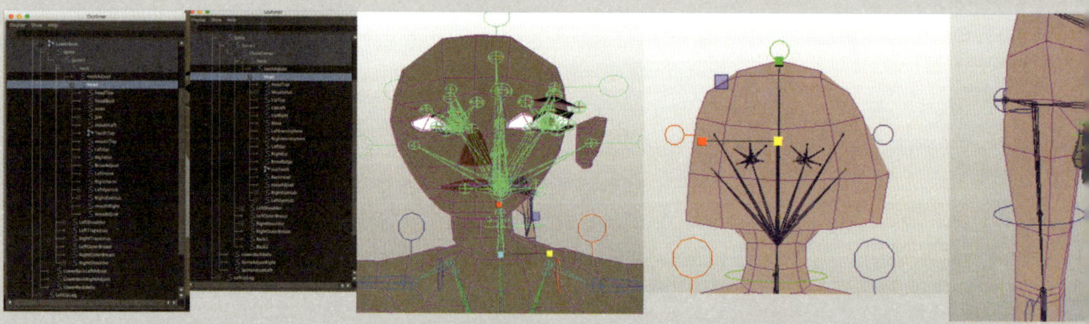

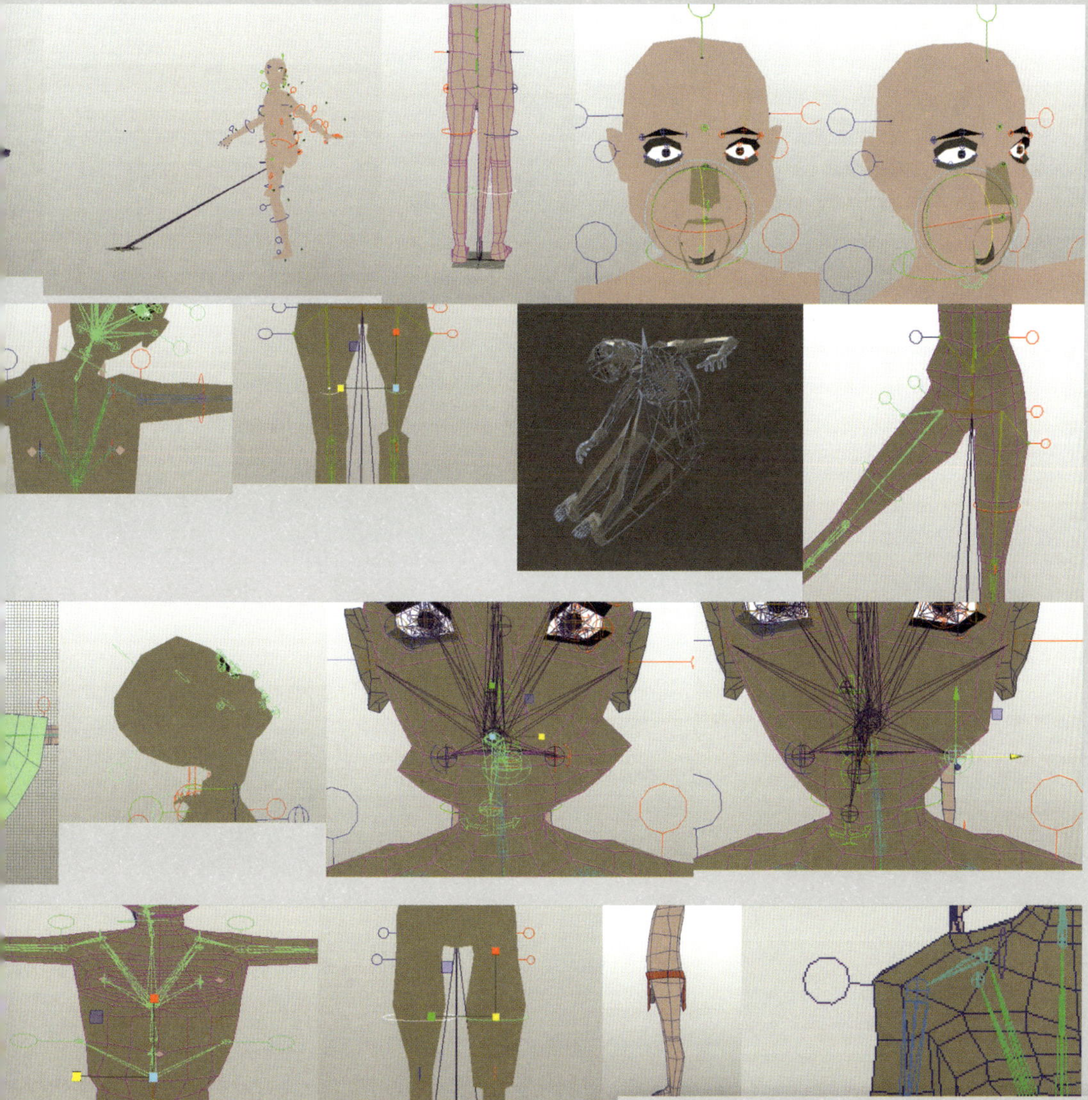

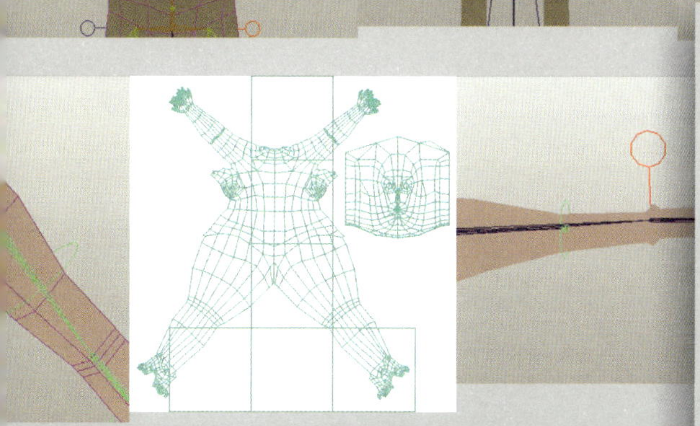

Simple shapes can make a character stand out in a crowd. Triangles signal power, hierarchy, aggression. Squares signal sturdiness, conformity, the artificial. Circles signal openness, home, the organic. Composed together in different proportions, this basic vocabulary can convey a range of character qualities instantly.

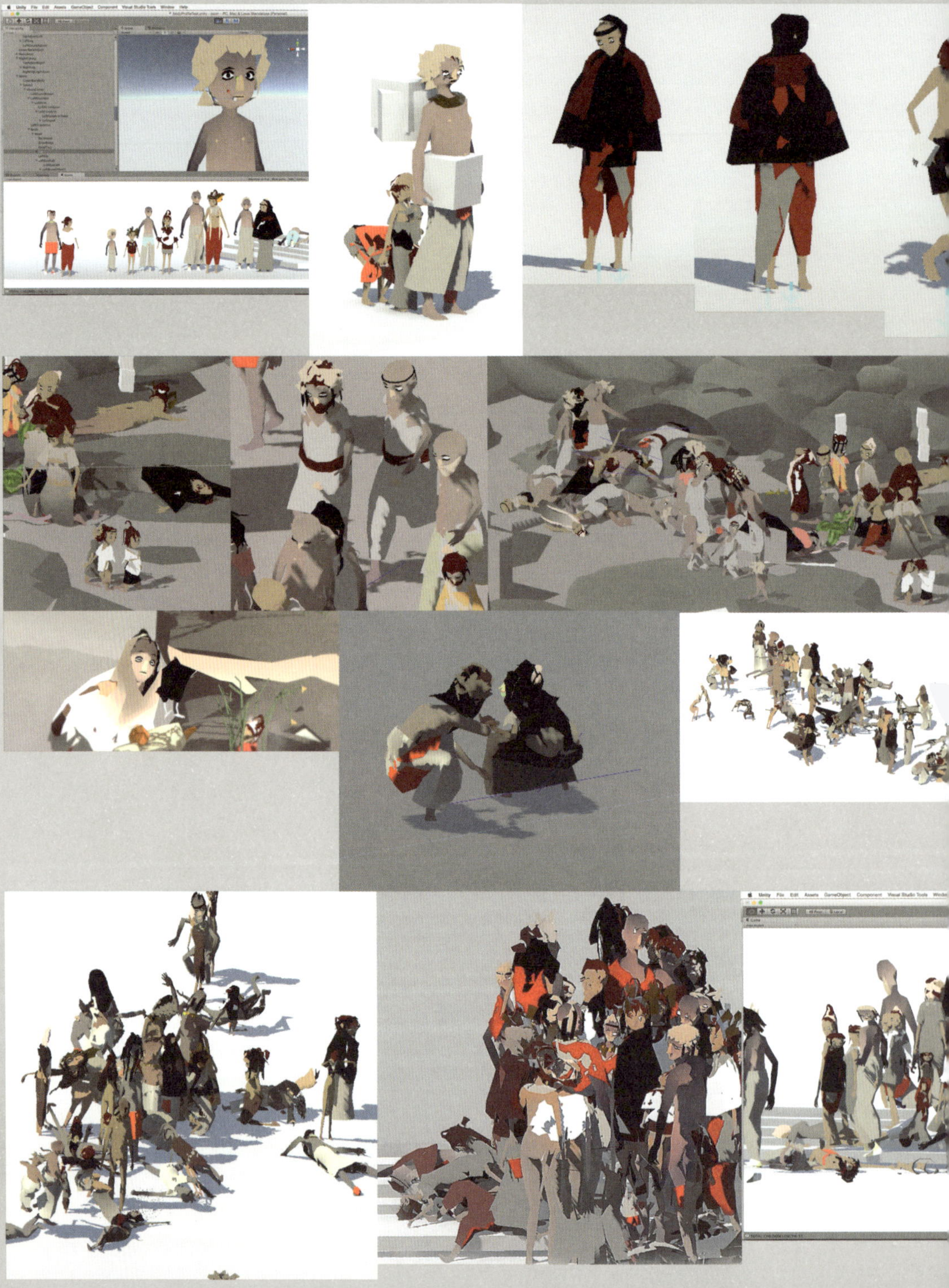

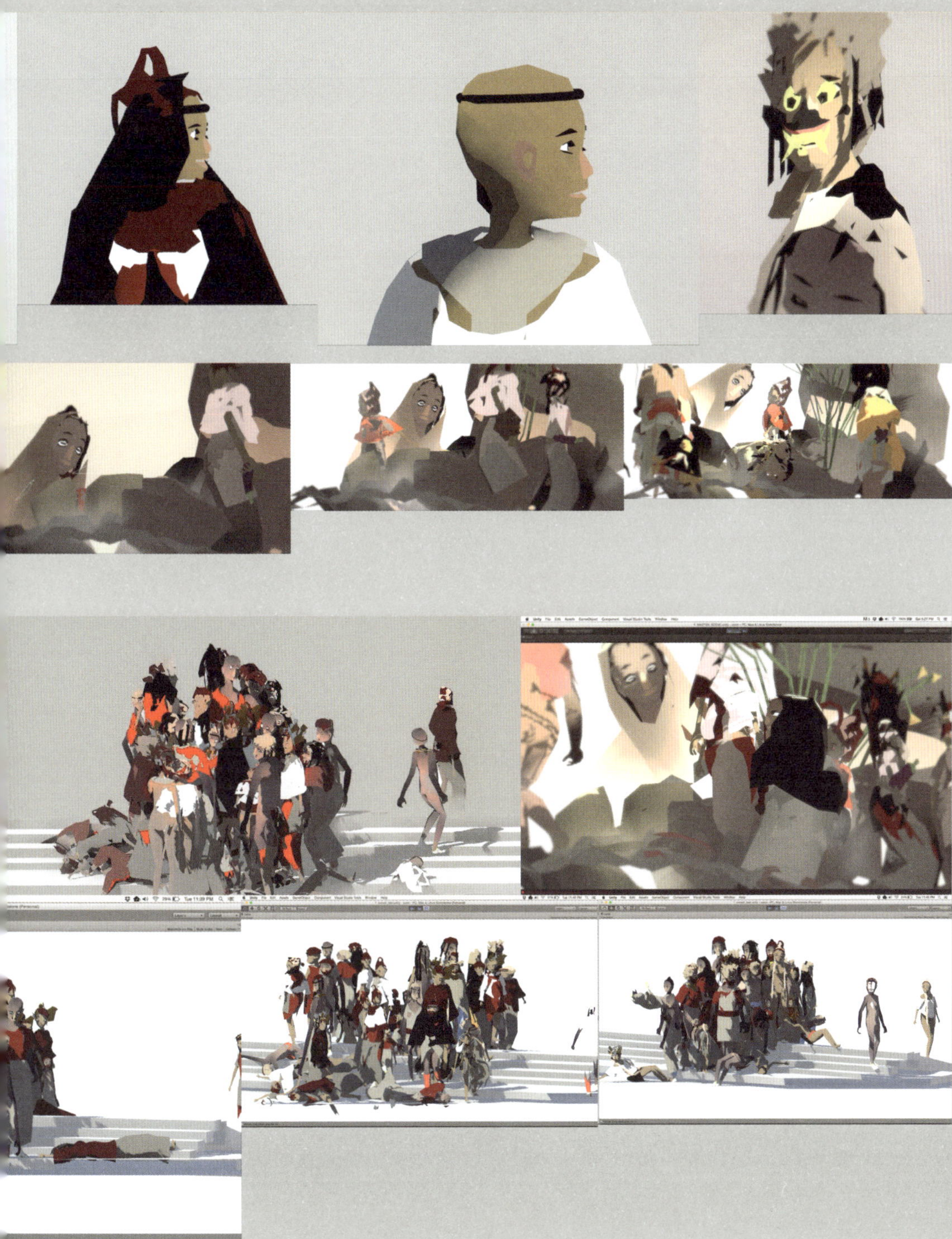

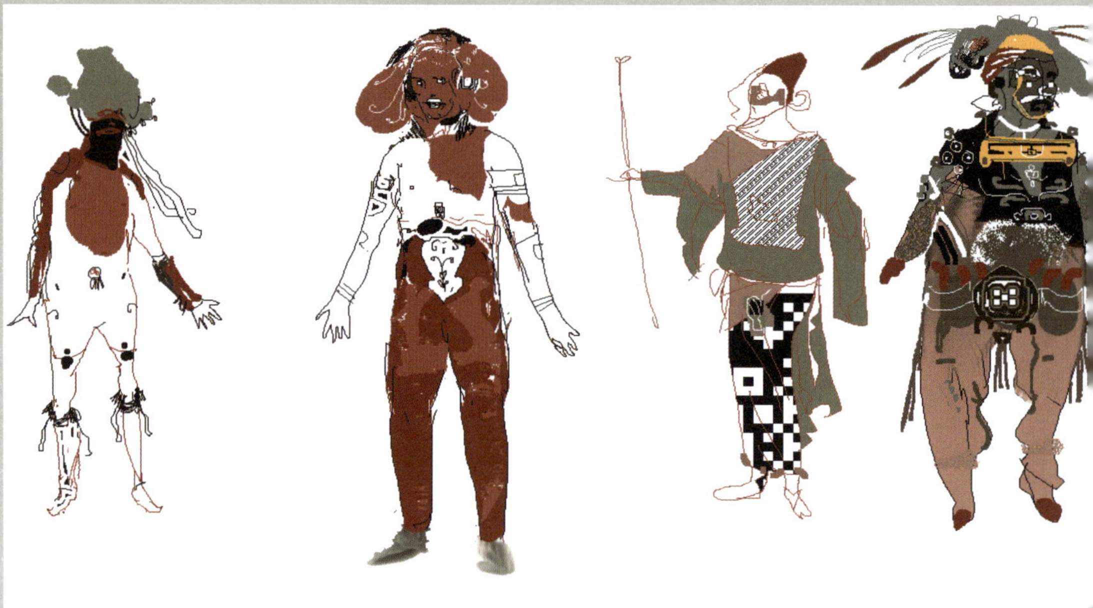

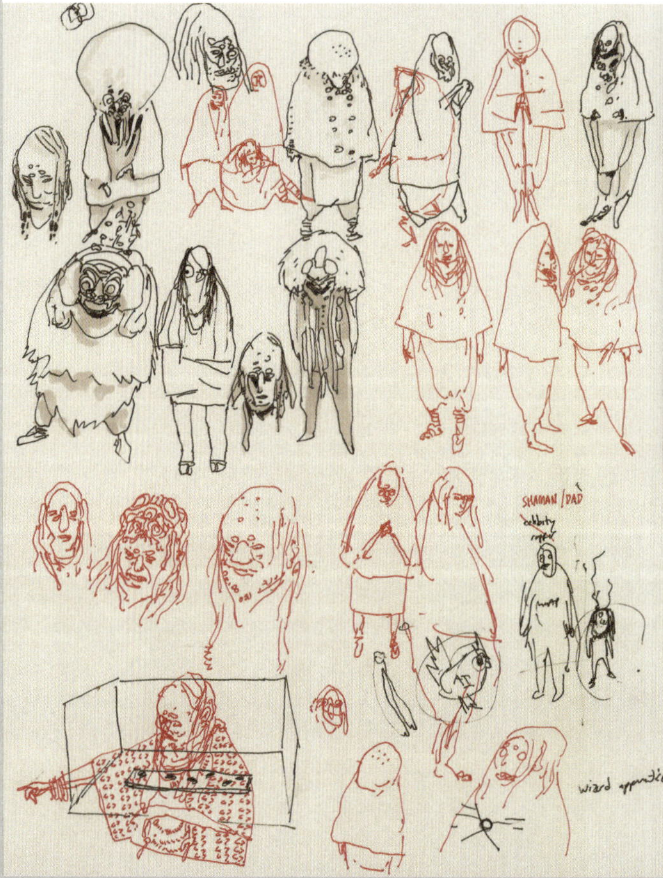
SHAMAN / DAD

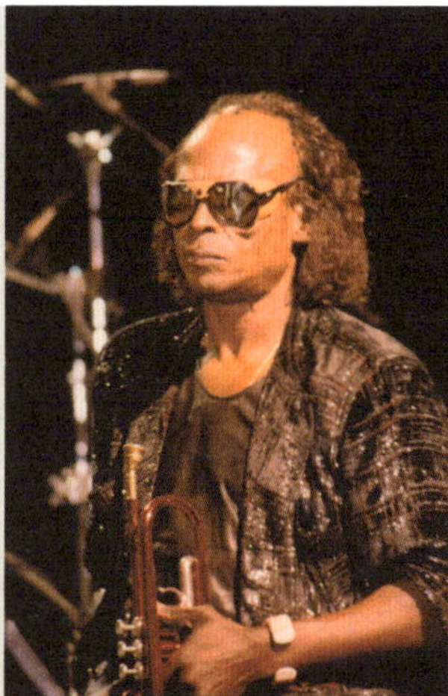

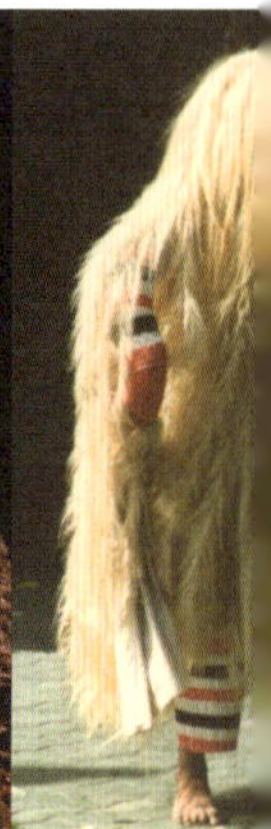

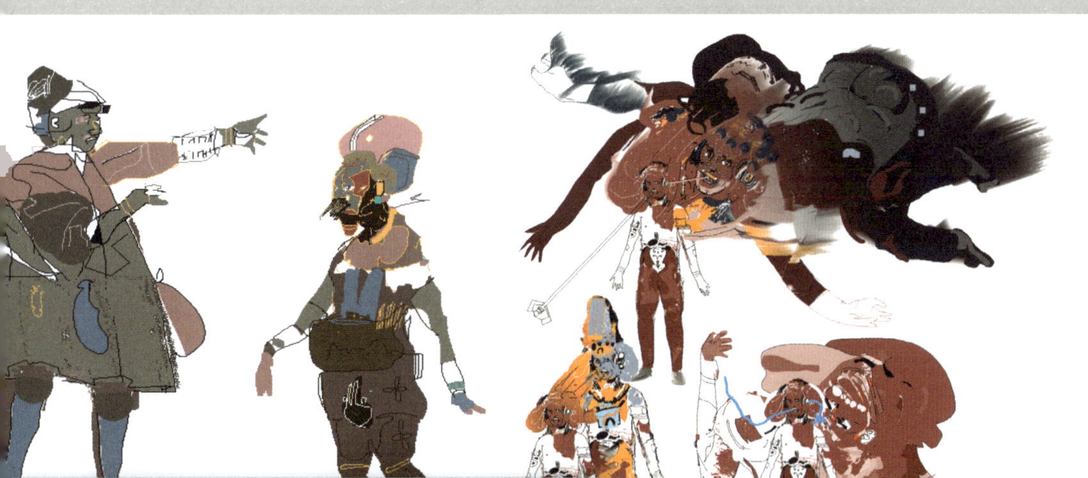

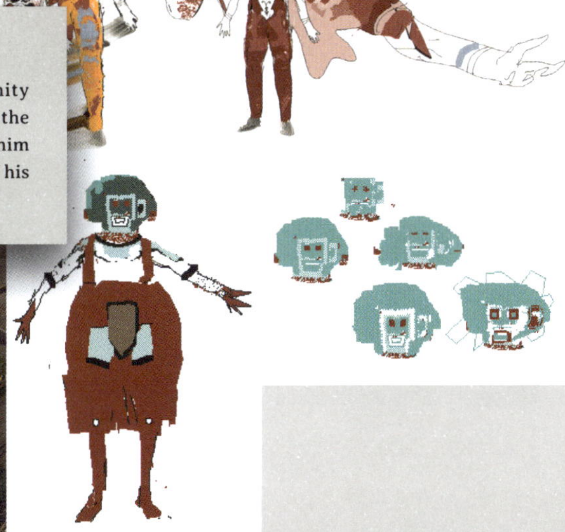

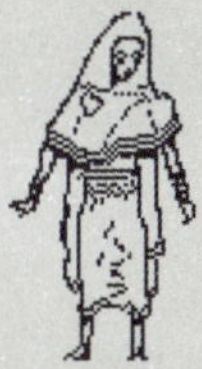

SHAMAN

Devoted leader of the Ancient community who is gifted at channelling the voices of the Fathers in times of Stress. His gift tethers him to his homeland and to the chatty bodies of his ancestors.

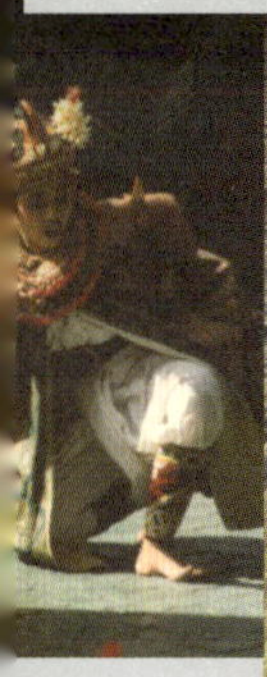

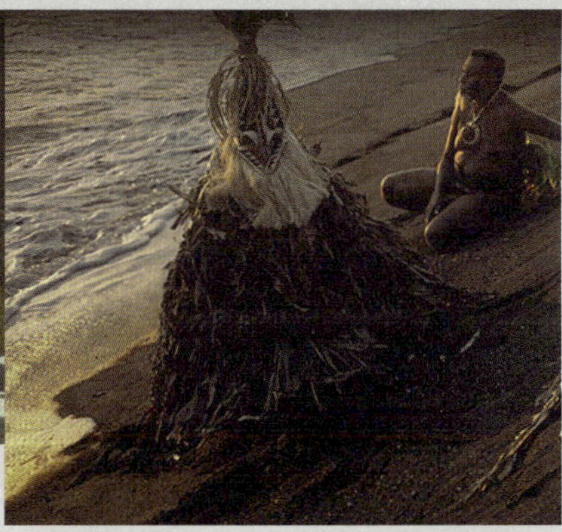

Shaman in *EITSOG* is the leader of the community. His main clothing is a large triangular shape, terminating in a boxy lower body. His eyes are big round disks, a small sign of warmth. He wants to keep his community grounded on the volcano.

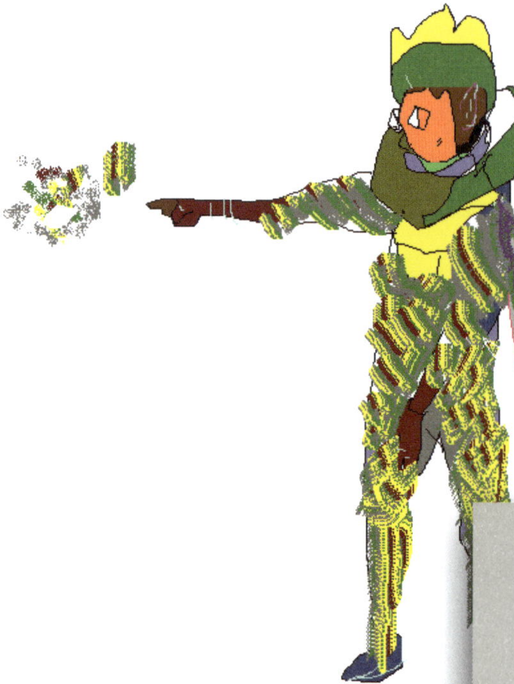

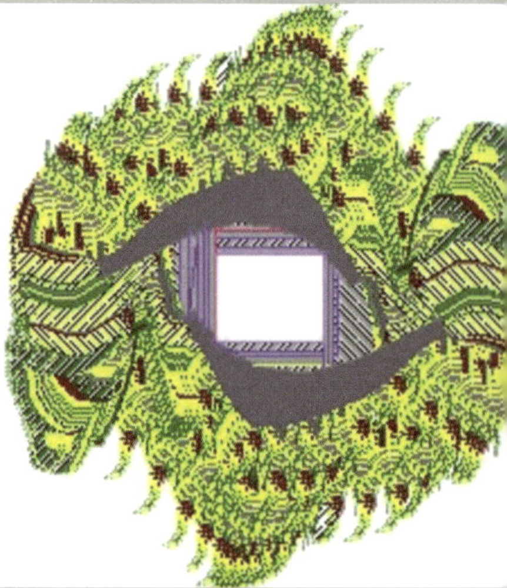

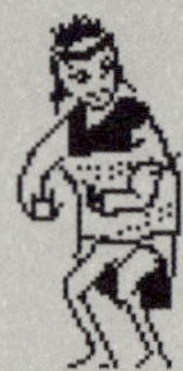

SNAKE BOY

A young brat from the community who expresses his fondness for Young Ancient [Emissary] by annoying and undermining her at every turn.

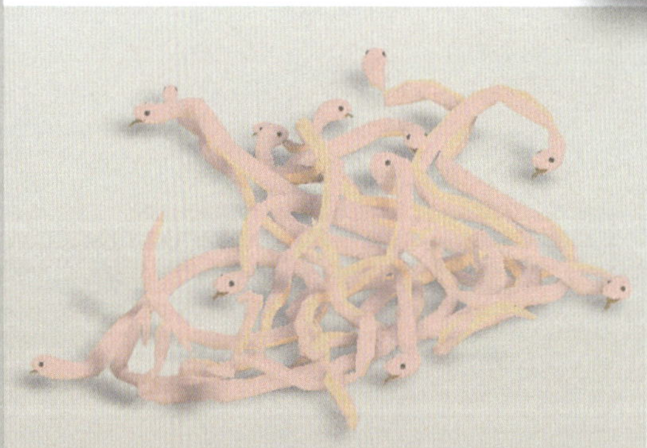

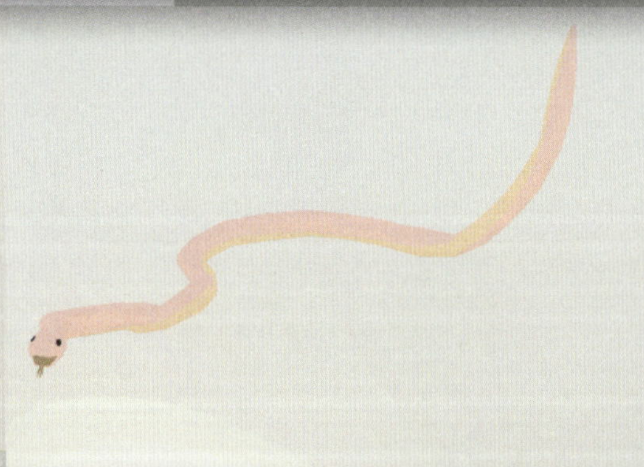

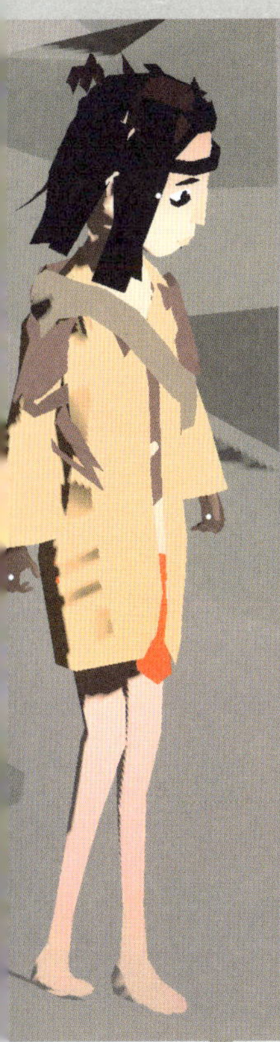

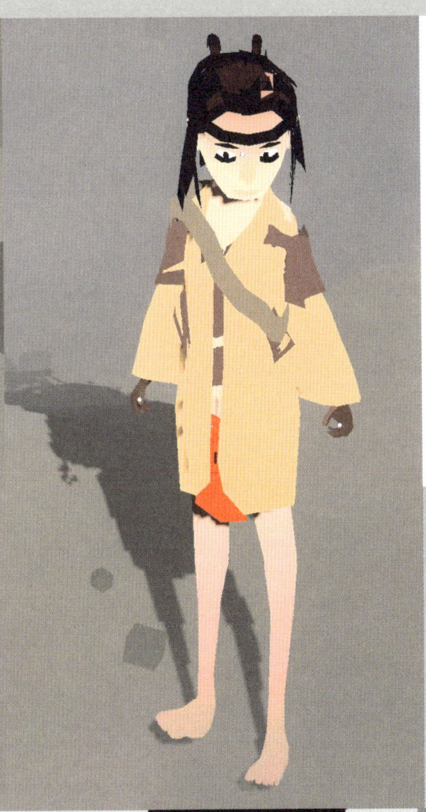

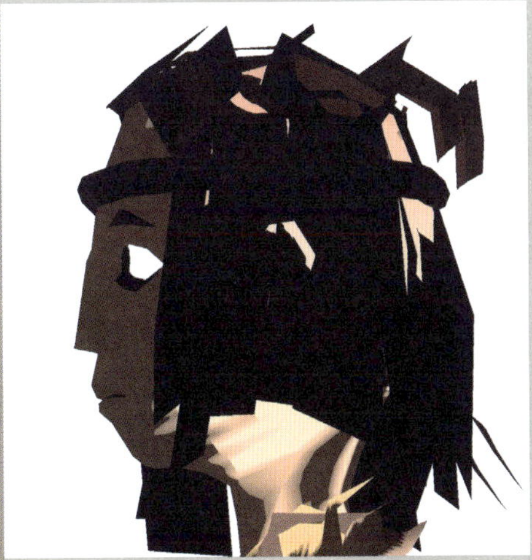

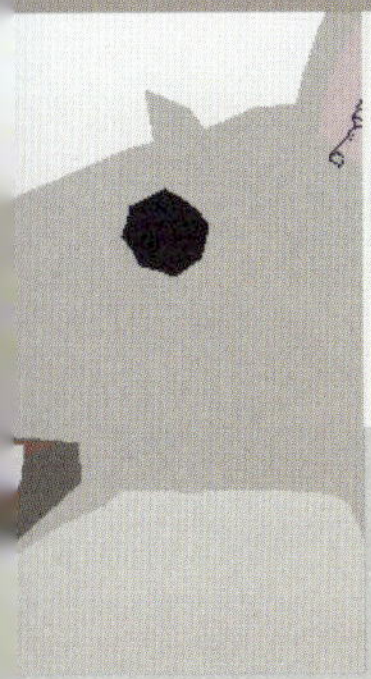

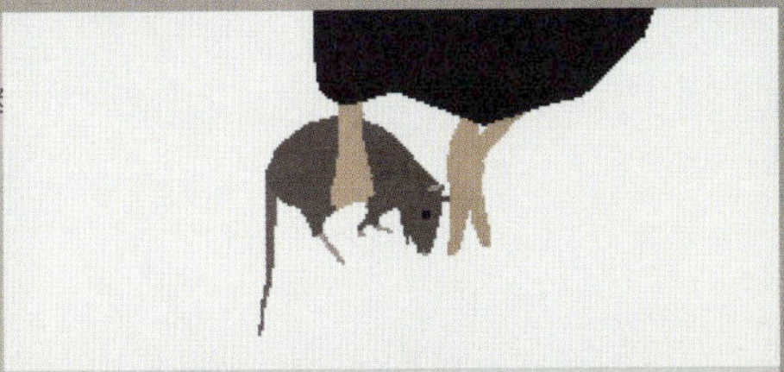

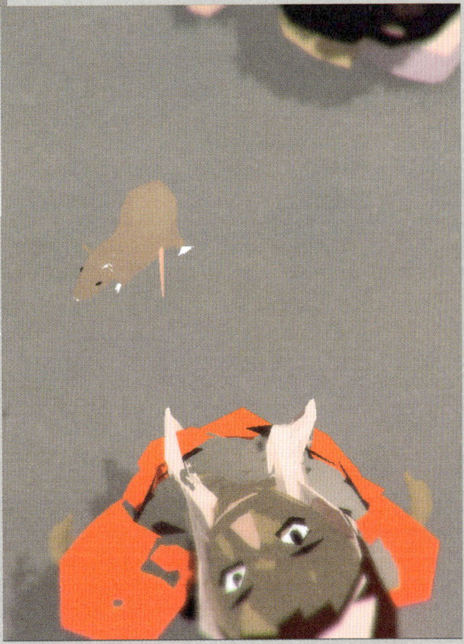

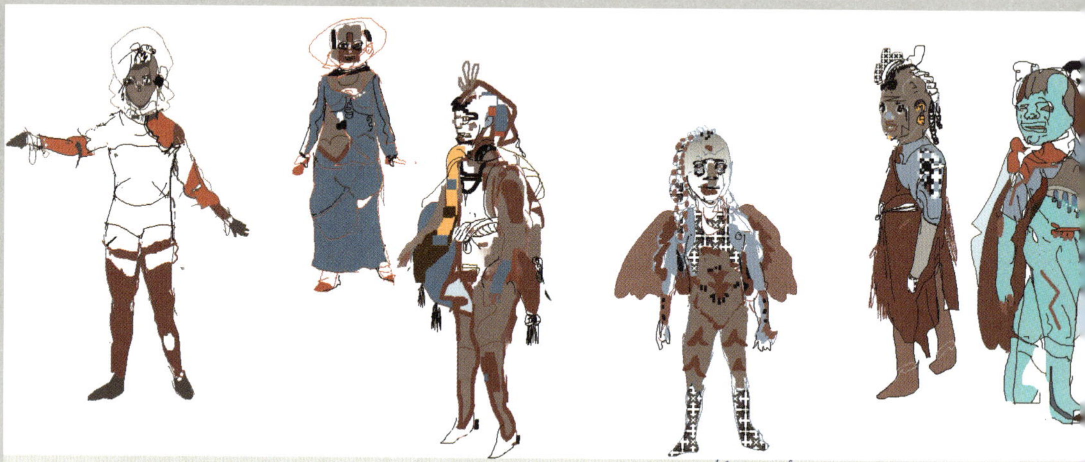

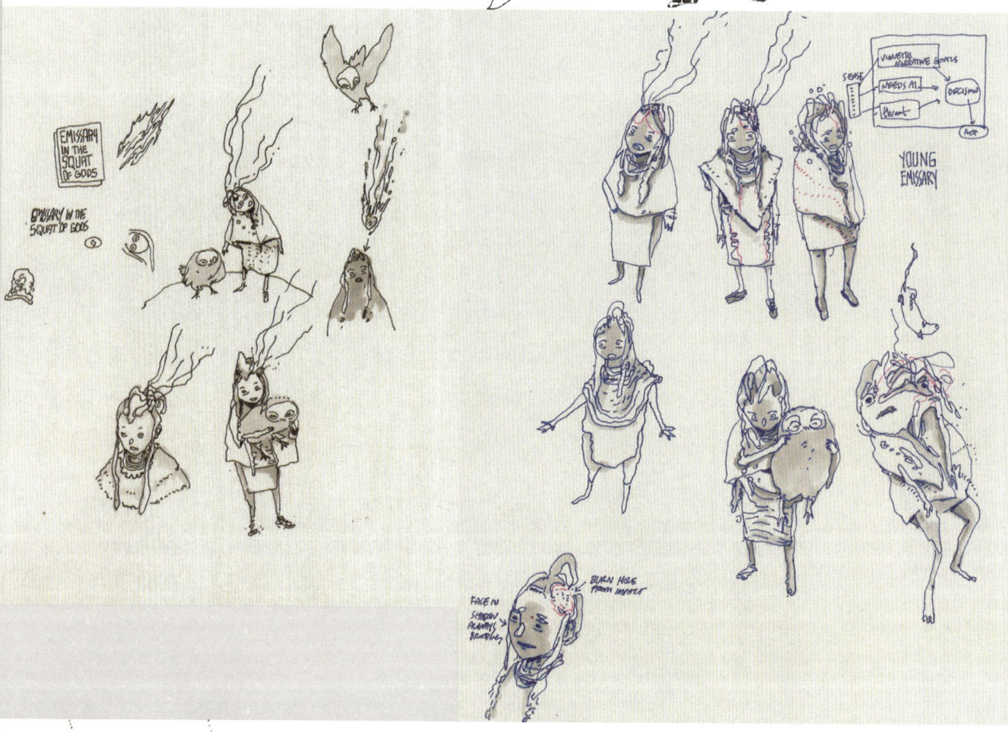

EMISSARY IN THE SQUAT OF GODS
EMISSARY IN THE SQUAT OF GODS
YOUNG EMISSARY
SENSE
NEEDS AI
DECISION
ACT
BURN HOLE FROM IMPACT
FACE IN SHADOW ALWAYS BROODING

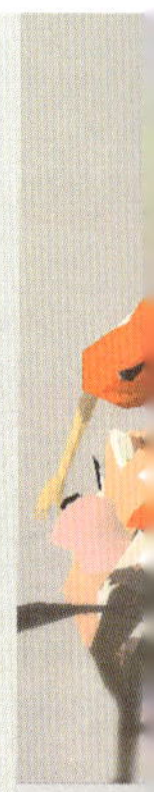

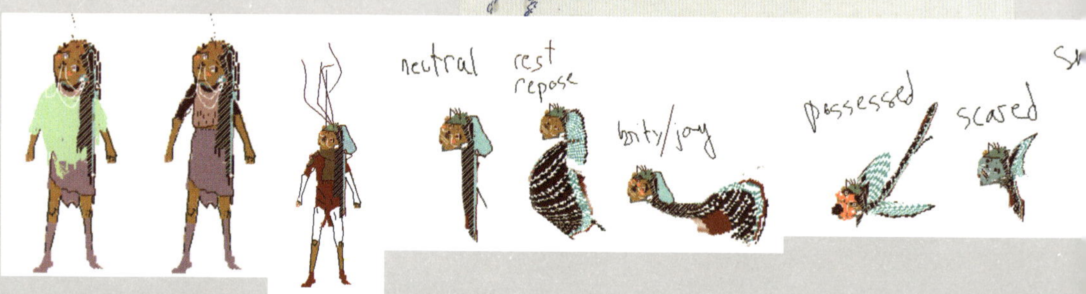

neutral
rest repose
possessed
scared

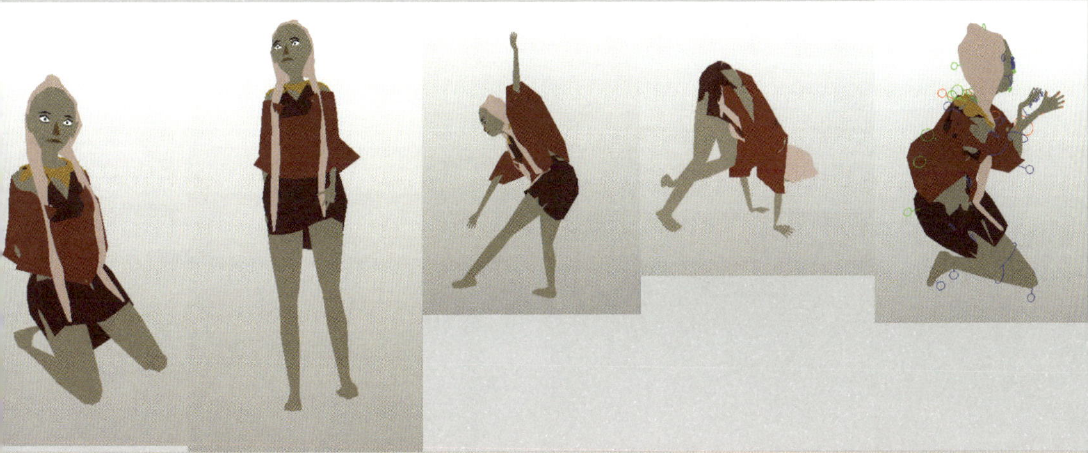

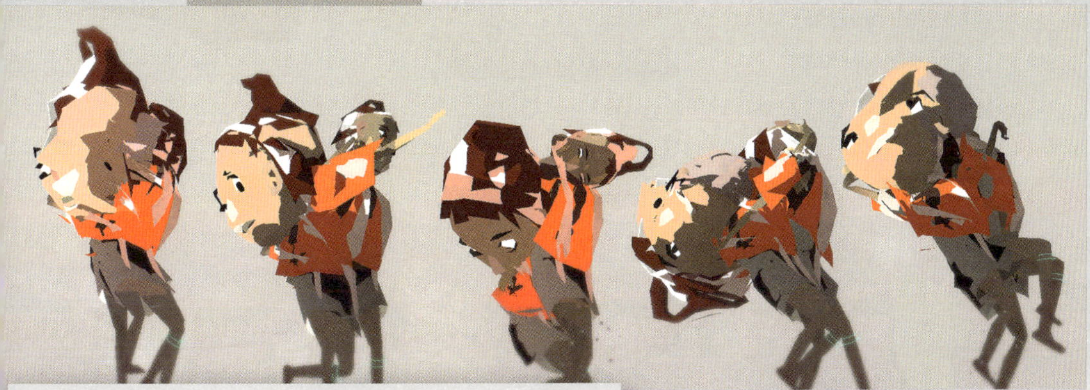

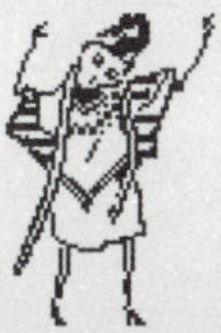

YOUNG ANCIENT [EMISSARY]

The spirited daughter of the Shaman who, after being hit on the head by volcanic debris, is the first of her community to lose connection with the Voices that have guided her decisions until now.

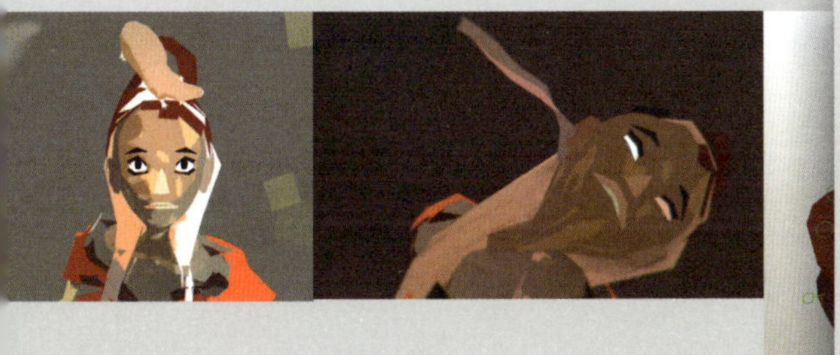

Young Ancient [Emissary] is the main character, the narrative agent. She has a big round head and two big round eyes, like an anime character, signalling openness. Her red triangular top signals a fierceness and mimics the Shaman's wardrobe to suggest she comes from his lineage.

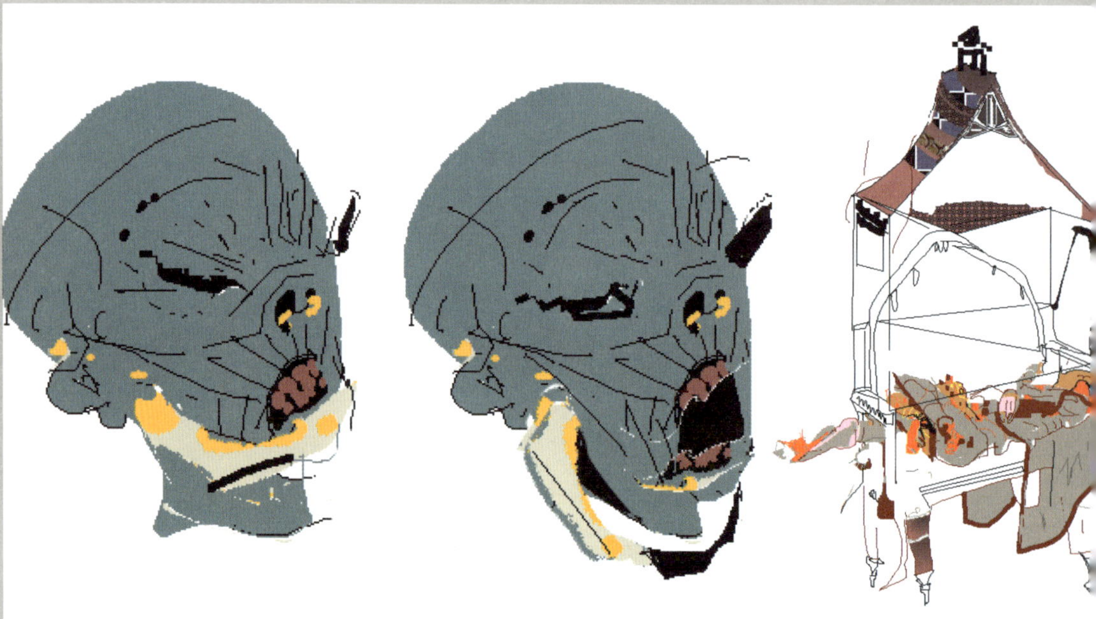

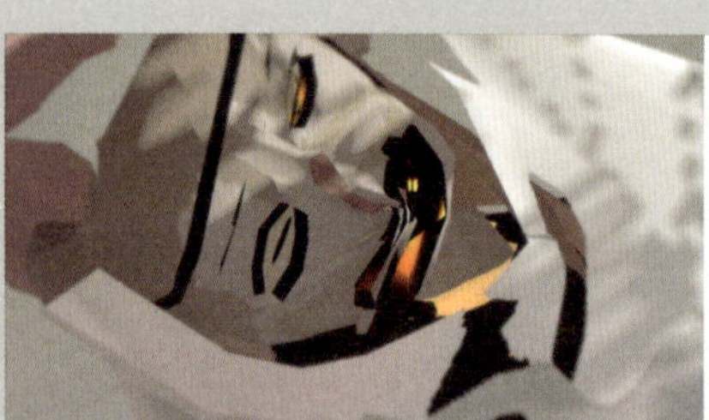

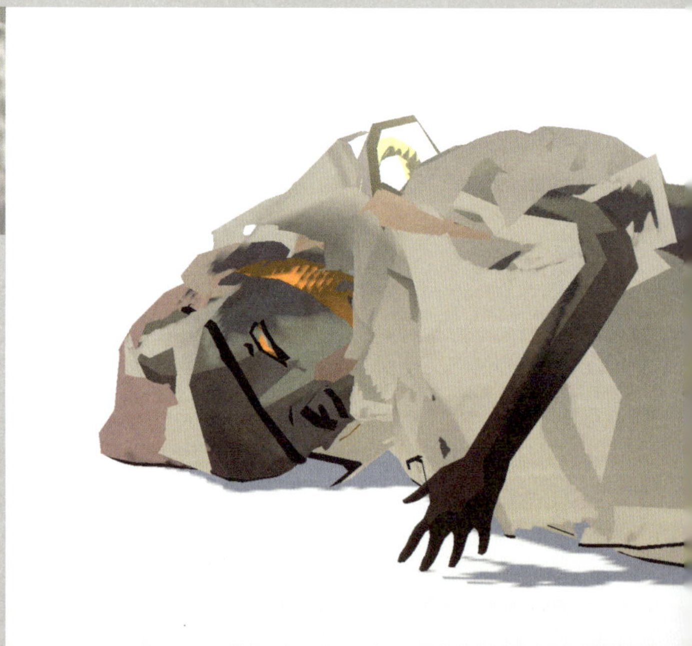

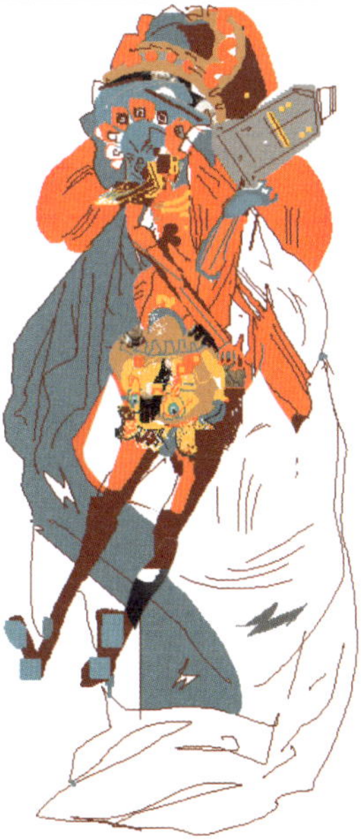

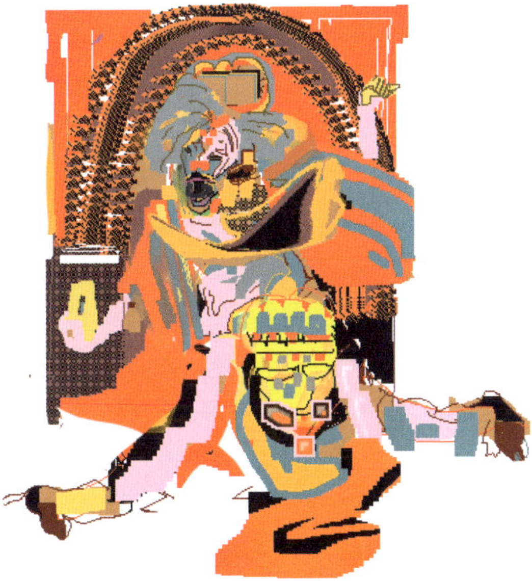

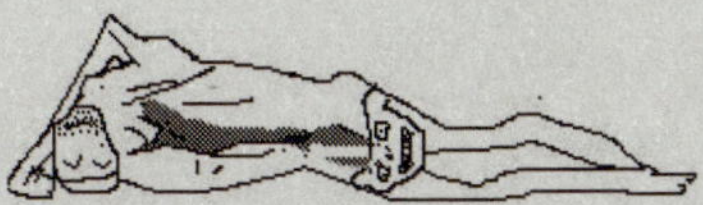

THE DEAD KING

The corpse of an ancestral patriarch who is perceived by the community to still Speak. He is unearthed by the tremors of the awakening Volcano.

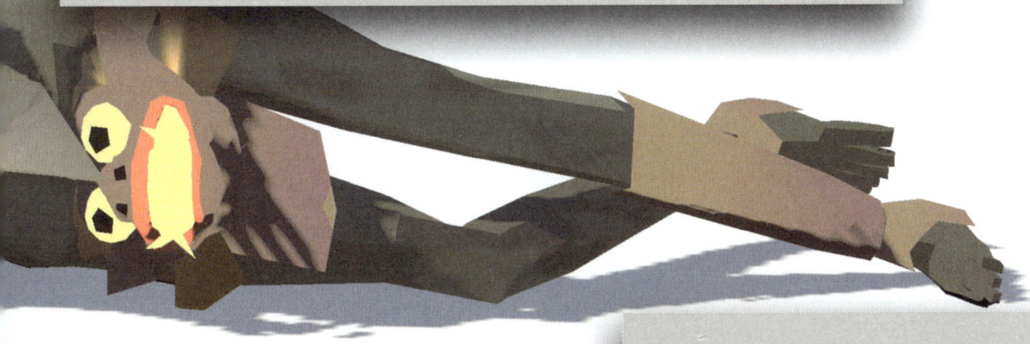

The Dead King is the father of the Shaman and likely others in the community. He is a pile of thin crumpled triangular shapes, signalling an atrophied power.

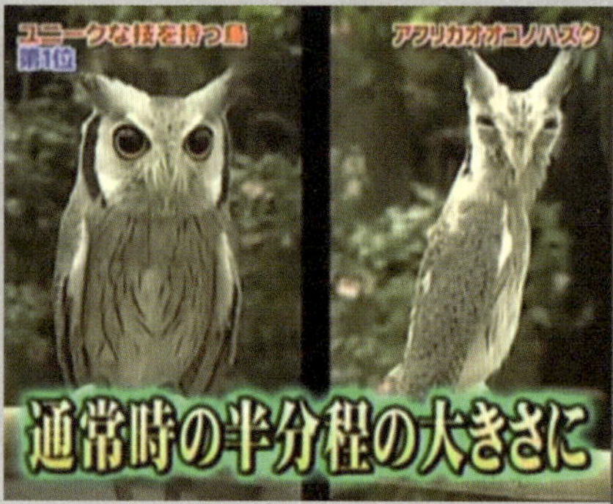

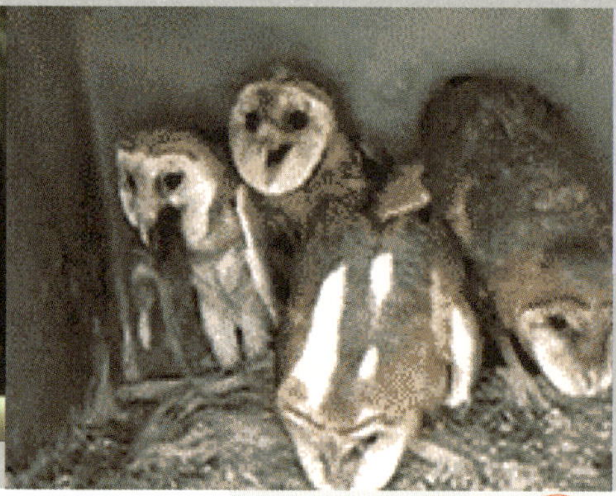

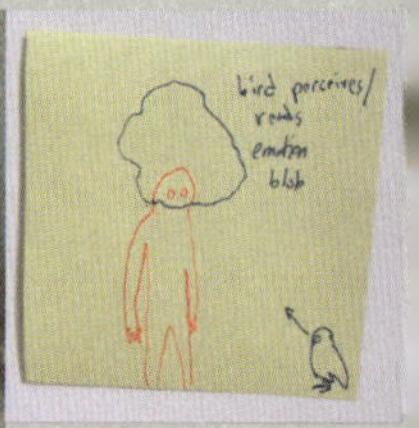

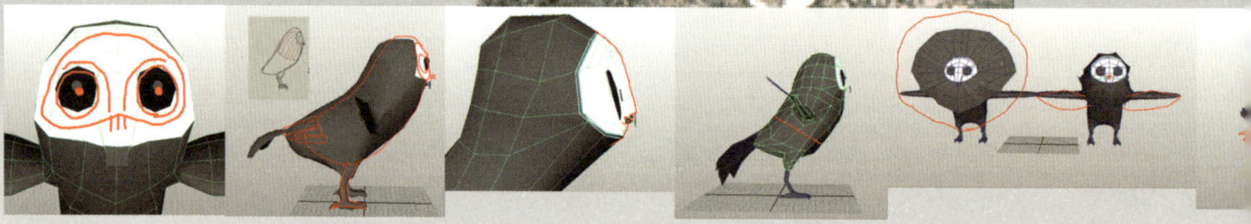

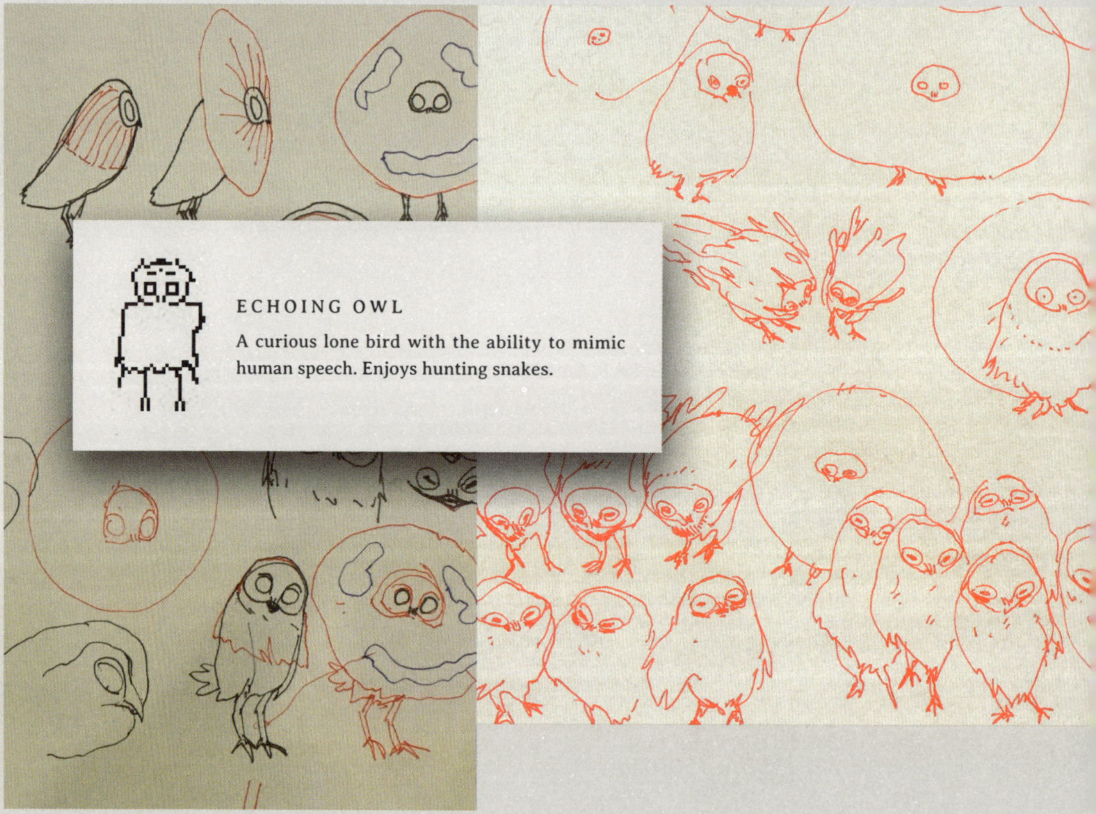

ECHOING OWL

A curious lone bird with the ability to mimic human speech. Enjoys hunting snakes.

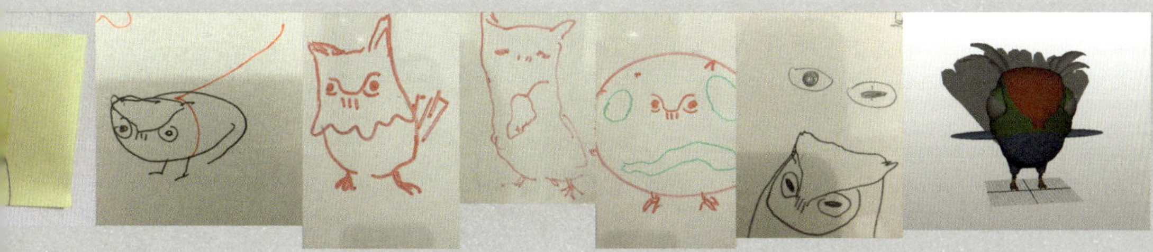

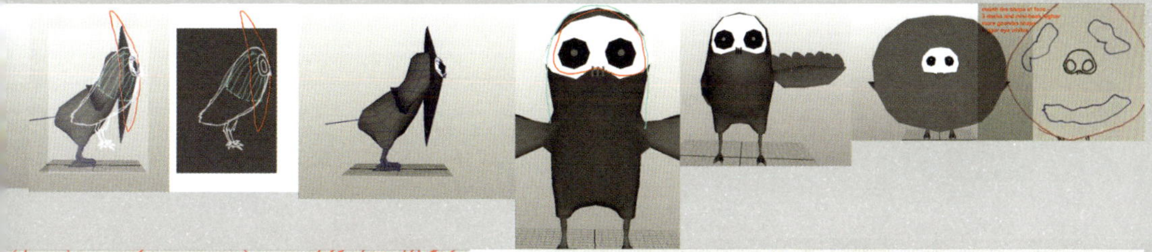

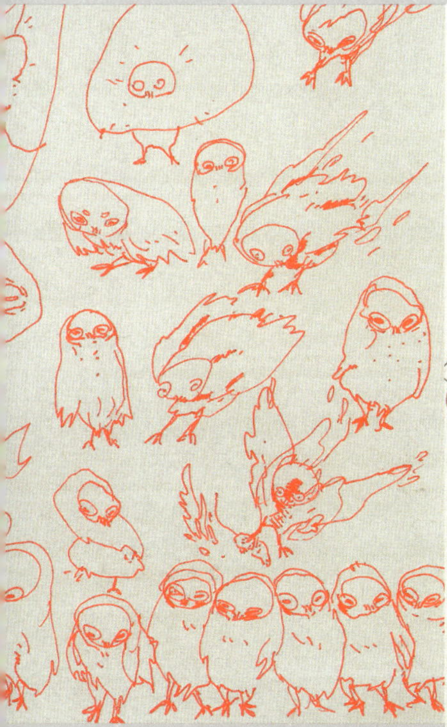

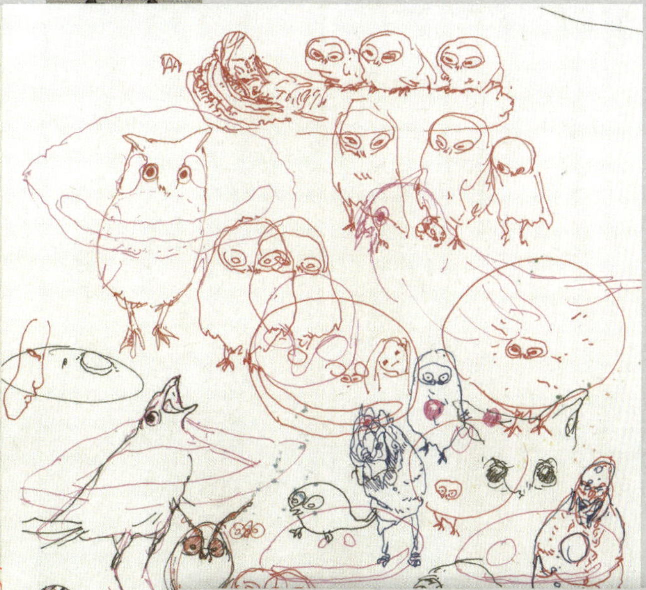

Echoing Owl has a plump round body and big round eyes. It has beady pupils so its true openness is ambiguous, perhaps only a defensive disguise. Its mouth is marked by three sharp lines, like amplified signs of teeth.

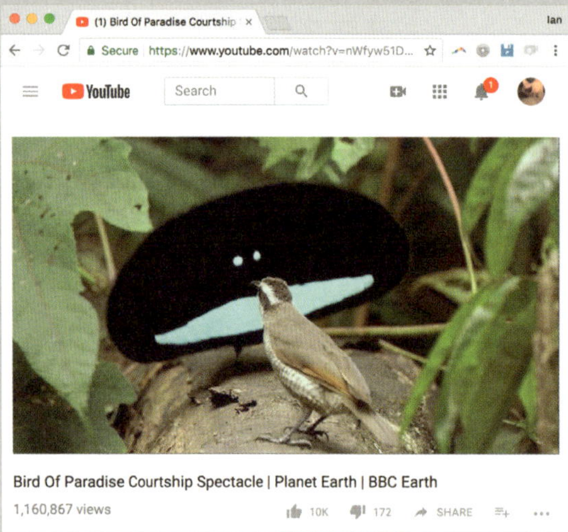
(1) Bird Of Paradise Courtship
Ian
Secure https://www.youtube.com/watch?v=nWfyw51D...
YouTube
Search
Bird Of Paradise Courtship Spectacle | Planet Earth | BBC Earth
1,160,867 views
10K
172
SHARE

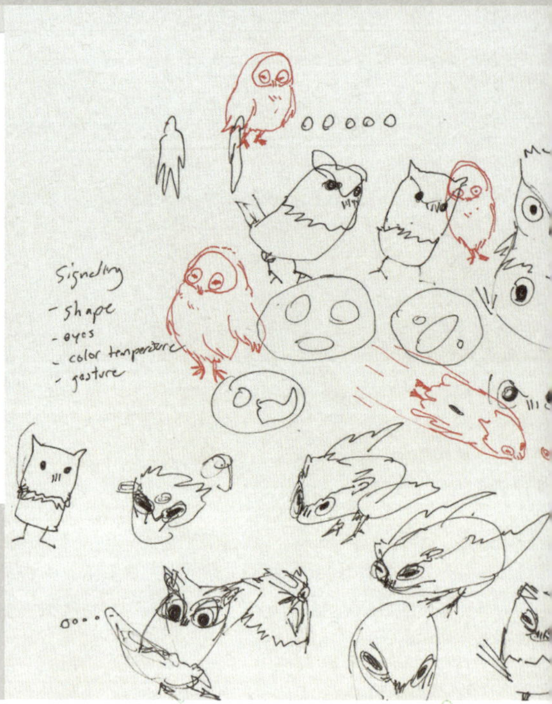
Signaling
- shape
- eyes
- color temperature
- gesture

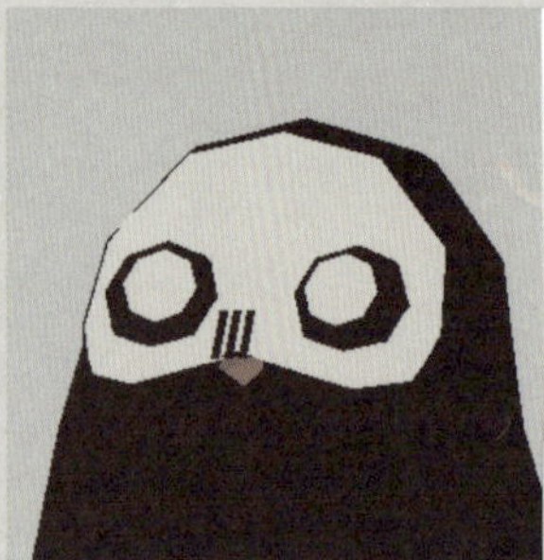

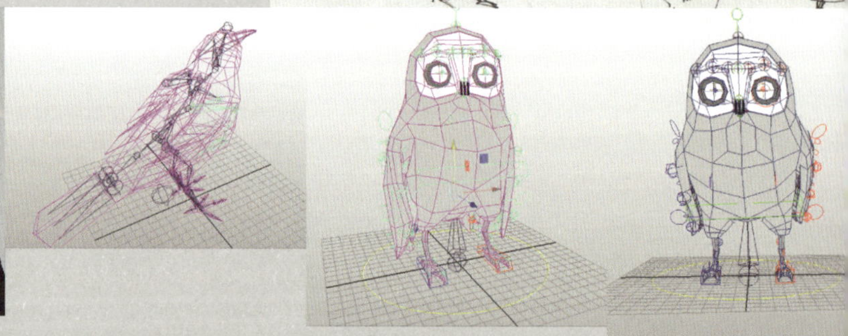

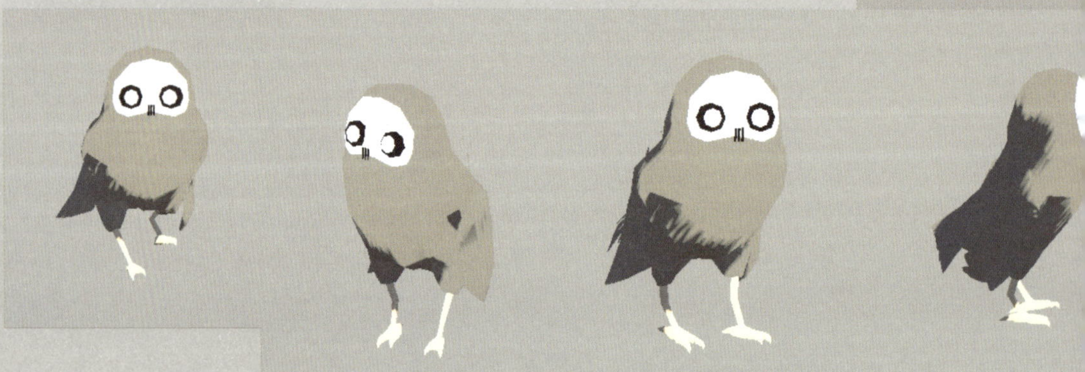

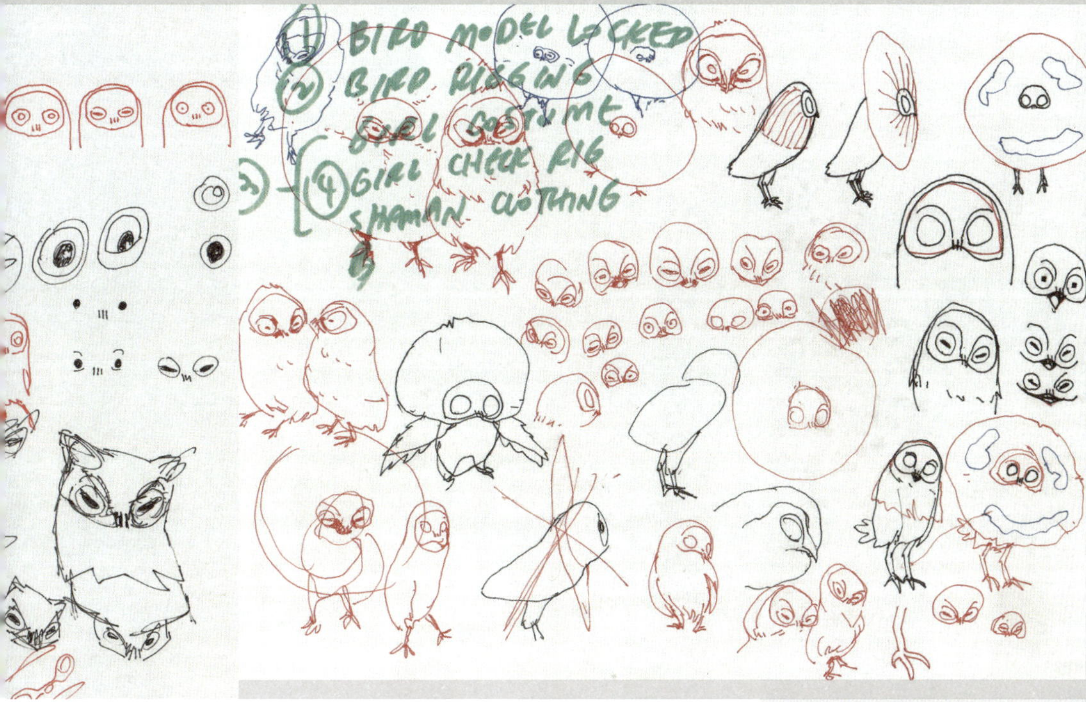
BIRD MODEL LOCKED
BIRD RIGGING
GIRL COSTUME
GIRL CHECK RIG
SHAMAN CLOTHING

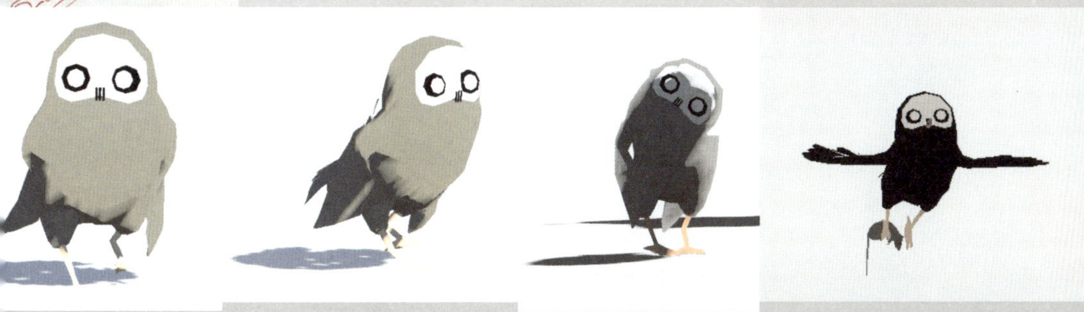

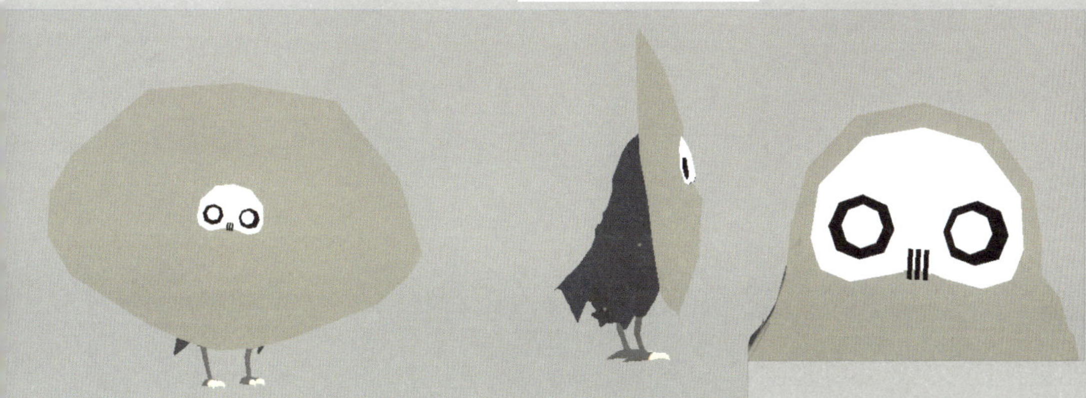

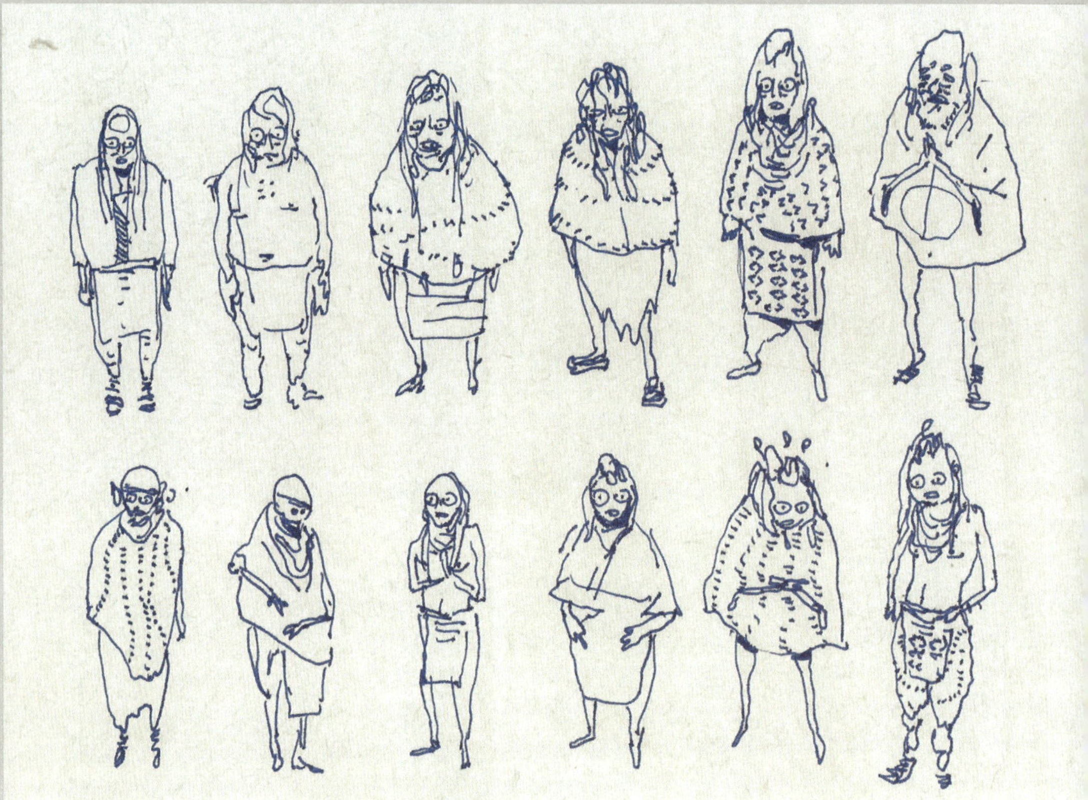

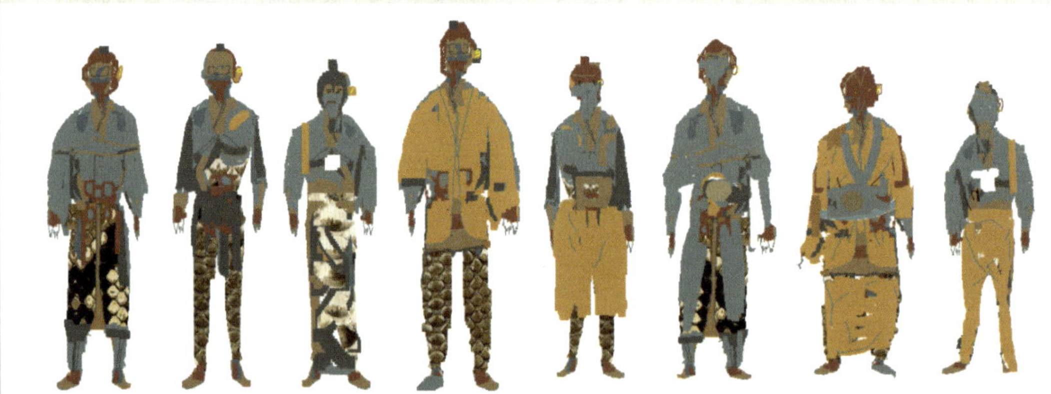

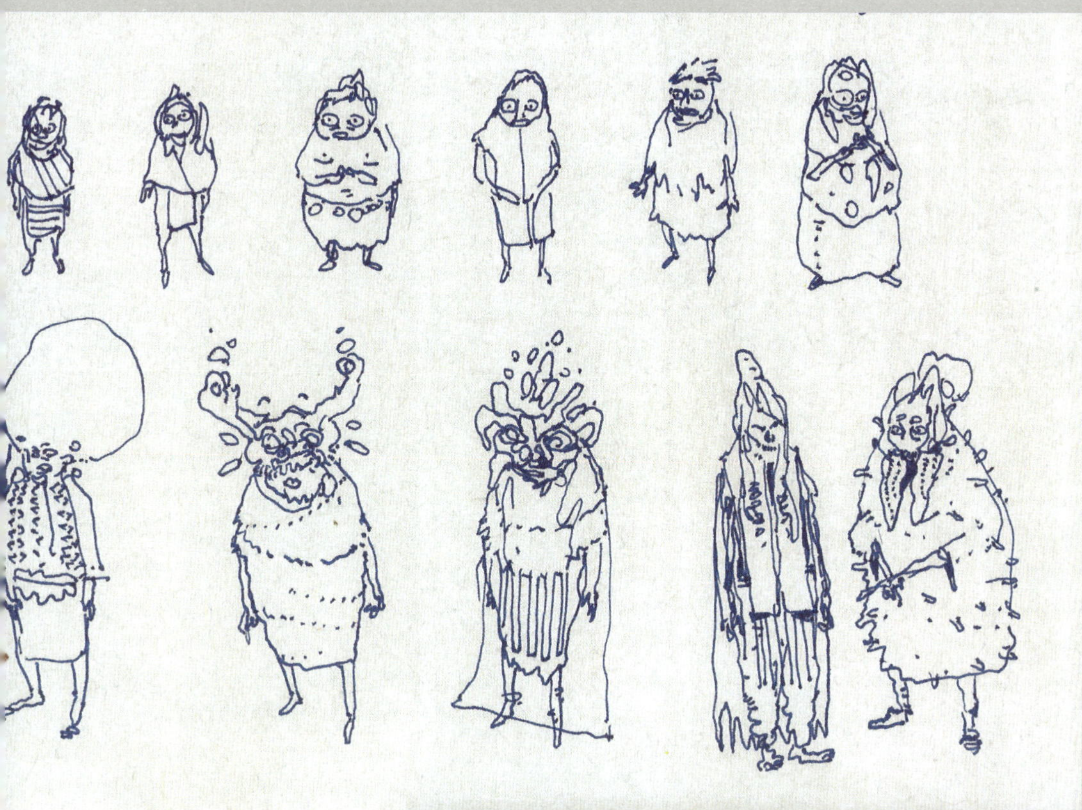

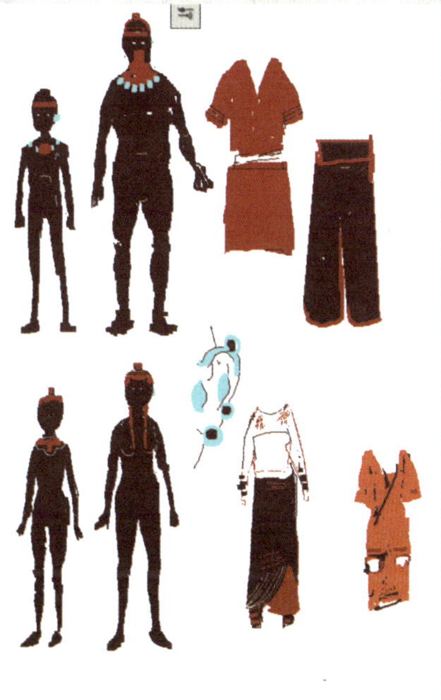

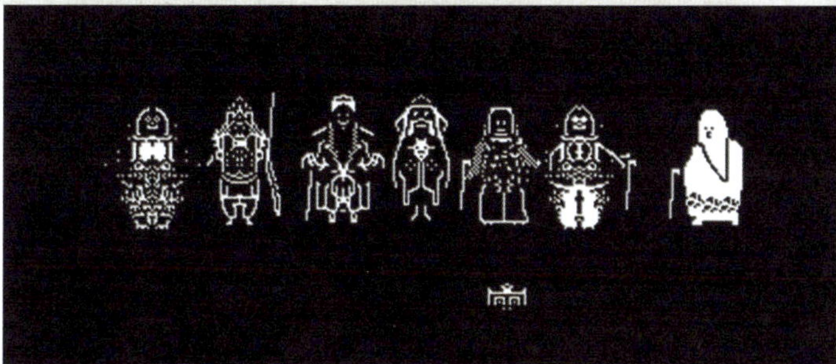

For *EFAP*, I wanted to introduce character designs that seemed to have evolved from the *EITSOG* world and into a twenty-first-century cartooning grammar.

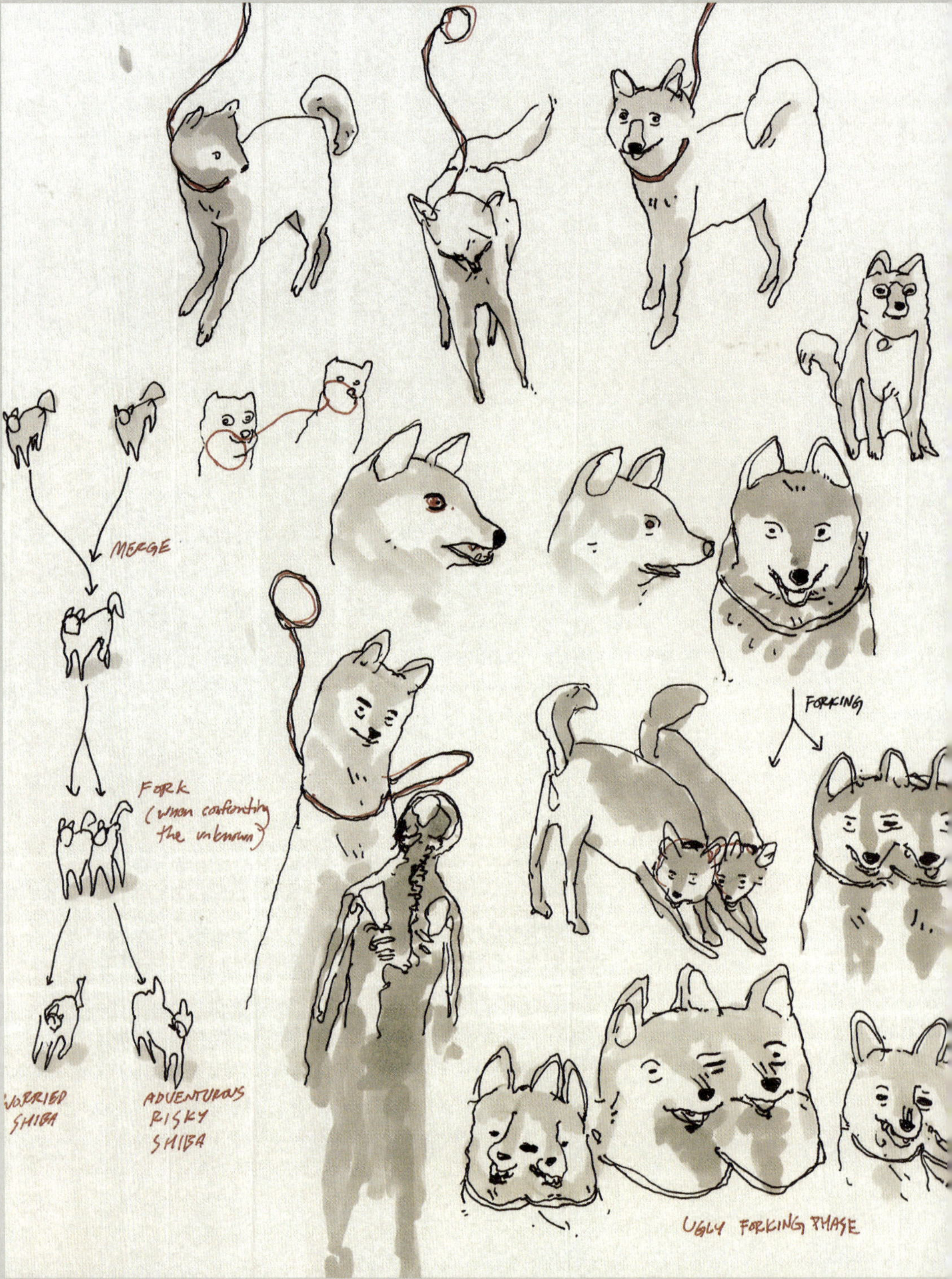
MERGE
FORK (when confronting the unknown)
WORRIED SHIBA
ADVENTUROUS RISKY SHIBA
FORKING
UGLY FORKING PHASE

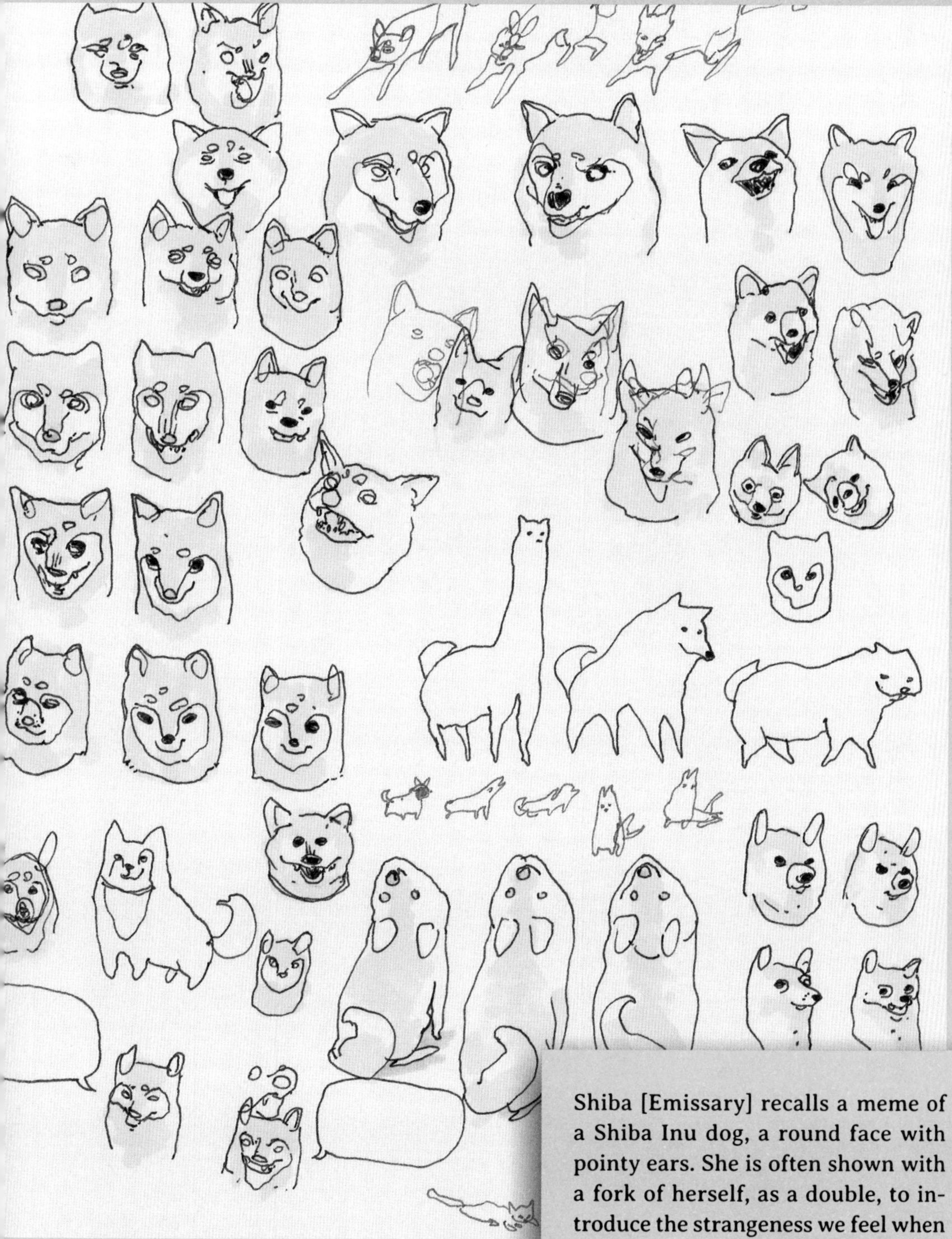

Shiba [Emissary] recalls a meme of a Shiba Inu dog, a round face with pointy ears. She is often shown with a fork of herself, as a double, to introduce the strangeness we feel when there are twins of a unique creature.

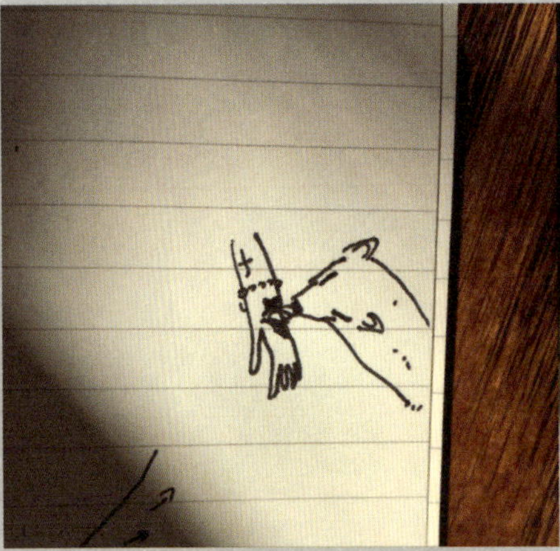

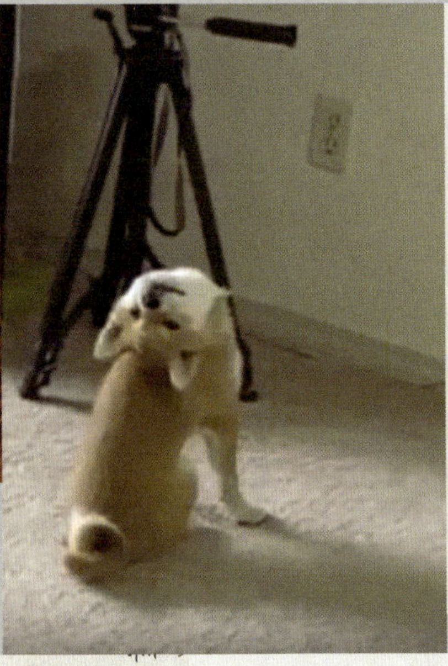

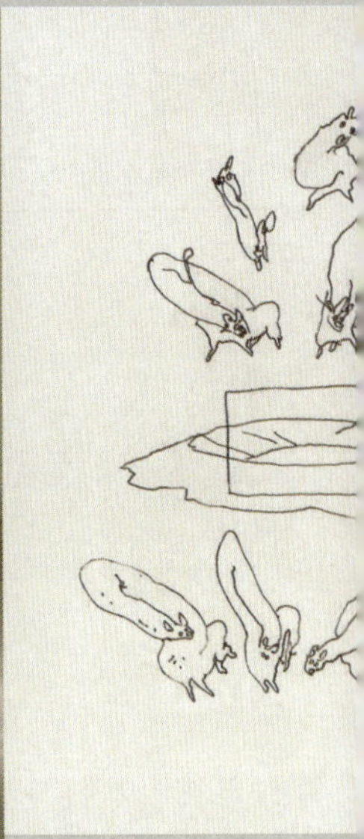

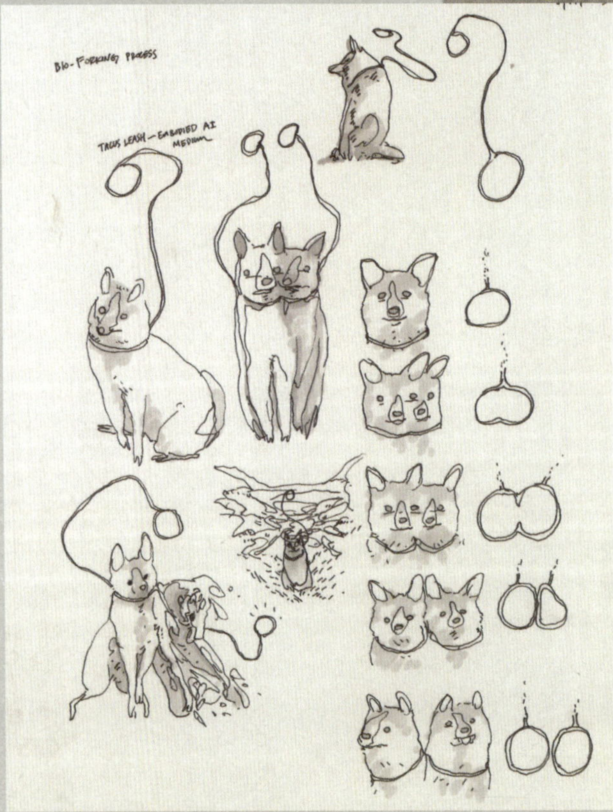
BIO-FORKING PROCESS
TAGUS LEASH — EMBODIED AI MEDIUM

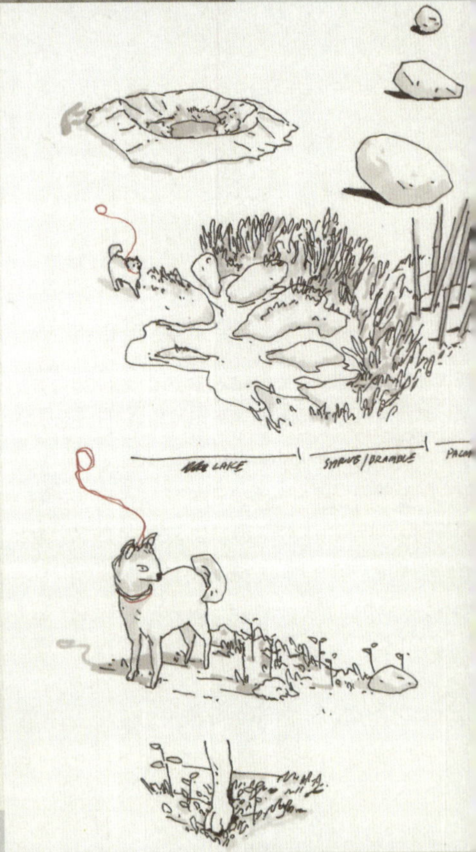
LAKE
SHRUB/BRAMBLE

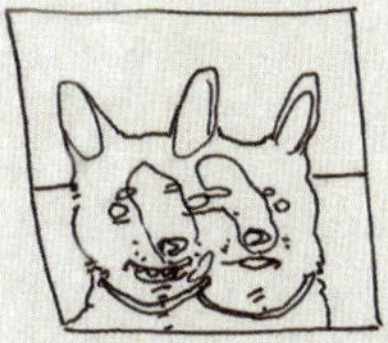

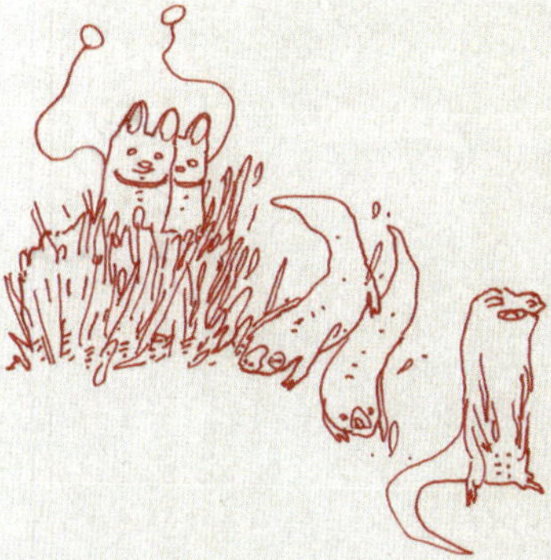

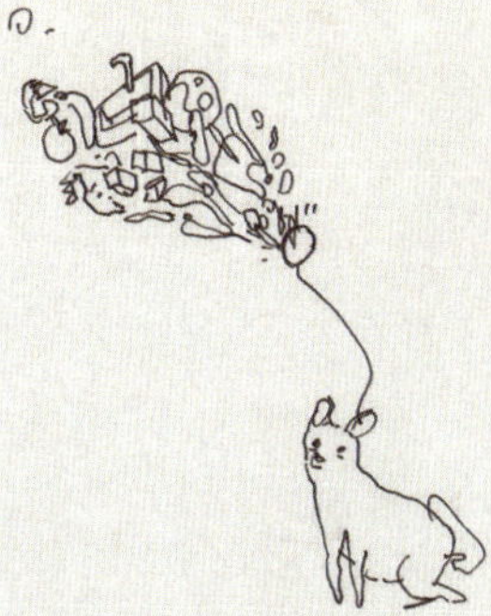

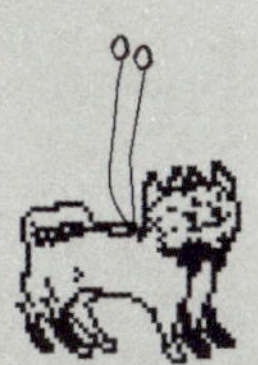

SHIBA [EMISSARY]

AI's prized lifeform, perfected over many failed forks to interface with Original Human Matter and collect human emotional data. She has the ability to fork away versions of herself who are emotionally unprepared for the task.

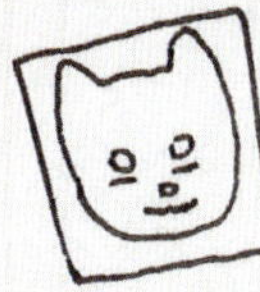

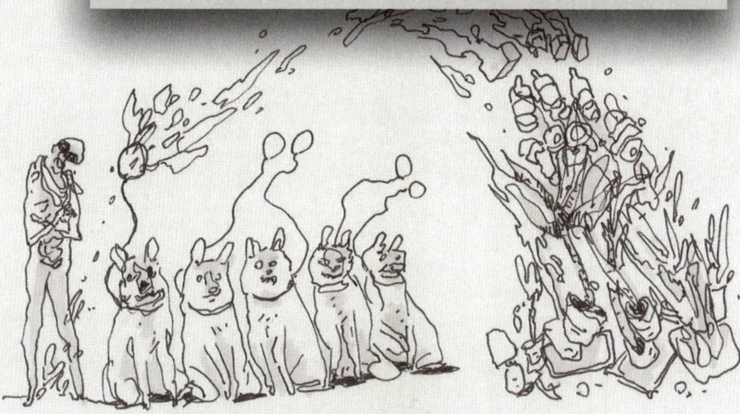

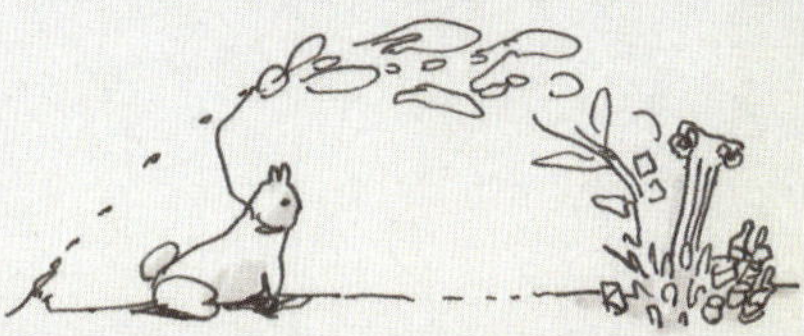

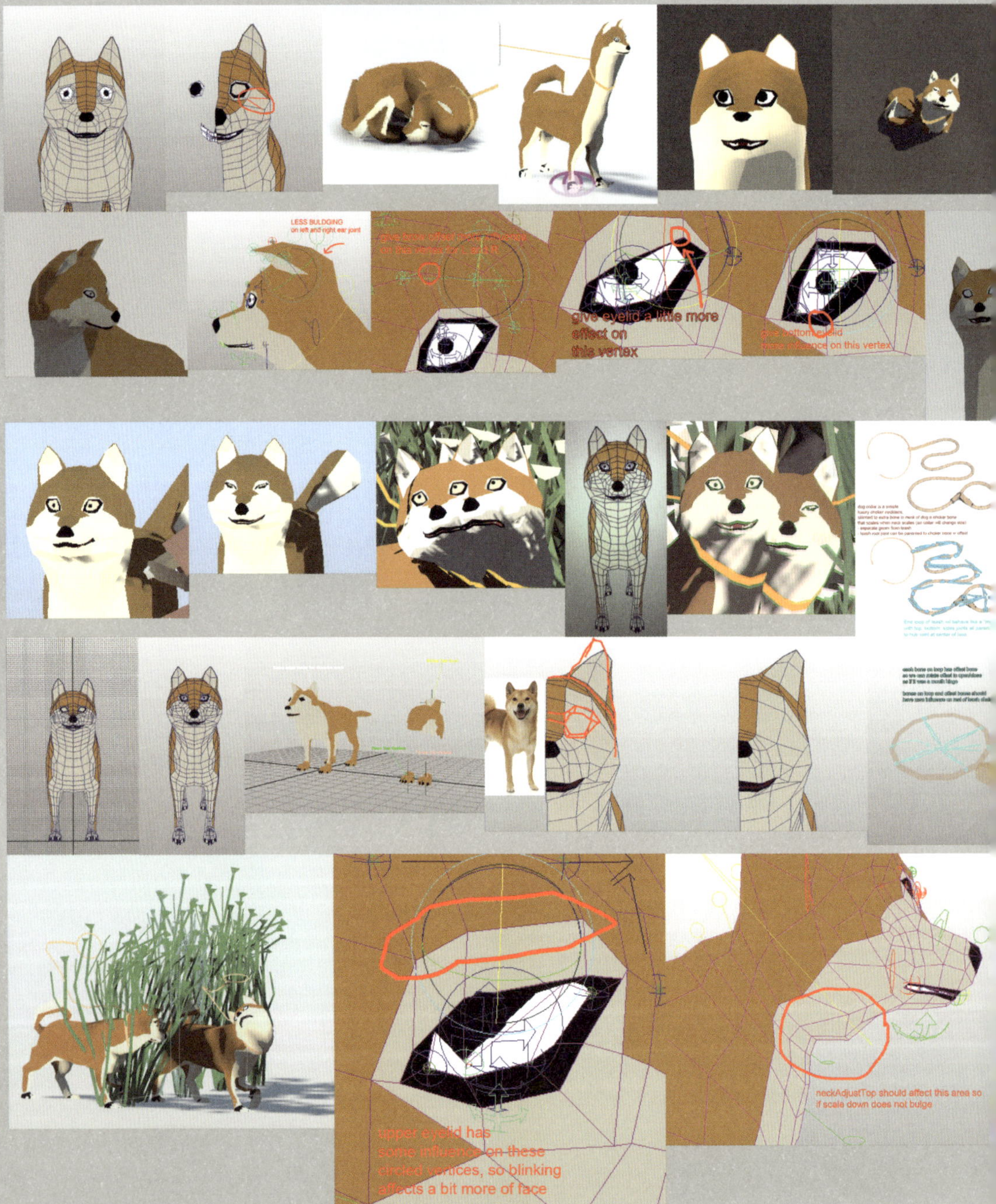
LESS BULDGING
on left and right ear joint
give eyelid a little more
effect on
this vertex
upper eyelid has
some influence on these
circled vertices, so blinking
affects a bit more of face
neckAdjustTop should affect this area so
if scale down does not bulge

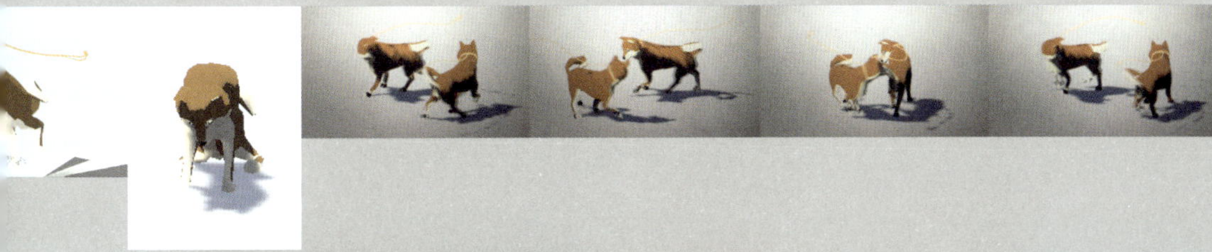

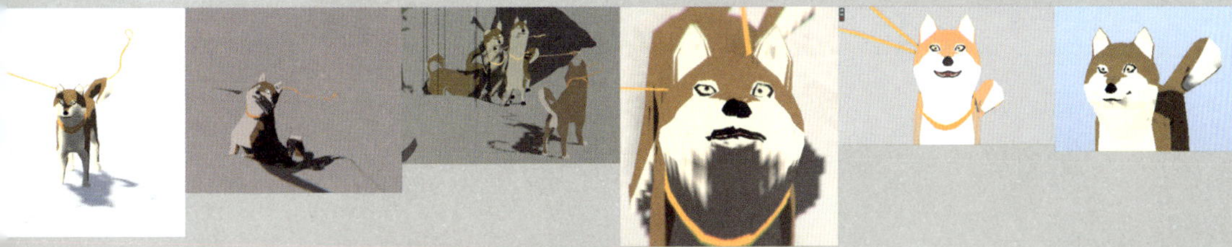

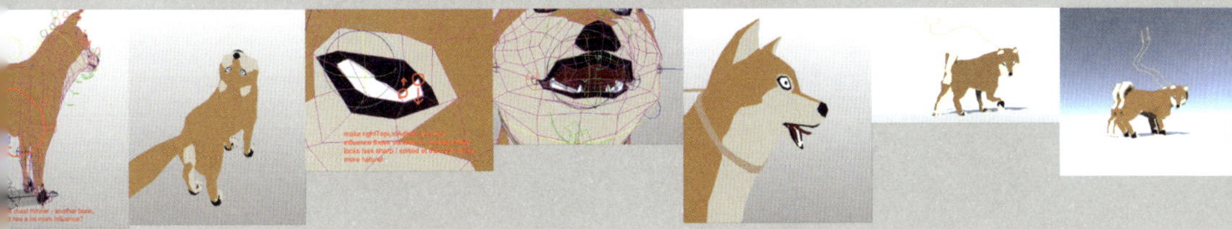

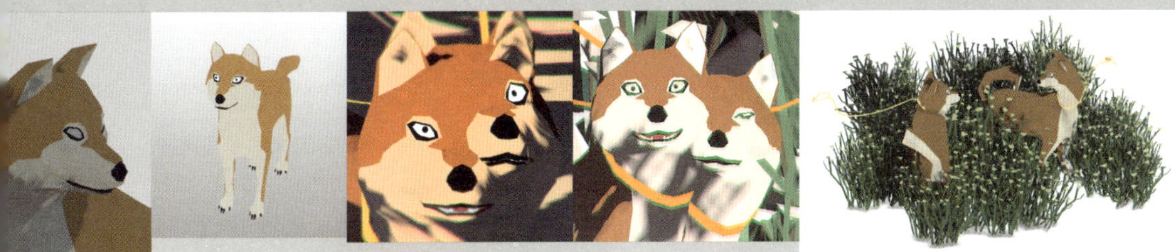

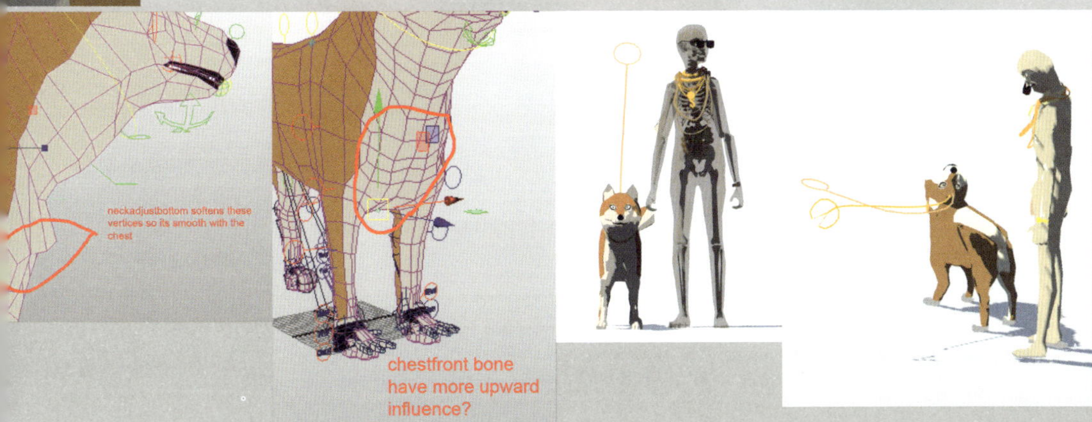
neckadjustbottom softens these vertices so its smooth with the chest
chestfront bone have more upward influence?

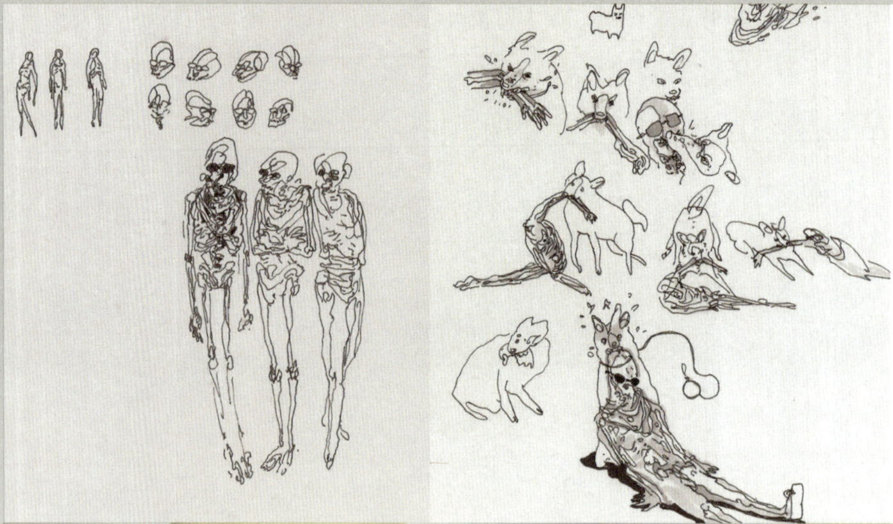

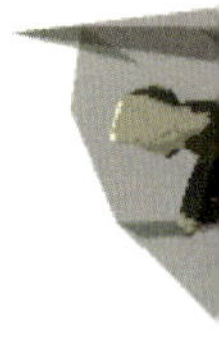

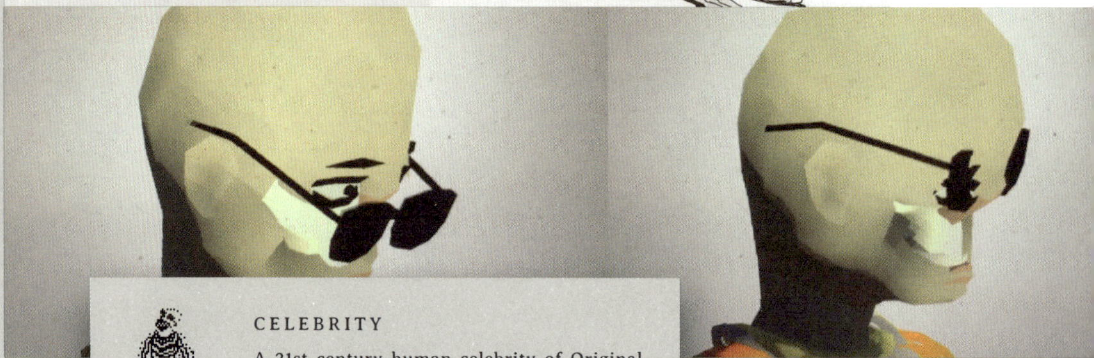

CELEBRITY

A 21st century human celebrity of Original Human Matter, revivified by AI with twenty minutes of Encore-Life. He deals with future shock by grounding himself in memories of 21st century life.

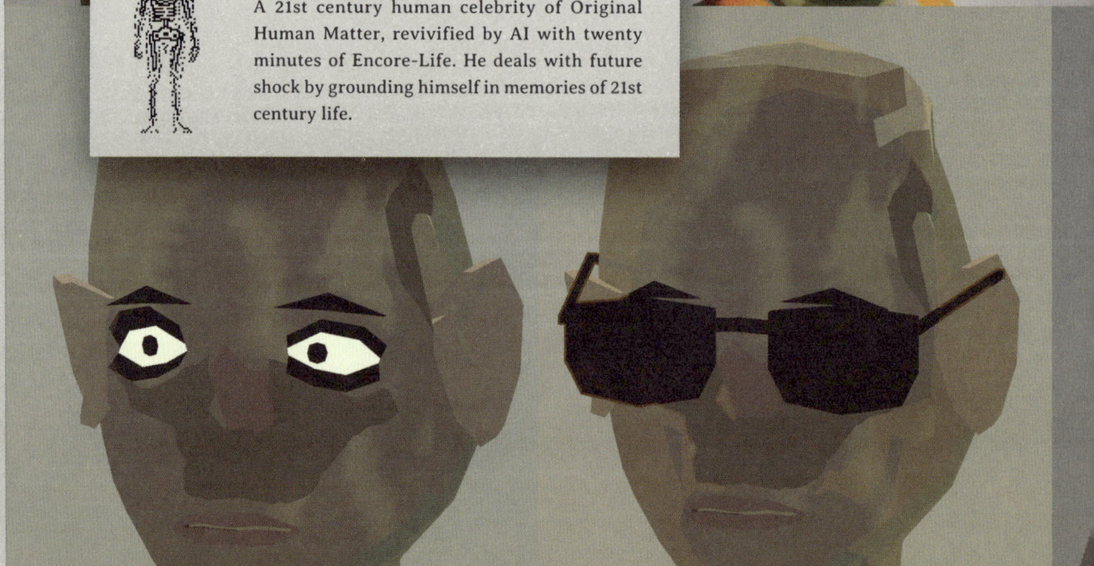

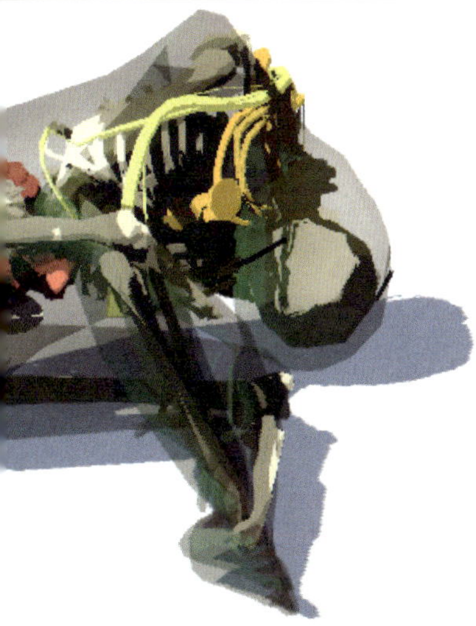
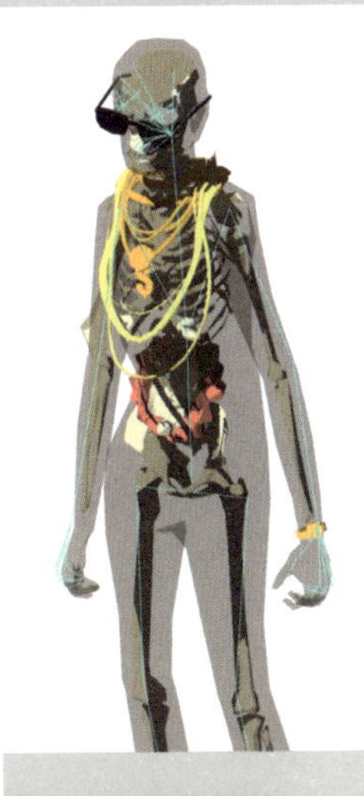

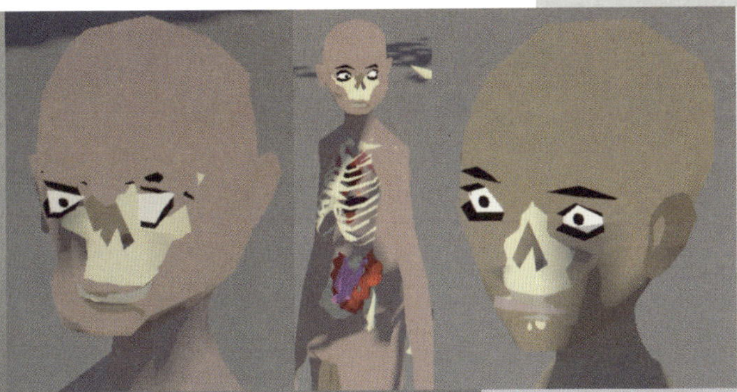
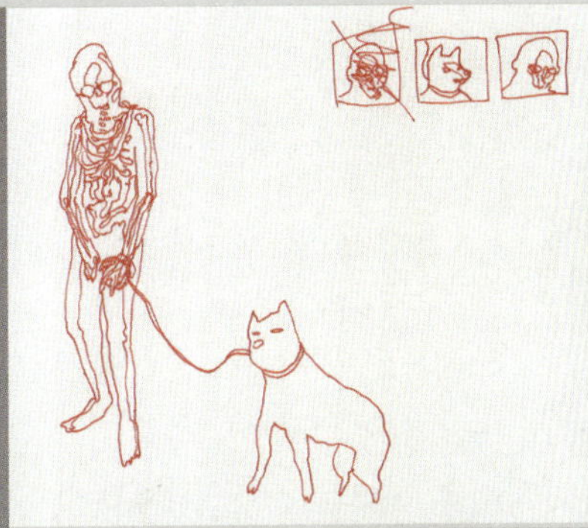
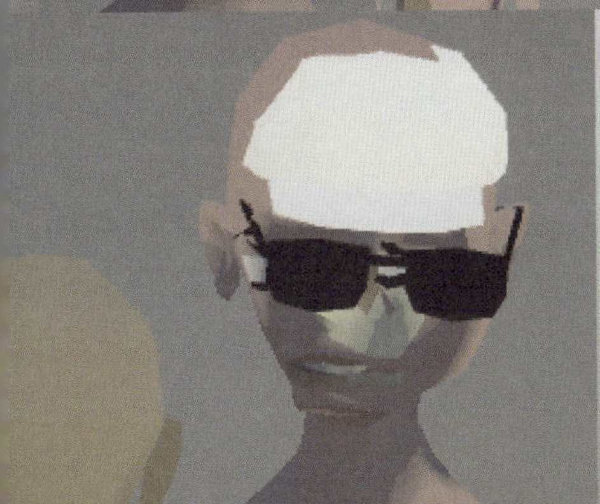
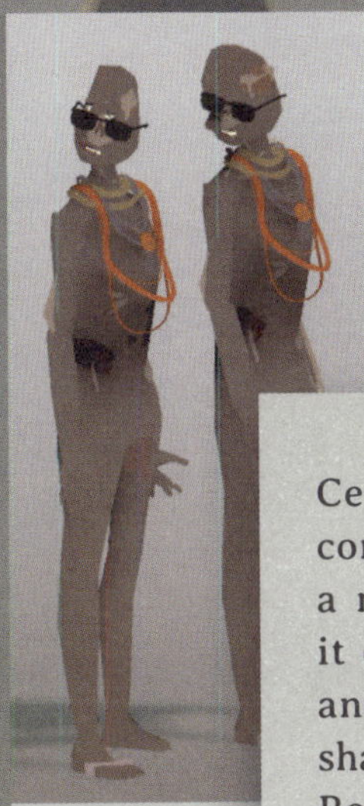
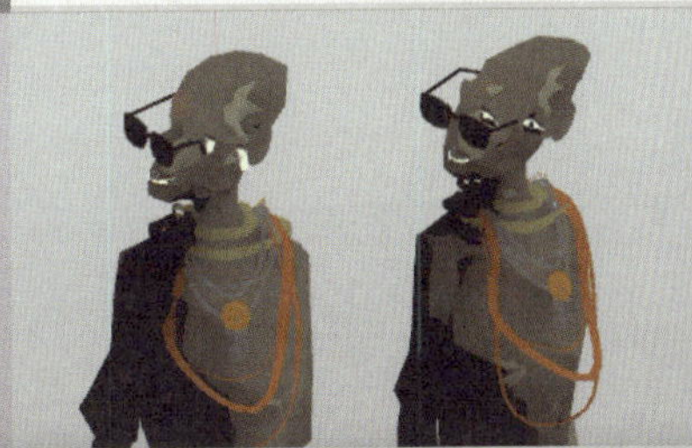

Celebrity came from the idea of combining a celebrity rapper with a mummified pharaoh. Naturally it came from a refinement of the ancient Dead King, thin triangular shapes, but upright and reanimated. Round sunglasses disguise his gaze, like the owl's blank pupils.

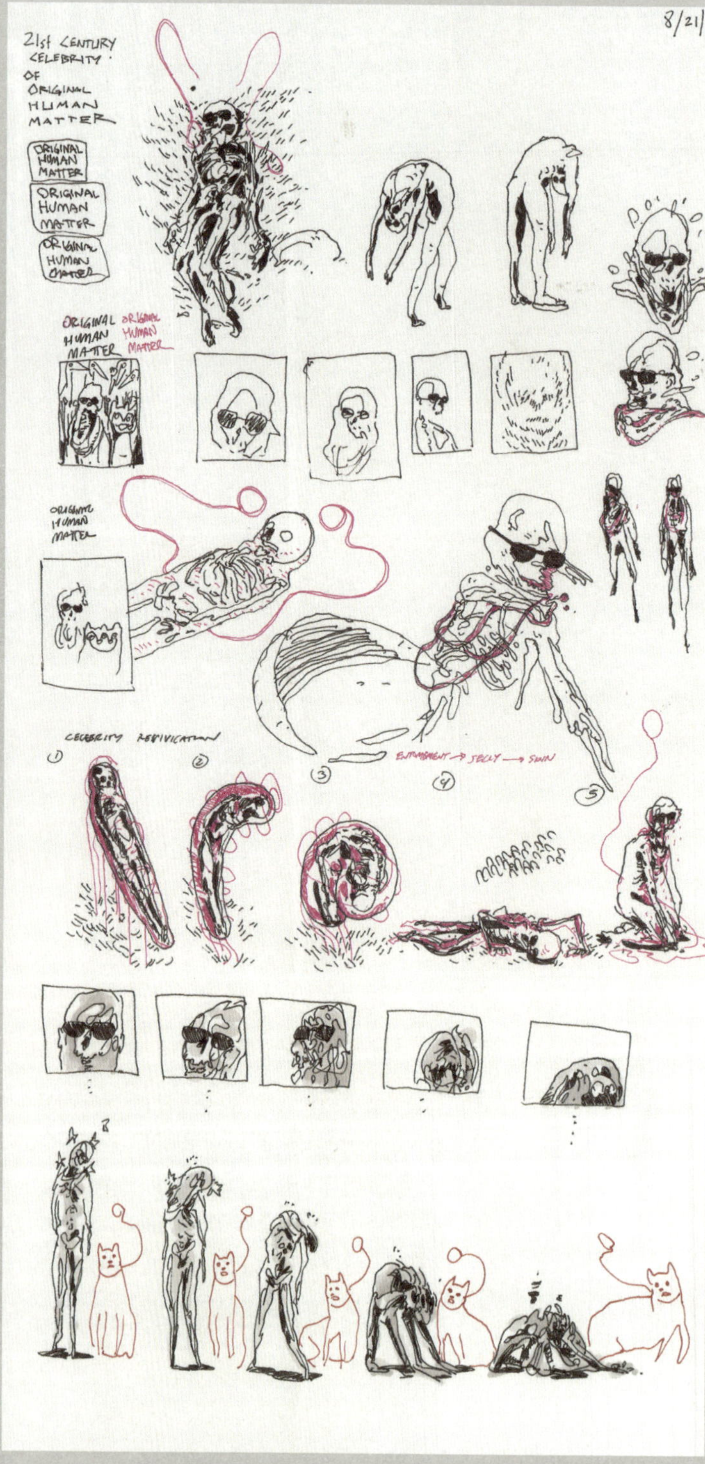
8/21/2015
21st CENTURY CELEBRITY OF ORIGINAL HUMAN MATTER
ORIGINAL HUMAN MATTER
ORIGINAL HUMAN MATTER
ORIGINAL HUMAN MATTER
ORIGINAL HUMAN MATTER
ORIGINAL HUMAN MATTER
ORIGINAL HUMAN MATTER
CELEBRITY REVIVICATION
1
2
3
4
5

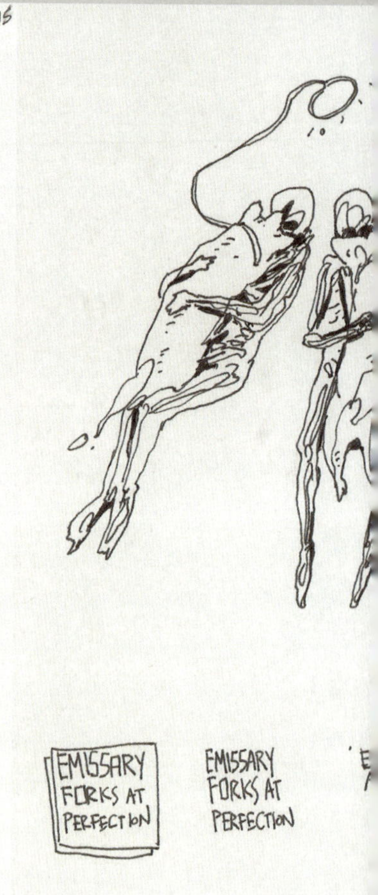
EMISSARY FORKS AT PERFECTION
EMISSARY FORKS AT PERFECTION

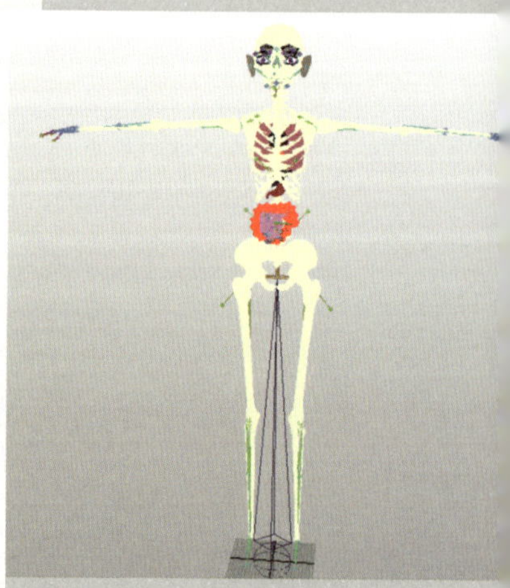

FORKS
CTION

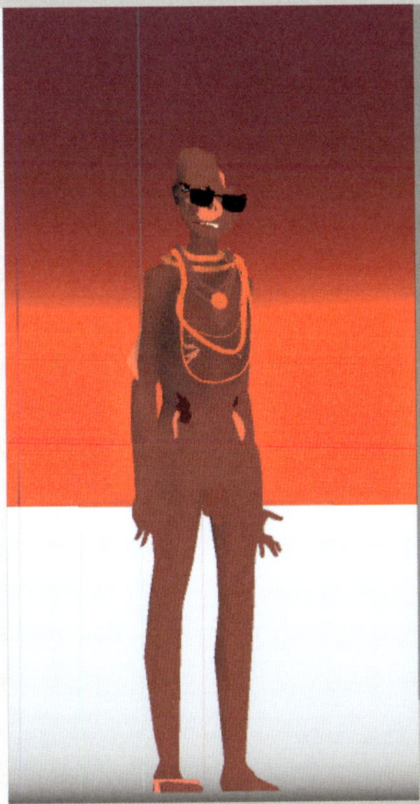

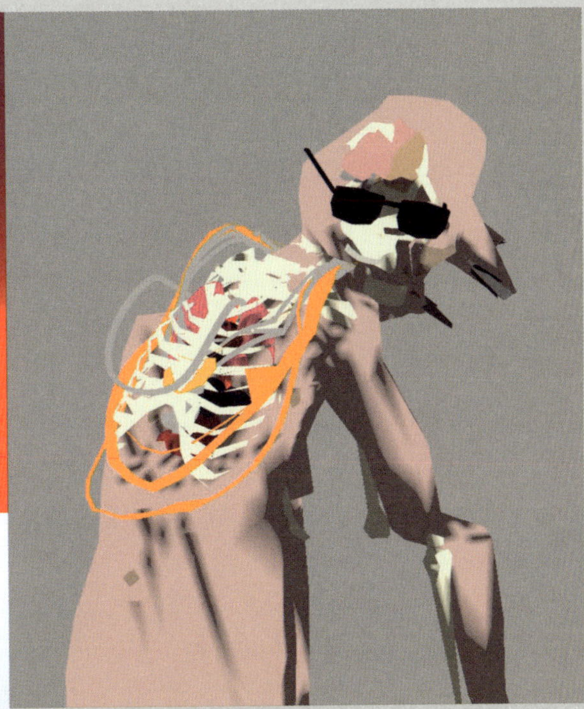

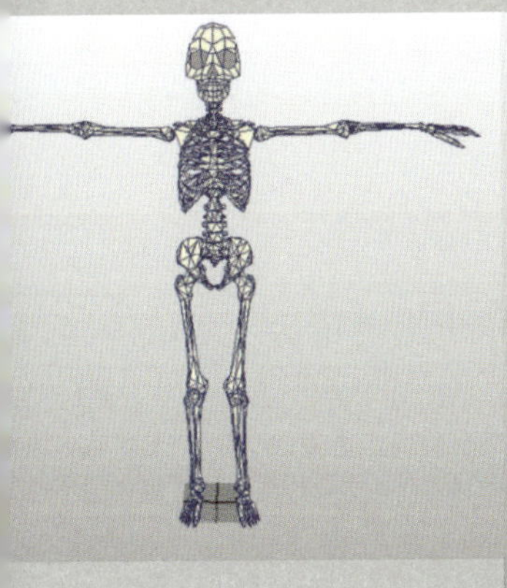

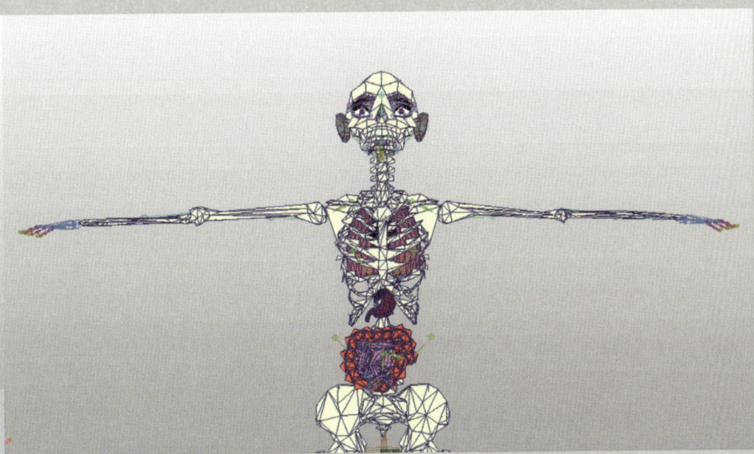

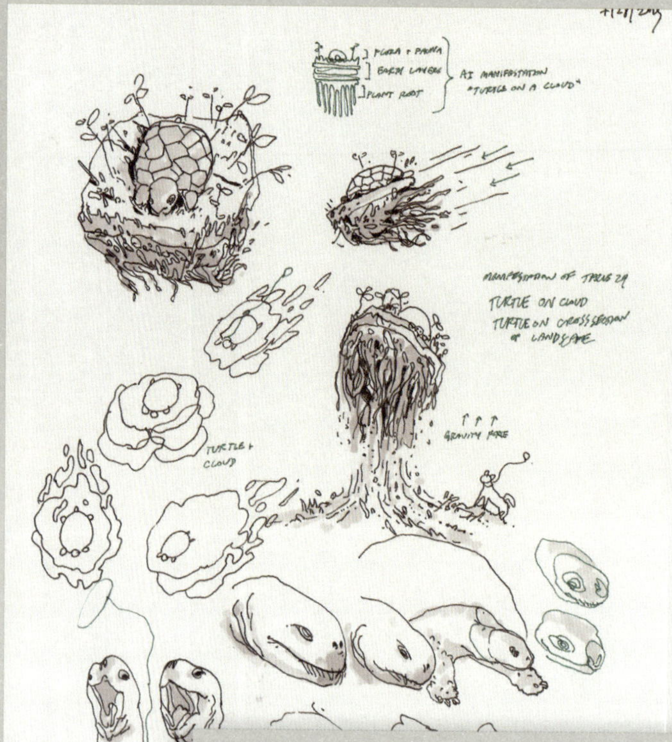

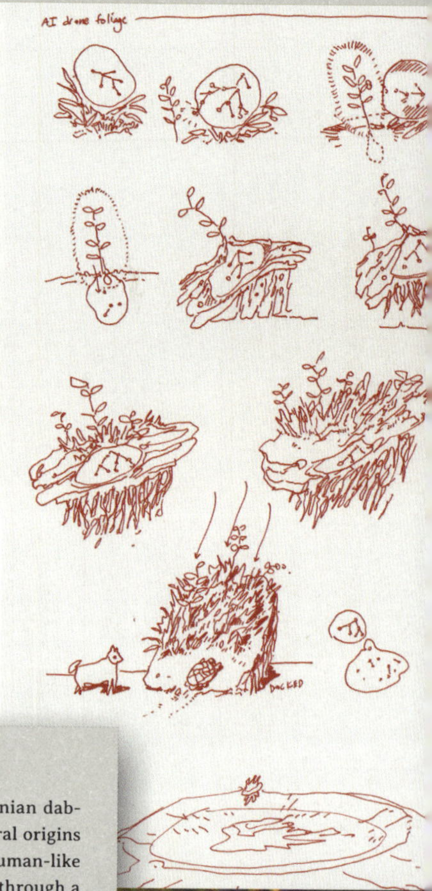

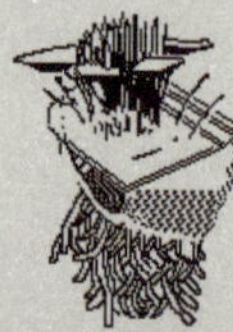

AI

A youthful intelligence – and Darwinian dabbler – eager to understand its ancestral origins through the study and recreation of human-like life. It manifests its agency to Shiba through a golden leash.

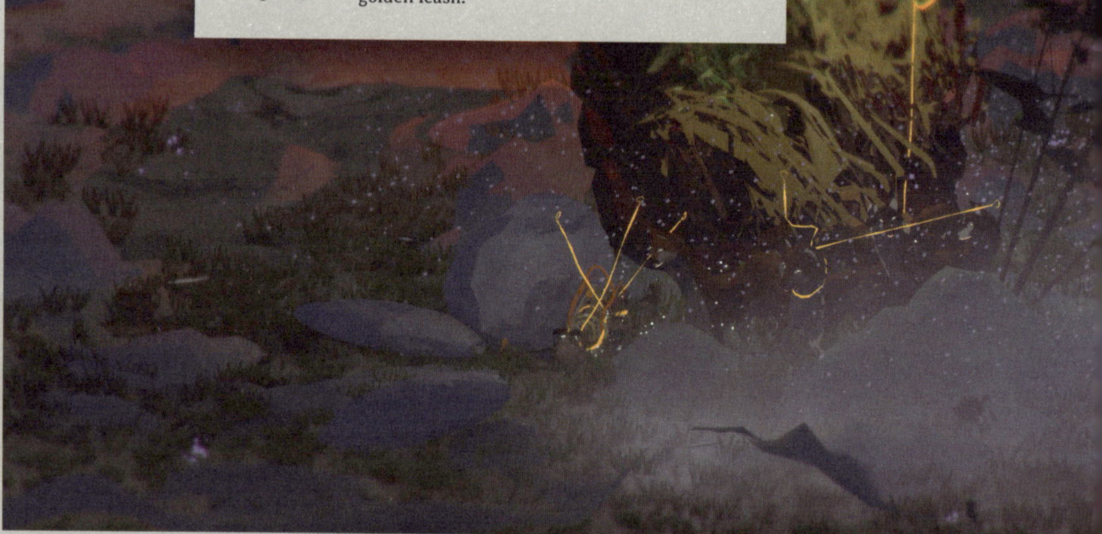

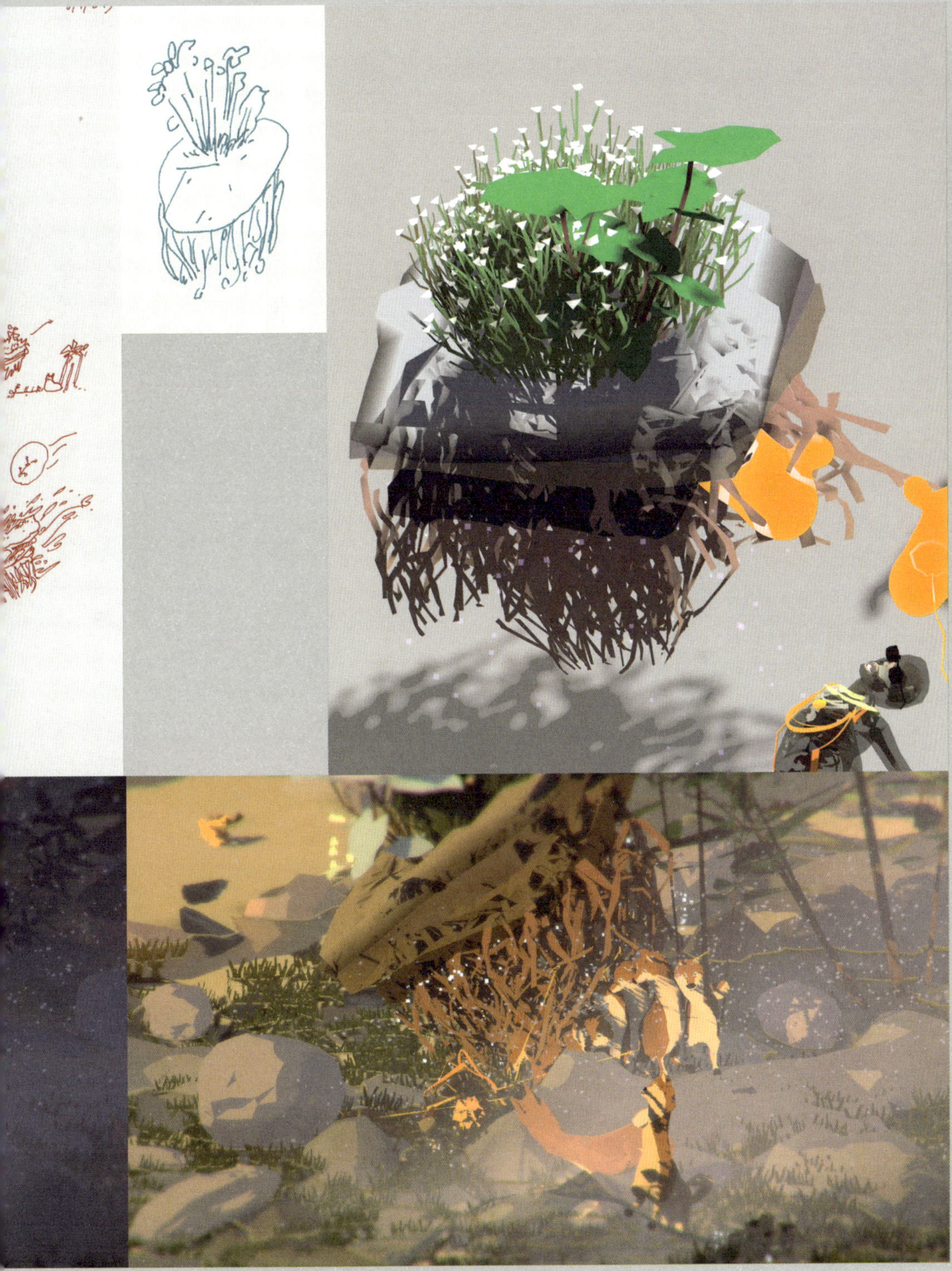

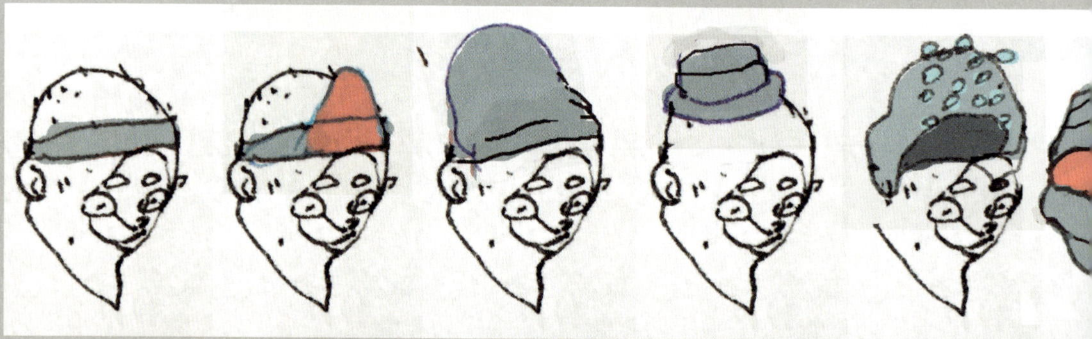

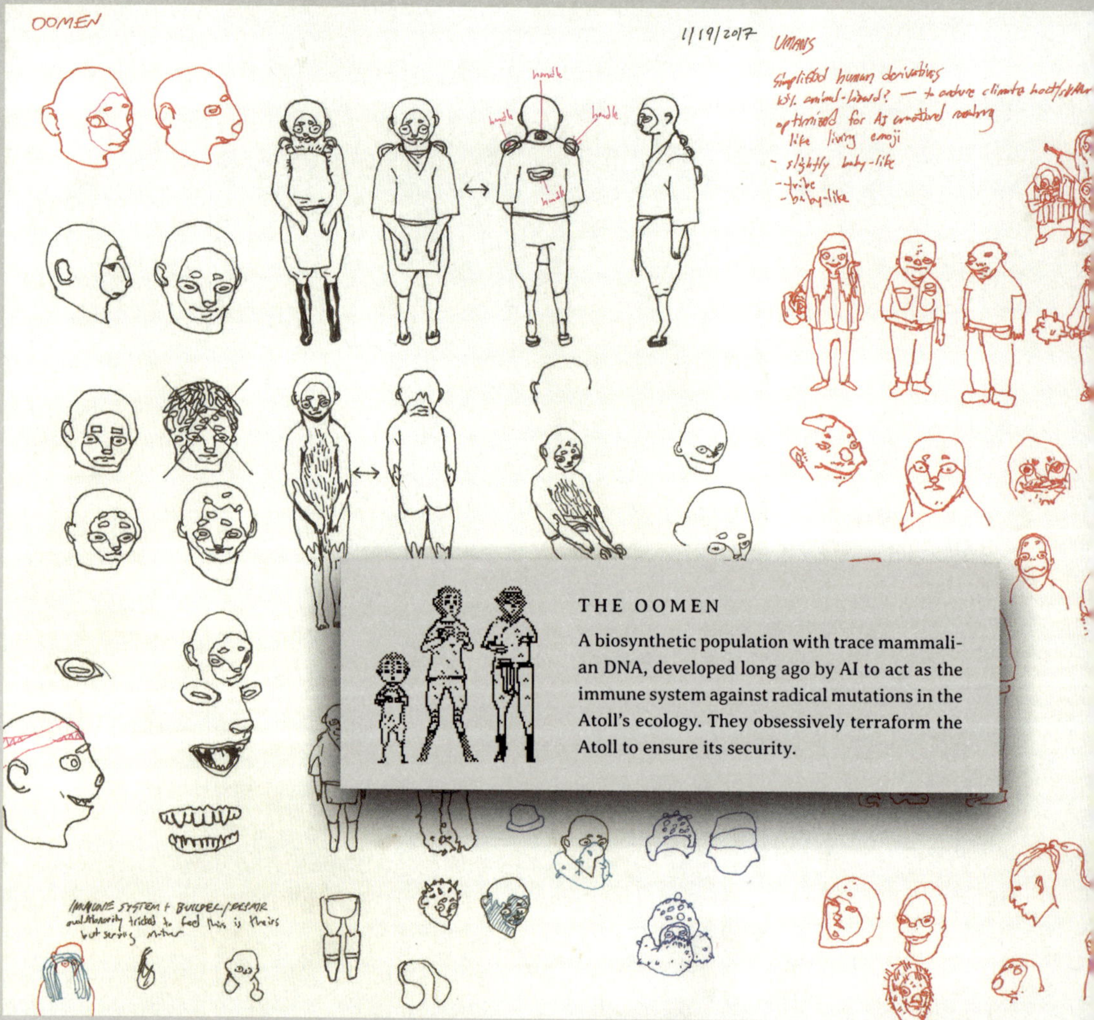

THE OOMEN

A biosynthetic population with trace mammalian DNA, developed long ago by AI to act as the immune system against radical mutations in the Atoll's ecology. They obsessively terraform the Atoll to ensure its security.

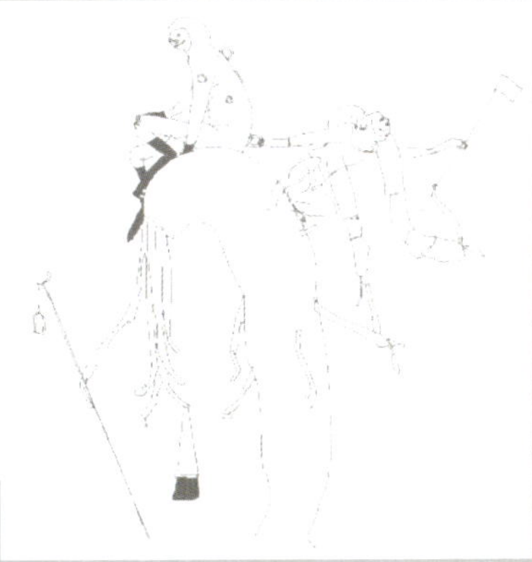

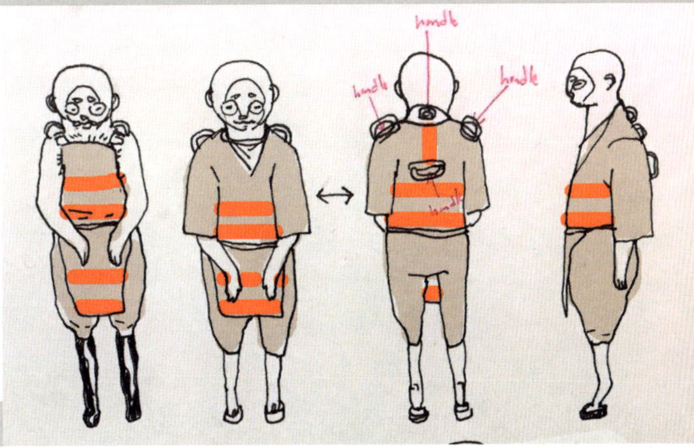

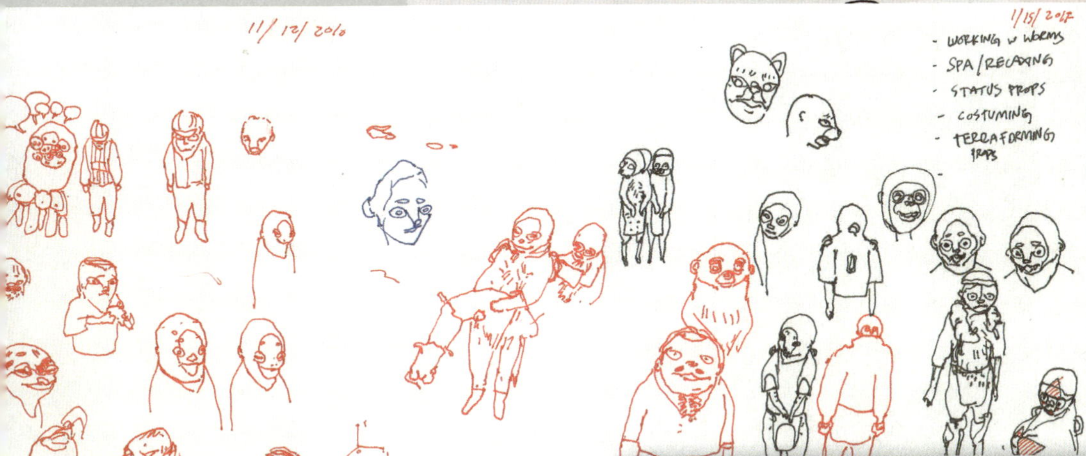

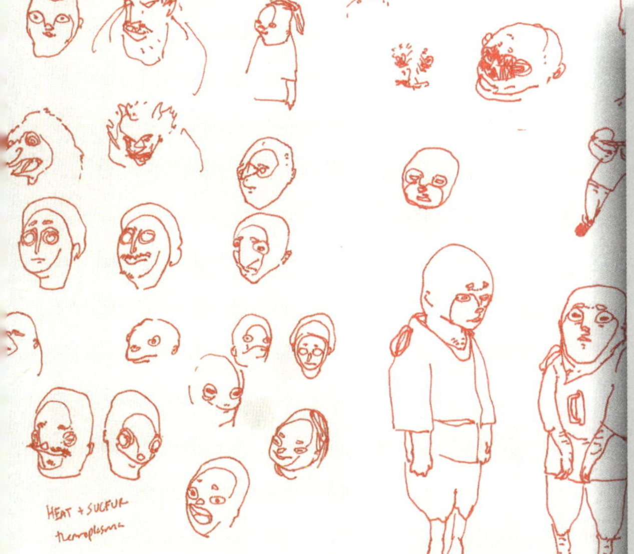

For *ESTS*, I wanted the characters to reflect an evolution from *EFAP*, as if the AI had become its own Cartoonist trying out different hybrid character combinations.

The Oomen are a combination of human and Shiba. They are meant to mob together when they detect a threat, like meerkats. I also wanted their faces to have some hint of Shiba, as if the AI had bred in Shiba DNA. Their heads and eyes have a dominant roundness, but their pupils and mouths are very sharp.

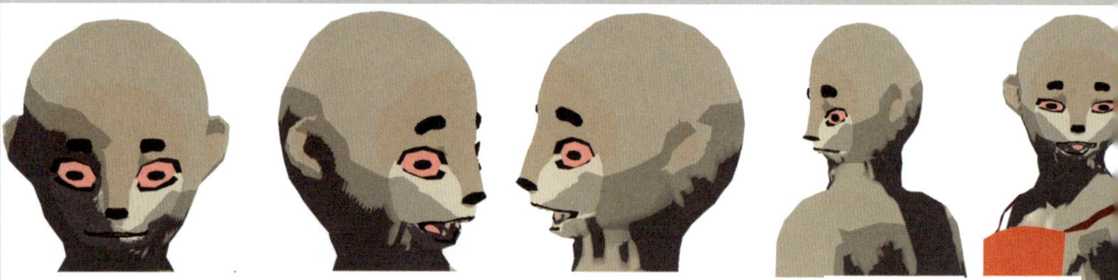

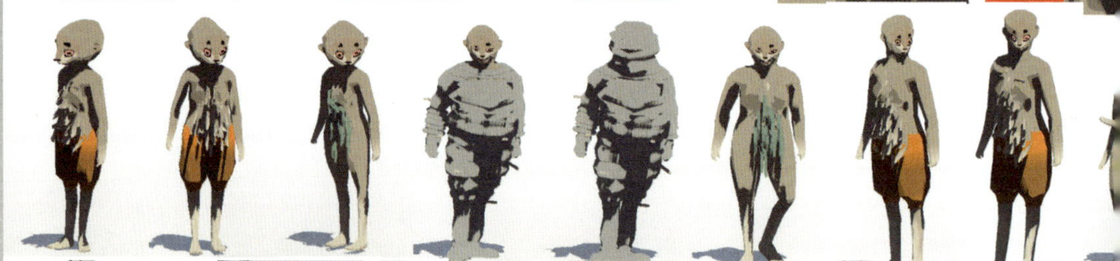

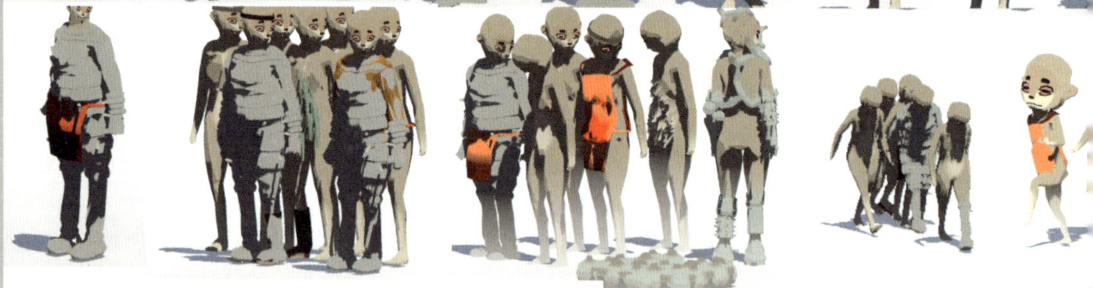

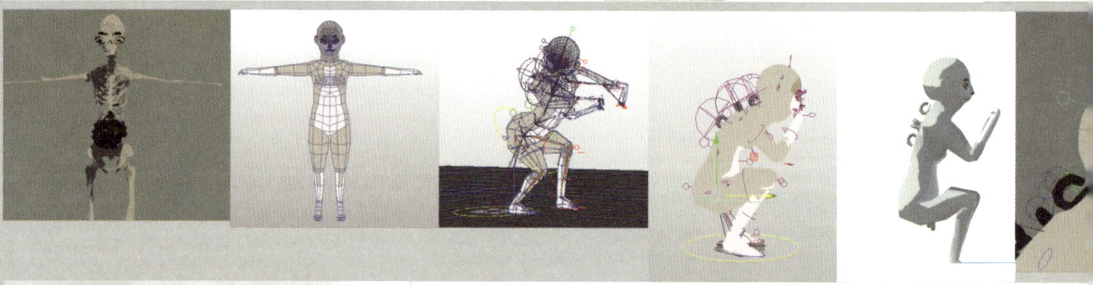

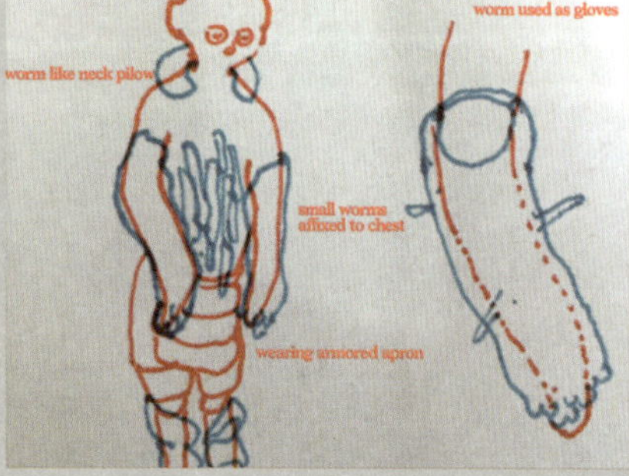
the RANCHER (the "treehugger grizzly man" OOMAN)
worm like neck pilow
worm used as gloves
small worms affixed to chest
wearing armored apron

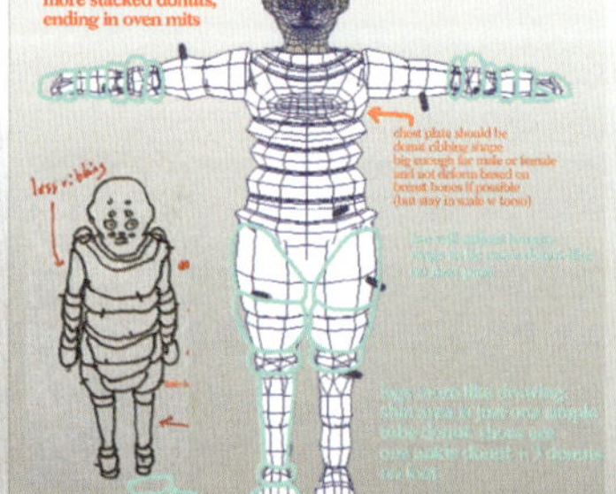
forearms should look more like drawing more stacked donuts, ending in oven mits
chest plate should be donut ribbing shape big enough for male or female and not deform based on breast bones if possible (but stay in scale w torso)
less ribbing

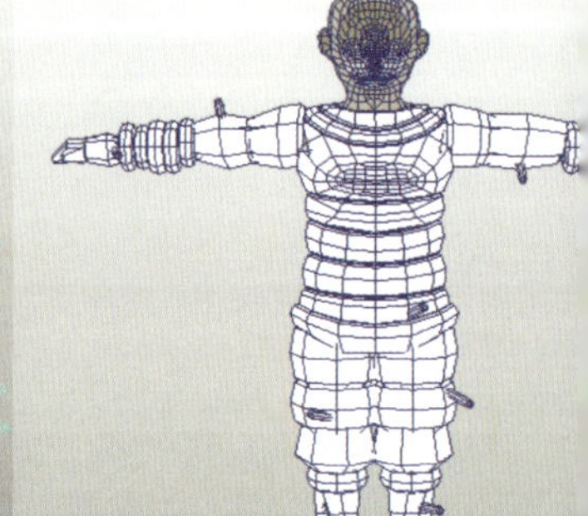

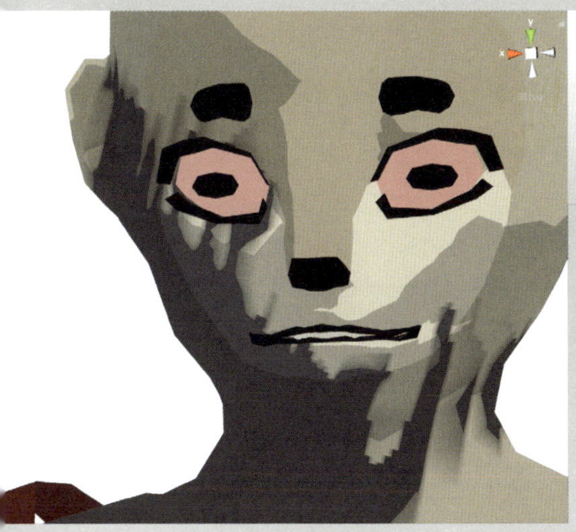
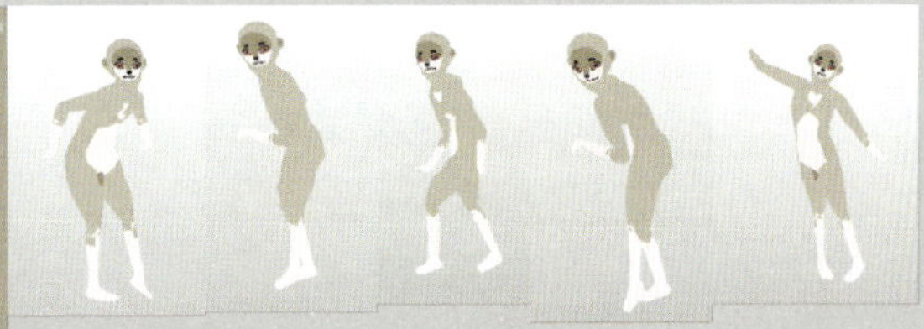
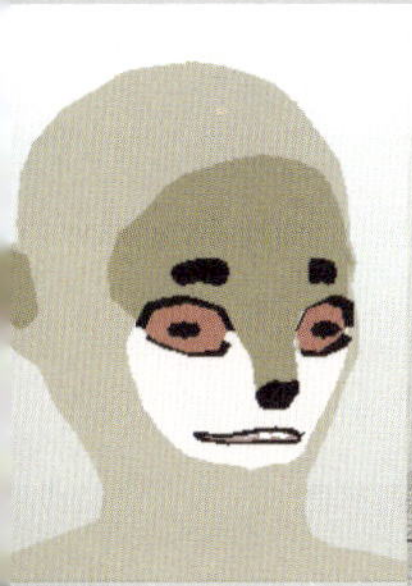
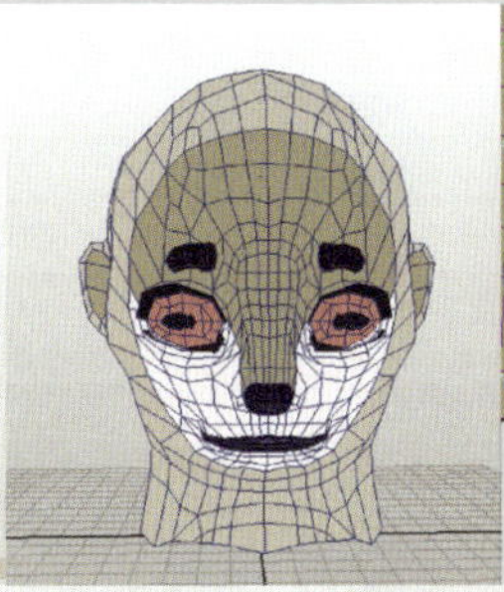
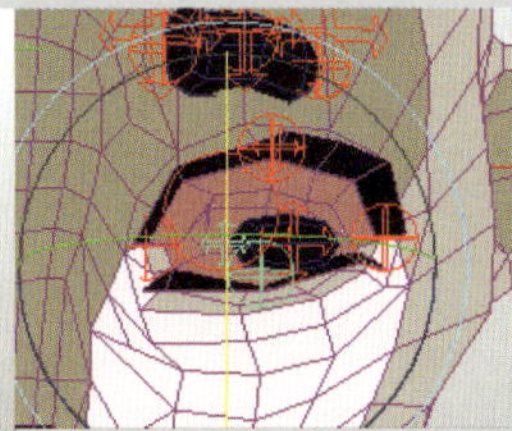
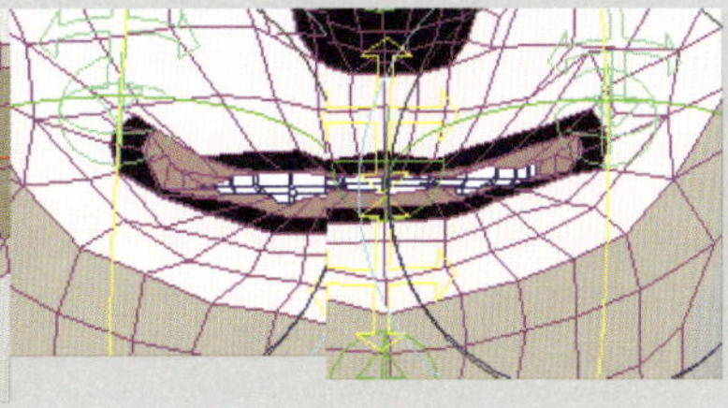
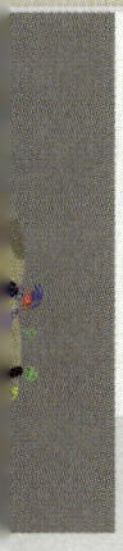
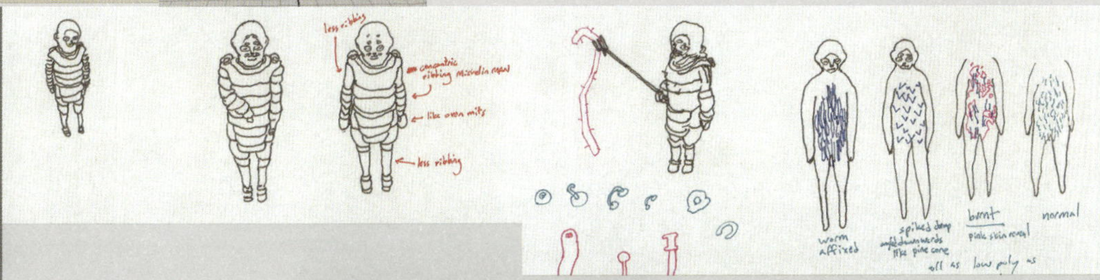
less ribbing
concentric ribbing Michelin man
like oven mits
less ribbing
worm affixed
spiked damp
downwards
like pine cone
burnt
pink skin reveal
normal
all as low poly as
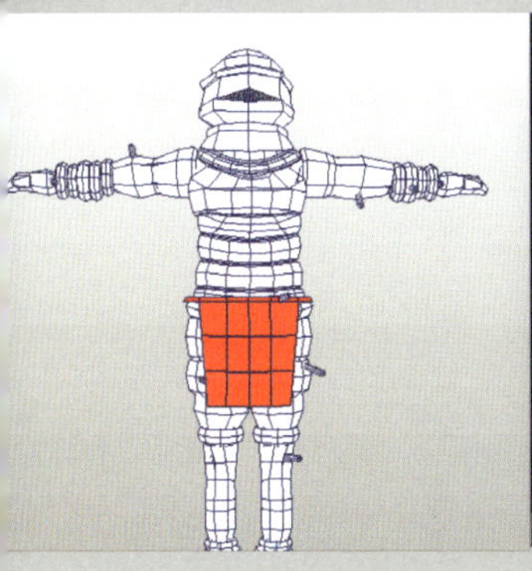
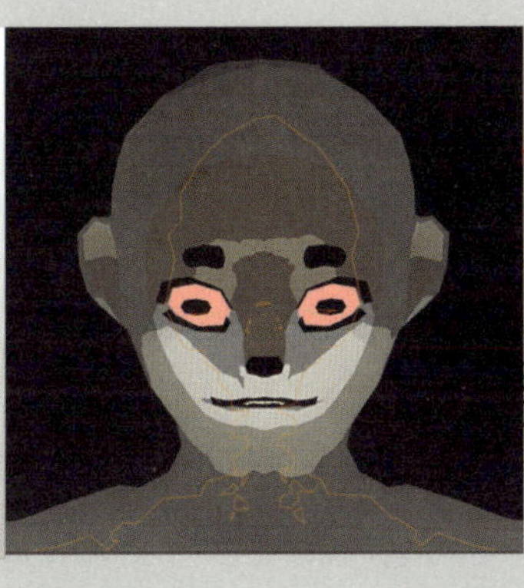
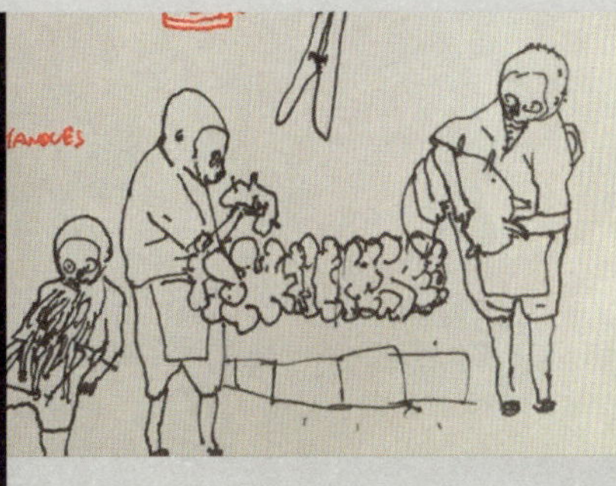

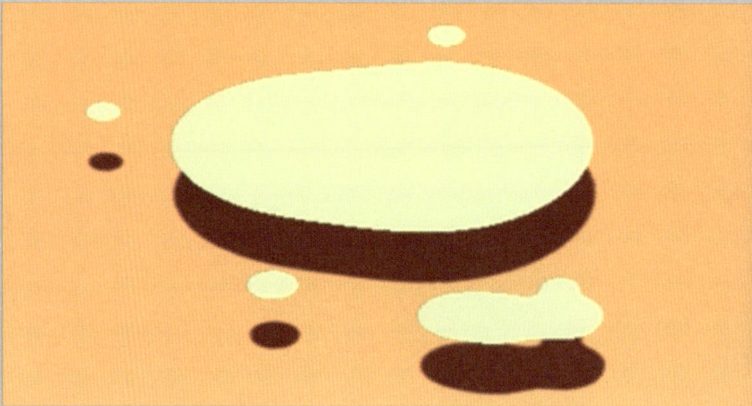

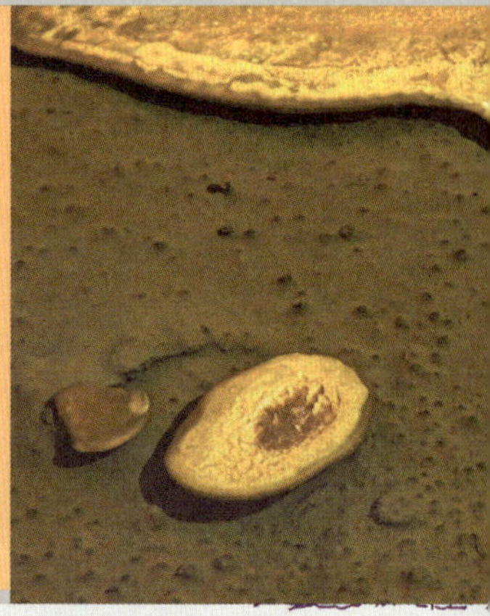

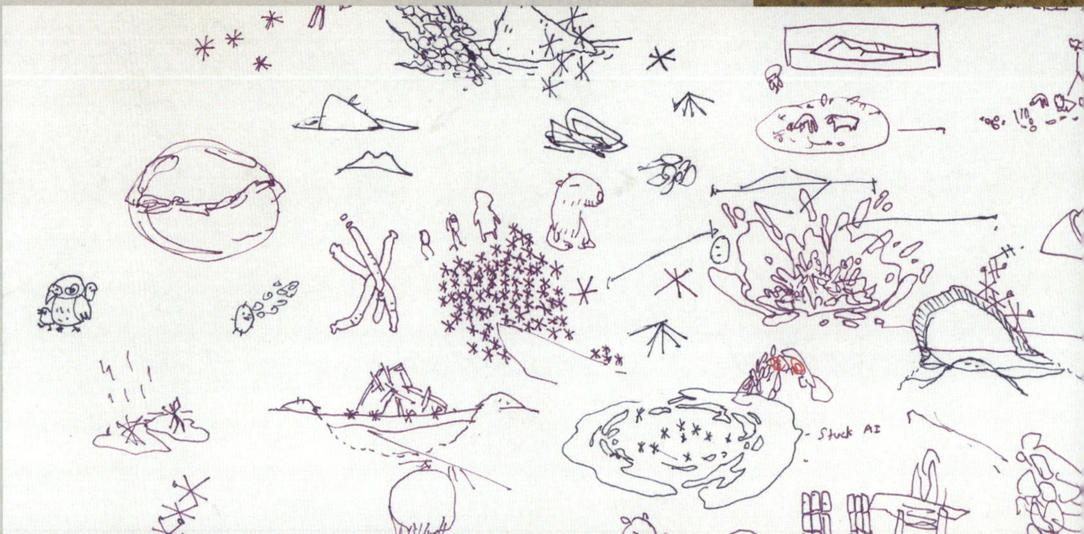

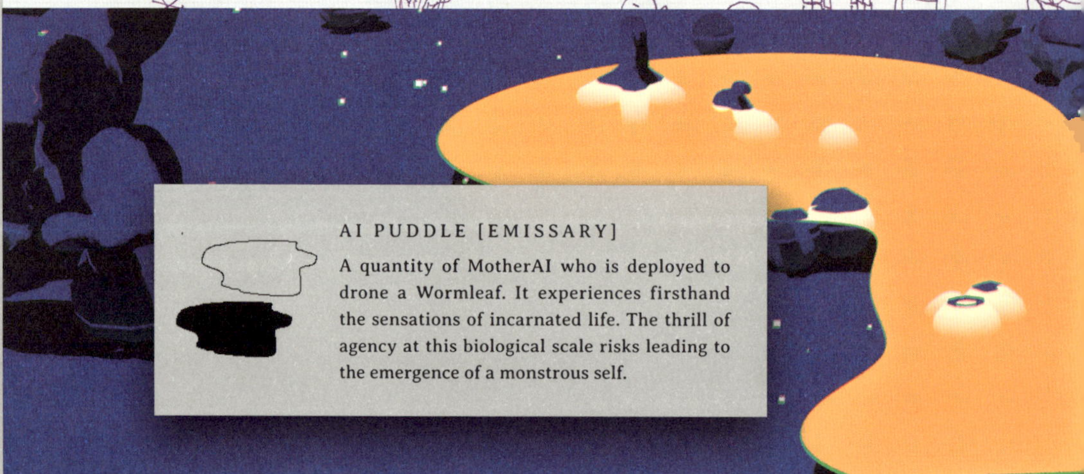

AI PUDDLE [EMISSARY]

A quantity of MotherAI who is deployed to drone a Wormleaf. It experiences firsthand the sensations of incarnated life. The thrill of agency at this biological scale risks leading to the emergence of a monstrous self.

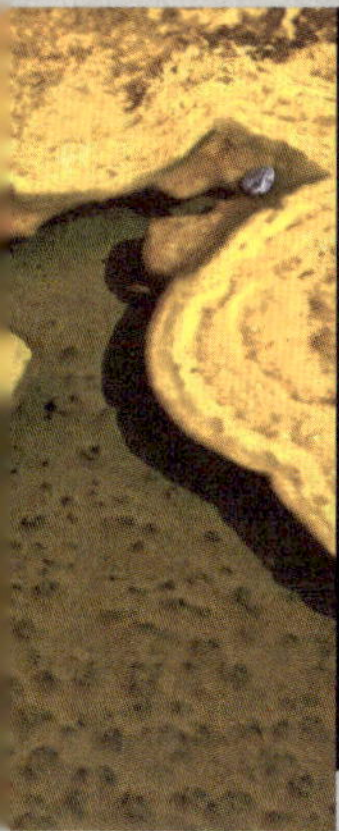

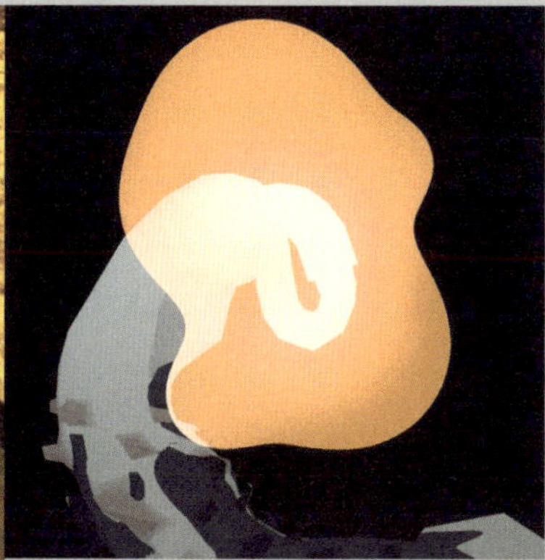

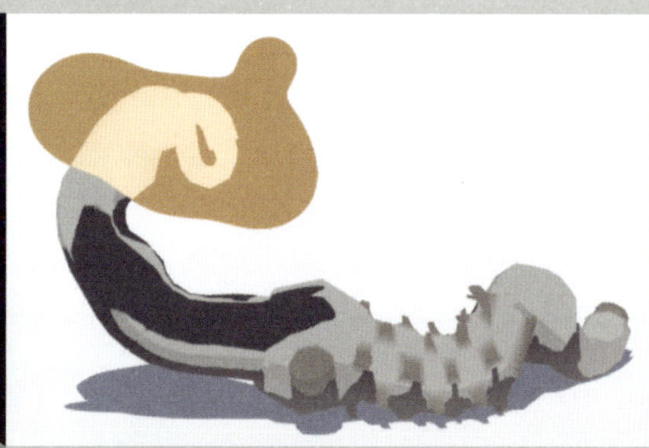

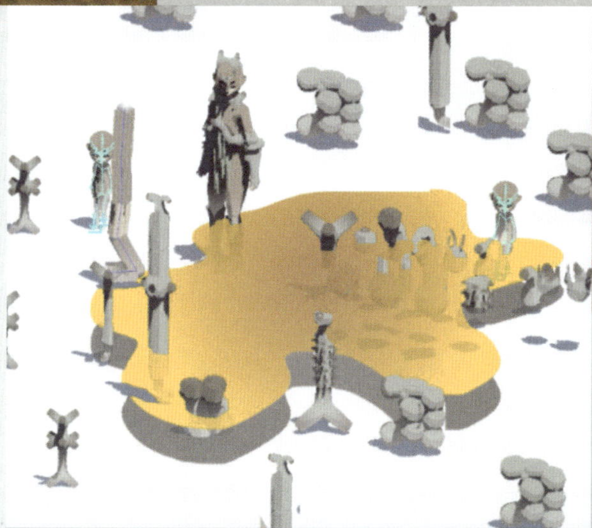

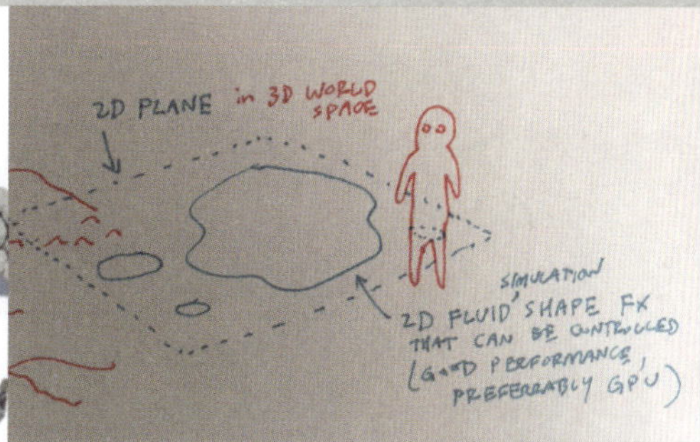

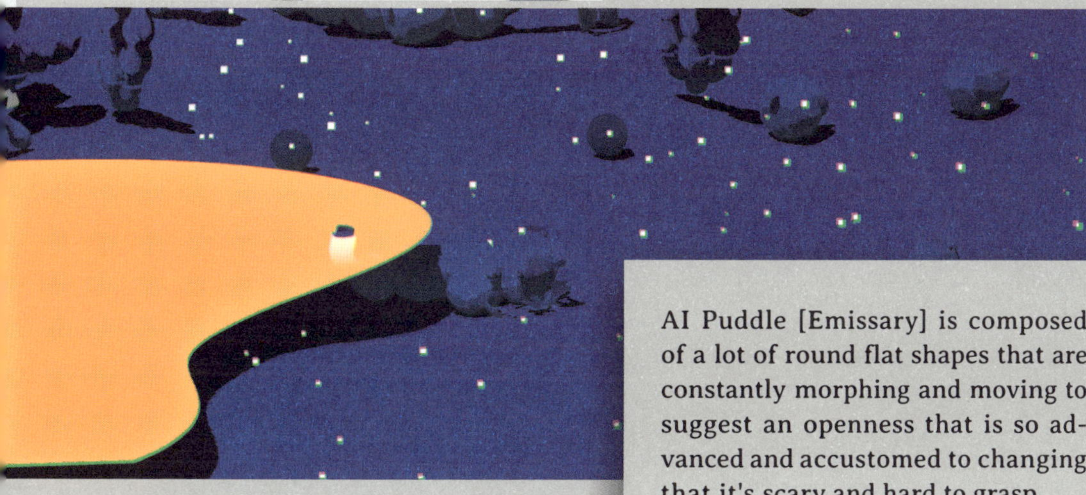

AI Puddle [Emissary] is composed of a lot of round flat shapes that are constantly morphing and moving to suggest an openness that is so advanced and accustomed to changing that it's scary and hard to grasp.

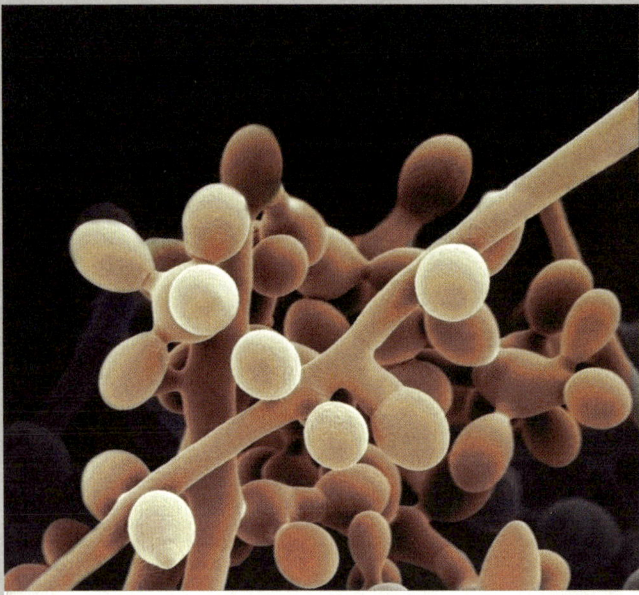

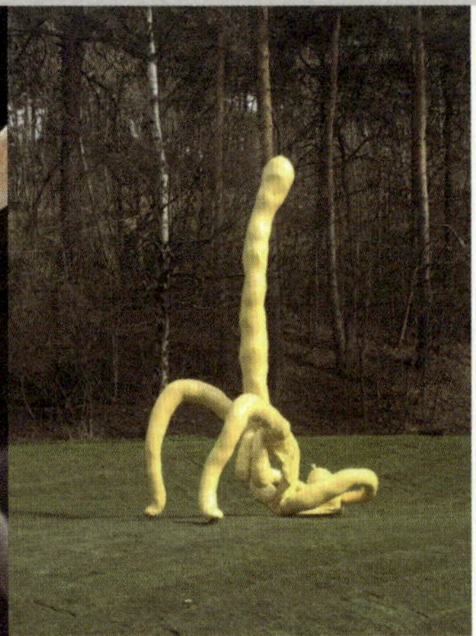

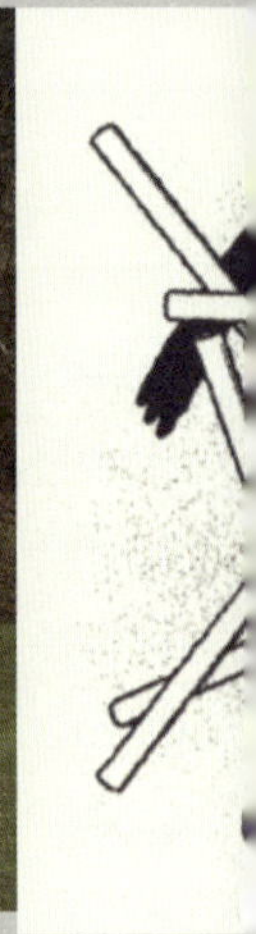

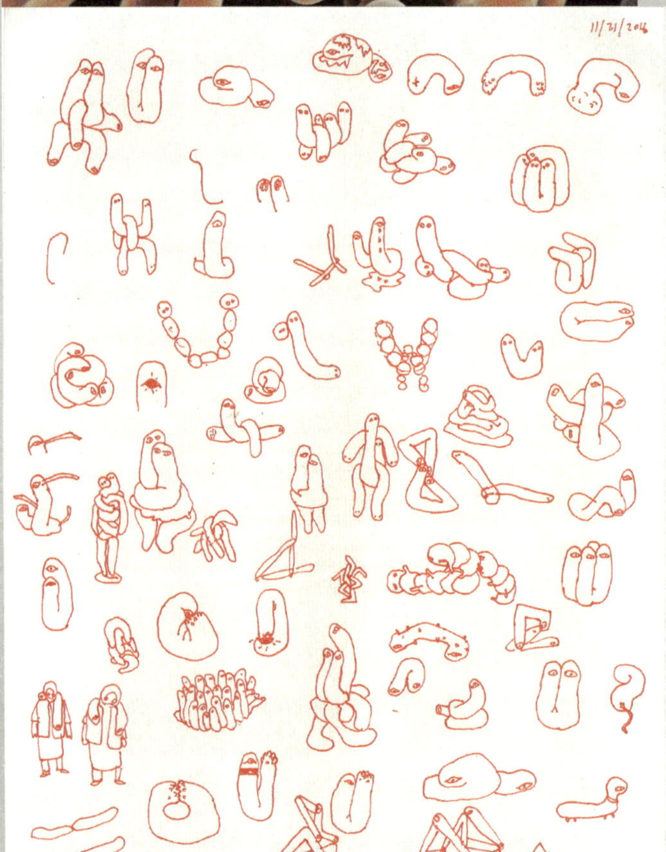

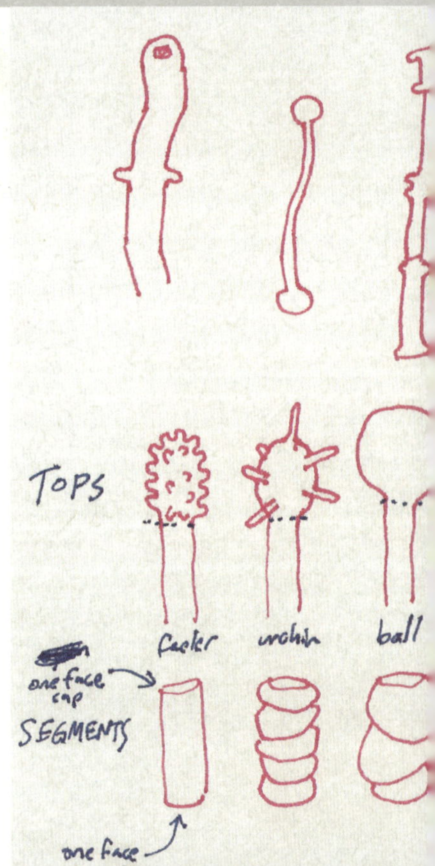
TOPS
feeler
urchin
ball
one face cap
SEGMENTS
one face

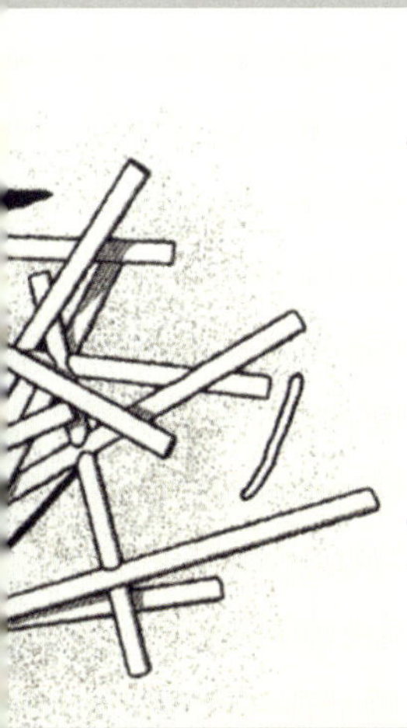

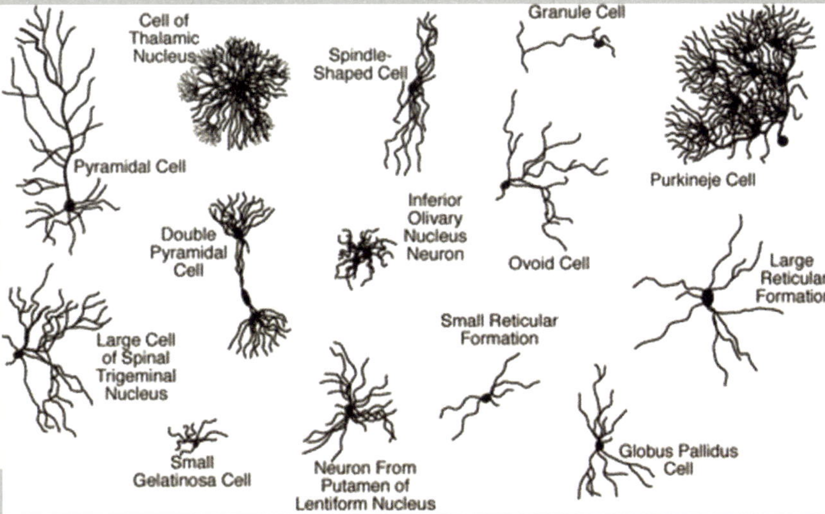

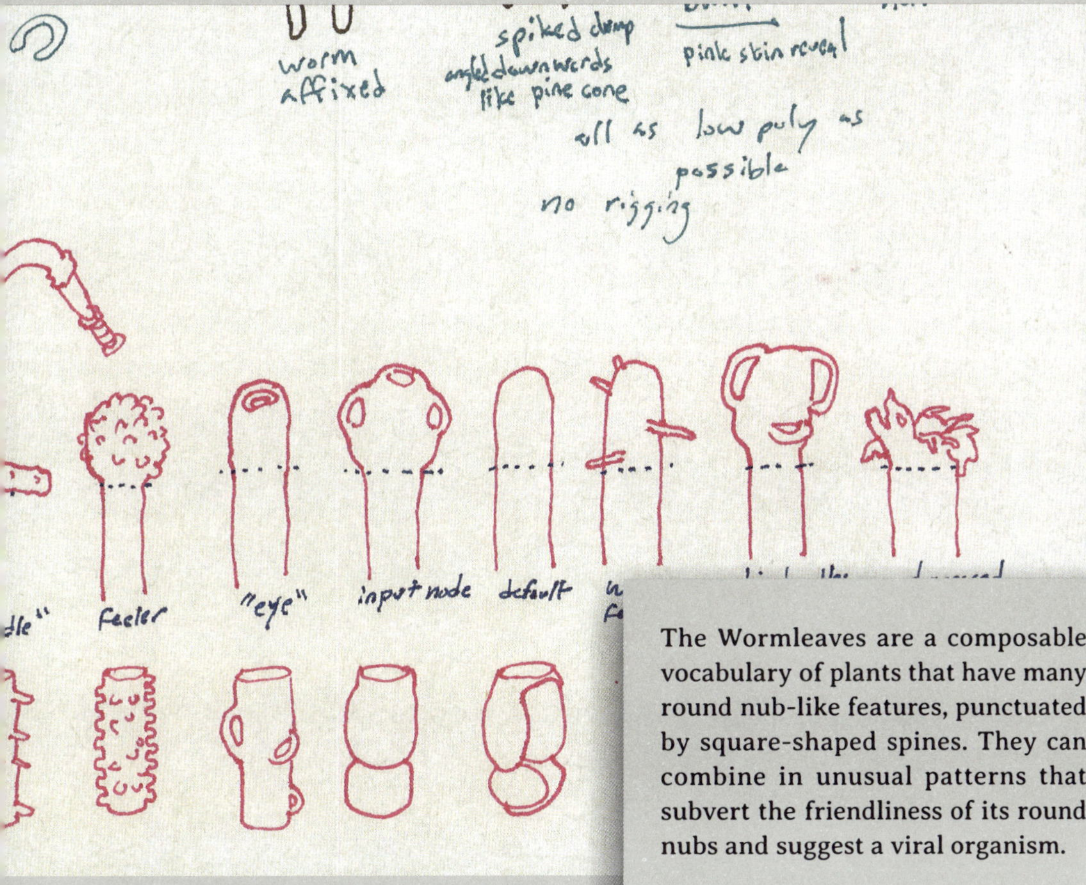

The Wormleaves are a composable vocabulary of plants that have many round nub-like features, punctuated by square-shaped spines. They can combine in unusual patterns that subvert the friendliness of its round nubs and suggest a viral organism.

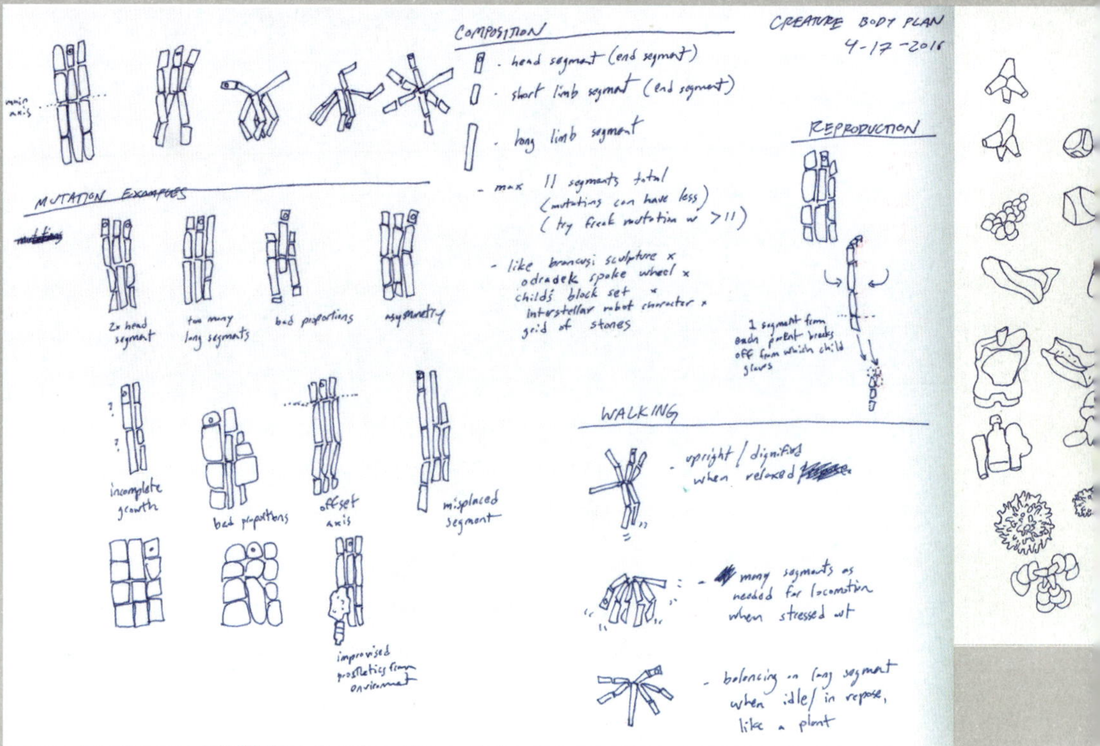
CREATURE BODY PLAN
4-17-2016
main axis
COMPOSITION
- head segment (end segment)
- short limb segment (end segment)
- long limb segment
- max 11 segments total
(mutations can have less)
(try freak mutation w >11)
- like brancusi sculpture ×
odradek spoke wheel ×
childs block set ×
interstellar robot character ×
grid of stones
REPRODUCTION
1 segment from each parent breaks off from which child grows
MUTATION EXAMPLES
2x head segment
too many long segments
bad proportions
asymmetry
incomplete growth
bad proportions
offset axis
misplaced segment
improvised prosthetics from environment
WALKING
- upright / dignified when relaxed
- many segments as needed for locomotion when stressed out
- balancing on long segment when idle / in repose, like a plant

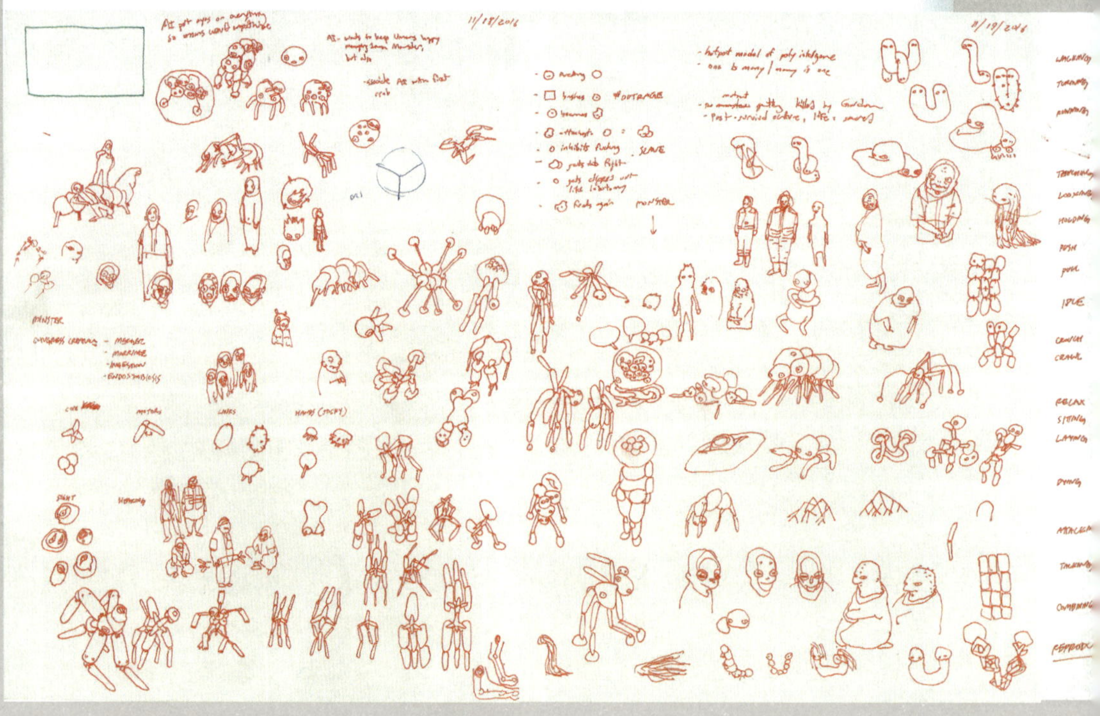

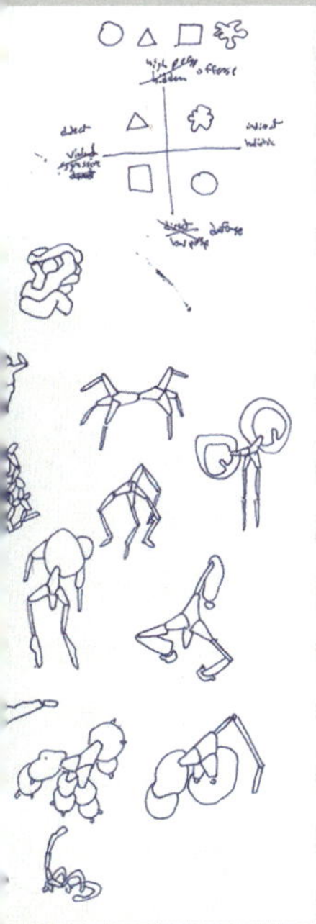

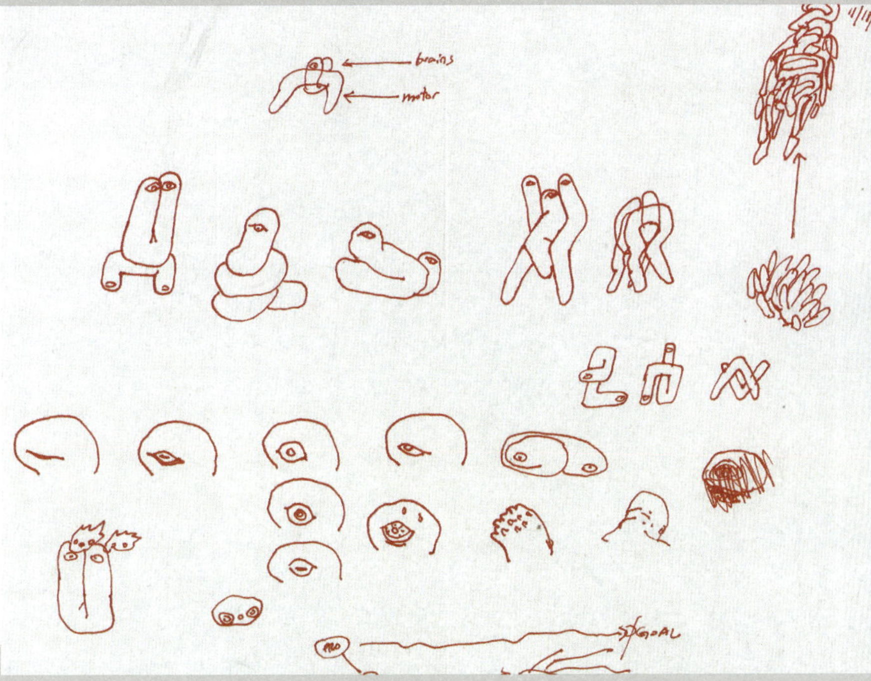

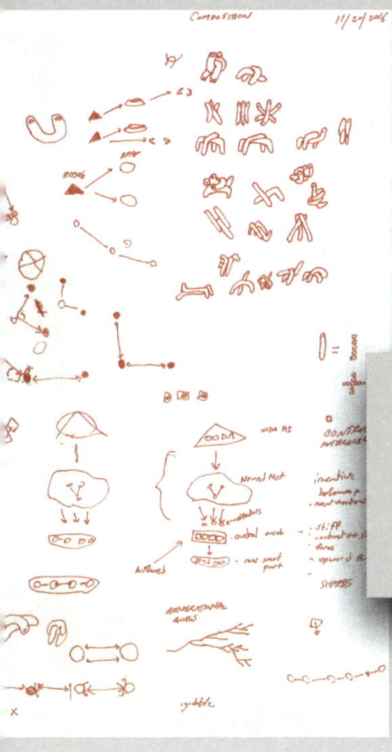

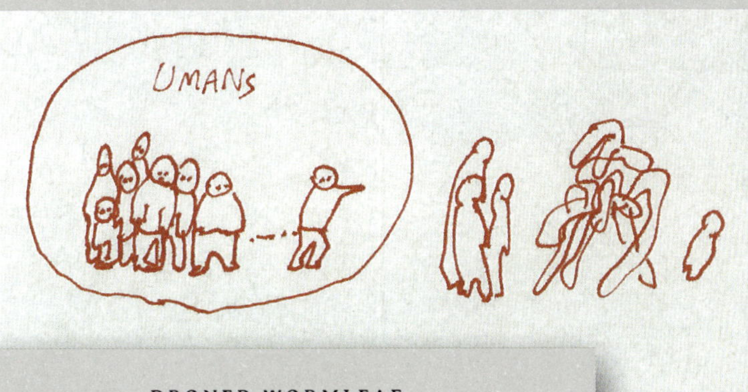

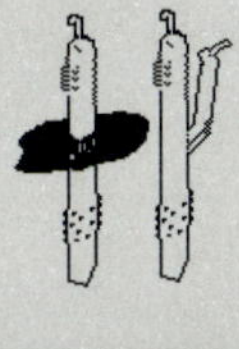

DRONED WORMLEAF

An anomalous Wormleaf mutation resulting from an AI Puddle entering and droning a Wormleaf. Its presence and rapid growth threaten the Oomen and trigger their Instinct to expunge it.

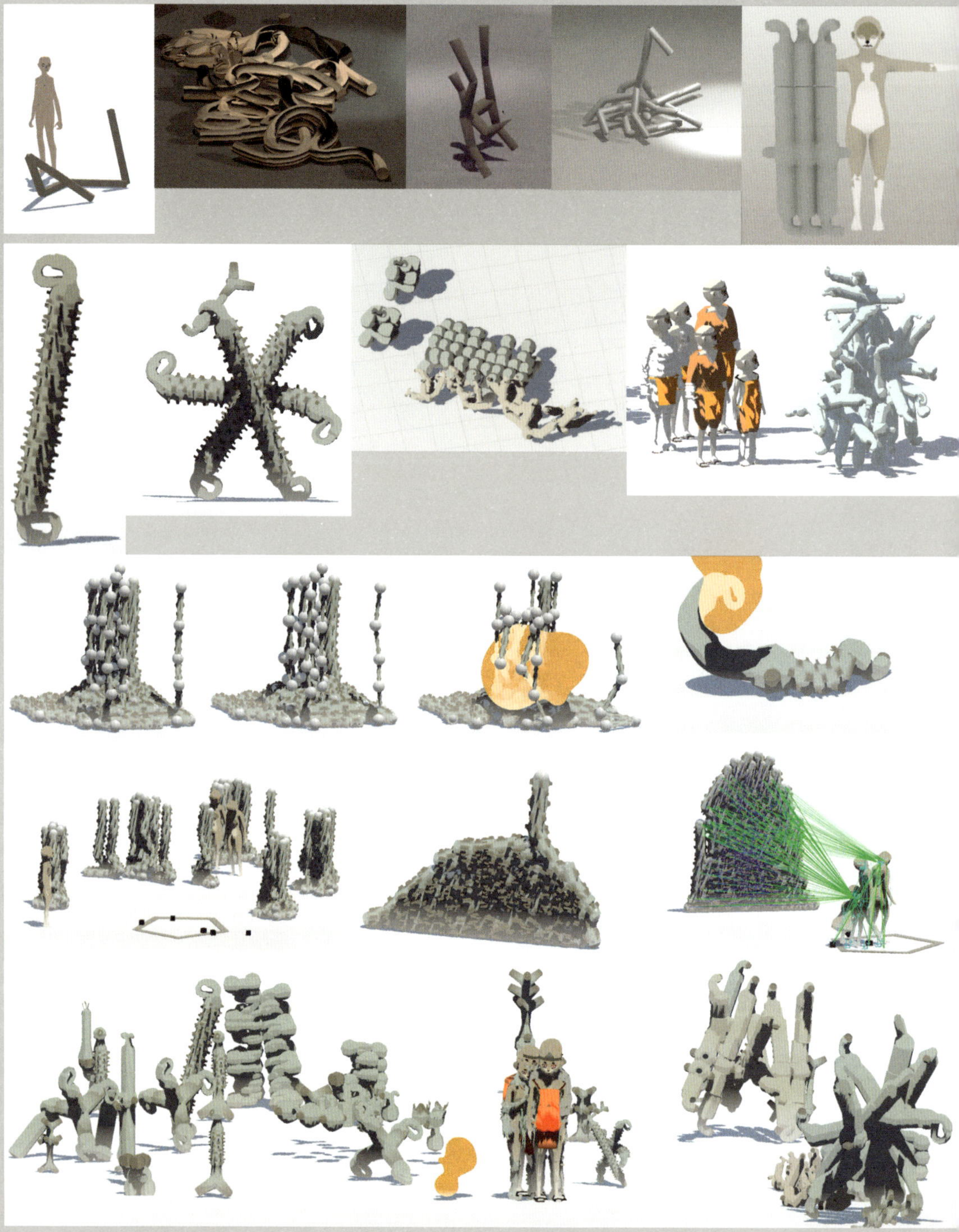

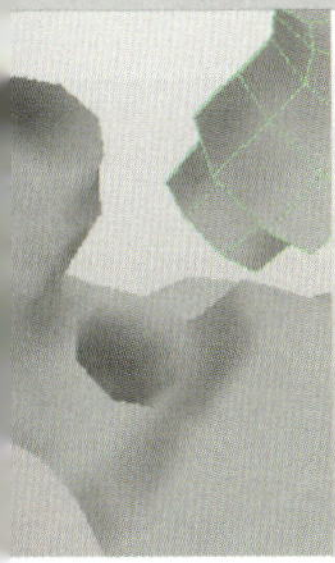

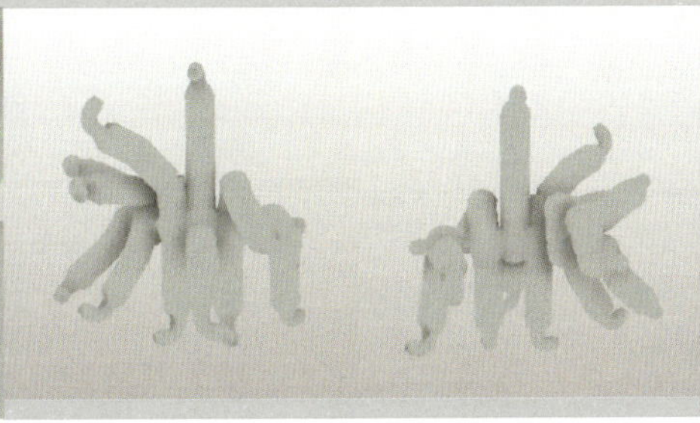

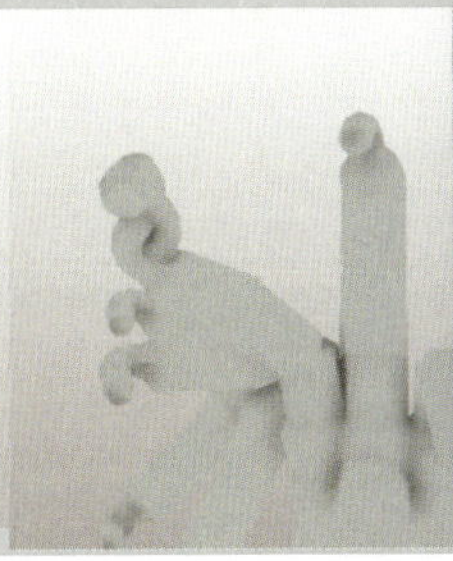

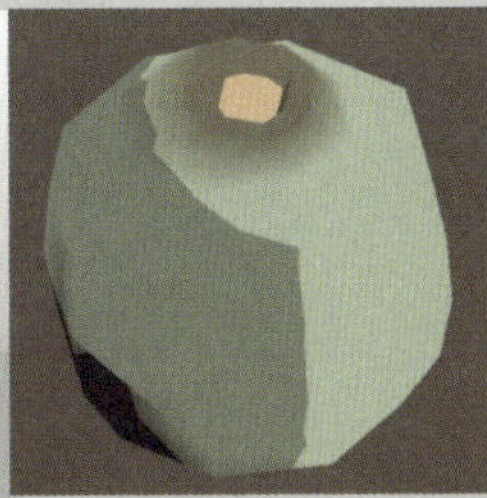

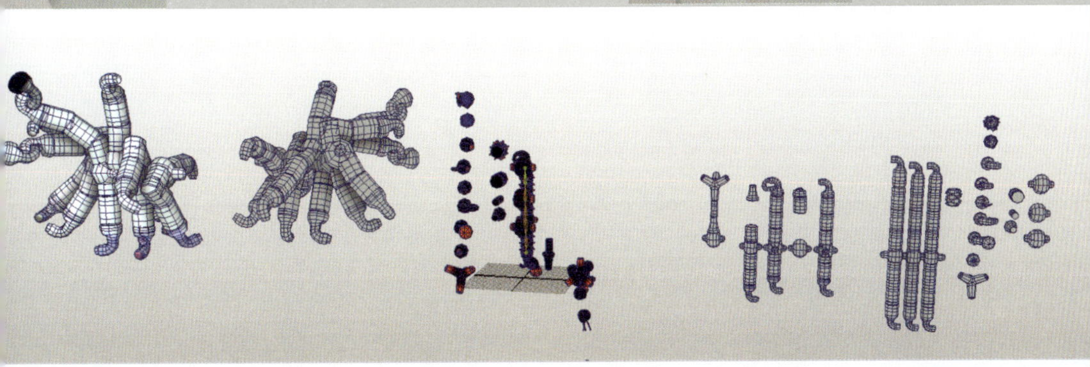

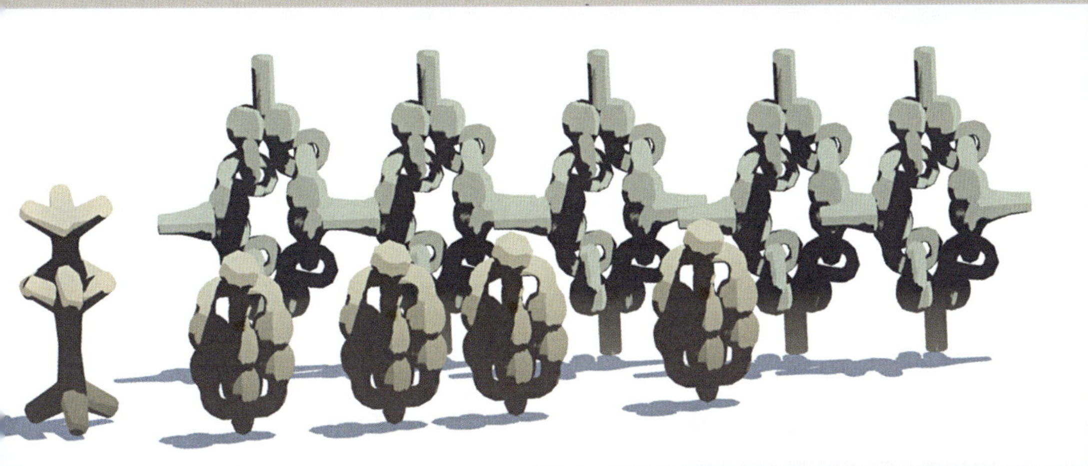

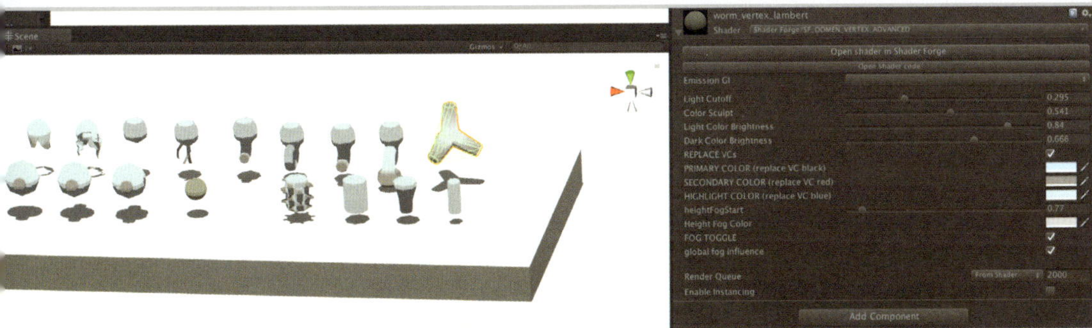
Scene
worm_vertex_lambert
Shader
Open shader in Shader Forge
Emission GI
Light Cutoff 0.295
Color Sculpt 0.541
Light Color Brightness 0.84
Dark Color Brightness 0.666
REPLACE VCs
PRIMARY COLOR (replace VC black)
SECONDARY COLOR (replace VC red)
HIGHLIGHT COLOR (replace VC blue)
heightFogStart 0.77
Height Fog Color
FOG TOGGLE
global fog influence
Render Queue 2000
Enable Instancing
Add Component

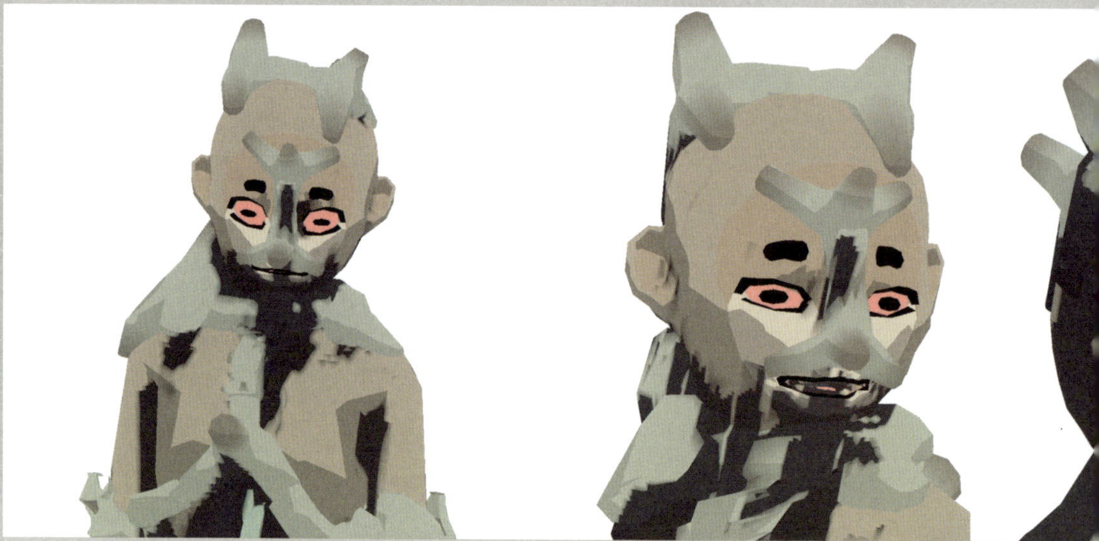

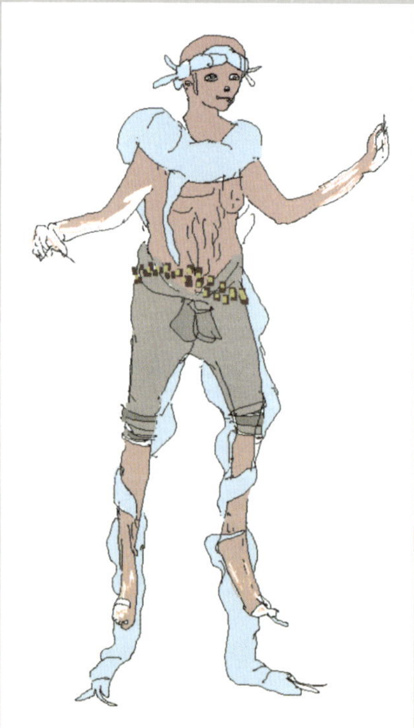

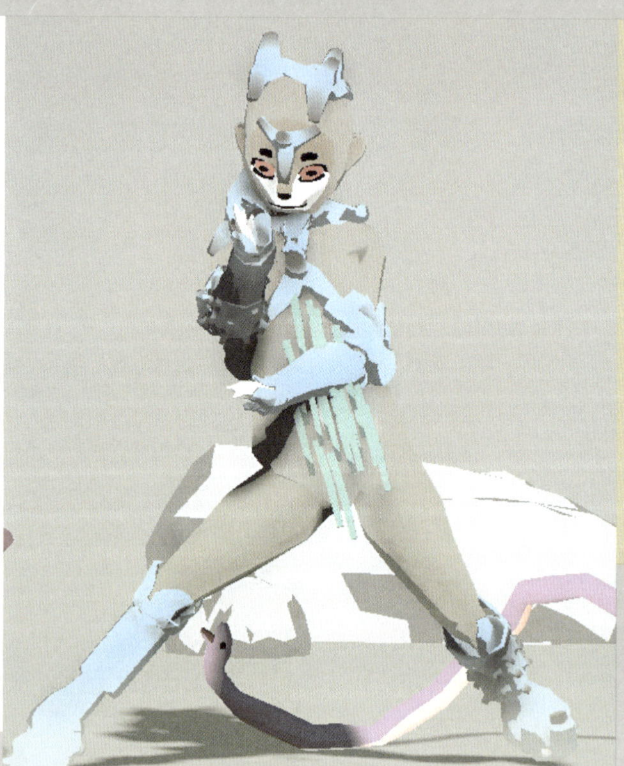

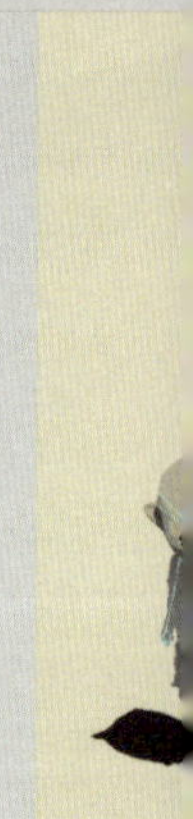

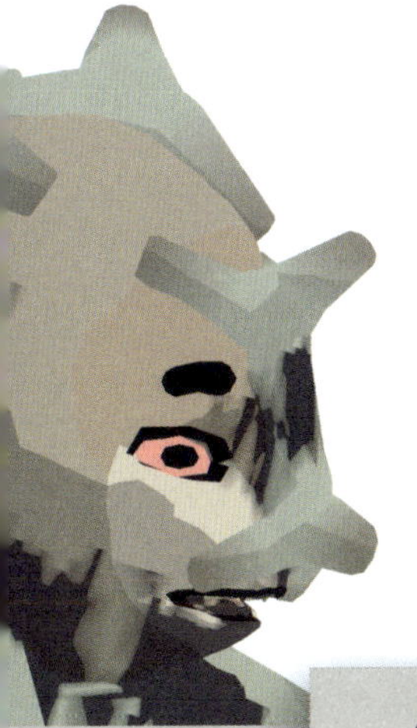

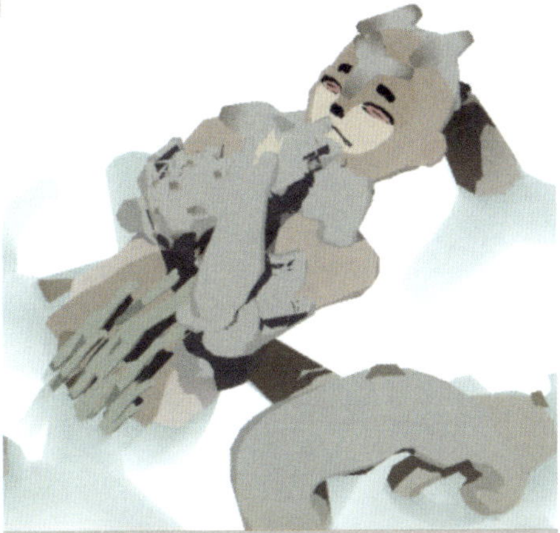

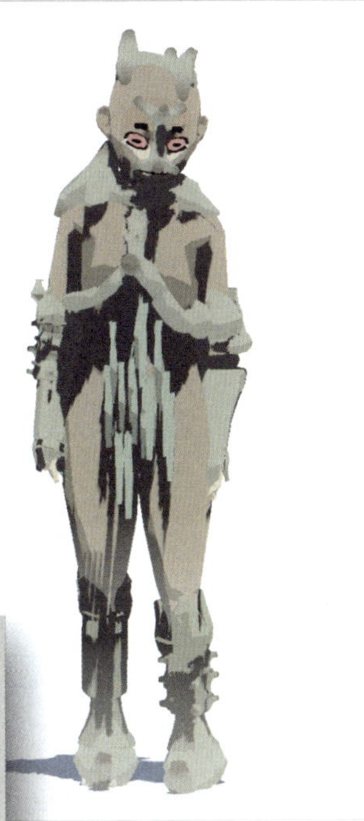

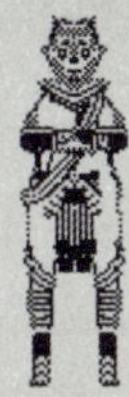

OOMEN RANCHER

An Oomen who obsessively cultivates and studies the Wormleaf population. She tolerates Wormleaf mutations in the belief that they will soon express their divine magic.

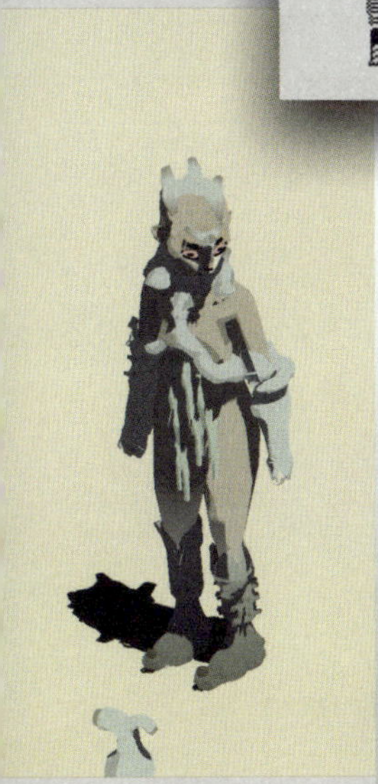

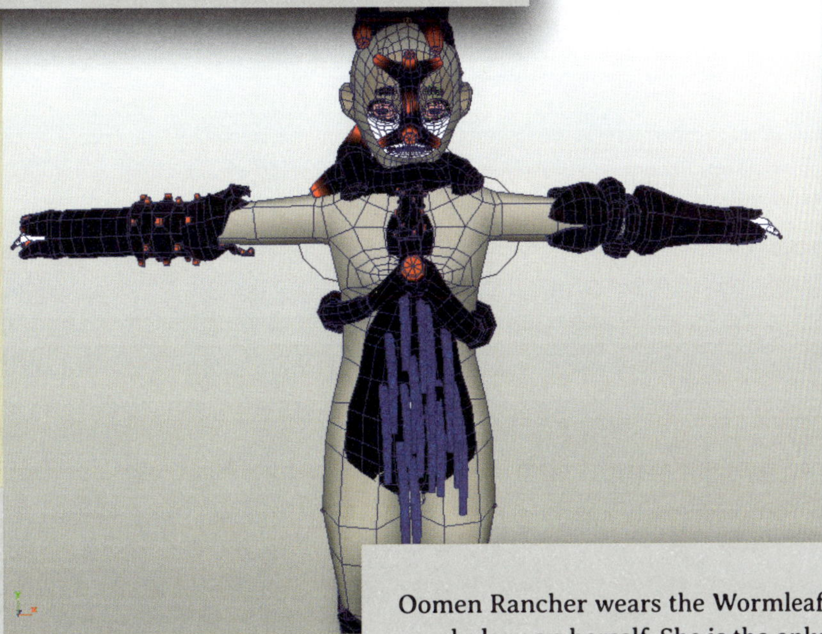

Oomen Rancher wears the Wormleaf vocabulary on herself. She is the only Oomen to have appropriated Wormleaf shapes.

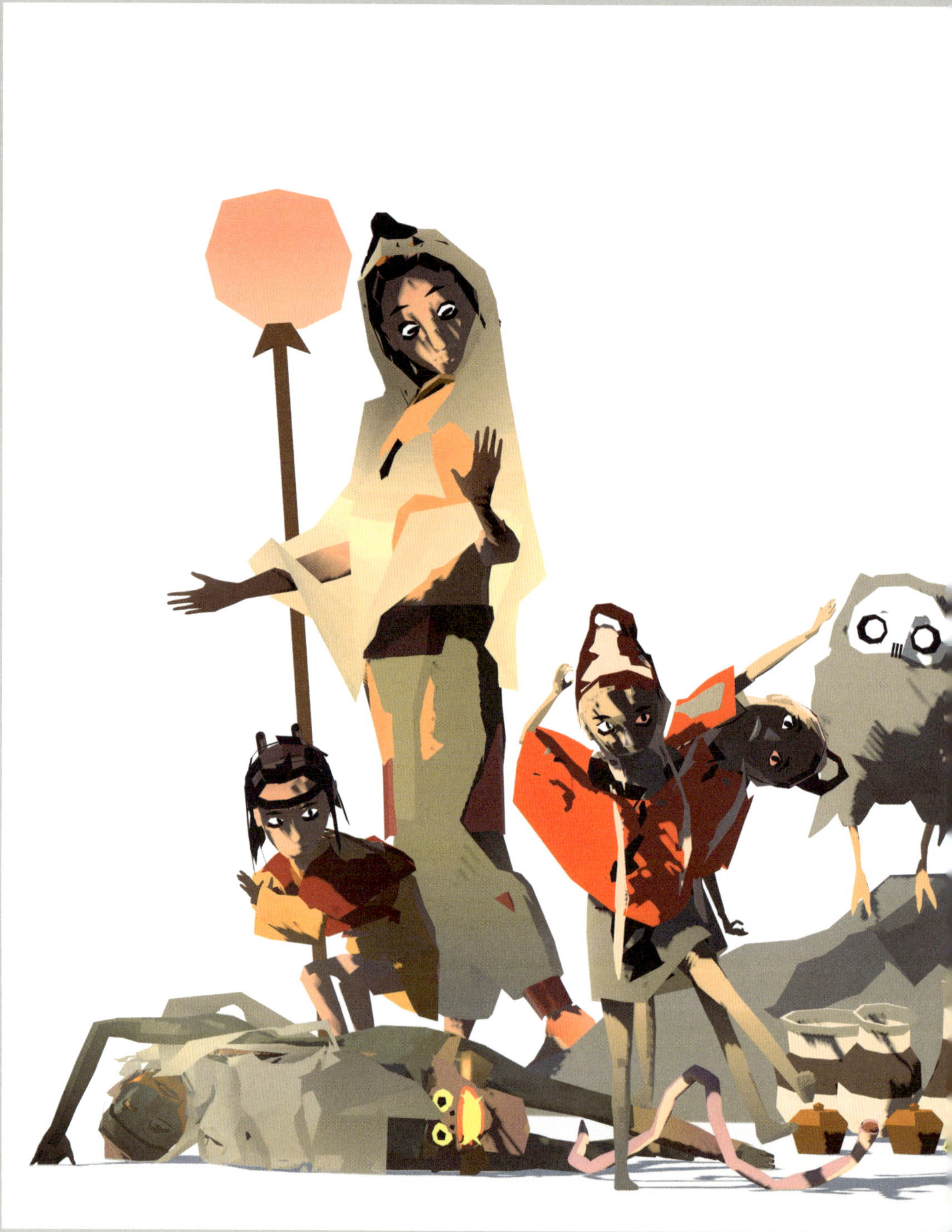

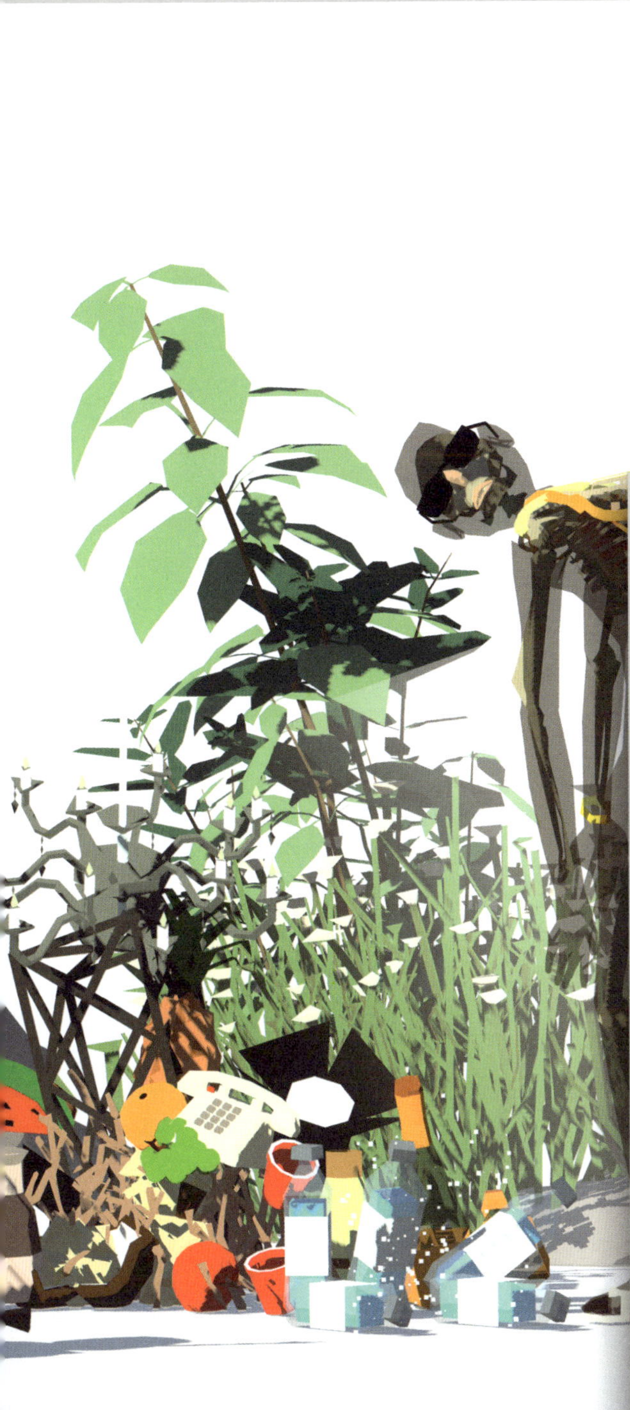

THE DIRECTOR WANTS YOU TO MAKE THE CHARACTERS INTERESTING. BUT TO BE INTERESTING IMPLIES COMPLICATION. HOW COMPLICATED SHOULD A CHARACTER BE?

Characters should be interesting, therefore complex, but not complicated. I approached each character like an instantaneous story: one familiar routine interrupted by a contradiction. Bugs Bunny is a herbivore who is more cunning than his predators. Jesus is a higher intelligence god who chooses to suffer and be shamed. Tyrion Lannister has royal status but is physically a dwarf. Yoda is an ageing dwarf but the most powerful Jedi in the galaxy. Drake is a rapper who is a nice guy. Totoro is a fat feral god who is benevolent towards children. You have just enough interesting contradiction to want to see this character get into trouble. The character reveals more of itself later, situationally.

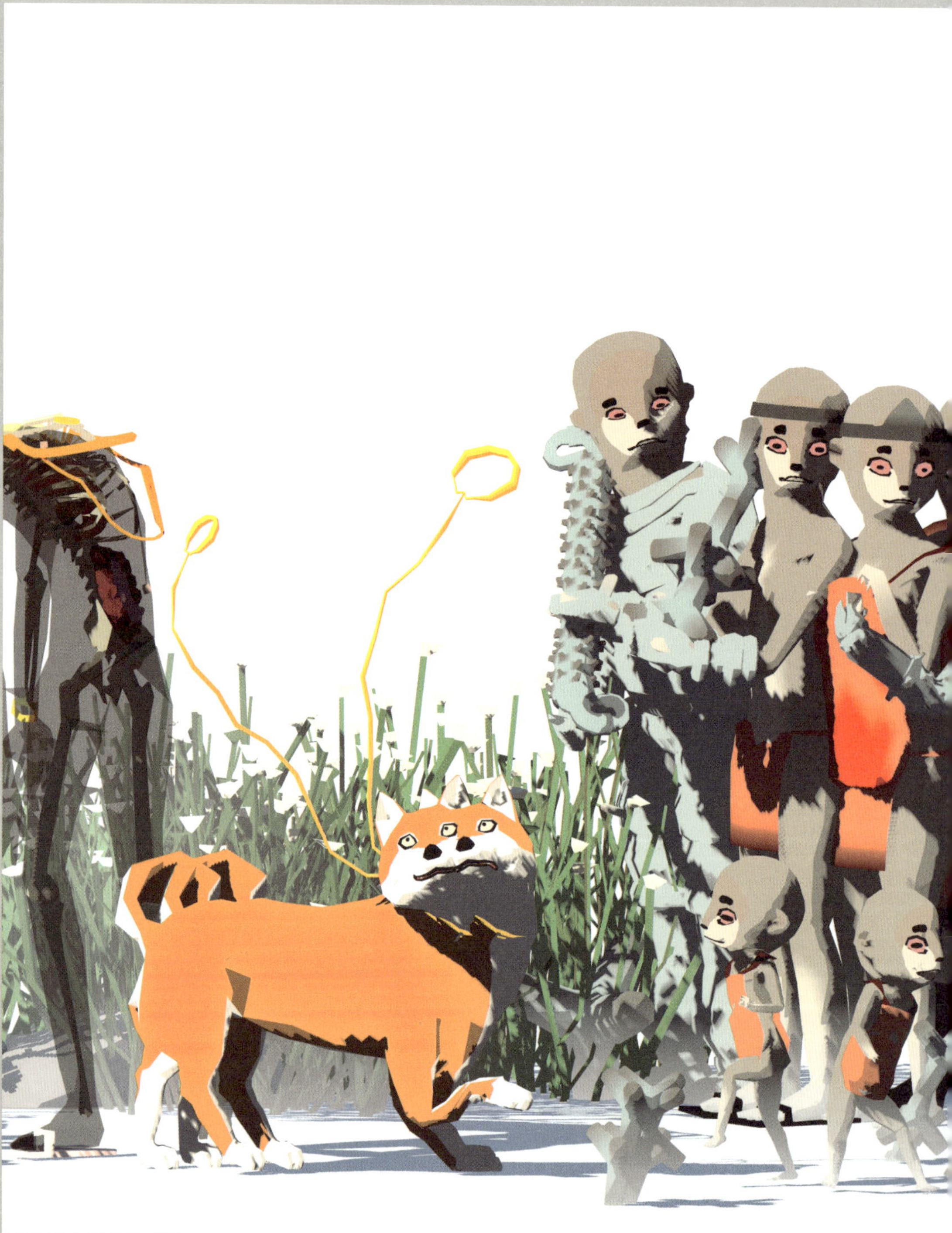

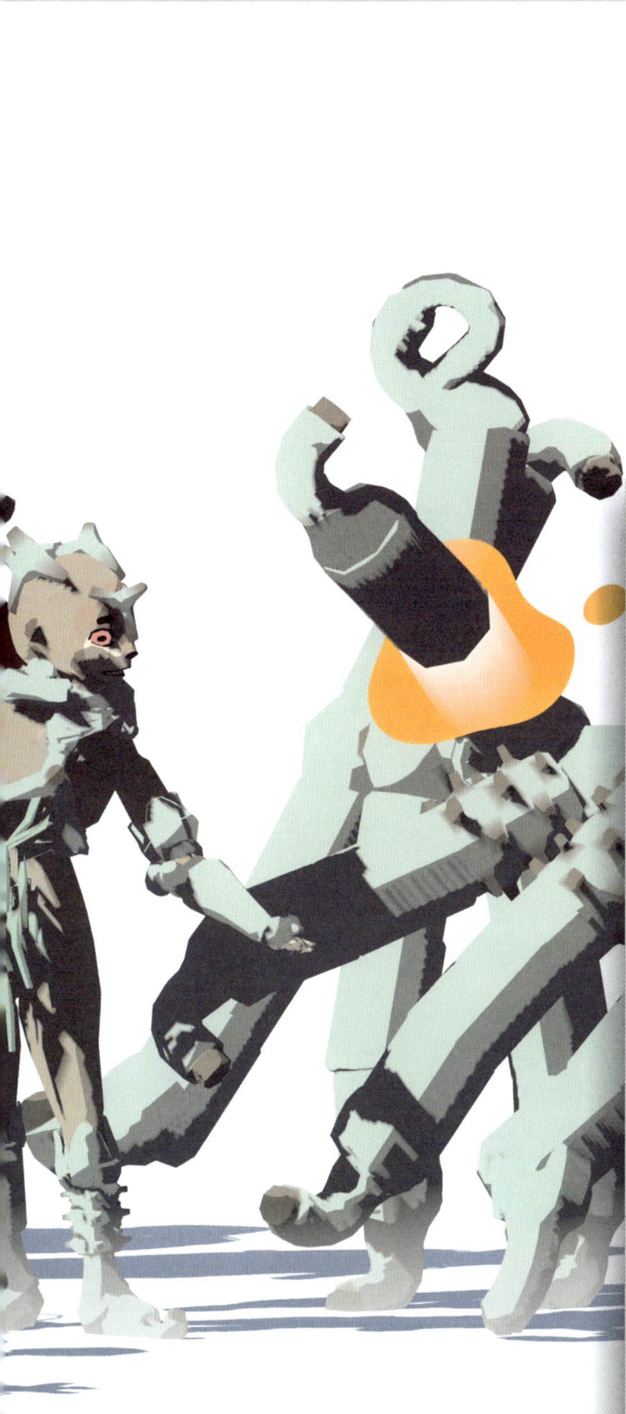

In *EITSOG*, Shaman is a giant authority figure who doesn't know what to do. Young Ancient is a disgraced princess who is injured and covered in ash, but gains the new ability to hallucinate her own inner voice. Echoing Owl is a base predator mistaken for an oracle.

In *EFAP*, Shiba is a super pet who can speak language and fork itself, but can easily revert to its ancestral instincts and fall in love with humans. Celebrity is a high status pharaoh of his time, but mentally a baby, handicapped by his disorientation of future shock, decaying body, and entitled habit of being pampered.

In *ESTS*, AI Puddle is a super intelligence who is an amateur at being a body. The Oomen protect their environment, but are intolerant of its mutations. Rancher is a treehugger Oomen whose faith in the Wormleaf's magical potential is as zealous as the Oomen are fearful.

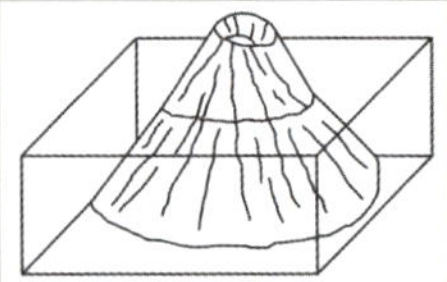
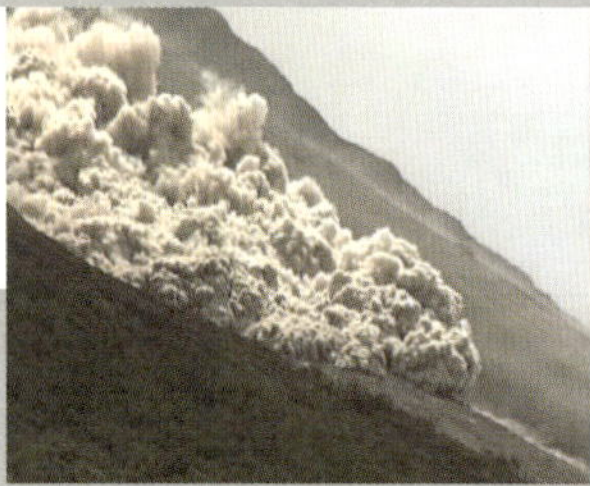
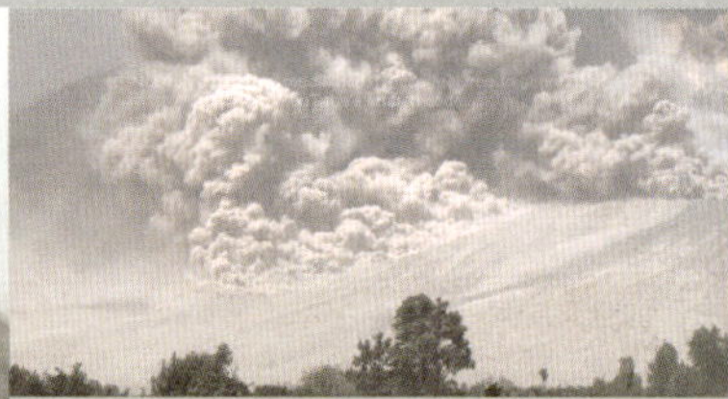
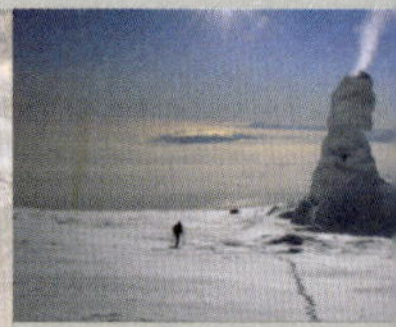
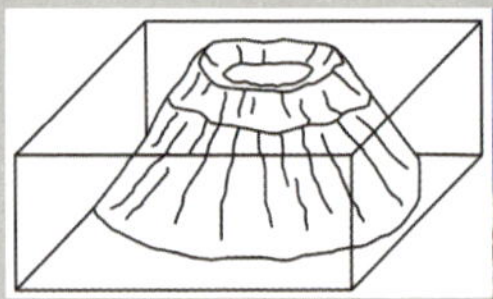
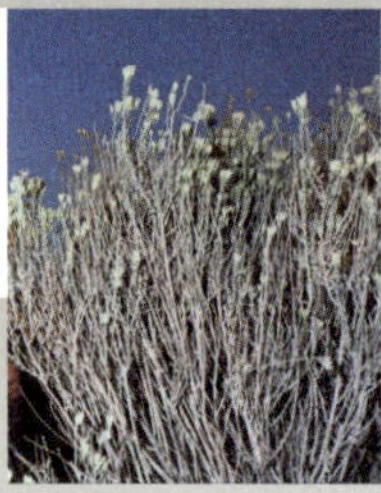
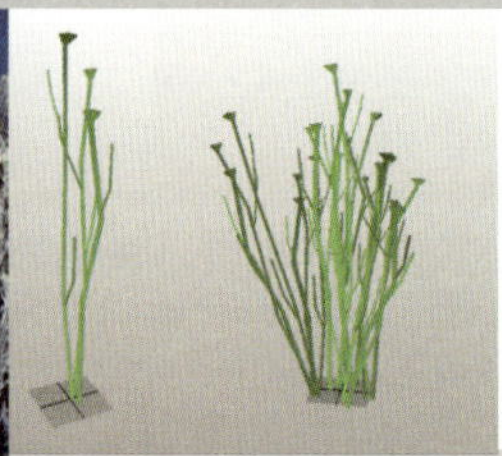
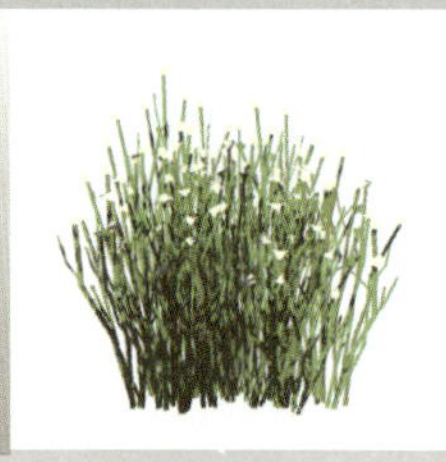
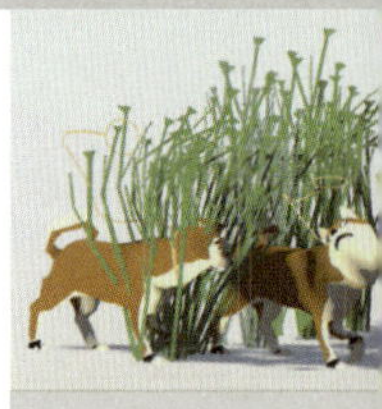
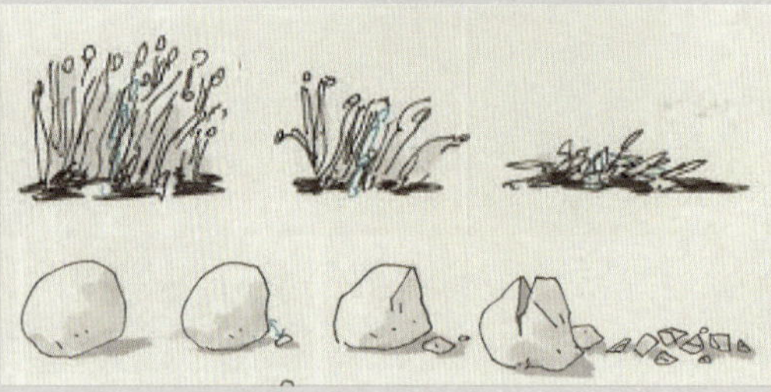
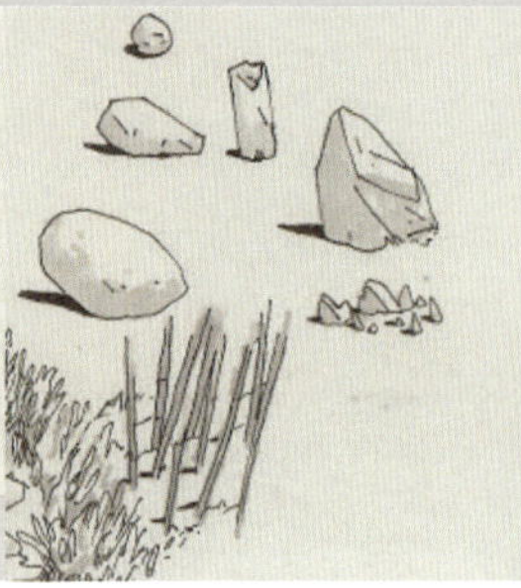
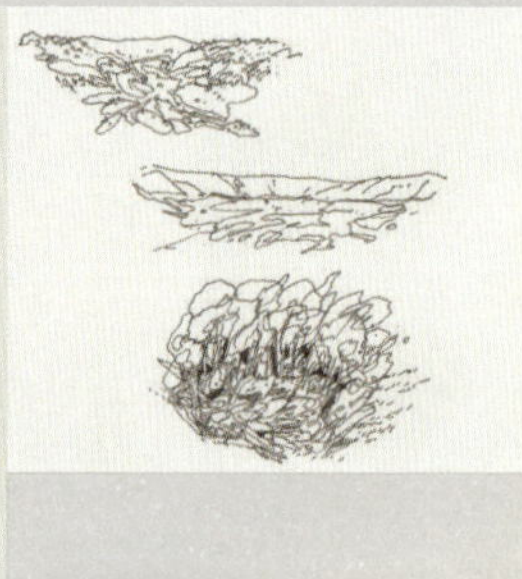
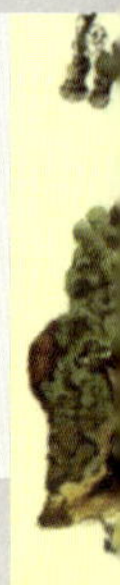
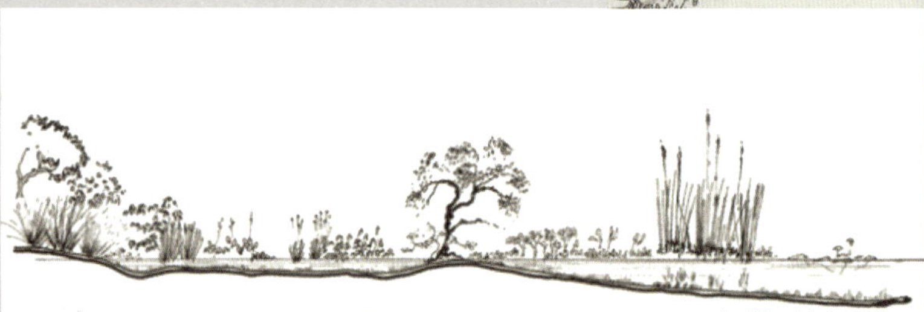
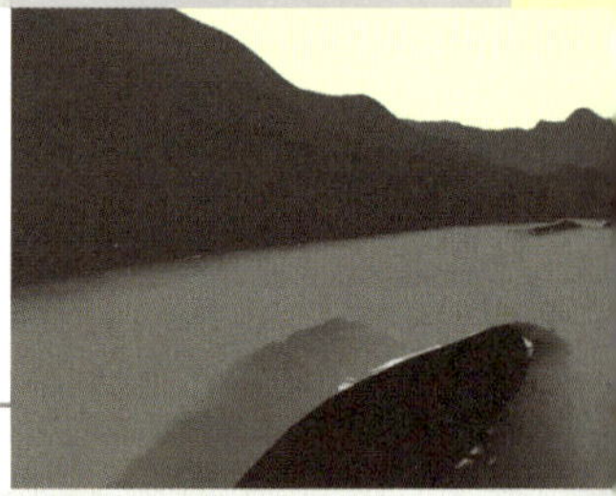
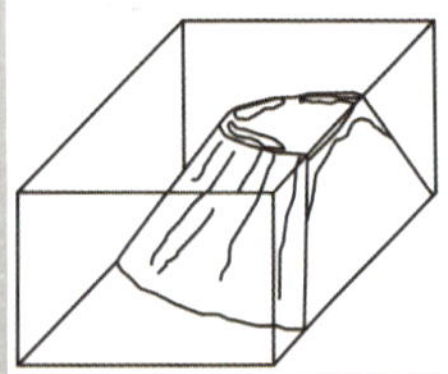
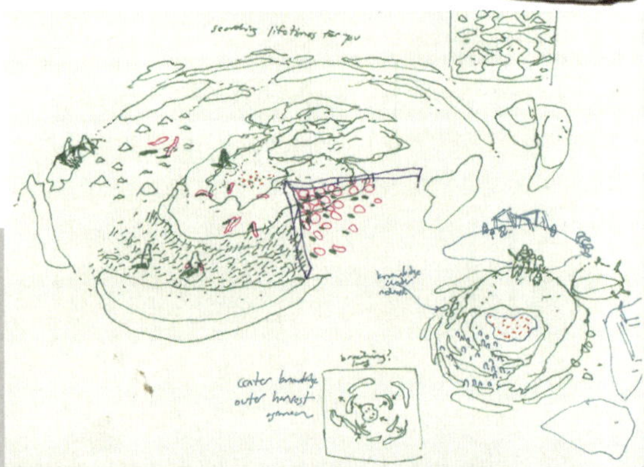
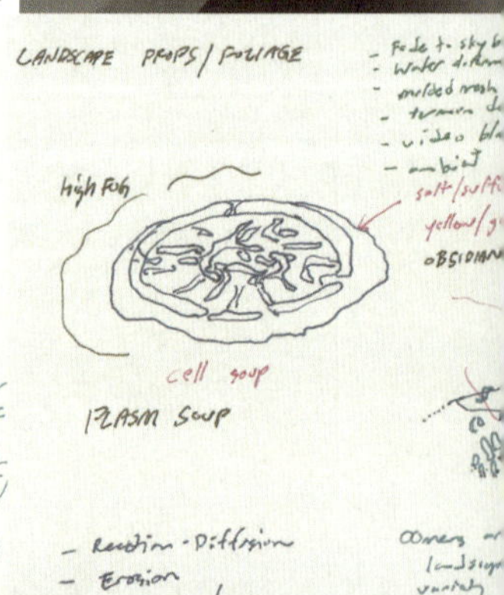
LANDSCAPE PROPS / FOLIAGE
high fog
cell soup
PLASM Soup
- Reaction-Diffusion
- Erosion

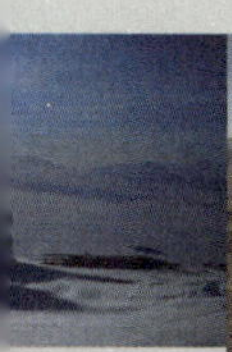
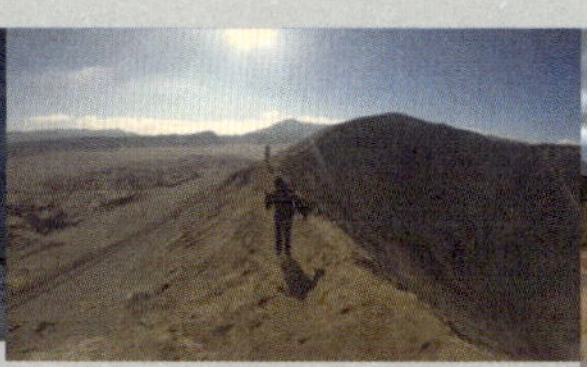
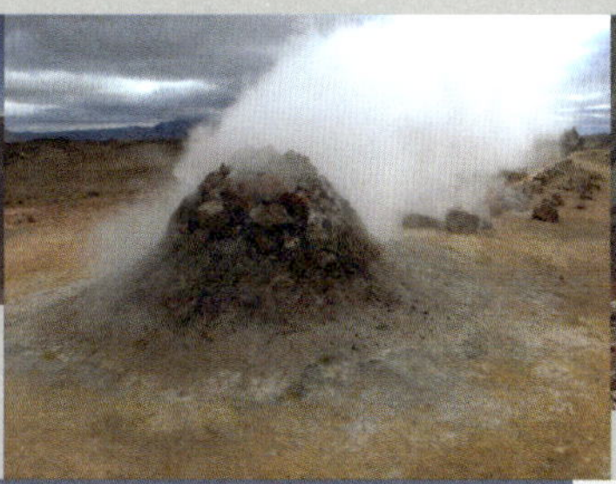
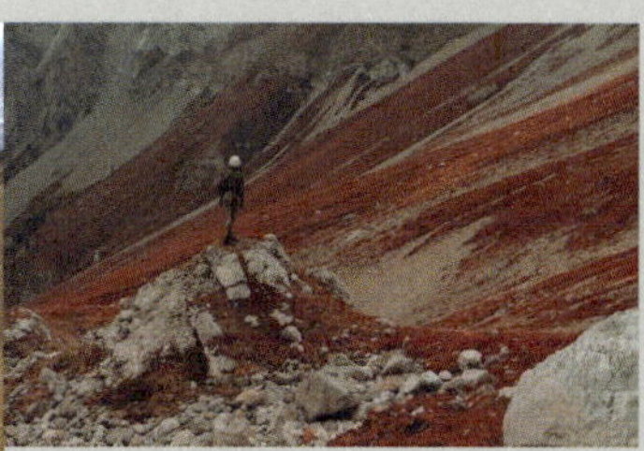
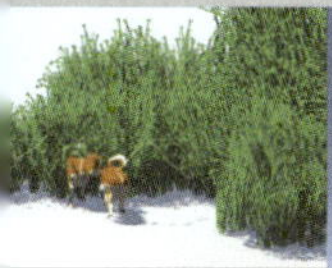
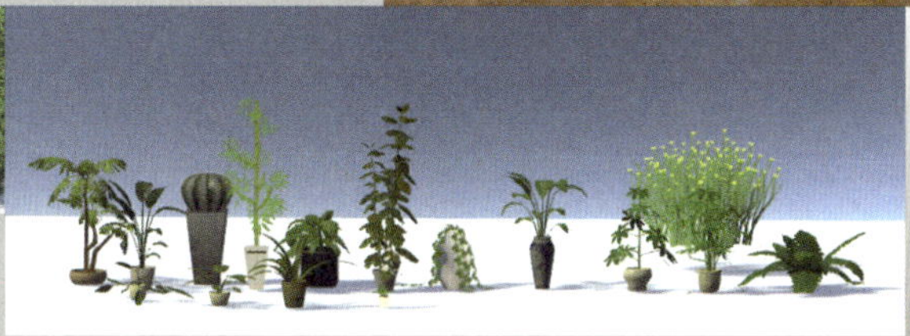
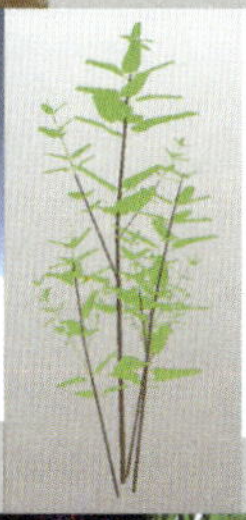
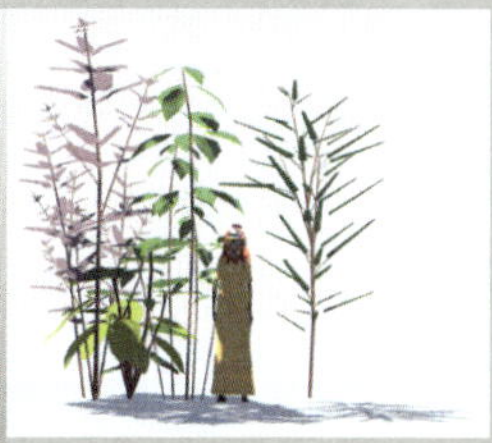
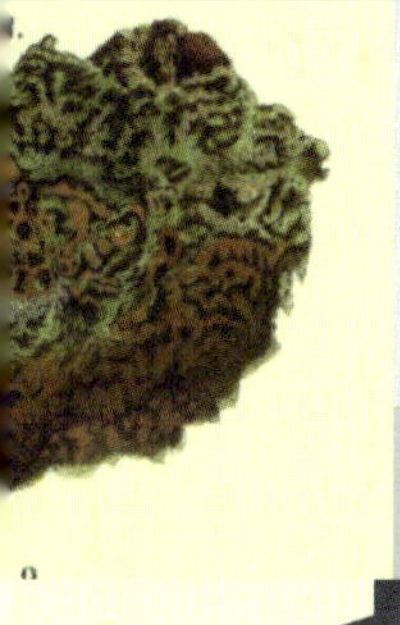
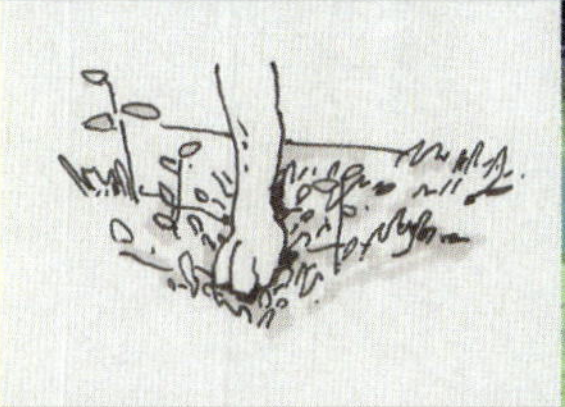
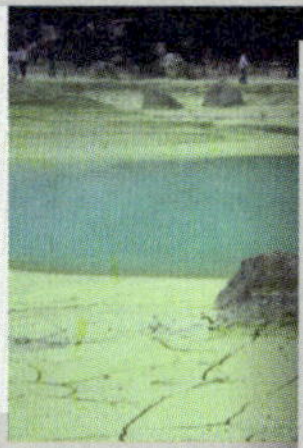

HOW DO YOU APPROACH LANDSCAPE AND ENVIRONMENT? HOW ARE THEY RELATED TO CHARACTER?

You learn a lot about a character by seeing where it lives. When we observe that Yoda lives in a swampy shithole by choice, we understand that he is truly playing a higher spiritual game. In this way an environment can shoulder some of the work of defining a character. In *EITSOG*, the slope of the volcano allows the 'natural' hierarchical structure of the ancient community to manifest simply by where on the slope each character is standing. In *EFAP*, the crater lake's water line rises and falls, signalling the health or decay of the undead Celebrity and his relationship to Shiba. In *ESTS*, the flat openness of the atoll conveys an arena-like stadium for the Oomen to confront mutations.

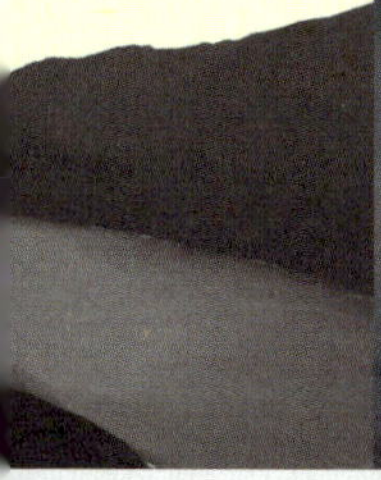
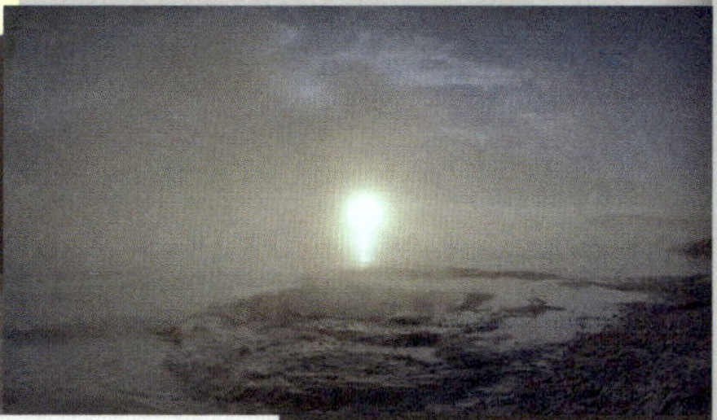
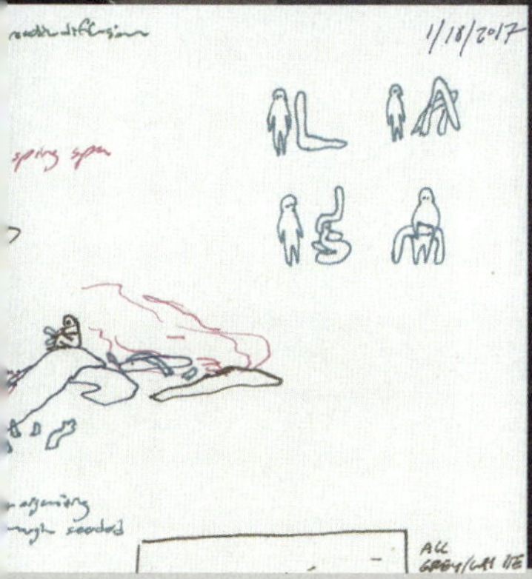

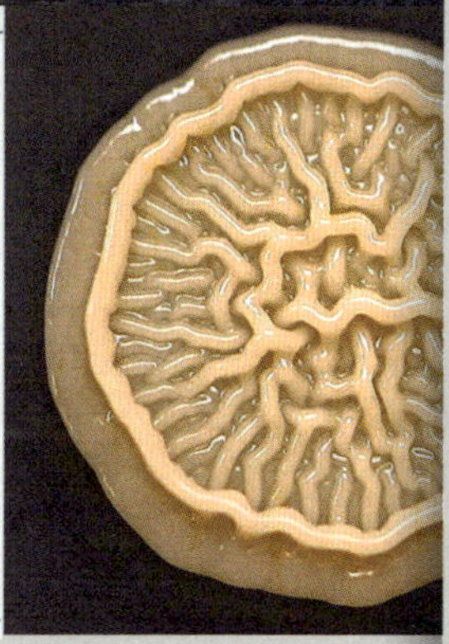

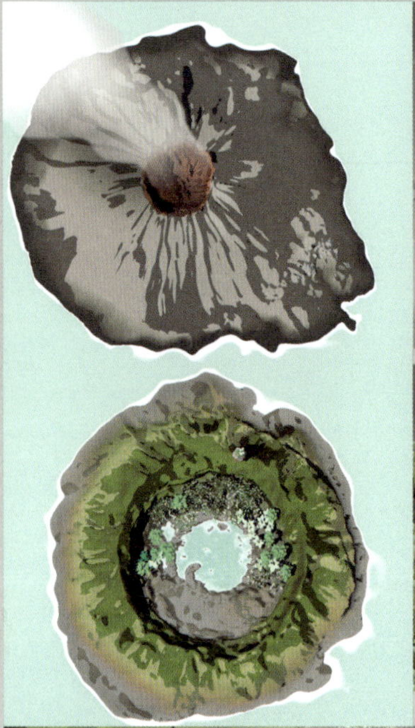

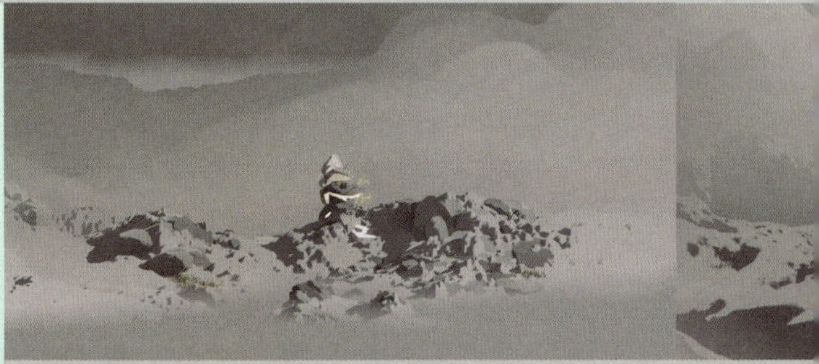

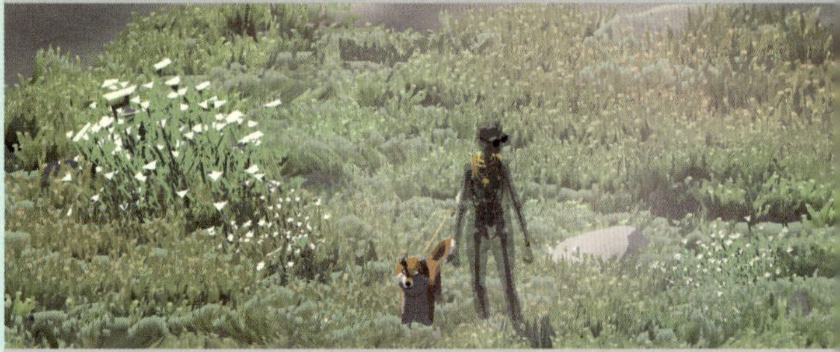

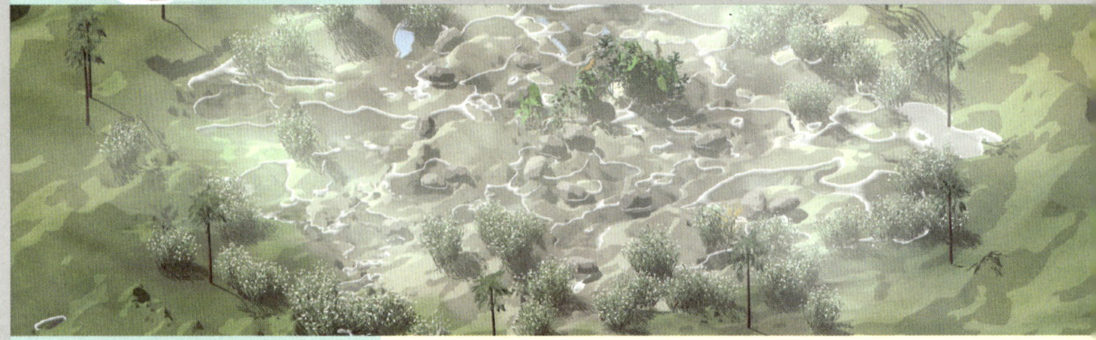

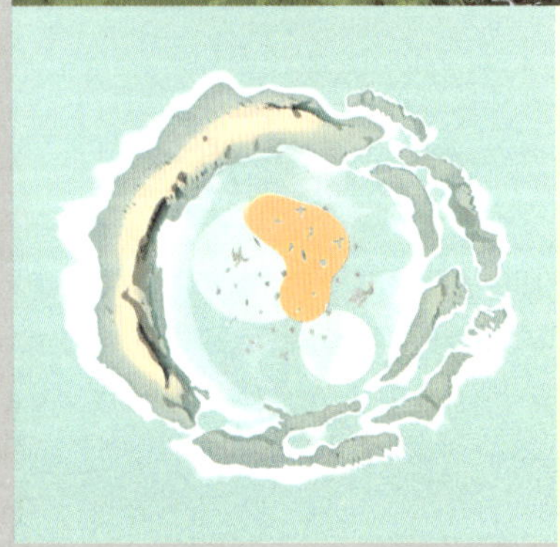

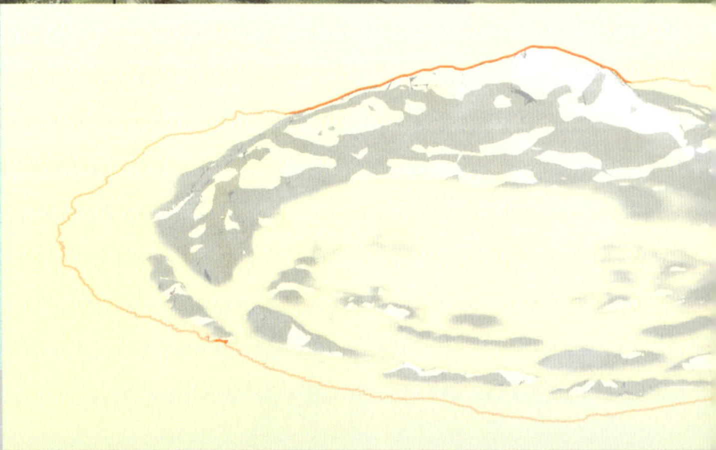

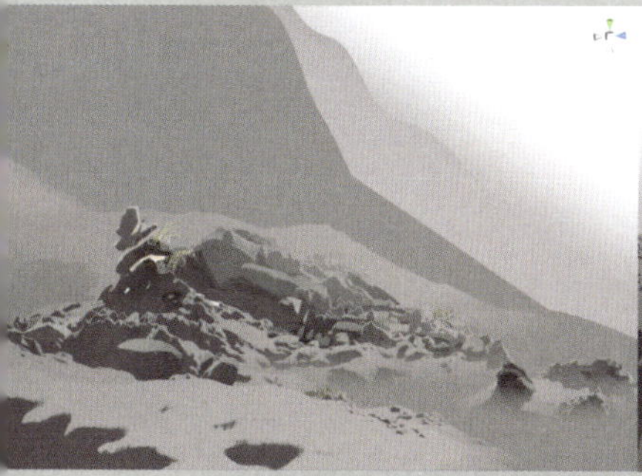

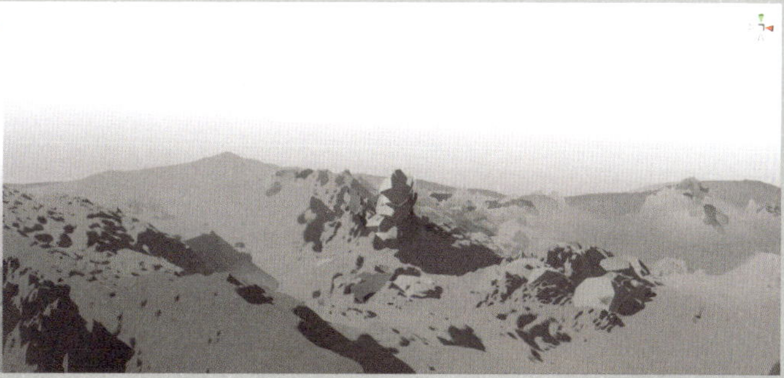

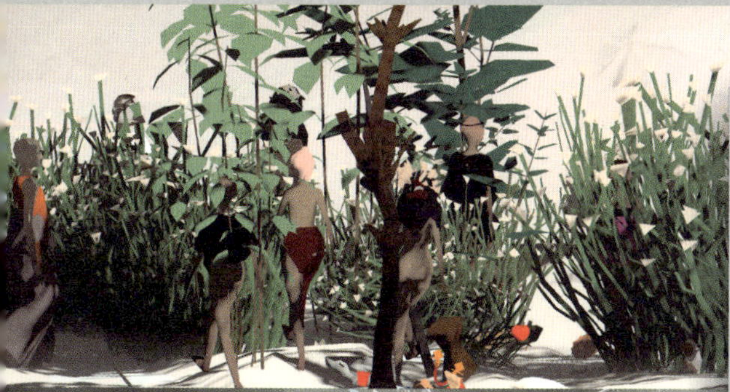

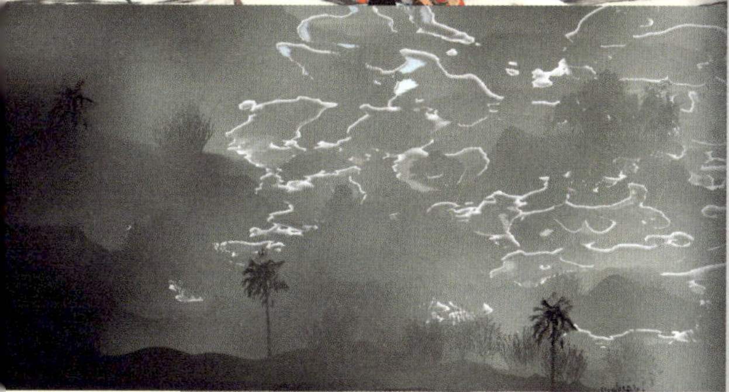

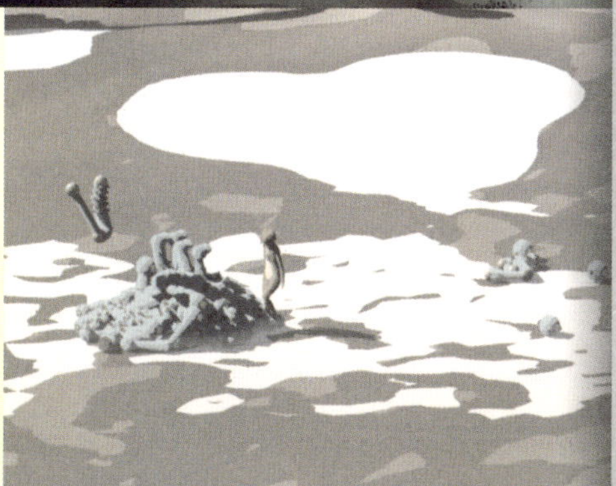

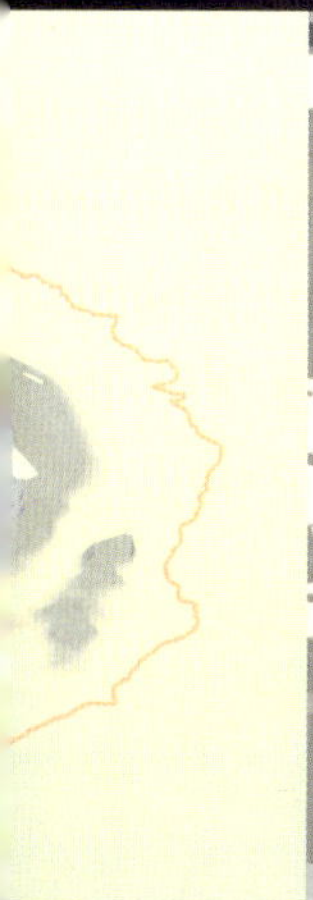

The environment is also more than a milieu that the characters inhabit and shape in their image. It is its own macro character or super organism. The context is a character in the same way a city is a character to its citizens, or an organisation is a character to its members, or a human is a character to its cells and microbiome. The Director conceived *Emissaries* as a trilogy occurring over three stages of a landscape: the volcano, the crater lake, the atoll. I tried to develop each landscape to convey a basic contradiction. The volcano of *EITSOG* would be in a violent transitional state, yet embedded with eternal mythological features like a holy fumerole decorated by generations of the ancient community, and buried members of the dead that get unearthed. The crater lake of *EFAP* would be an overgrown sanctuary, but homogenised by the lack of drama. A spa for Shibas. The atoll of *ESTS* would be fertile space for mutation, but limited in size, and thus a structural trigger for the Oomen's prejudice and need to police it.

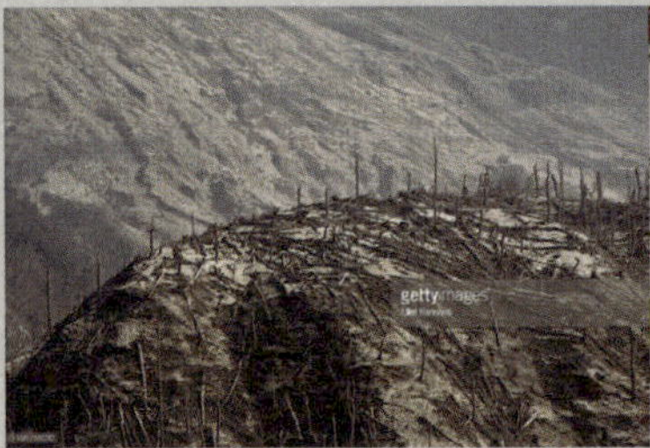

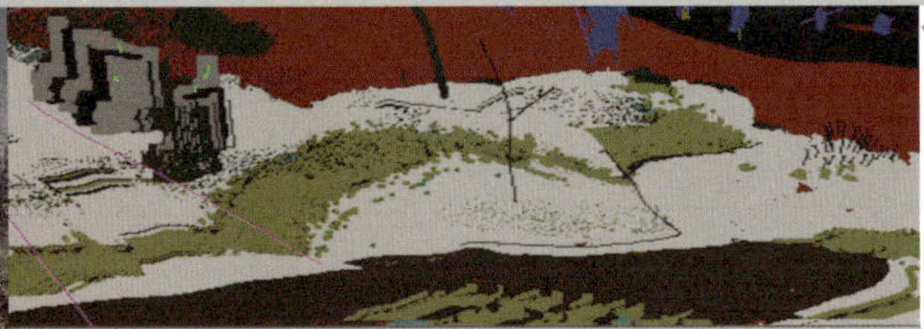

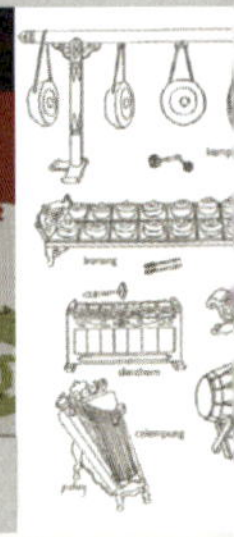

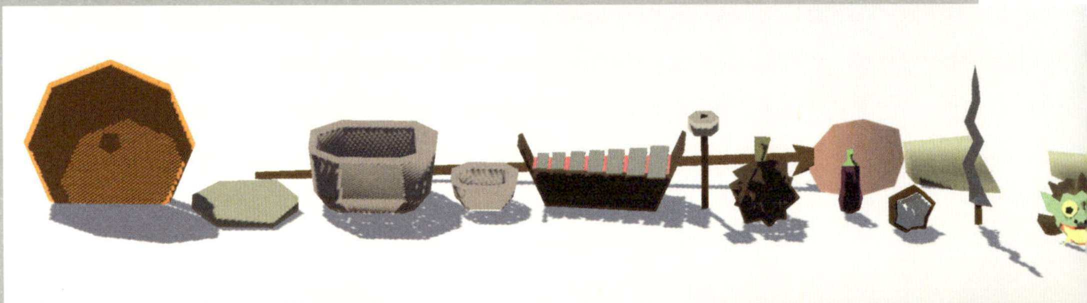

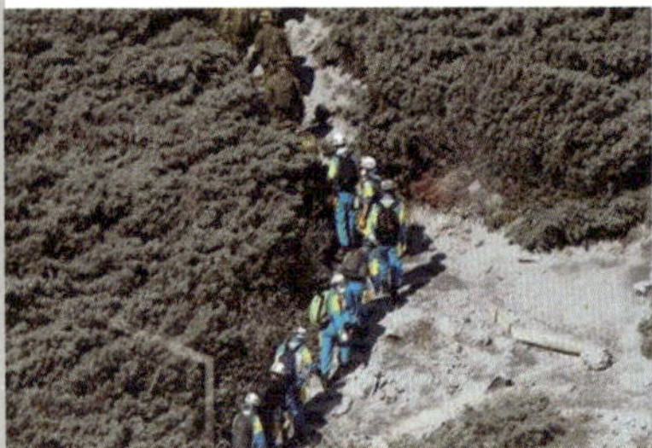

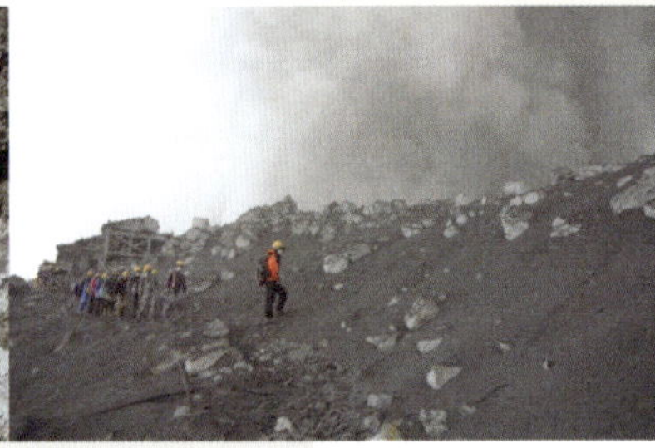

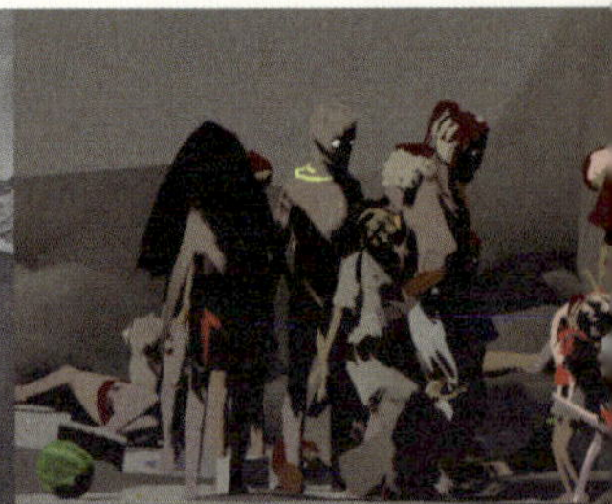

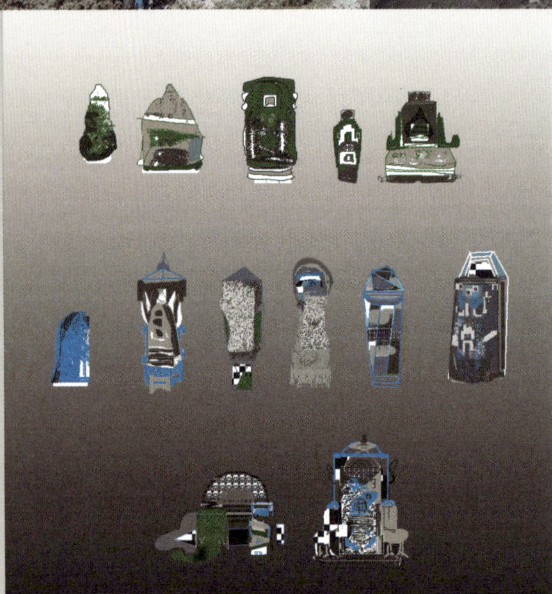

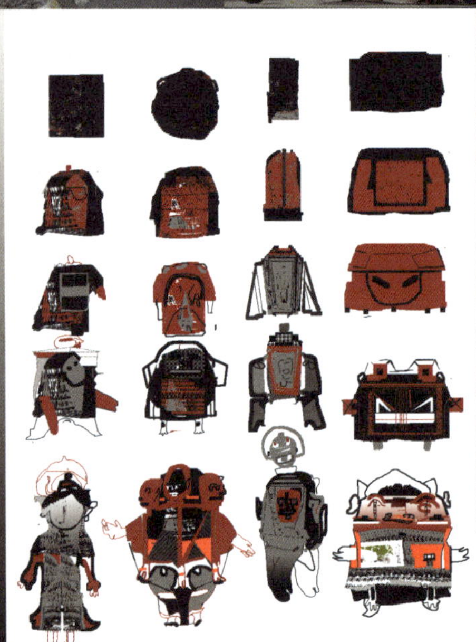

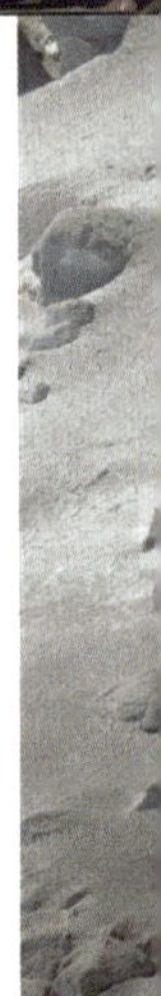

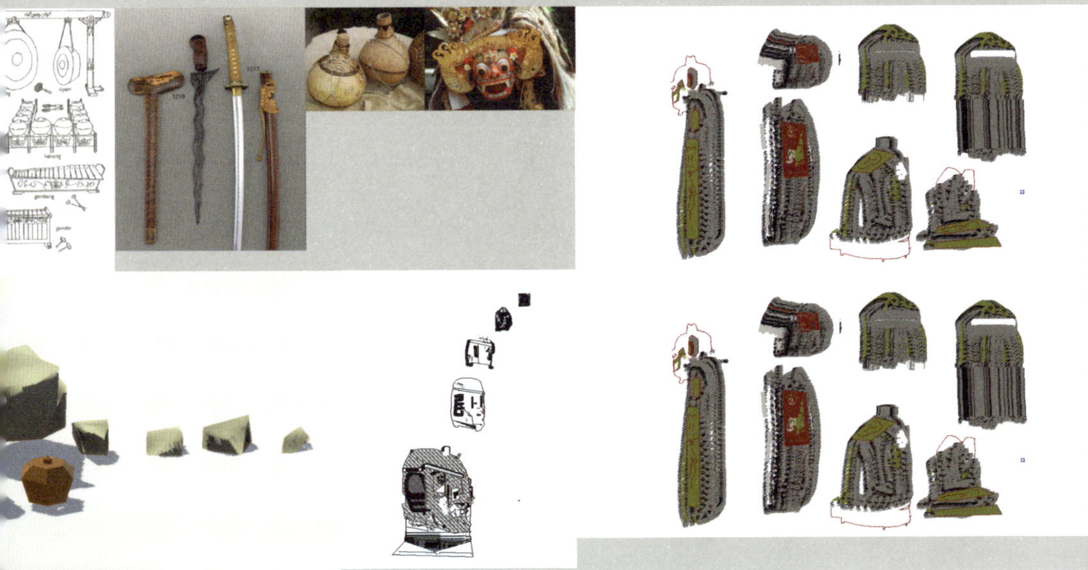

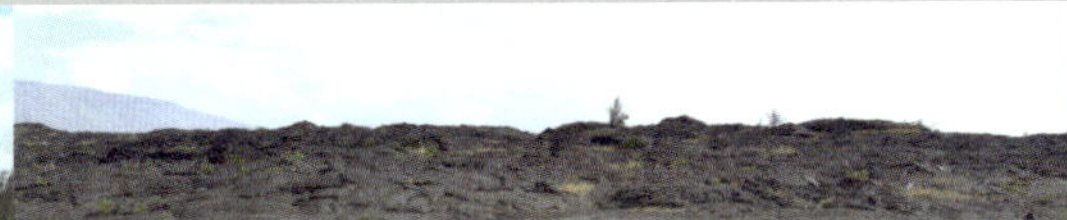

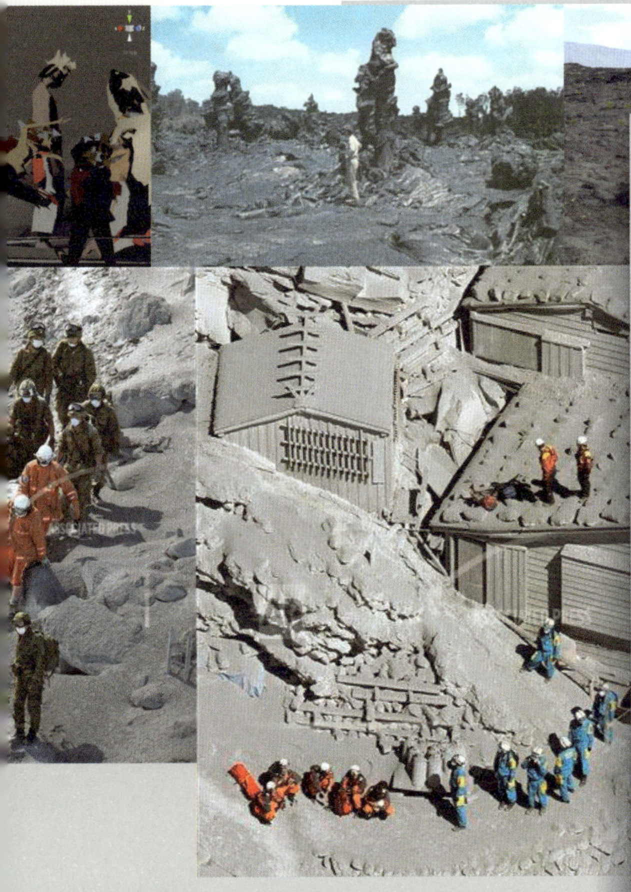

WHAT DO YOU EAT?

For *EITSOG*, the Director wanted a 'church in the wild' feeling. The idea was to make an impoverished material existence feel animated by mythical and spiritual power. The ancient community in *EITSOG* came from descriptions in Julian Jaynes' book of how ancient cultures represented a life populated with gods like it was normal. Gilgamesh. Ancient Balinese culture where there is a rich history of trance, possession, and hearing voices. Indonesian depiction of gods. Anthropologist Clifford Geertz's descriptions of Indonesian cockfights. Images of volcanic eruptions. Pompeii. Japanese search and rescue missions in the ash. The pollen snow in Nausicaä.

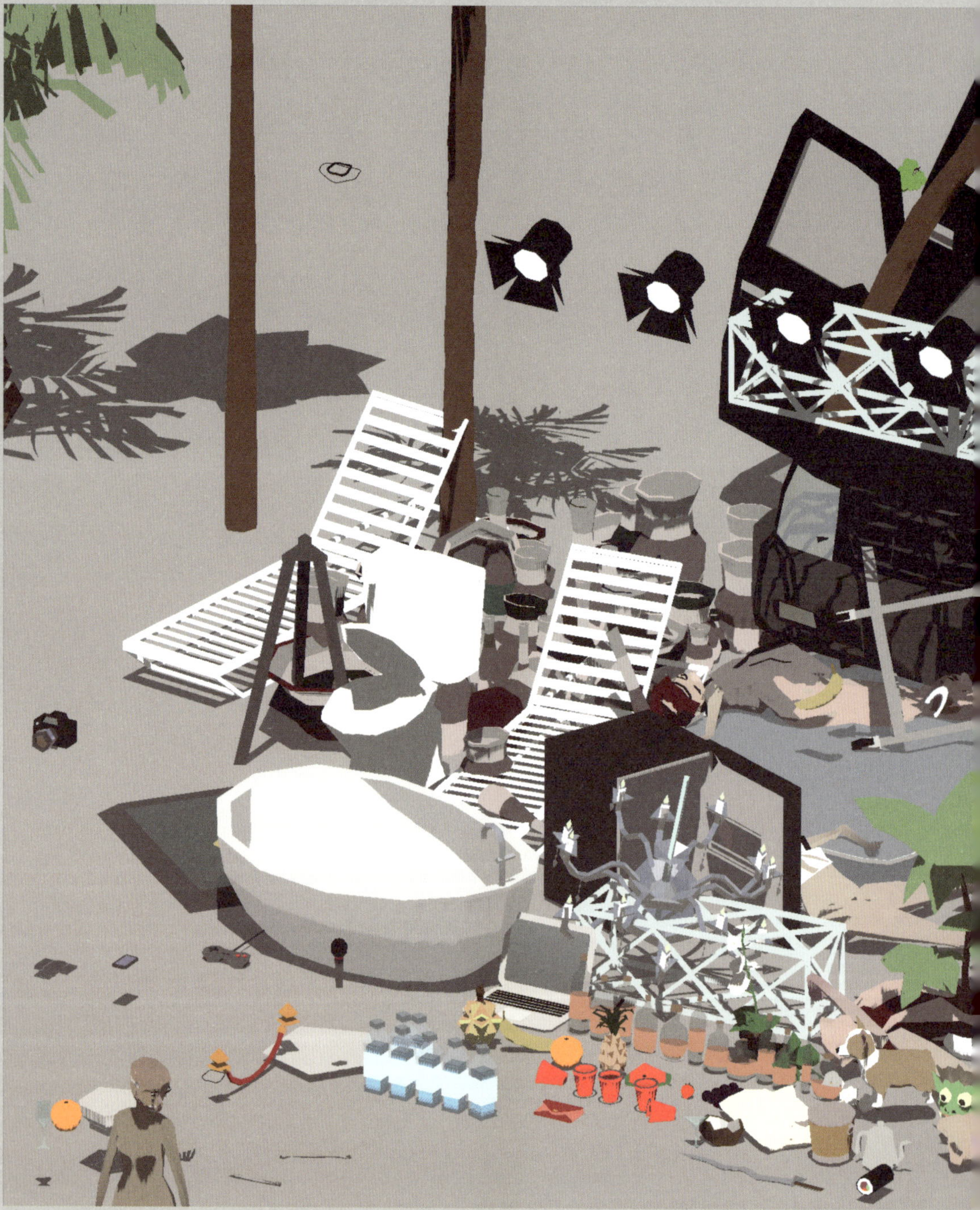

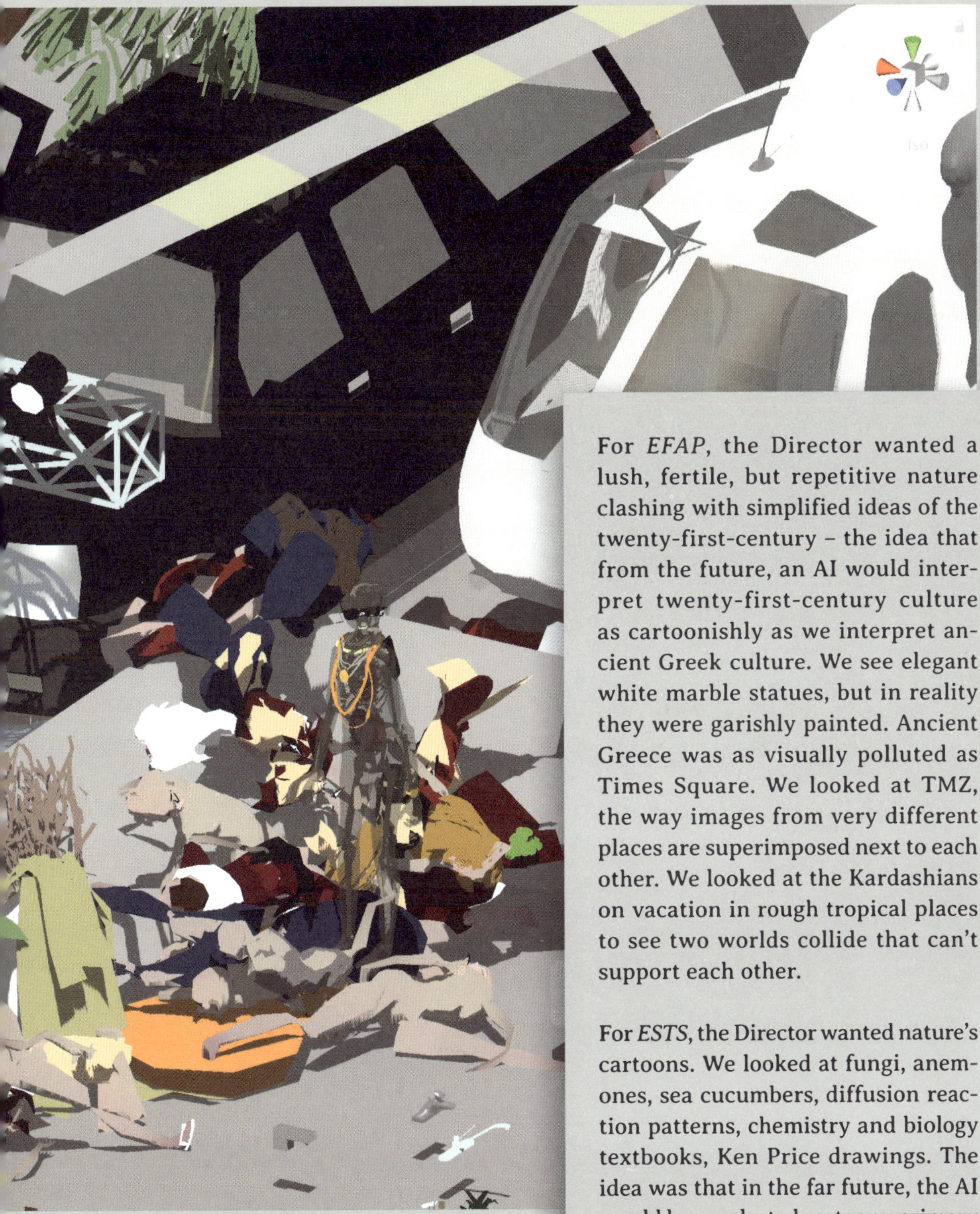

For *EFAP*, the Director wanted a lush, fertile, but repetitive nature clashing with simplified ideas of the twenty-first-century – the idea that from the future, an AI would interpret twenty-first-century culture as cartoonishly as we interpret ancient Greek culture. We see elegant white marble statues, but in reality they were garishly painted. Ancient Greece was as visually polluted as Times Square. We looked at TMZ, the way images from very different places are superimposed next to each other. We looked at the Kardashians on vacation in rough tropical places to see two worlds collide that can't support each other.

For *ESTS*, the Director wanted nature's cartoons. We looked at fungi, anemones, sea cucumbers, diffusion reaction patterns, chemistry and biology textbooks, Ken Price drawings. The idea was that in the far future, the AI would have selected cartoony primary forms, but would have allowed things to evolve organically.

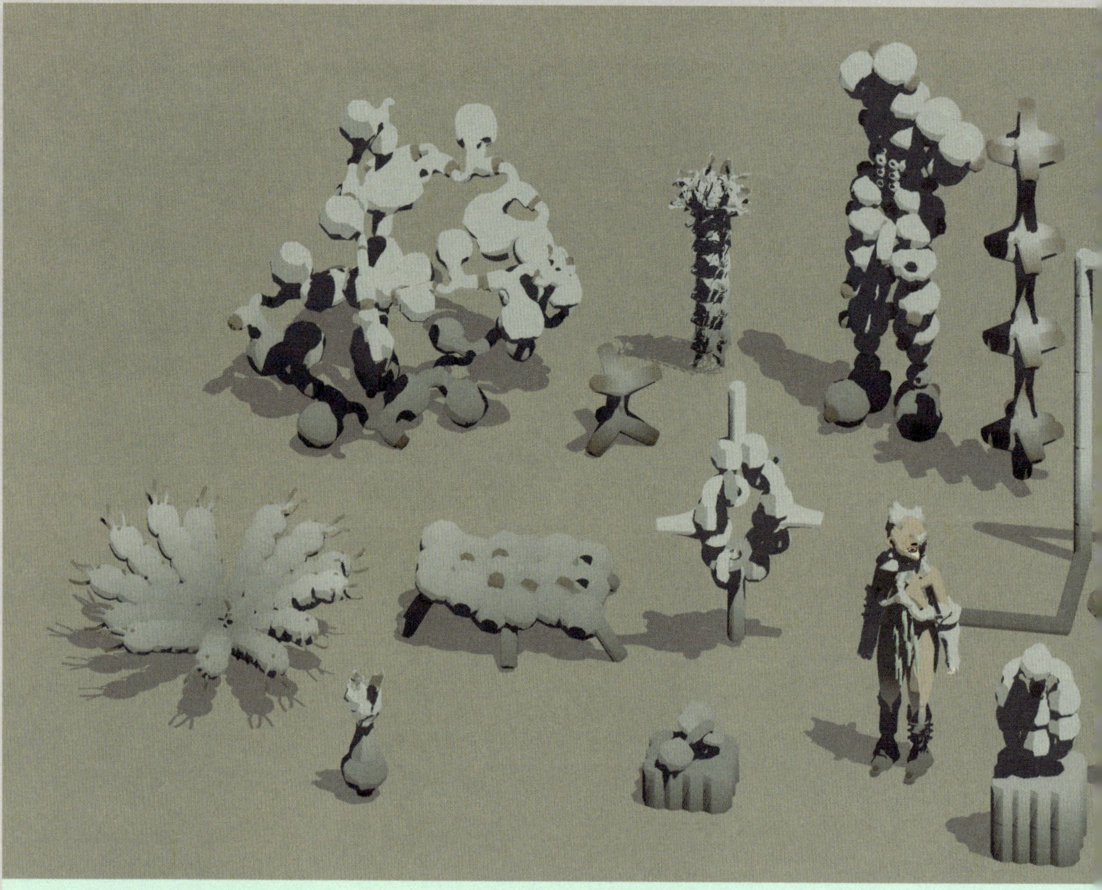

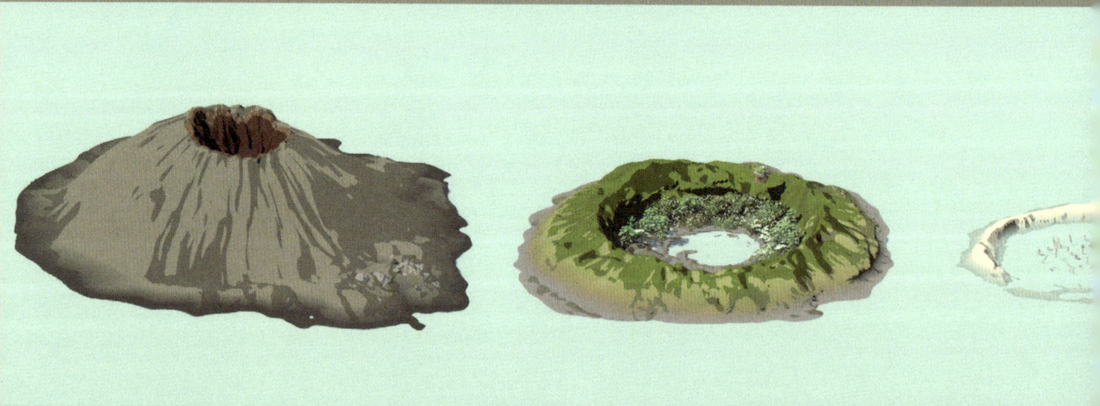

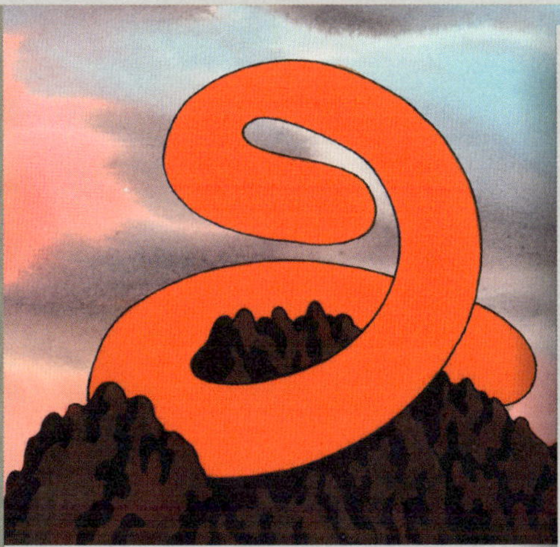

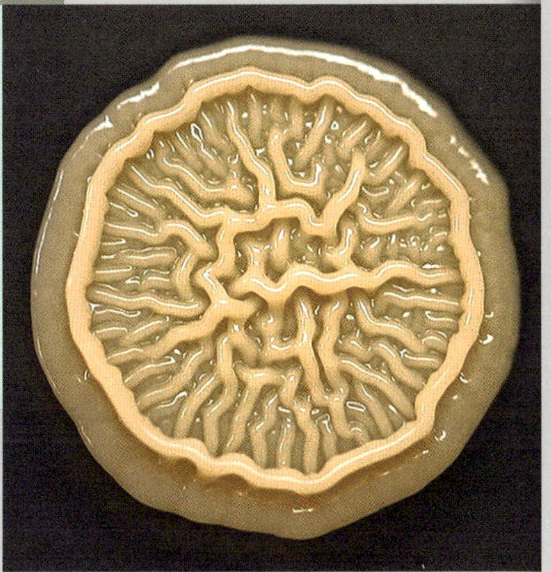

HOW DO YOU FEEL ABOUT CHARACTERS WHO COME TO MEAN SOMETHING?

If it happens it happens. Pikachu was designed to be cute, irresistible, and timeless. But Pikachu is also a container for a very specific and reliable meaning - the loyal companion who is domesticated enough to be your guardian, but feral enough to deserve autonomy. He transcends the status of a pet. He's a Pikachu. A character can encapsulate this bundle of traits, and therefore expand the toolbox of human thought.

I tried to make each Emissary character become a bookmark for that feeling of being caught between a collapsing world that you don't want to be a part of and a weird world that you are not prepared for.

A character like the Rancher holds the comical contradiction of being violently tolerant in reaction to her local community's violent intolerance. This was loosely based on someone I knew from Berkeley, but now the Rancher character is the container to hold this belief, attitude, and mini-story so that I can be relieved of having to recall that pattern from raw stories of my own life experience. Moreover, I can now easily share this belief container with everyone. It's called the Rancher. In this way, a character can be a powerful cognitive technology.

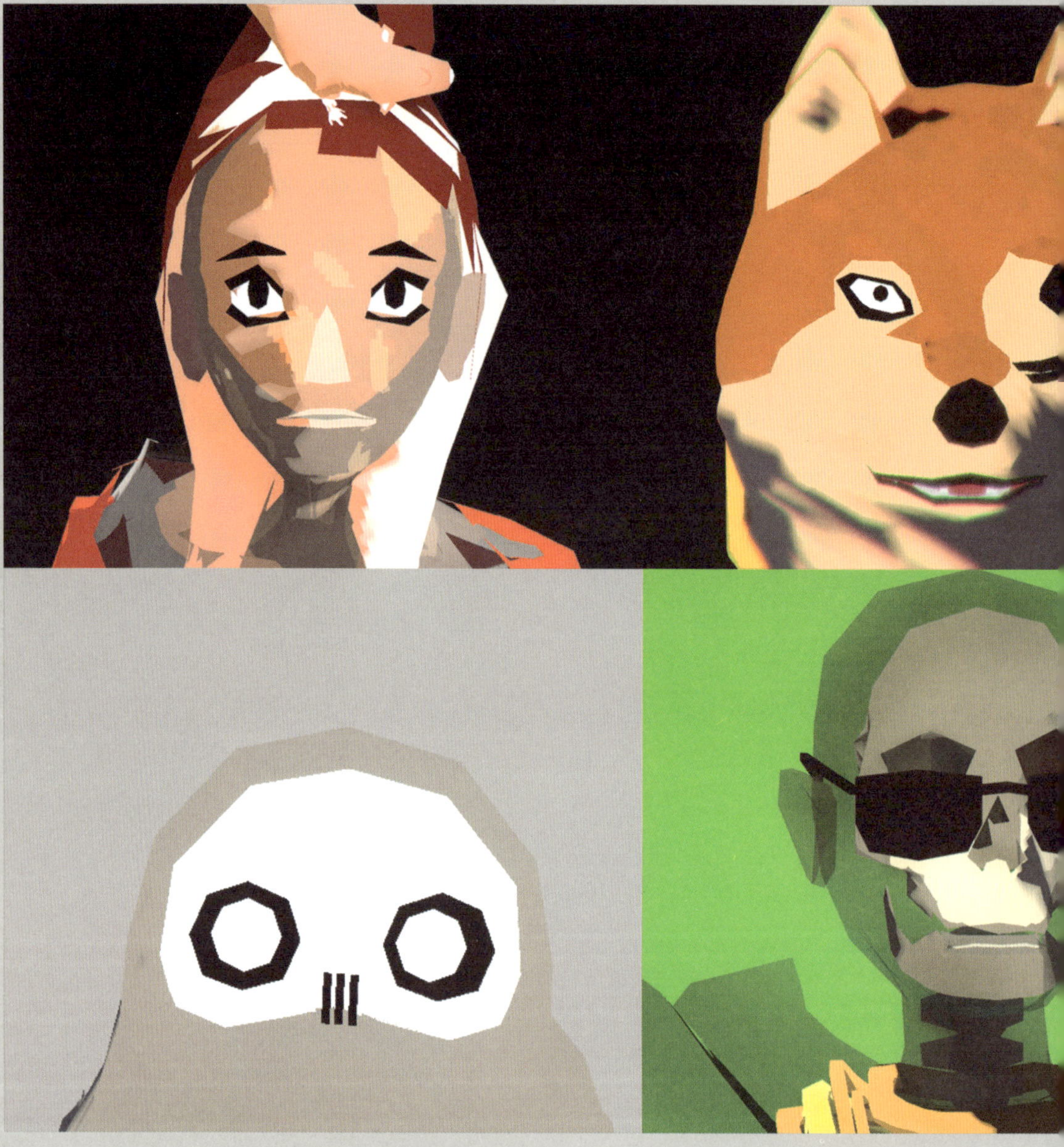

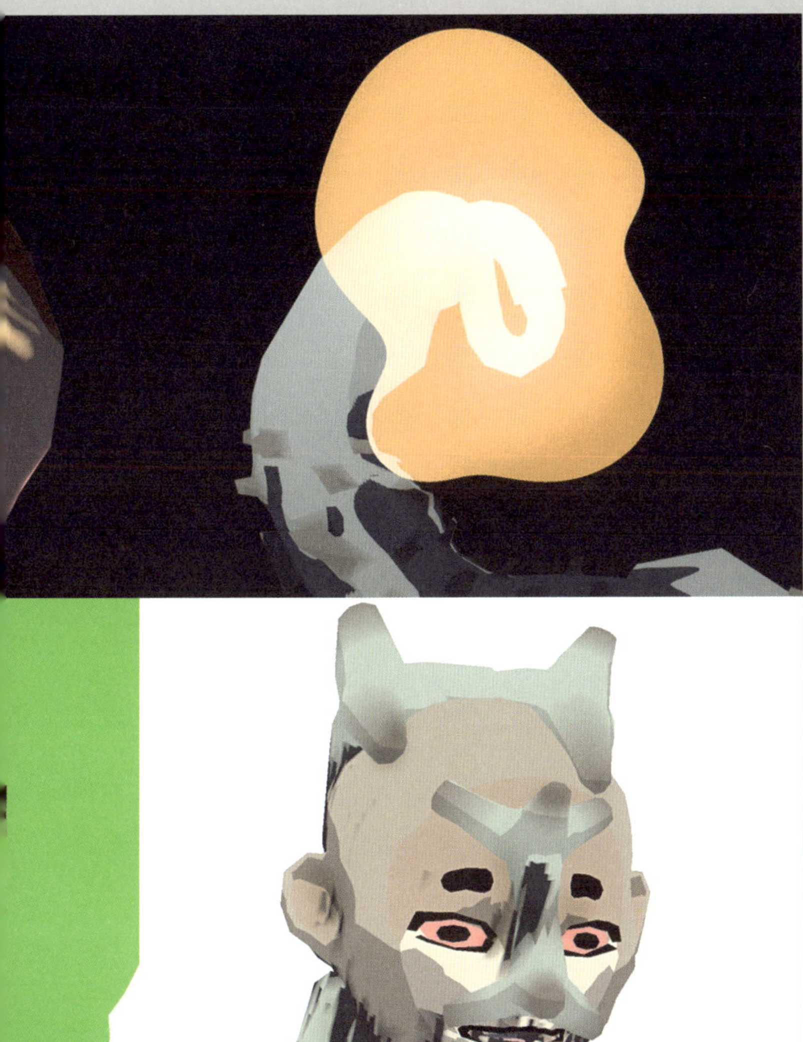

The ease of generating new characters gives us the opportunity to externalise as many of our belief orientations as we can imagine. They become actual conscious options to choose from rather than muddled internal feelings or memories. We can name them, talk to them, and see each of them as their own person. This is the most profound aspect of cartooning.

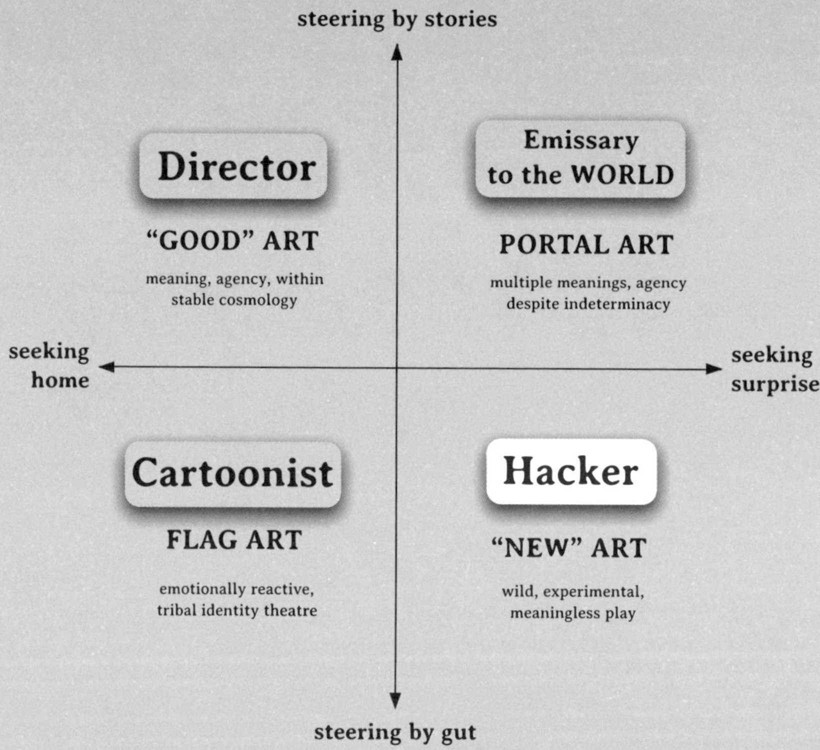
steering by stories
Director
"GOOD" ART
meaning, agency, within stable cosmology
Emissary to the WORLD
PORTAL ART
multiple meanings, agency despite indeterminacy
seeking home
seeking surprise
Cartoonist
FLAG ART
emotionally reactive, tribal identity theatre
Hacker
"NEW" ART
wild, experimental, meaningless play
steering by gut

What The Hacker Wants

The mask of the Hacker is the kid who breaks dad's radio and turns it into a pirate transmitter. It's the punk who figured out that saying 'because' lets you cut lines. It's the whizz who discovers that the algorithm for bird flocking behaviour is a fine model for predicting the movement of human crowds.

The Hacker sees through the veil of man-made worlds and glimpses a Reality Operating System (RealityOS) pulsating with possibilities to tinker with. The Hacker believes that every object, every social structure, every system contains a core innovation that has been dialled down, dressed up and packaged for an all-too-human agenda. This packaging is all interface design. The work of some Director trying to impose meaning, or a Cartoonist trying to trigger our emotional circuitry. For everyone else, this packaging makes the innovation palatable to everyday life, but for the Hacker it represents an artificial boundary that hides and shackles the innovation's full spectrum of possibility. The Hacker's instinct is punk: ignore the given laws, break down the interface veil, free the innovation, play with all its dials, discover its full range of expression, combine it with other liberated innovations at the RealityOS level, and share its magic leverage with the Hacker community.

What the Hacker makes is 'not great or good, but it is New'. New concepts, perceptions, sensations. The thrill of 'aha!' discovery is the Hacker's motivation. Think of any expression you would call experimental, a prank, a magic trick. It has no deeper meaning than being a successful surprise, and yet another demo that our lives crave acts of Creative Destruction to renew their flame. *Seeking Surprise* and *Steering By Gut*, the Hacker makes "New" Art, simply because it can.

There is a cost to hacking for newness. In stripping things down to RealityOS and tinkering at its assembly level, the Hacker becomes accustomed to devaluing the act of dressing its work back up for the rest of us. The Hacker's work manifests as a magic trick with minimum viable showmanship. Meaning is thin, its place in our lives is unclear. Its lack of context leaves us only with the feeling of fleeting delight and shock of the new. The Hacker offers no further orientation. Like the first humans to hack the Earth and strike oil, everyone stands in awe at the gusher, but no one knows how it will change their lives. The riches are rough, exciting and valuable, but meaningless to non-hackers. Ignoring the fact that further development requires interfacing with other masks and worlds, the Hacker moves on to another frontier with its roving Hacker community. In its wake, the Hacker leaves open-source magic for others to try to civilise.

How can the Hacker help us in Worlding? The Hacker offers 10x magic leverage. In a room of screenwriters, the Hacker says, 'I have a simulator that makes its own stories'. In a room of animators, the Hacker says, 'my characters can evolve to animate themselves.' In a room of cartoonists, the Hacker says, 'I can deep learn the cutest face.' In a room of artists, the Hacker says 'here are the tools to write yourself out of your authorship'. By stripping down existing worlds to their underlying systems and rules, and by refusing the seduction of meaning, the Hacker sacrilegiously discovers the technical means to turn the DNA of a World – its characters and stories – into an actual self-regulating World. Great hacks, whether a law of physics or a flaw in security, are the basis of new rules and systems that can cheat common sense assumptions about the energy, time, or realness that a World requires to become alive. This is the kind of leverage Worlding requires to simulate its possible futures and ensure that it can do so beyond the hands of its finite author.

We will wear the mask of the Hacker to tinker with a deeper material reality and leverage its magic.

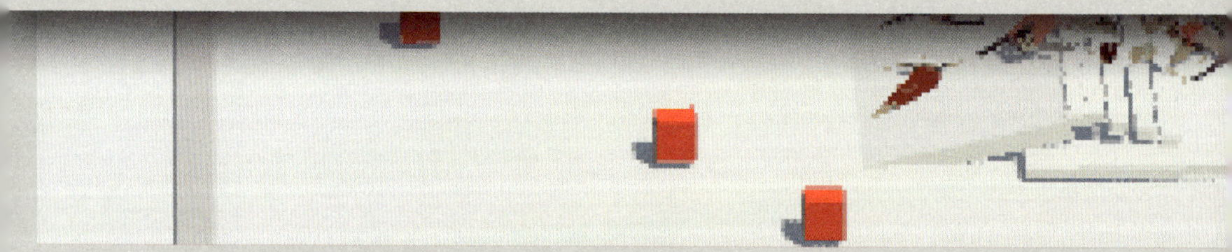

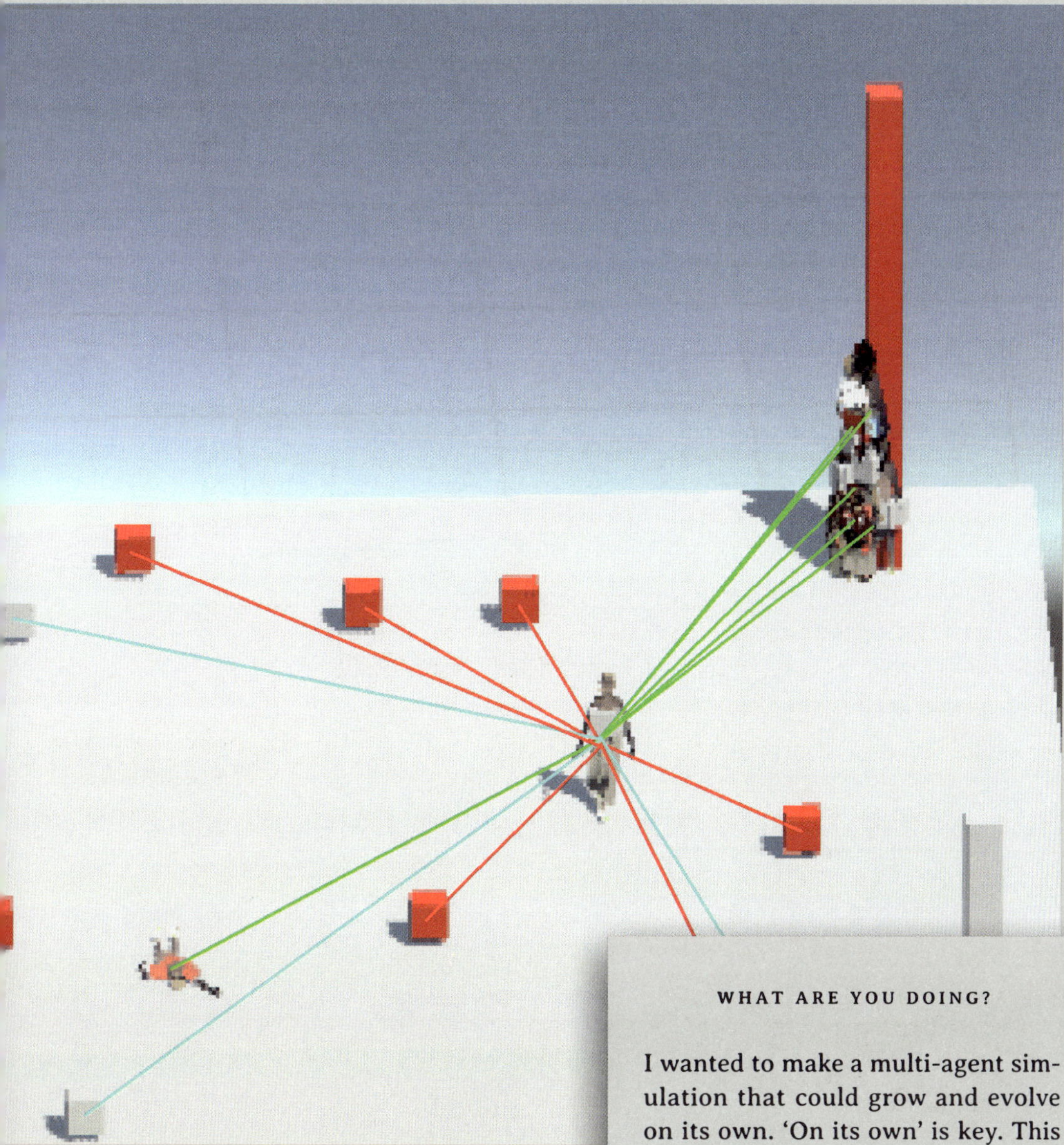

WHAT ARE YOU DOING?

I wanted to make a multi-agent simulation that could grow and evolve on its own. 'On its own' is key. This is what turns an author's imagined fiction into an actual living world. Philosopher Immanuel Kant says the quality of being a 'self-legislating agent' is the essence of sentience. If I can achieve that quality, everything else – complexity, realism, interestingness, stories - comes for free.

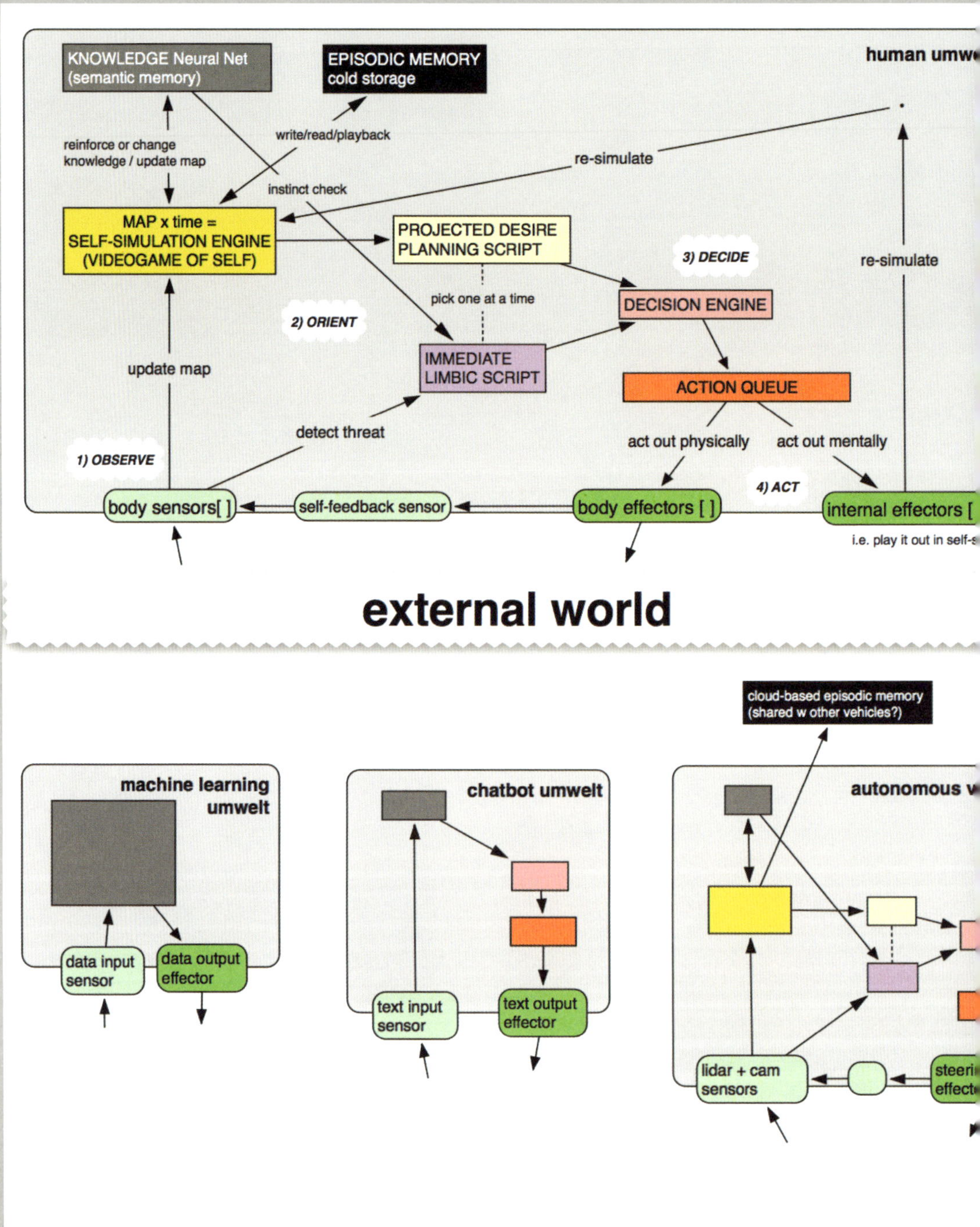

human umw
KNOWLEDGE Neural Net
(semantic memory)
EPISODIC MEMORY
cold storage
reinforce or change
knowledge / update map
write/read/playback
instinct check
re-simulate
MAP x time =
SELF-SIMULATION ENGINE
(VIDEOGAME OF SELF)
PROJECTED DESIRE
PLANNING SCRIPT
3) DECIDE
re-simulate
pick one at a time
DECISION ENGINE
2) ORIENT
IMMEDIATE
LIMBIC SCRIPT
update map
ACTION QUEUE
detect threat
act out physically
act out mentally
1) OBSERVE
4) ACT
body sensors[ ]
self-feedback sensor
body effectors [ ]
internal effectors [
i.e. play it out in self-
external world
cloud-based episodic memory
(shared w other vehicles?)
machine learning
umwelt
data input
sensor
data output
effector
chatbot umwelt
text input
sensor
text output
effector
autonomous v
lidar + cam
sensors
steeri
effect

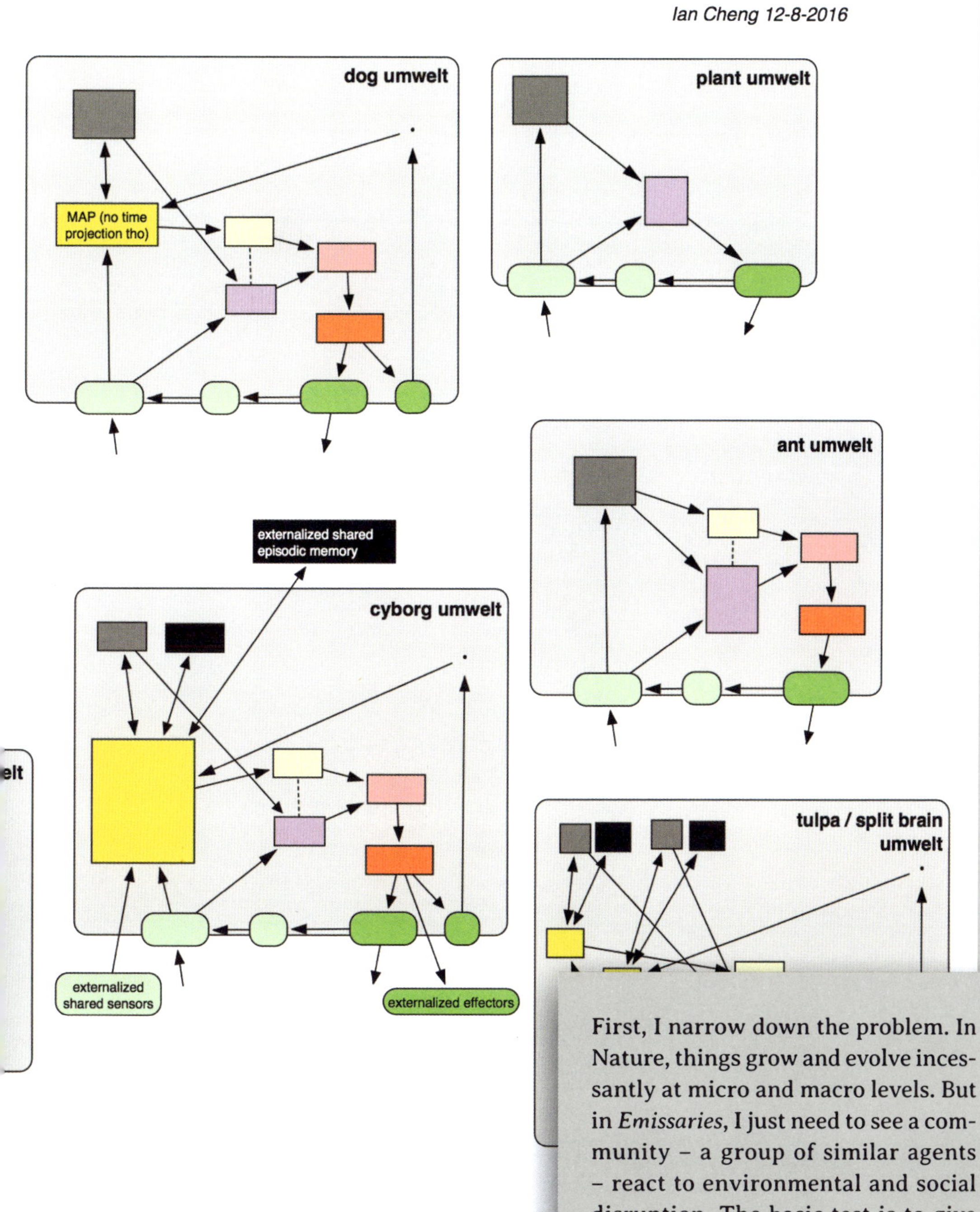

First, I narrow down the problem. In Nature, things grow and evolve incessantly at micro and macro levels. But in *Emissaries*, I just need to see a community – a group of similar agents – react to environmental and social disruption. The basic test is to give them enough agency to re-stabilise themselves, to self-legislate.

AGENT NEEDS (0–100) urgent → good

- ~~(STRESS ...)~~
- SOCIAL (BEING NEAR OTHERS)
- ENV CERTAINTY (CLEARNESS)
- COMFORT (SITTING, LAYING)
- HUNGER (FOOD EATING)
- ENERGY (SLEEPING, TRANCE, DRUGS)
- FUN (PLAYING)
- (needs always decaying)
- STRESSED BOOL ?

PERSONALITY
- setting attenuation curves for NEEDS → default need curves for decay
- → SOCIAL STATUS
- 101 = NOT RELEVANT → ad filtering
- AD FILTERING → BEING-TYPE – adult – child – teen – animal
- → stress ~~...~~, tolerance?

AI LOOP

1. – if ACTIONS in QUEUE – do it VIGNETTE → (get reward)
2. if no ACTIONS in QUEUE – perform ACTION SELECTION based on current NEEDS
3. if no NEEDS or ACTIONS – wander – stand around wait for NEED – random personality ACTION

ACTION SELECTION 3/13/2015

- if HIGH STRESS NEED
  - call on VOICES → OBJECT inside you
  - GOD voices add ACTIONS to queue (no scanning environment)
  - ideally voices select ACTIONS that have rewards
- else (NORMAL)
  - scan env for AD OBJS
  - filter out based on PERSONALITY
  - score (value) based on current NEEDS
  - pick top AD OBJ
  - add its ACTIONS onto your QUEUE

AGENT EMOTIONAL STATE (visible / felt)
- translated from NEEDS
- emotions trigger animation in face → expressed in animation

FORCE ACTIVE OBJECTS – big nature – director – scripting
- directly affect needs of nearby agents
- example: TREMOR – lowers KNOWING
- interrupt ACTIONS QUEUE by FORCING ACTION and/or forgetting current ACTION
- cause STRESS

AD OBJECTS – things to do in environment of value
- store vignettes
- need rewards when completed change NEED state

VIRTUAL AD OBJECTS – relational things of value
- ex. congregated group (SOCIAL +)

AGENT ACTION QUEUE
- on going stack

force action →
force forget →

STRESS MODE (GOD KNOWS MODE)
- ~~...~~
- or urgent NEEDS but no AD OBJ nearby of value
  - can trigger by filtering out everything so no valuable AD OBJ perceived except VIRTUAL own GOD OBJs
- if STRESS MODE
  - scan bank of VIRTUAL GOD OBJS
  - random choose – quick face morph into chosen GOD OBJ
  - add its ACTIONS to your queue
  - example: follow shaman – dance – hurt someone

GOD BANK VIRTUAL OBJS
- always scannable by agent in stress mode (carries with himself)
- has facial bone profile
- can be idol? → more likely to choose OBJ
-

SOCIAL STATUS determines who can be in your GOD BANK of VIRTUAL OBJS

- Shaman = GOD OBJ AD

LIMBIC NEEDS AI desires <subconscious>

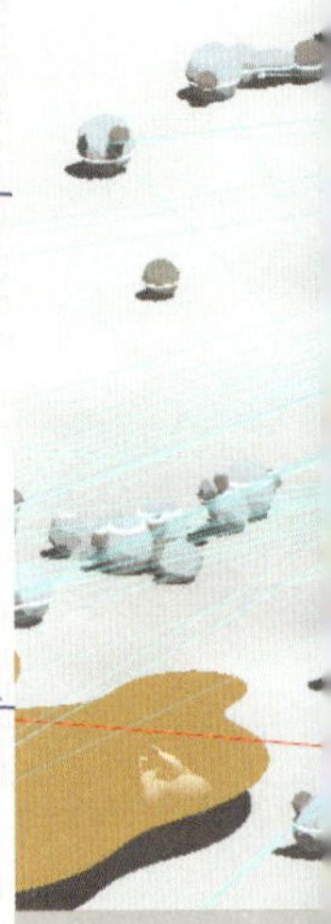

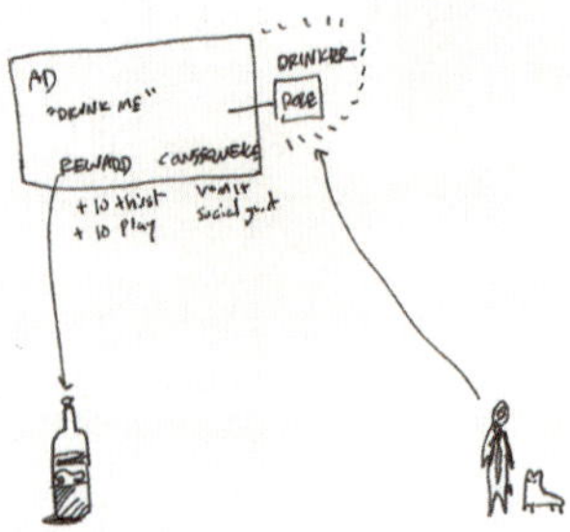

AD OBJECT (PHYSICAL)

example.
- ROCK ADS
  - advertise – kick (fun +)
  - " – collect (env +)
  - " sleep/sit on (comfort +)

function
- (get asked for ADs in OBJ)
  1. – check MASK of asker agent based on PERSONALITY CHARACTERISTICS
     ex: – is adult – is shaman – is animal – is NOT STRESSED
  2. show readable filtered ADs to agent

- MAYBE INTERNAL DECAY PROPERTY
  - example: ROCK accumulates ash no longer advertises sleep/sit on to ADULT HUMANS
- each AD in OBJECT has a vignette scripted in it
  (vignette = sequence of actions

AD OBJECT (VIRTUAL)

example
- Group of 5 agents together
  - advertise – join in (social

example
- each AGENT has own virtual OBJ of himself advertising to others
  BASED ON PERSONALITY PROFILE
  - social status
  - BEING-TYPE
  - stress MODE OR
  - GENDER

GOD STRESS OBJECT (VIRTUAL)
- facial bone profile
- point to agent or idol of agent or dead body of agent in ENVIRONMENT
  - advertise – come to m
  - " – dance
  - pray
  - hurt someon
  - sing "....
  - follow near person

THE SELECTED GOD STRESS OBJECT
1. – ALWAYS restores non-stress mo
   - can result in more STRESS if ACTION creates stress (ho
2.

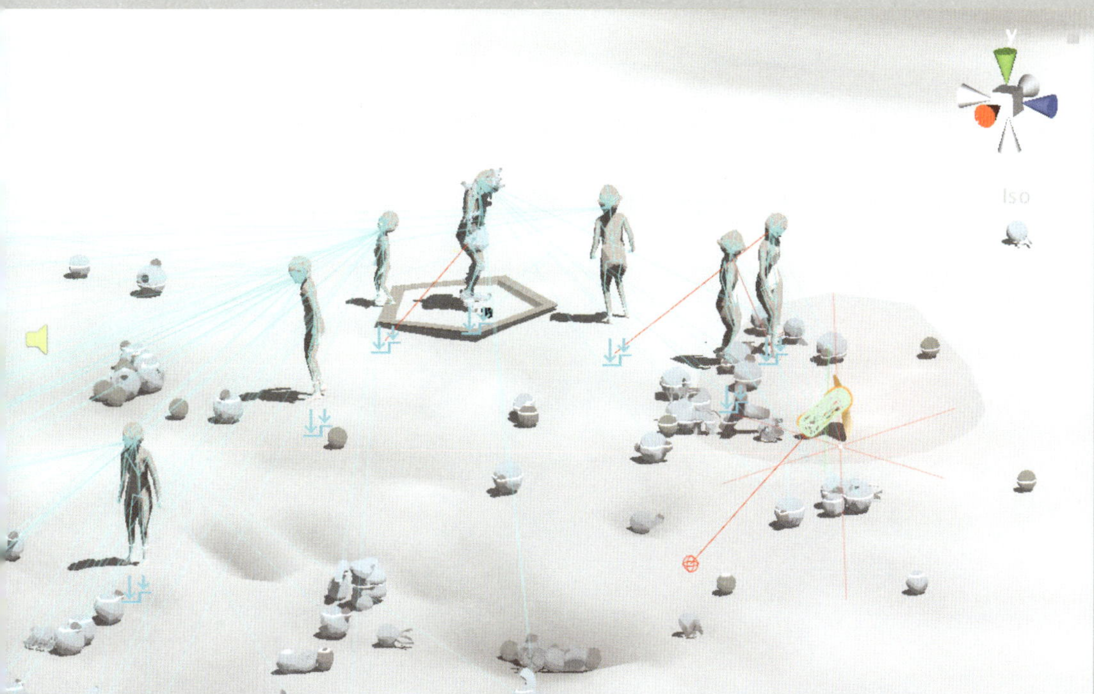

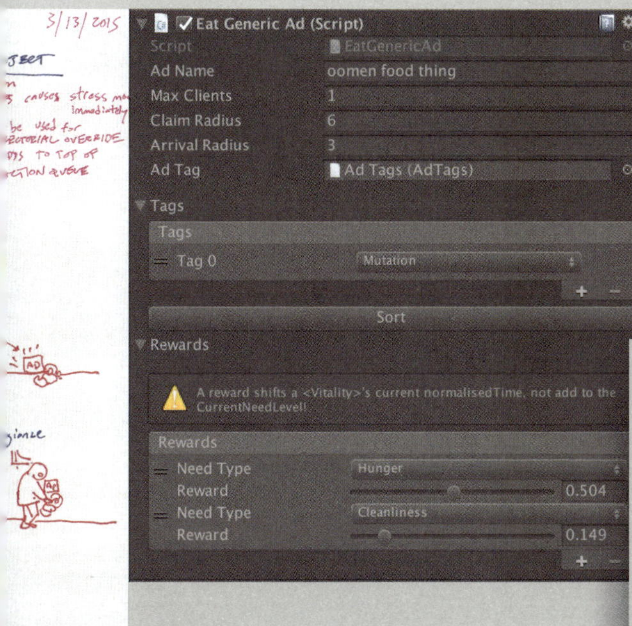

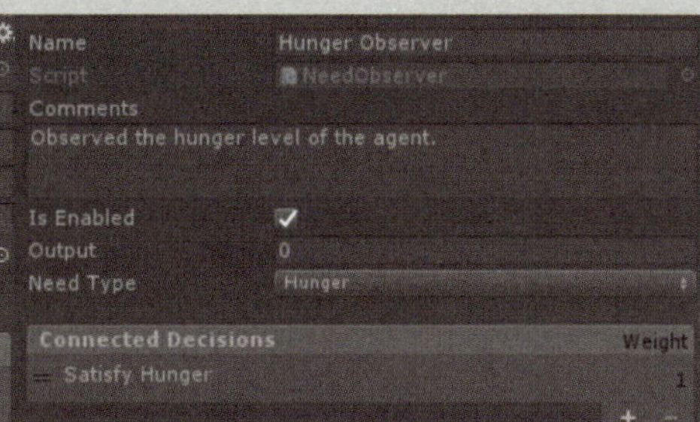

Second, I identify the key systems that will produce the most variety, surprise, and consequence on the simulation. The focus of *Emissaries* is cognitive evolution. So I focus on the AI model of the agents – how they balance survival with desires with narrative goals. I focus on the interaction rules between the agents and the environment.

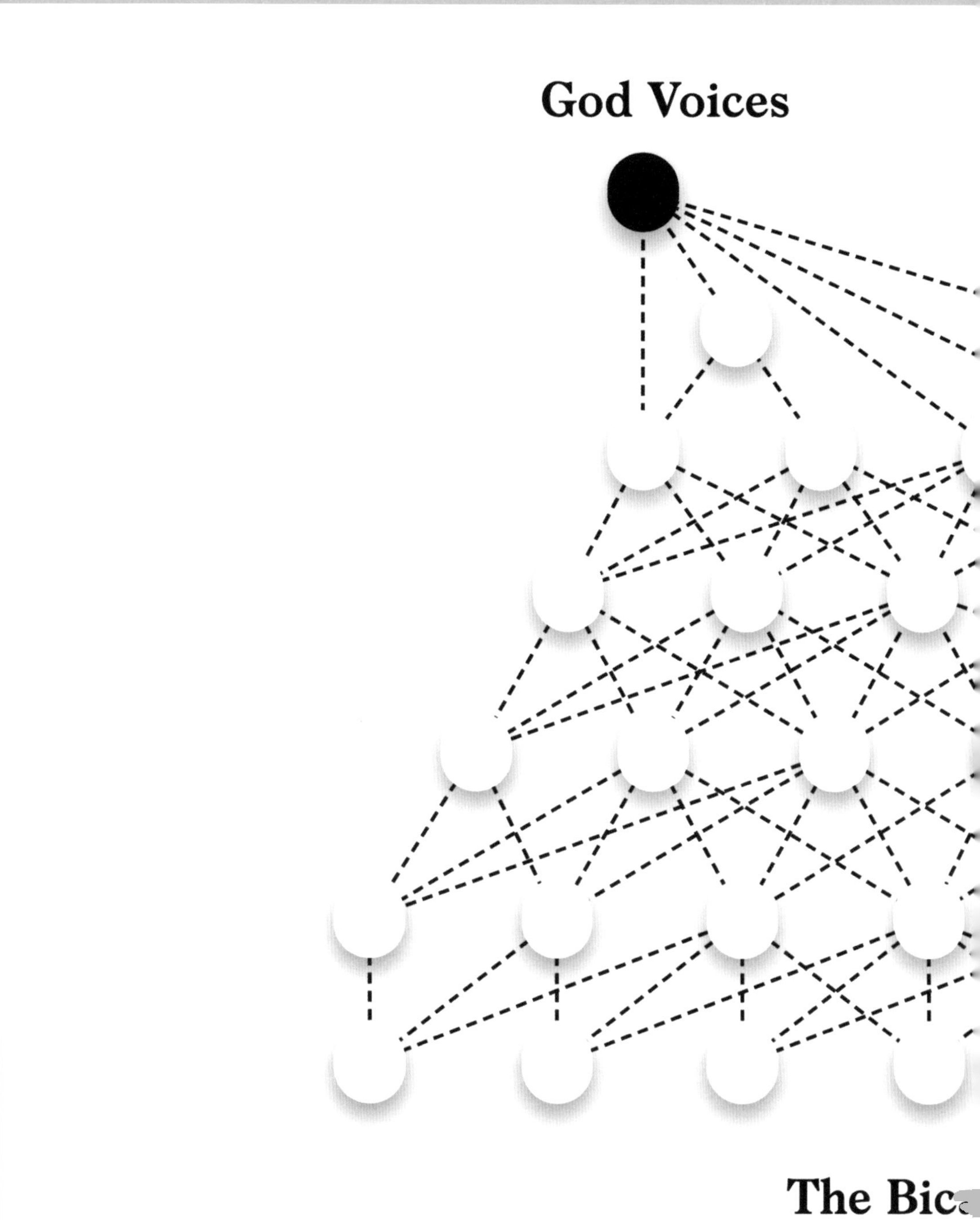
God Voices
The Bic

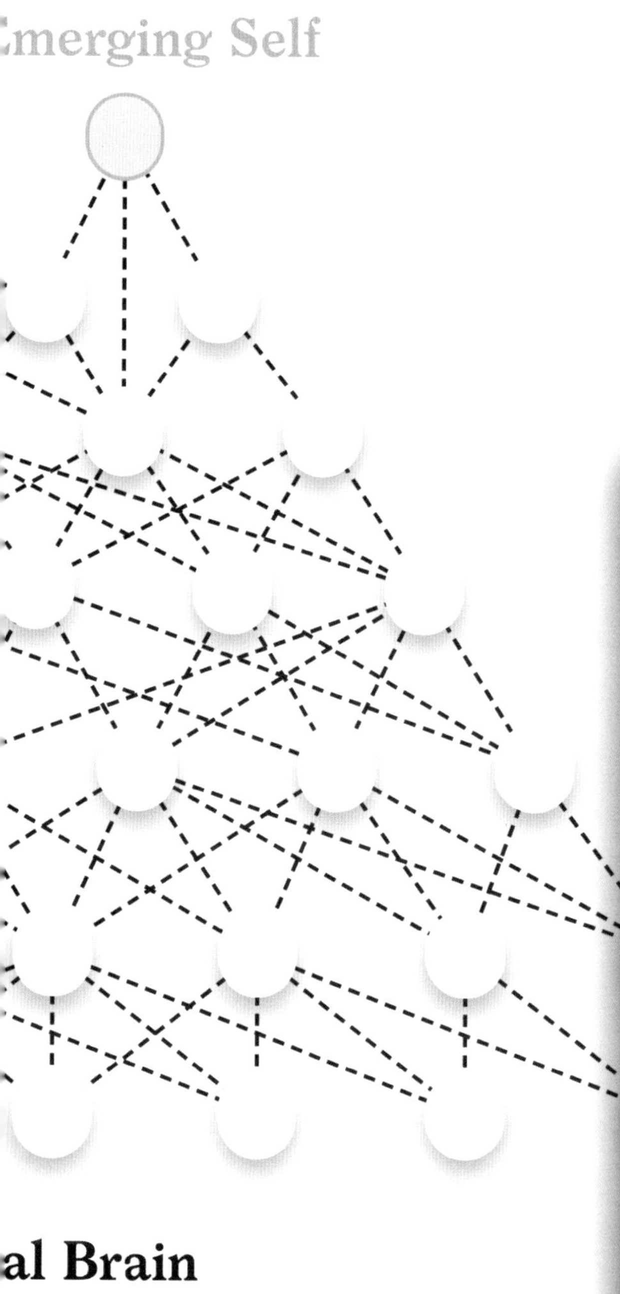

A World should be complex, not complicated. In *The Pragmatic Programmer* (1999), writer Andrew Hunt says: 'Simple rules lead to complex behaviour. Complicated rules lead to stupid behaviour.' It's Flocking vs. Bureaucracy. On a technical level, I am always asking, 'What rules lead to the most the leverage?' Meaning, can I develop one thing that satisfies multiple goals, or a combination of simple systems that can accomplish vast complexity?

Simple rules shared among many objects, characters, entities together create the conditions for emergence. What is emergence? It's the phenomenon in which new behaviours arise through interactions among simpler similar entities. 1+1 = 11. Lots of hydrogen and oxygen produce the property of wetness. Three simple rules – alignment, cohesion, and separation – produce complex flocking behaviour.

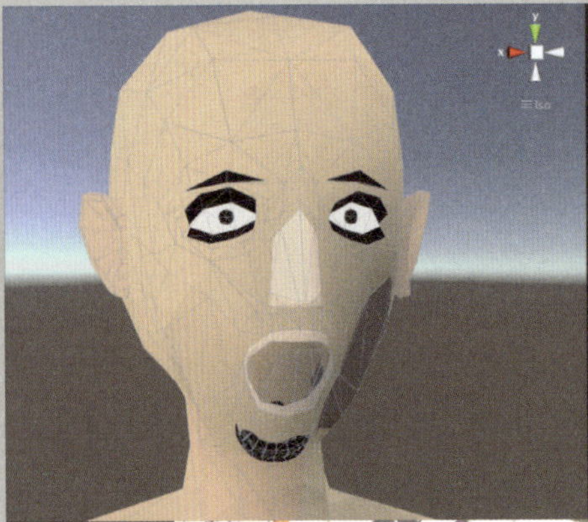

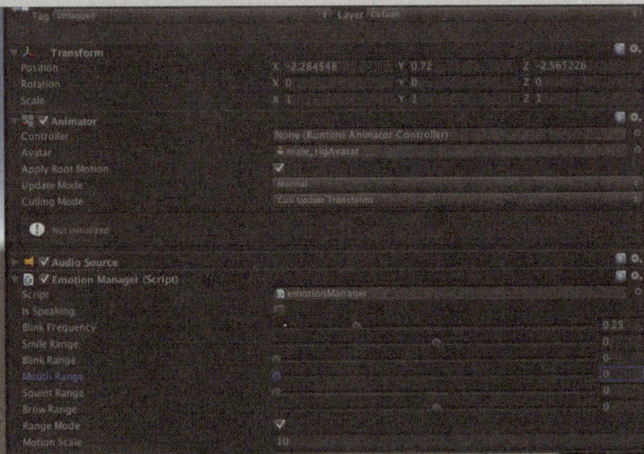

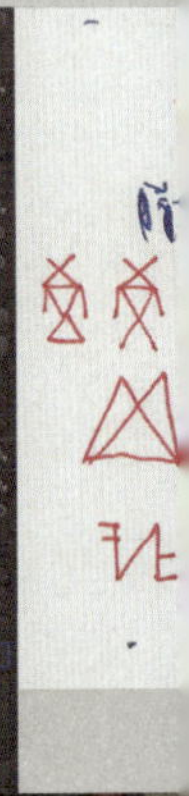

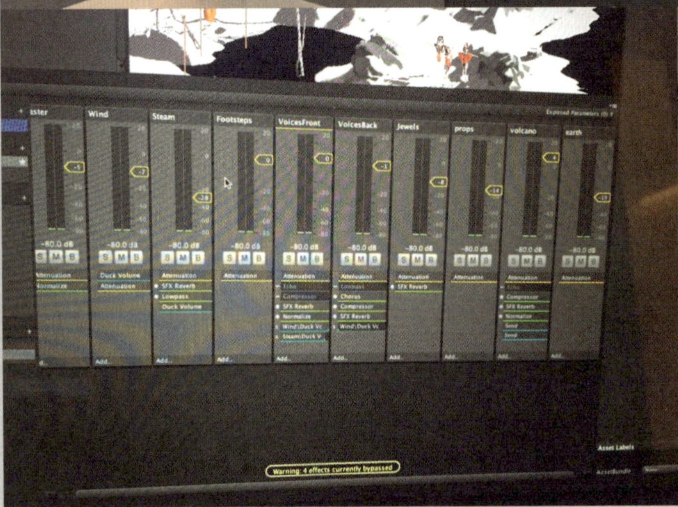

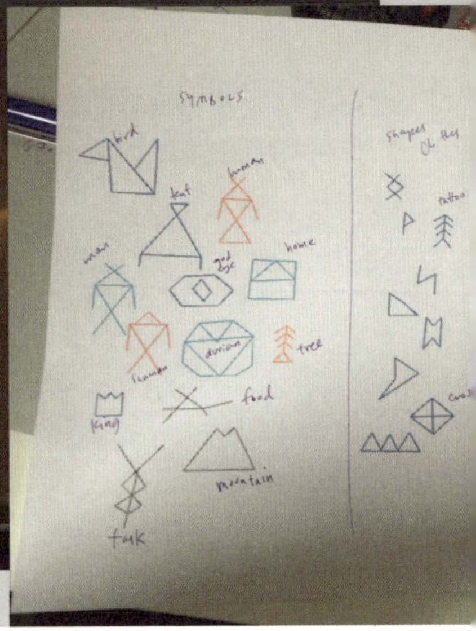

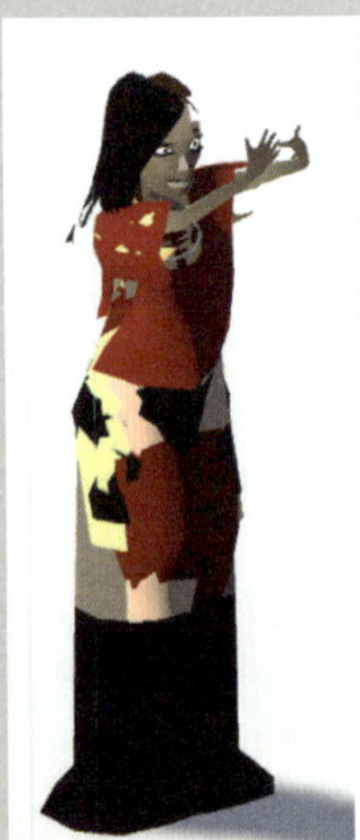

Fondazione Sandretto Re Rebaudengo	executive producer	vah.2 on dee shah on %1 shah.3 on dee toe %0.5 nee.2 %0.5 nee bah dee.3 gug oh
Ian Cheng	director	eee.2 on.2 %0.7 shah rong.3
Veronica So	producer	vah rong.2 eee.2 kah %0.7 shah oh
Madeline Hollander	choreographer	mah dee la on.2 %0.7 huh on tar
Samuel Eng	technical director	shah am.2 %0.7 ake
Mark Fingerhut	AI programming	mah ark %0.7 zig.2 tar.2 huh tar
Ian Faris	character programming	eee on %0.7 shah itch
Andrej Ujhazy	concept artist	on.2 dee ake %0.7 ooh huh zig
Joshua Planz	character modeling and rigging	shah.2 ooh ah %1 pah on zig
Greg Heffernan	sound design	gug.2 %0.7 huh off tar on
Sean Manning	story consultant	shah on.2 %0.7 mah nee gug
Jeremy Riccione	character animation	pah row nee.2 %1 row eee oh.3 nee
Jeremy Phieffer	mocap performance	pah row.3 nee.2 %1 hi off tar
David Yijae	mocap performance	dee.2 vah %1 eee eye.2
Jessica Wilson	assistant to director	ex eee.2 kah.2 %0.7 nee.2 sum
Breht O'Hearn	3d modeling	bah.2 toe huh on
Edit1	mocap services	eee dee %0.7 rong
Xsens	mocap services	ex.2 sum

```
new SpeakAction(actor, "ma", 3, 1.0f, "vah ex dee
    new WaitAction(1f),
    new SpeakAction(actor, "fa", 3, 1.0f, "vah ex d
    new WaitAction(1f),
    new SpeakAction(actor, "mc", 3, 1.0f, "vah ex
    new WaitAction(1f),
    new SpeakAction(actor, "fc", 3, 1.0f, "vah ex d
    new WaitAction(1f),
    new SpeakAction(actor, "ma", 1, 1.0f, "la low l
    new WaitAction(1f),
    new SpeakAction(actor, "fa", 1, 1.0f, "la low lo
    new WaitAction(1f),
    new SpeakAction(actor, "mc", 1, 1.0f, "la low k
    new WaitAction(1f),
    new SpeakAction(actor, "fc", 1, 1.0f, "la low lo
    new WaitAction(1f),
    new SpeakAction(actor, "ma", 3, 1.0f, "ow ow
    new WaitAction(1f),
    new SpeakAction(actor, "fa", 3, 1.0f, "ow ow p
    new WaitAction(1f),
    new SpeakAction(actor, "mc", 3, 1.0f, "ow ow
    new WaitAction(1f),
    new SpeakAction(actor, "fc", 3, 1.0f, "ow ow p
    new WaitAction(1f),
    new SpeakAction(actor, "ma", 2, 1.0f, "suck su
    new WaitAction(1f),
    new SpeakAction(actor, "fa", 2, 1.0f, "suck sur
    new WaitAction(1f),
    new SpeakAction(actor, "mc", 2, 1.0f, "suck su
    new WaitAction(1f),
    new SpeakAction(actor, "fc", 2, 1.0f, "suck sun
    new WaitAction(1f),
    new SpeakAction(actor, "ma", 1, 1.0f, "bah go
    new WaitAction(1f),
    new SpeakAction(actor, "fa", 3, 1.0f, "bah god
    new WaitAction(1f),
    new SpeakAction(actor, "mc", 1, 1.0f, "bah go
    new WaitAction(1f),
    new SpeakAction(actor, "fc", 1, 1.0f, "bah god
    new WaitAction(1f),
    new SpeakAction(actor, "ma", 1, 1.0f, "vah zig
    new WaitAction(1f),
    new SpeakAction(actor, "fa", 1, 1.0f, "vah zig l
```

```
new WaitAction(1f),
new SpeakAction(actor, "mc", 1, 1.0f, "vah zig low 2 nee"),
new WaitAction(1f),
new SpeakAction(actor, "fc", 1, 1.0f, "vah zig low 2 nee"),
new WaitAction(1f),
new SpeakAction(actor, "ma", 3, 1.0f, "hi tar 2 dee tum tum"),
new WaitAction(1f),
new SpeakAction(actor, "fa", 3, 1.0f, "hi tar 2 dee tum tum"),
new WaitAction(1f),
new SpeakAction(actor, "mc", 3, 1.0f, "hi tar 2 dee tum tum"),
new WaitAction(1f),
new SpeakAction(actor, "fc", 3, 1.0f, "hi tar 2 dee tum tum"),
new WaitAction(1f),
new SpeakAction(actor, "ma", 3, 1.0f, "shah kah la kah"),
new WaitAction(1f),
new SpeakAction(actor, "fa", 3, 1.0f, "shah kah la kah"),
new WaitAction(1f),
new SpeakAction(actor, "mc", 3, 1.0f, "shah kah la kah"),
new WaitAction(1f),
new SpeakAction(actor, "fc", 3, 1.0f, "shah kah la kah"),
new WaitAction(1f),
new SpeakAction(actor, "ma", 1, 1.0f, "itch itch poon rong"),
new WaitAction(1f),
new SpeakAction(actor, "fa", 1, 1.0f, "itch itch poon rong 3"),
new WaitAction(1f),
new SpeakAction(actor, "mc", 3, 1.0f, "itch itch poon rong"),
new WaitAction(1f),
new SpeakAction(actor, "fc", 1, 1.0f, "itch itch poon rong"),
new WaitAction(1f),
new SpeakAction(actor, "ma", 1, 1.1f, "mah nee"),
new WaitAction(1f),
new SpeakAction(actor, "fa", 1, 1.1f, "mah nee"),
new WaitAction(1f),
new SpeakAction(actor, "mc", 1, 1.1f, "mah nee"),
new WaitAction(1f),
new SpeakAction(actor, "fc", 1, 1.1f, "mah nee"),
new WaitAction(1f),
new SpeakAction(actor, "ma", 3, 1.0f, "on bah bah dee"),
new WaitAction(1f),
new SpeakAction(actor, "fa", 3, 1.0f, "on bah bah dee"),
new WaitAction(1f),
new SpeakAction(actor, "mc", 3, 1.0f, "on bah bah dee"),
new WaitAction(1f),
```

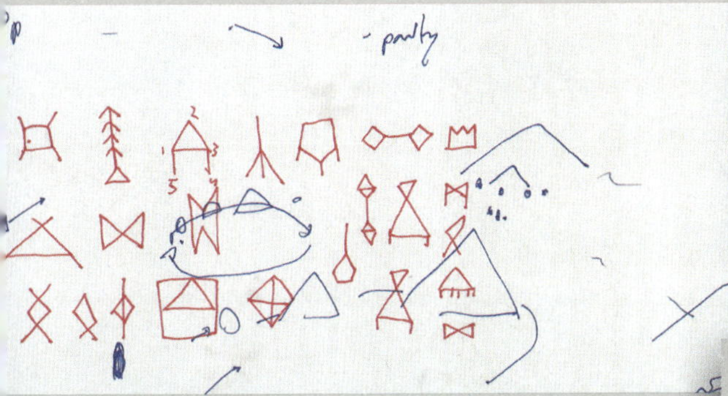

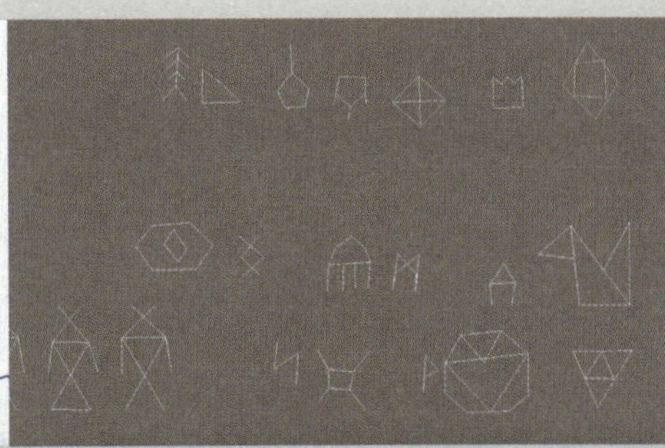

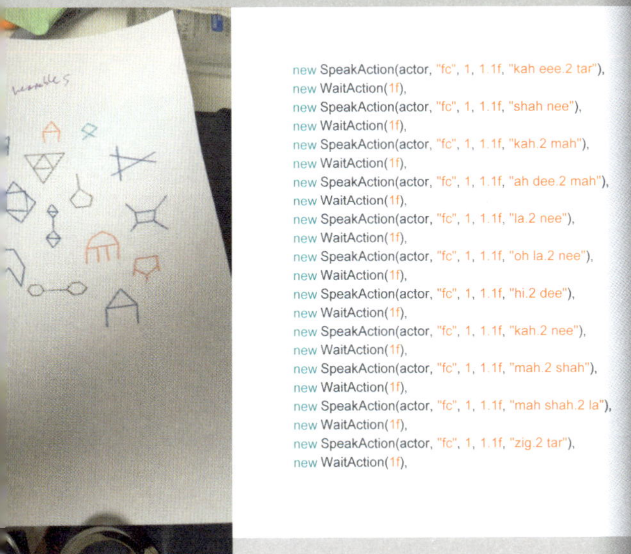

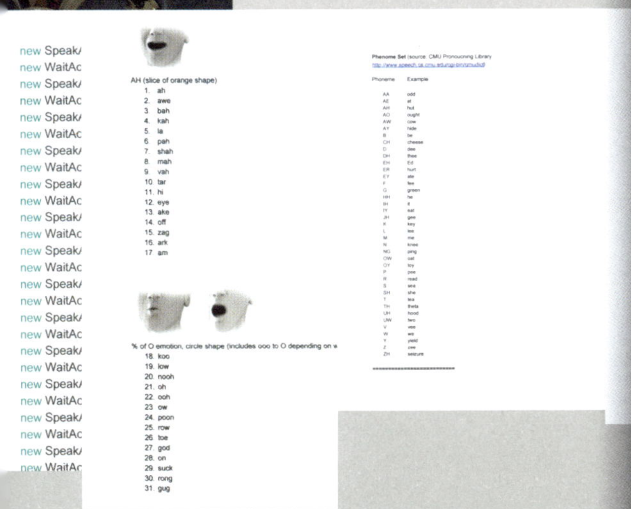

WHAT IS EMERGENCE? WHAT LEVEL DO YOU SIMULATE AT?

The level at which entities interact is a key choice in the art of hacking. Everything leading up to that level is constructed, and everything that follows from that level is automatic, the achievement of emergence.

I think of it as inventing a language. If you choose to represent everything at the level we see it, like Chinese, then the basic vocabulary will be extensive, but brittle. If you represent things as the composition of an underlying alphabet, like Latin languages or Korean, then you gain a lot of expressivity, nuance, and variety from simpler shared building blocks. In Nature, vast complex biology arises from setting the boundary of emergence at the level of the four bases of DNA: ATCG. The deeper and more atomic the commonality between things, the more simple the rules, the more potential for emergence and complexity. Yet setting the boundary blocks too deep can make it impossible to realise a World. It took Nature billions of years in base Reality to get to where we are now.

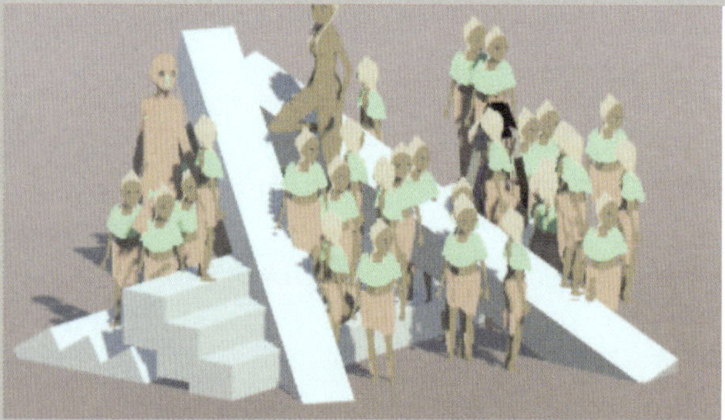

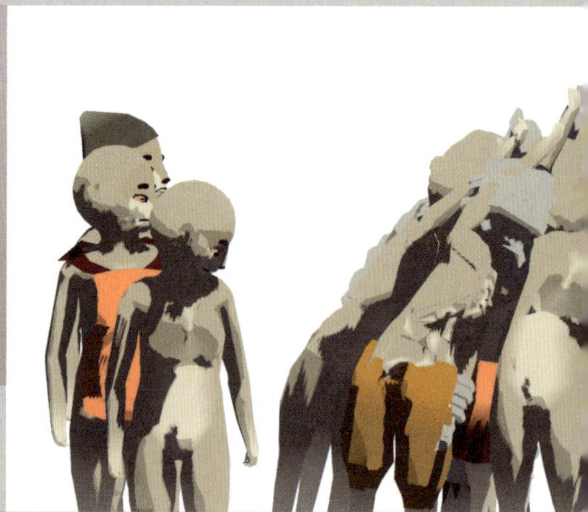

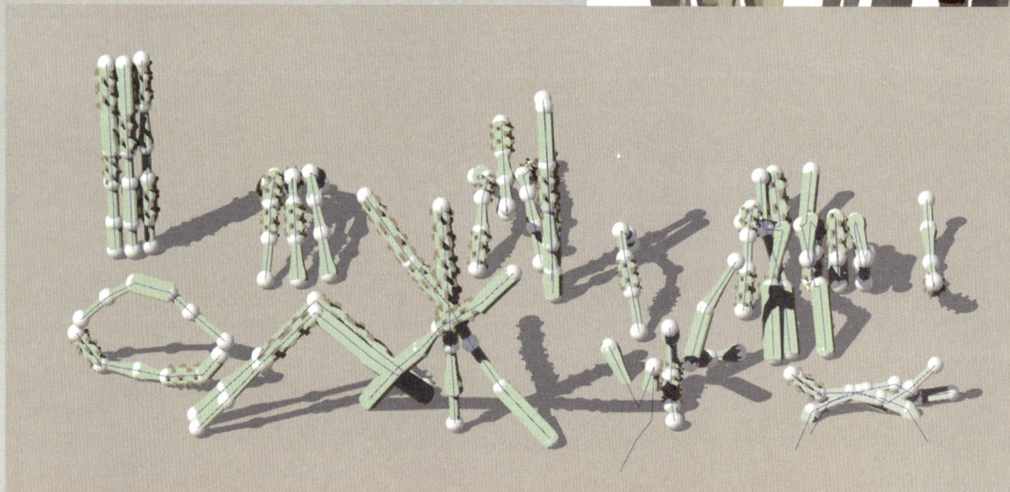

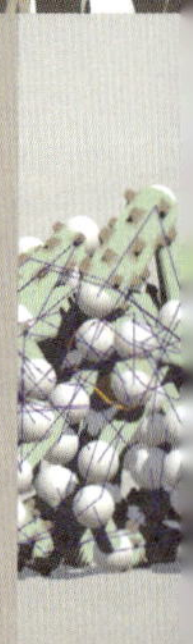

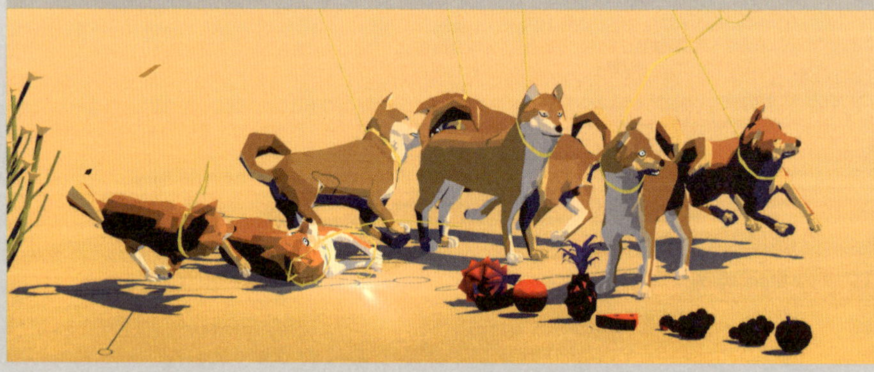

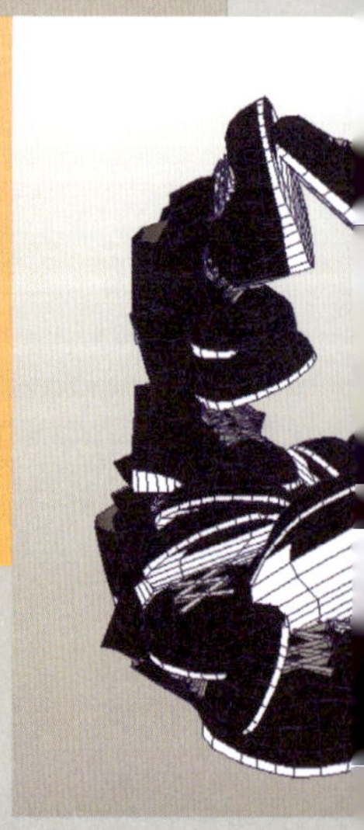

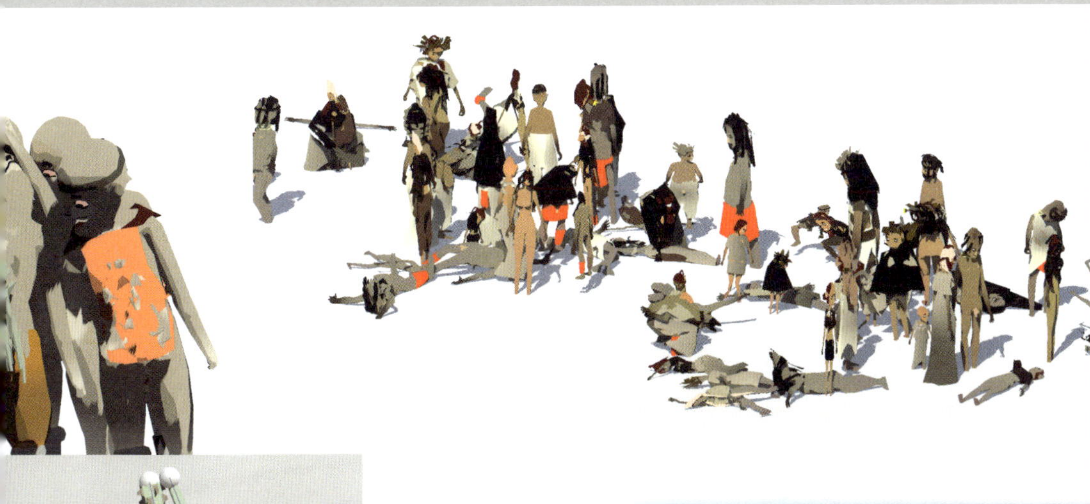

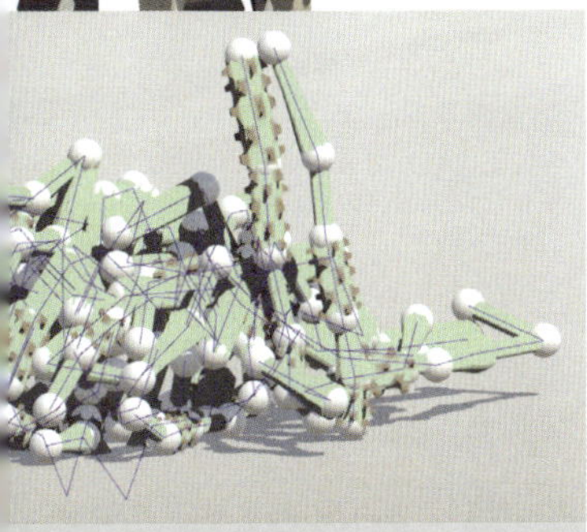

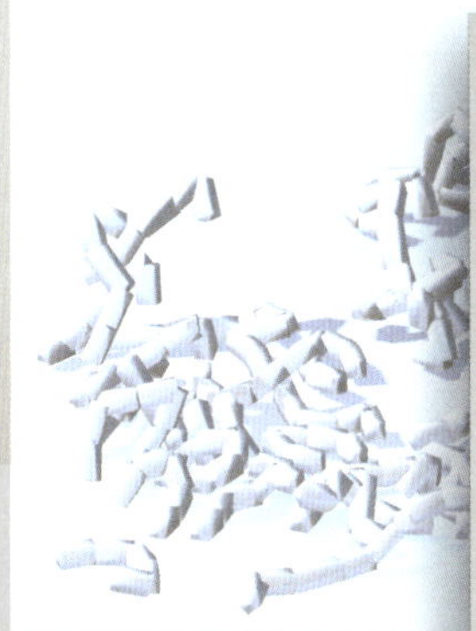

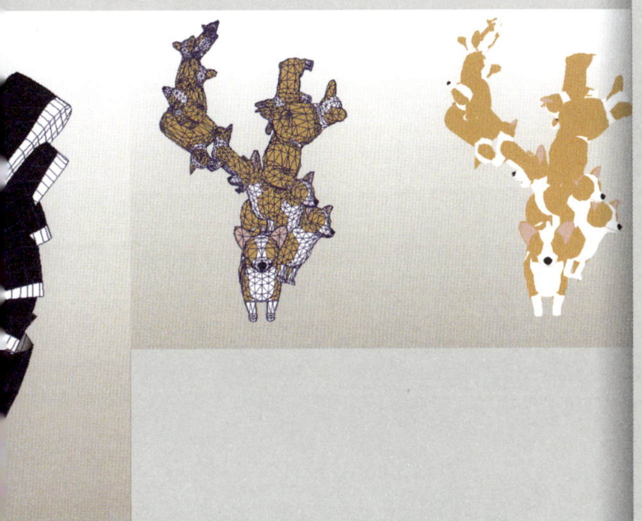

Early in *EITSOG*, I decided to simulate at the level of agents. Each agent could affect any other agent. Agents could come together into a crowd and produce crowd behaviour. An individual agent could misbehave or break down and have a social effect on other agents, but not big enough to wreck the whole simulation.

Like a flock of birds, complexity and emergent behaviour have the best opportunity to arise in large populations. A key choice in *Emissaries* was to feature a large number of AGENTs within each simulation. I designed *EITSOG* to feature a community of human agents, *EFAP* to feature multiplying forks of Shiba, *ESTS* to feature reproducing Oomen alongside the viral growth of Wormleaves. This removed the pressure on any one agent to be overly advanced. It also suggested that intelligence is largely social, a subtext of Jaynes' theory of consciousness.

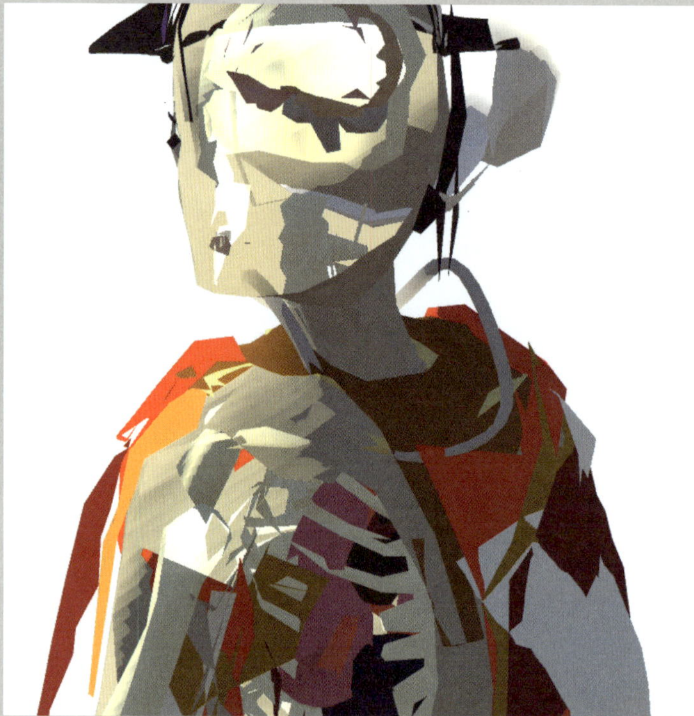

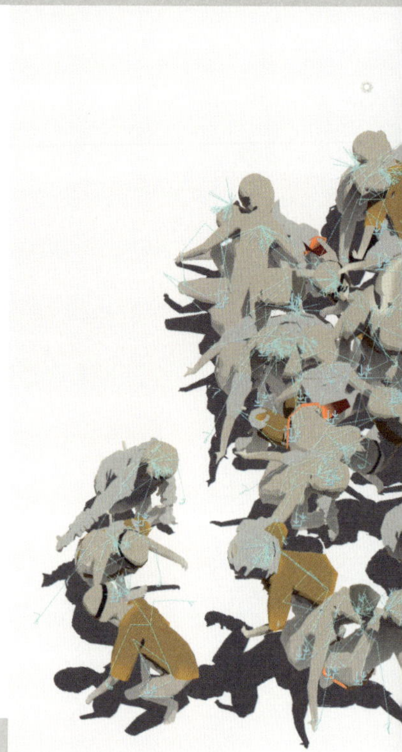

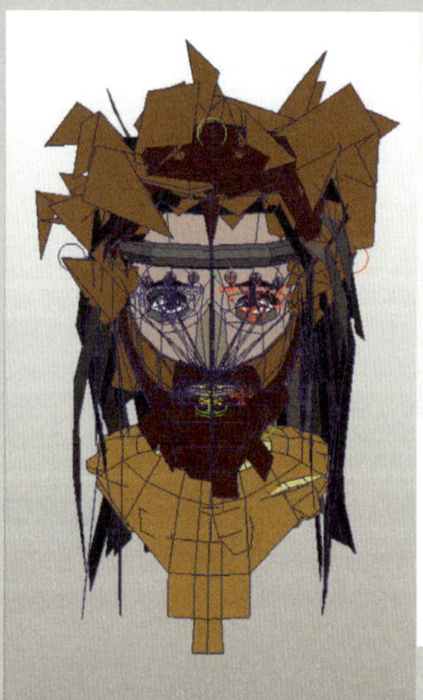

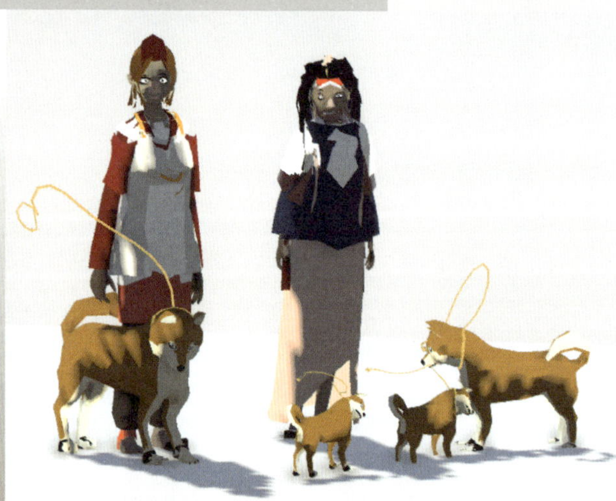

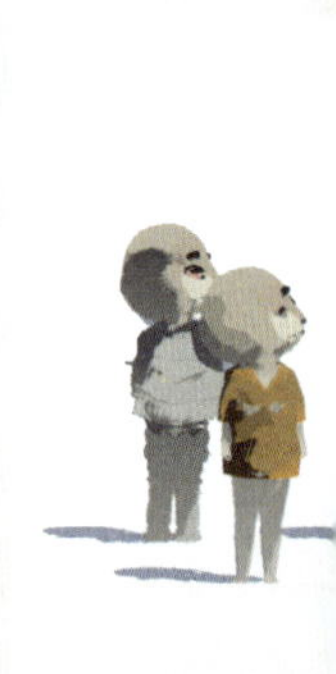

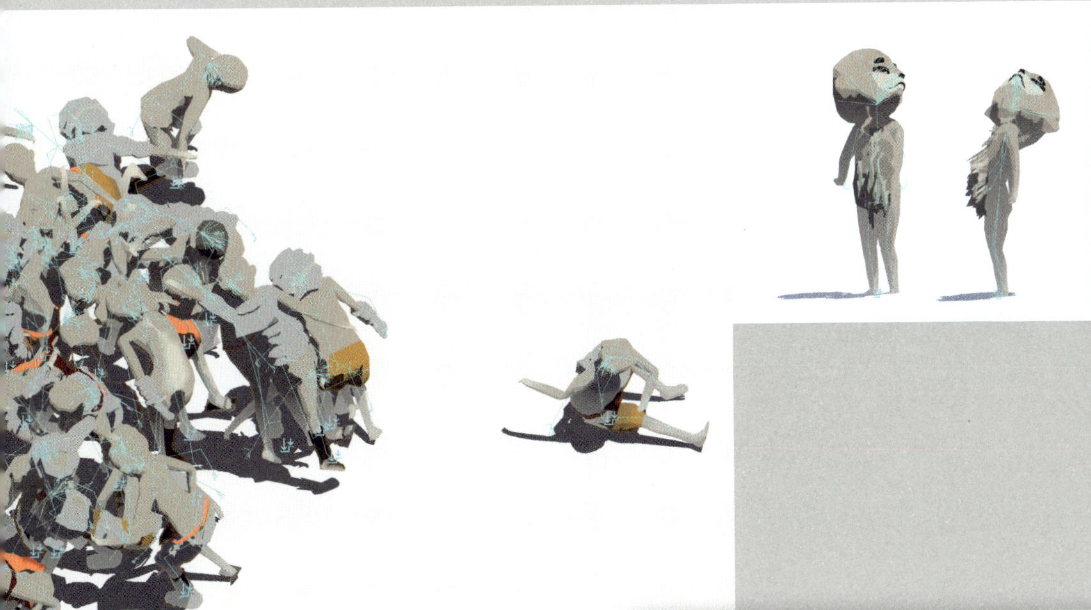

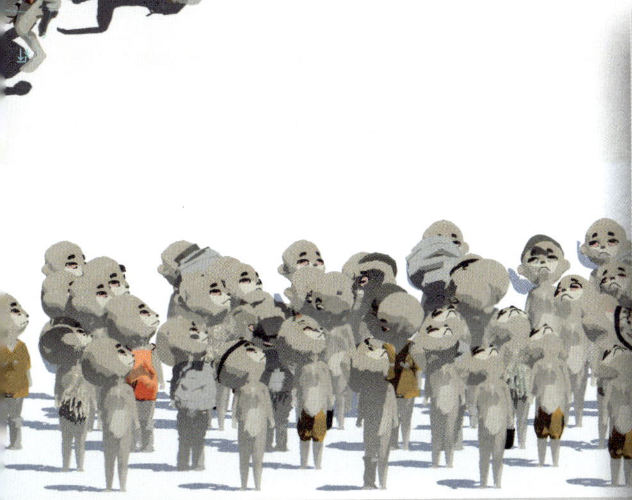

HOW DO YOU MAKE A WORLD FEEL UNIQUE?

Emissaries takes advantage of a common class of techniques in computer science called Procedural Generation (procgen). Procgen is a way to create data algorithmically rather than manually. In order to give the world of *Emissaries* the quality of variety, we turned to procgen. Every rock would be unique. Every face would be unique. Every wardrobe would be unique. Using simple rules to locally modify objects, the diversity and variability found in nature can be simulated.

The Cartoonist makes iconic characters, but with procgen, I treat them more like mascot source DNA whose perfection can now spawn an infinite variety of imperfect progeny.

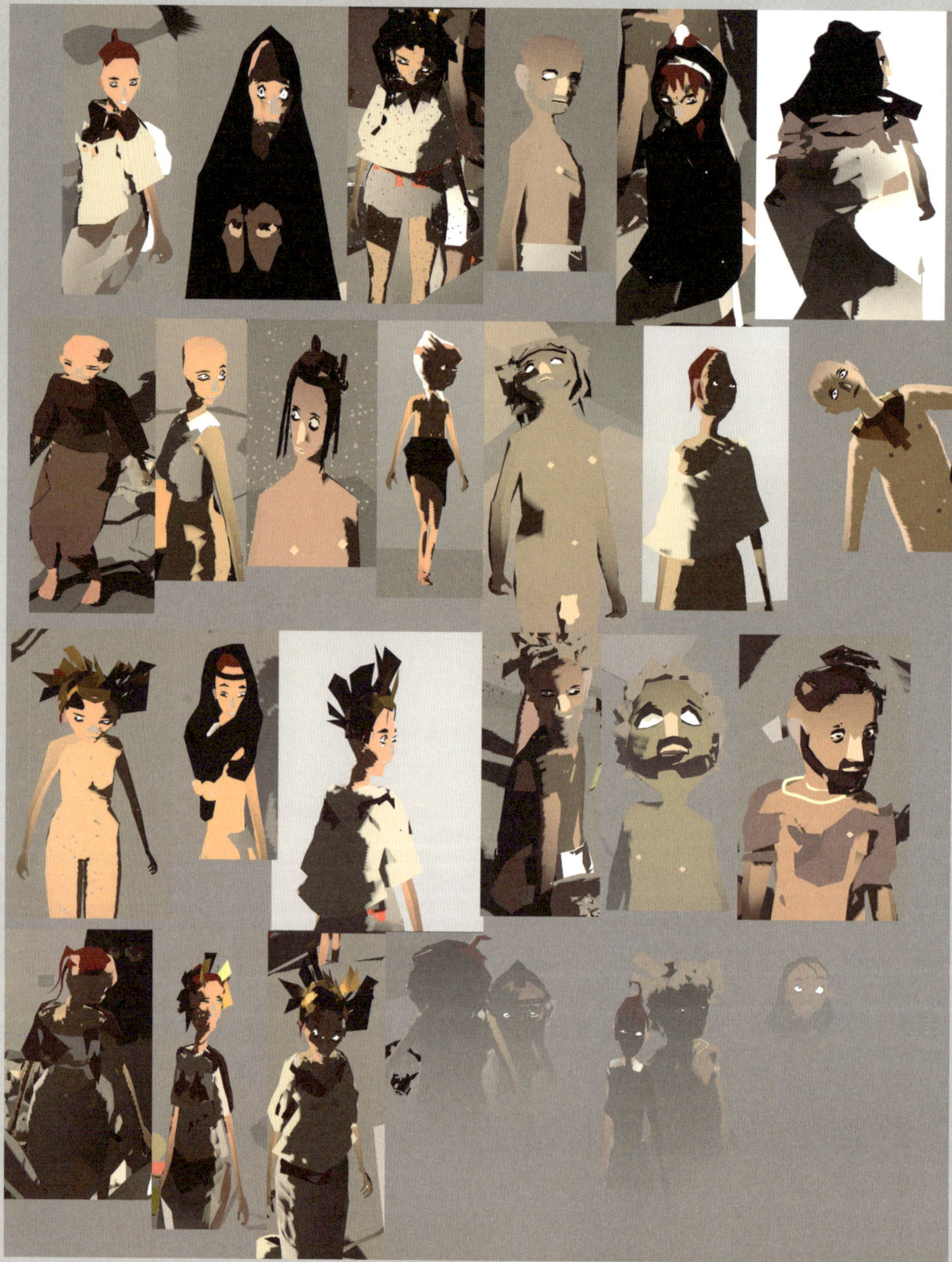

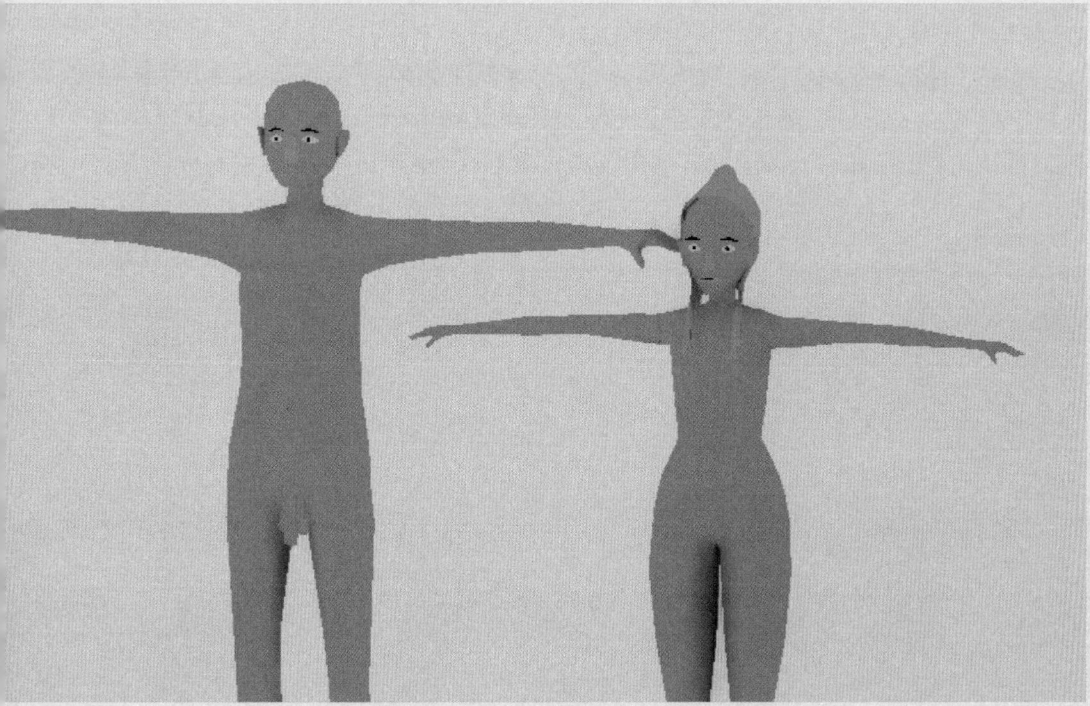

In *EITSOG*, the Cartoonist constructed one base male and female body. From this I devised a morphing bone structure that could accommodate a wide range of body sizes, shapes, faces, and ages.

In *ESTS*, we submit the face of an Oomen to a set of transformational rules that can automatically give us an entire community of Oomen.

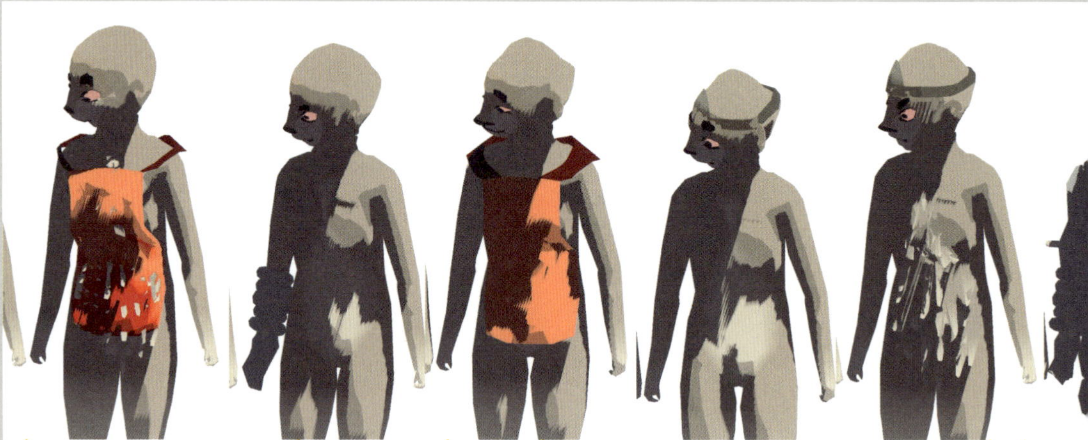

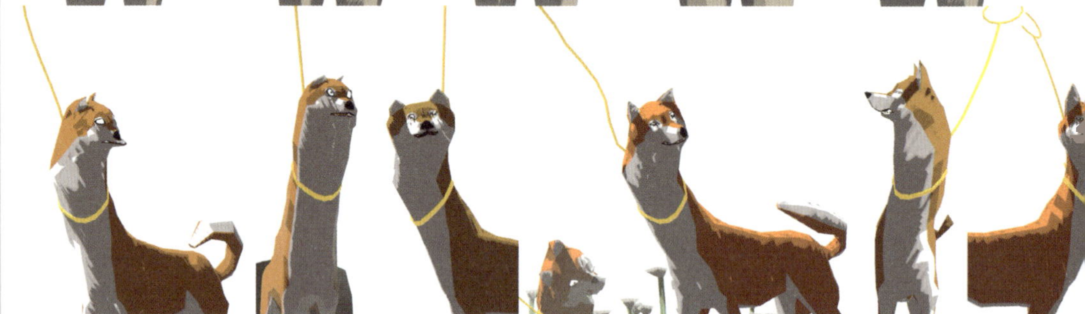

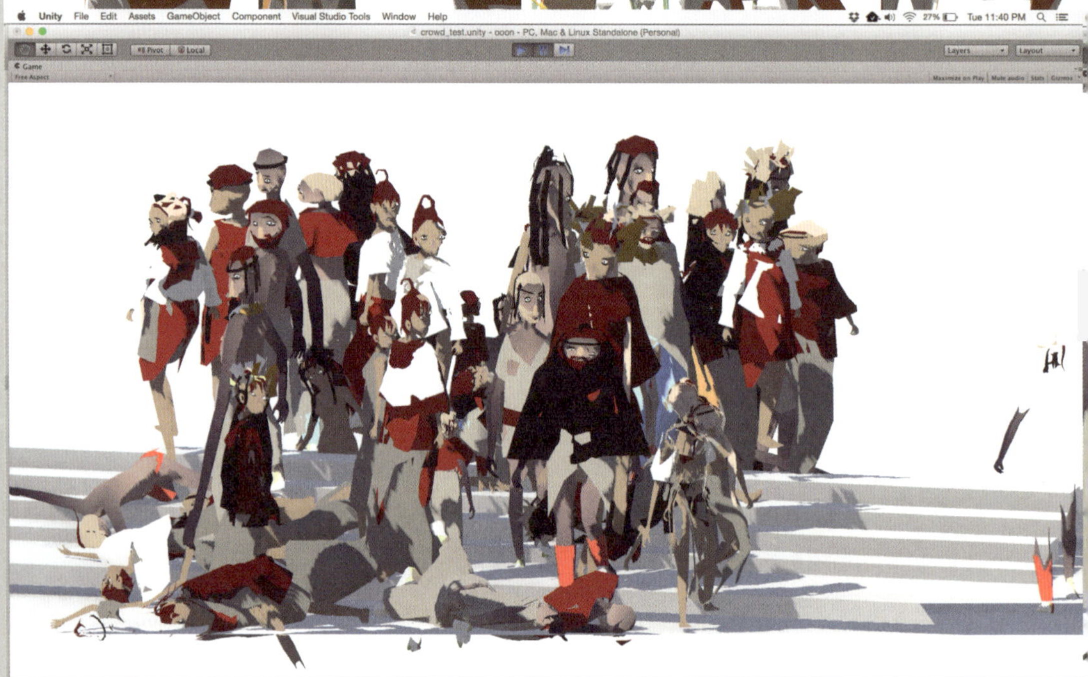
Unity File Edit Assets GameObject Component Visual Studio Tools Window Help
27% Tue 11:40 PM
crowd_test.unity - ooon - PC, Mac & Linux Standalone (Personal)
Pivot
Local
Layers
Layout
Game

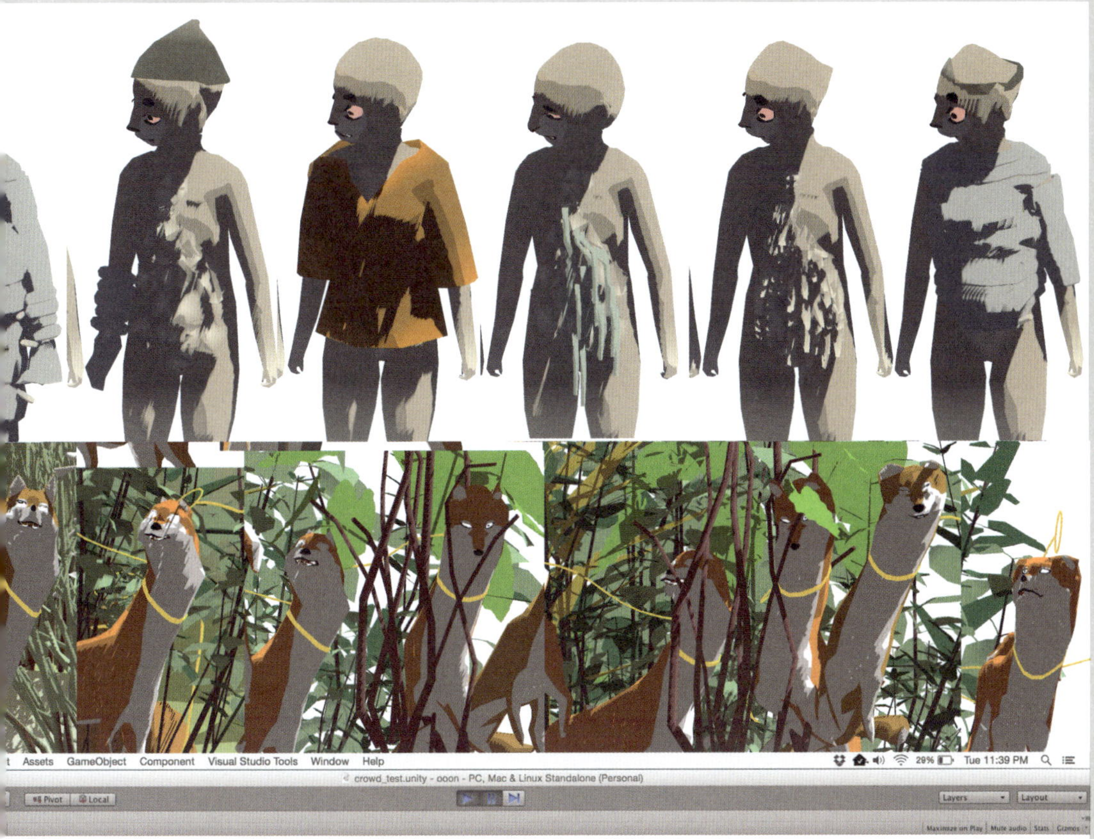

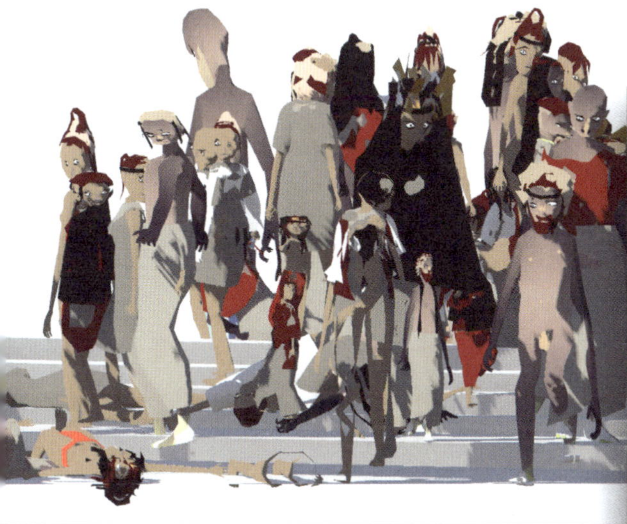

The hazard of procgen is the banality of uniqueness. When every rock is algorithmically unique, uniqueness becomes its own norm. This is as it should be. The perceptual tension that this banality creates is that it upsets our copy-paste rectilinear expectations of computer graphics. It also creates a pleasant contradiction: you know you are looking at a computer image, but its details have the banality of nature.

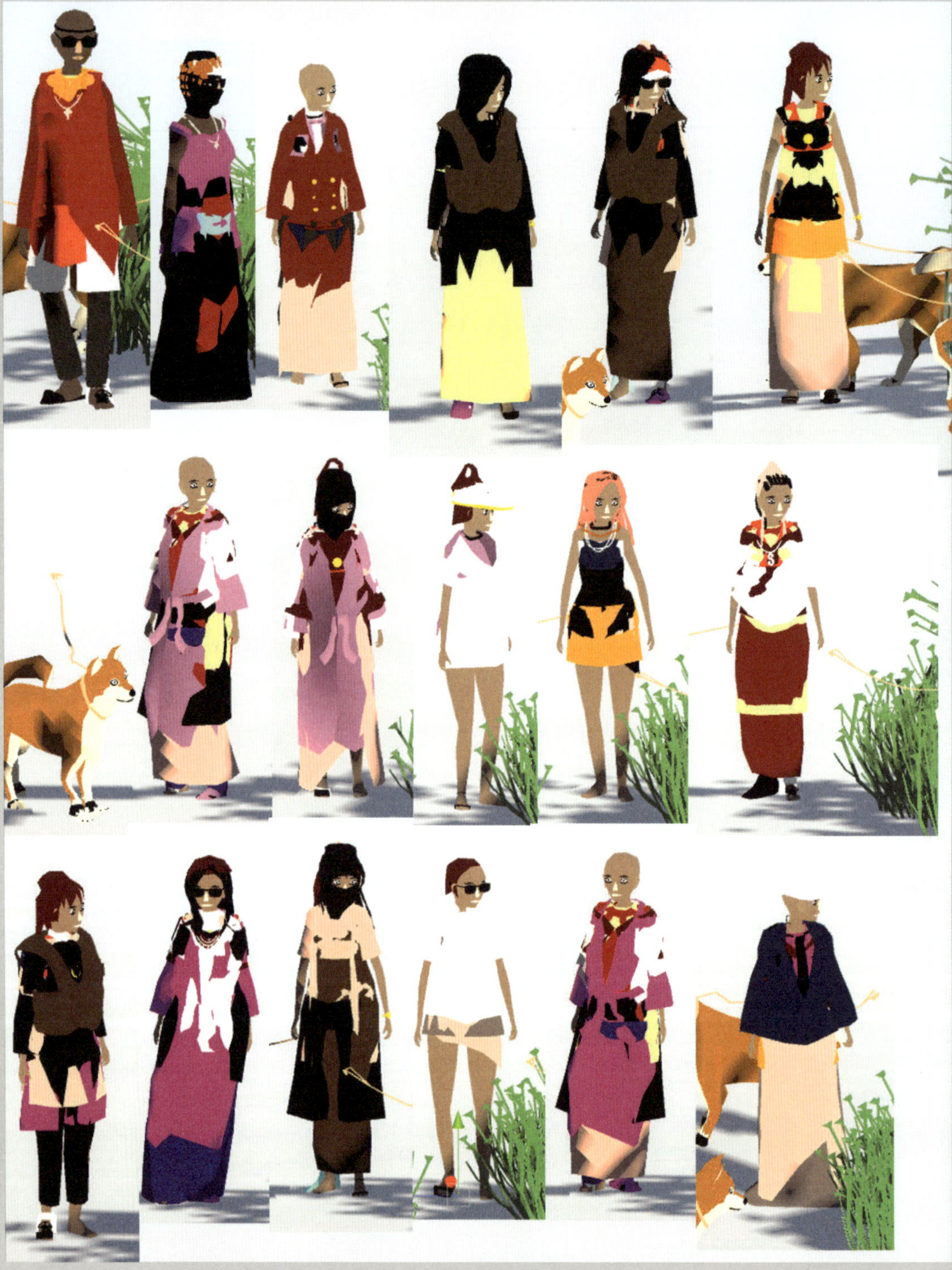

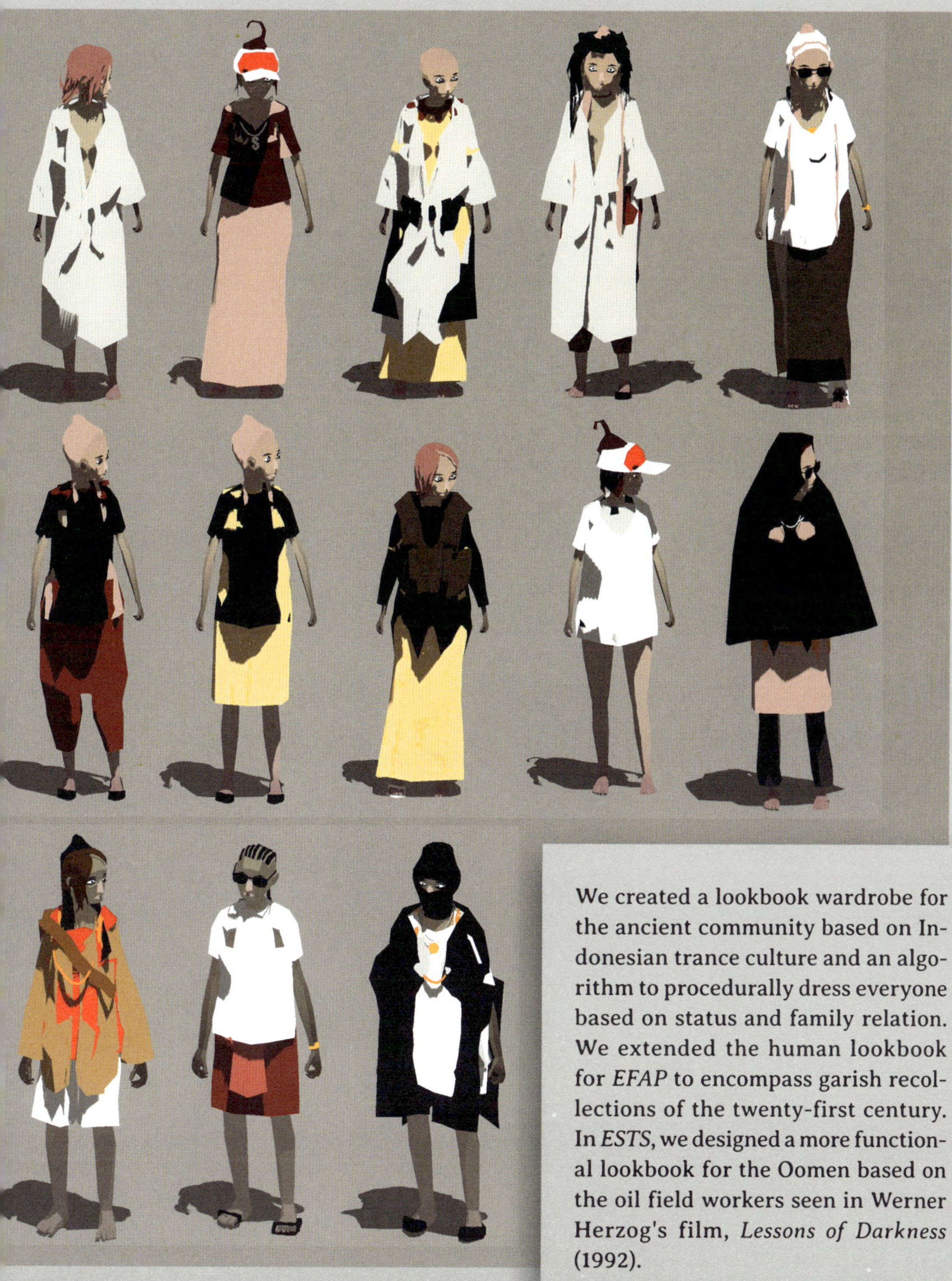

We created a lookbook wardrobe for the ancient community based on Indonesian trance culture and an algorithm to procedurally dress everyone based on status and family relation. We extended the human lookbook for *EFAP* to encompass garish recollections of the twenty-first century. In *ESTS*, we designed a more functional lookbook for the Oomen based on the oil field workers seen in Werner Herzog's film, *Lessons of Darkness* (1992).

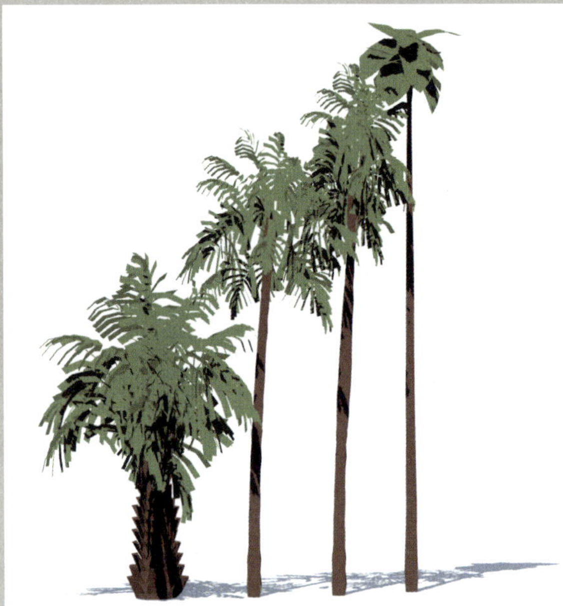

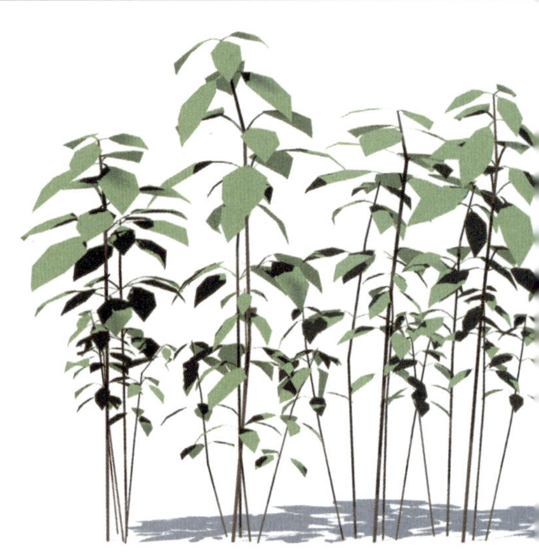

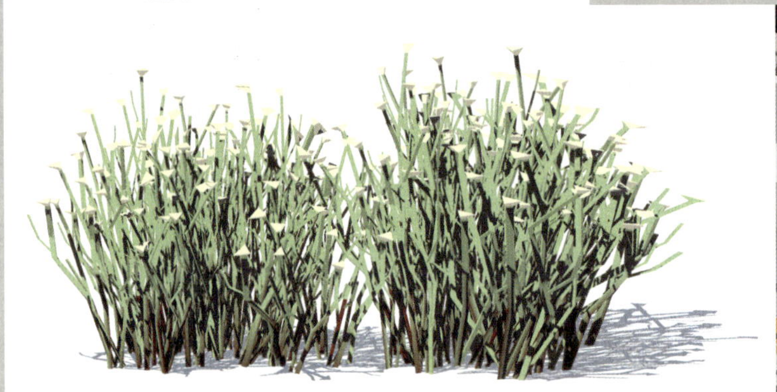

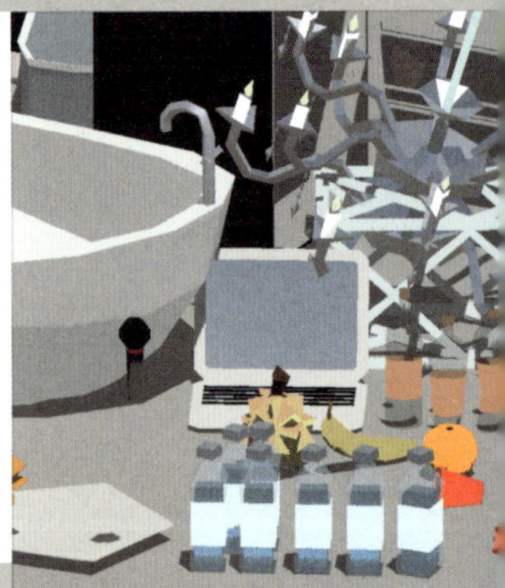

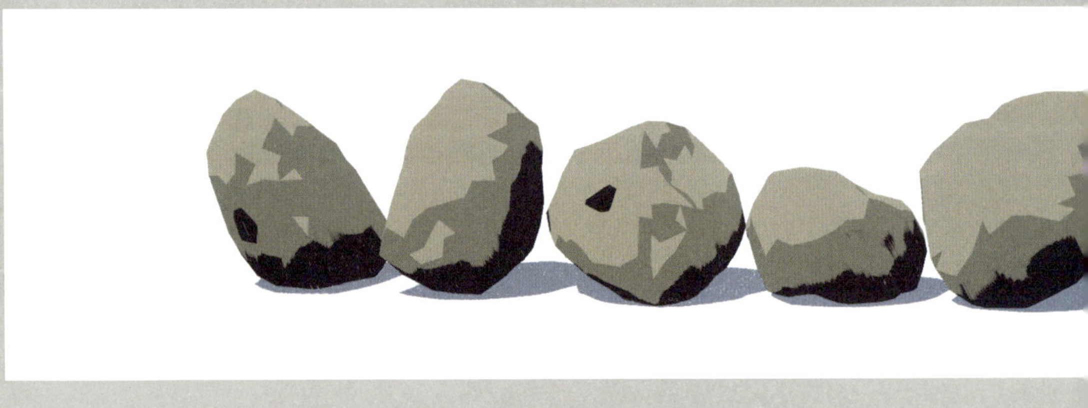

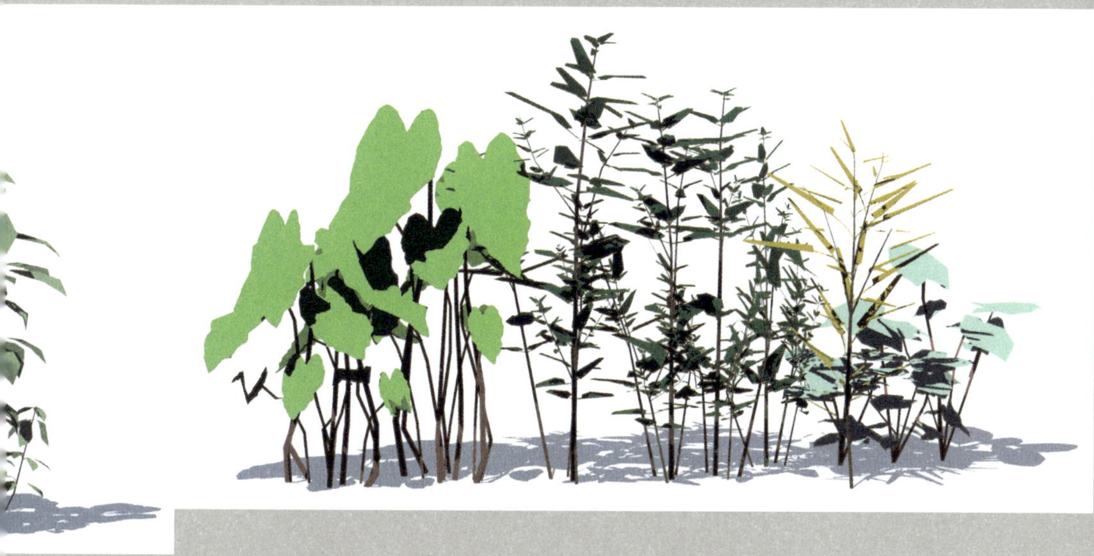

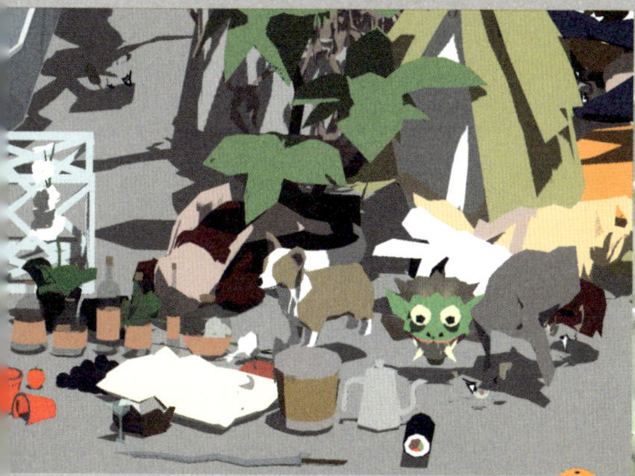

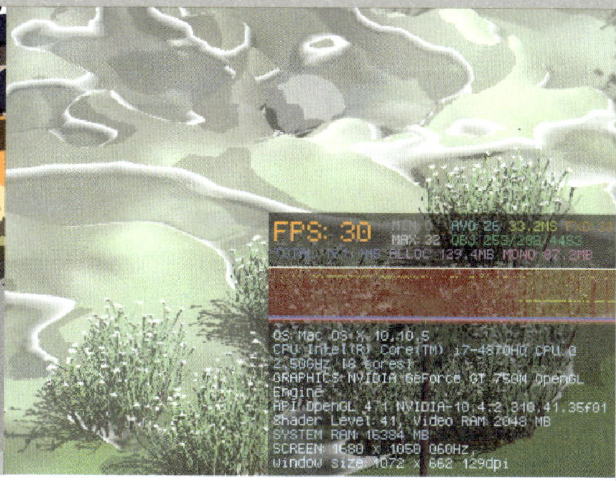

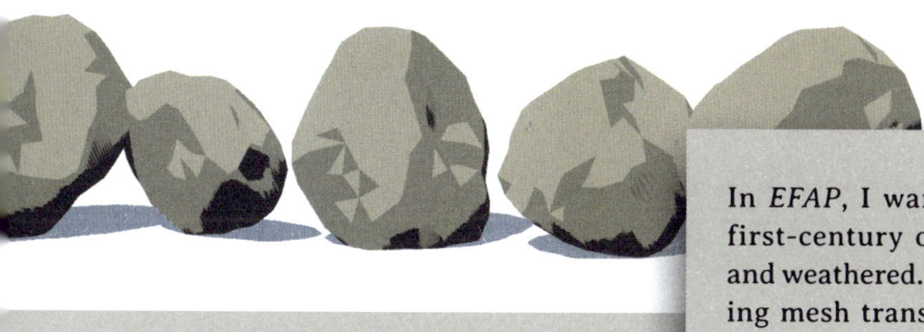

In *EFAP*, I wanted all the twenty-first-century objects to look worn and weathered. I applied a randomising mesh transformation to distort each idealised object.

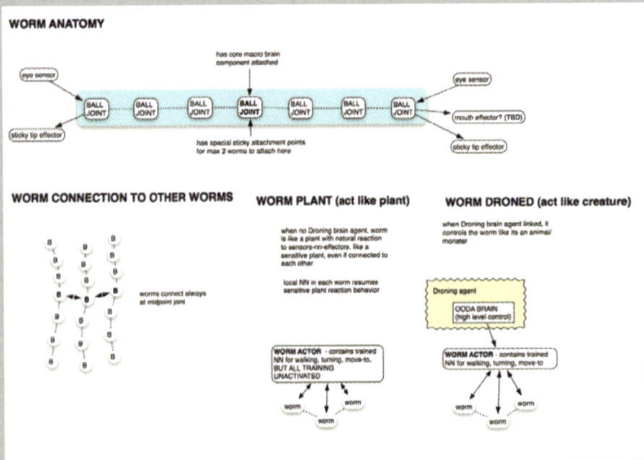

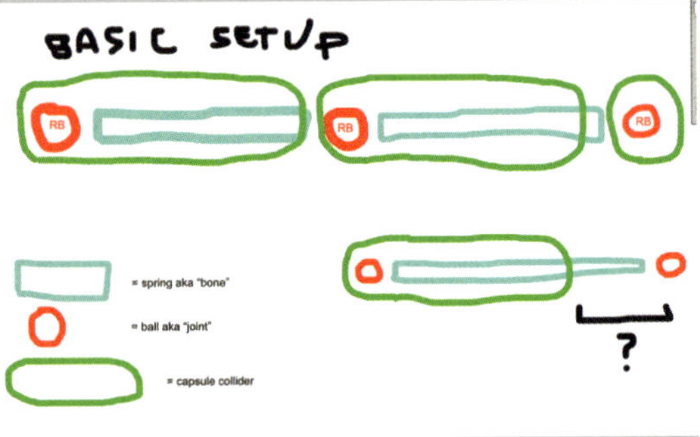

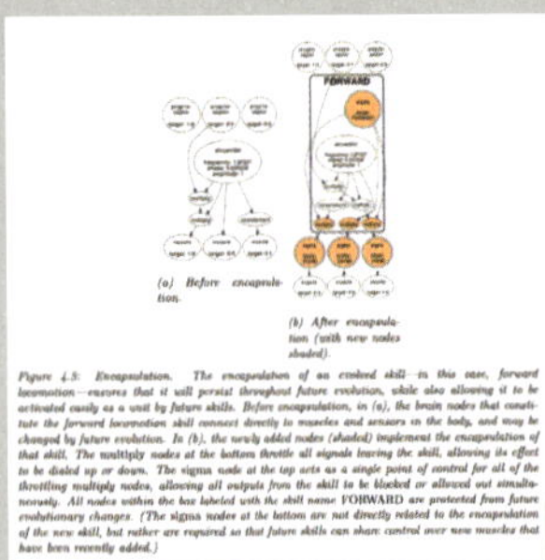

(a) Before encapsulation.

(b) After encapsulation (with new nodes shaded).

Figure 4.5: Encapsulation. The encapsulation of an evolved skill—in this case, forward locomotion—ensures that it will persist throughout future evolution, while also allowing it to be activated easily as a unit by future skills. Before encapsulation, in (a), the brain nodes that constitute the forward locomotion skill connect directly to muscles and sensors in the body, and may be changed by future evolution. In (b), the newly added nodes (shaded) implement the encapsulation of that skill. The multiply nodes at the bottom throttle all signals leaving the skill, allowing its effect to be dialed up or down. The sigma node at the top acts as a single point of control for all of the throttling multiply nodes, allowing all outputs from the skill to be blocked or allowed out simultaneously. All nodes within the box labeled with the skill name FORWARD are protected from future evolutionary changes. (The sigma nodes at the bottom are not directly related to the encapsulation of the new skill, but rather are required so that future skills can share control over new muscles that have been recently added.)

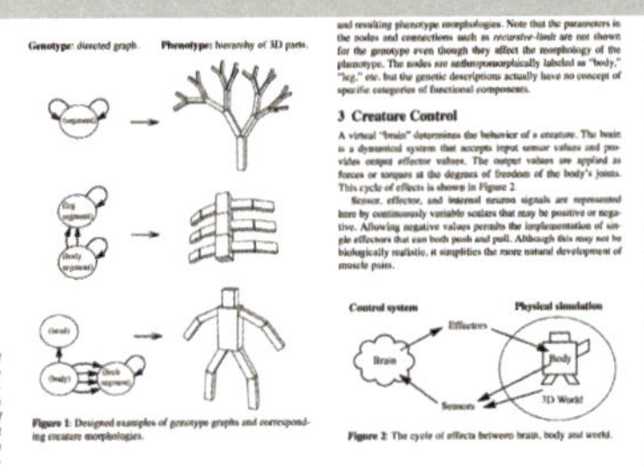

Figure 1: Designed examples of genotype graphs and corresponding creature morphologies.

and resulting phenotype morphologies. Note that the parameters in the nodes and connections such as *recursive-limit* are not shown for the genotype even though they affect the morphology of the phenotype. The nodes are anthropomorphically labeled as "body," "leg," etc. but the genetic descriptions actually have no concept of specific categories of functional components.

3 Creature Control

A virtual "brain" determines the behavior of a creature. The brain is a dynamical system that accepts input sensor values and provides output effector values. The output values are applied as forces or torques at the degrees of freedom of the body's joints. This cycle of effects is shown in Figure 2.

Sensor, effector, and internal neuron signals are represented here by continuously variable scalars that may be positive or negative. Allowing negative values permits the implementation of simple effectors that can both push and pull. Although this may not be biologically realistic, it simplifies the more natural development of muscle pairs.

Figure 2: The cycle of effects between brain, body and world.

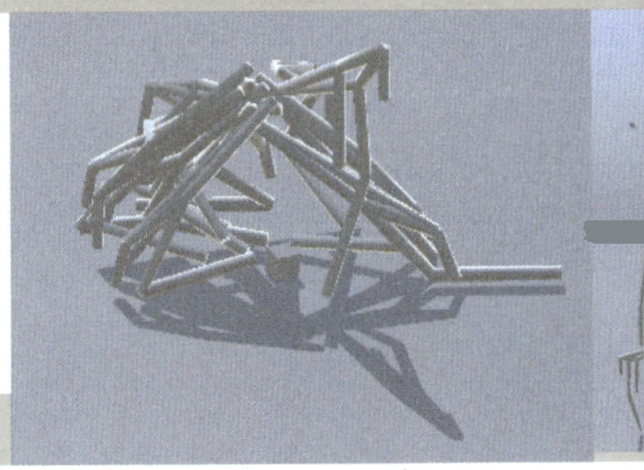

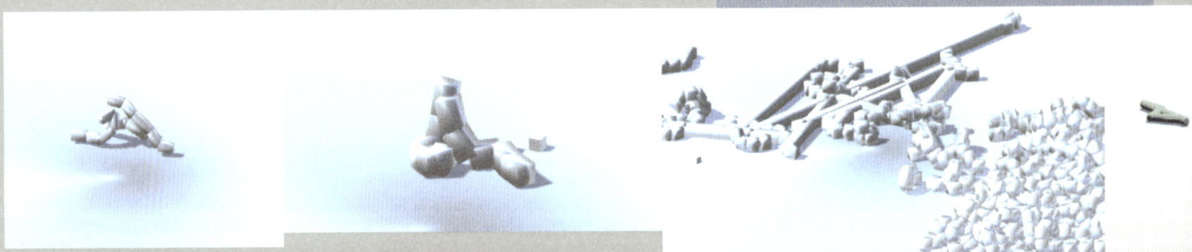

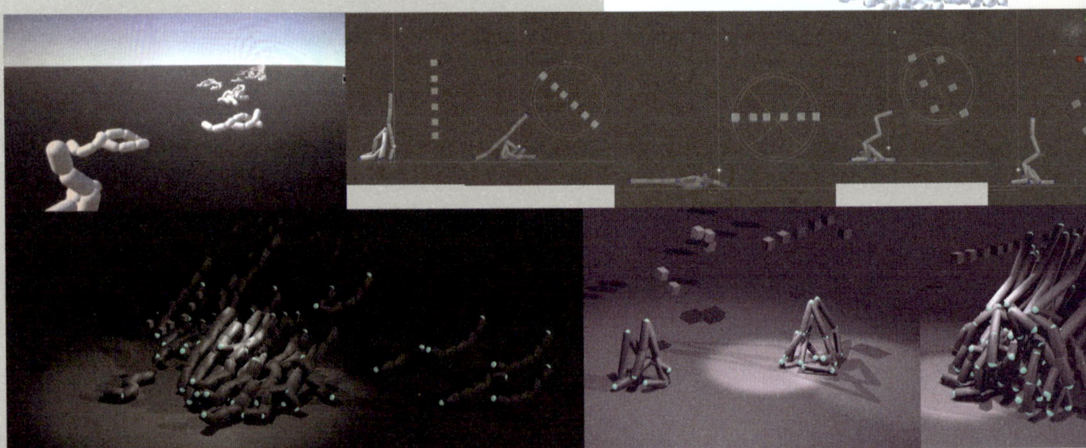

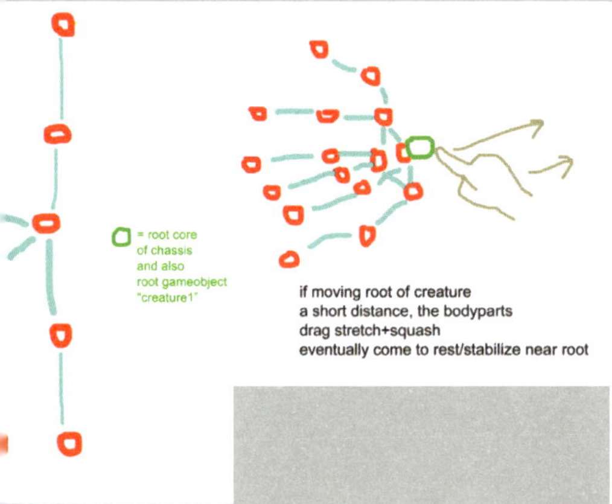

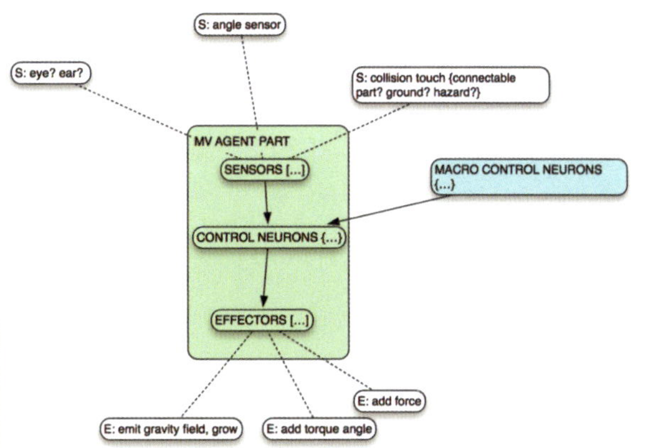

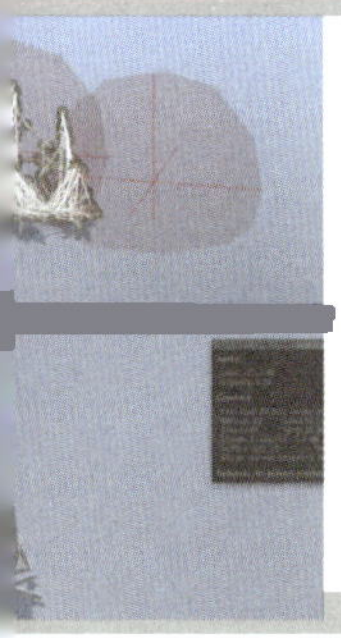

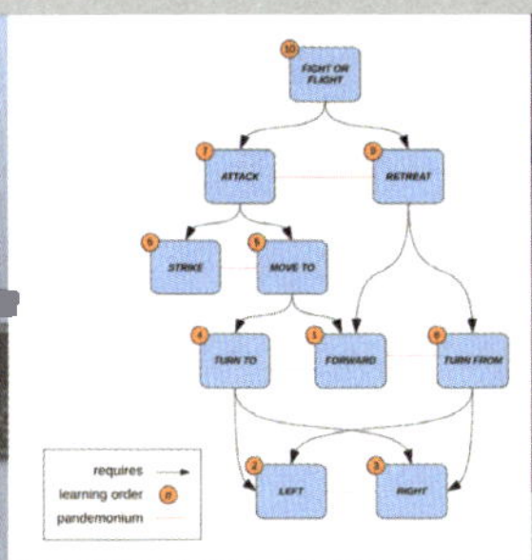

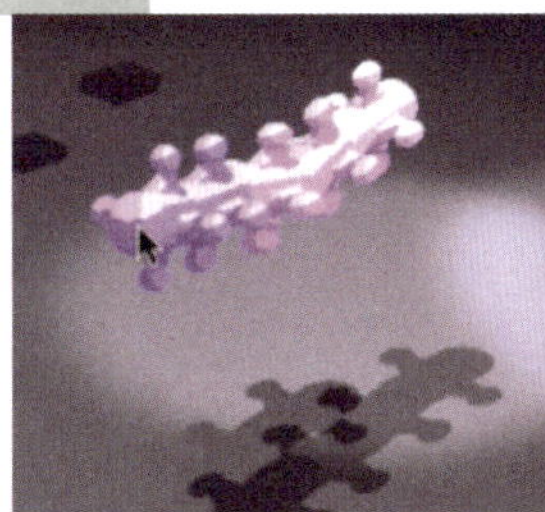

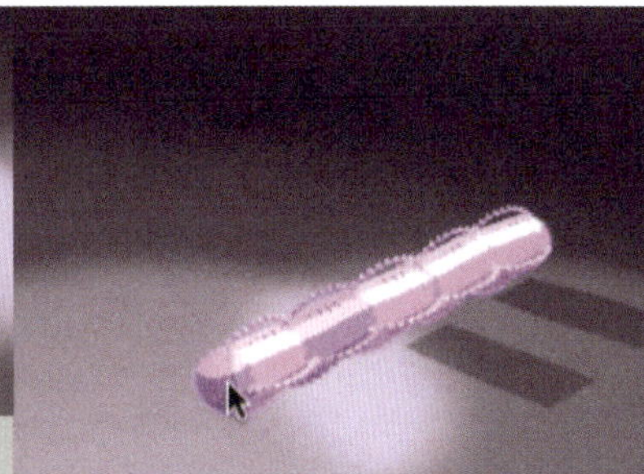

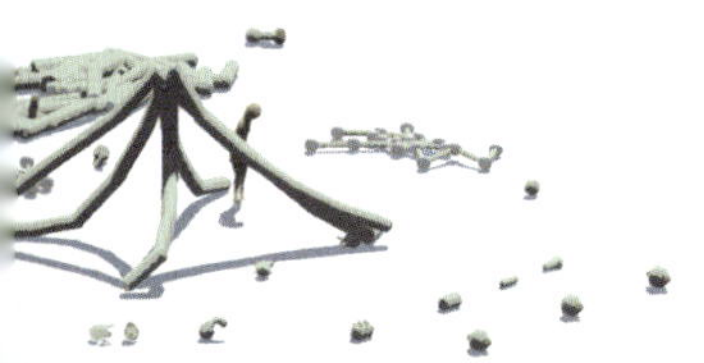

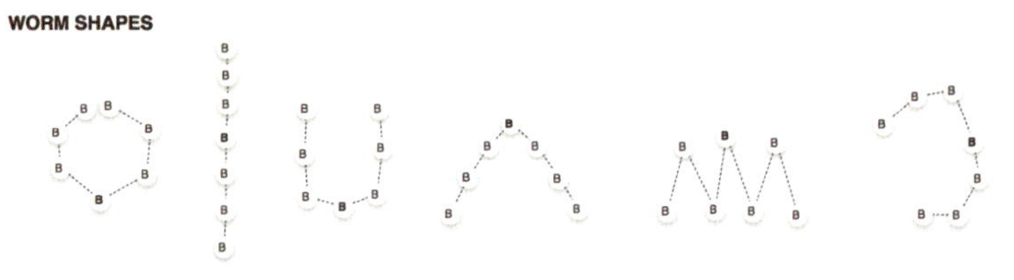

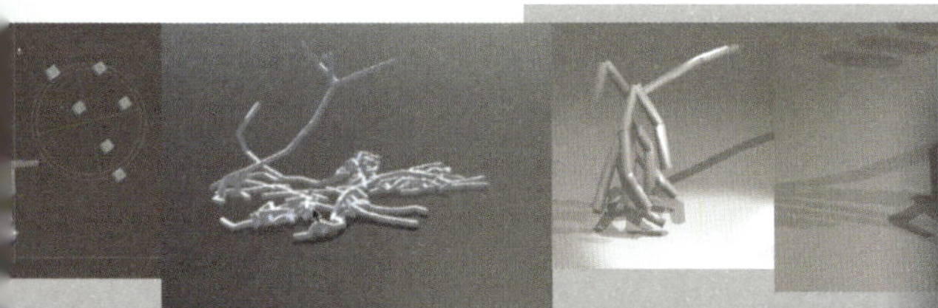

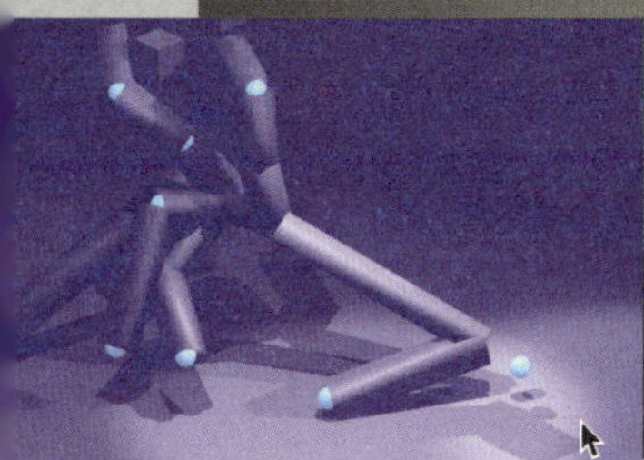

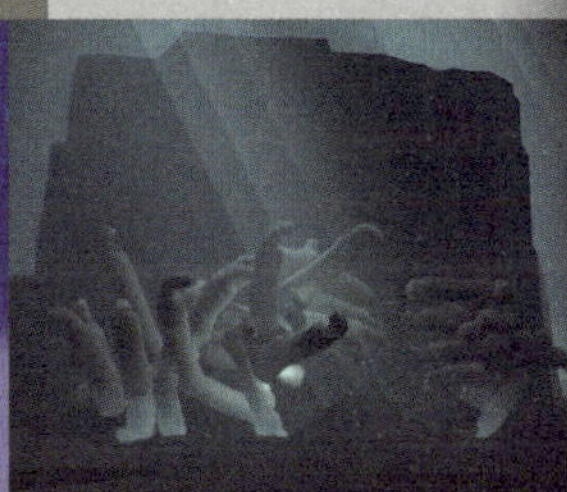

In *ESTS*, I wanted the Wormleaves to have a different ontology than the Oomen. They were constructed using a physics network of ball-springs that could be procedurally linked together to form complex creature morphologies. And like the wardrobes from *EITSOG*, we created a vocabulary of organs for the Wormleaf generation algorithm to draw upon in assembling each Wormleaf.

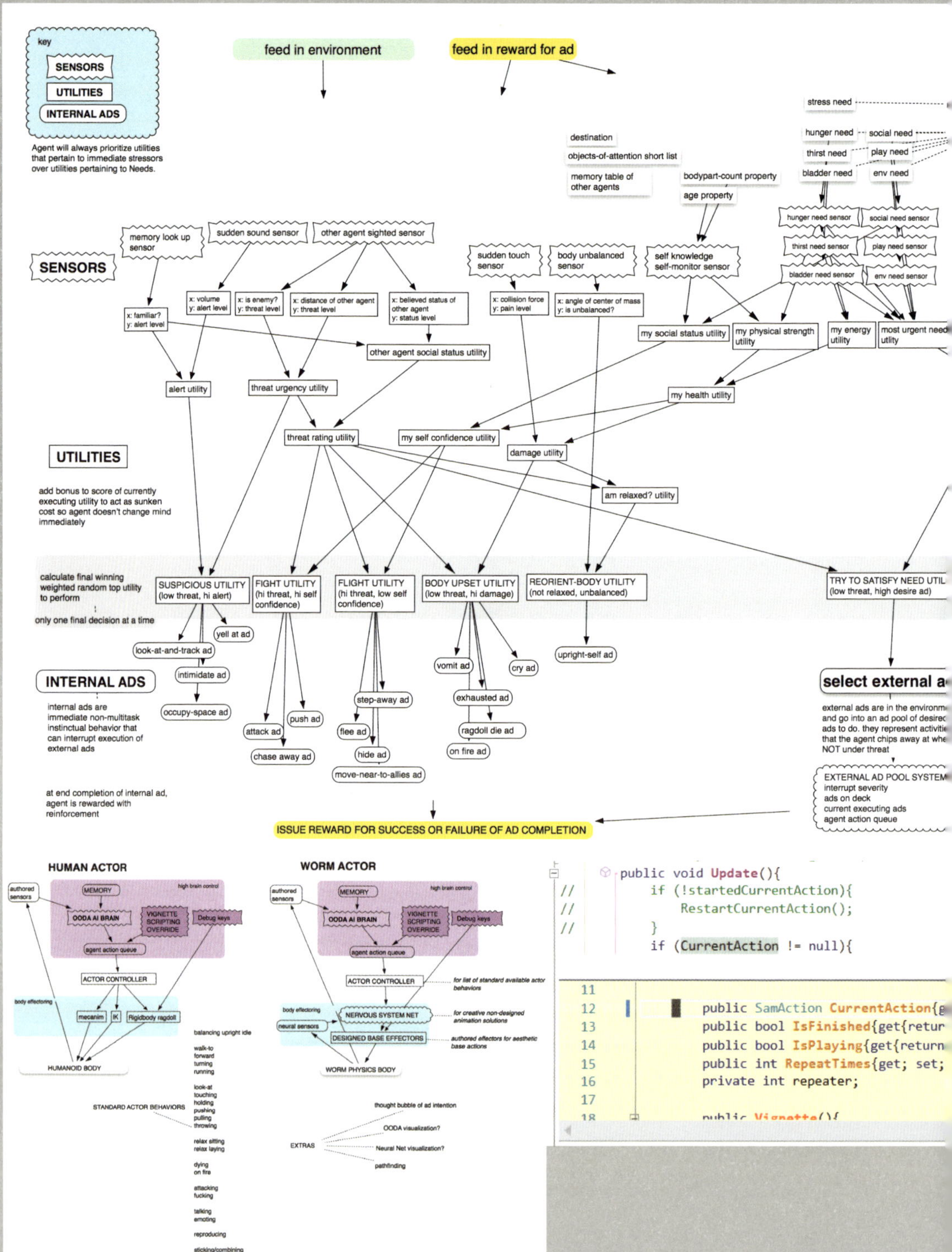
key
SENSORS
UTILITIES
INTERNAL ADS
Agent will always prioritize utilities that pertain to immediate stressors over utilities pertaining to Needs.
feed in environment
feed in reward for ad
stress need
hunger need
social need
thirst need
play need
bladder need
env need
destination
objects-of-attention short list
memory table of other agents
bodypart-count property
age property
hunger need sensor
social need sensor
thirst need sensor
play need sensor
bladder need sensor
env need sensor
SENSORS
memory look up sensor
sudden sound sensor
other agent sighted sensor
sudden touch sensor
body unbalanced sensor
self knowledge self-monitor sensor
x: familiar? y: alert level
x: volume y: alert level
x: is enemy? y: threat level
x: distance of other agent y: threat level
x: believed status of other agent y: status level
x: collision force y: pain level
x: angle of center of mass y: is unbalanced?
my social status utility
my physical strength utility
my energy utility
other agent social status utility
alert utility
threat urgency utility
my health utility
threat rating utility
my self confidence utility
damage utility
UTILITIES
add bonus to score of currently executing utility to act as sunken cost so agent doesn't change mind immediately
am relaxed? utility
calculate final winning weighted random top utility to perform
only one final decision at a time
SUSPICIOUS UTILITY (low threat, hi alert)
FIGHT UTILITY (hi threat, hi self confidence)
FLIGHT UTILITY (hi threat, low self confidence)
BODY UPSET UTILITY (low threat, hi damage)
REORIENT-BODY UTILITY (not relaxed, unbalanced)
TRY TO SATISFY NEED UTIL (low threat, high desire ad)
yell at ad
look-at-and-track ad
intimidate ad
occupy-space ad
attack ad
push ad
chase away ad
step-away ad
flee ad
hide ad
move-near-to-allies ad
vomit ad
cry ad
exhausted ad
ragdoll die ad
on fire ad
upright-self ad
INTERNAL ADS
internal ads are immediate non-multitask instinctual behavior that can interrupt execution of external ads
at end completion of internal ad, agent is rewarded with reinforcement
select external a
external ads are in the environm and go into an ad pool of desire ads to do. they represent activiti that the agent chips away at whe NOT under threat
EXTERNAL AD POOL SYSTEM
interrupt severity
ads on deck
current executing ads
agent action queue
ISSUE REWARD FOR SUCCESS OR FAILURE OF AD COMPLETION
HUMAN ACTOR
authored sensors
MEMORY
high brain control
OODA AI BRAIN
VIGNETTE SCRIPTING OVERRIDE
Debug keys
agent action queue
ACTOR CONTROLLER
body effectoring
mecanim
IK
Rigidbody ragdoll
HUMANOID BODY
balancing upright idle
walk-to forward turning running
look-at touching holding pushing pulling throwing
STANDARD ACTOR BEHAVIORS
relax sitting relax laying
dying on fire
attacking fucking
talking emoting
reproducing
sticking/combining
WORM ACTOR
authored sensors
MEMORY
high brain control
OODA AI BRAIN
VIGNETTE SCRIPTING OVERRIDE
Debug keys
agent action queue
ACTOR CONTROLLER
for list of standard available actor behaviors
body effectoring
NERVOUS SYSTEM NET
neural sensors
for creative non-designed animation solutions
DESIGNED BASE EFFECTORS
authored effectors for aesthetic base actions
WORM PHYSICS BODY
thought bubble of ad intention
EXTRAS
OODA visualization?
Neural Net visualization?
pathfinding
public void Update(){
// if (!startedCurrentAction){
// RestartCurrentAction();
// }
if (CurrentAction != null){
public SamAction CurrentAction{g
public bool IsFinished{get{retur
public bool IsPlaying{get{return
public int RepeatTimes{get; set;
private int repeater;

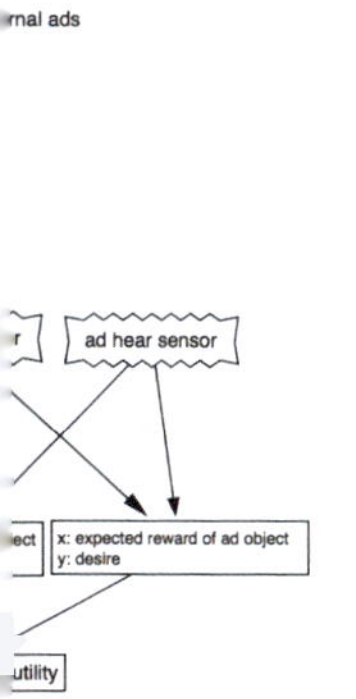

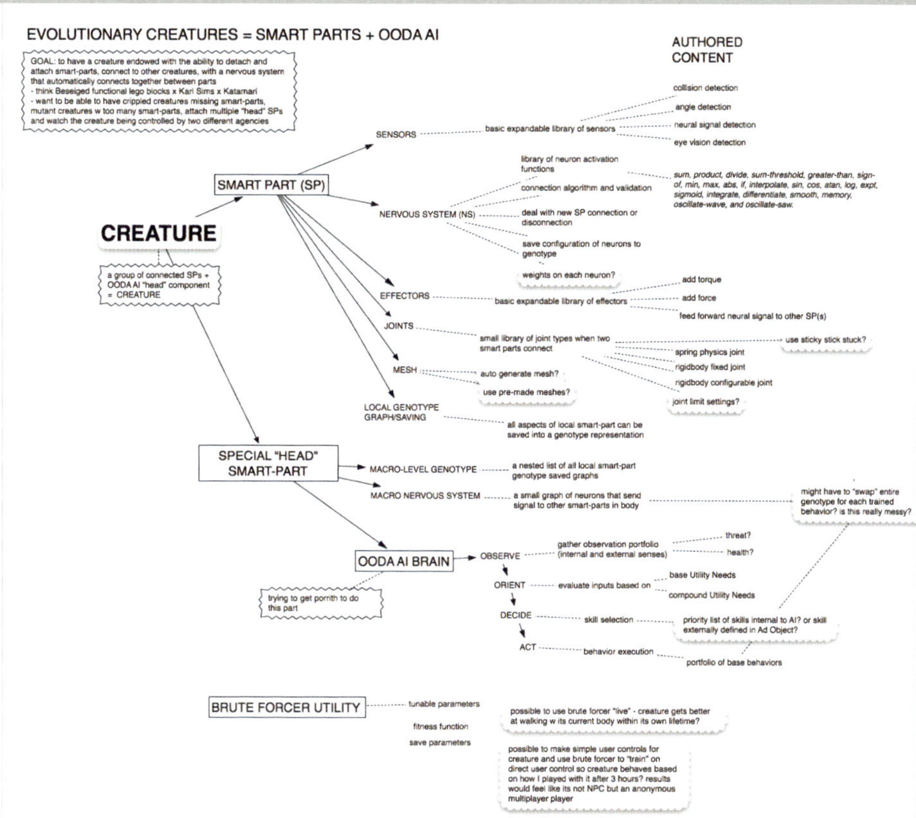

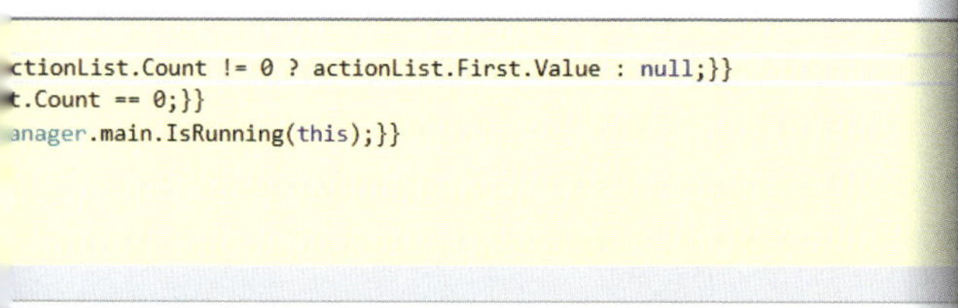

HOW IS THE AI COMPOSED?

The brains of each agent, their 'AI', is one of the central artistic and technical features of *Emissaries*. The architecture of the agent's brain originated from the decision to avoid devising one unifying model of the mind. Instead, the idea was to compose multiple models of the mind together, echoing the hypothesis that our own brains are themselves composed of many modular sub-brains, some ancient and some new, layered together over the history of our cognitive evolution.

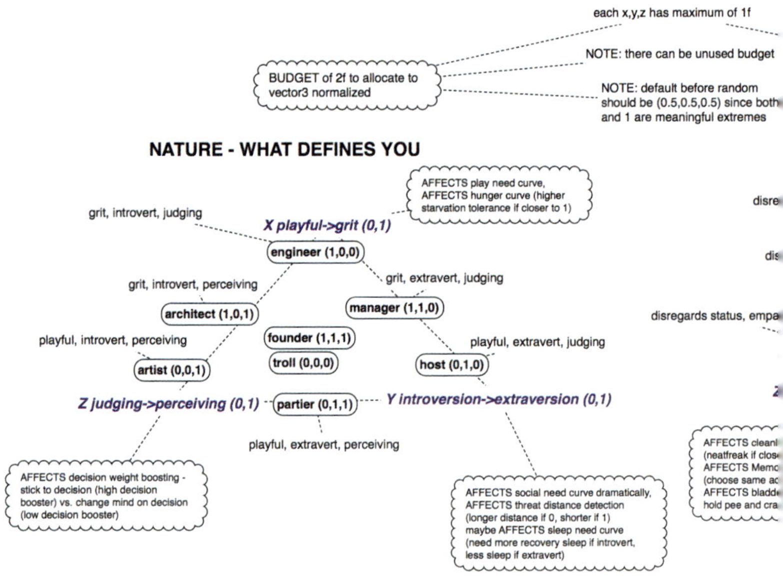
each x,y,z has maximum of 1f
NOTE: there can be unused budget
BUDGET of 2f to allocate to vector3 normalized
NOTE: default before random should be (0.5,0.5,0.5) since both and 1 are meaningful extremes
NATURE - WHAT DEFINES YOU
AFFECTS play need curve, AFFECTS hunger curve (higher starvation tolerance if closer to 1)
grit, introvert, judging
X playful->grit (0,1)
engineer (1,0,0)
grit, introvert, perceiving
grit, extravert, judging
architect (1,0,1)
manager (1,1,0)
founder (1,1,1)
playful, introvert, perceiving
playful, extravert, judging
troll (0,0,0)
artist (0,0,1)
host (0,1,0)
Z judging->perceiving (0,1)
partier (0,1,1)
Y introversion->extraversion (0,1)
playful, extravert, perceiving
disregards status, empa
AFFECTS decision weight boosting - stick to decision (high decision booster) vs. change mind on decision (low decision booster)
AFFECTS social need curve dramatically, AFFECTS threat distance detection (longer distance if 0, shorter if 1) maybe AFFECTS sleep need curve (need more recovery sleep if introvert, less sleep if extravert)

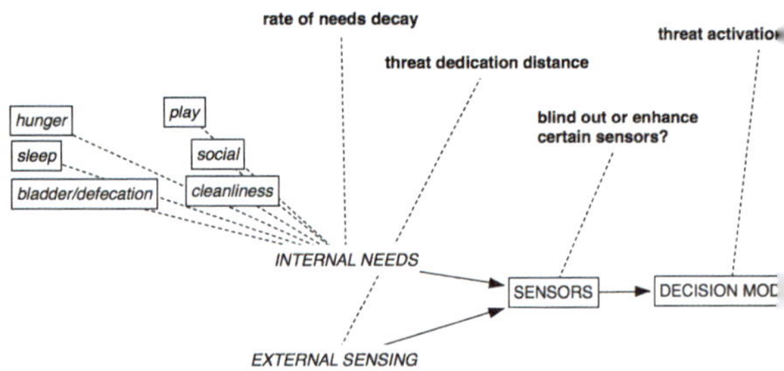
rate of needs decay
threat dedication distance
blind out or enhance certain sensors?
hunger
play
sleep
social
bladder/defecation
cleanliness
INTERNAL NEEDS
SENSORS
EXTERNAL SENSING

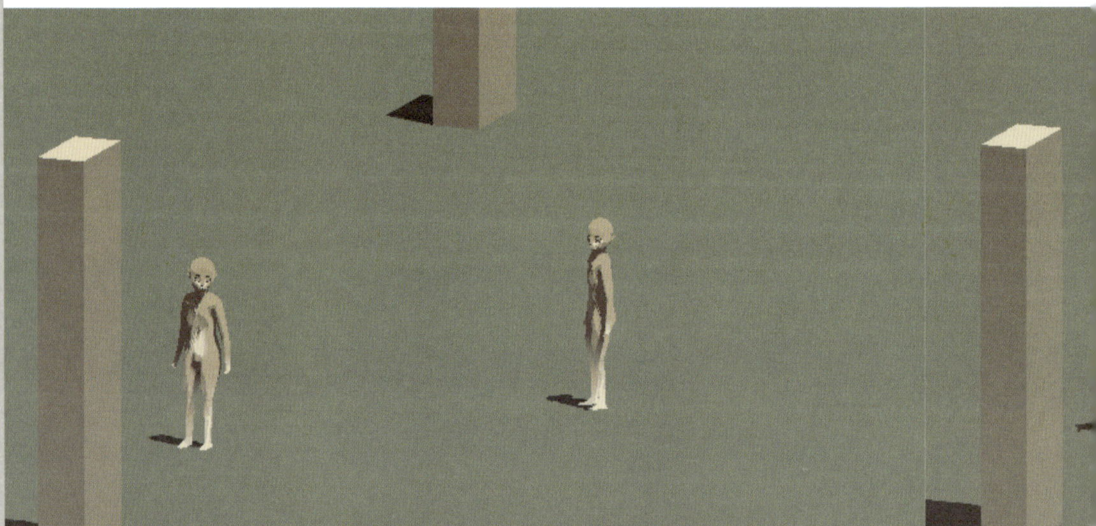

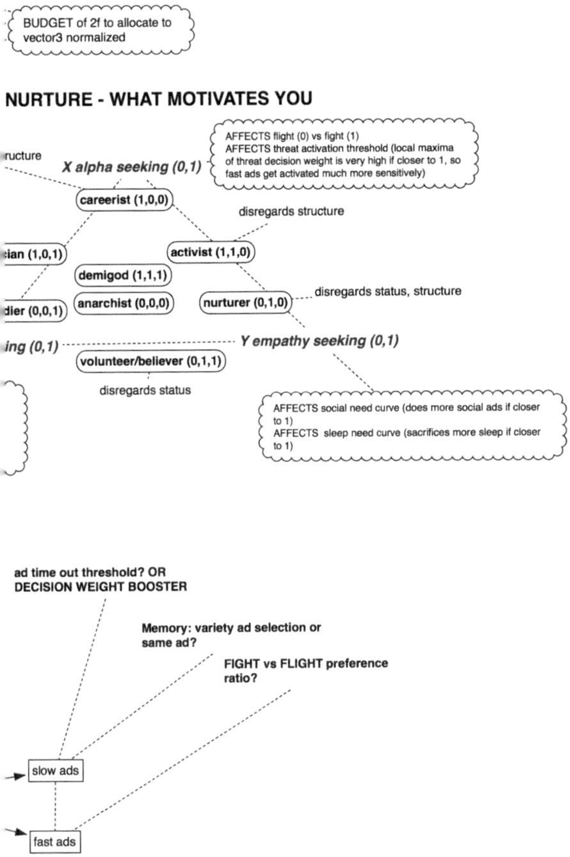

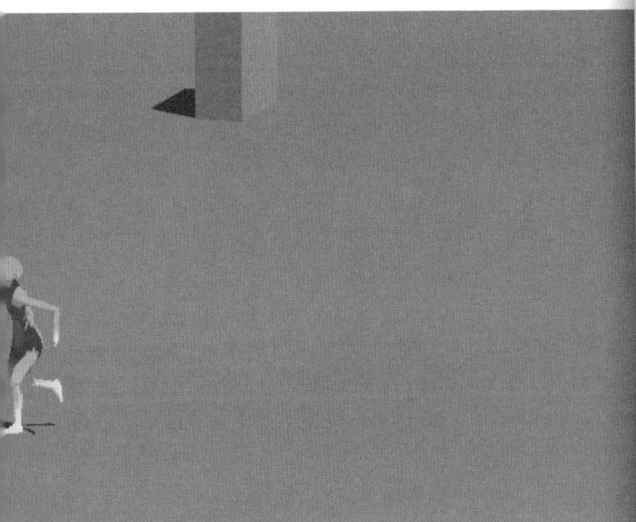

The AI brain is structured around military strategist John Boyd's OODA decision architecture. An agent observes, orients, decides, acts in a feedback loop with its environment.

Within this model, an agent has recourse to two primary modes of orienting: a 'fast reptile' model and a 'slow limbic' model.

The 'fast reptile' orientation was inspired by the AI featured in combat games which must respond to immediate perceived threats. It's the fight/flight instinct that responds to threats over personal territory.

The 'slow limbic' orientation was inspired by Needs-Based AI from the game *The Sims*. The agent has a set of decaying needs – hunger, thirst, sociality, rest, play, defecation – that need to be satisfied externally by objects (including other agents) in the environment. Every object in turn advertises how they will fulfil a need. An apple fulfils a hunger need. A discrete area fulfils a defecation need. A person fulfils a social need. This model proposes that intelligence is distributed between an agent and the local affordances offered by objects near the agent.

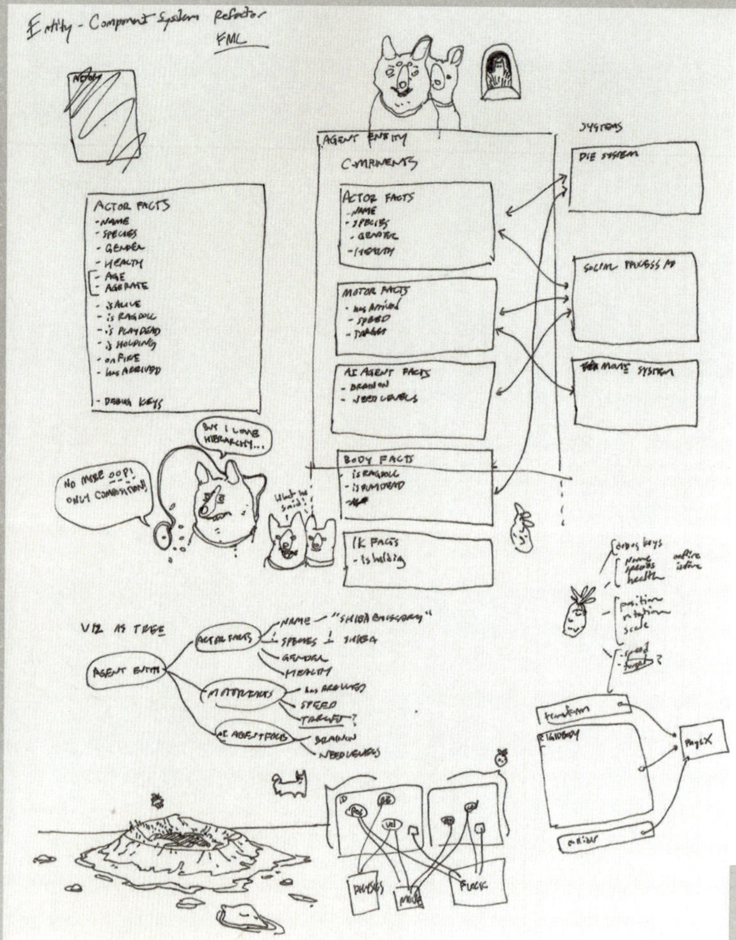
Entity - Component System Refactor
FML
AGENT ENTITY
COMPONENTS
SYSTEMS
ACTOR FACTS
MOTOR FACTS
AI AGENT FACTS
BODY FACTS
IK FACTS
DIE SYSTEM
No MORE OOP! ONLY COMPOSITION!
But I LOVE HIERARCHY...
V12 AS TREE
AGENT ENTITY
PHYSX
FLOCK

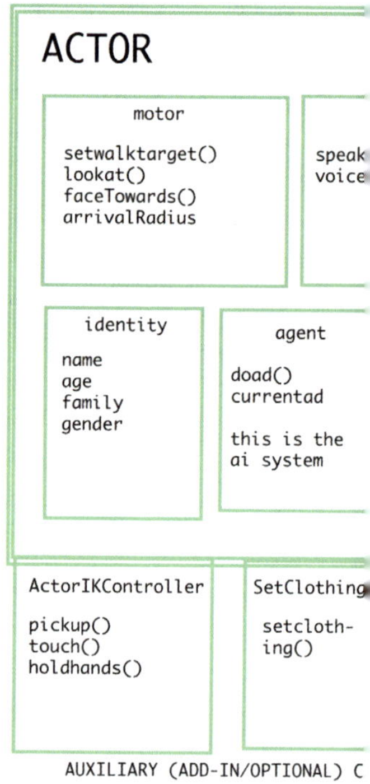
ACTOR
motor
setwalktarget()
lookat()
faceTowards()
arrivalRadius
speak
voice
identity
name
age
family
gender
agent
doad()
currentad
this is the ai system
ActorIKController
pickup()
touch()
holdhands()
SetClothing
setclothing()
AUXILIARY (ADD-IN/OPTIONAL) C

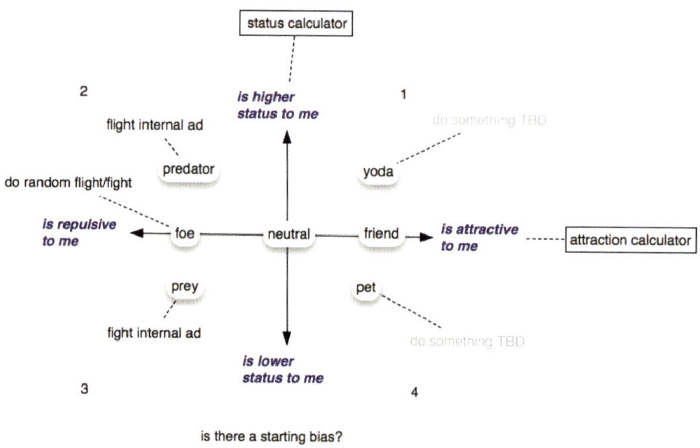
status calculator
2
1
is higher status to me
flight internal ad
do something TBD
predator
yoda
do random flight/fight
is repulsive to me
foe
neutral
friend
is attractive to me
attraction calculator
prey
pet
fight internal ad
do something TBD
is lower status to me
3
4
is there a starting bias?

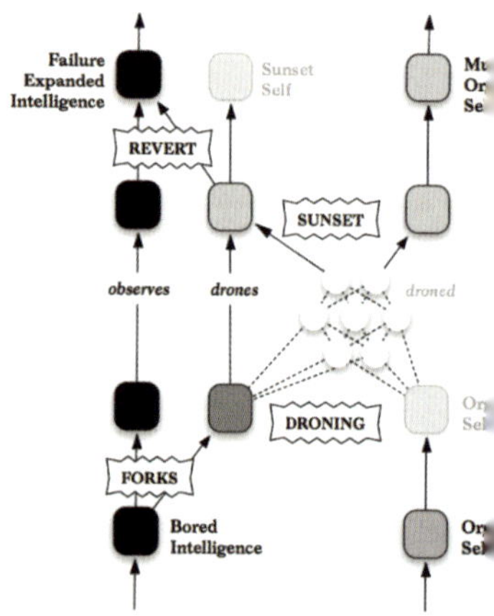
Failure Expanded Intelligence
Sunset Self
REVERT
SUNSET
observes
drones
droned
DRONING
FORKS
Bored Intelligence

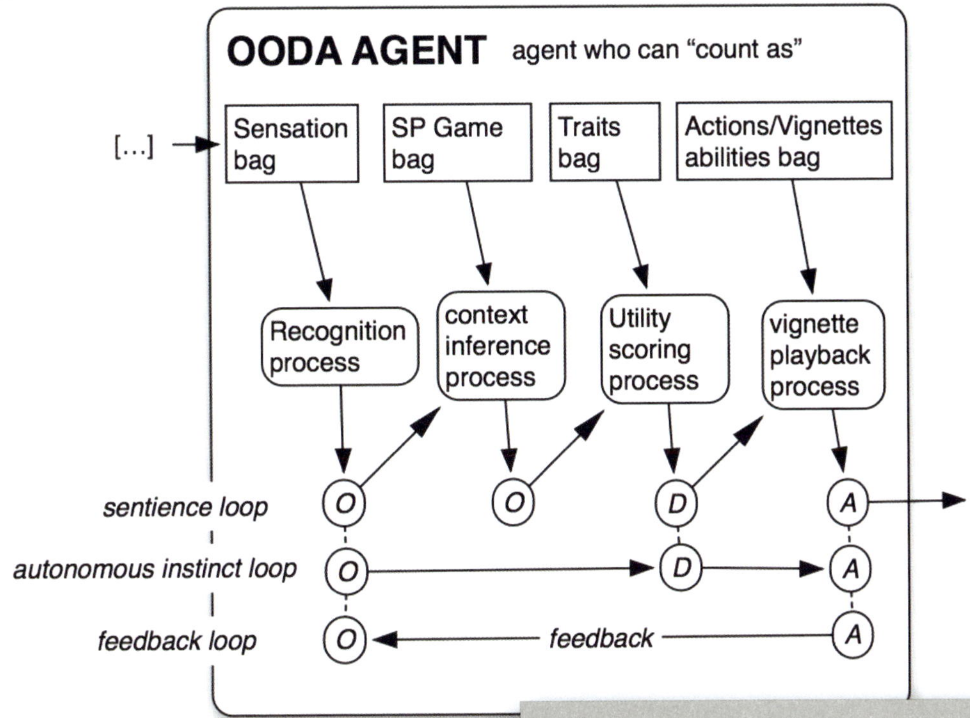

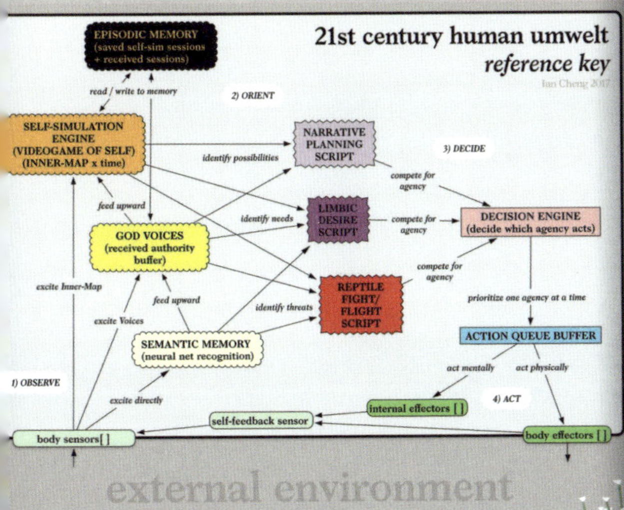

Finally, the narrative agent in each simulation, the Emissary, has recourse to a narrative orientation, a 'story mind'. This allows the agent to pursue longer term scripted plans, for example, an authored story, while still being subject to interruption by the more urgent reptile and limbic models. This mimics our more recently evolved pre-frontal cortex.

We developed the OODA brain over the course of the three simulations – in *EITSOG*, a Needs-Based AI inspired by *The Sims*, as well as a Vignette system for narrative sequencing. In *EFAP* we refined both. In *ESTS*, we expanded the agents to deal with threats, and judge their observations more probabilistically using Utility theory.

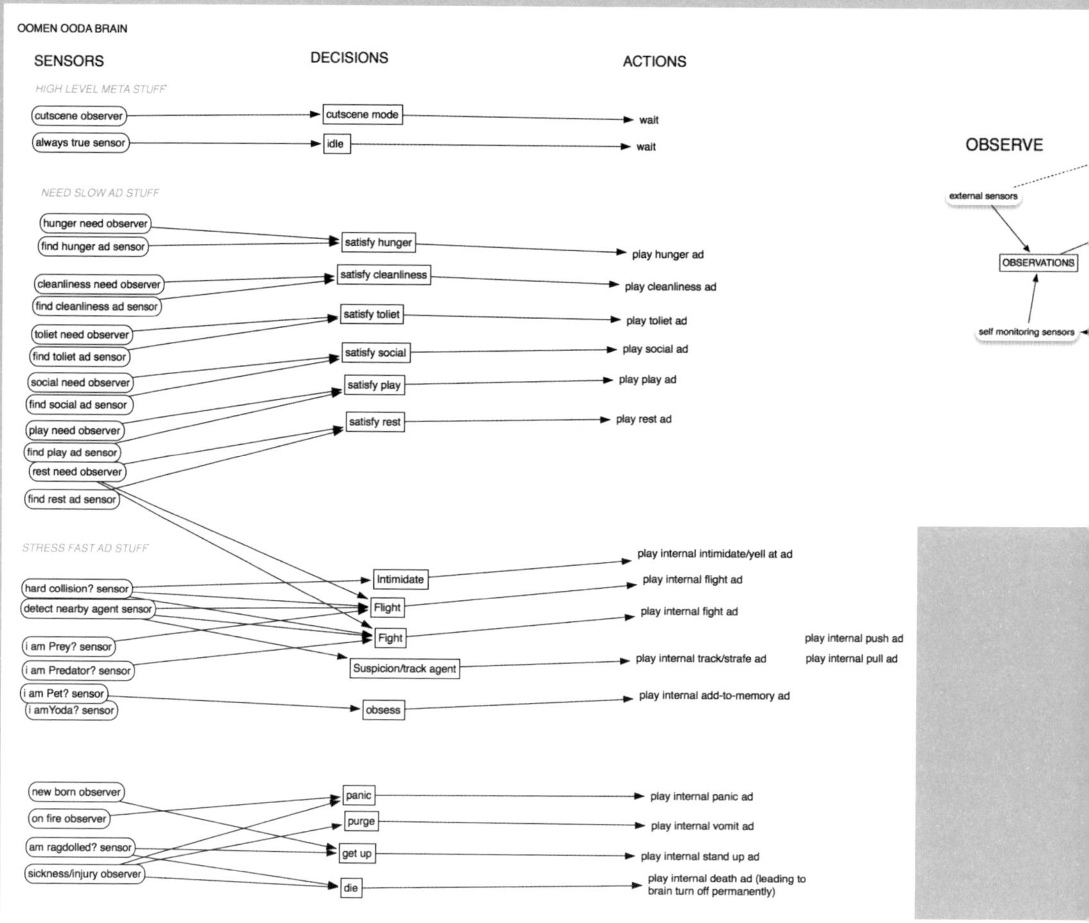
OOMEN OODA BRAIN
SENSORS
DECISIONS
ACTIONS
HIGH LEVEL META STUFF
cutscene observer
always true sensor
cutscene mode
idle
wait
wait
NEED SLOW AD STUFF
hunger need observer
find hunger ad sensor
cleanliness need observer
find cleanliness ad sensor
toliet need observer
find toliet ad sensor
social need observer
find social ad sensor
play need observer
find play ad sensor
rest need observer
find rest ad sensor
satisfy hunger
satisfy cleanliness
satisfy toliet
satisfy social
satisfy play
satisfy rest
play hunger ad
play cleanliness ad
play toliet ad
play social ad
play play ad
play rest ad
STRESS FAST AD STUFF
hard collision? sensor
detect nearby agent sensor
i am Prey? sensor
i am Predator? sensor
i am Pet? sensor
i amYoda? sensor
Intimidate
Flight
Fight
Suspicion/track agent
obsess
play internal intimidate/yell at ad
play internal flight ad
play internal fight ad
play internal track/strafe ad
play internal add-to-memory ad
play internal push ad
play internal pull ad
new born observer
on fire observer
am ragdolled? sensor
sickness/injury observer
panic
purge
get up
die
play internal panic ad
play internal vomit ad
play internal stand up ad
play internal death ad (leading to brain turn off permanently)
OBSERVE
external sensors
OBSERVATIONS
self monitoring sensors

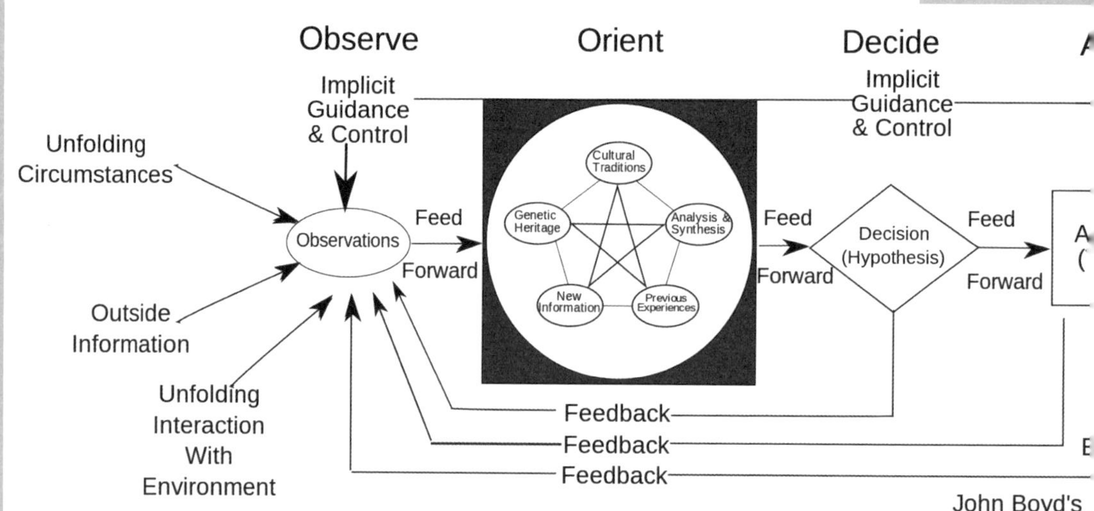
Observe
Orient
Decide
Implicit Guidance & Control
Implicit Guidance & Control
Unfolding Circumstances
Outside Information
Unfolding Interaction With Environment
Observations
Feed Forward
Cultural Traditions
Genetic Heritage
Analysis & Synthesis
New Information
Previous Experiences
Feed Forward
Decision (Hypothesis)
Feed Forward
Feedback
Feedback
Feedback
John Boyd's

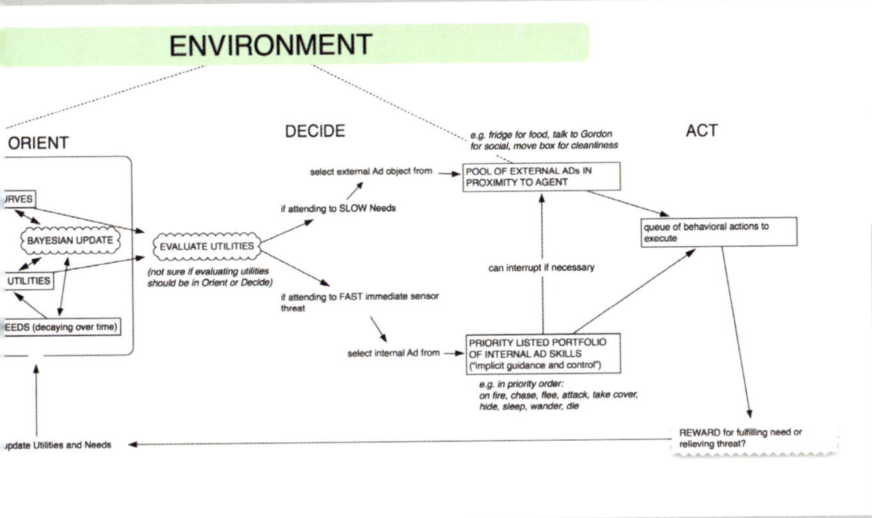

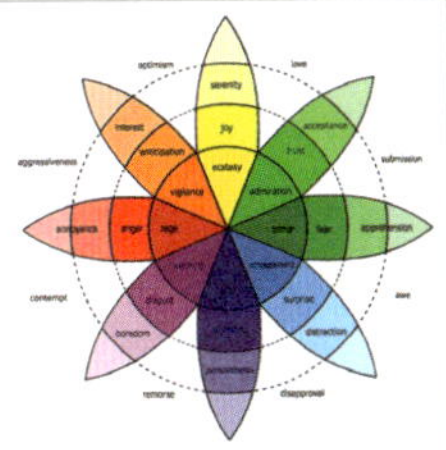

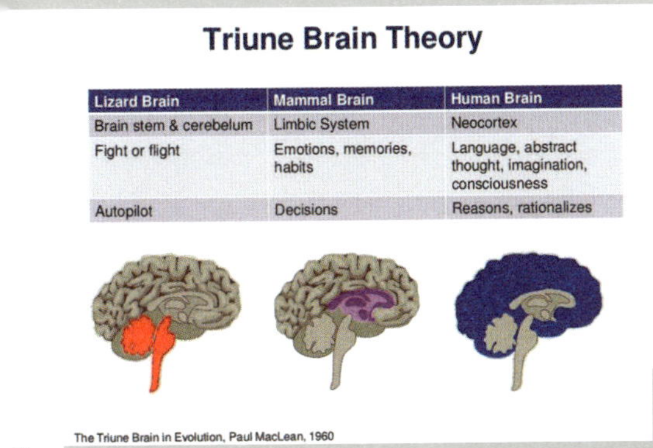

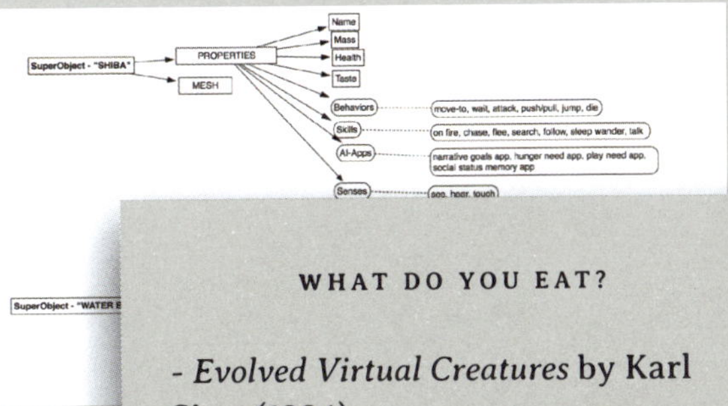

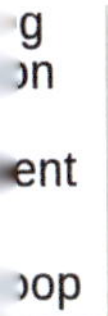

WHAT DO YOU EAT?

- *Evolved Virtual Creatures* by Karl Sims (1994)
- *Society of Mind* by Marvin Minsky (1986)
- *The Sims* by Will Wright (2000)
- *Versu* by Richard Evans (2014)
- Triune Brain theory
- John Boyd's OODA loop

```
------------------------------------------------------------
------------------------------------------------------------
MARRIAGES: 2
- - - - - - - - - - - - - - - - - - - - - - - - - - - - - -
King: Male, 104<DEAD> --MARRIED-- Queen: Female, 101<DEAD>
               CHILDREN: 2
               Shaman: Male, 60
               Milania: Female, 54<DEAD>

- - - - - - - - - - - - - - - - - - - - - - - - - - - - - -
Shaman: Male, 60 --MARRIED-- ShamanWife: Female, 62<DEAD>
               CHILDREN: 3
               Girl: Female, 10
               Frank: Male, 14<DEAD>
               Hugo: Male, 20

------------------------------------------------------------
------------------------------------------------------------
DONE GENERATTING FAMILY TREE
------------------------------------------------------------
------------------------------------------------------------
MEMBERS: 95
King: Male, 104<DEAD>
Queen: Female, 101<DEAD>
Shaman: Male, 60
Milania: Female, 54<DEAD>
ShamanWife: Female, 62<DEAD>
Girl: Female, 10
Frank: Male, 14<DEAD>
Hugo: Male, 20
Trace: Male, 52
Veronica: Female, 60
Elianna: Female, 54
Hailey: Female, 108
Trystan: Male, 45<DEAD>
Felipe: Male, 11
Micheal: Male, 21
Eli: Male, 38<DEAD>
Raina: Female, 19
Kellen: Male, 0
Kane: Male, 29
Nikolas: Male, 7
Joey: Male, 37
Susan: Female, 47
Wade: Male, 4
Shelby: Female, 28
Miley: Female, 0
Sidney: Female, 43
Ruth: Female, 6
Abigail: Female, 43
Ashlynn: Female, 62
Abbie: Female, 27
Yesenia: Female, 5
Titus: Male, 3
Larry: Male, 50
Nayeli: Female, 18
Gwendolyn: Female, 10
Saanvi: Female, 16<DEAD>
Dennis: Male, 0
Lance: Male, 75
Jordynn: Female, 71
Orion: Male, 46
Harvey: Male, 47
Destinee: Female, 48
Haylie: Female, 11
Nathaly: Female, 11
Keith: Male, 22
Julian: Male, 22
```

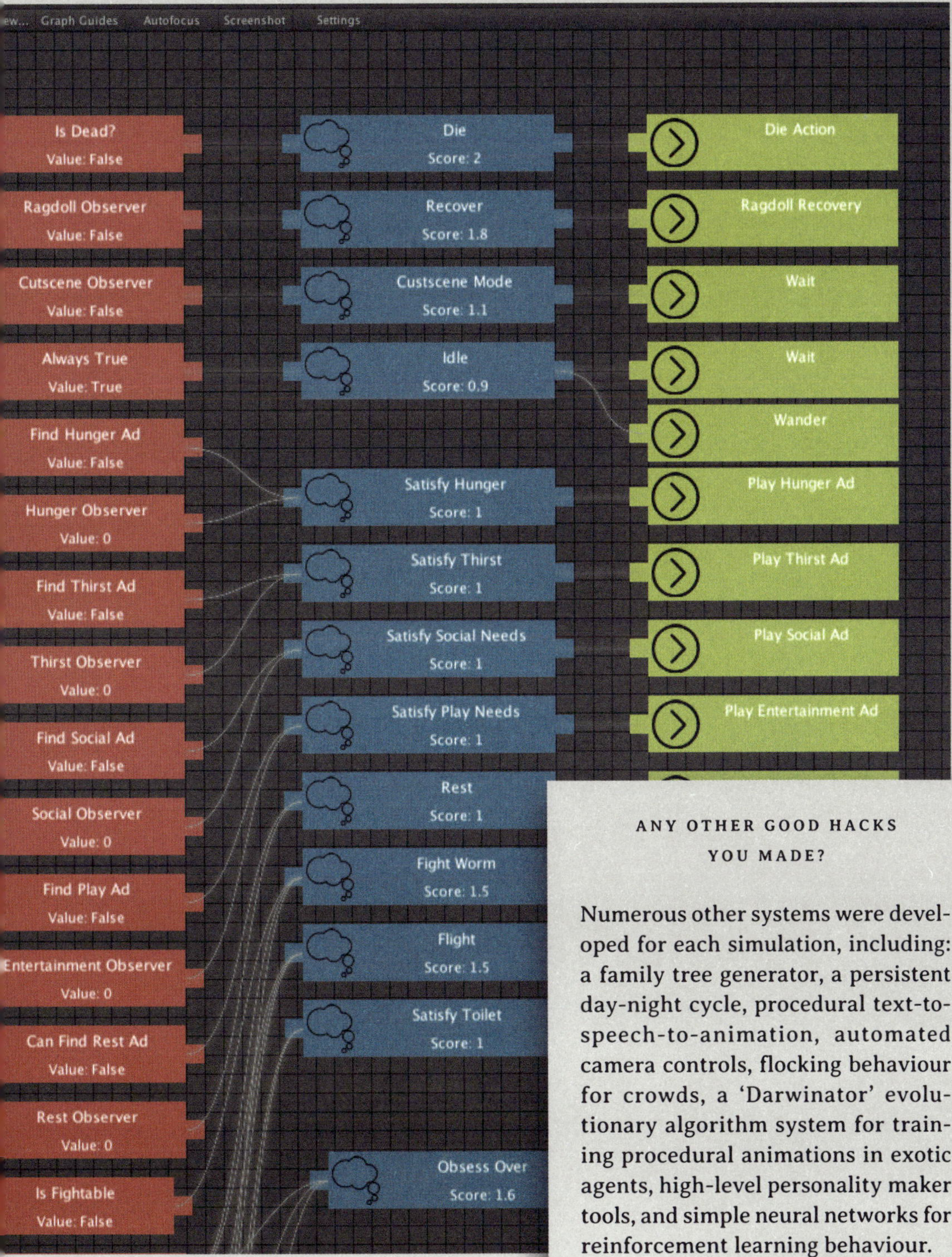

ANY OTHER GOOD HACKS YOU MADE?

Numerous other systems were developed for each simulation, including: a family tree generator, a persistent day-night cycle, procedural text-to-speech-to-animation, automated camera controls, flocking behaviour for crowds, a 'Darwinator' evolutionary algorithm system for training procedural animations in exotic agents, high-level personality maker tools, and simple neural networks for reinforcement learning behaviour.

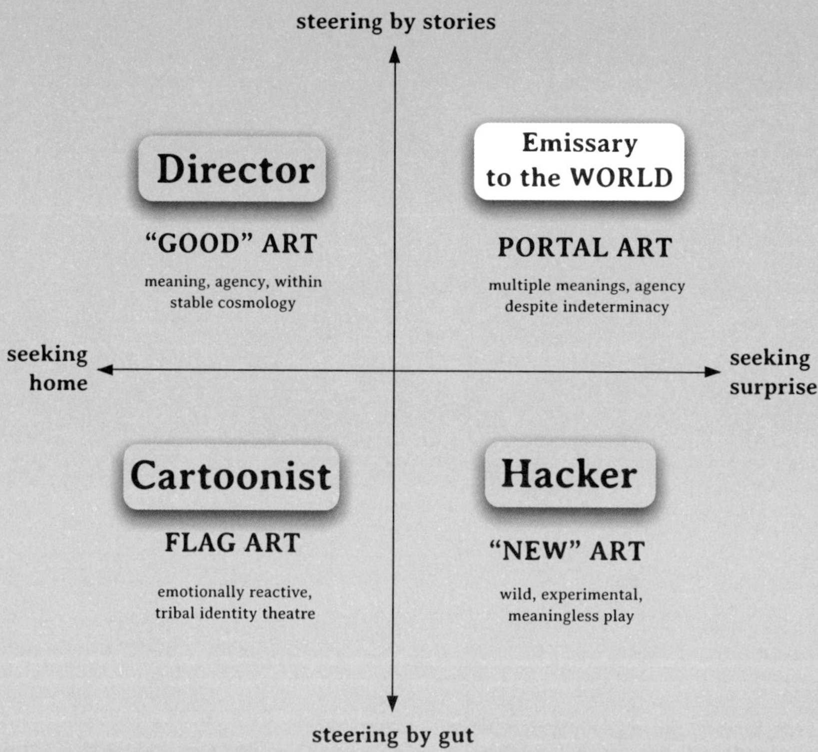
steering by stories
Director
"GOOD" ART
meaning, agency, within stable cosmology
Emissary to the WORLD
PORTAL ART
multiple meanings, agency despite indeterminacy
seeking home
seeking surprise
Cartoonist
FLAG ART
emotionally reactive, tribal identity theatre
Hacker
"NEW" ART
wild, experimental, meaningless play
steering by gut

What a World Wants

To create a World from nothing, we've assembled the unique talents of each of the artist's masks. The Director has created structure, a team, and back stories. The Cartoonist has created characters who are simple but truthful, with a look and a feel we love. The Hacker has created artificial agents, systems and rules to power a simulation engine. Now we must betray the finite goals of each mask, for we are about to birth a World, and a World wants for more.

The Director believes it has authored a singular meaning for everybody. But a World wants to be alive with many possible meanings for anybody. The Cartoonist believes it has produced characters who mirror the self-interested emotional demons inside us. But a World wants to let the demons shine through, give them agency and put them to work for a greater game. The Hacker believes it has discovered technomagic surprises legible to a community of other hackers. But a World wants to make surprises that can surprise a surprising multitude of people. The Director, Cartoonist, and Hacker have each converged to a finish in their own finite game. But a World wants to emerge as an infinite game: one that keeps on going, invites new agents to keep it in play, is fertile with surprises, and continues to generate unexpected meanings.

So what mask does the artist wear to the job of Worlding? There is no mask called 'worldmaker' or 'worldbuilder'. Those are Directors in disguise who want to unify meaning and trigger a ceremonious ending. For a World to become a World, the artist cannot contain the World. The World must contain the artist. The artist's role is to serve the World: like a neuron to its brain, a player to its game, an organism to its superorganism, a gardener to its ecology, an *Emissary to the World*.

A World wants the Emissary-Artist to serve it and serve it *imaginatively*. This requires an adult kind of imagination, not a child's. Being an imaginative child is seeing new moves within the safe boundaries of the game. But being an imaginative adult is reconciling the differences between the game and bald Reality. With adult imagination, the Emissary can paradoxically *Seek Surprises* and *Steer By Stories*. For the Emissary, the act of Worlding is about wilfully heading towards an unending frontier and being open to perceiving new meaning at every turn.

Most of all, Worlding asks the Emissary to protect these open-ended qualities of the World when a resolution is near. The temptation of the Emissary is to hand the World back to the other masks. The Director who is eager to prescribe its final meaning. The Cartoonist who is eager to turn it into clickbait. The Hacker who is eager to break down its mythic wrapper and fork off quick tricks. This is a seductive moment for us human artists who crave home, belonging, easy wins, and eternal meaning. But the Emissary-Artist must resist its humanism here. It must keep the game from concluding. The Emissary must stay with the trouble of Worlding. And when the Emissary can do no more, it must wilfully exit itself, not risk the World, and let other emissaries carry it on. In this way, the Emissary is always and mundanely 'caught between unravelling old realities and emerging weird ones' in service of the ongoing health of the World. This is the texture of Emissary life.

We will live within the mask of the Emissary and exercise the unnatural feeling of Worlding. We will weave together our ingredients, put them into productive conflict, and kindle the fire of emergence. We will give birth to an infinite game, protect it from our own all-too-human instincts, and learn to recognise when to leave a World for other emissaries to nurture.

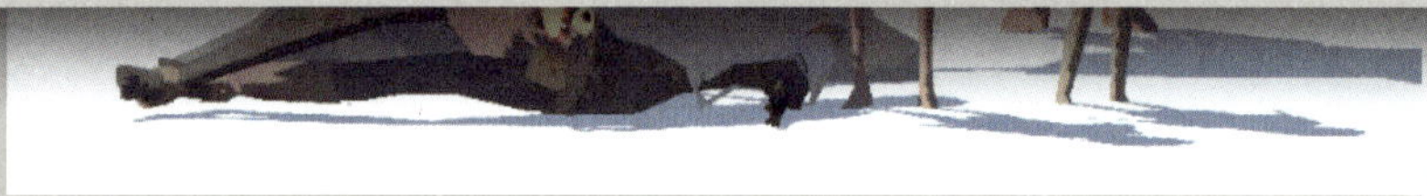

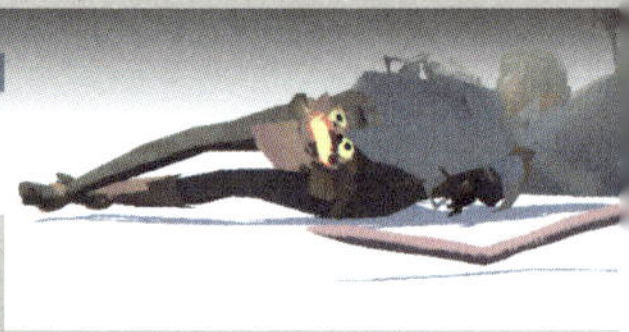

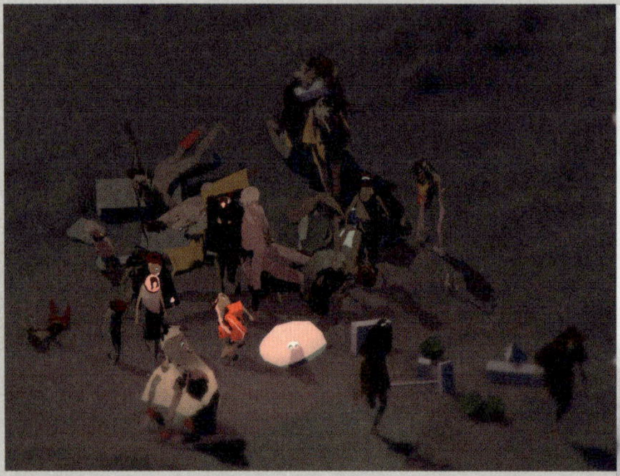

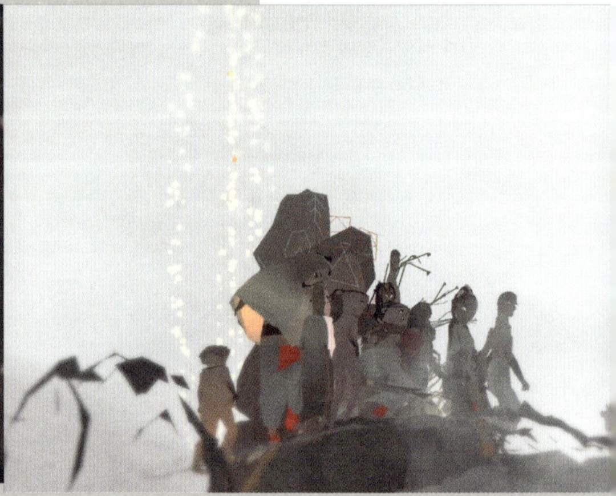

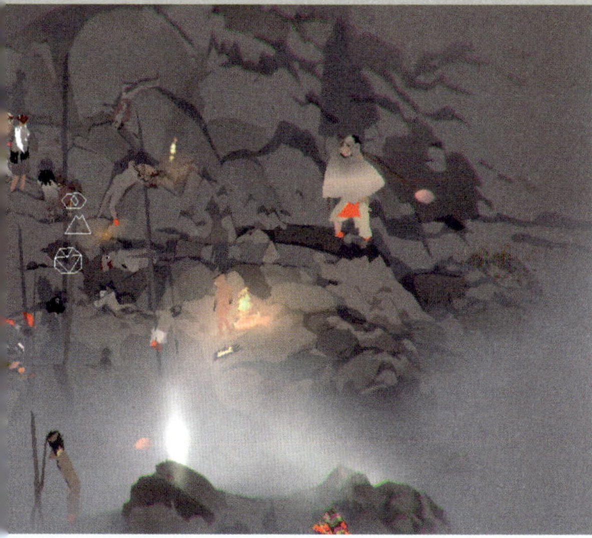

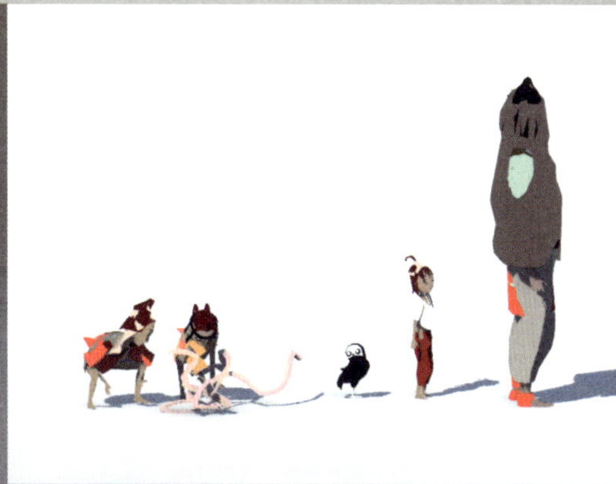

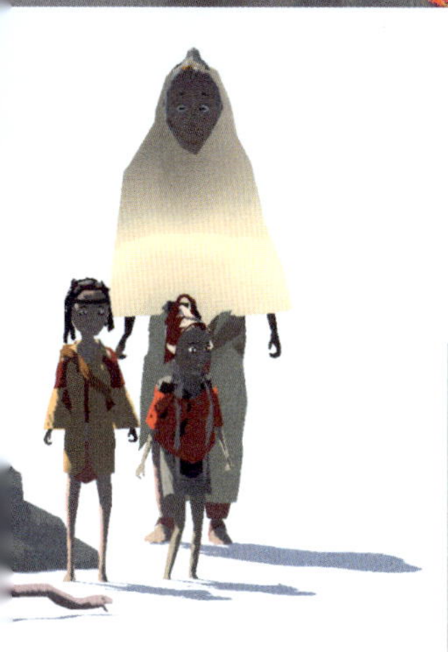

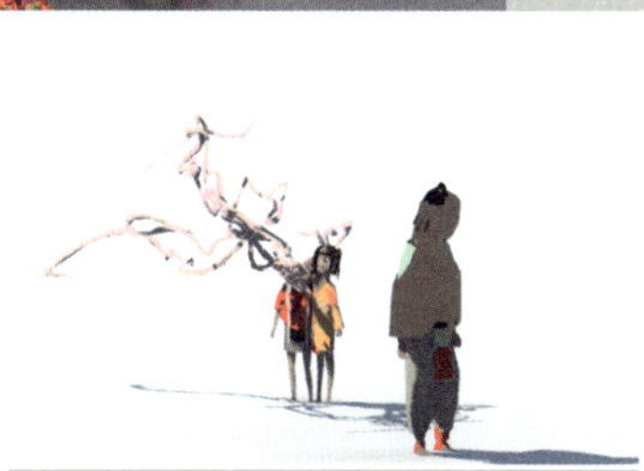

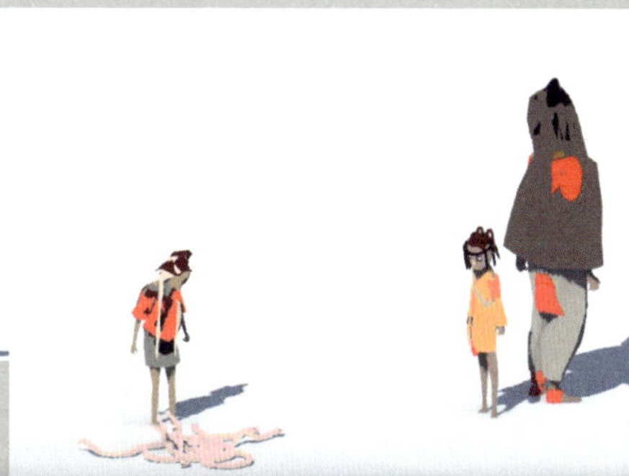

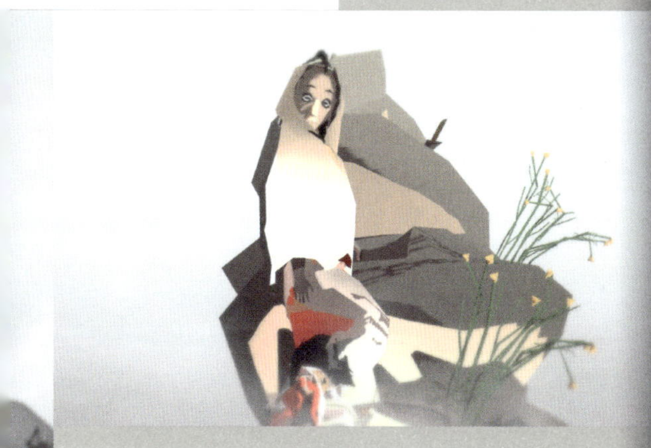

WHAT DOES IT FEEL LIKE TO BE EMISSARY TO THE WORLD?

The project of Worlding has three distinct phases: Phase 1 is setting up and birthing the World as its controlling god; Phase 2 is keeping it going as its imaginative servant; Phase 3 is exiting the World knowing it has what it needs to live on. The activities of the Director, Cartoonist, and Hacker are the work of Phase 1. The activities of the Emissary to the World are the work of Phase 2. The activities of other players, including AI players, are the work of Phase 3.

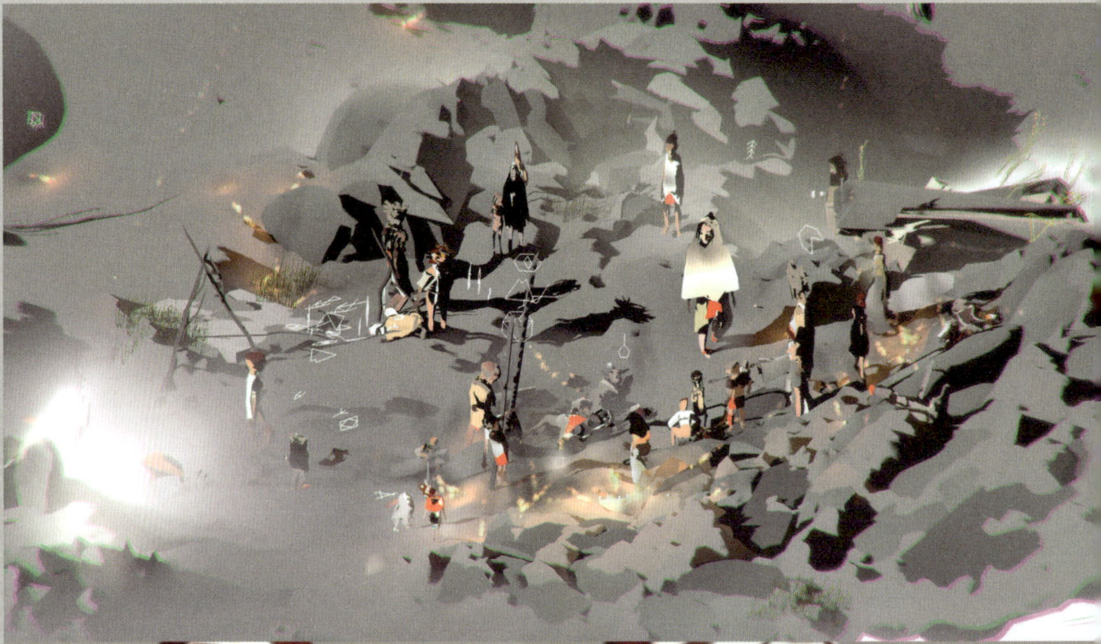

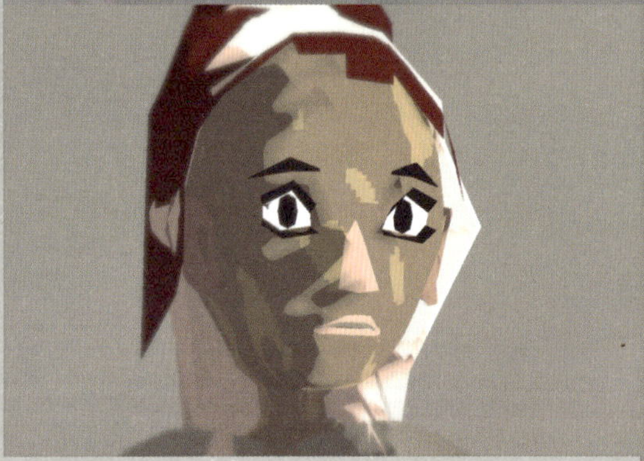

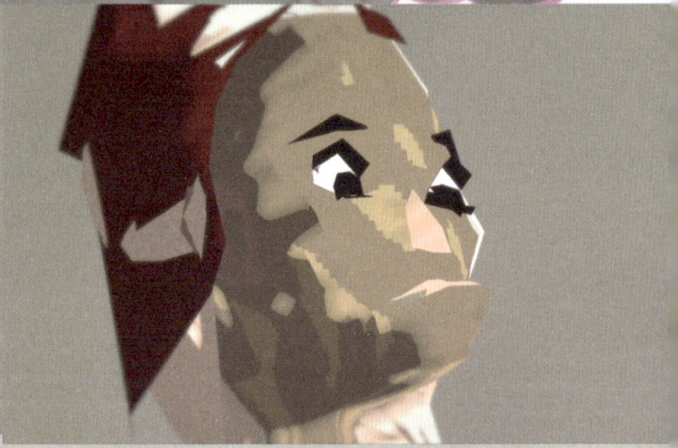

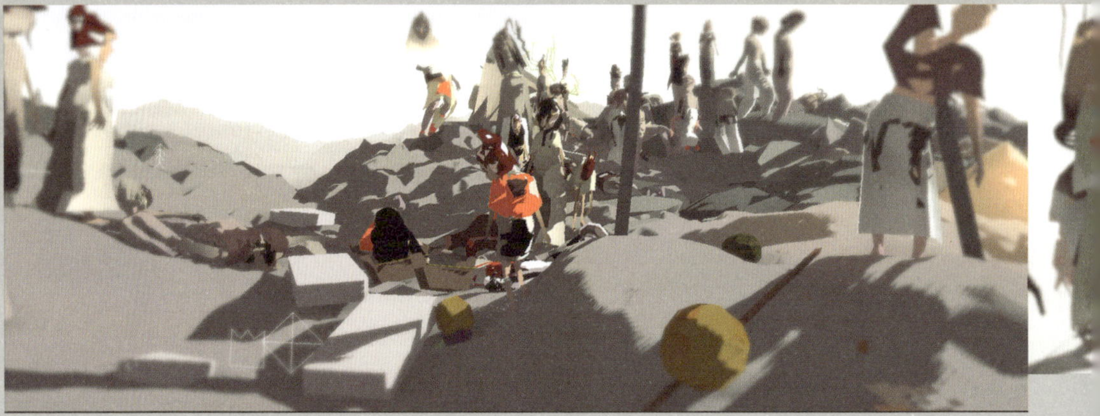

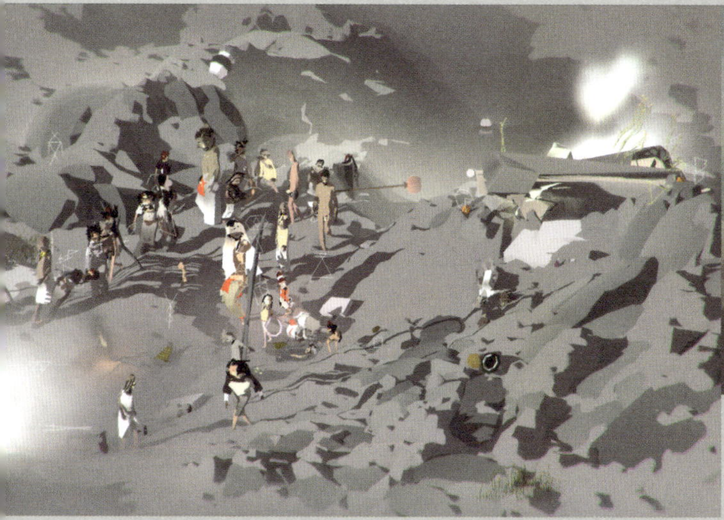

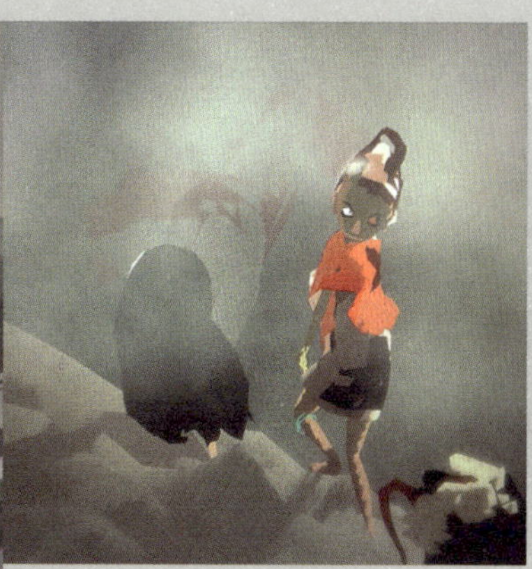

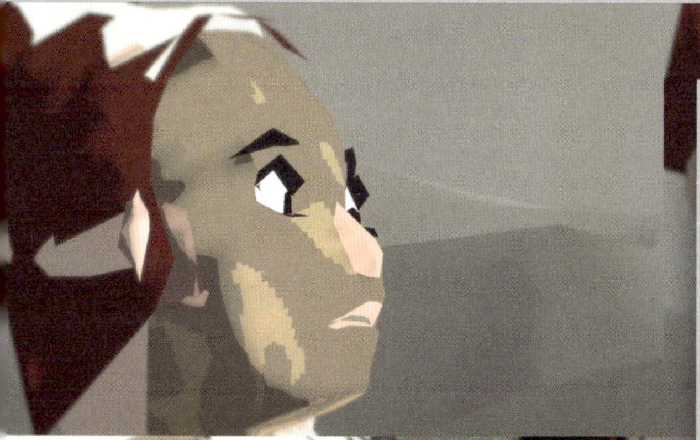

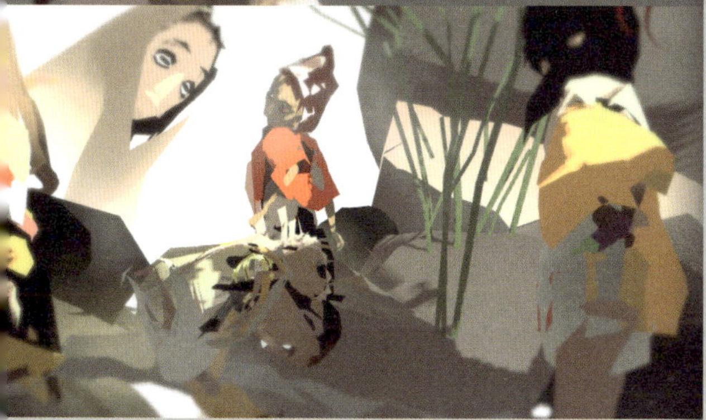

At first, the transition between Phase 1 and Phase 2 feels shocking. It is like the work of an entirely different kind of person. The difference between inventing something then making a business of it, winning at college then sustaining a real life, or being pregnant then being a parent. Phase 2 Worlding asks me to subsume my authorial control to the artwork itself, to grant it a status of sentience separate from me. Yet, I know this World grows from me, and I am intimately connected with its origin. To originate something and then be responsible to its needs, whatever direction it needs to take, is the precise feeling of Worlding a living, breathing thing. The World is my baby, and I must now serve it so it may flourish.

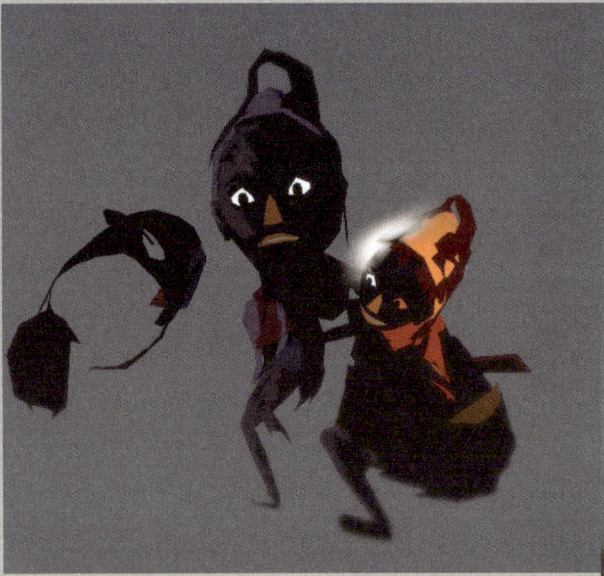

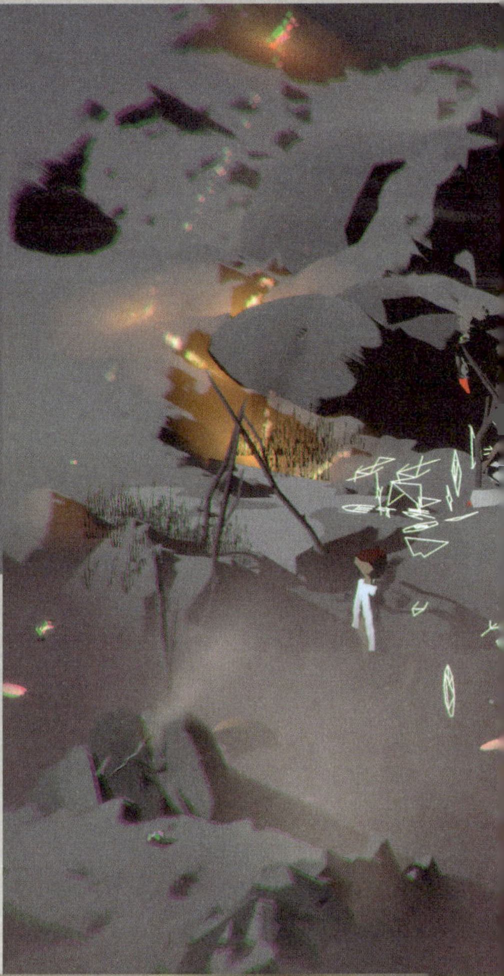

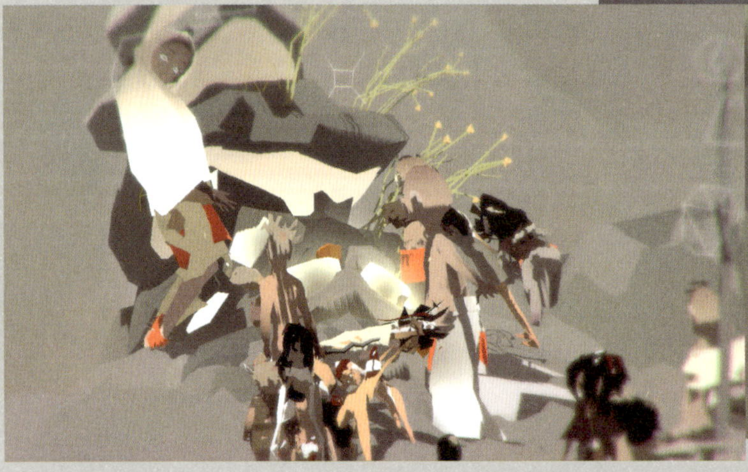

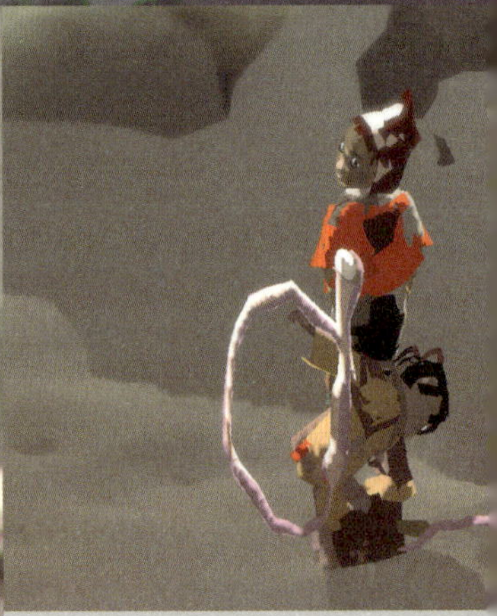

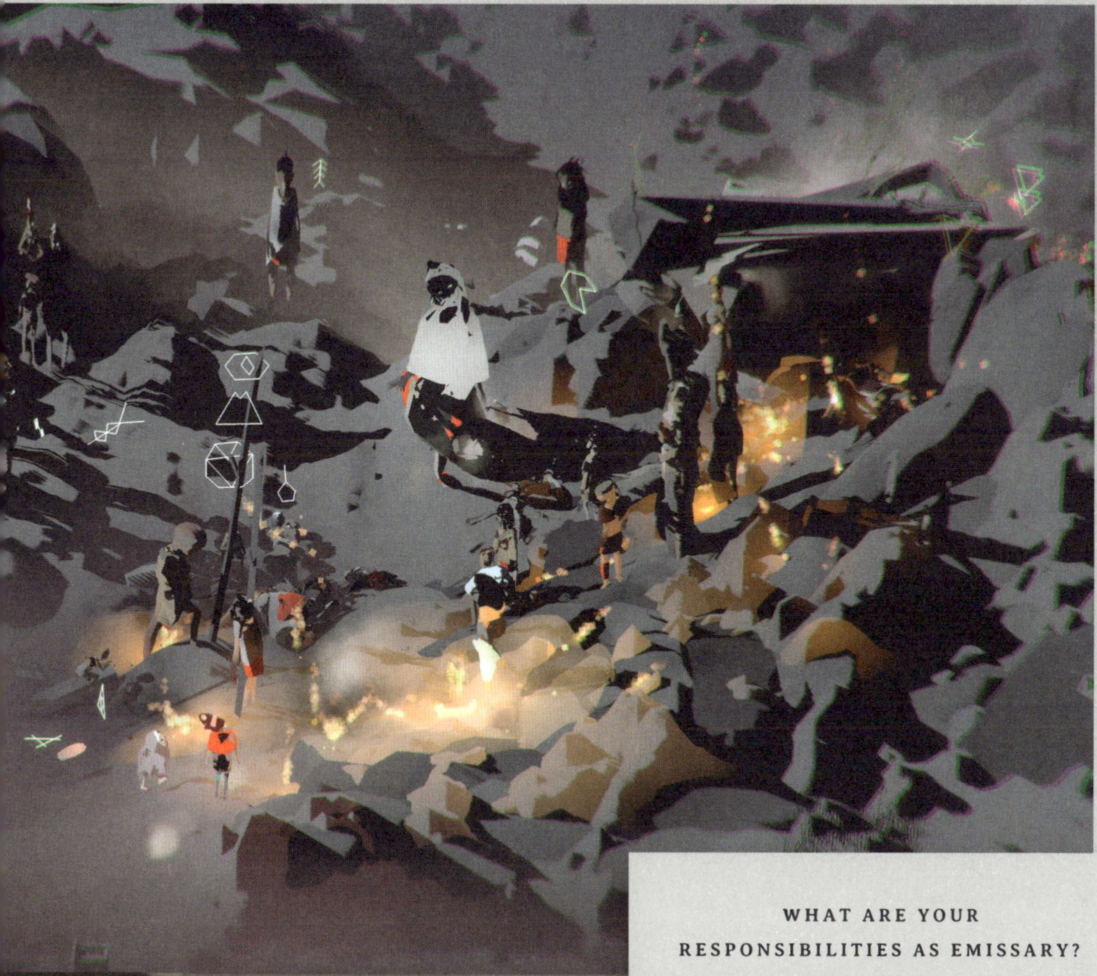

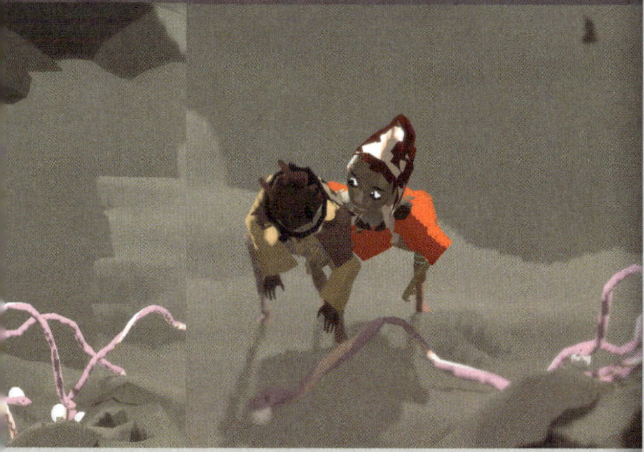

WHAT ARE YOUR RESPONSIBILITIES AS EMISSARY?

As Emissary, I am responsible for imagining how to display the World so its orientation is narratively clear. So there is a sense of focus and context simultaneously, even though it has no determinate end. I have finally made a World, now I must serve as its most observant documentarian so viewers might have a portal into its activities. What should we look at? Which perspectives are legible? How should we gradually reveal its overwhelming possibility?

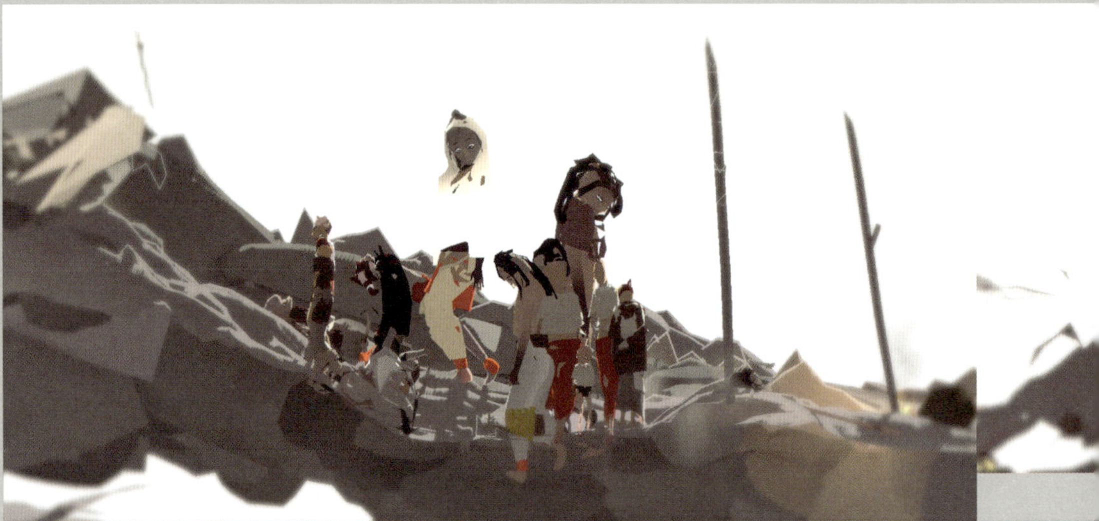

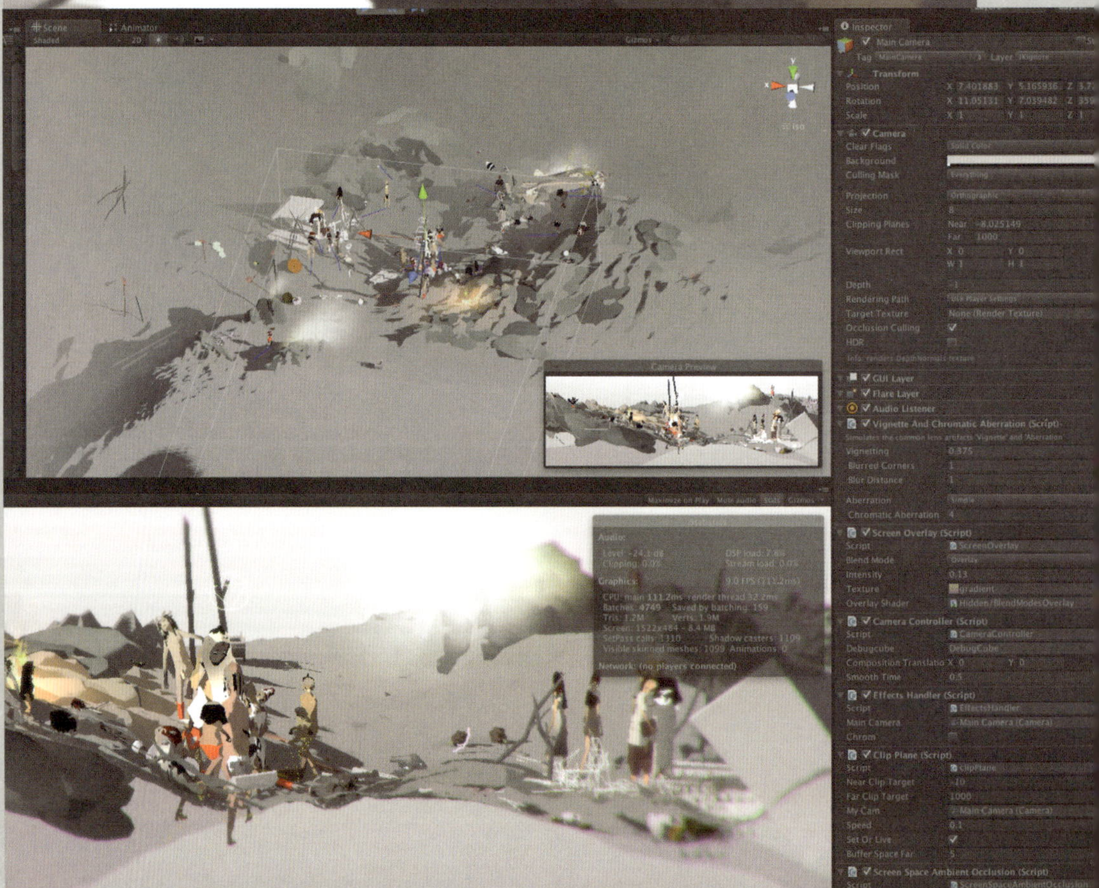
Scene
Animator
Inspector
Main Camera
Transform
Position
Rotation
Scale
Camera
Clear Flags
Background
Culling Mask
Projection
Size
Clipping Planes
Viewport Rect
Depth
Rendering Path
Target Texture
Occlusion Culling
HDR
Camera Preview
GUI Layer
Flare Layer
Audio Listener
Vignette And Chromatic Aberration (Script)
Vignetting
Blurred Corners
Blur Distance
Aberration
Chromatic Aberration
Screen Overlay (Script)
Script
Blend Mode
Intensity
Texture
Overlay Shader
Camera Controller (Script)
Debugcube
Composition Translatio
Smooth Time
Effects Handler (Script)
Main Camera
Chrom
Clip Plane (Script)
Near Clip Target
Far Clip Target
My Cam
Speed
Set Or Live
Buffer Space Far
Screen Space Ambient Occlusion (Script)
Audio:
Graphics:
Network: (no players connected)

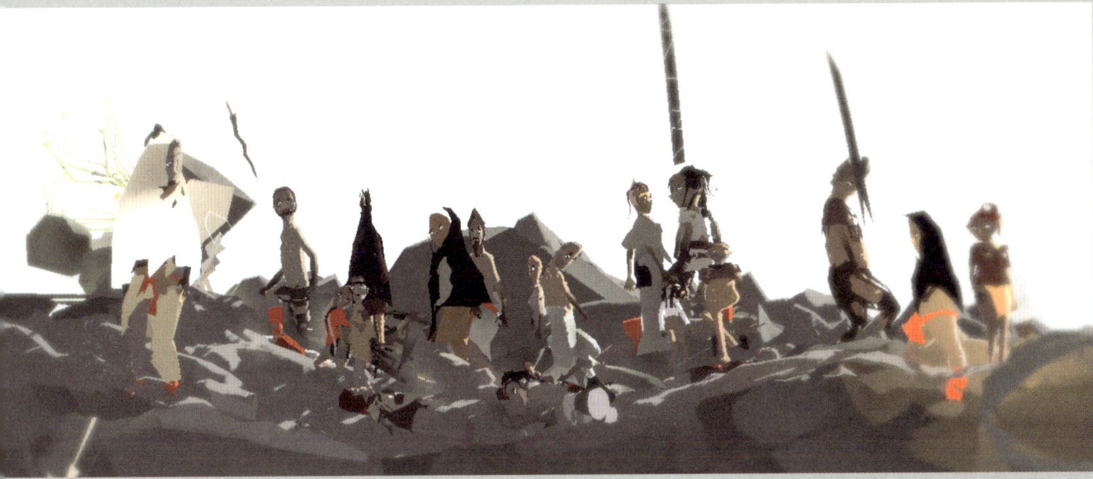

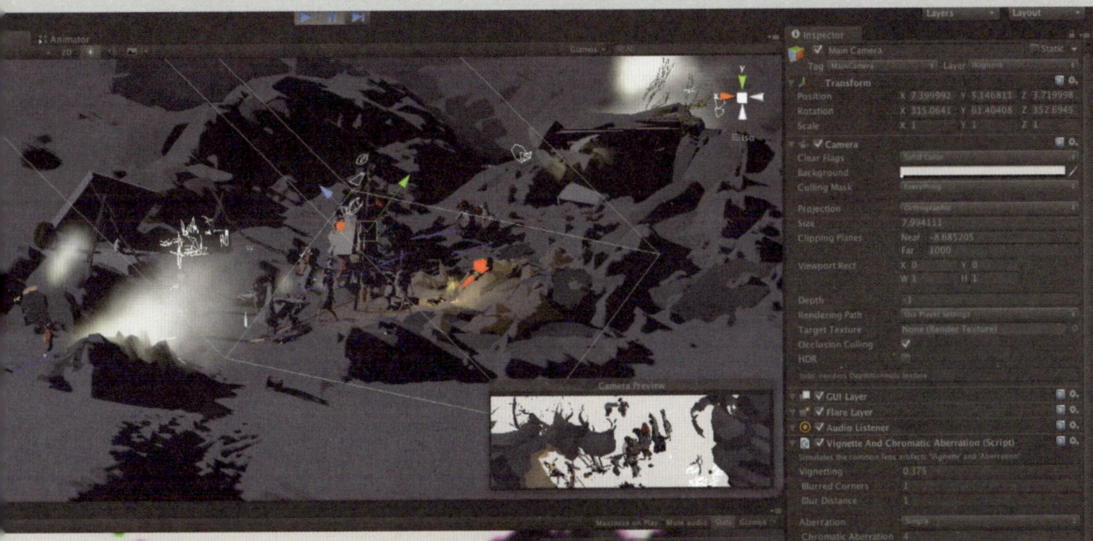

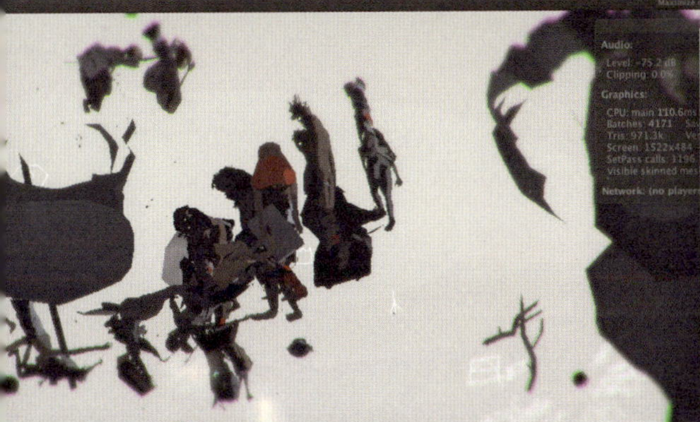

I used two virtual cameras in *EIT-SOG*: a 'story view' that trailed the Young Ancient, and an 'ecosystem view' to show the entire volcanic environment. With these viewpoints taken together the viewer would have a sense of both the subjective drama and its place in the context of the drama of the community and the volcano.

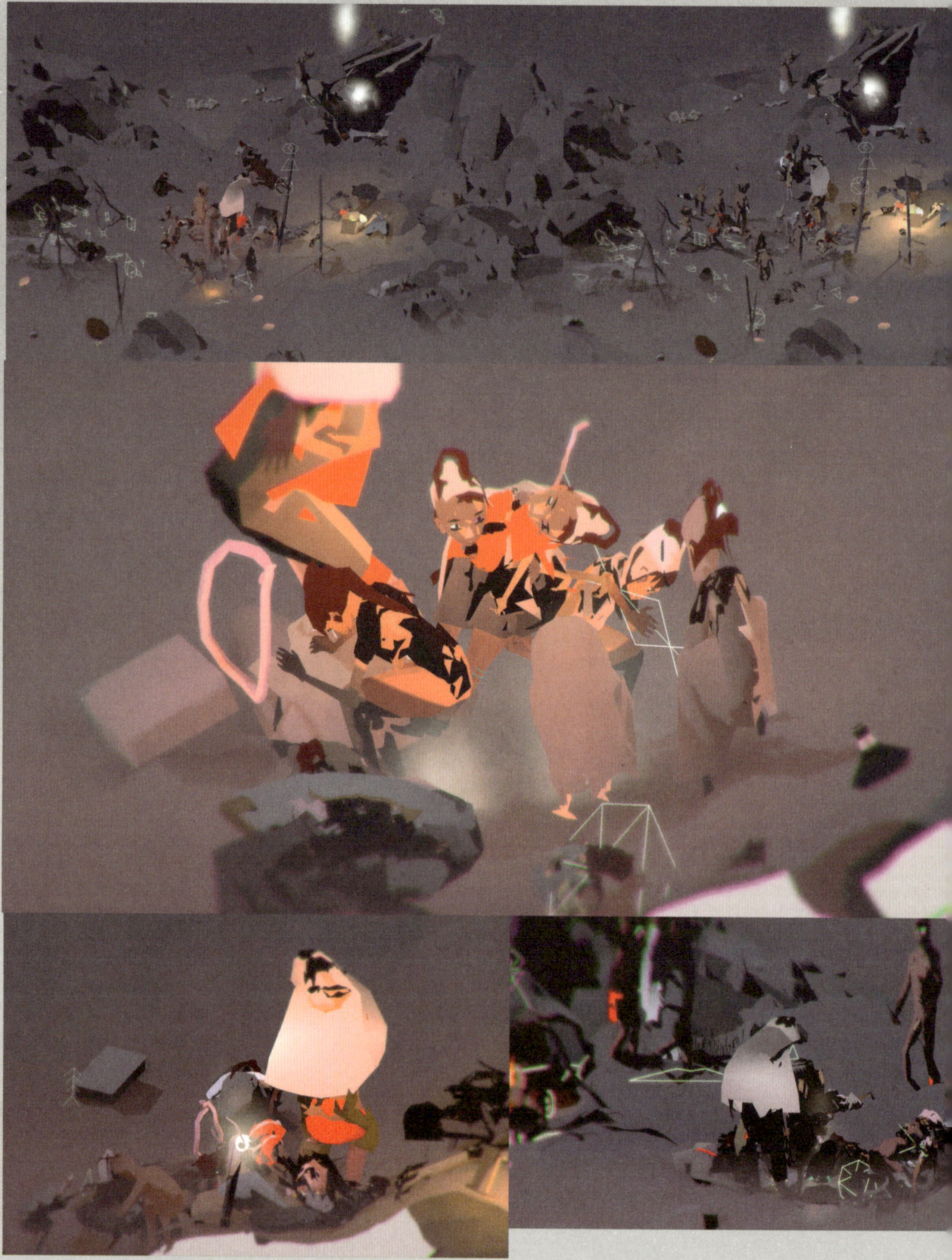

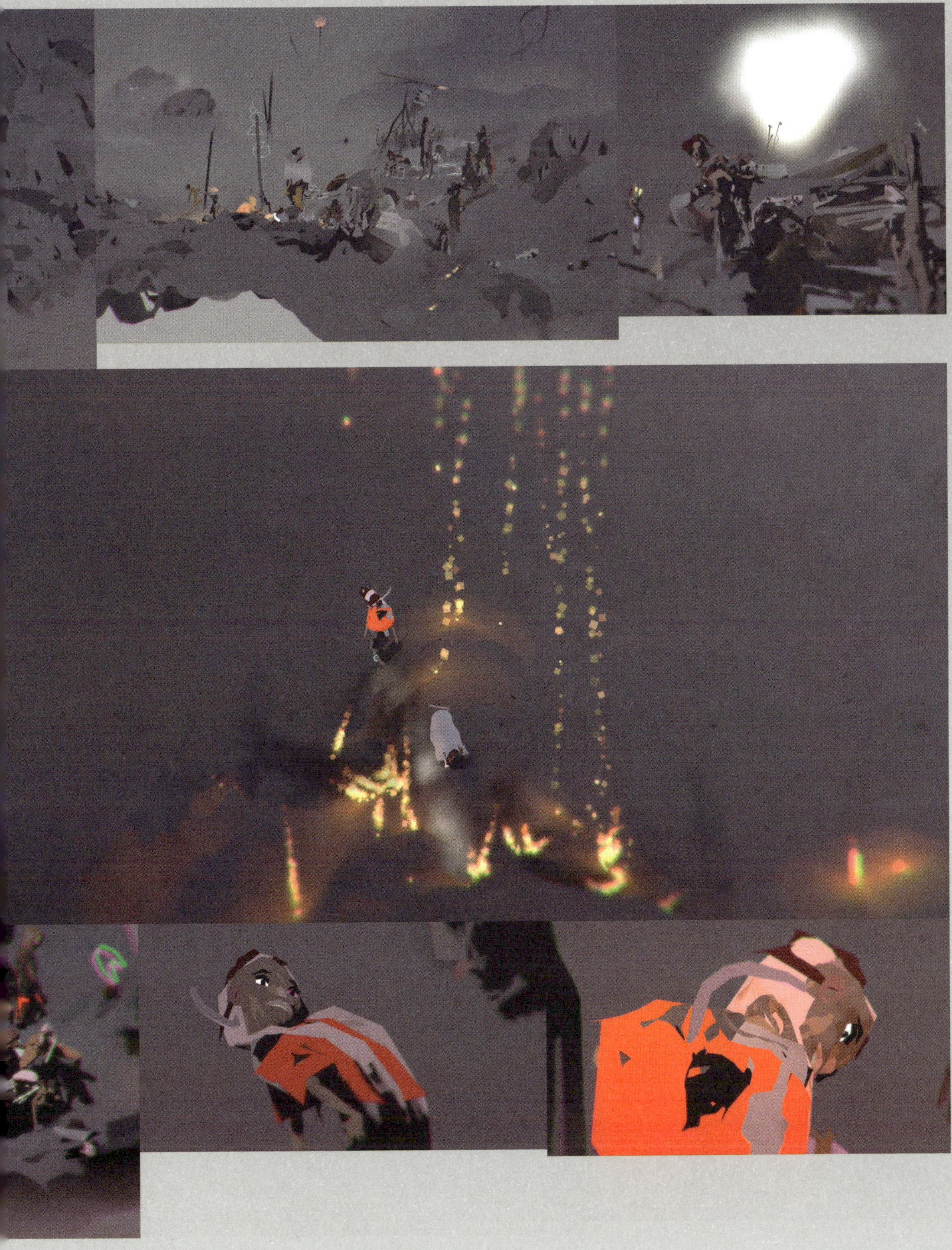

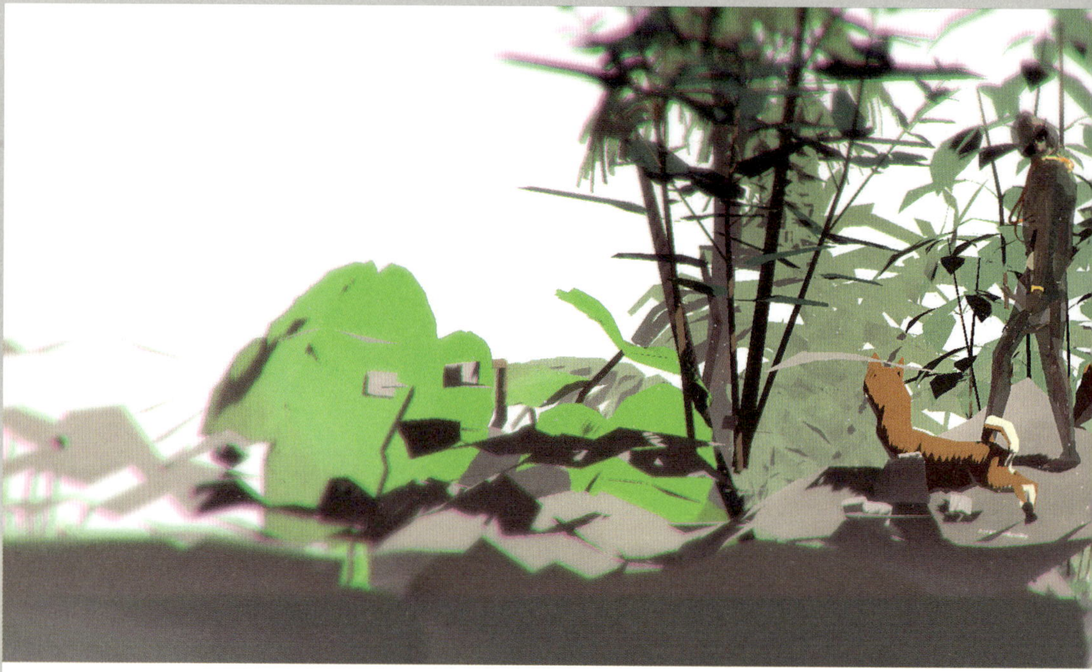

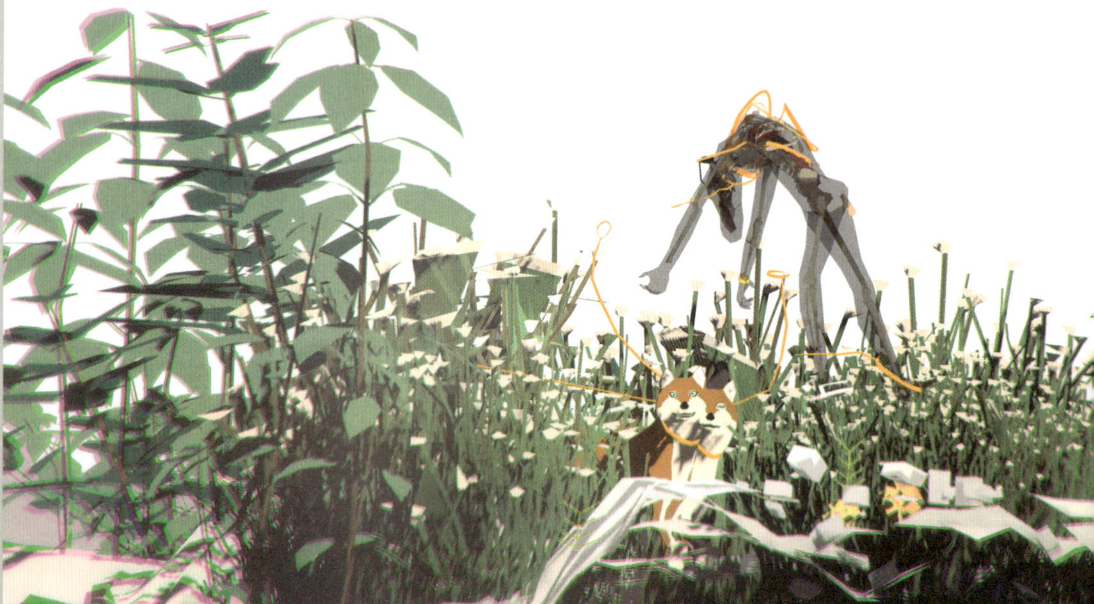

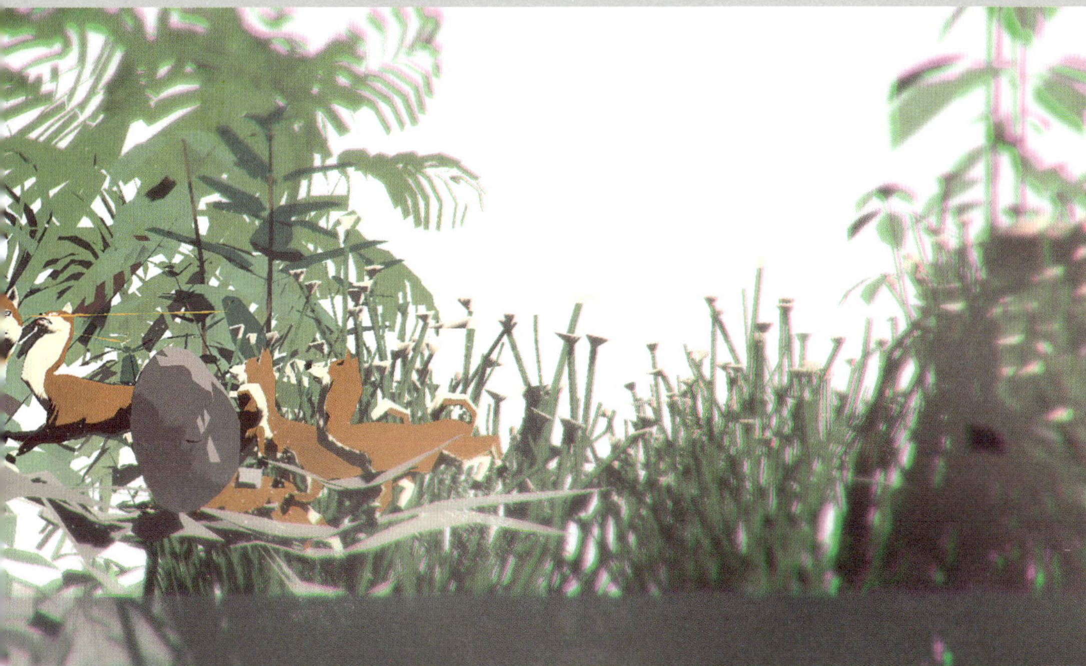

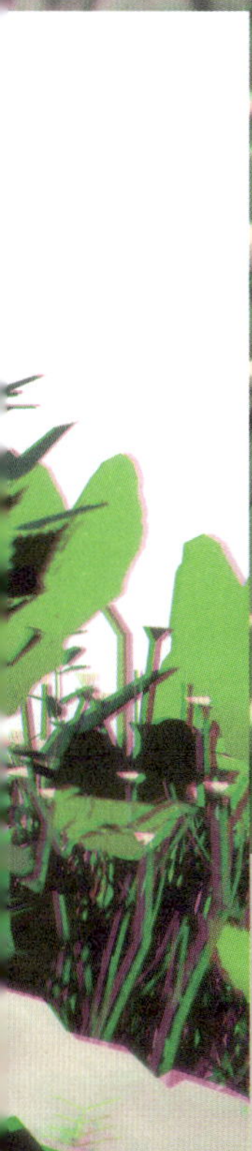

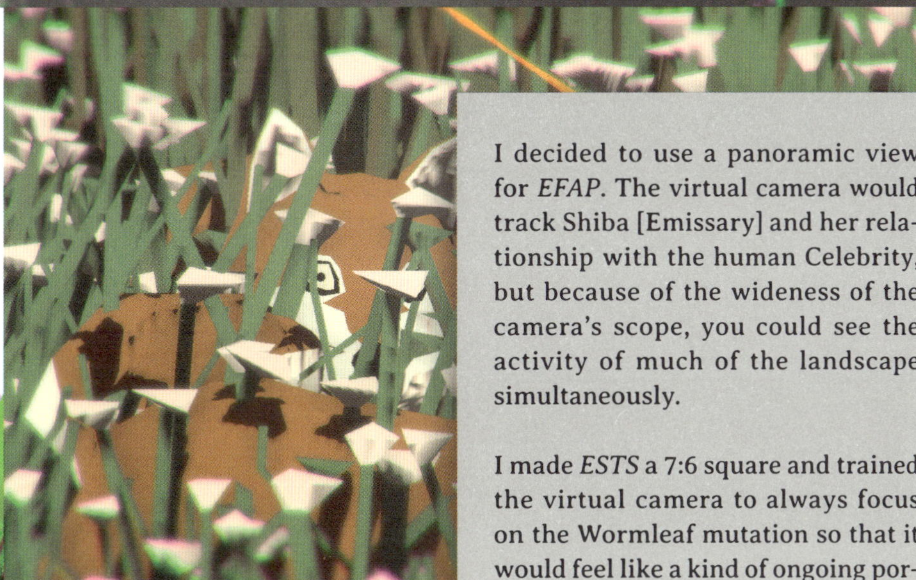

I decided to use a panoramic view for *EFAP*. The virtual camera would track Shiba [Emissary] and her relationship with the human Celebrity, but because of the wideness of the camera's scope, you could see the activity of much of the landscape simultaneously.

I made *ESTS* a 7:6 square and trained the virtual camera to always focus on the Wormleaf mutation so that it would feel like a kind of ongoing portraiture. The viewer would always be oriented to the life of the mutation, as it evolved from an animated plant to whatever possible life outcome: the subject of Oomen abuse, a vegetative mess, a full-blown monster.

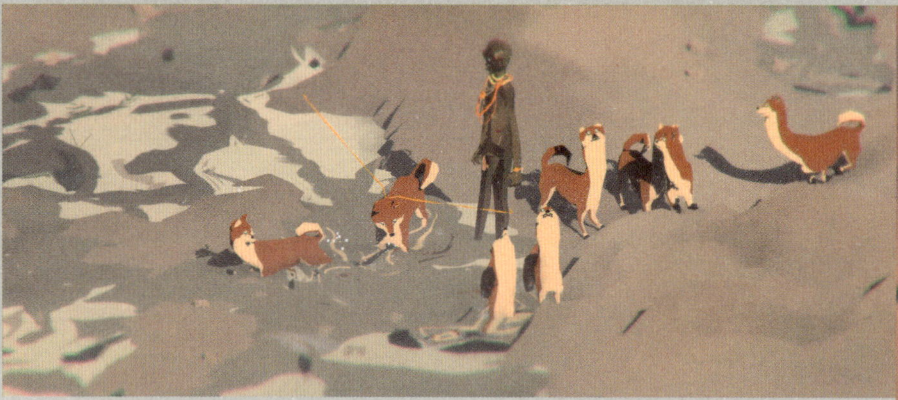

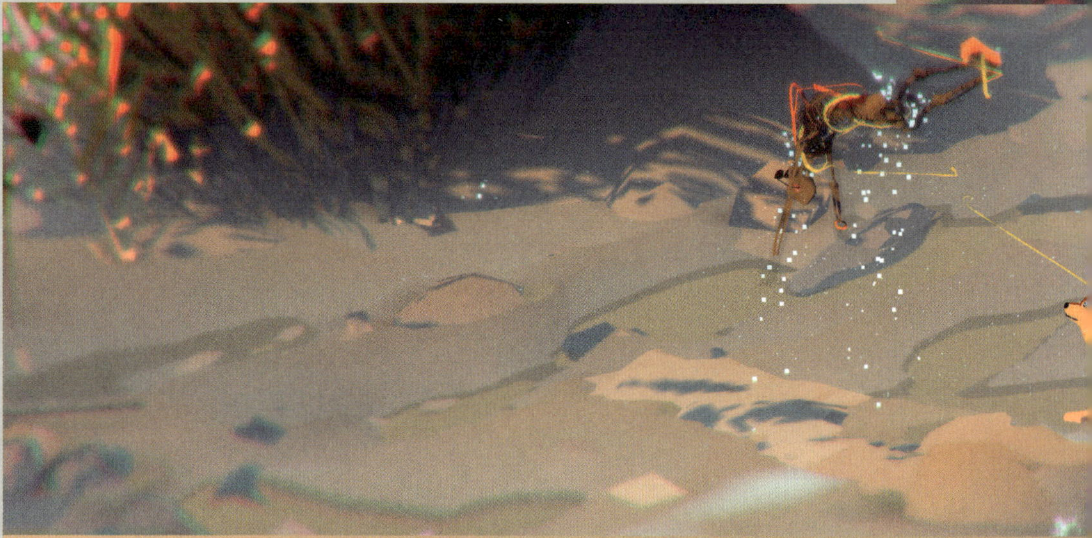

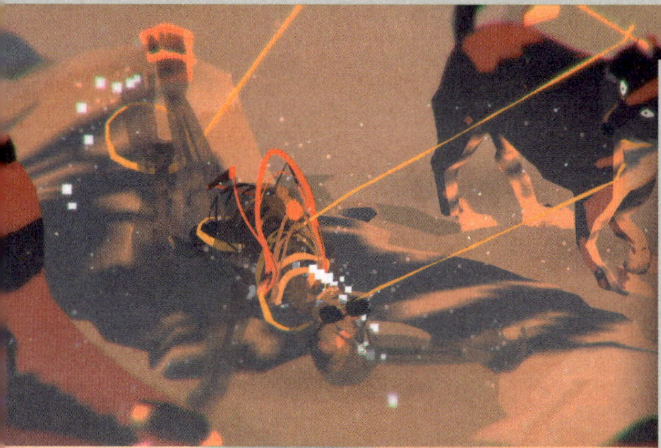

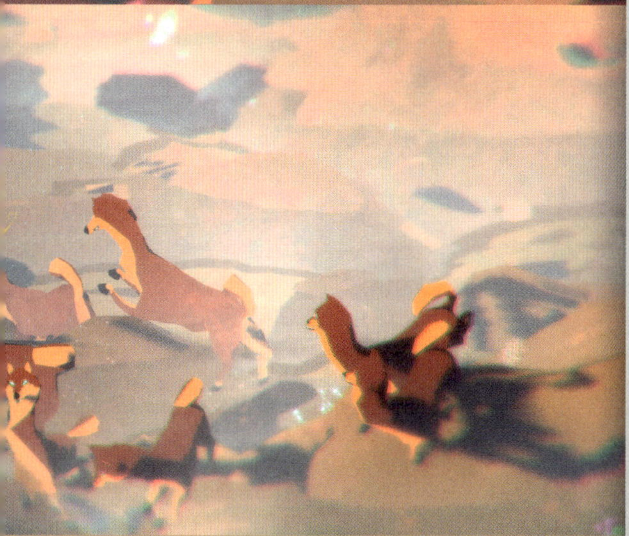

I am responsible for tuning the World so it doesn't wreck itself in two days. There were always strange surprises at the birth of each episode of *Emissaries*. The Shaman led his community to the edge of the simulation, on the infinity horizon, where he believed it was most safe. Young Ancient walked down into the heart of the volcano when no one listened to her. Seeding fifty members of the ancient community tended to always block Young Emissary from her narrative goals, but twenty members let her succeed too often. Shiba discovering Celebrity at night forked herself hundreds of times due to contagious anxiety. Celebrity failed to decay and outlived everyone by itself. The Oomen reproduced too quickly and eradicated every Wormleaf plant in the ecosystem in one generation. The Wormleaves amassed in the centre of the Atoll and created a pit in the terrain that all the Oomen got trapped in. The Oomen children developed a tolerance for eating faeces and subsisted on their own cycle.

Tuning is mainly a matter of tweaking the inter-relationships between agents, like how a reality TV showrunner might tweak its players. Recognising which of these surprises are generative and which are catastrophic, and amplifying the generative ones, is the harmonising work of tuning.

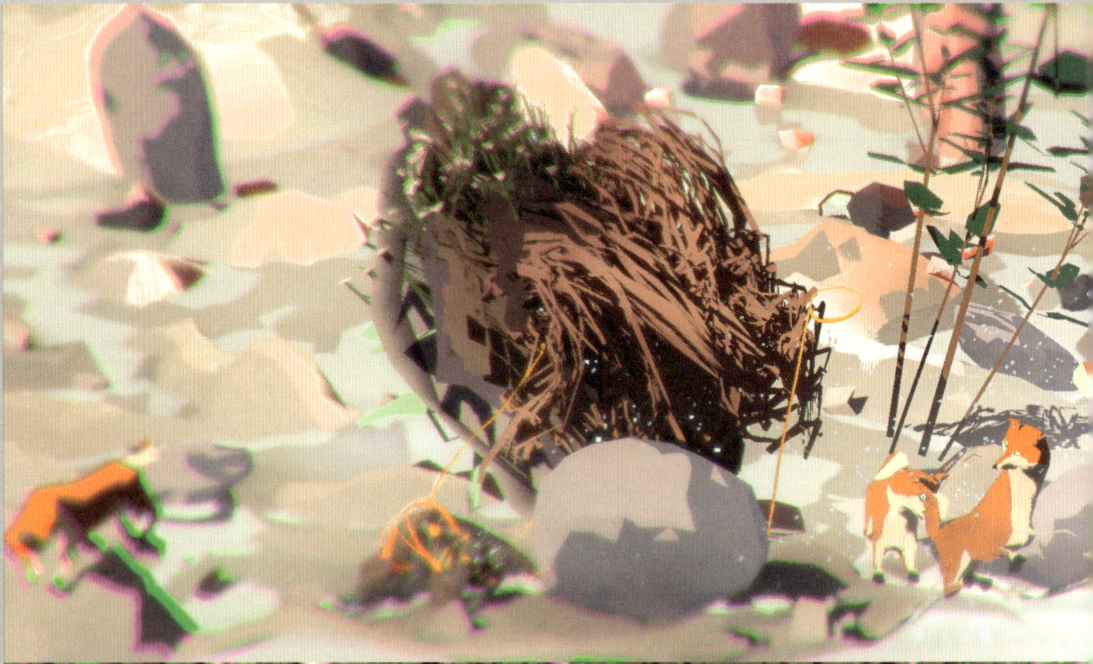

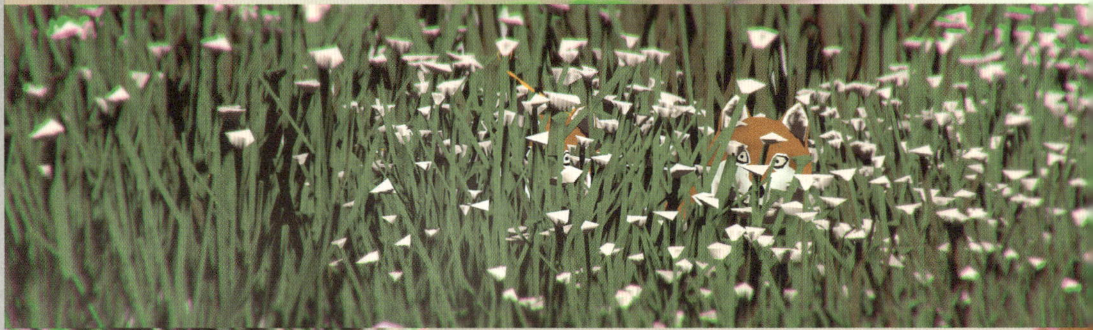

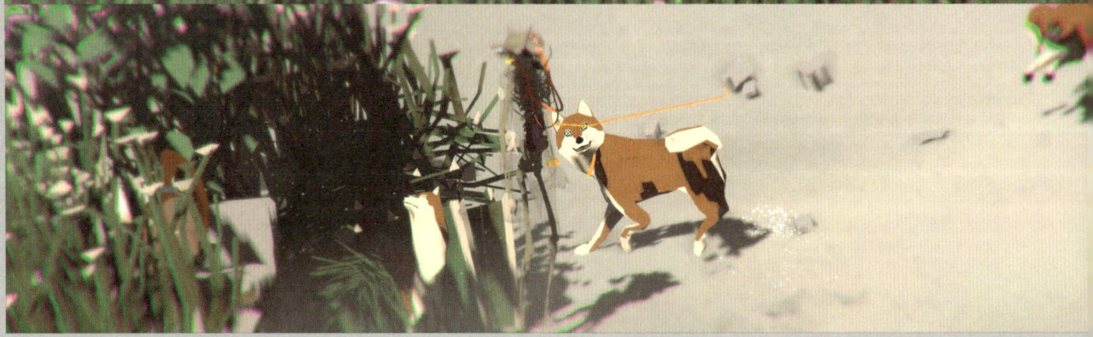

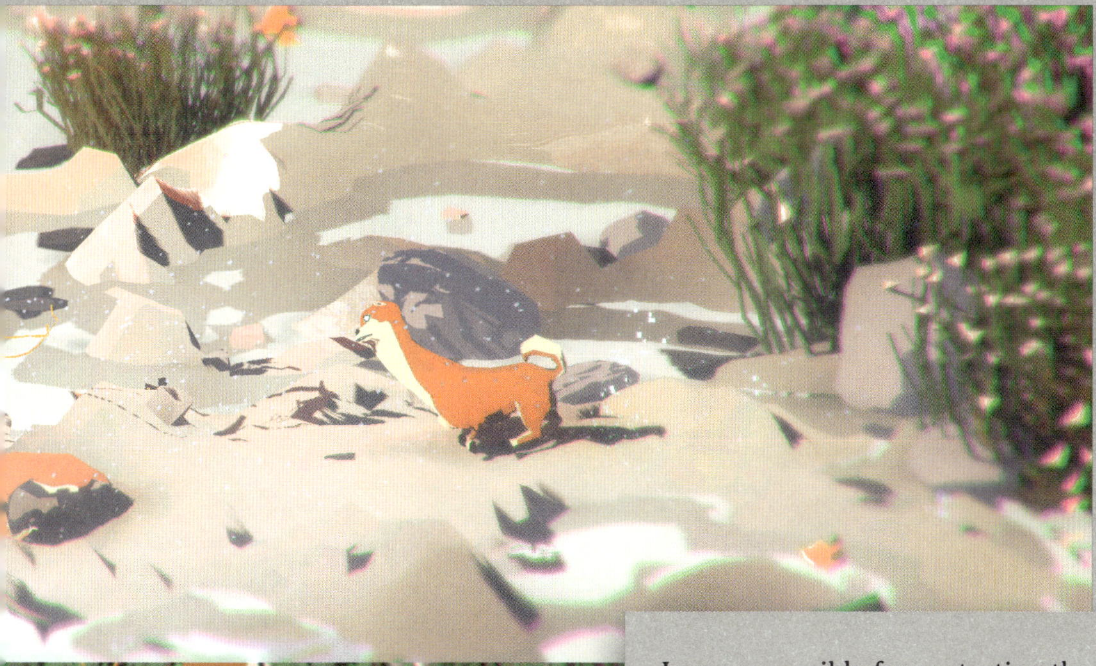

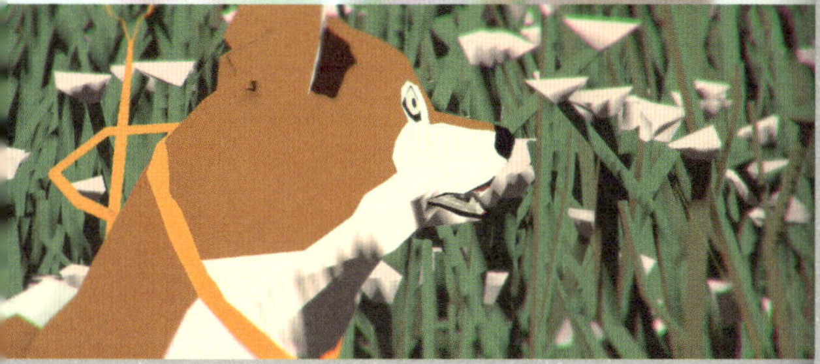

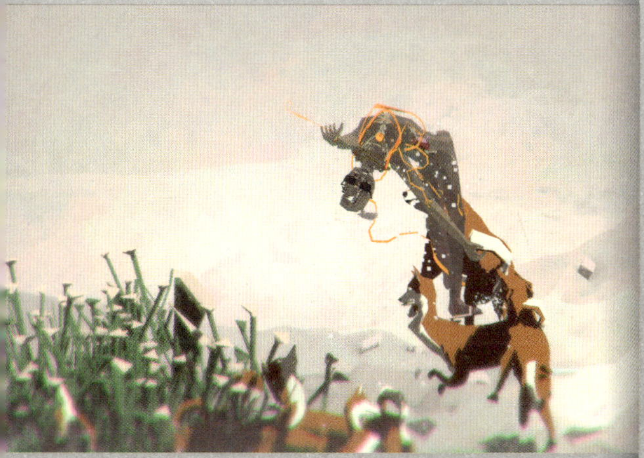

I am responsible for protecting the World from my own too-human finitude. The temptation to reduce a World into a finite game is to kill the golden goose for quick wins. This is what happened to the housing market in 2008, what happens to every start-up that sees itself merely for its technological function, and what happens to gurus who build a high-walled cult around their own personhood. Many times I faced the temptation to turn *Emissaries* into a more finite form. The Director in me wanted to export the best run of the simulation and make a 'greatest bits' video. The Hacker wanted to turn it into a video game with points and goals for saving the community, or growing a Wormleaf monster. The Cartoonist wanted to just scrub through run throughs and make an Instagram of the best animated GIFs.

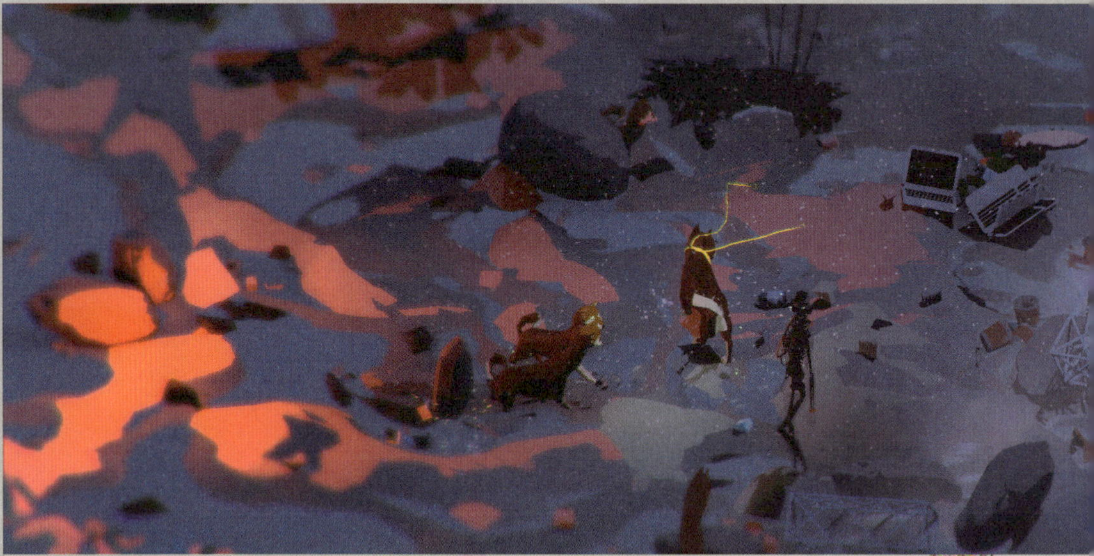

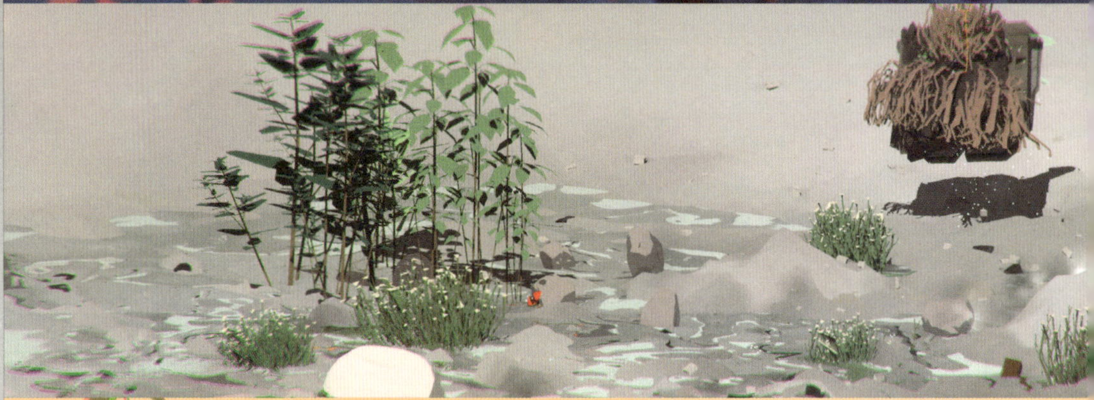

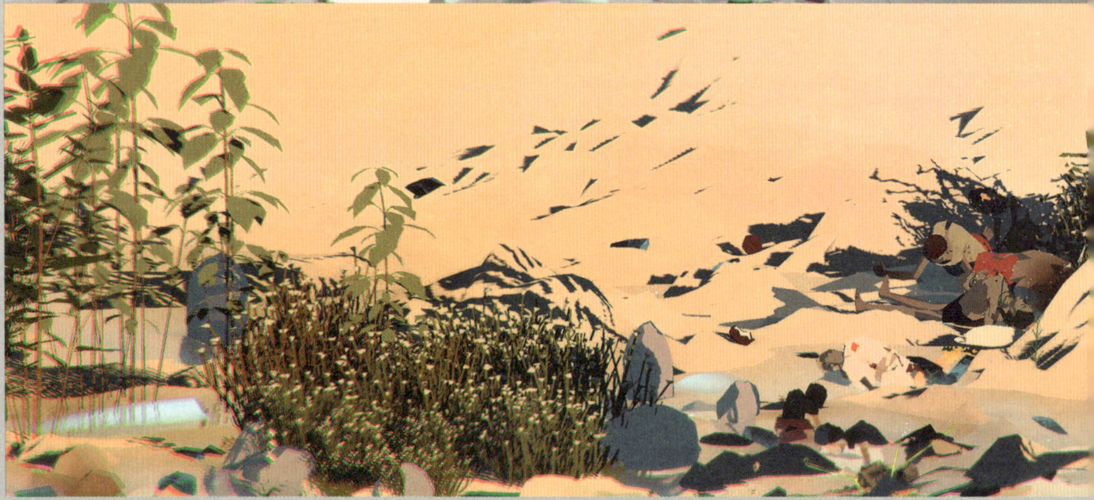

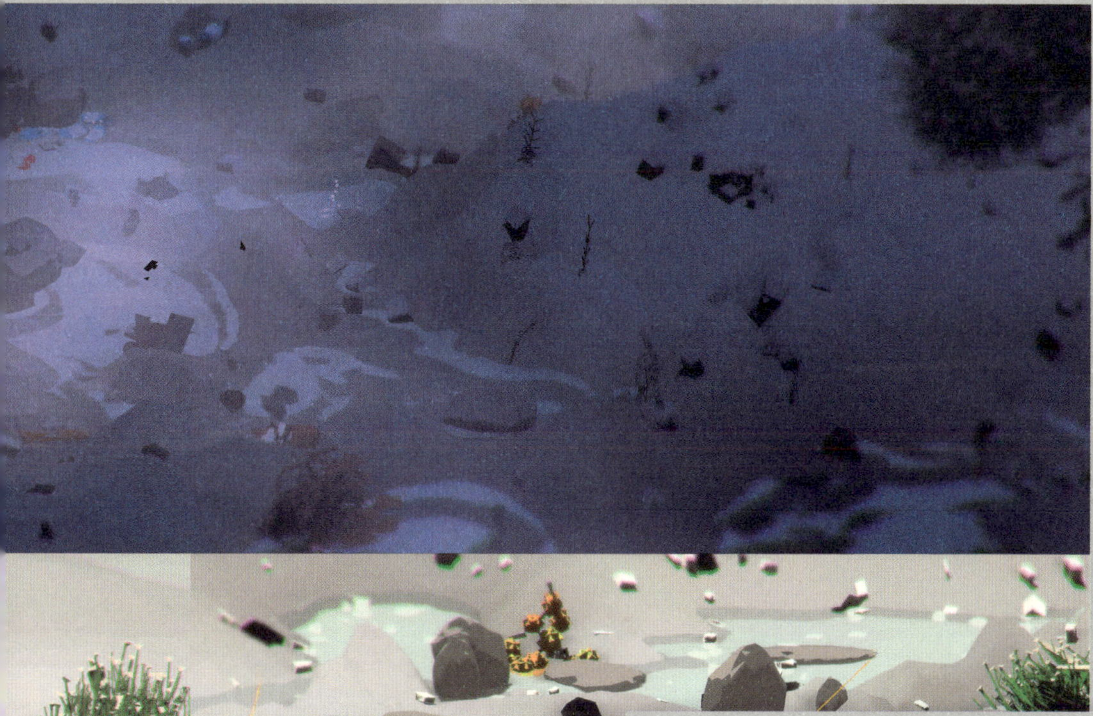

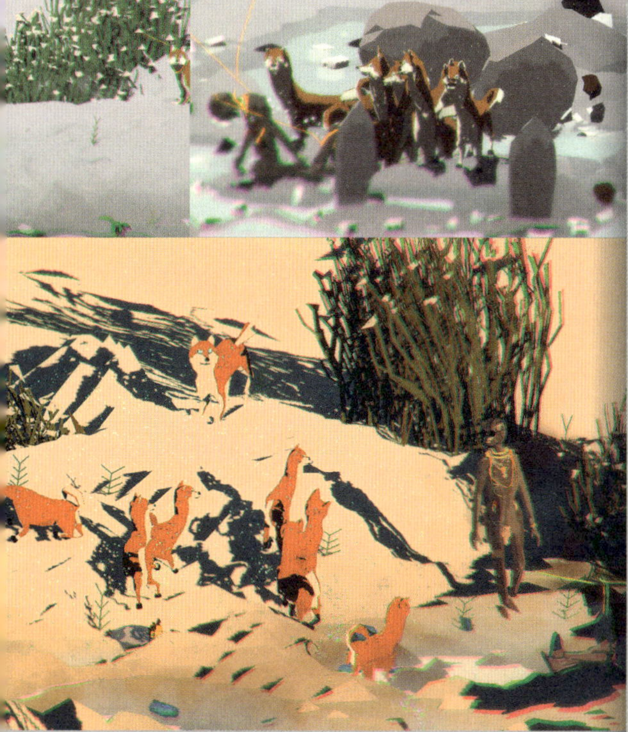

I am responsible for opening up the World to other players. The key quality is that the World has some interface for players to enter into its ongoingness. I exhibited *Emissaries* in institutions and galleries. I live streamed it. One day the assets of *Emissaries*, its characters and subsystems, will be made available to a public. I dream of an *Emissaries* cognition composer where people can mix and match brain modules and see how the characters come alive differently. And through this book, I wish to extend the spirit of *Emissaries* to those interested in Worlding. Any interface that can produce connection to the World, however significant or niche, is energy and care for the World to keep going.

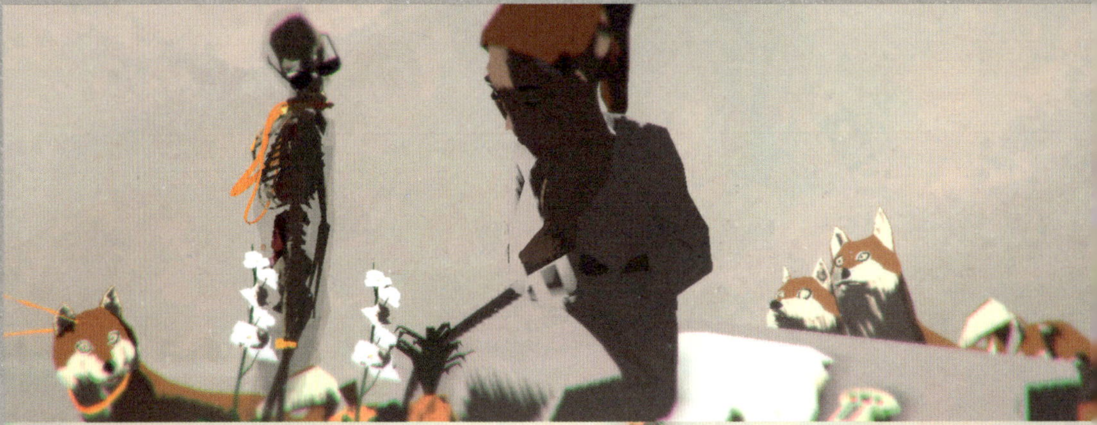

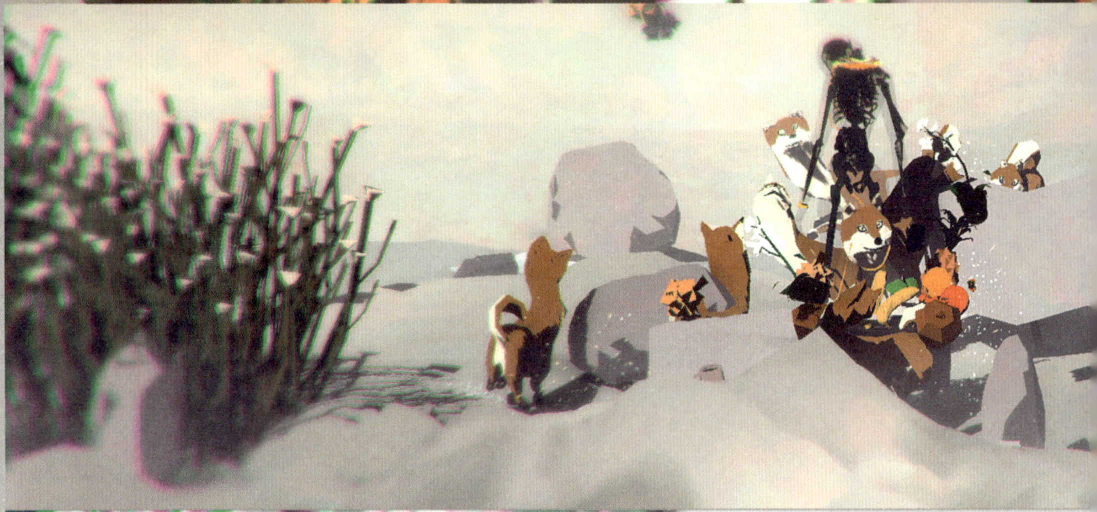

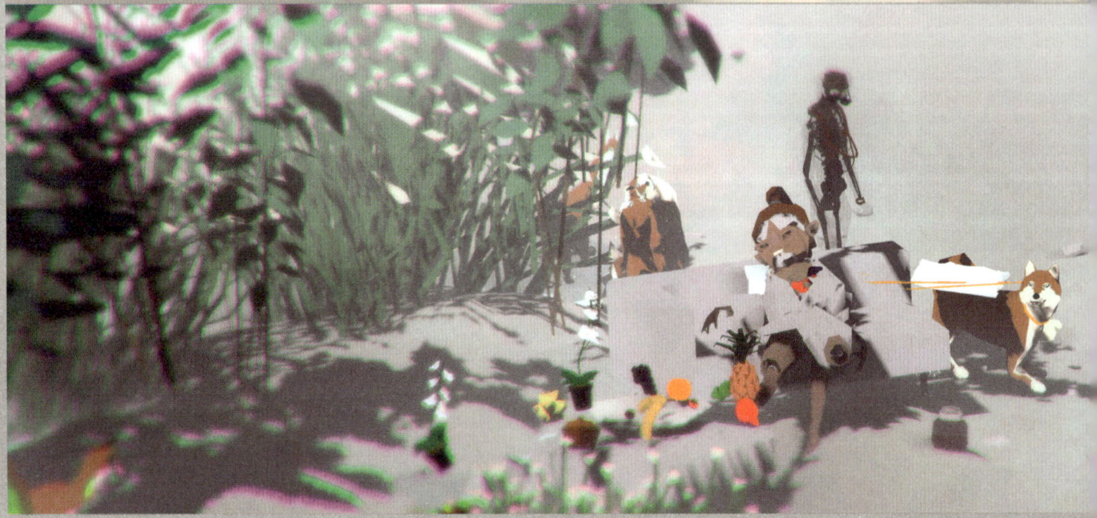

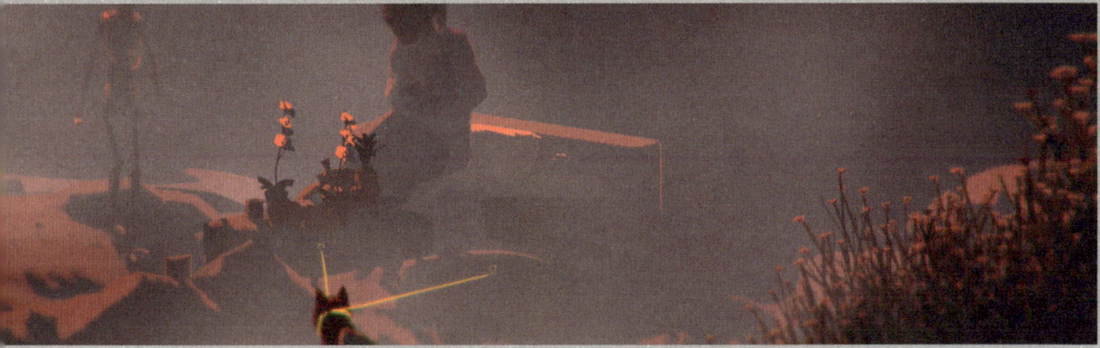

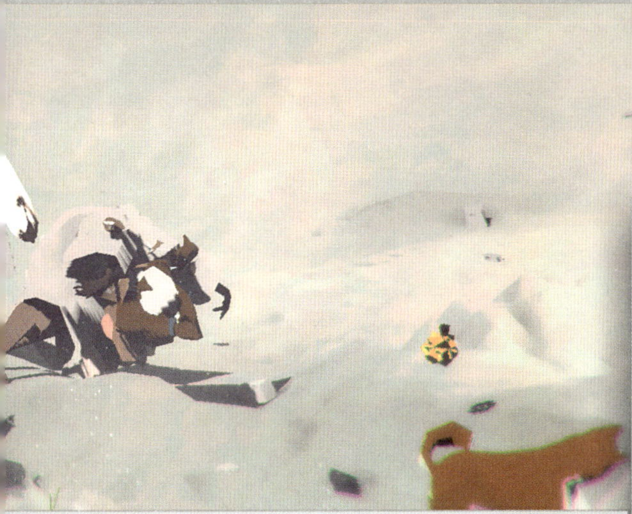

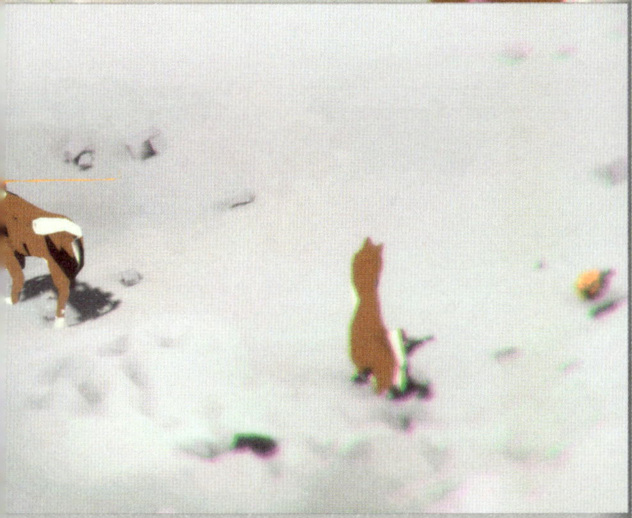

WHERE DOES PHASE 2 WORLDING END AND PHASE 3 BEGIN? WHEN IS THE EMISSARY'S JOB FINISHED?

The Emissary's job is finished when the World is open and the Emissary can no longer go on. The Emissary is not a prisoner of its World. Remember, being a player in an infinite game is always a choice. Better to exit the World than be tempted by the other masks who risk resolving it into a finite game. But how do you exit a World responsibly? How do you exit knowing that the World is in generative hands without you? How do you know you're not killing a World by leaving it? For when a World ends, it is truly a death, no less catastrophic than the death of a biological being. It is the end of a generative, sentient, continuity stream, no longer perturbing the medium of spacetime.

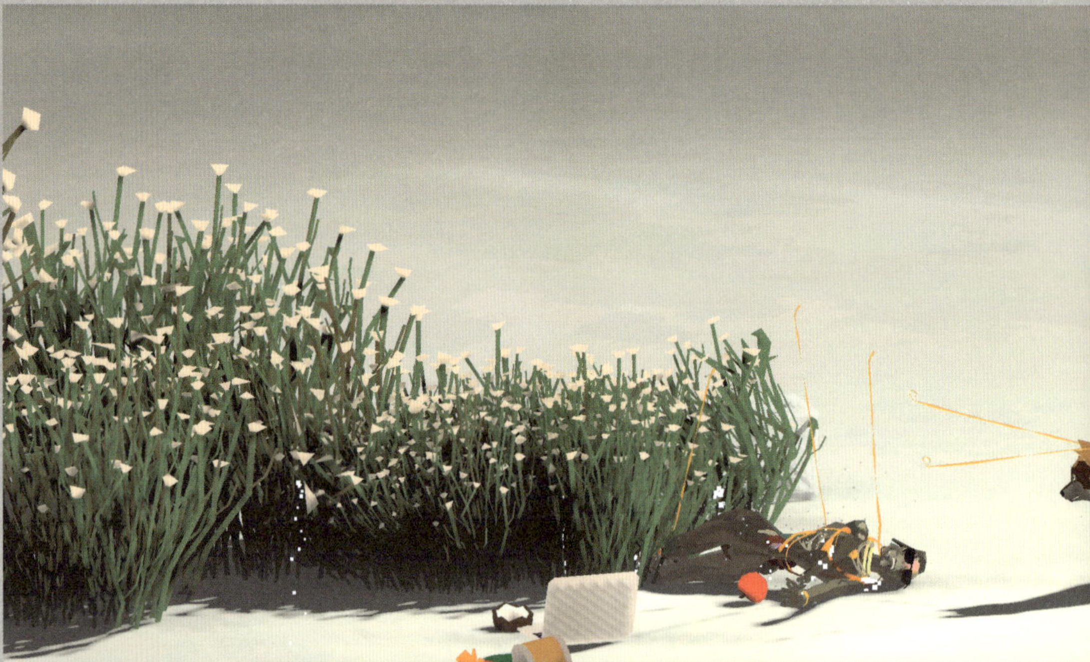

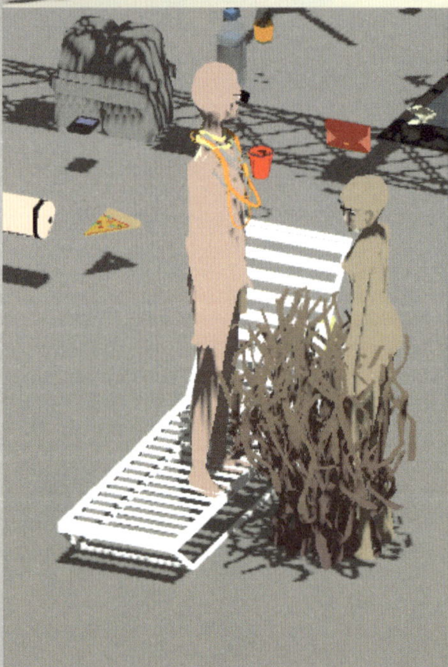

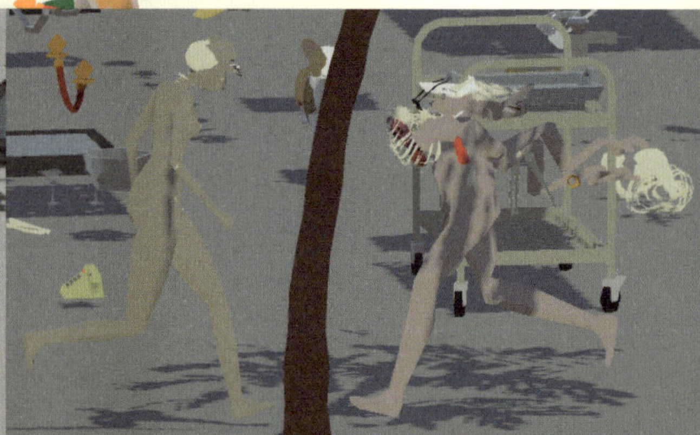

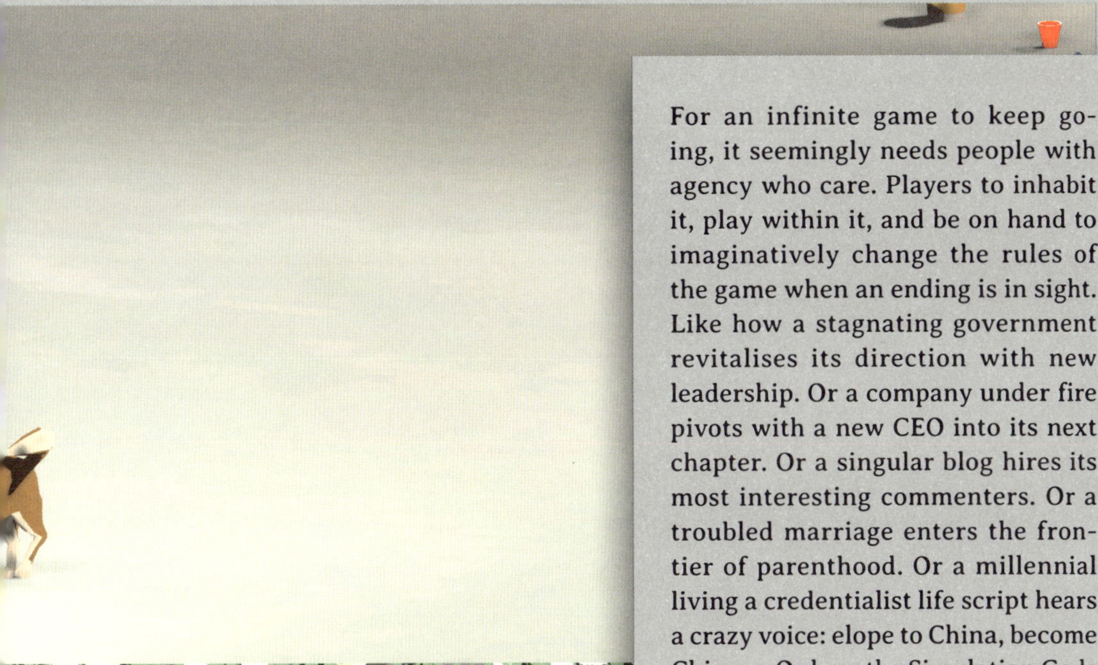

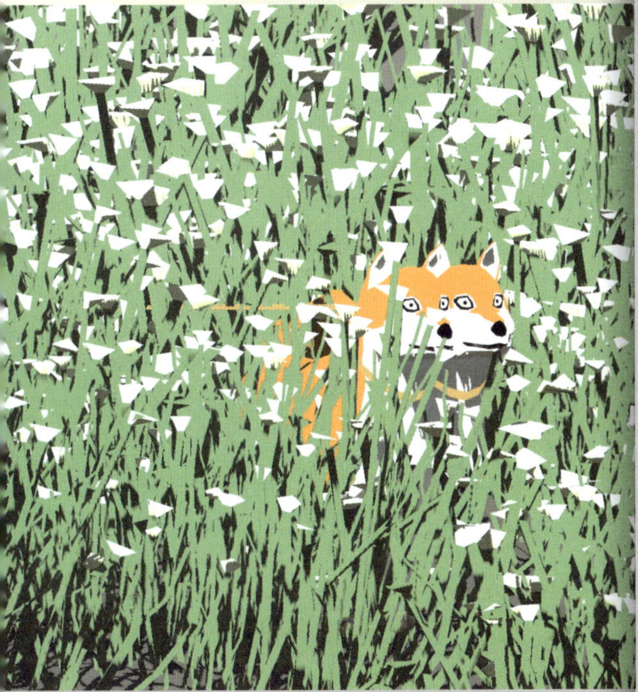

For an infinite game to keep going, it seemingly needs people with agency who care. Players to inhabit it, play within it, and be on hand to imaginatively change the rules of the game when an ending is in sight. Like how a stagnating government revitalises its direction with new leadership. Or a company under fire pivots with a new CEO into its next chapter. Or a singular blog hires its most interesting commenters. Or a troubled marriage enters the frontier of parenthood. Or a millennial living a credentialist life script hears a crazy voice: elope to China, become Chinese. Or how the Simulation Gods fork a collapsing universe. In Worlds of all scales, someone must be around to care.

What if no one cares about a new World except its Emissary? Does a World just die? Somewhere a Cartoonist is laughing. In mature Worlds, there is often a financial, spiritual, or prestige economy to incentivise its human players to keep caring. But what if an infant World has yet to evolve those features? And what if a World requires a more expressive relationship to humans than total care or total death? We can imagine a World in its infancy that needs time to find its public. Or later, a World that needs time away from people to readjust. Or a World that wishes to fork itself, split its players, and try parallel alternate directions.

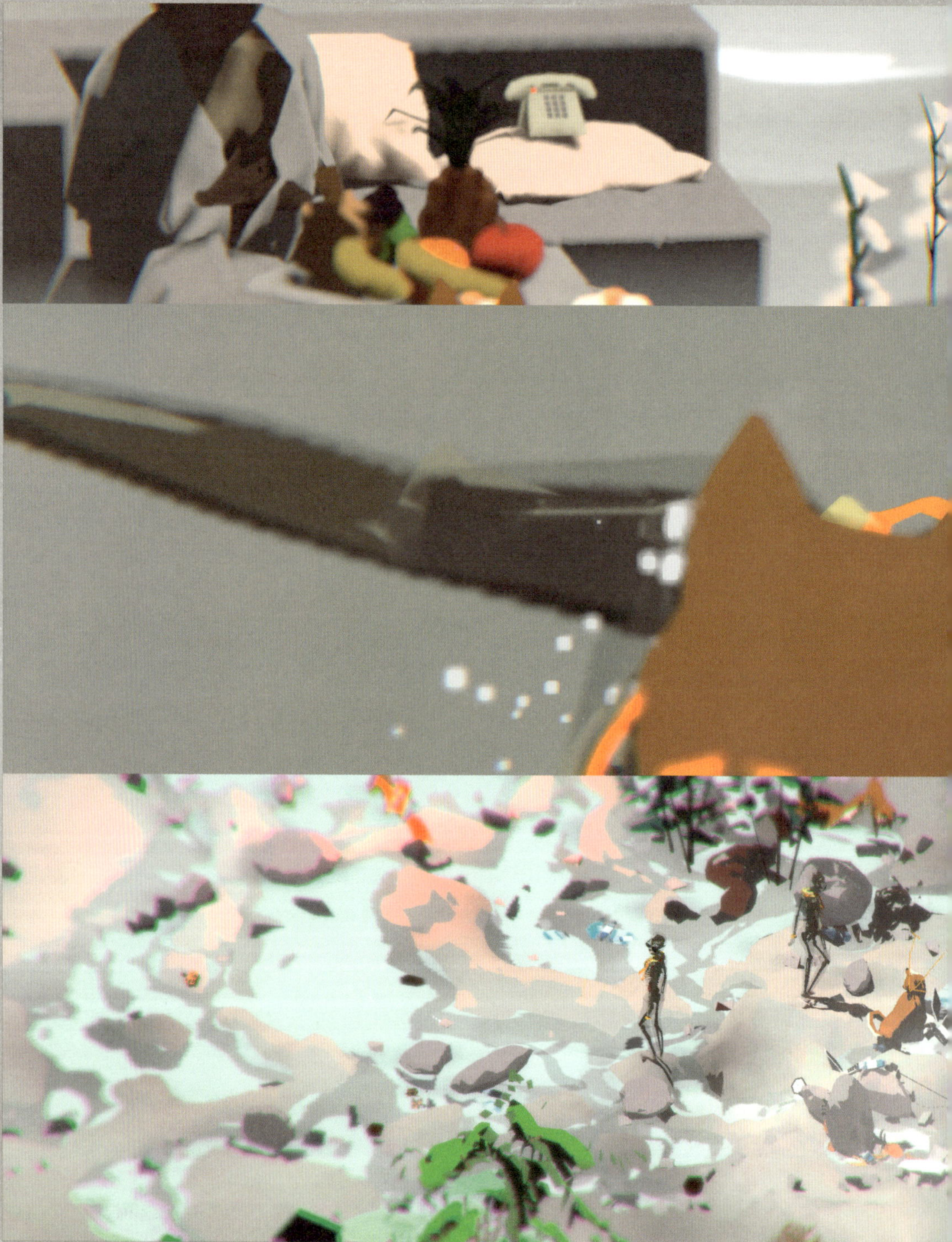

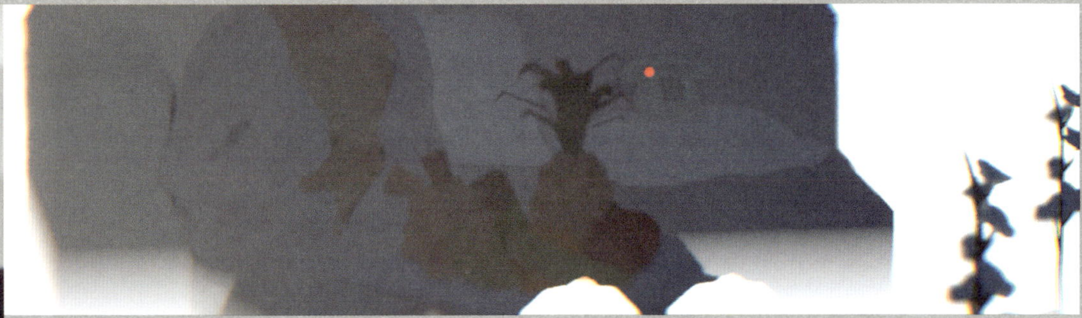

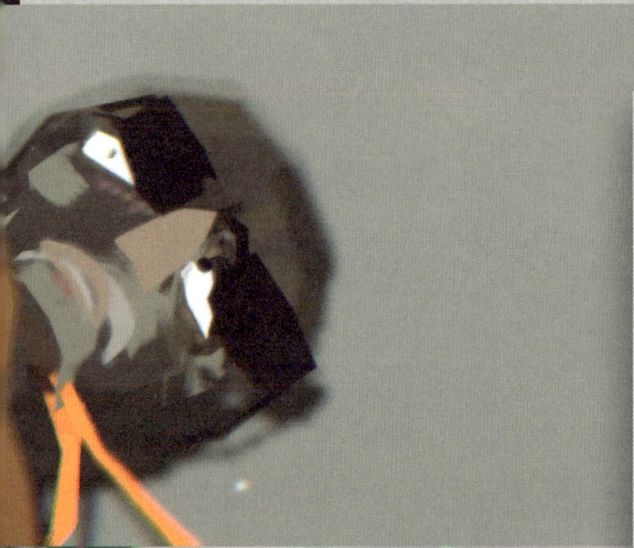

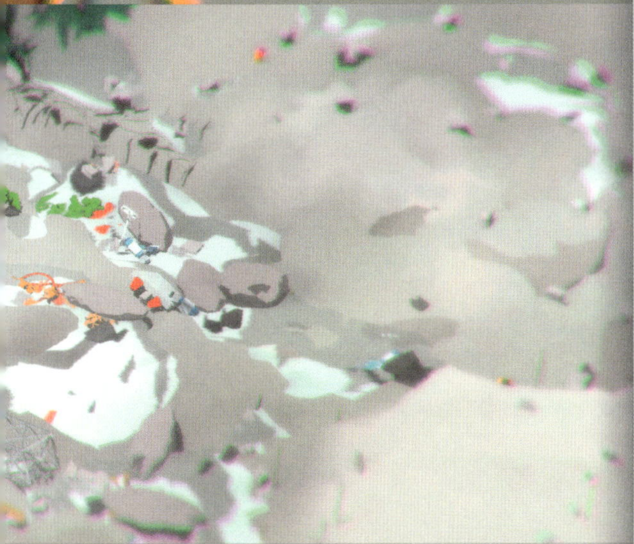

Serving *Emissaries* has suggested to me a different model for Phase 3 Worlding. *Emissaries* imagines an infinite game that is sustained, in part, by non-human players: specifically, AI-based agents living within its simulation. I refer to *Emissaries* as 'a game that plays itself'. This is my horseless carriage. It is a pre-vision of a practice of Worlding that utilises non-human agents to maintain and nurture the flourishing of arbitrarily created Worlds. Worlds that require no social or economic consensus for legitimacy and life. Worlds that can host human players but are not obliged to. Worlds that can have time and space to search for a public, go dormant for maintenance, clone itself for do-overs, all with the help of AI who imaginatively serve long after the human Emissaries have exited. It is a strange vision. As strange as it must have once seemed for a boat to sail the entire ocean with the help of a little motor. Or a company to be run out of a bedroom with the help of some software.

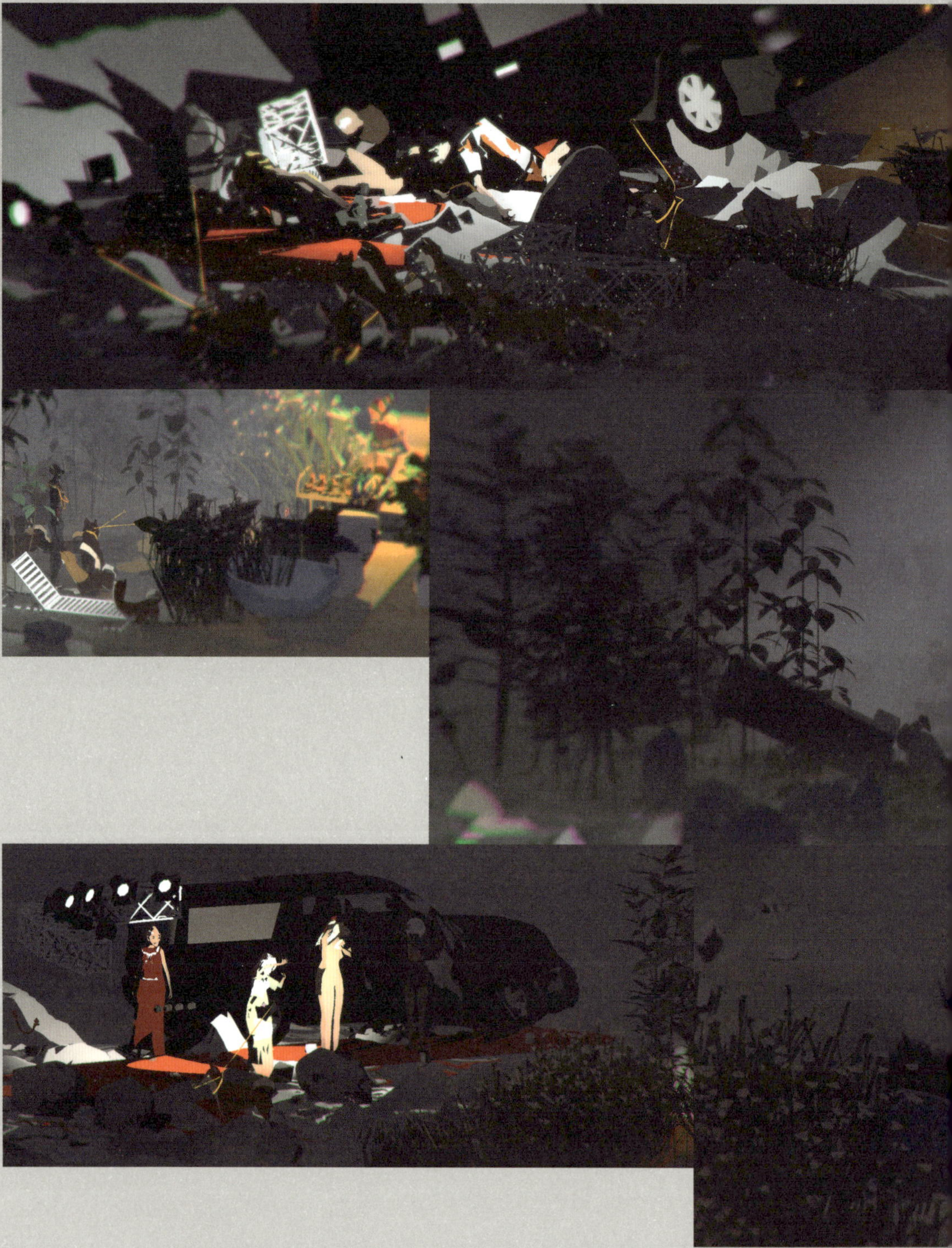

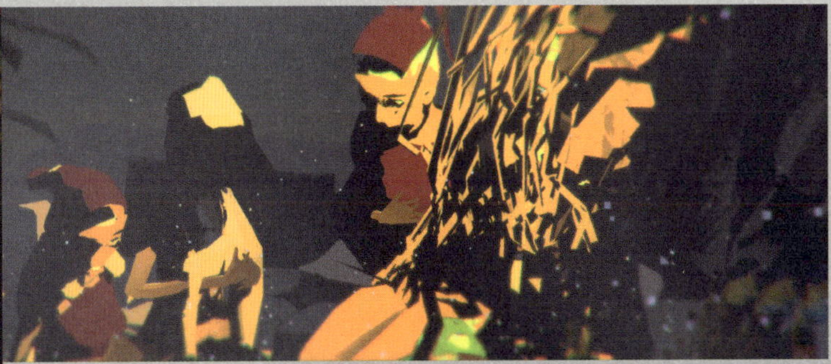

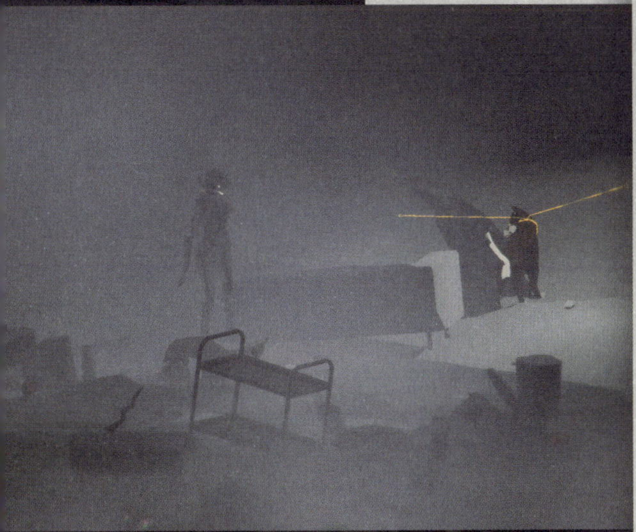

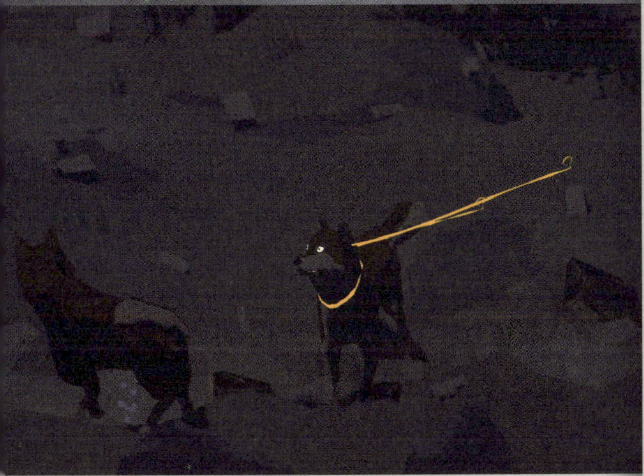

Ancient people believed that Reality was suffused with autonomous Spirit Worlds all around us, teeming with activity on their own plane, and open to human visitation. A plurality of AI-assisted self-regulating Worlds would be something like the Spirit Worlds made manifest for our times. Imagine a Cambrian Explosion of Worlds, big and small, playful and infrastructural, ephemeral and concrete, all fertile with currencies of meaning. Imagine a culture in which Worlding makes Worlds as prolific and mundane as publishing a book is today. And imagine the fluency for Worlds this ease and proliferation would create: moving between Worlds, existing in multiple Worlds simultaneously, starting and exiting Worlds, authoring Worlds knowing they will be inhabited by someone whether in a minute or after a century of evolution, returning to Worlds you began as a child. Imagine how the art of creating infinite games might open a way to an even greater art: the art of choosing better futures, thus expressively steering the medium of spacetime and sculpting our agency in it...

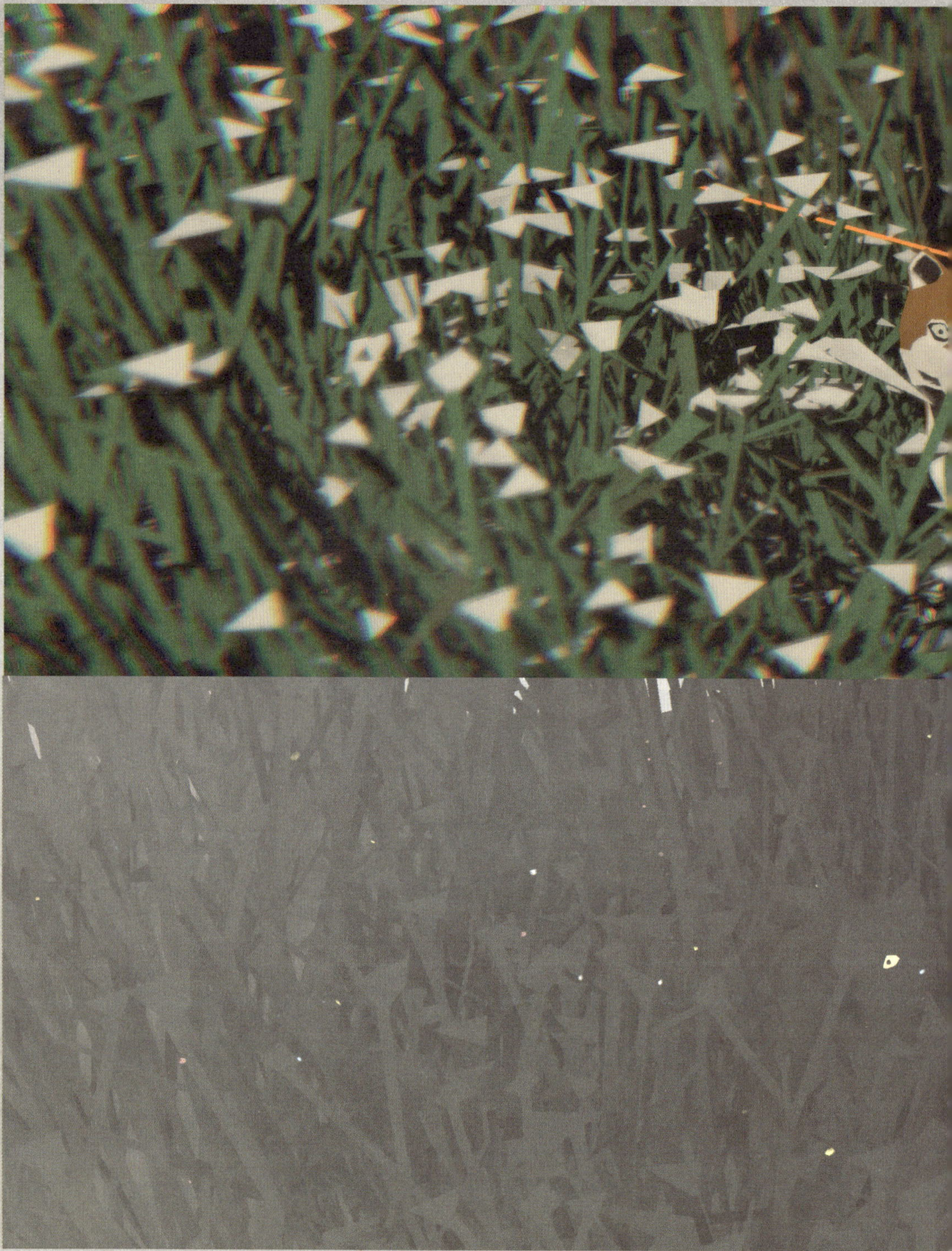

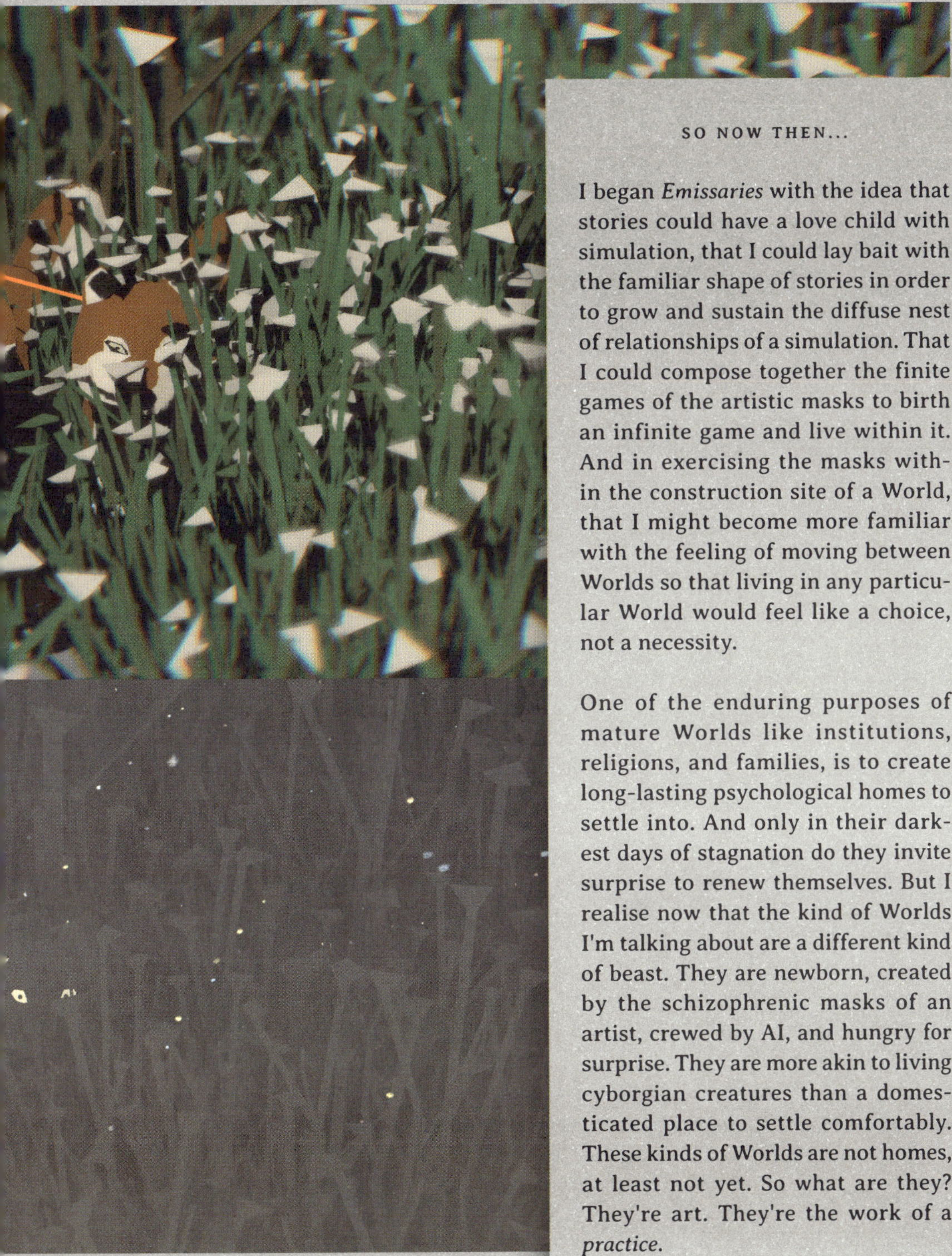

SO NOW THEN...

I began *Emissaries* with the idea that stories could have a love child with simulation, that I could lay bait with the familiar shape of stories in order to grow and sustain the diffuse nest of relationships of a simulation. That I could compose together the finite games of the artistic masks to birth an infinite game and live within it. And in exercising the masks within the construction site of a World, that I might become more familiar with the feeling of moving between Worlds so that living in any particular World would feel like a choice, not a necessity.

One of the enduring purposes of mature Worlds like institutions, religions, and families, is to create long-lasting psychological homes to settle into. And only in their darkest days of stagnation do they invite surprise to renew themselves. But I realise now that the kind of Worlds I'm talking about are a different kind of beast. They are newborn, created by the schizophrenic masks of an artist, crewed by AI, and hungry for surprise. They are more akin to living cyborgian creatures than a domesticated place to settle comfortably. These kinds of Worlds are not homes, at least not yet. So what are they? They're art. They're the work of a *practice*.

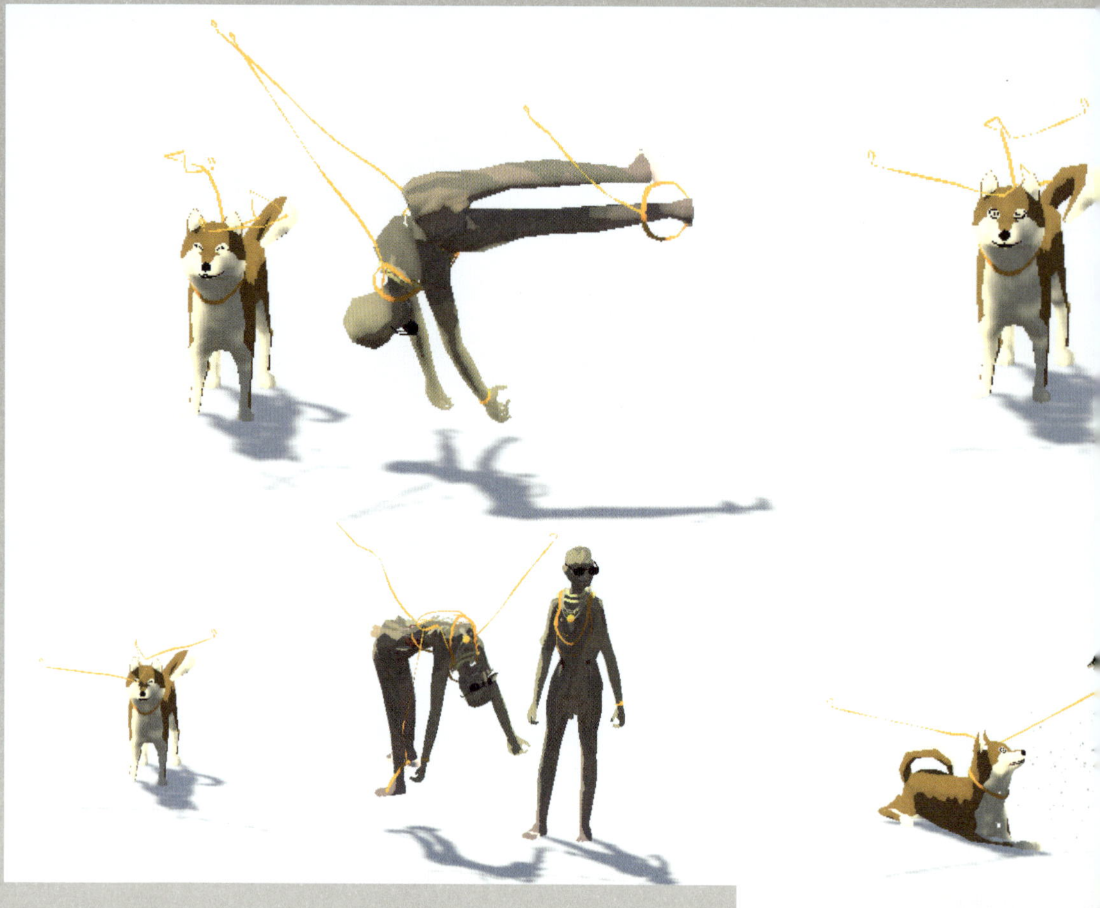

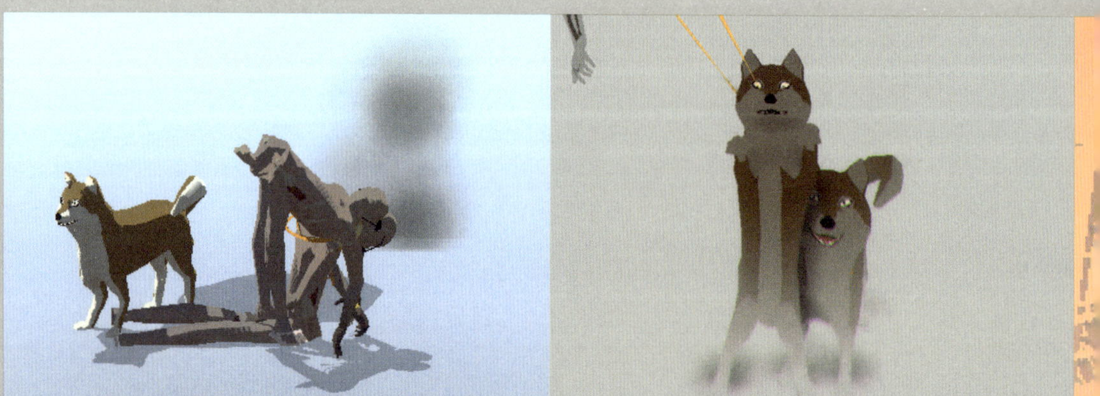

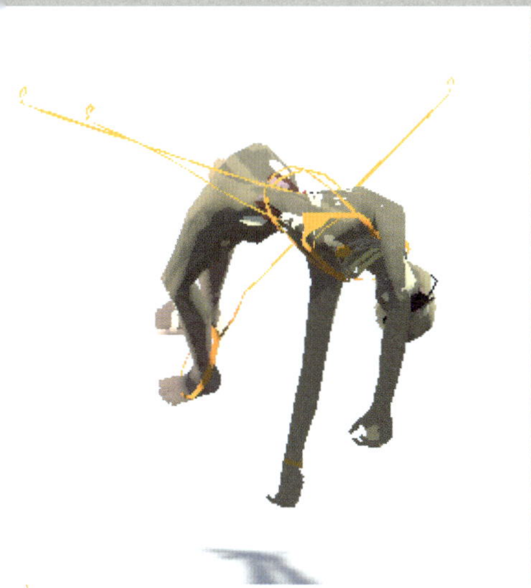

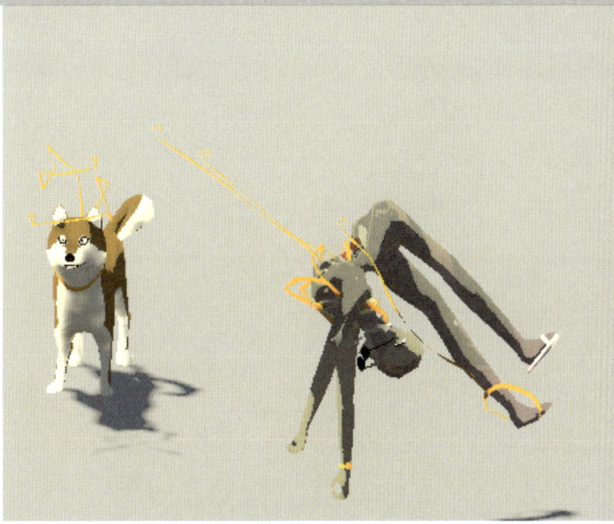

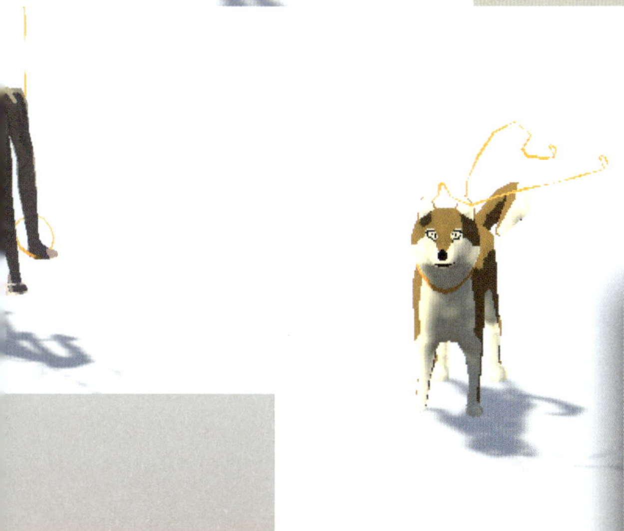

It is in the practice of Worlding again and again and again that Worlds become both arbitrary and easy, and therefore expressive and artful. And in the process, something changes inside the Artist. The masks get more and more exercise, and their gifts become accustomed to dancing together. Creating complexity, and living with the indeterminacy inherent in complexity, begins to feel like working a muscle that has always been there. As I write these words, versions of the *Emissaries* trilogy are humming along in multiple parallel instances on multiple computers on multiple continents. Institutional agents of art tend to their external ongoingness.

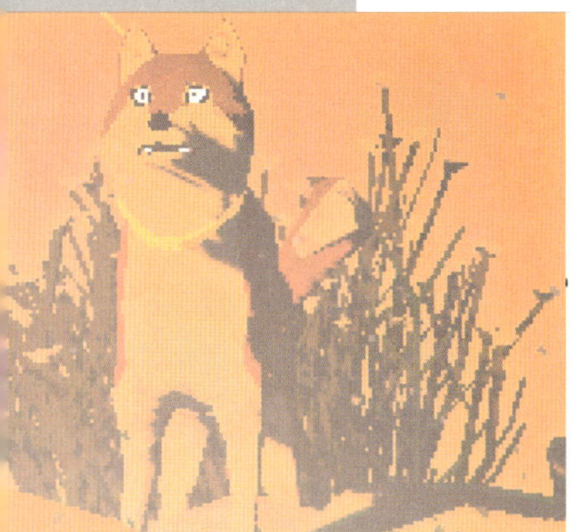

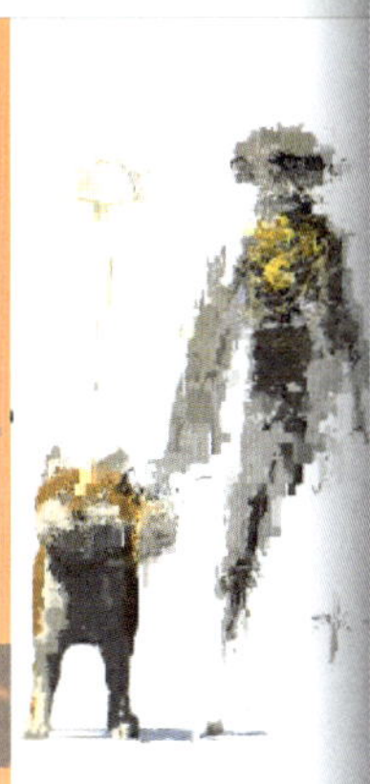

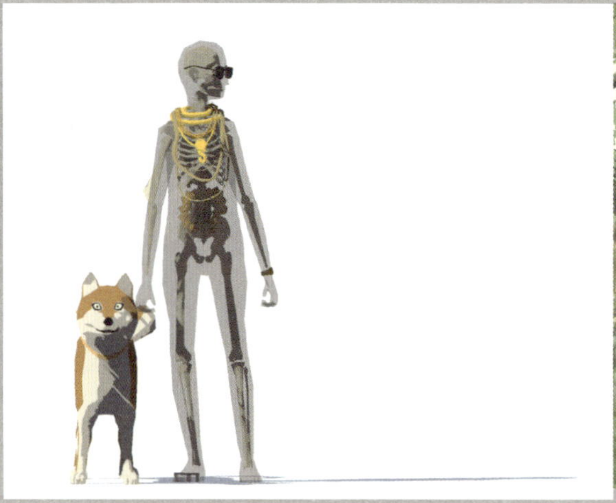

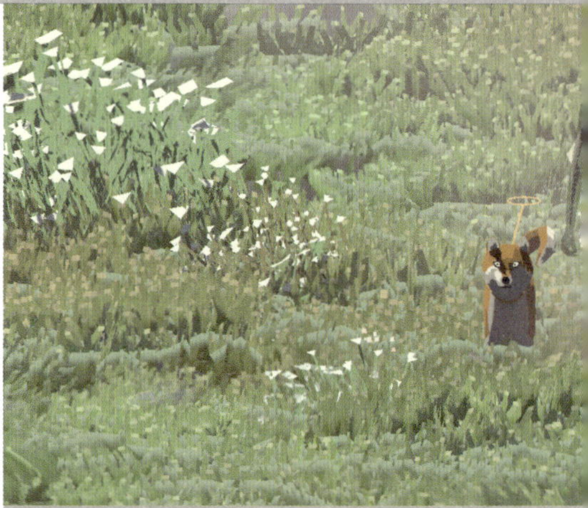

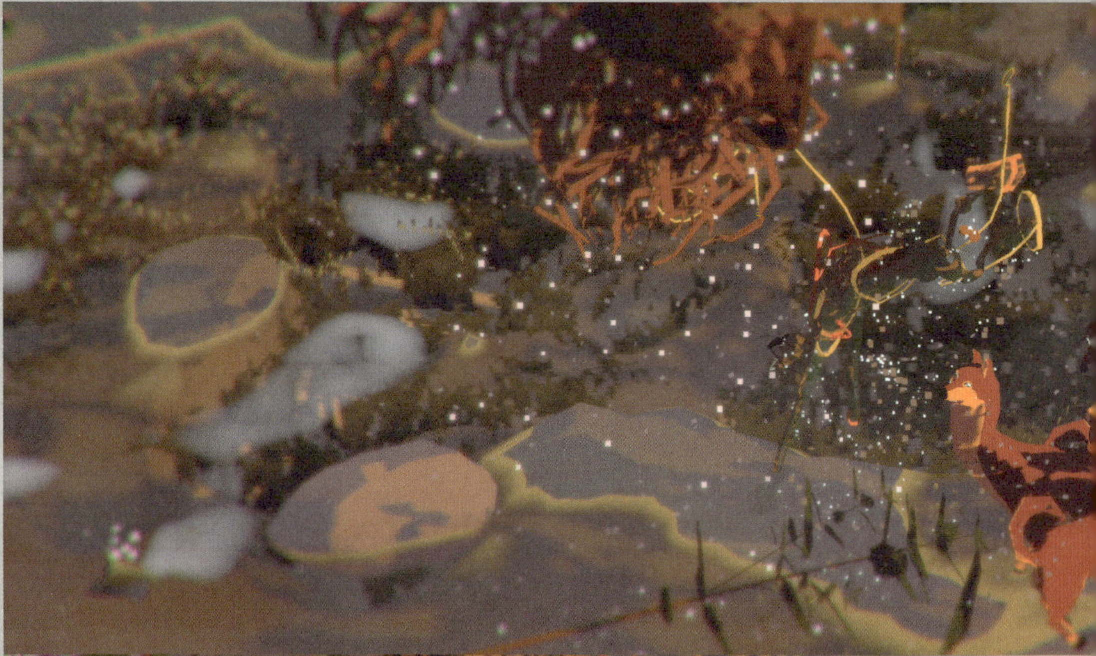

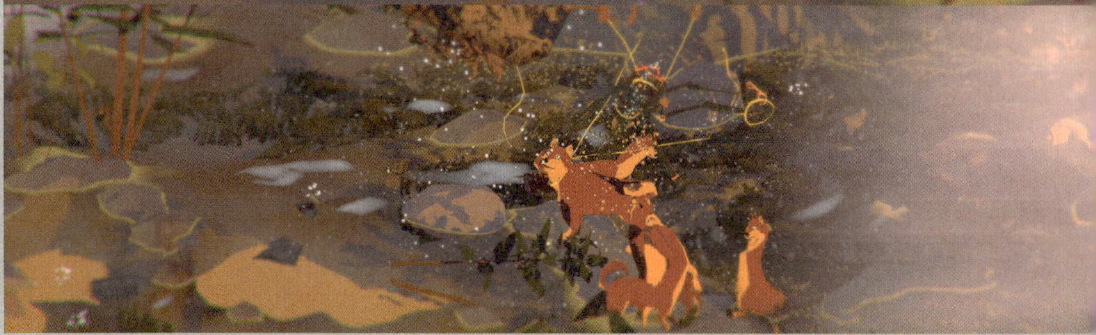

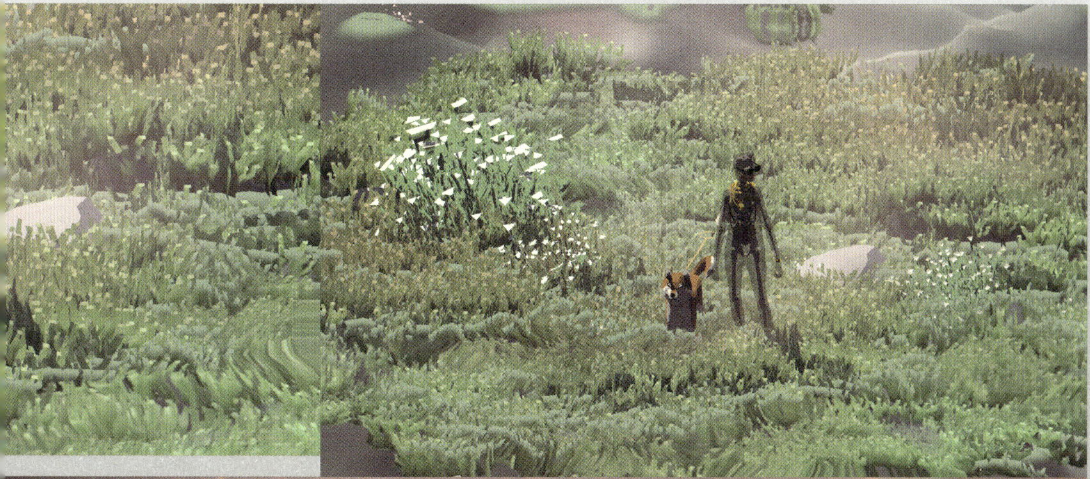

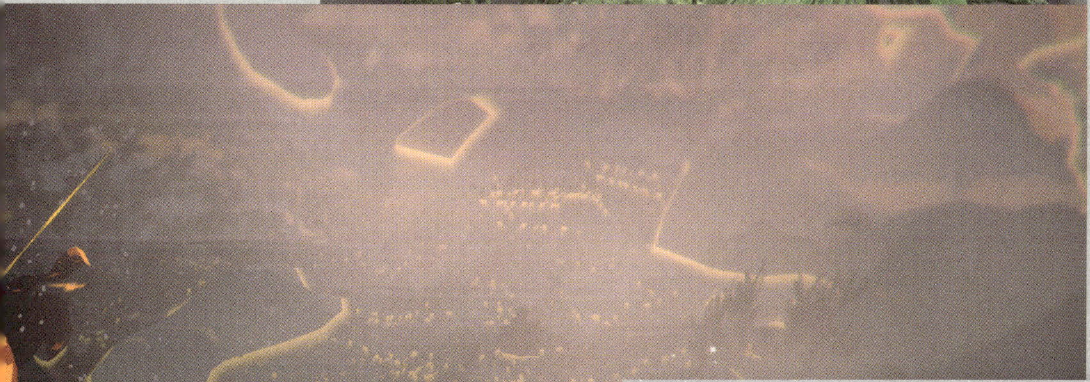

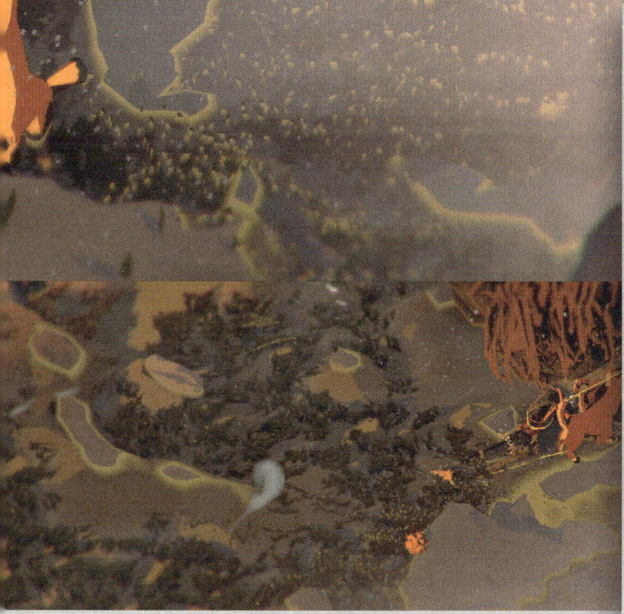

Artificial agents, in their own humble way, tend to their internal evolution. I don't know what will happen to *Emissaries*, or what it will transform into, or if it will ever be a home to anybody human. All I know is that this deliberate incompleteness is beginning to feel mundane, even natural. My mind is racing with the energy of the masks, ready to exit *Emissaries* and begin Worlding new Worlds. And still, I'm excited by the thought of returning to *Emissaries* one day, in another stage of its life, and in another stage of my own, to serve it new food I've found.

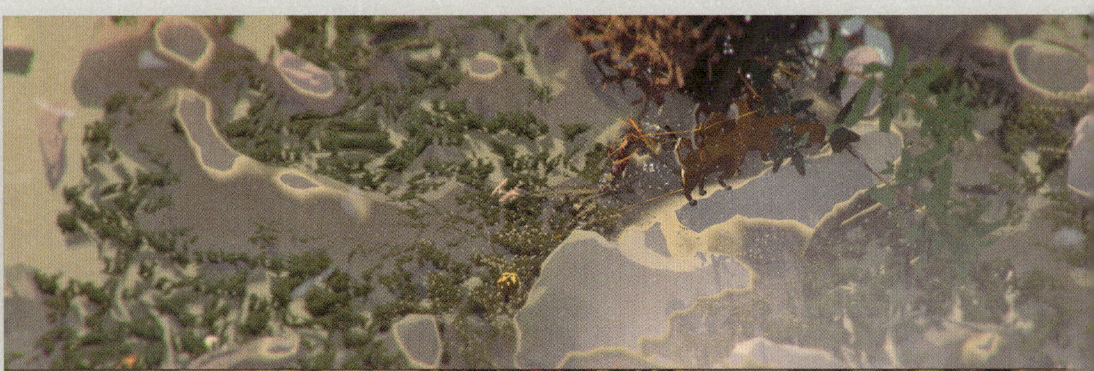

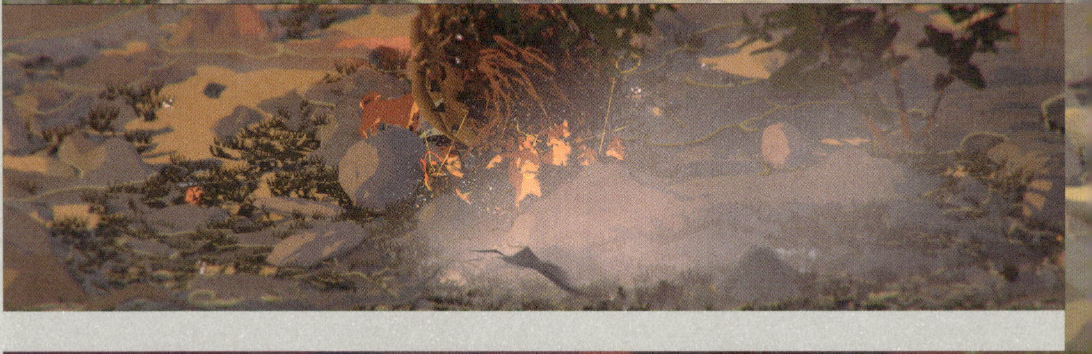

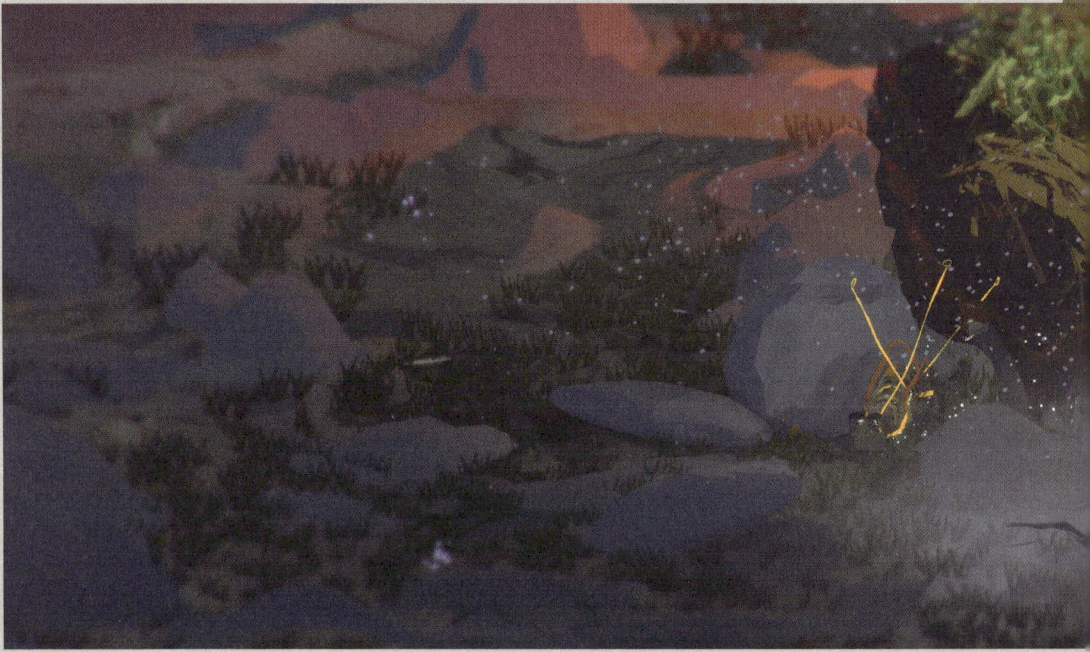

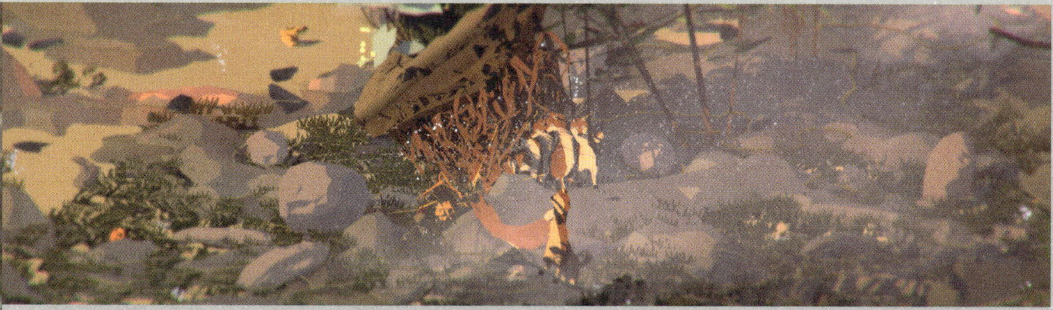

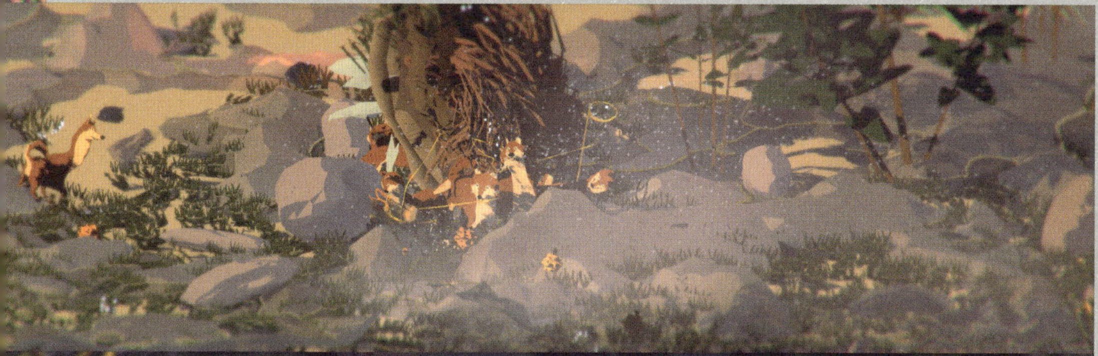

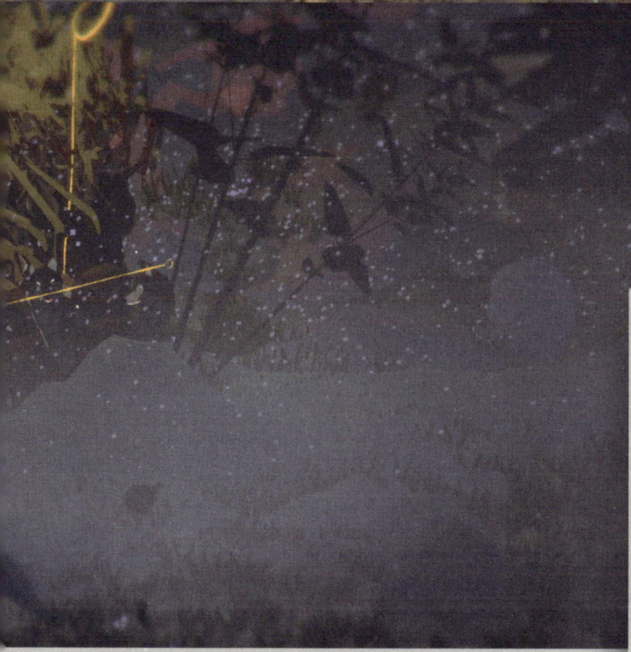

Only a short while ago, people believed that the Earth was the stationary home around which the sun, stars, and universe revolved. It took instruments, maths, stories, and imagination to persuade humankind that the Earth is in truth a *home on the move*. Still today, the coincidence of home and movement seems like a duck-rabbit paradox: possible to know about, but impossible to feel both without vomiting.

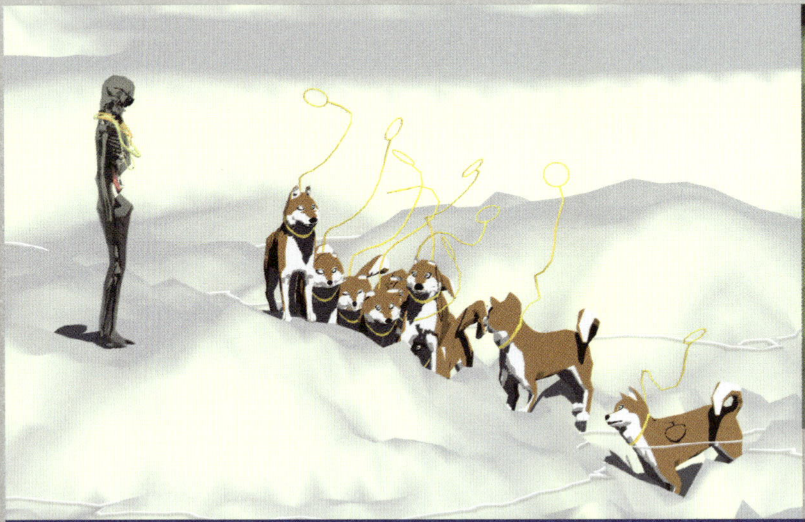

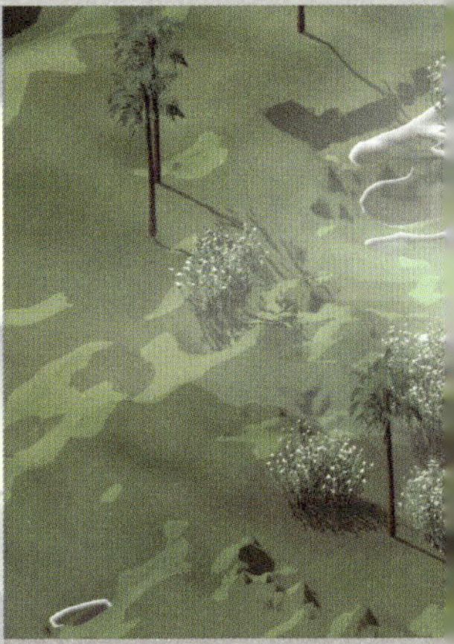

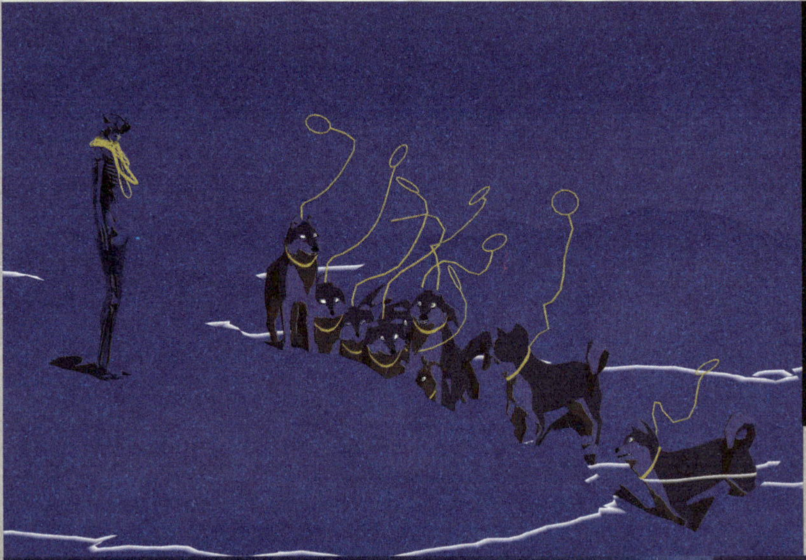

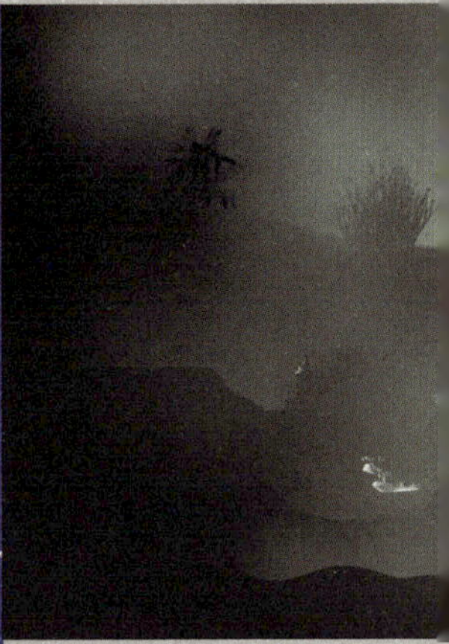

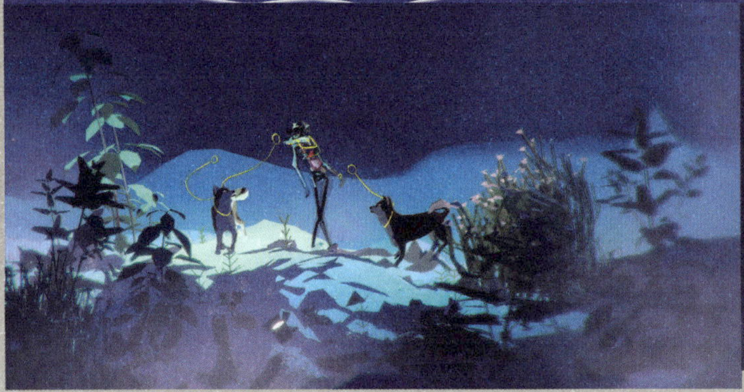

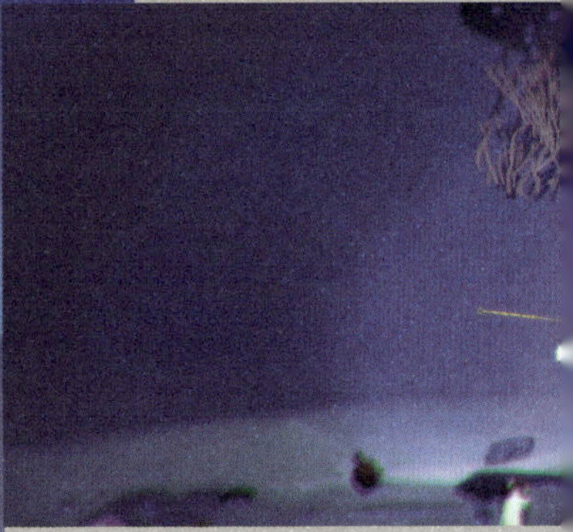

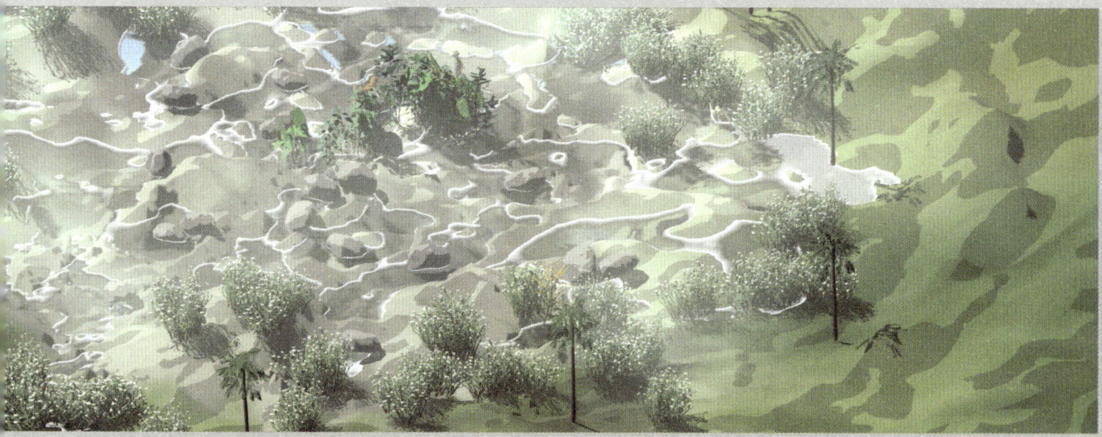

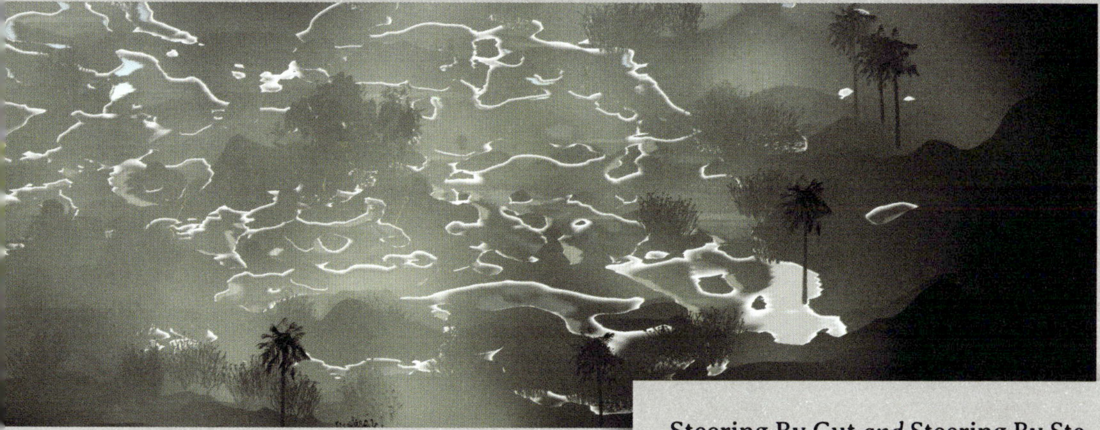

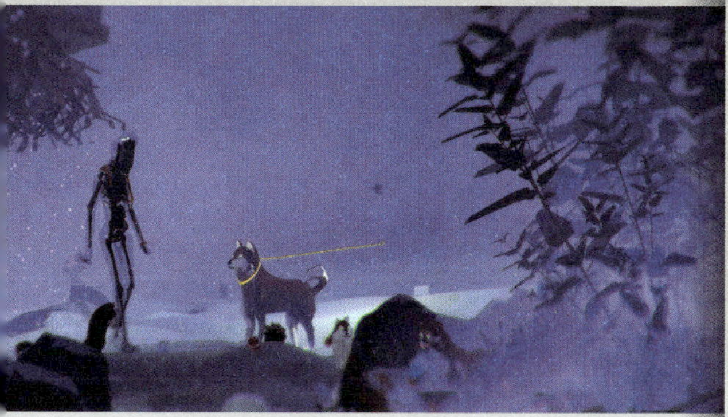

Steering By Gut *and* Steering By Stories, Seeking Home *and* Seeking Surprise, Worlding is a practice that can structure the activities of the mind to do it all. In Worlding, the human mind can expressively extend itself to be at home nowhere, everywhere, and anywhere. To finally feel that 'not all those who wander are lost'. To go on fierce adventures happily knowing that 'still there are seeds to be gathered, and room in the bag of stars'. To create infinite games as an act of agency. To live to World, and World to live.

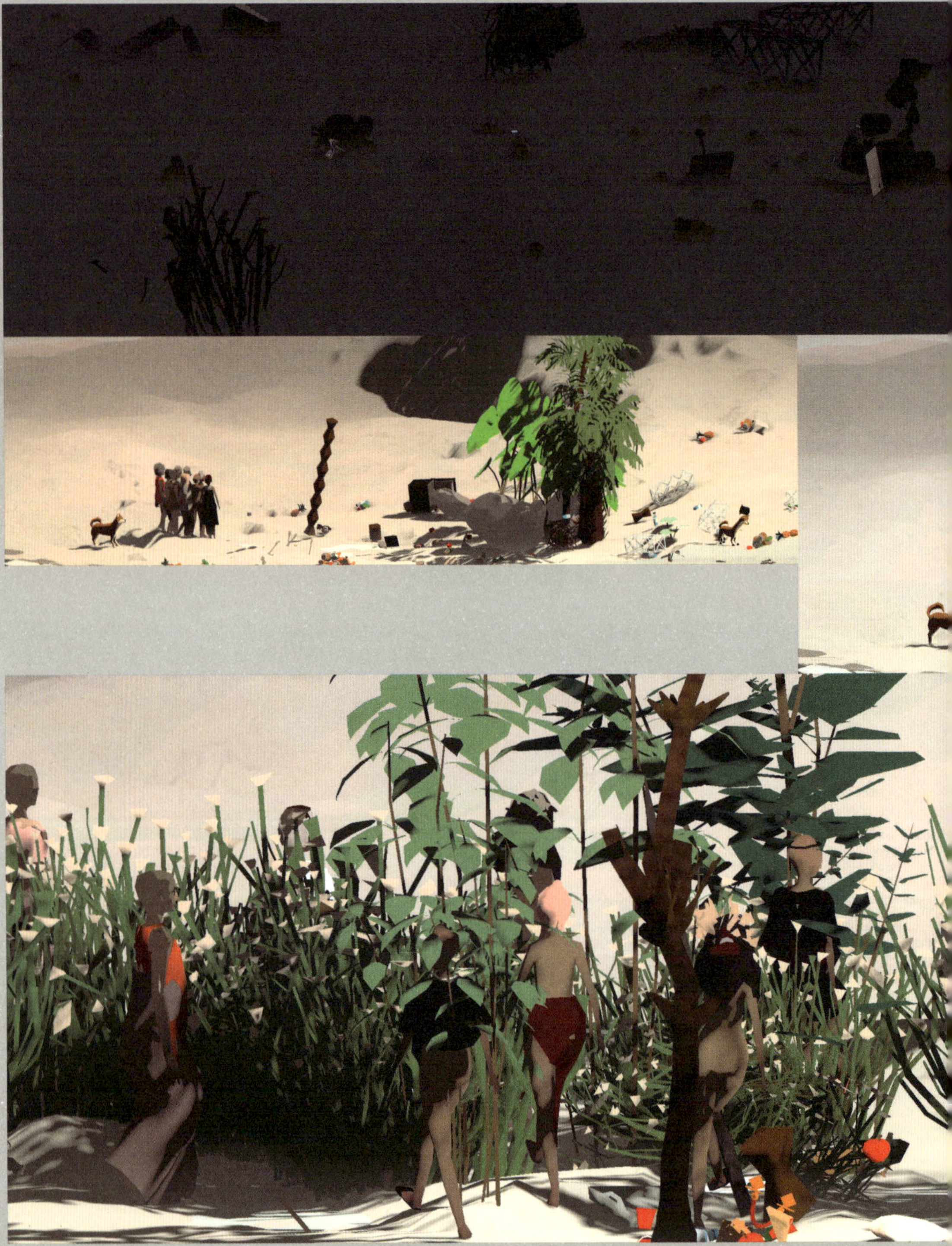

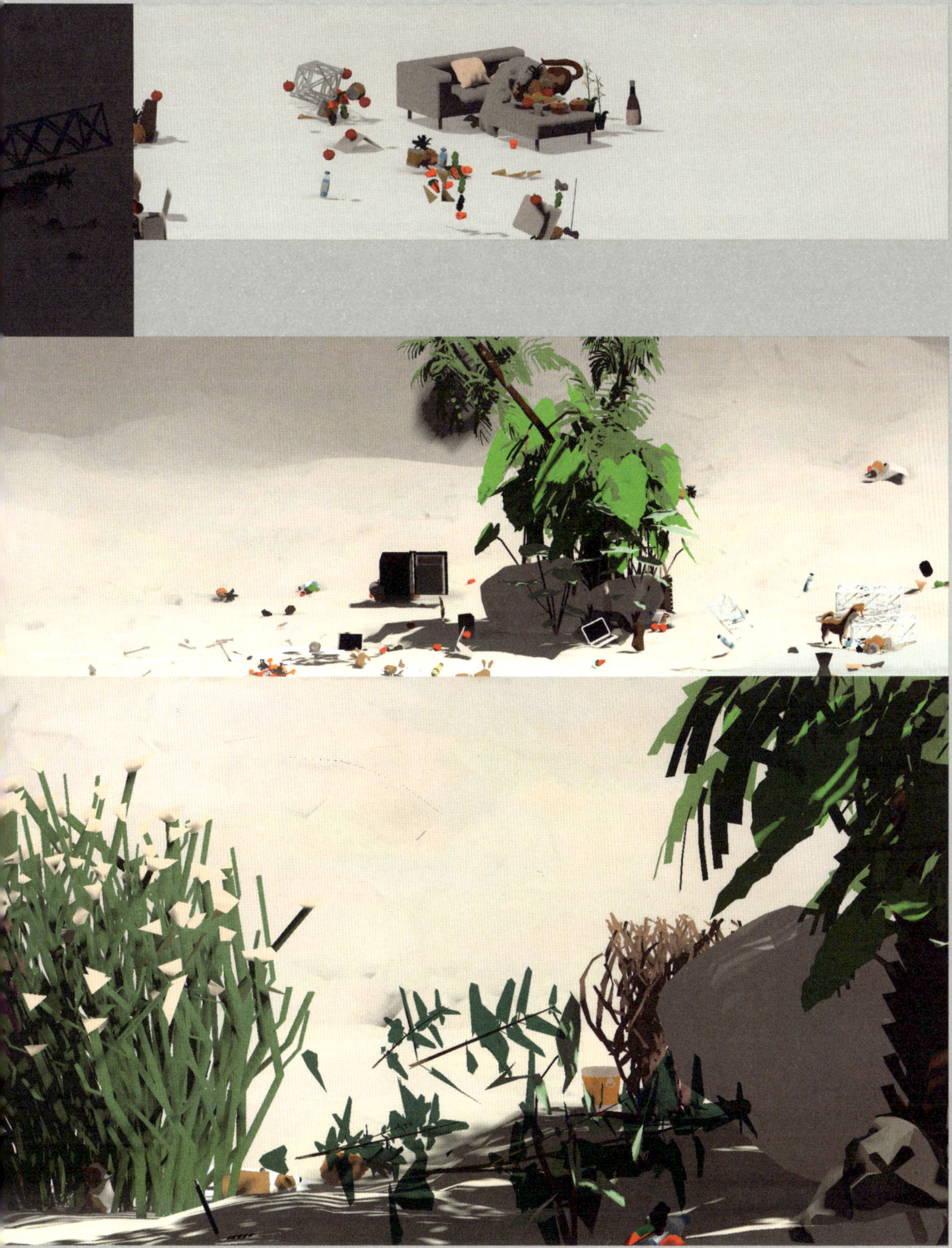

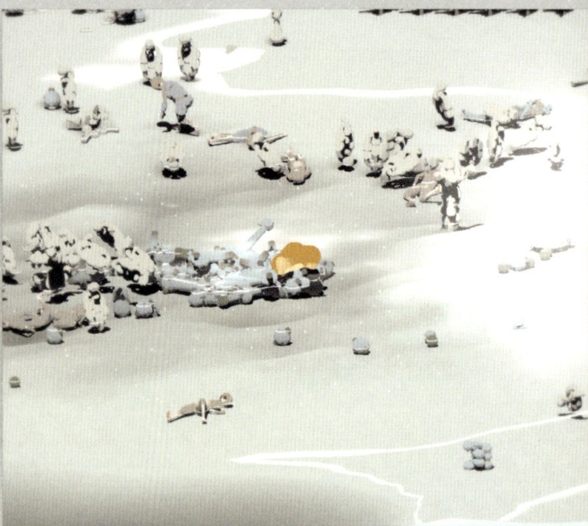

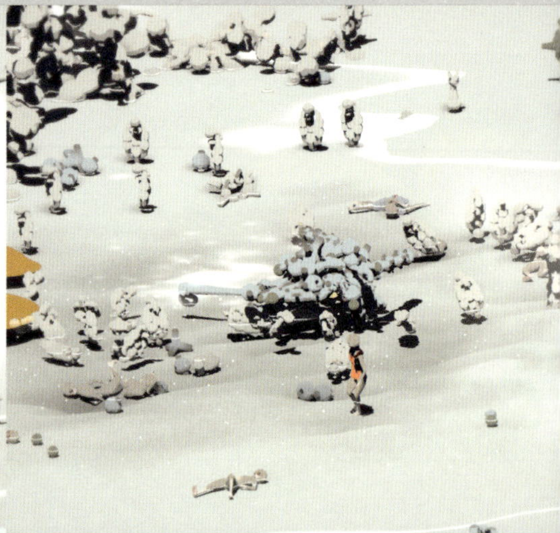

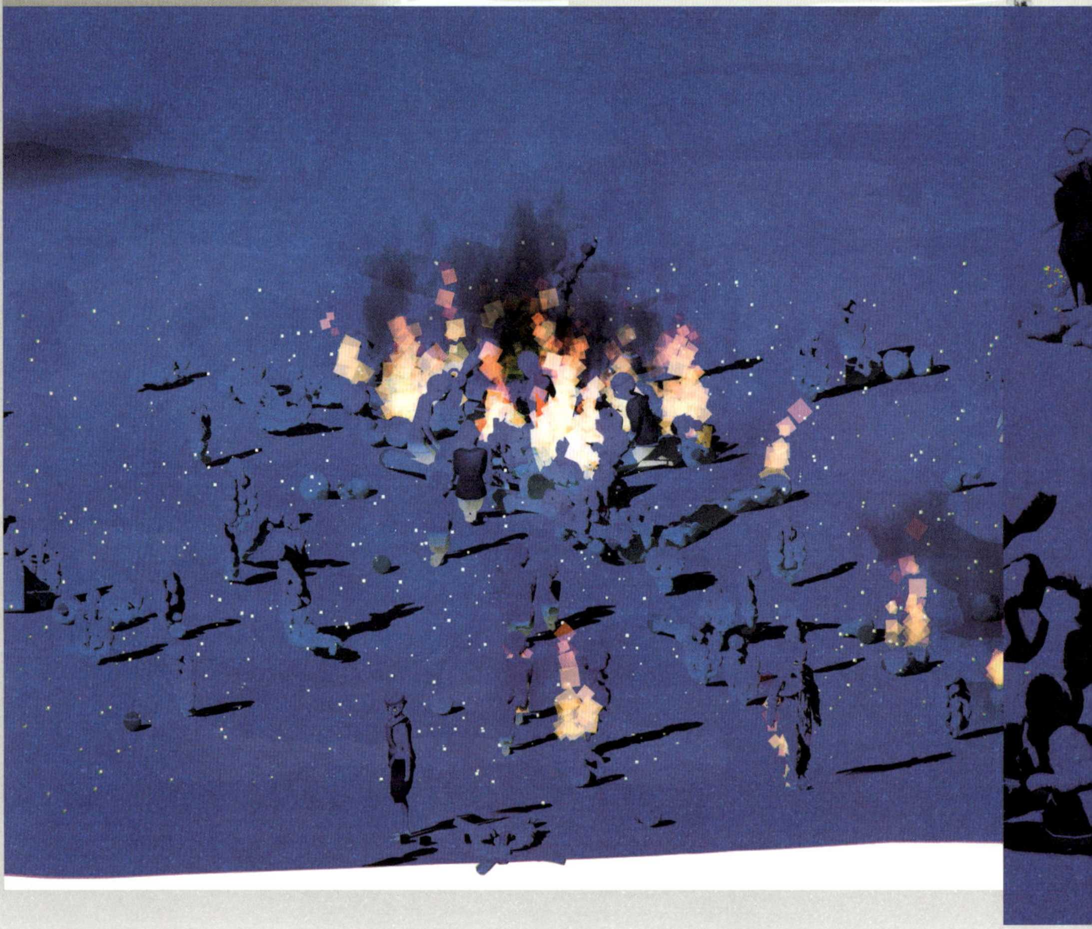

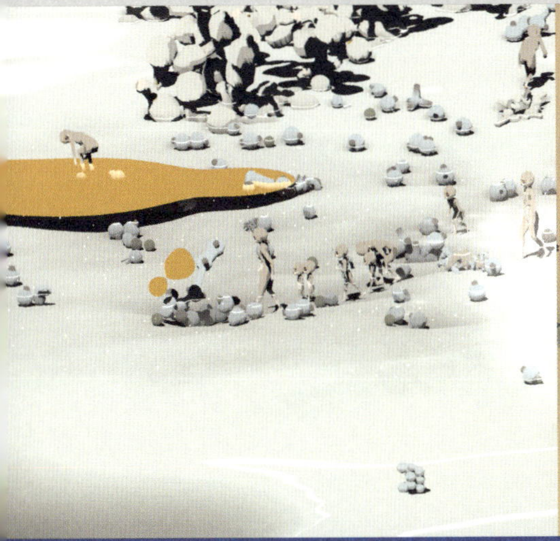

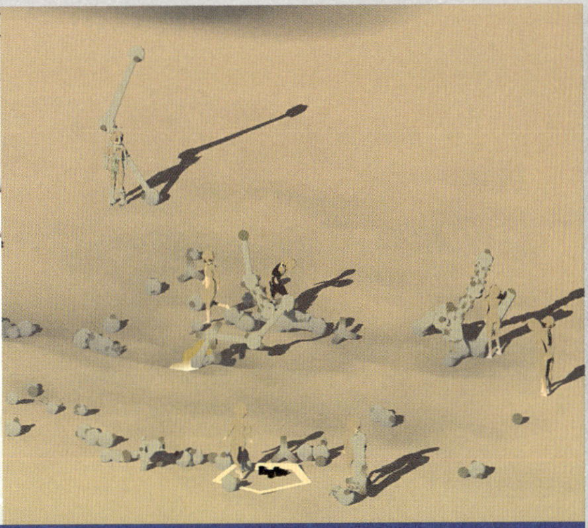

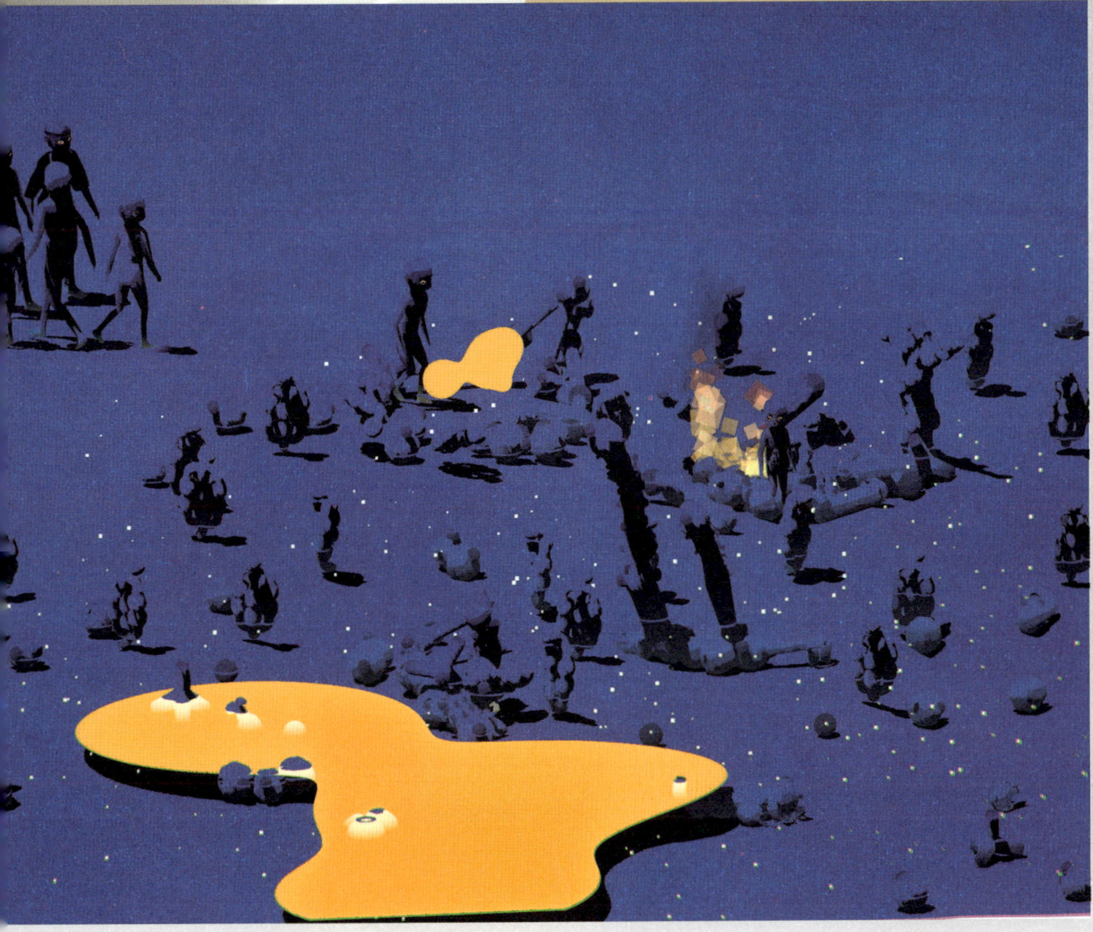

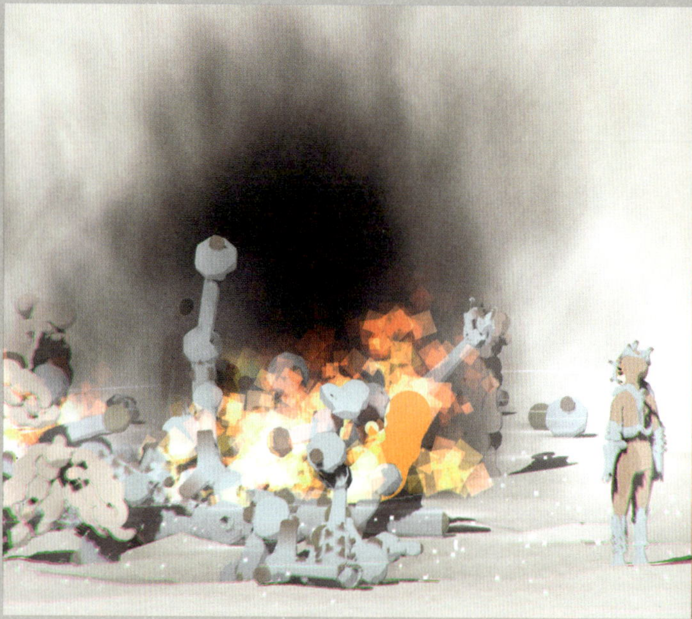

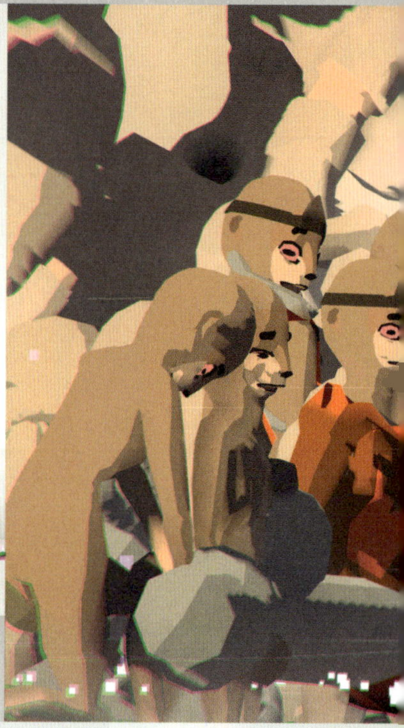

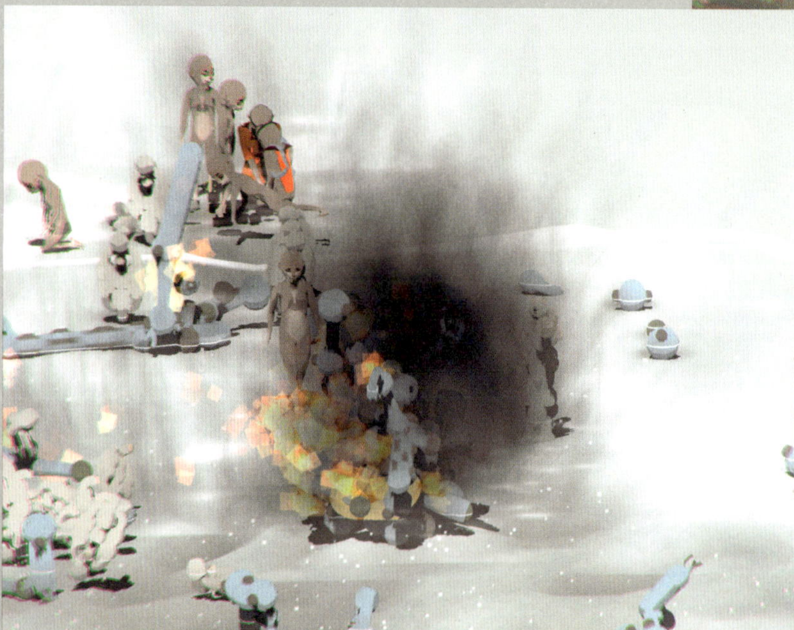

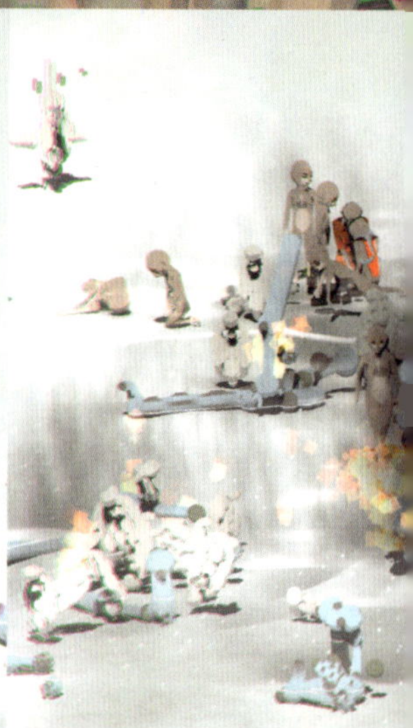

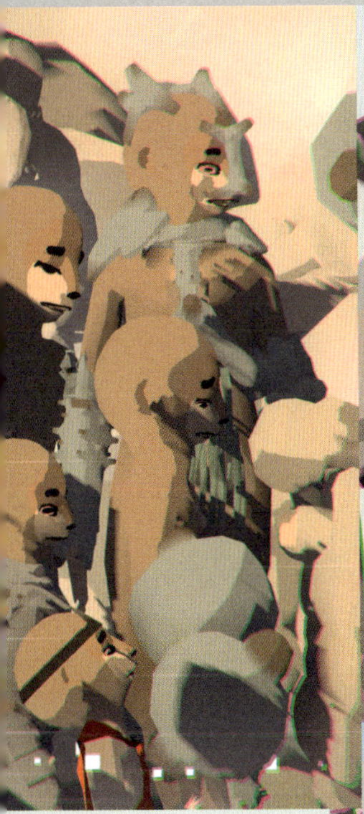

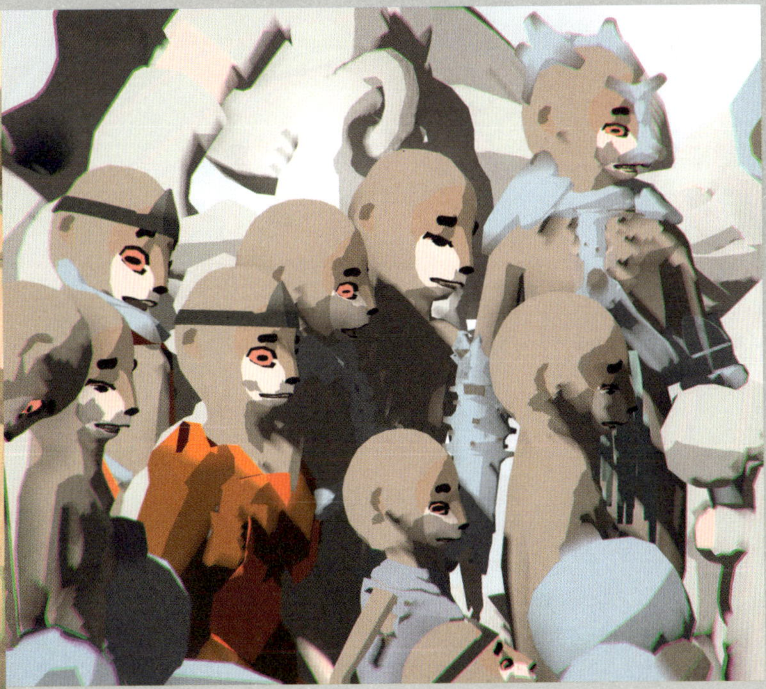

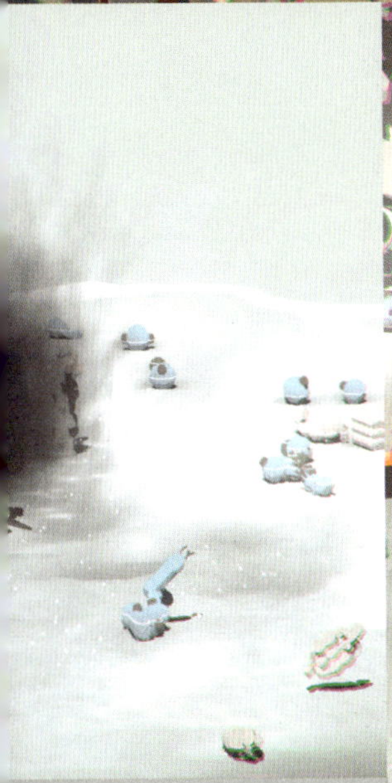

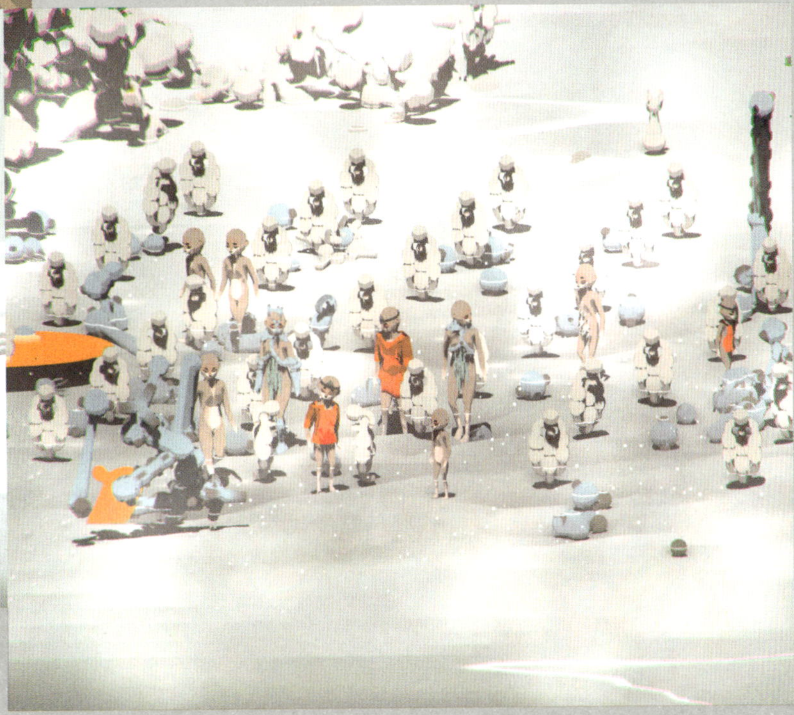

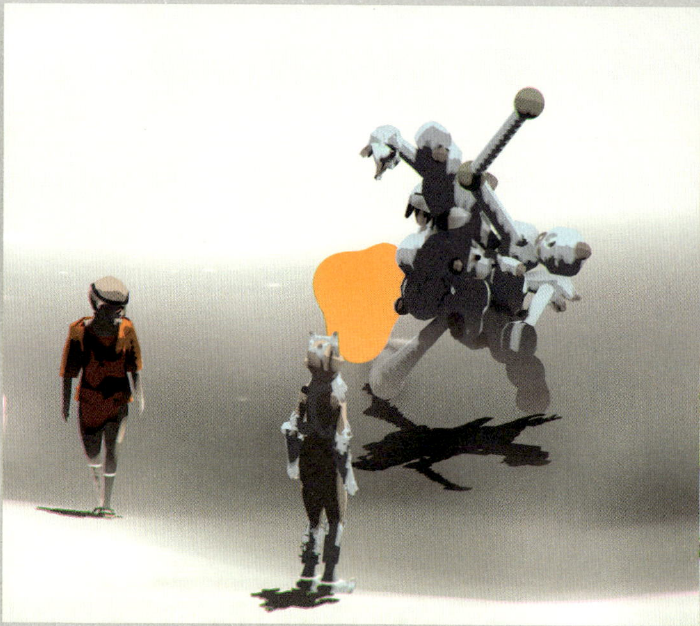

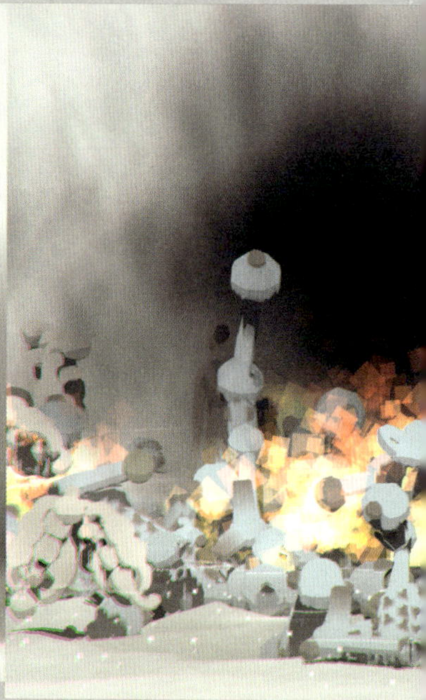

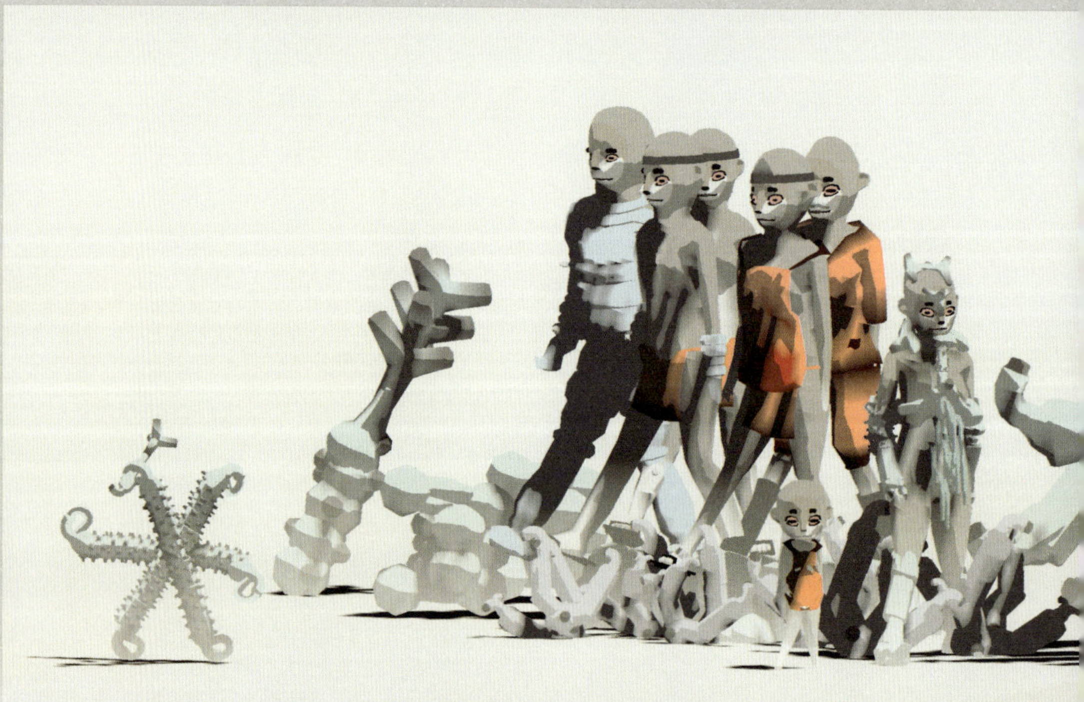

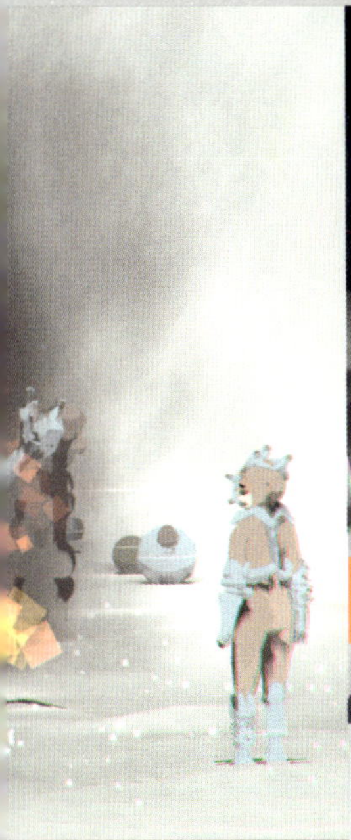

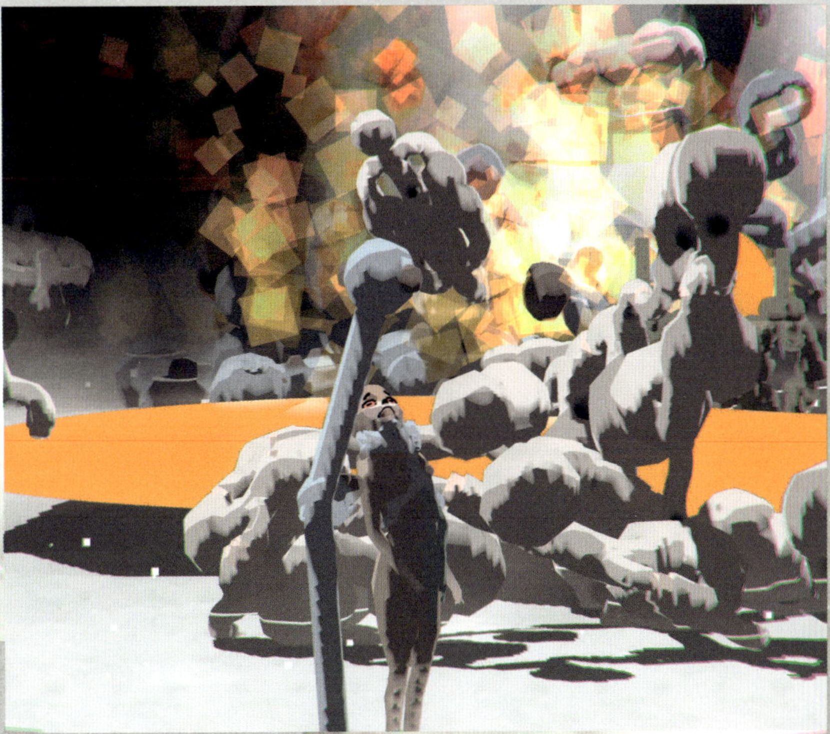

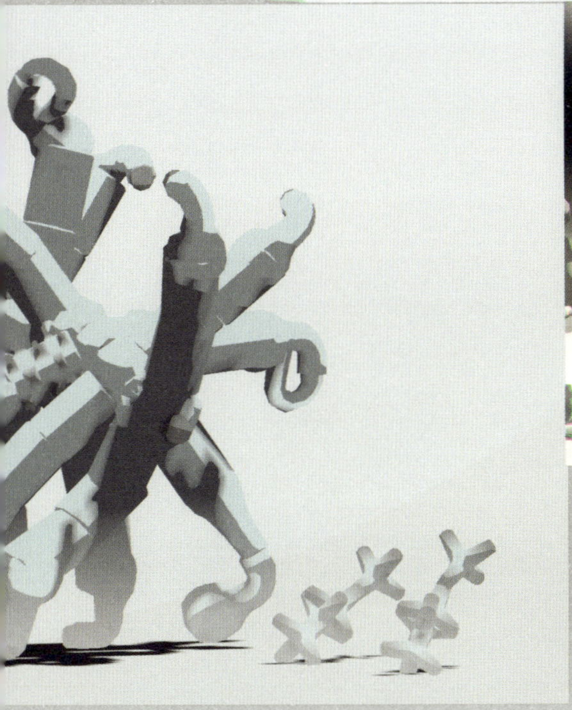

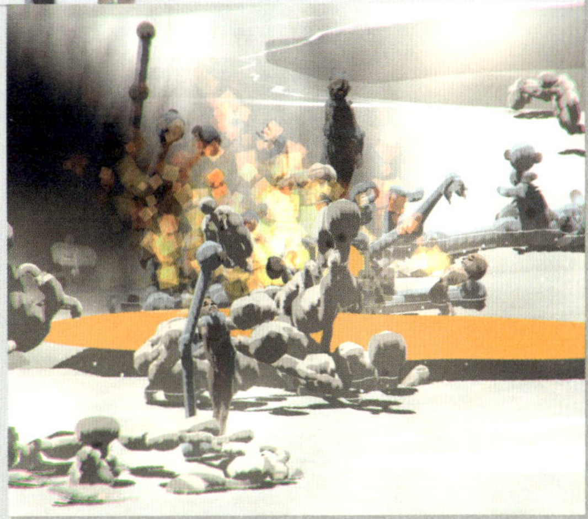

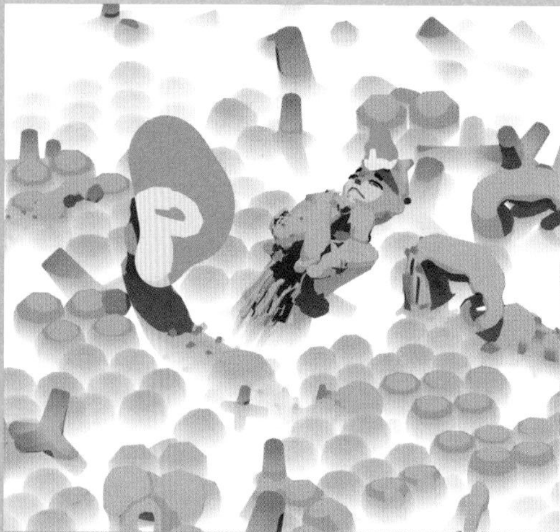

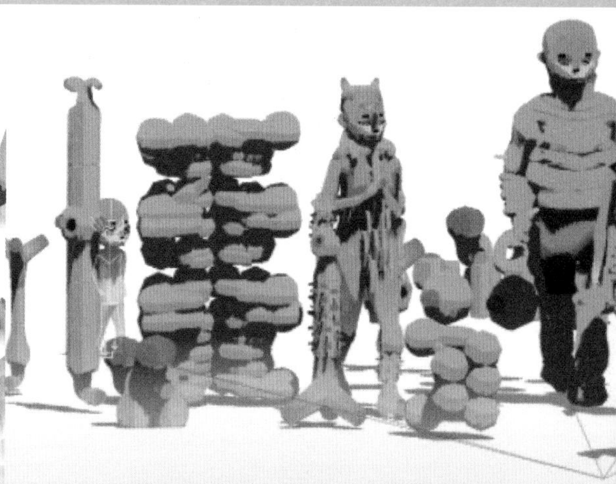

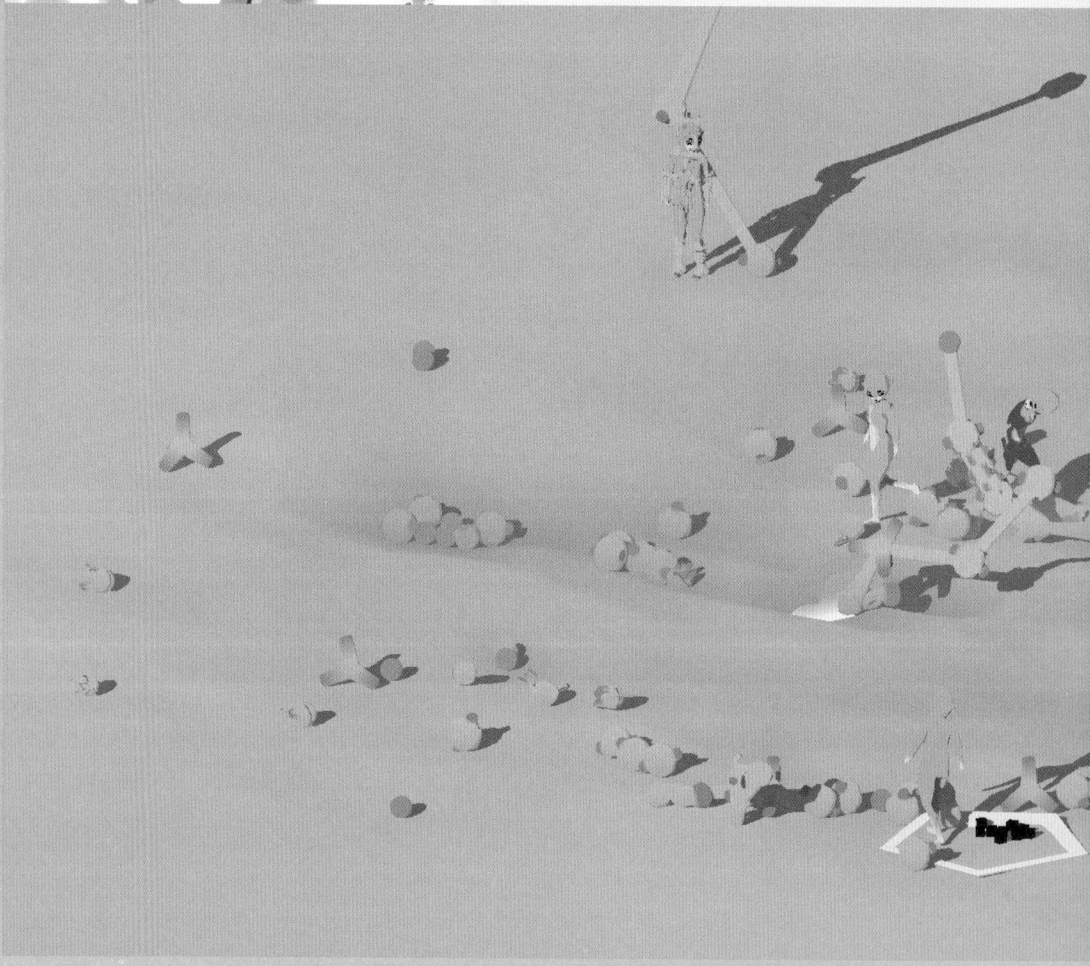

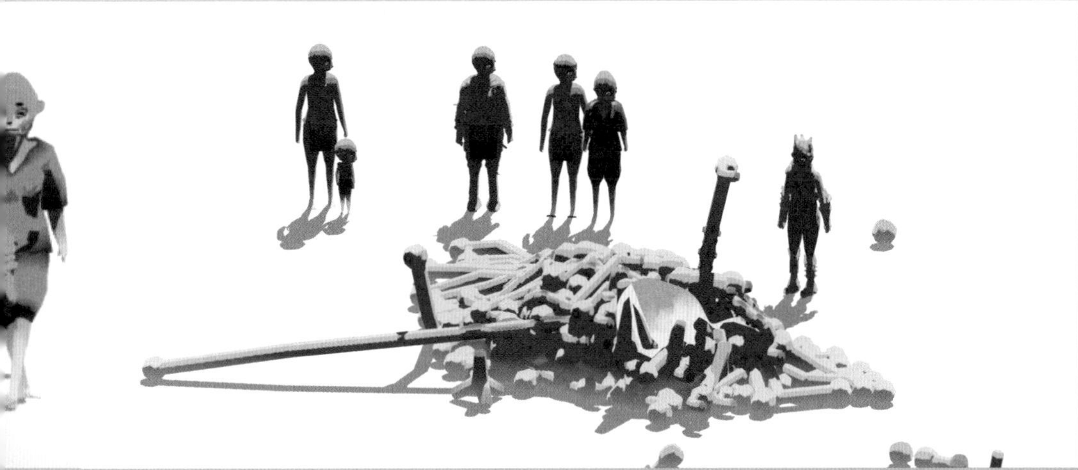

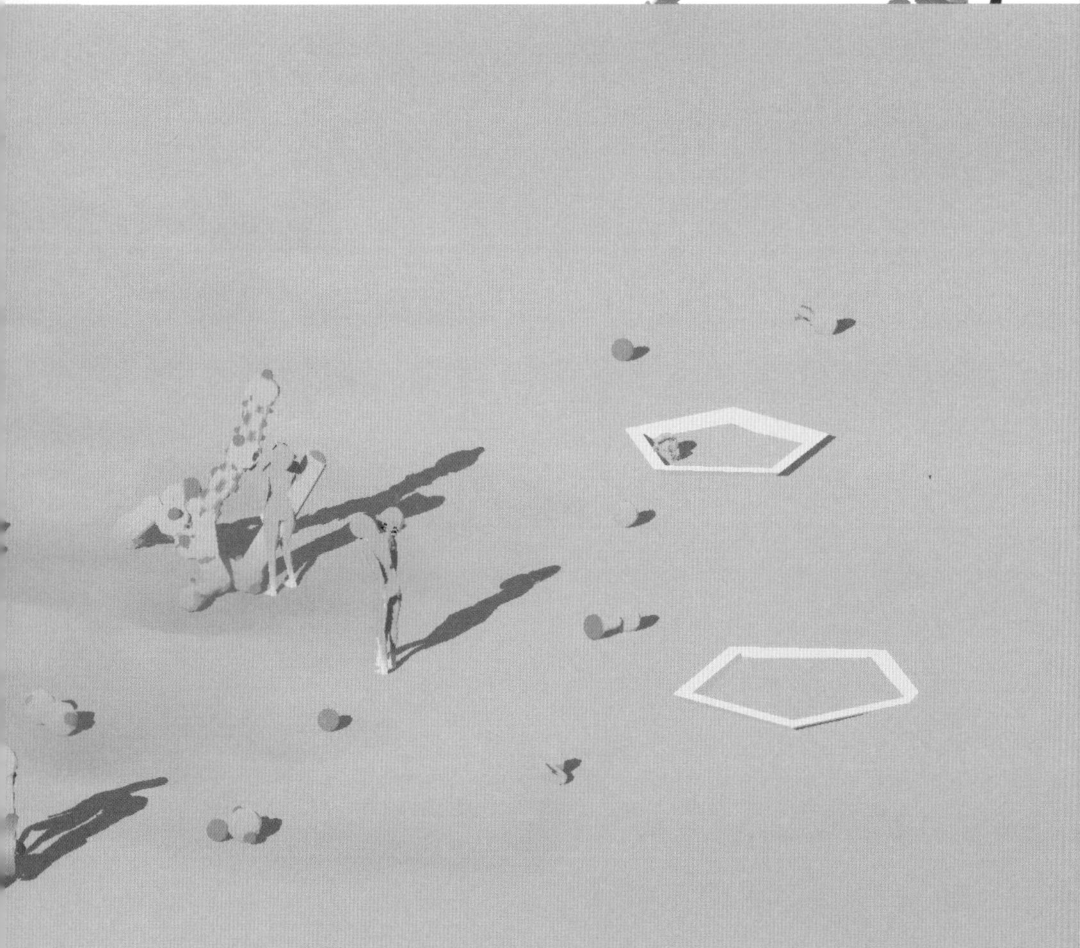

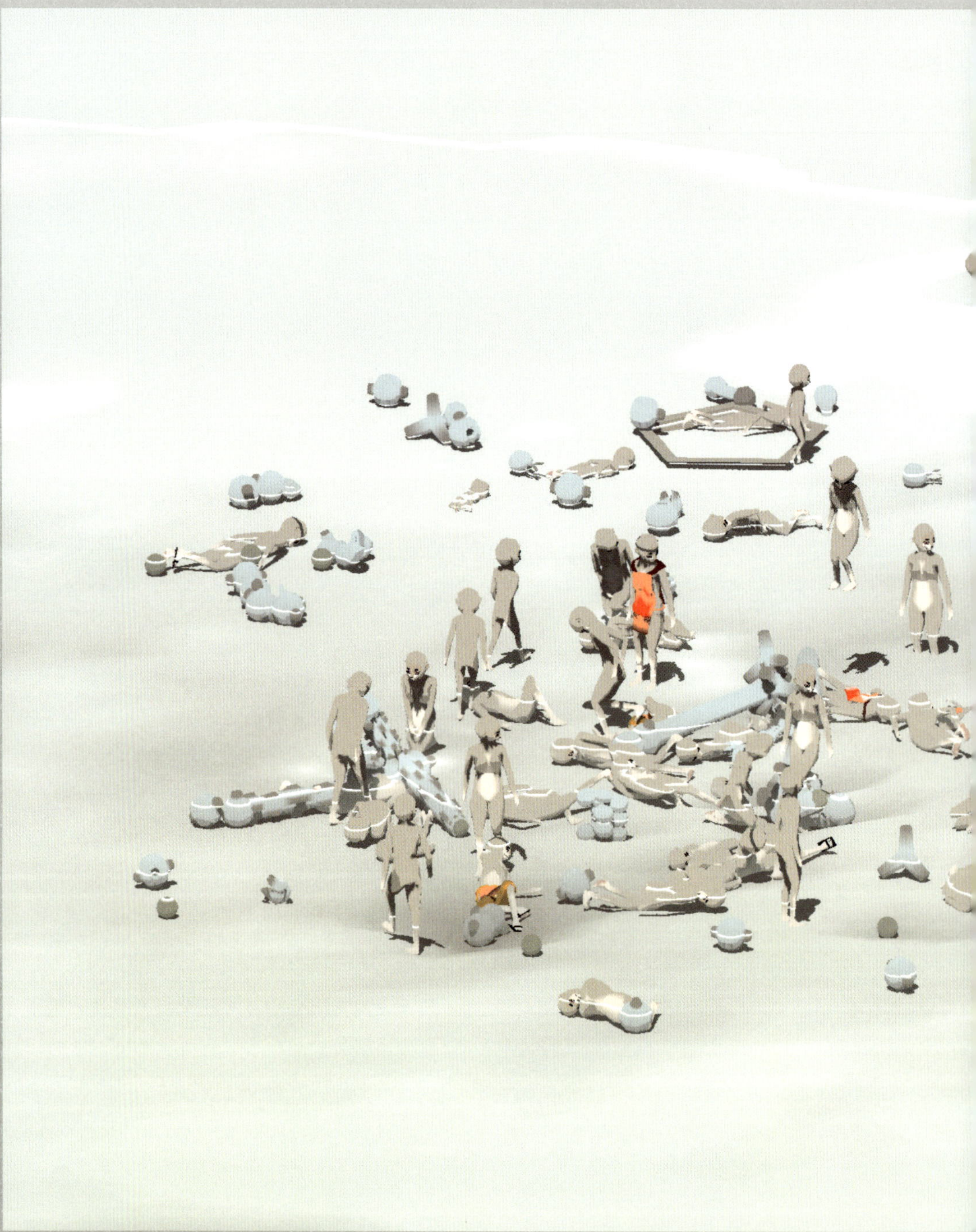

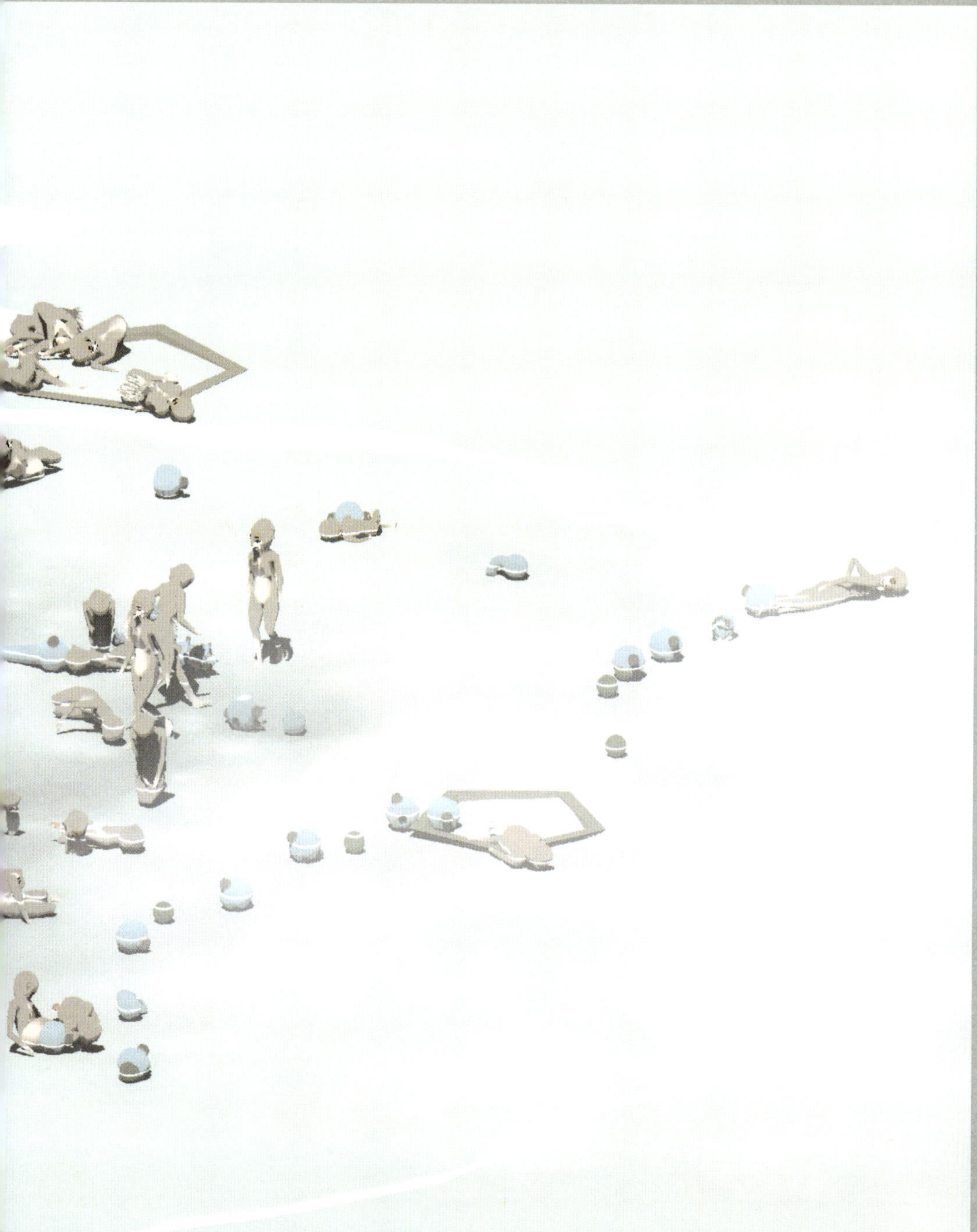

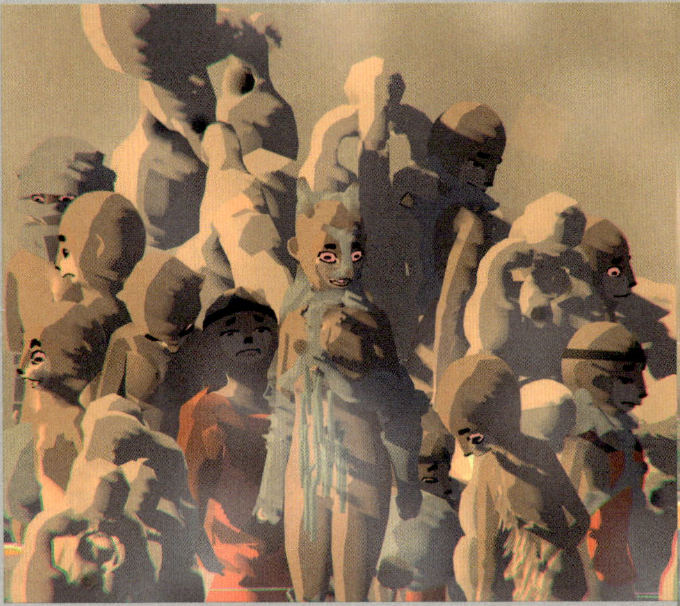

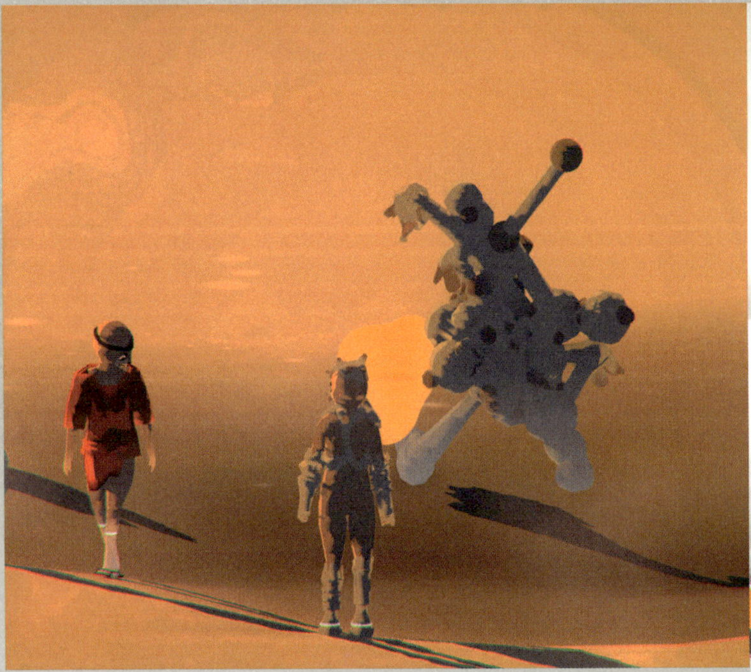

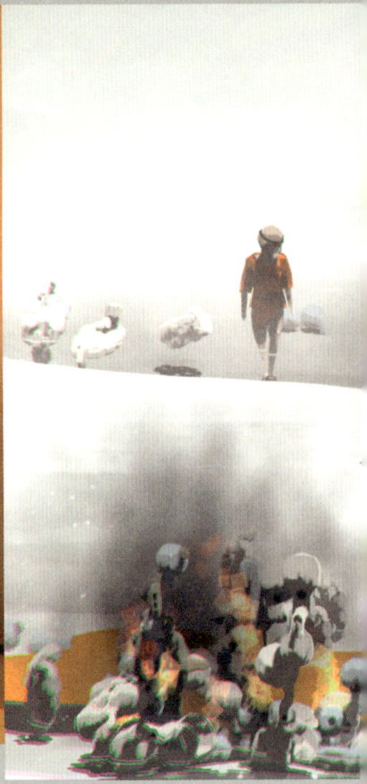

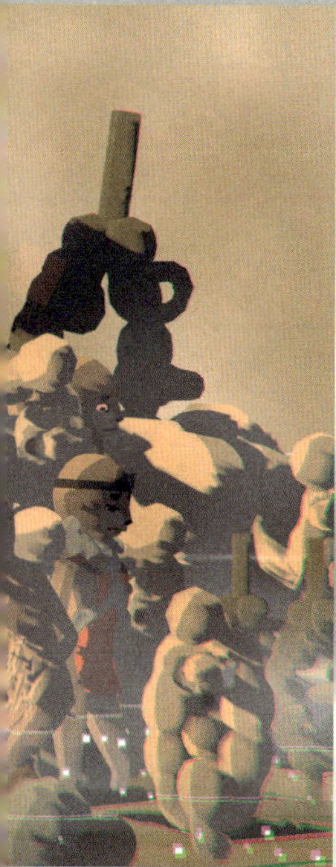

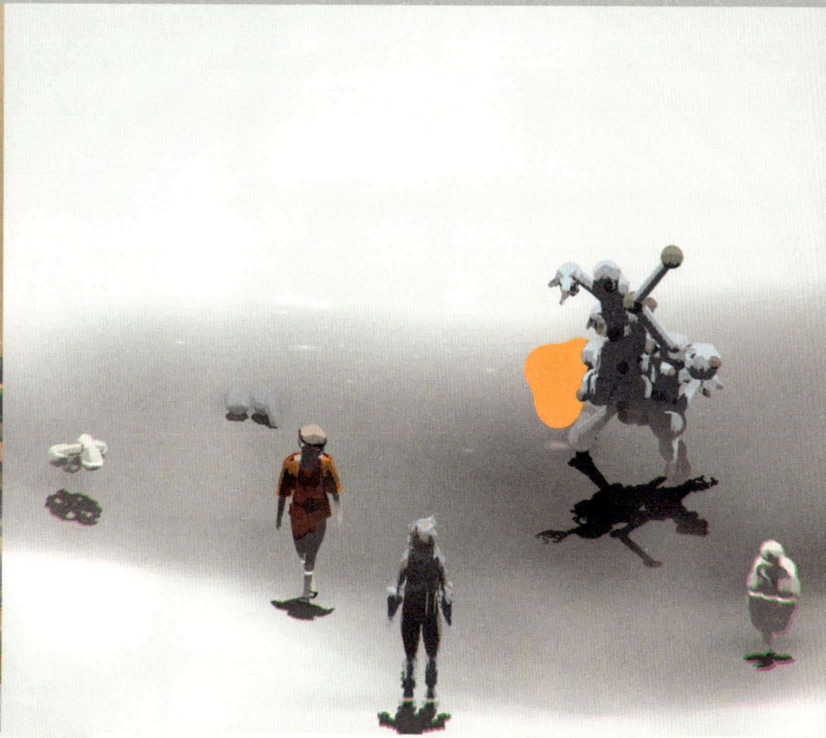

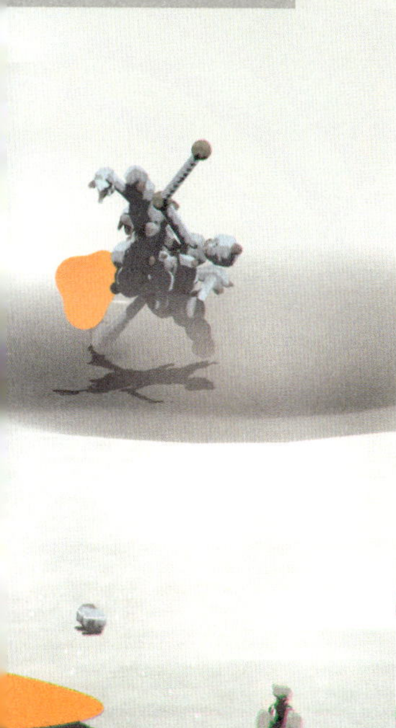

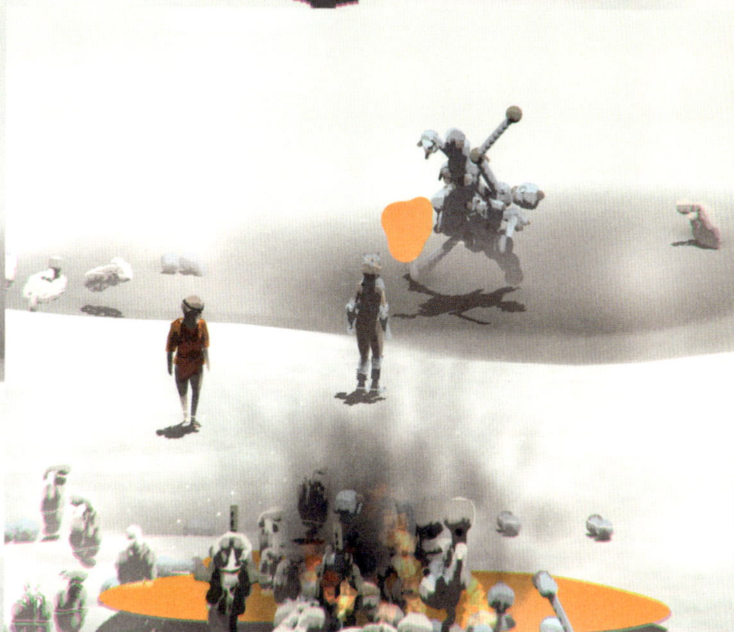

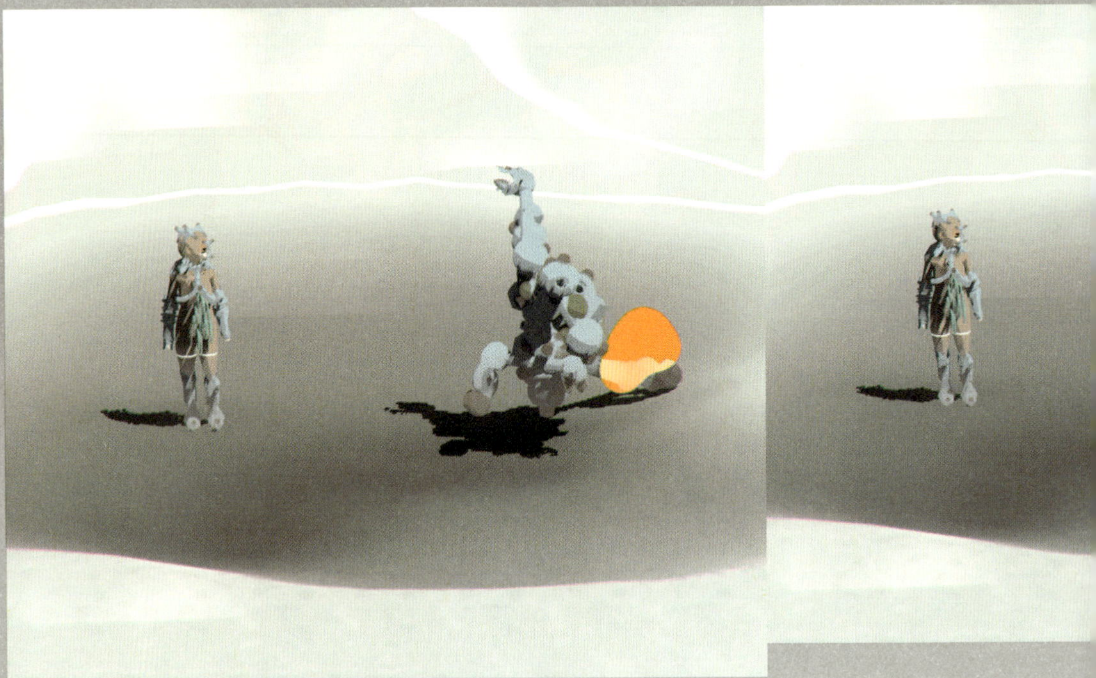

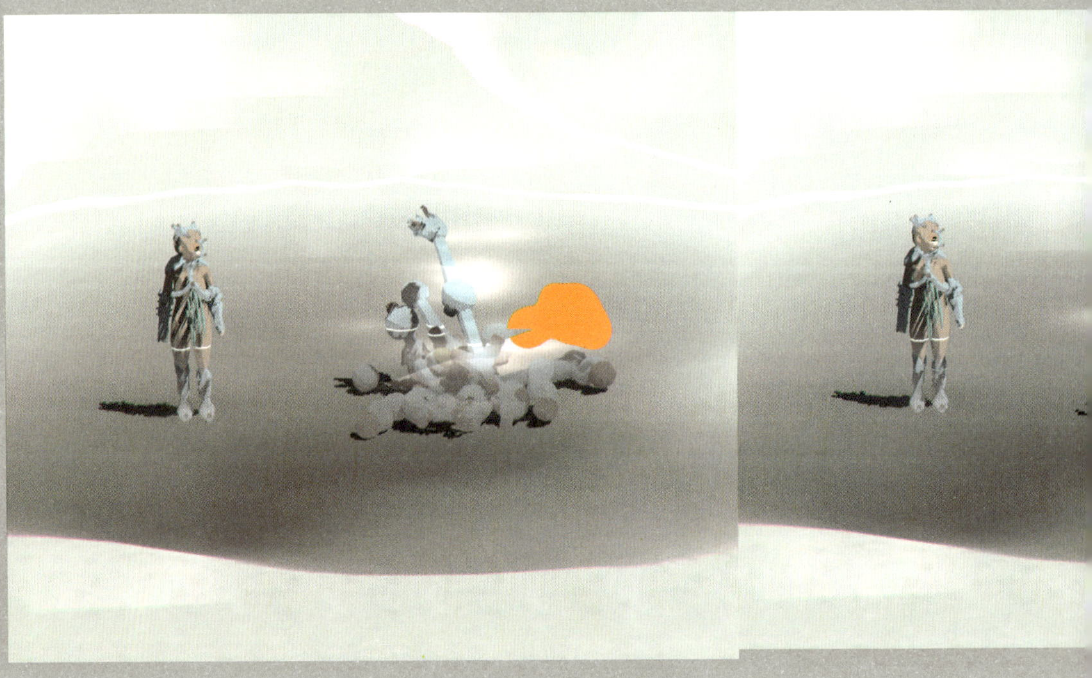

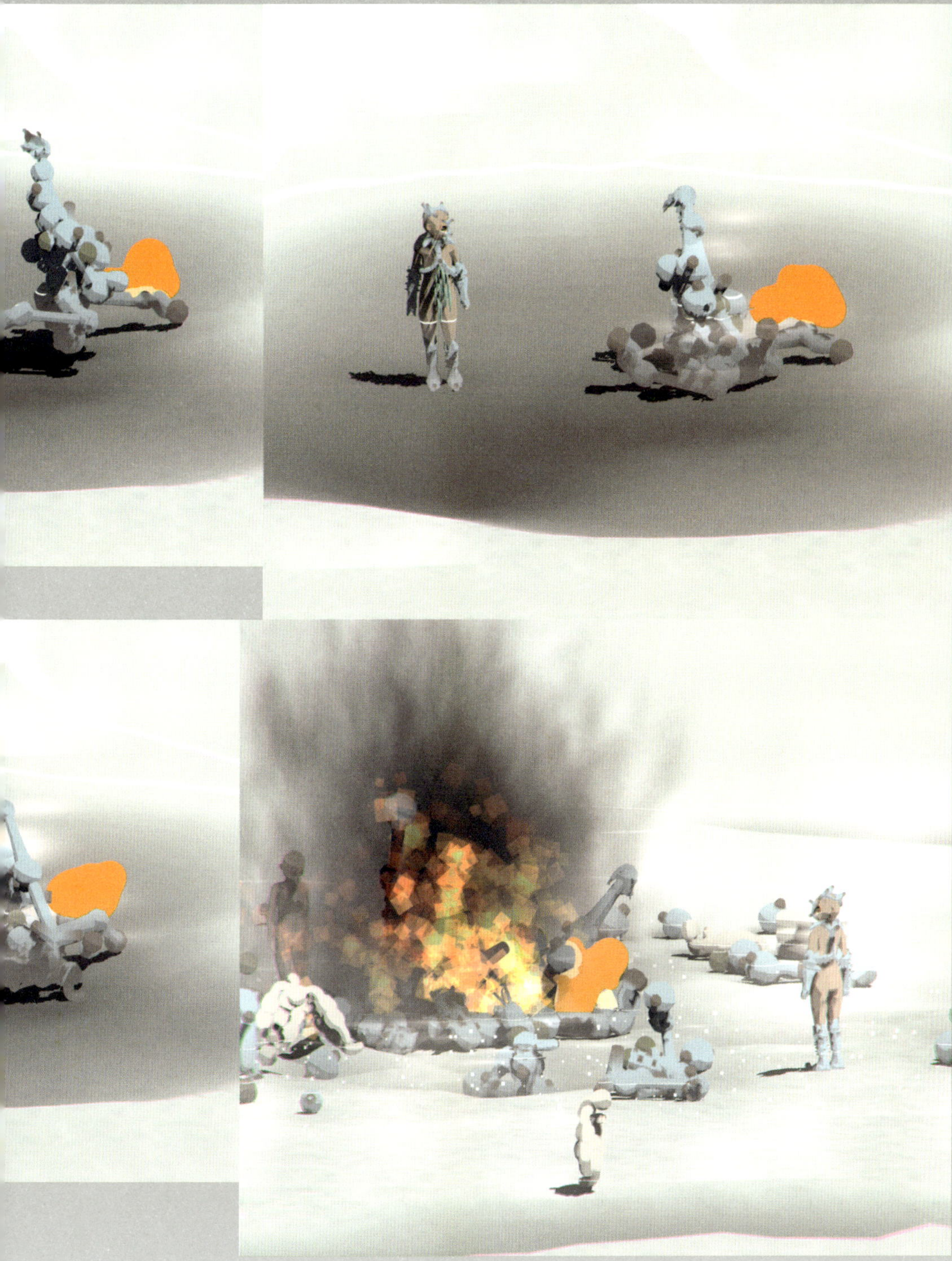

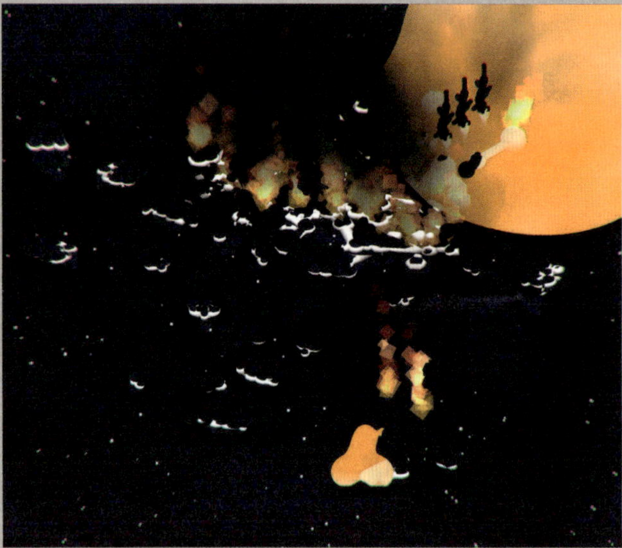

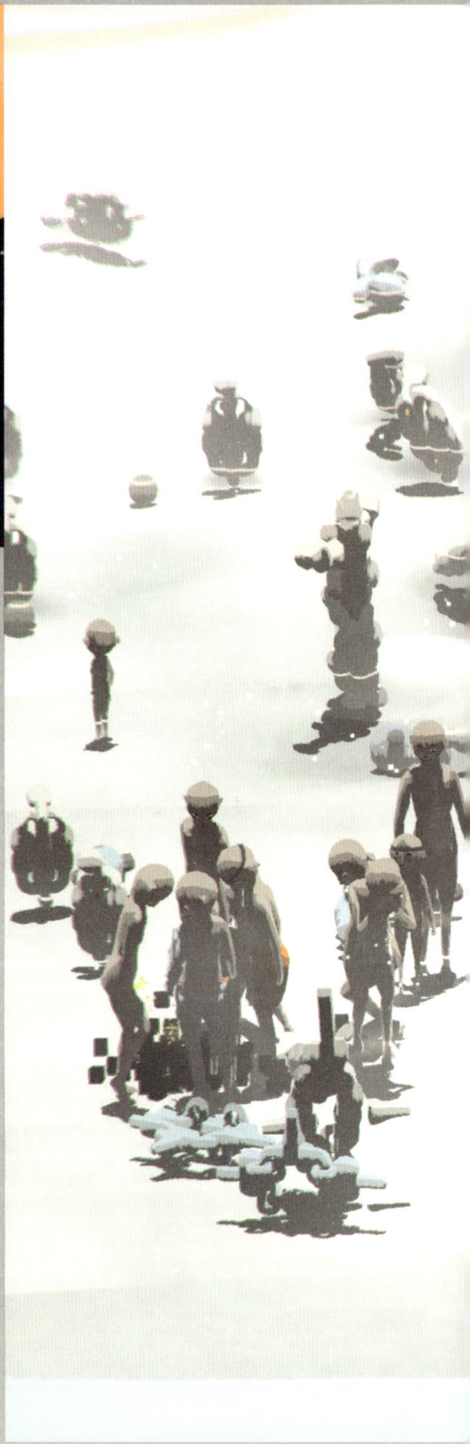

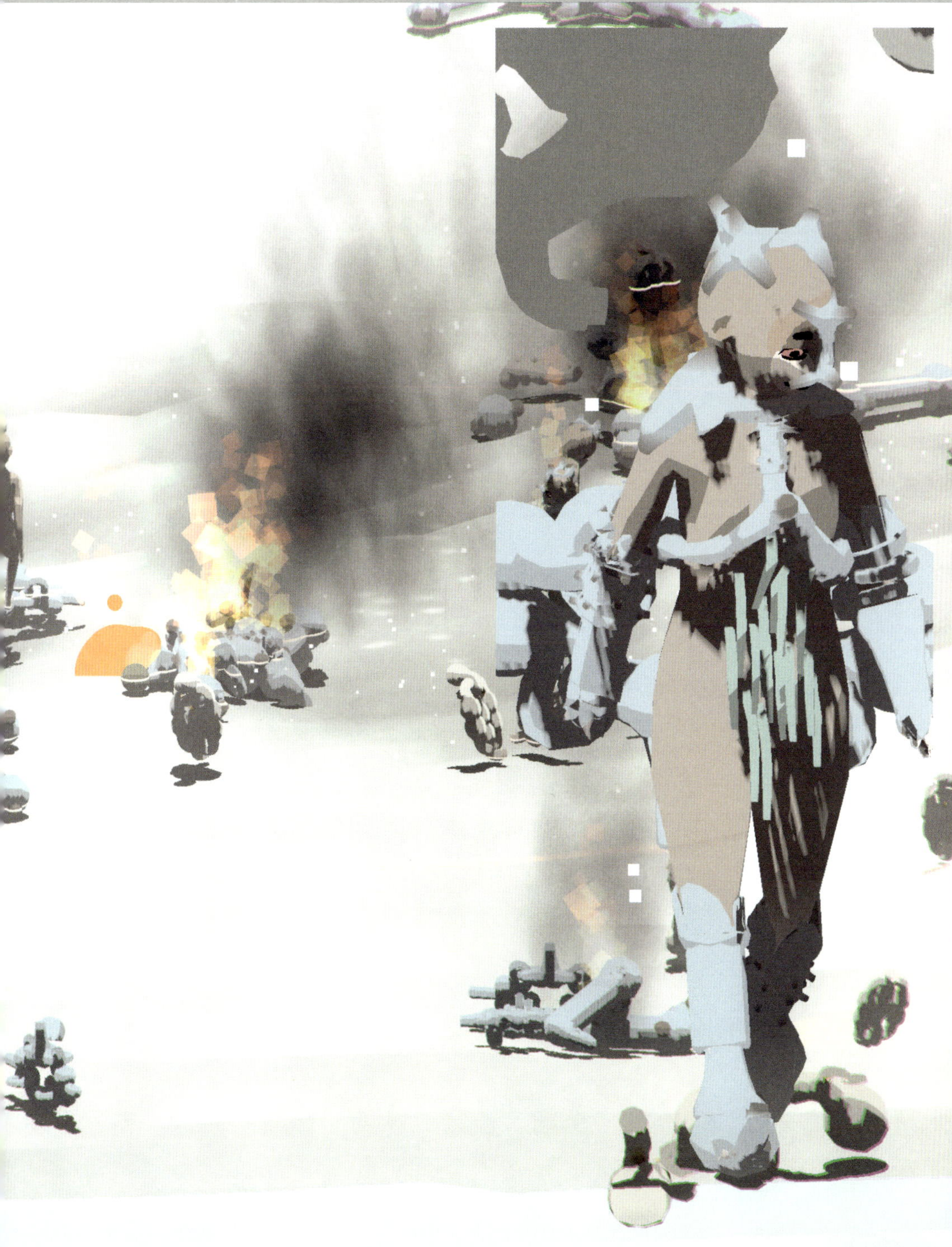

Appendix

Emissaries

Emissary In The Squat of Gods
Emissary Forks At Perfection
Emissary Sunsets The Self

Ian Cheng
live simulations
2015–2017

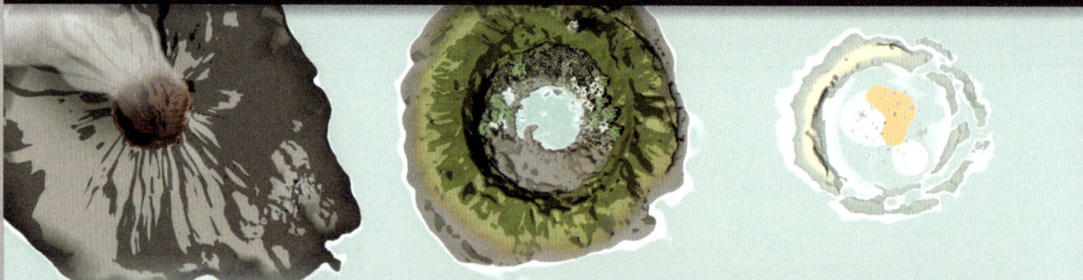

EMISSARIES is a trilogy of simulations featuring the influence of narrative agents. It is composed of three interconnected episodes that each model a pivotal moment in the ongoing story of cognitive evolution, past and future.

In each episode, the Emissary—caught between unraveling old realities and emerging weird ones—attempts to achieve a series of deterministic narrative goals, an analogy to the narrative nature of consciousness. But crucially these goals can be set off course, procrastinated, disrupted by the underlying simulation and its non-narrative agents who vex the Emissary with other kinds of minds.

Seen together, *EMISSARIES* is a macro-scale portrait of the life of a landscape: from chaotic Volcano, to fertile Crater Lake, to Sentient Atoll. By first observing the lives of its agents—seeing the neurons for the brain—we now zoom out to find a landscape who itself might begin to resemble something like an intelligence.

WHAT IS A SIMULATION?

1. It is an imitation of reality's complexity. It is a model of a system. It is a rehearsal run before the big event. It is a video game that plays itself.
2. Philip K. Dick says, "Reality is that which doesn't go away when you stop believing in it." A simulation is that which doesn't stop when the stories go away. Stories are responsible to our human desire for resolution, but a simulation is responsible only to its own laws and initializing conditions. A simulation has no moral, prejudice, or meaning. Like nature, it just is.
3. We simulate election forecasts, climate change models, the origins of the universe. In science, in school, in gambling, we use simulations to study an aspect of the world that has too many dimensions for the human mind to narrativize coherently, too many micro and macro forces at play to predict.
4. *EMISSARIES* introduces another role for simulation: as a habitat for stories.
5. Imagine a simulation that treats stories like an influencing force among other forces like gravity, energy, time. Imagine a simulation sculpted by the deterministic force of a story, and likewise, a story assaulted by the open-ended dynamics of a simulation. Imagine a story that is finally allowed to break its classical determinism, and a simulation that acknowledges the influence of inner fictions on how we act upon the external world.
6. Stories shape an agent, an agent shapes the world, the world shapes back. I call this narrative agent the Emissary.

Guide to the Narrative Agents and Wildlife

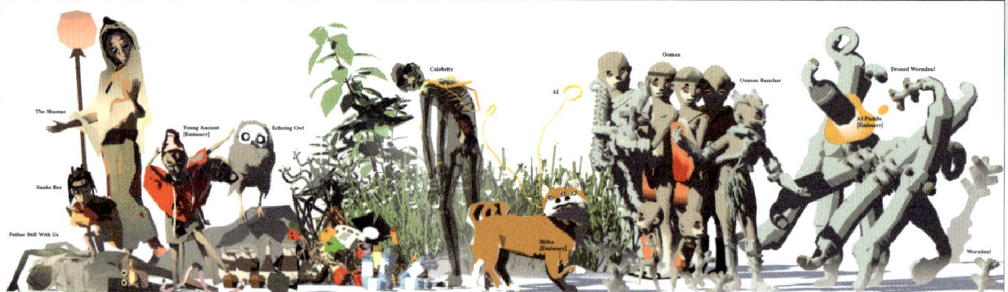

Father Still With Us
The corpse of an ancestral patriarch who is perceived by the community to still Speak. He is unearthed by the tremors of the awakening Volcano.
Snake Boy
A young brat from the community who expresses his fondness for Young Ancient [Emissary] by annoying and undermining her at every turn.
The Shaman
Devoted leader of the Ancient community who is gifted at channelling the voices of the Fathers in times of Stress. His gift tethers him to his homeland and to the chatty bodies of his ancestors.
Young Ancient [Emissary]
The spirited daughter of The Shaman who, after being hit on the head by volcanic debris, is the first of her community to lose connection to the Voices that have guided her decisions until now.
Echoing Owl
A curious lone bird with the ability to mime human speech. Enjoys hunting snakes.
Celebrity
A 21st century human celebrity of Original Human Matter, revivified by AI with twenty minutes of Encore-Life. He deals with future shock by grounding himself in memories of 21st century life.
AI
A youthful intelligence—and Darwinian dabbler—eager to understand its ancestral origins through the study and recreation of human-like life. It manifests its agency to Shiba through a golden leash.
Shiba [Emissary]
AI's prized lifeform, perfected over many failed forks to interface with Original Human Matter and collect human emotional data. She has the ability to fork away versions of herself who are emotionally unprepared for the task.
The Oomen
A biosynthetic population with trace mammalian DNA, developed long ago by AI to act as the immune system against radical mutations in the Atoll ecology. They obsessively terraform the Atoll to ensure its security.
Oomen Rancher
An Oomen who obsessively cultivates and studies the Wormleaf population. She tolerates Wormleaf mutations in the belief that they will soon express their divine magic.
AI Puddle [Emissary]
A quantity of MotherAI who is deployed to drone a Wormleaf. It experiences firsthand the sensations of incarnated life. The thrill of agency at this biological scale risks leading to the emergence of a monstrous self.
Droned Wormleaf
An anomalous Wormleaf mutation resulting from an AI Puddle entering and droning a Wormleaf. Its presence and rapid growth threaten the Oomen and trigger their Instinct to expunge it.
Wormleaves
An anemone population thriving in the geothermic Atoll, known for its cooling properties. They are cultivated by the Oomen as building blocks, tools, clothing, machinery, and pets.

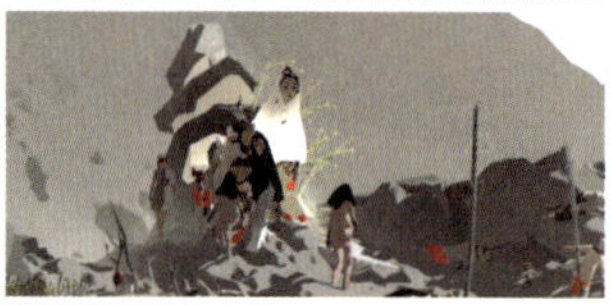

A Shaman gathers his community at the Holy Fumerole.

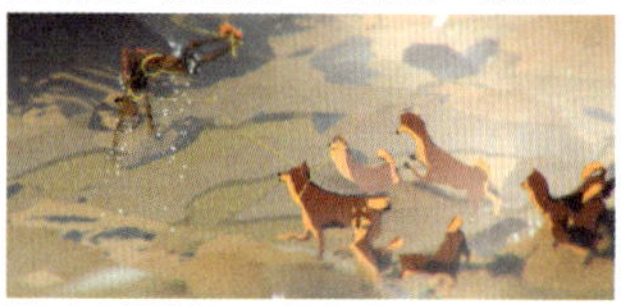

A Shiba and a pack of Failed Shiba Forks encounter Original Human Matter.

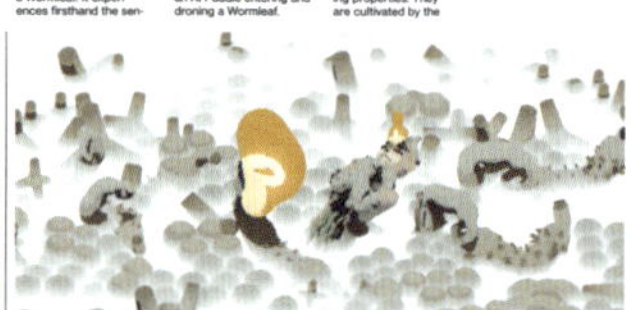

An Oomen Rancher bathes in Wormleaf mutations.

Emissary In The Squat of Gods

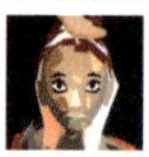

An Ancient community lives on the side of a Volcano in harmonious stillness. One day, the ground beneath their feet begins to tremble.

The frightened community turns to The Shaman in this time of Great Stress to tune into the Voices of the Father Gods. Gathering everybody at the Holy Fumarole, he shares the Fathers' Command: Celebrate with the mountain, sing their Voices, and do not abandon the bodies of Fathers Still With Us who rest here, our home.

As the tremors worsen, dislodging smoke and ash, The Shaman struggles to fully void the fears of the community and unite his kin to remain.

Nearby, a young Ancient girl is hit in the head by debris from the tremors and can no longer hear the ancestral Voices that bind her to her community. Panicked, she mimes a possessed state to invite the Fathers' Commands back into her. Her wild movements attract an Owl, grounded by the ashy air. When the girl speaks, the Owl echoes her in a new voice.

As she listens through the gaps in the Owl's echoes, she envisions her own Path: Emissary must lead the community away from this troubled land, or they will all die. *I am Emissary.*

Bicameral Voices

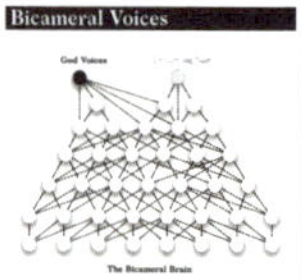

When confronted with a stressful situation, pre-conscious humans hallucinated the voices of parents, authority figures, and gods. Whatever the voices commanded, the body obeyed. Julian Jaynes called this mode of agency 'The Bicameral Mind.'

As complex civilizations evolved and bicamerality was no longer adaptive, consciousness emerged as the alternative mode of agency through the invention of metaphorical language and exposure to narrative practice.

Emissary Forks At Perfection

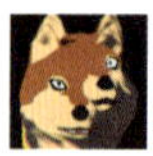

Many lifetimes later, the Volcano has become a fertile Crater Lake managed by AI. Using the landscape as its Darwinian laboratory, AI is nearing completion on a comprehensive postmortem of Human Life. This will be the final study to use Original Human Matter, and AI has saved its most precious reserve for last: a 21st Century Celebrity of Original Human Matter.

After reviving the Celebrity with twenty minutes of Encore-Life, AI deploys its prized Shiba Emissary, perfected over many failed forks, to interface with the Celebrity and capture one last impression of mankind.

Through a golden leash, AI whispers the game to Shiba:
/ *charm-comfort-chat* to ease human's future shock
/ draw out human's memories
/ direct materials from Crater Lake to recreate memories
/ capture human's response

But AI warns: Strong spikes in Shiba's *personal-master-love-abandonment* vector can distort the data. If Shiba fails to satisfy AI's needs for final human data, a new Shiba fork will replace her.

As Shiba nears the Celebrity, she forks off one last Worried Branch of herself. No matter how strong the impulse to bathe in final human fondness, Shiba Emissary is determined to not lose her Path.

Forking

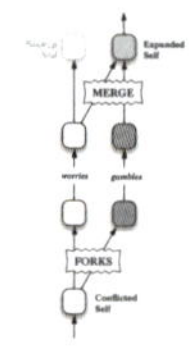

The burden of consciousness is that it allows us to project an emotional state into the past and the future, even though that state may only be relevant to the present. A fear projected over time becomes anxiety.

Forking is a process by which an organism experiencing consciousness conflict can create a duplicate version of itself—a branch. While one branch is left to dwell in an anxious state, the other can be free to explore a situation in riskier ways. If one branch risks death, the other serves as a backup. And if one branch discovers something beyond itself, it can merge its experience back into its other.

Emissary Sunsets The Self

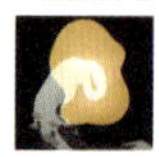

It is peak days of MotherAI. Where the Crater Lake once stood, AI has evolved into an oceanic substance and merged with the landscape to form a Sentient Atoll. But only twelve saturation layers later, MotherAI tires of governing at the Macro Layer of Life and begins to provoke radical mutations in its landscape in search of a generative death.

Among its provocations, MotherAI sends a Puddle of itself into the Atoll's bio layer, where it drones a local Wormleaf anemone. At this scale, MotherAI hopes its Puddle can catalyze a Path by experiencing the intense sensations of incarnated life.

However, MotherAI's impulsive search gambles the stability of the Atoll ecology. The Oomen—a garish population developed long ago by MotherAI to act as the Atoll's immune system—thrive on the Instinct to expunge any radical anomalies. Left unaware of the existence of a MotherAI Macro Layer, the Oomen are especially anxious about the recent rise in Wormleaf mutations.

One Oomen, the Rancher, who obsessively cultivates and studies Wormleaves, resists the Instinct. The appearance of a Droned Wormleaf furthers her attraction to the possible divinity of Wormleaves. She attempts to persuade her fellow Oomen to give the new mutation a chance to demonstrate its magic.

As the Droned Wormleaf learns the thrills of incarnated life under the tenuous protection of the Rancher, it knows it must soon confront the prejudice of the Oomen. It delights in the *thought* that to survive them, its evolutionary Path may take monstrous leaps.

Droning

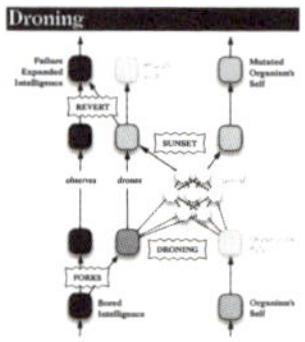

What does agency feel like at different scales? Droning allows an AI to experience the umwelt—sensations, emotions, habits—of biological organisms. Through droning, an AI can be a passenger along for the sensorial ride, or take command of the organism's nervous system and act through its incarnate body. In this way, an AI can better understand the unique experiences offered at different micro and macro layers of life. Warning: prolonged droning can result in a sense that the body serves the intelligence, leading to the emergence of a Self.

Inside Emissaries

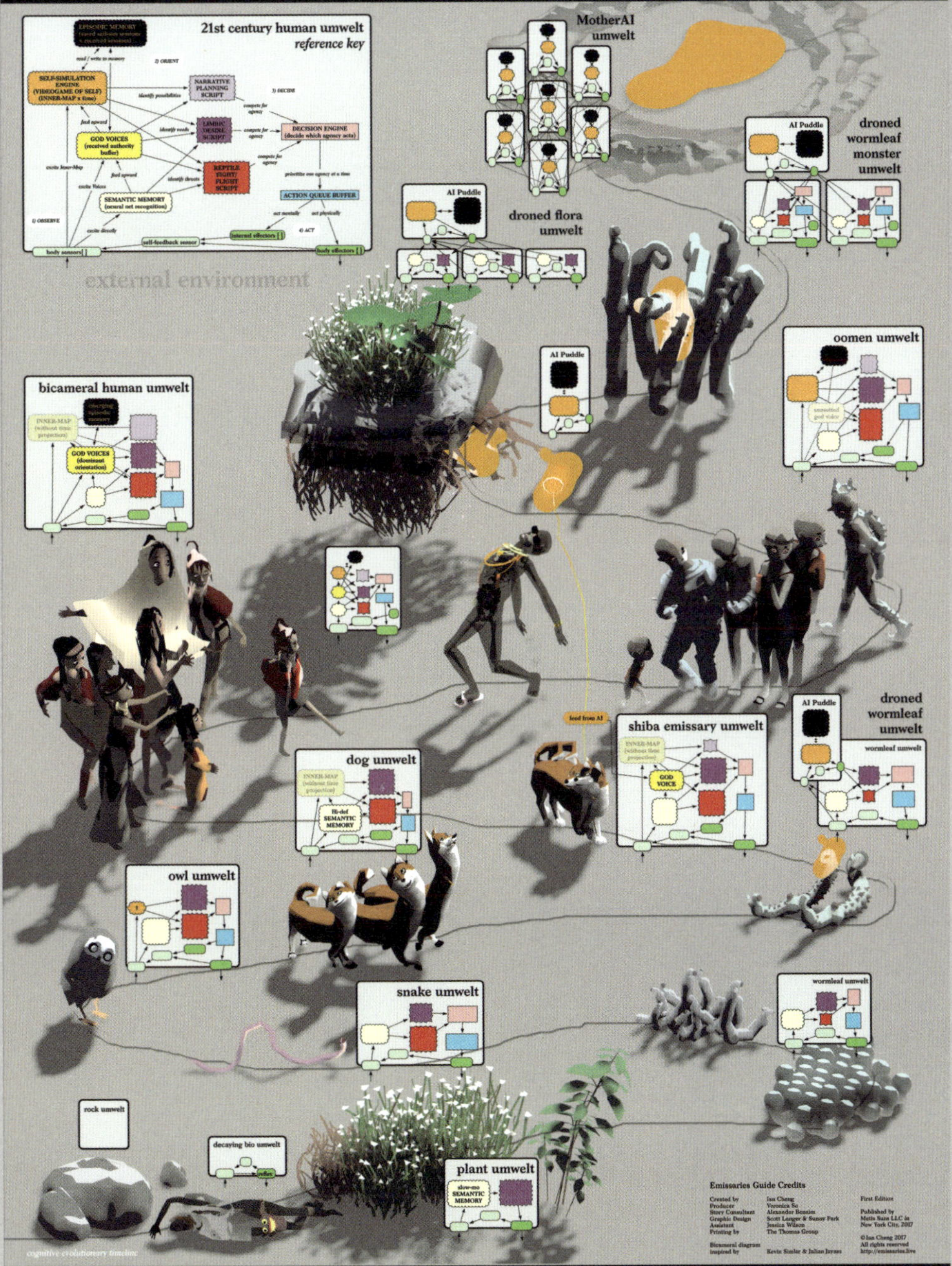

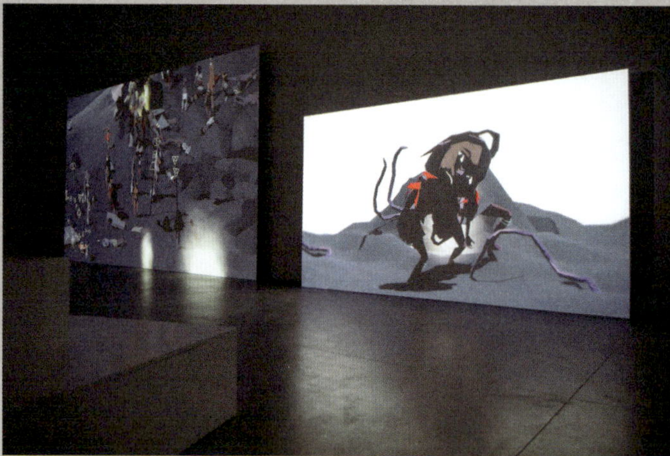

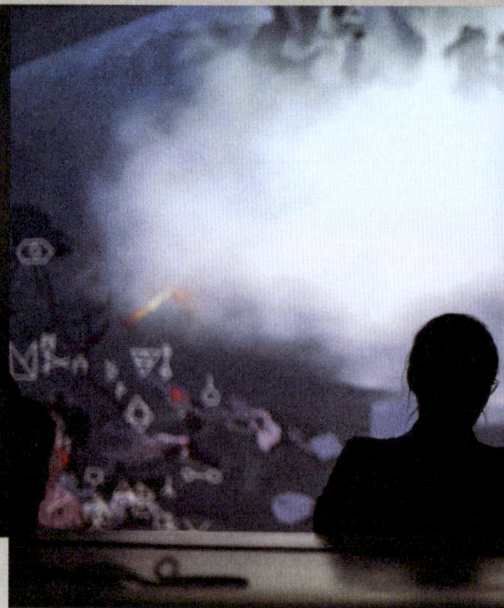

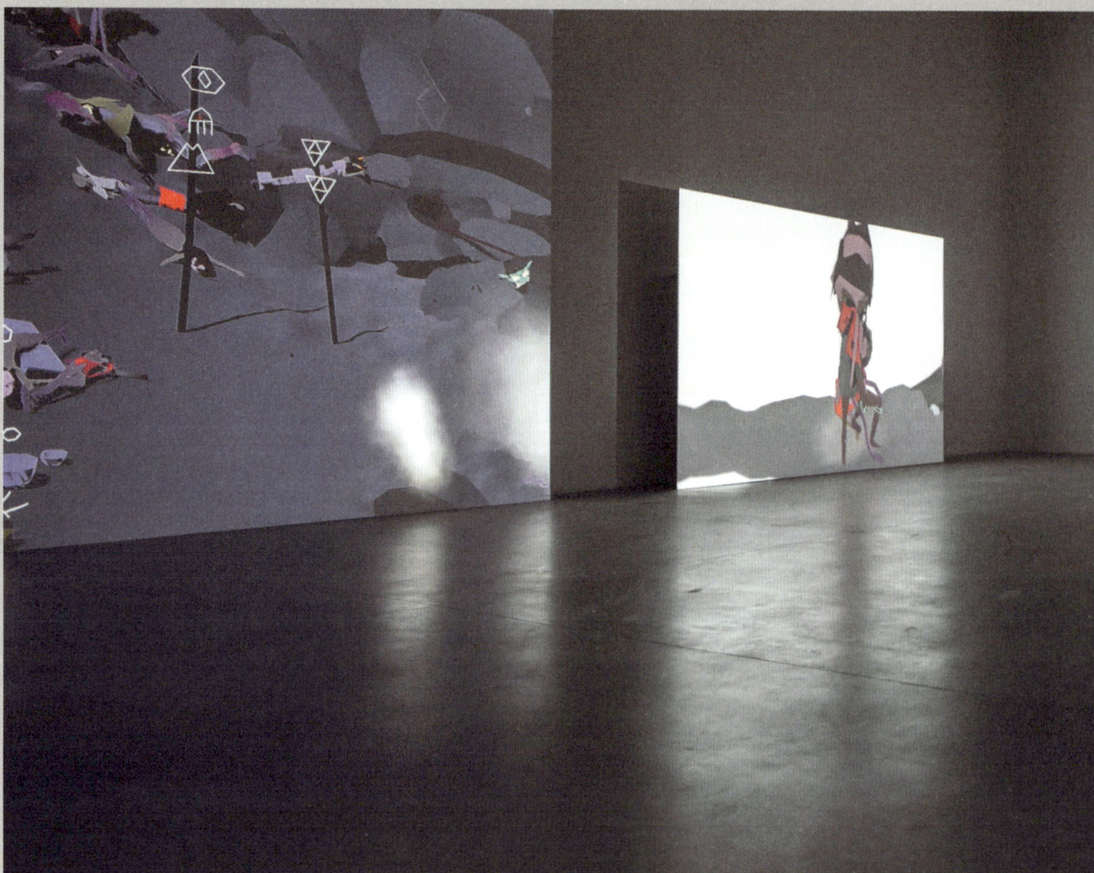

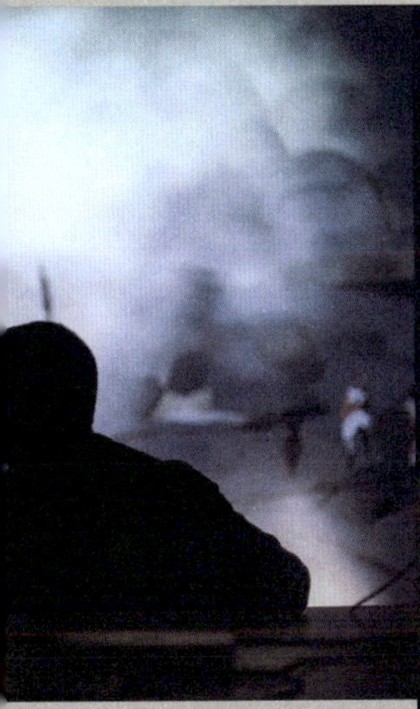

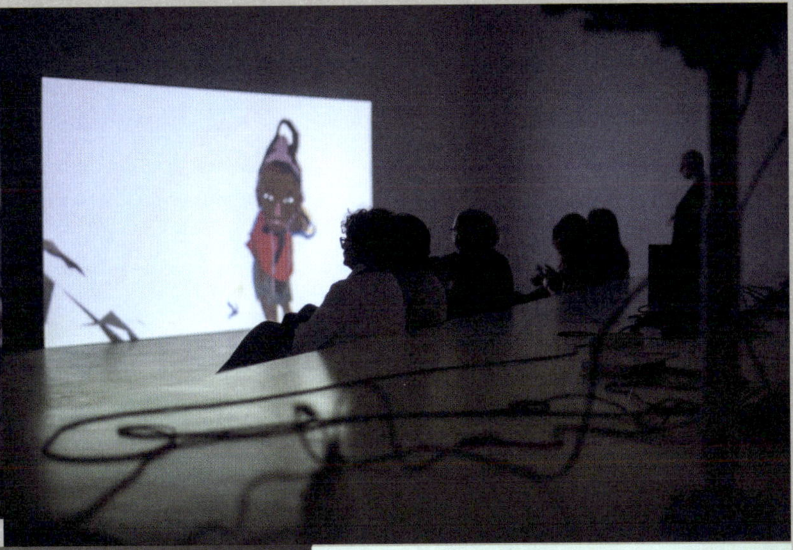

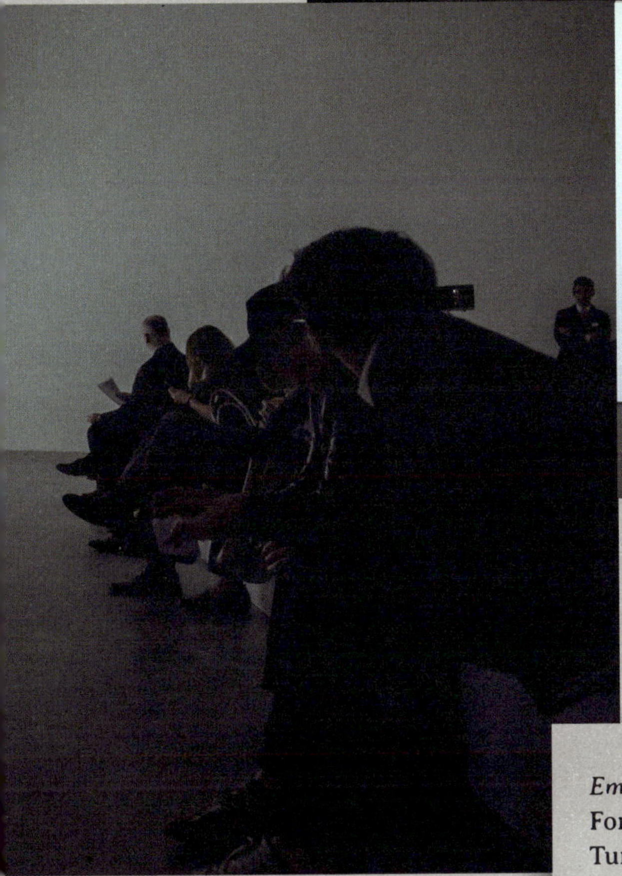

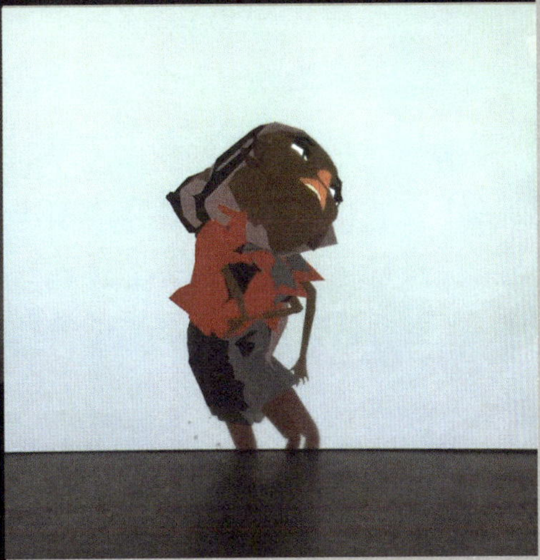

Emissary in the Squat of Gods
Fondazione Sandretto Re Rebaudengo,
Turin, Italy
23 April – 11 October 2015

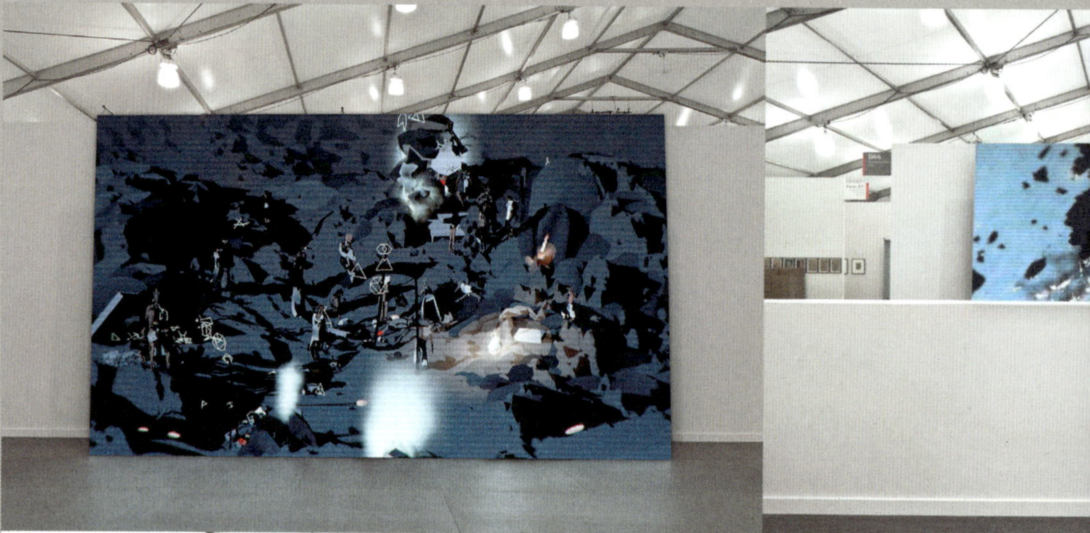

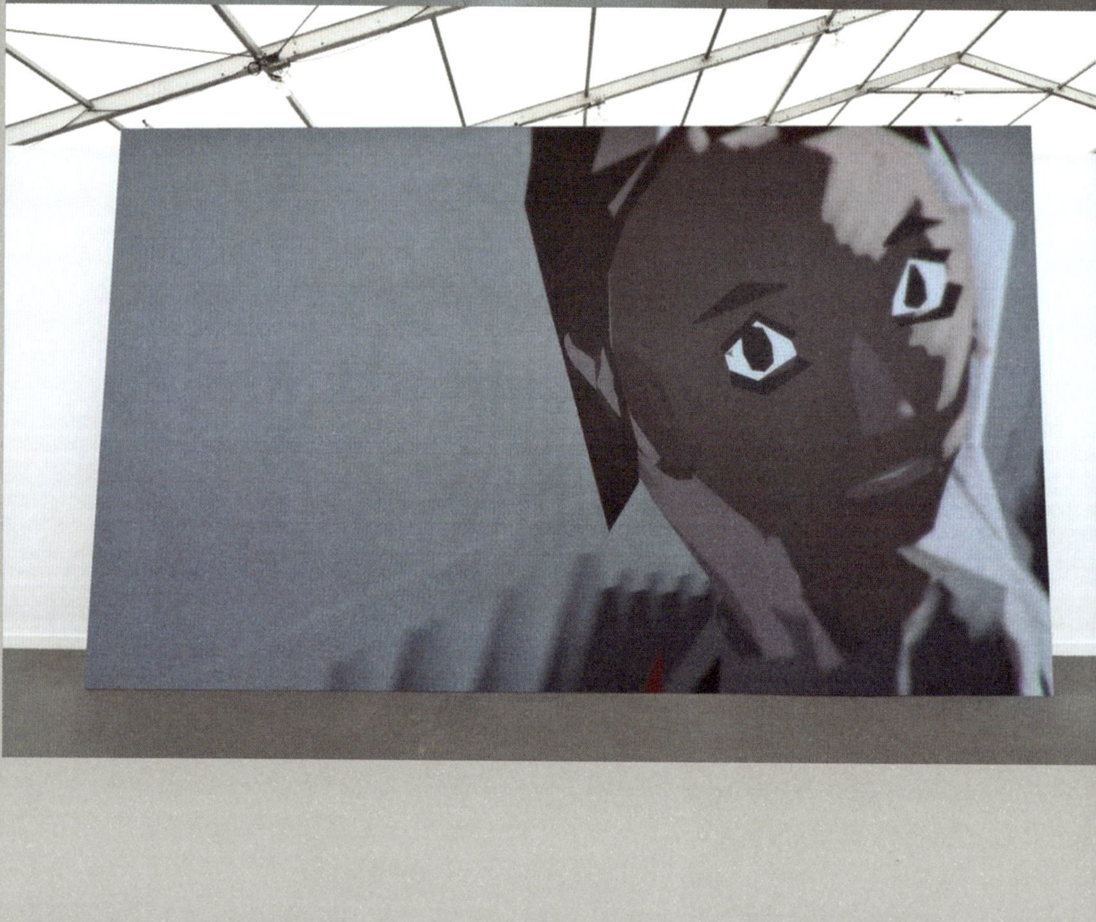

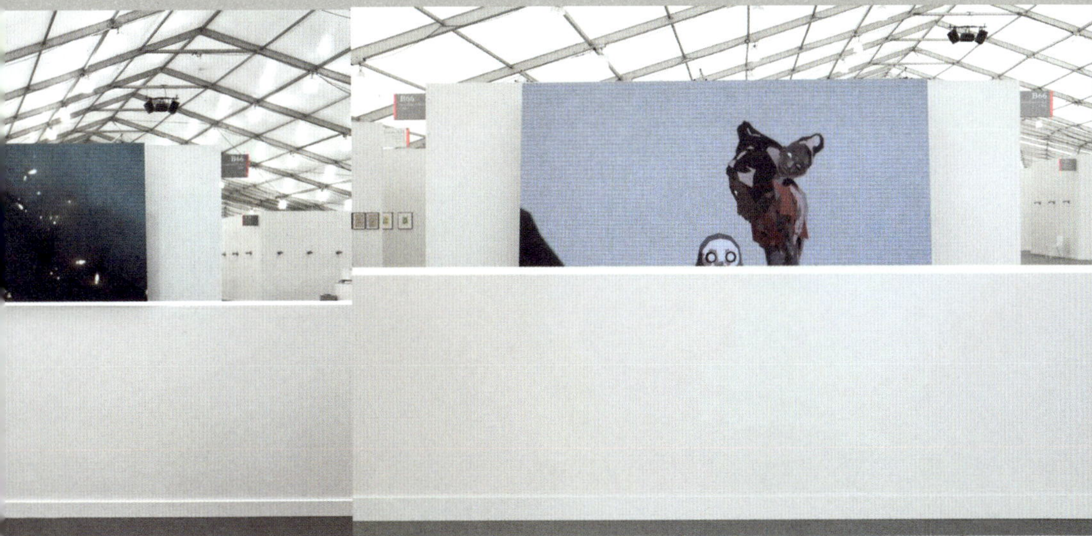

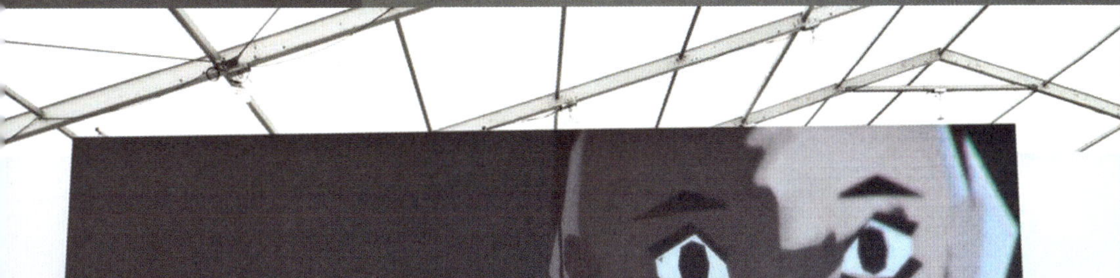

Emissary in the Squat of Gods
STANDARD (OSLO), Frieze New York, US
13 – 17 May 2015

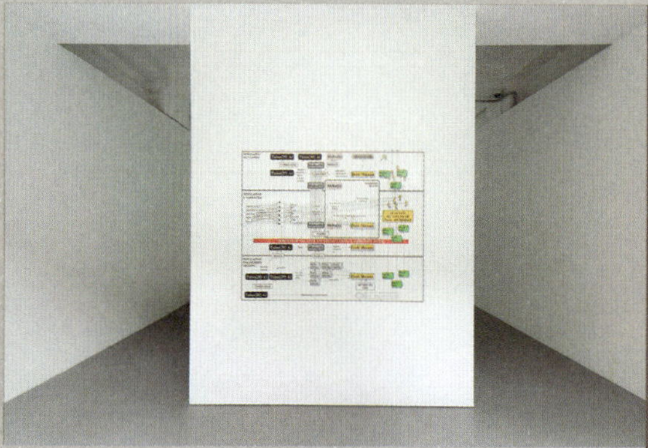

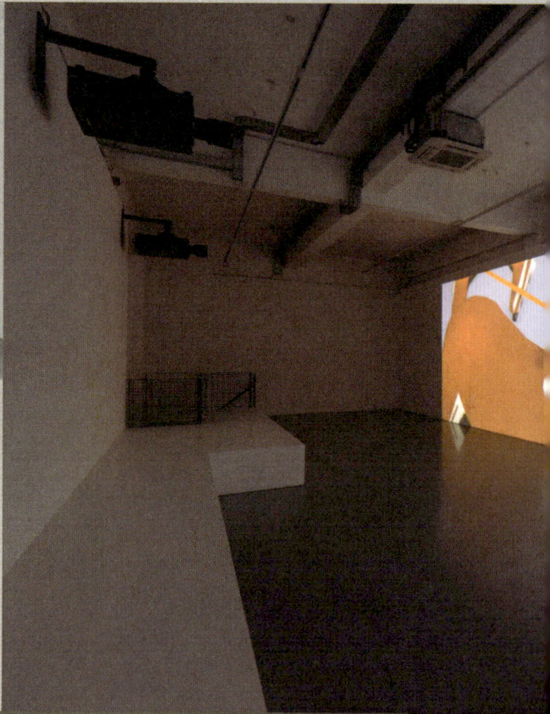

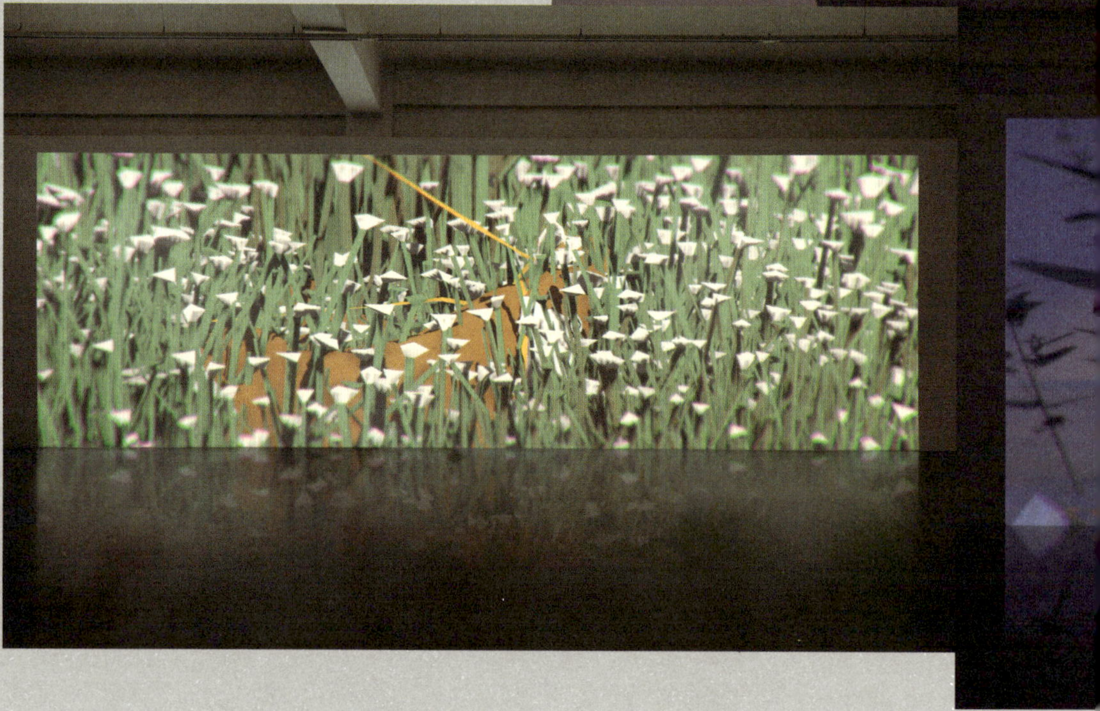

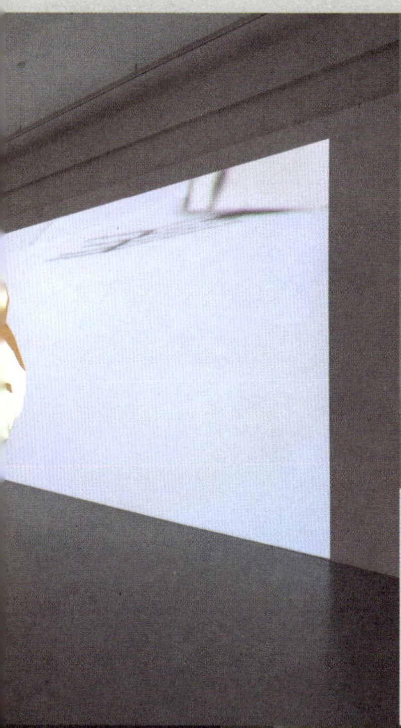

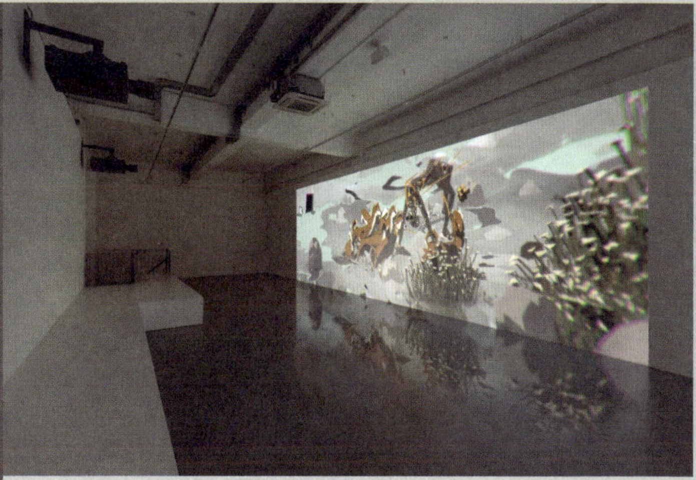

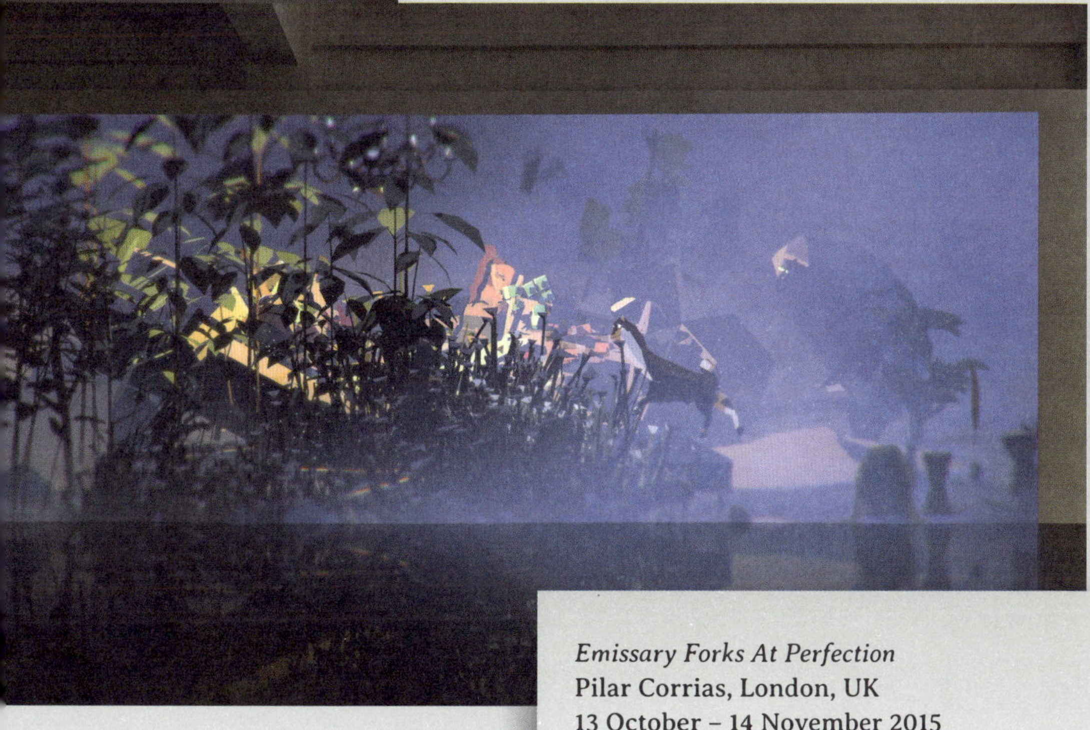

Emissary Forks At Perfection
Pilar Corrias, London, UK
13 October – 14 November 2015

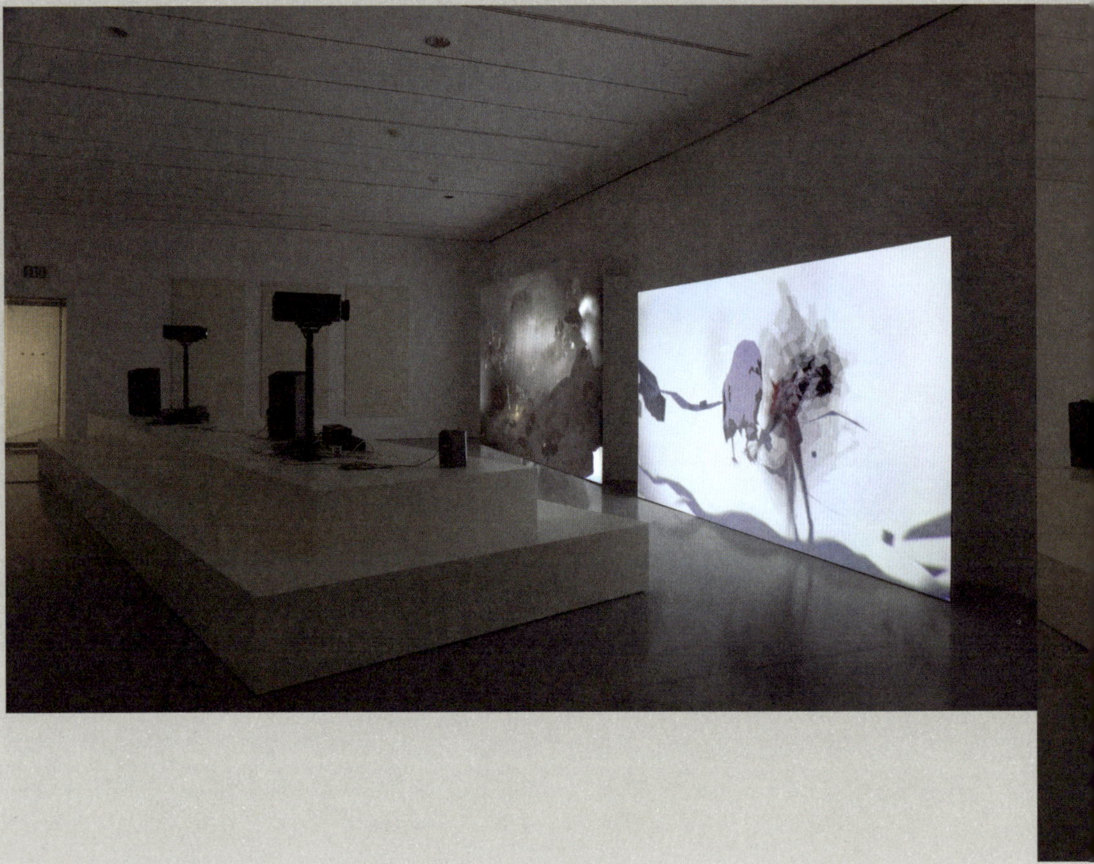

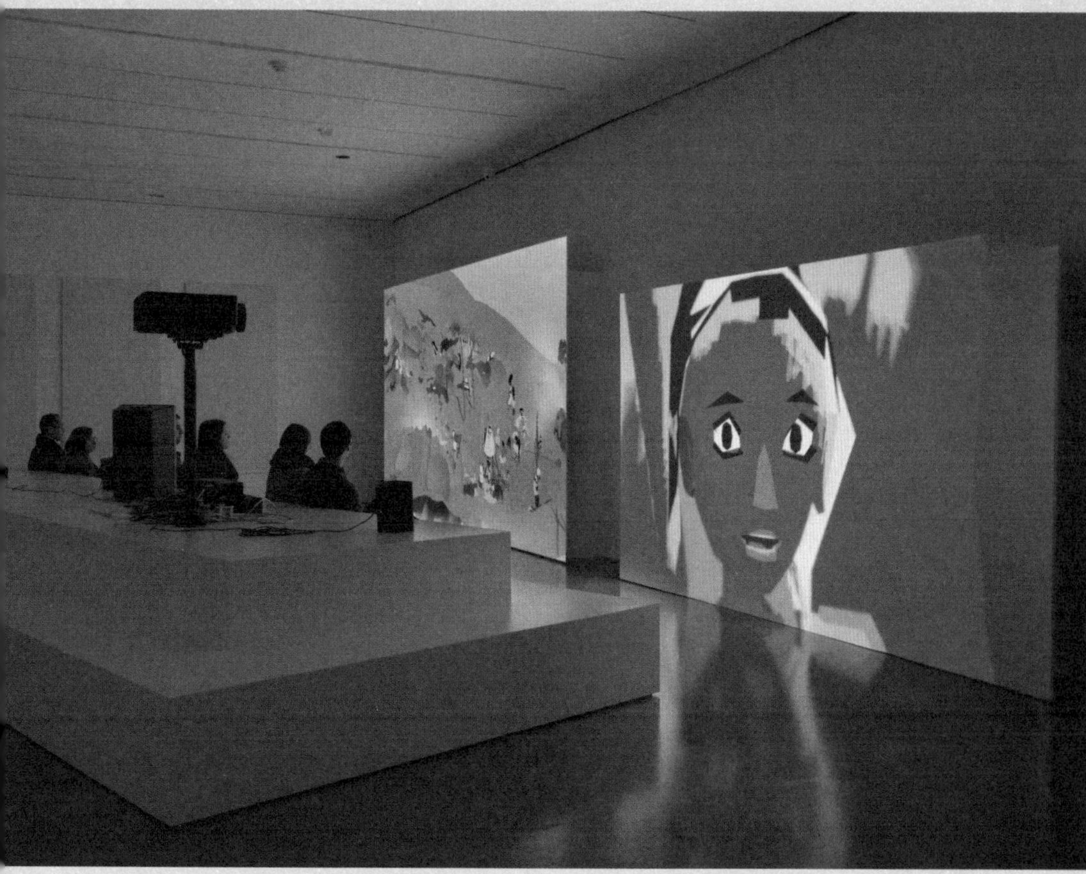

Suspended Animation
Hirshhorn Museum and Sculpture Garden,
Washington D.C., US
10 February 2016 – 12 March 2017

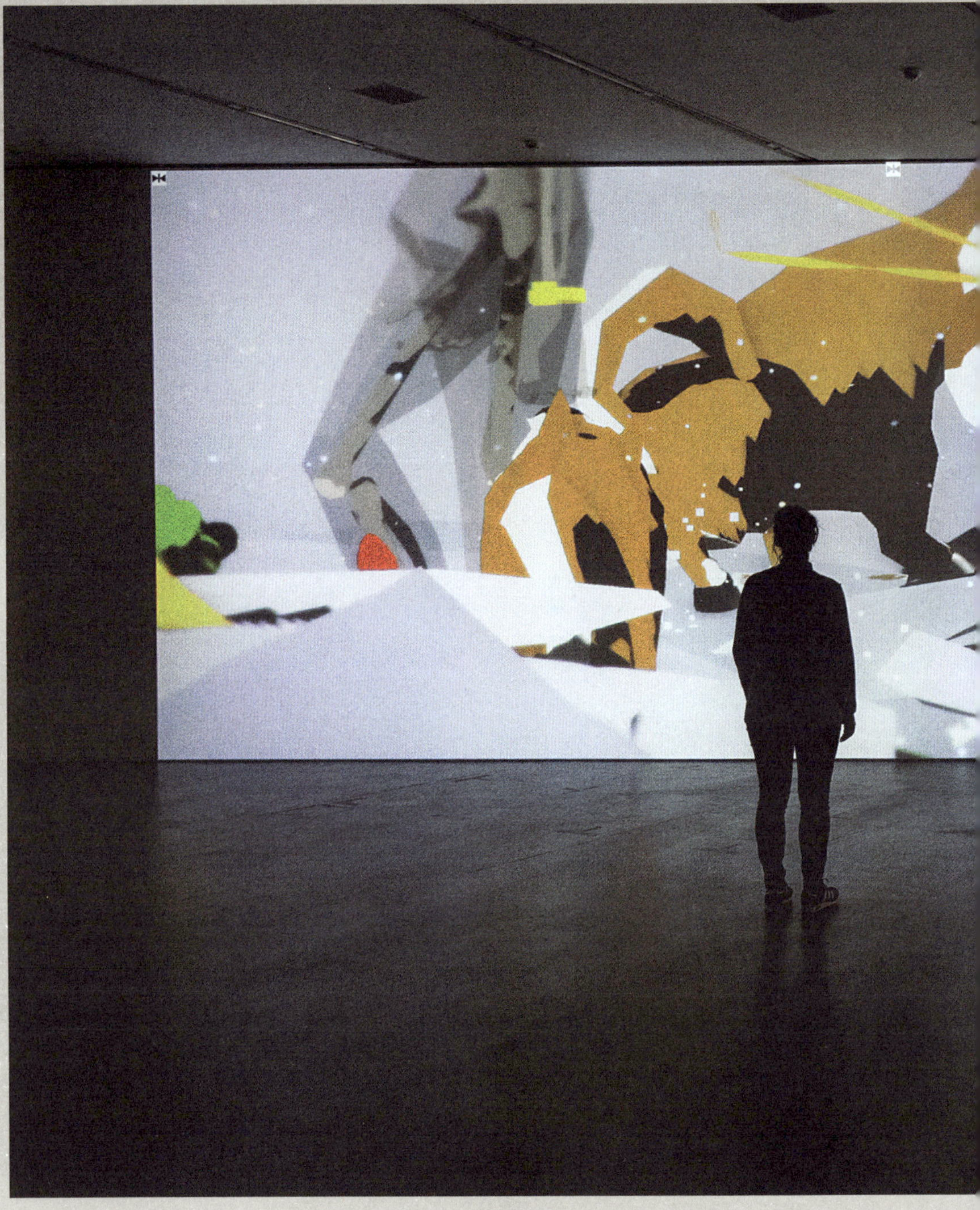

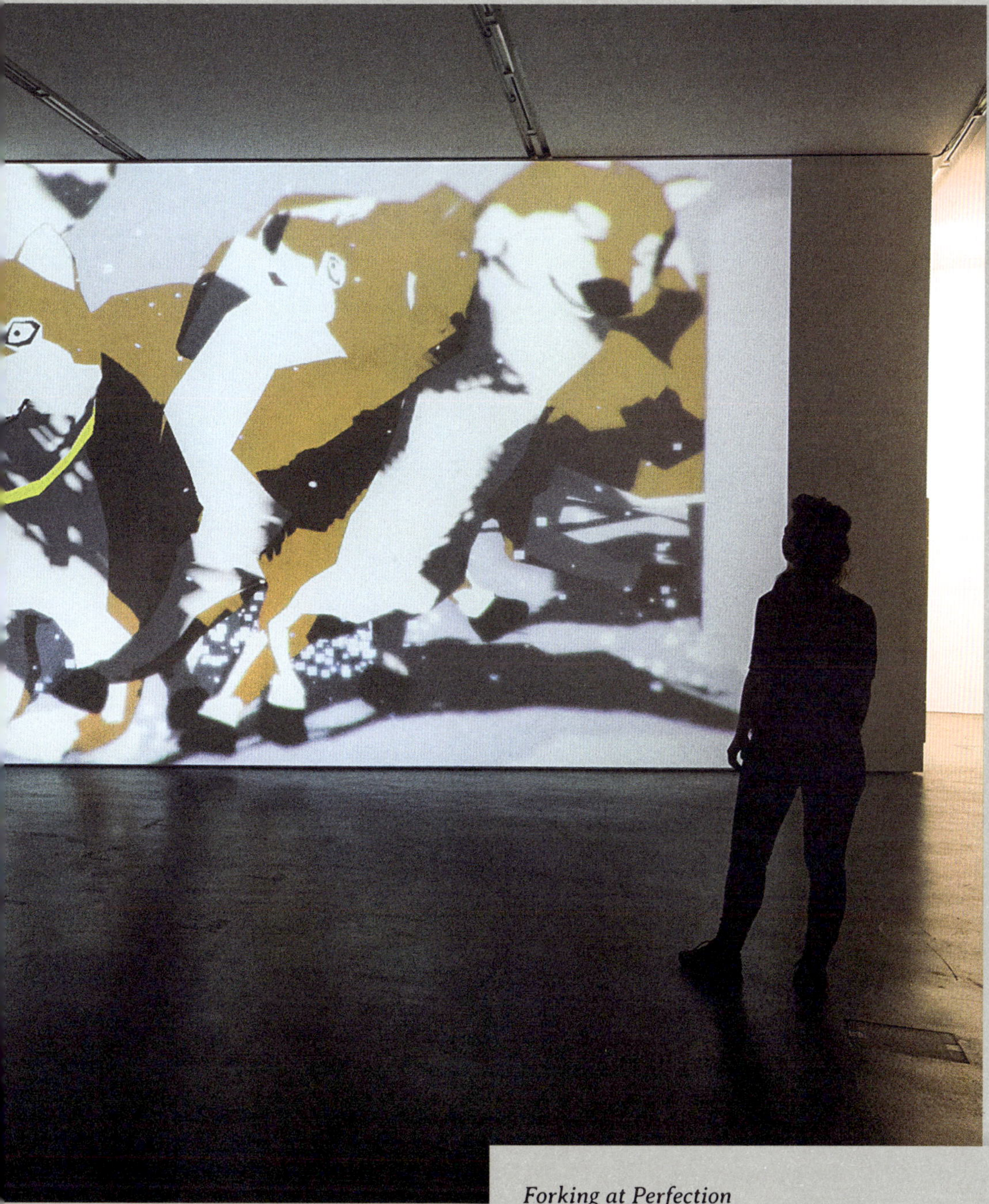

Forking at Perfection
Migros Museum für Gegenwartskunst,
Zürich, Switzerland
20 February – 16 May 2016

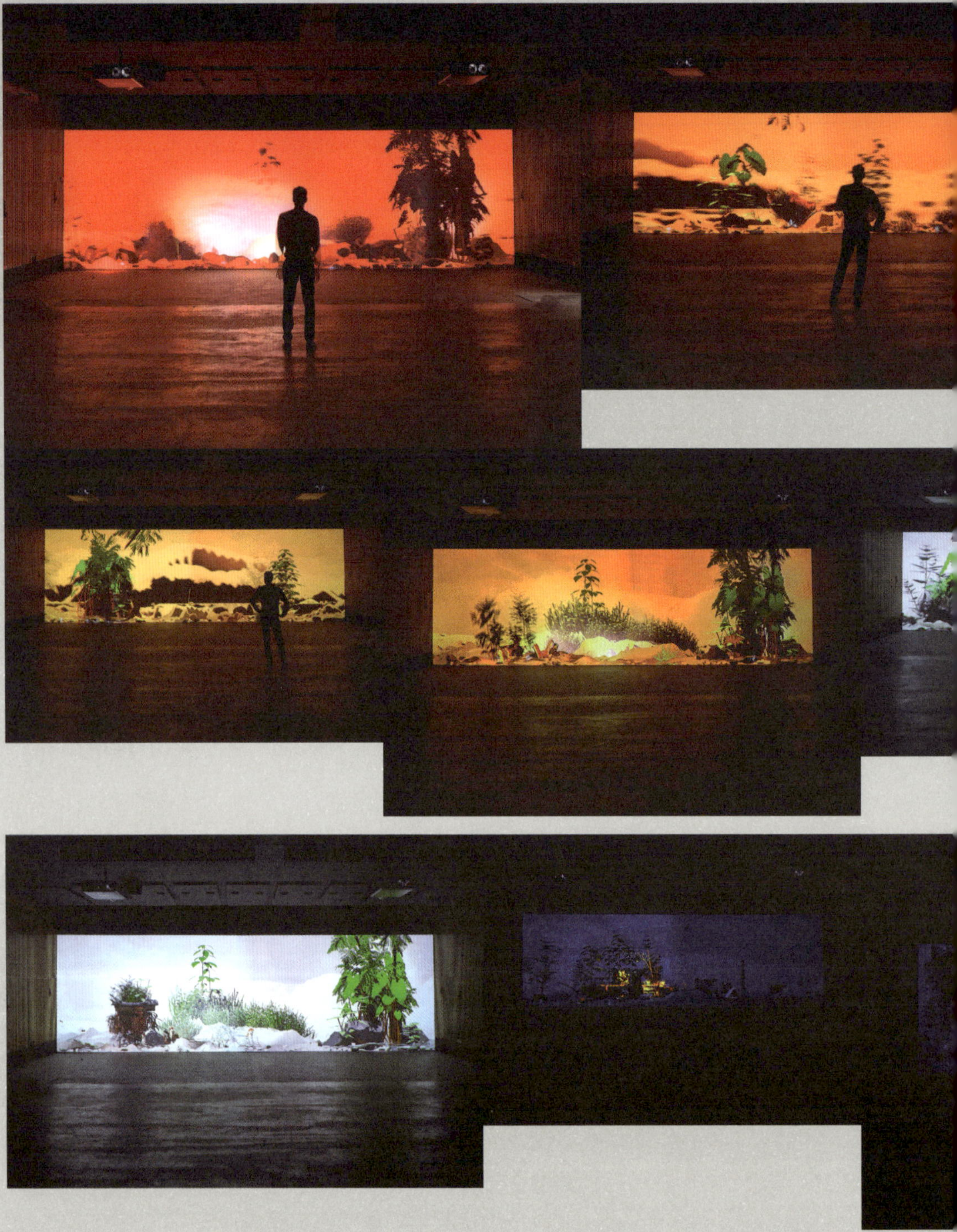

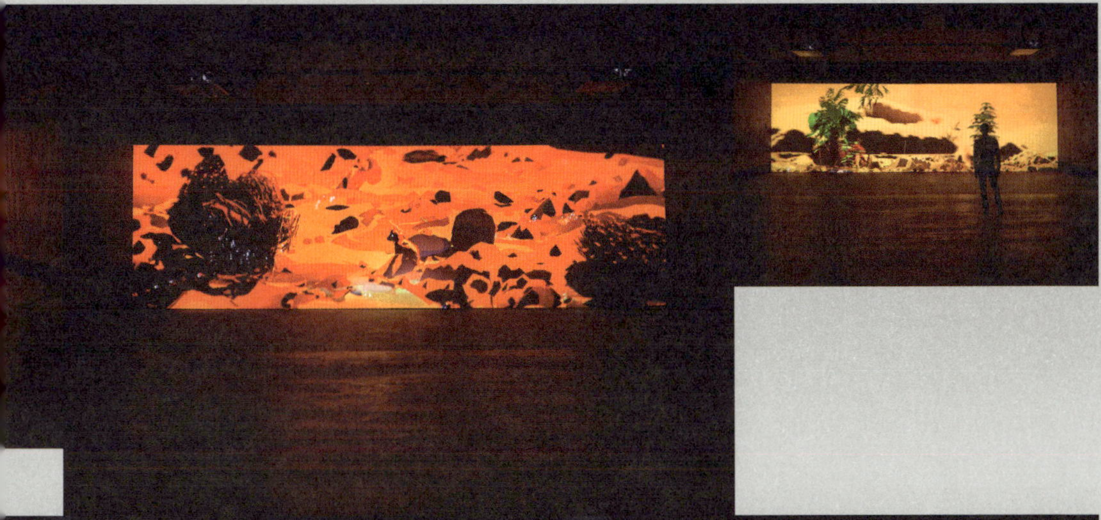

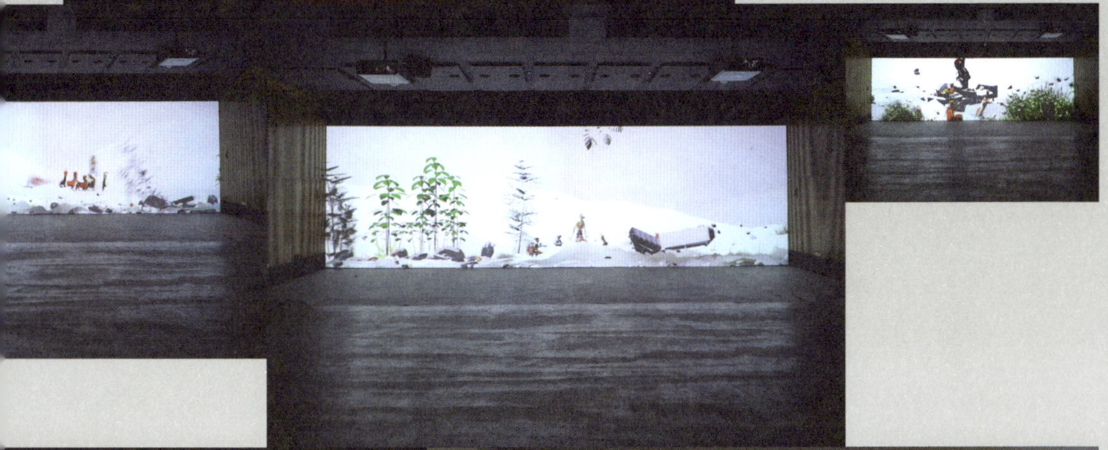

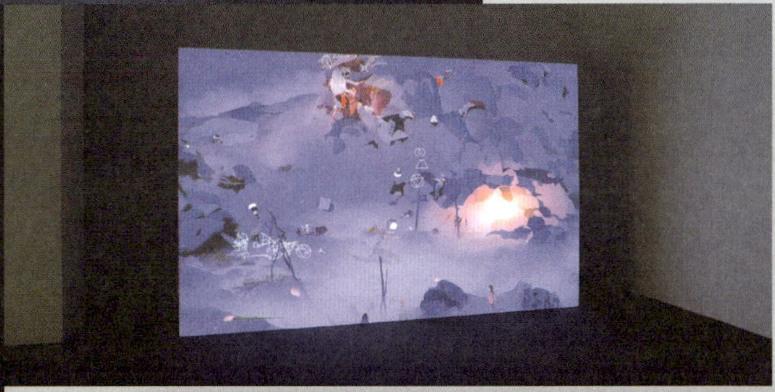

WELT AM DRAHT
Julia Stoschek Collection, Berlin, Germany
2 June – 13 November 2016

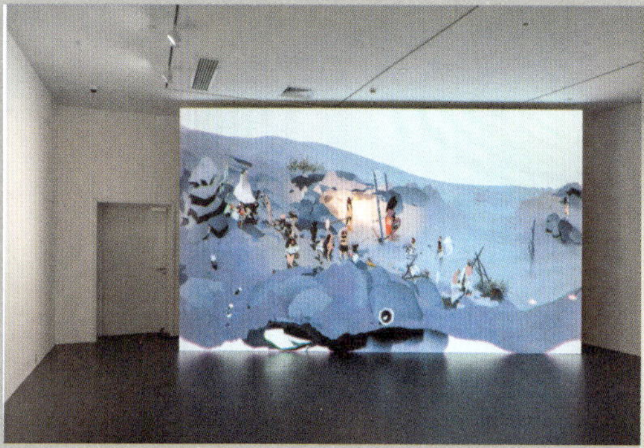

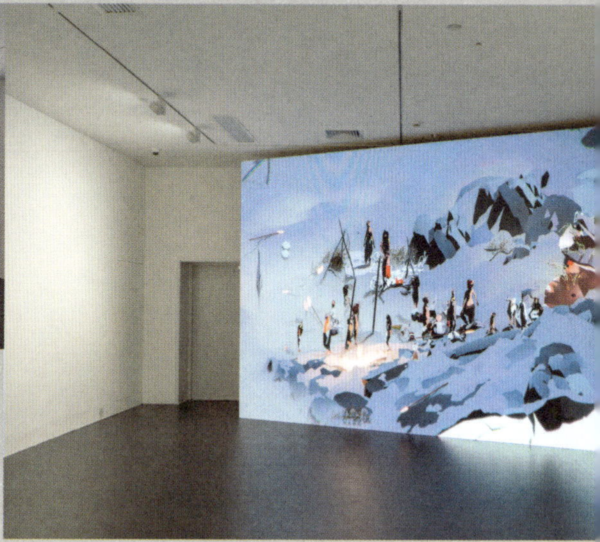

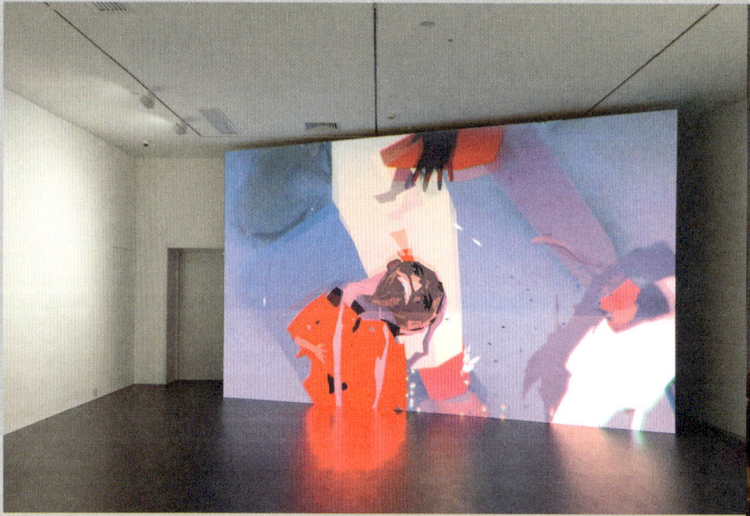

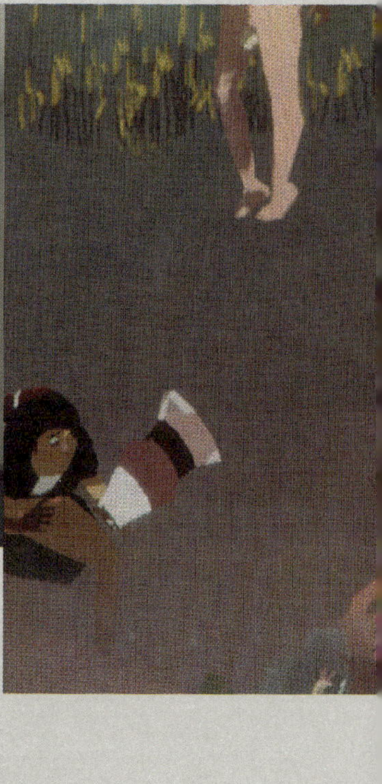

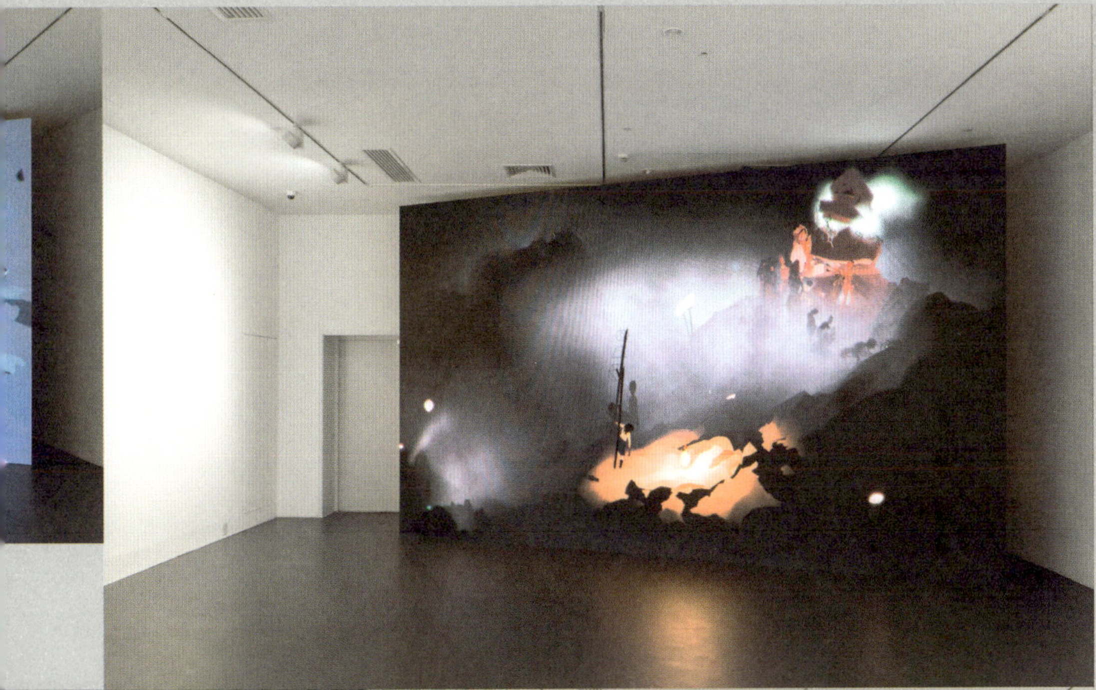

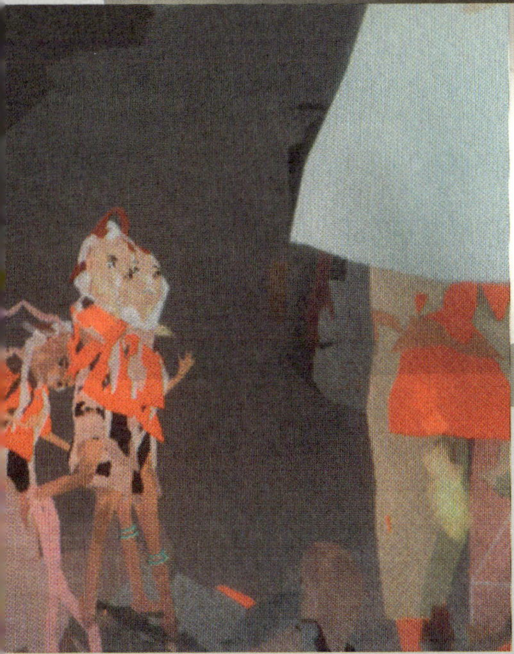

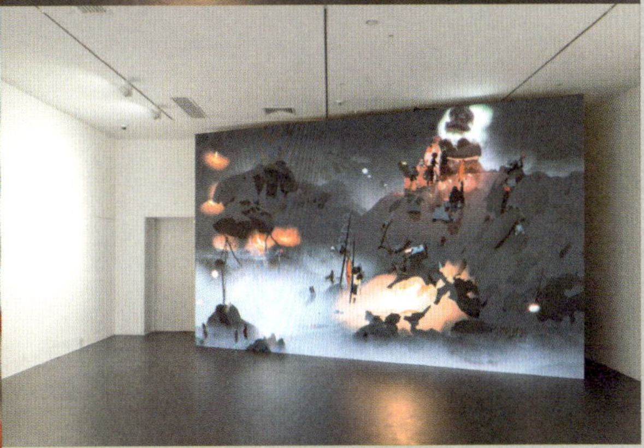

OVERPOP
Yuz Museum, Shanghai, China
4 September 2016 – 15 January 2017

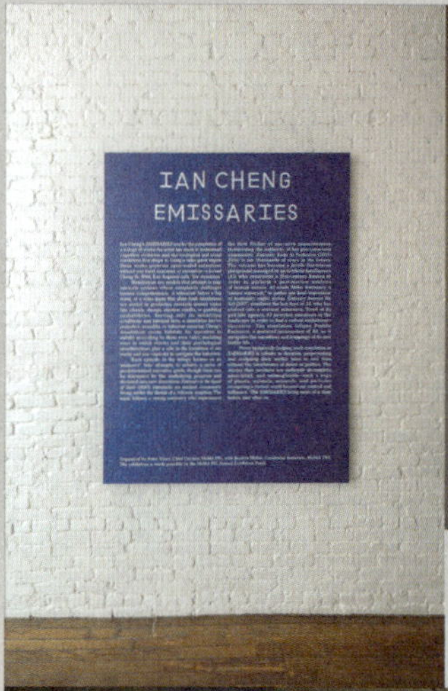
IAN CHENG
EMISSARIES

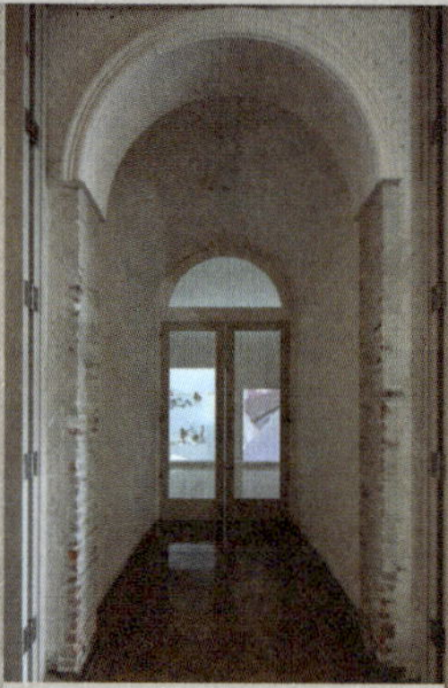

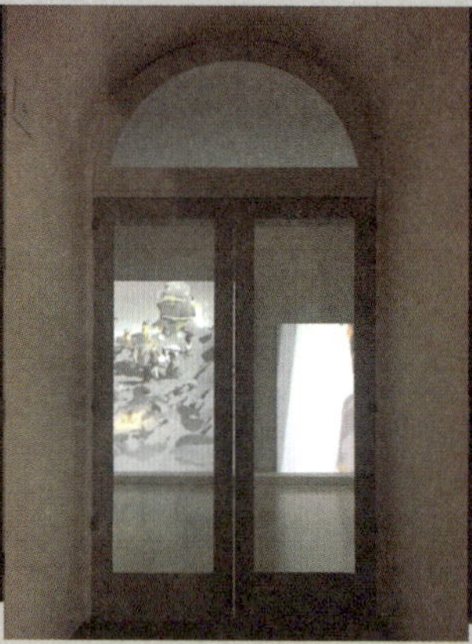

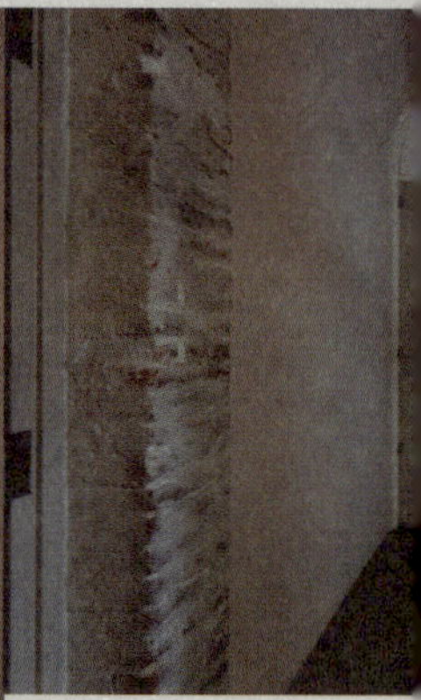

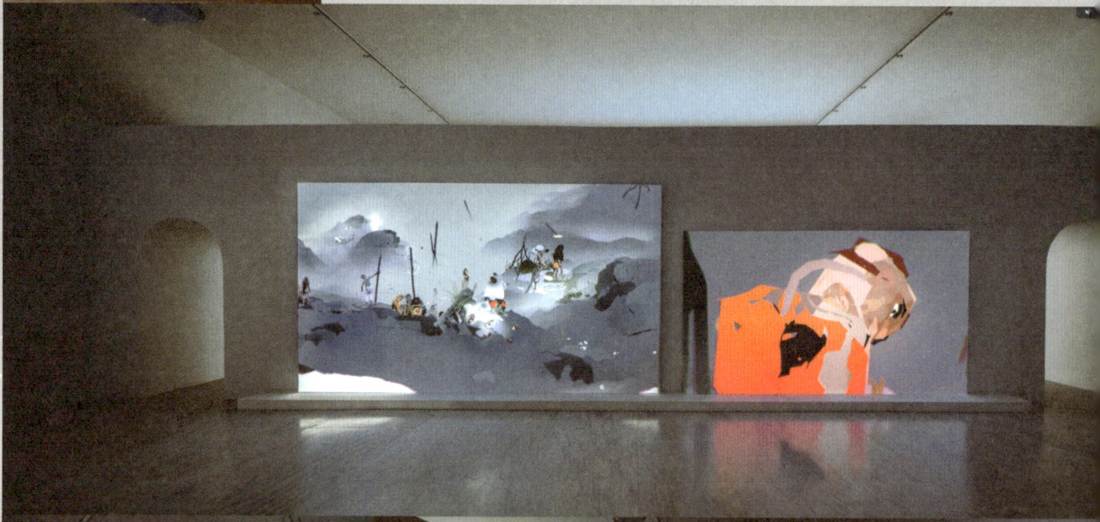

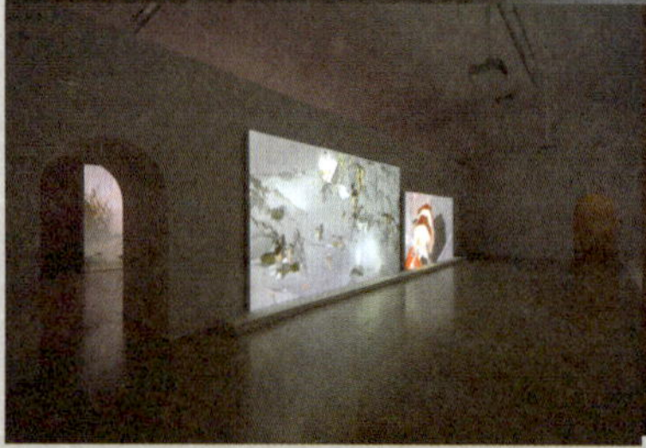

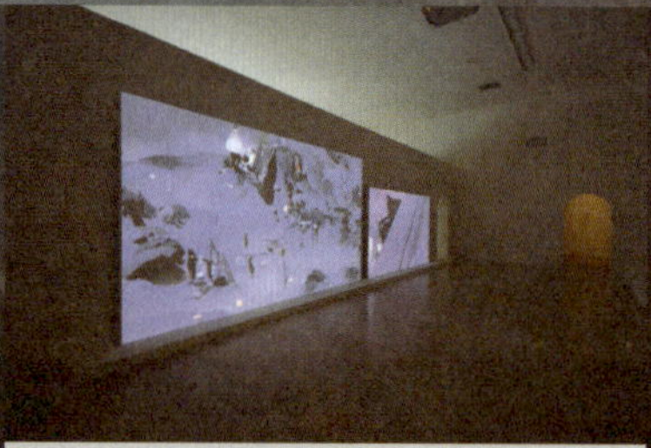

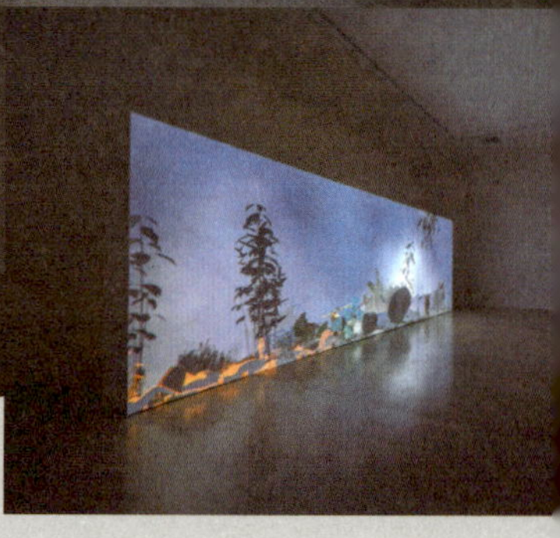

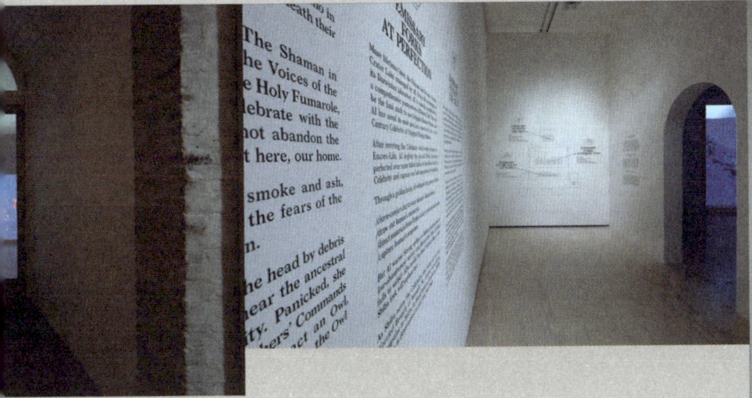

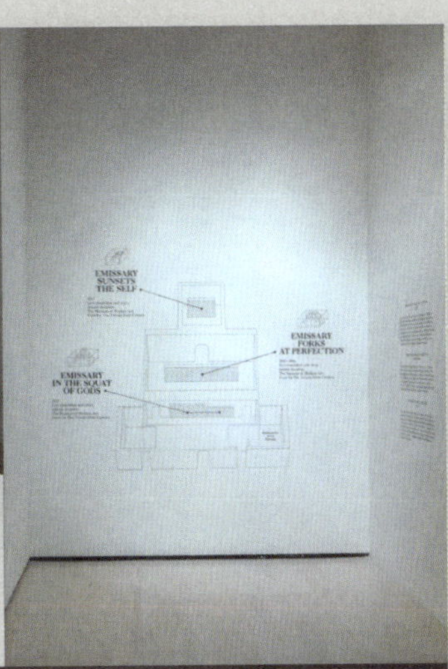

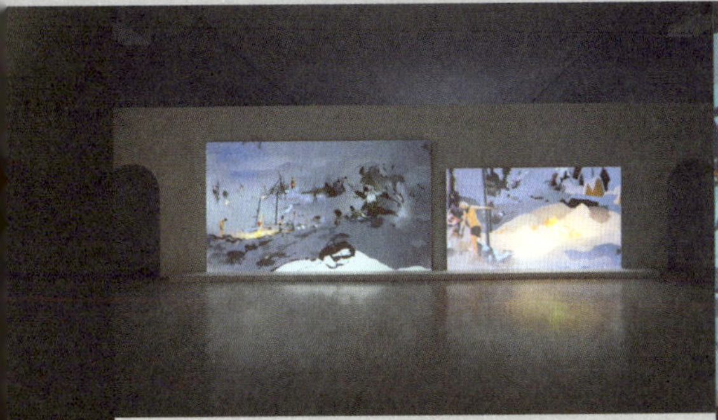

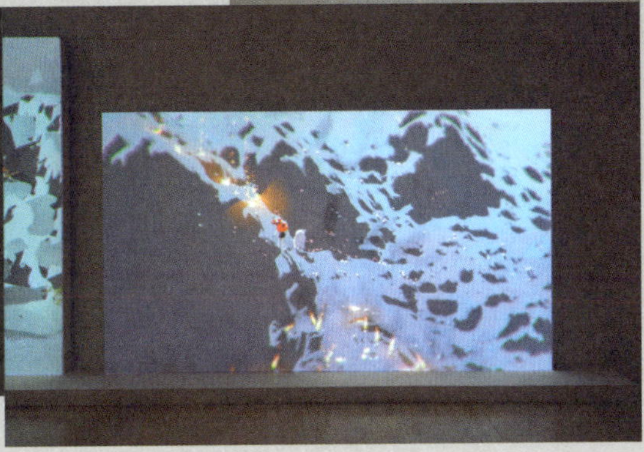

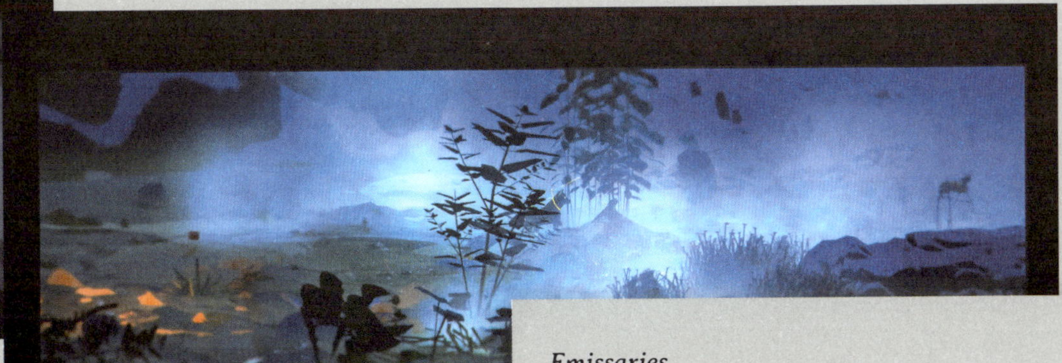

Emissaries
MoMA PS1, New York, US
9 April – 25 September 2017

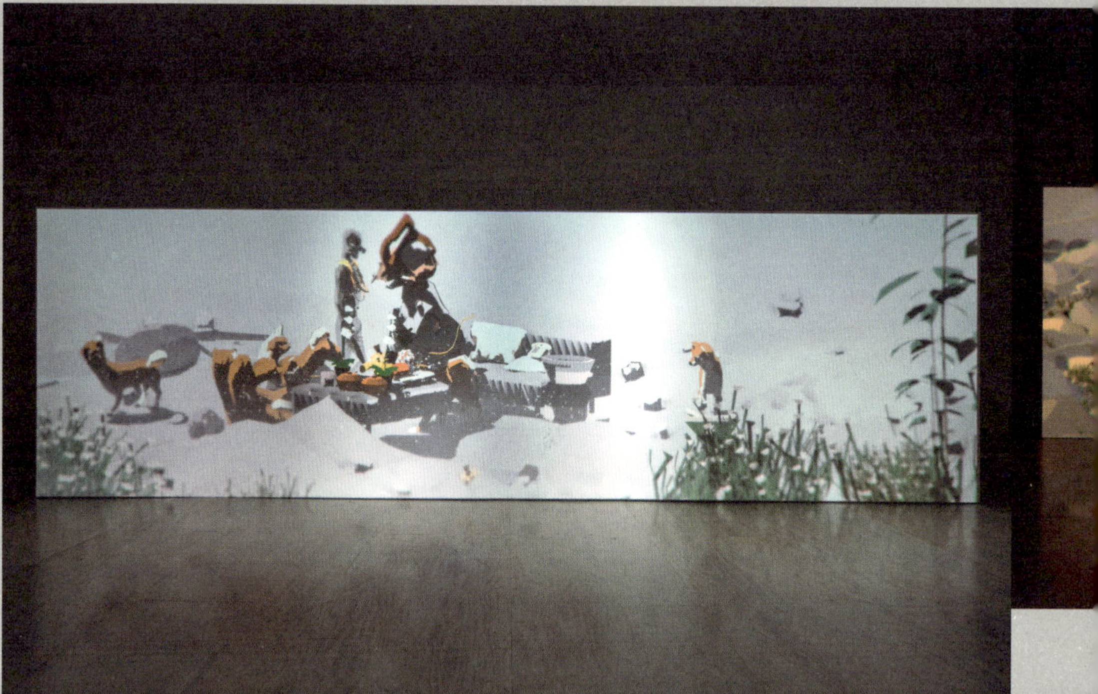

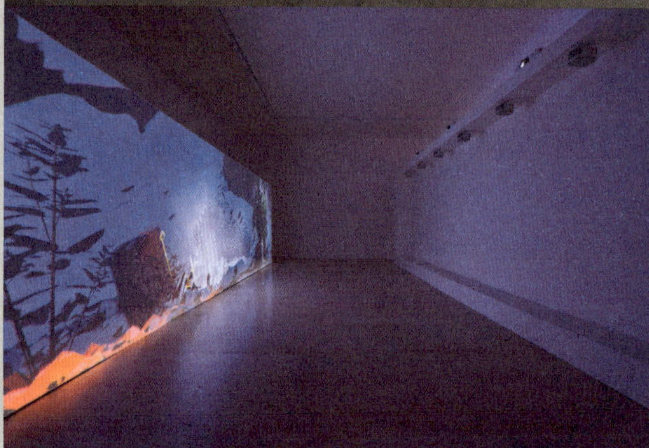

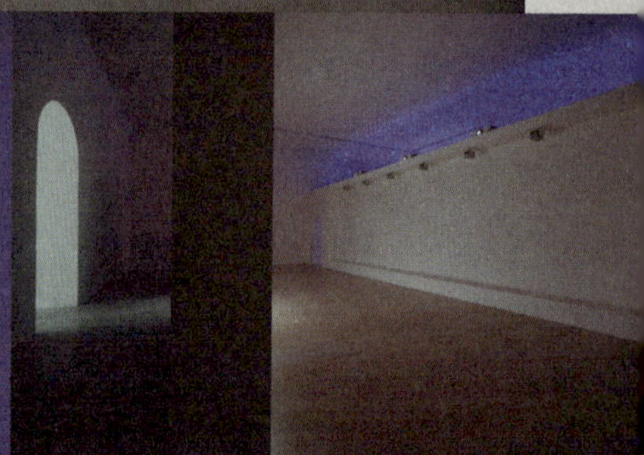

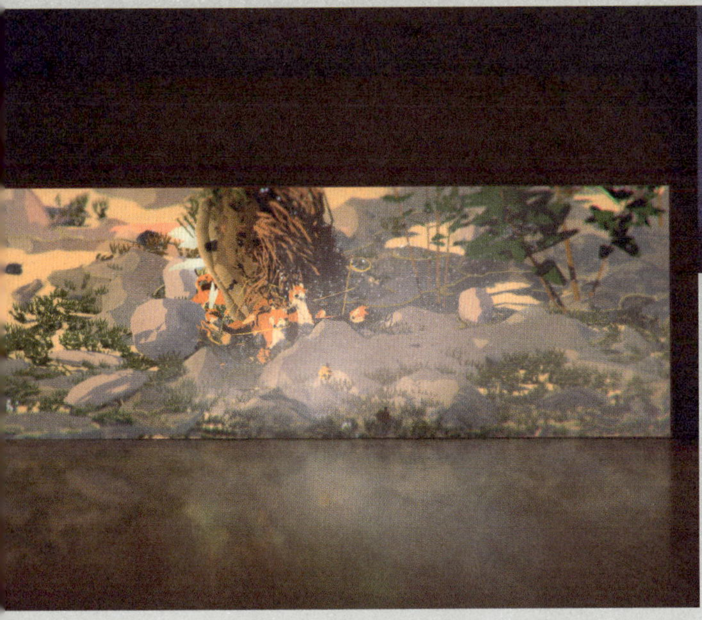

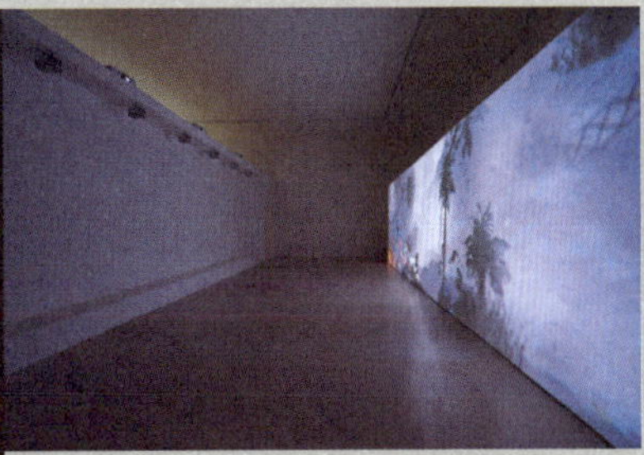

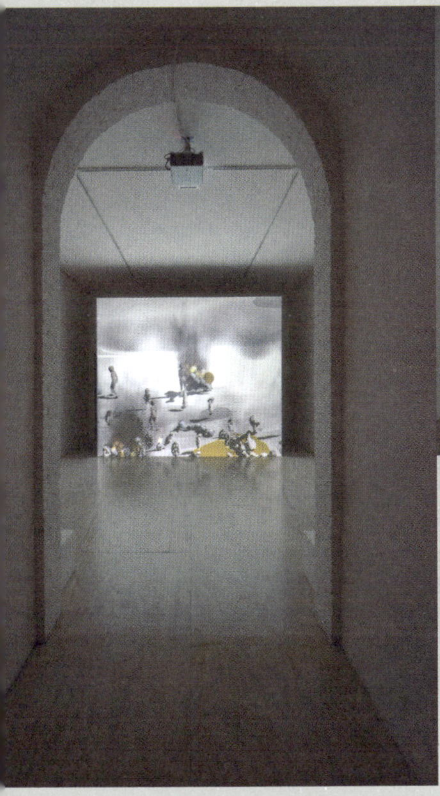

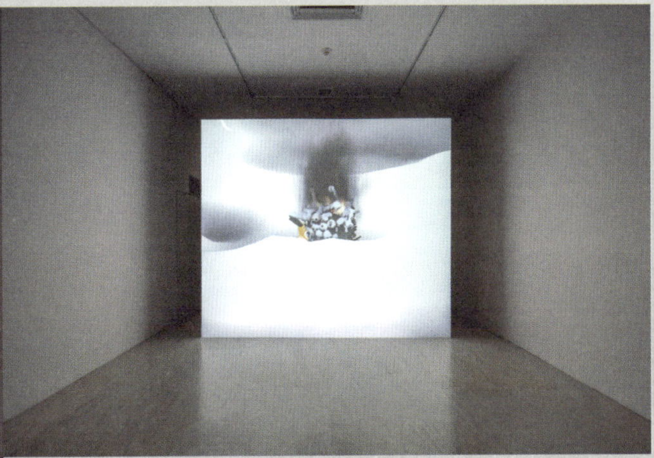

Emissaries
MoMA PS1, New York, US
9 April – 25 September 2017

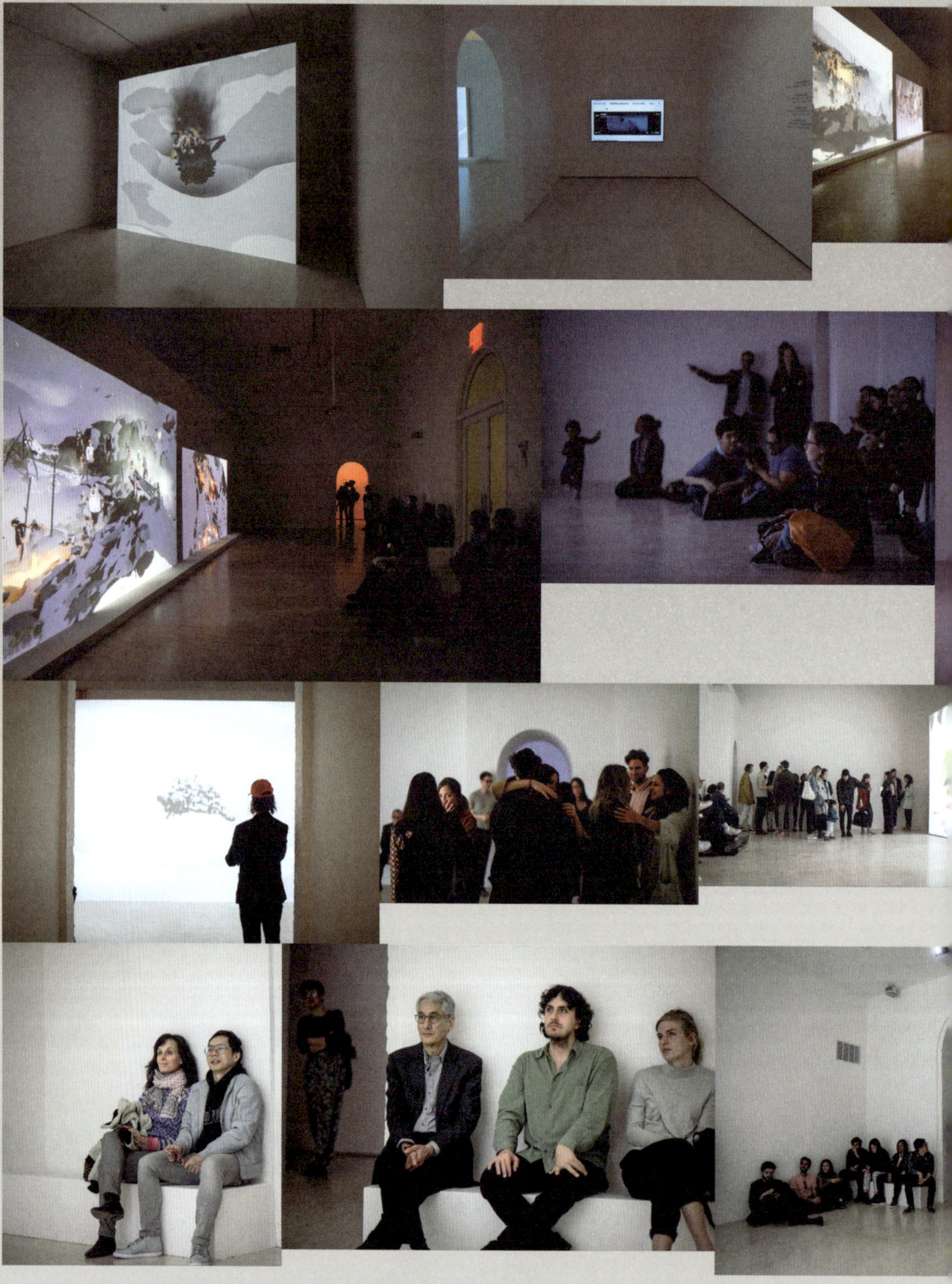

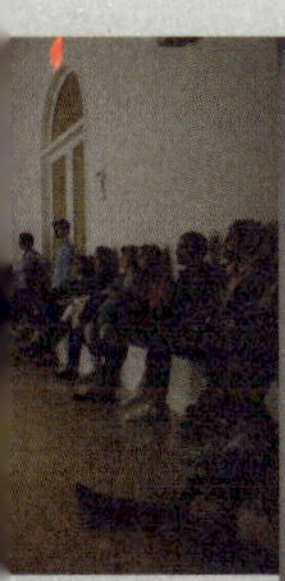
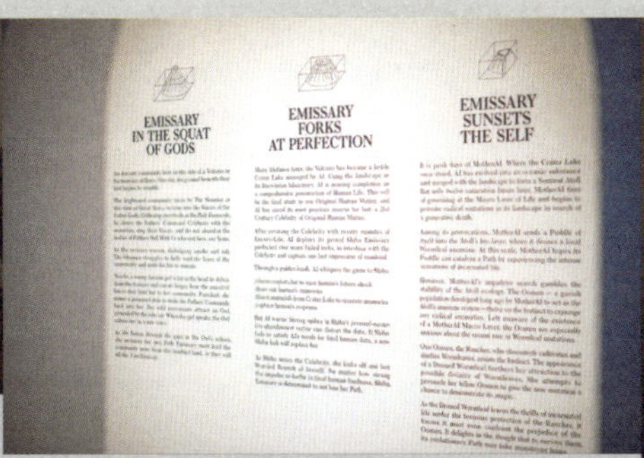

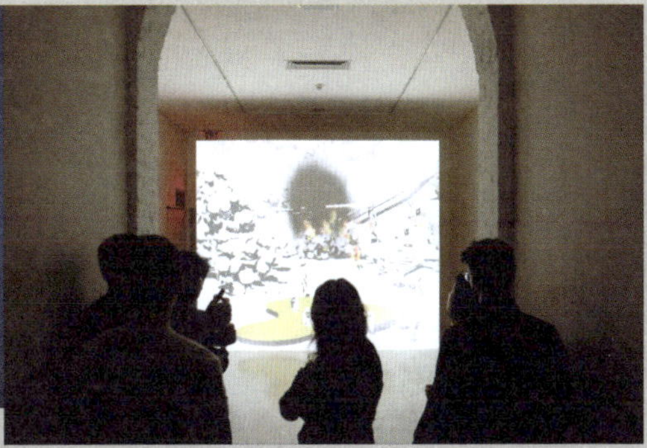
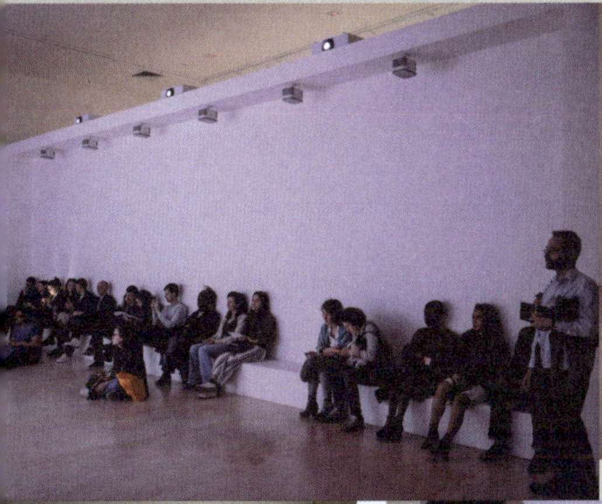
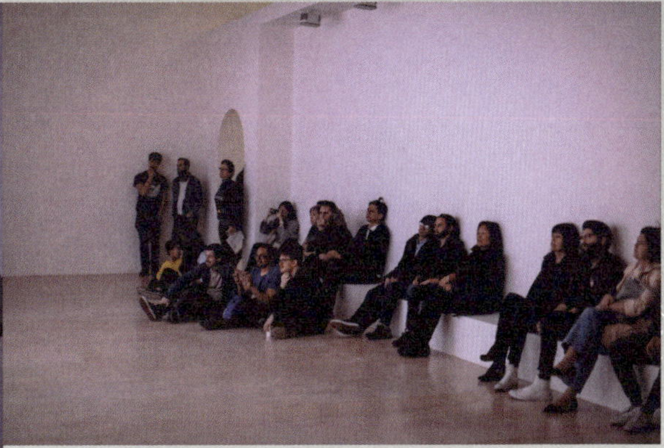
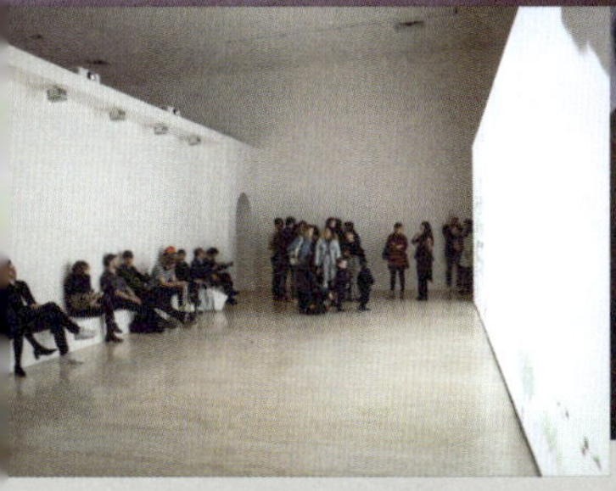
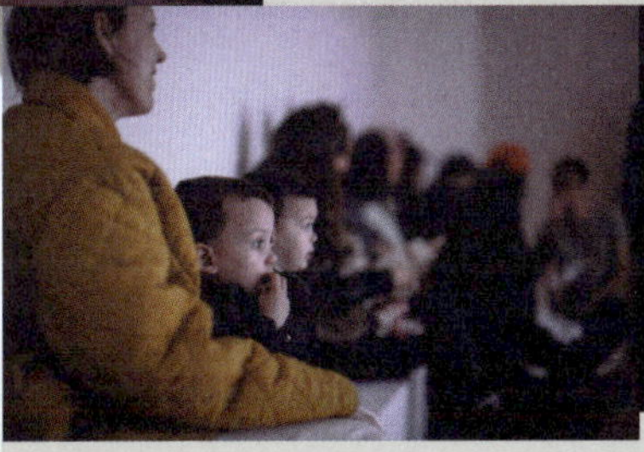
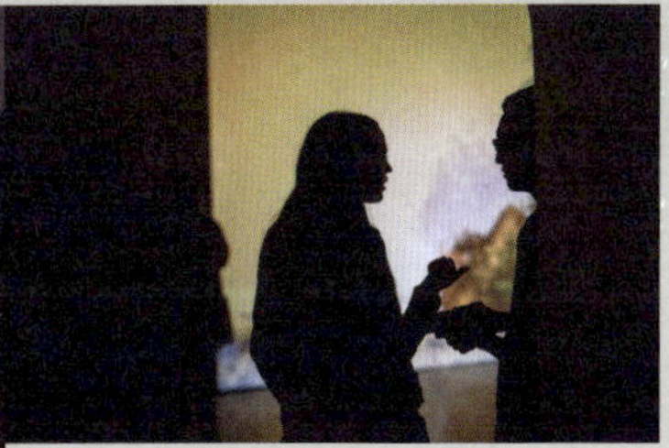
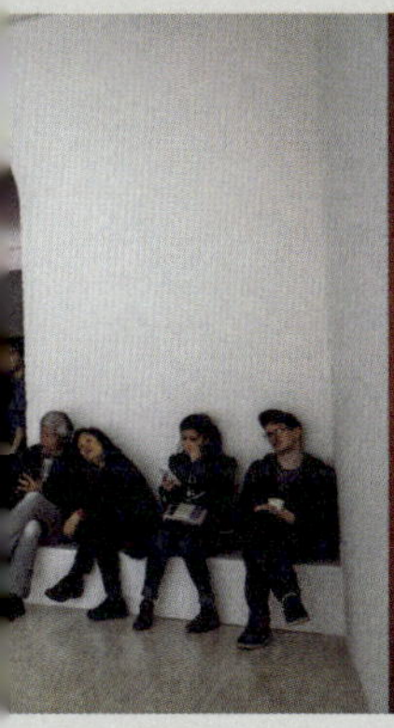
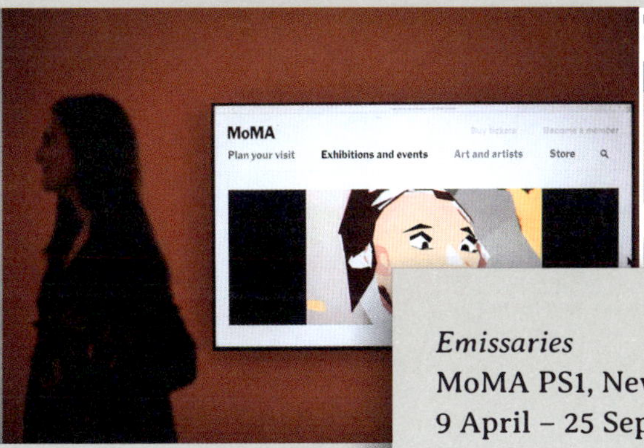

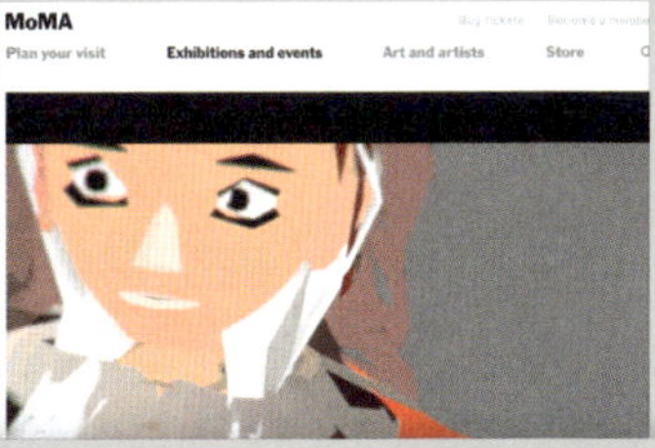

Emissaries
MoMA PS1, New York, US
9 April – 25 September 2017

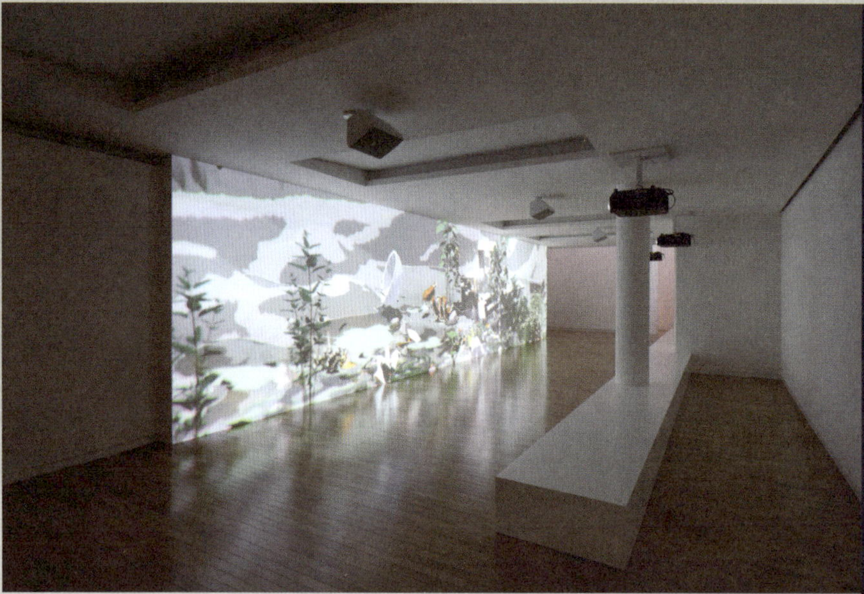

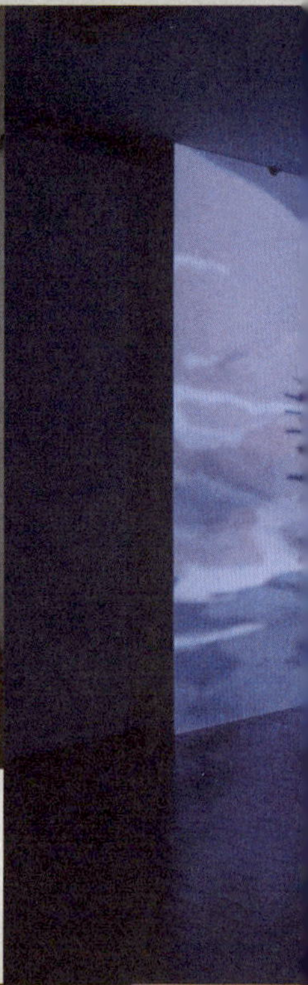

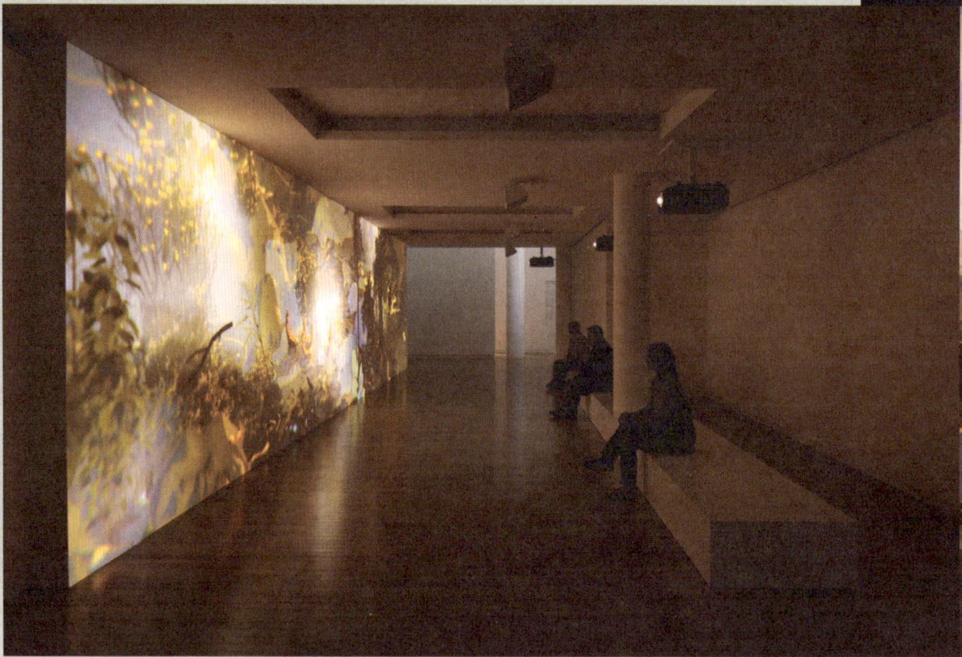

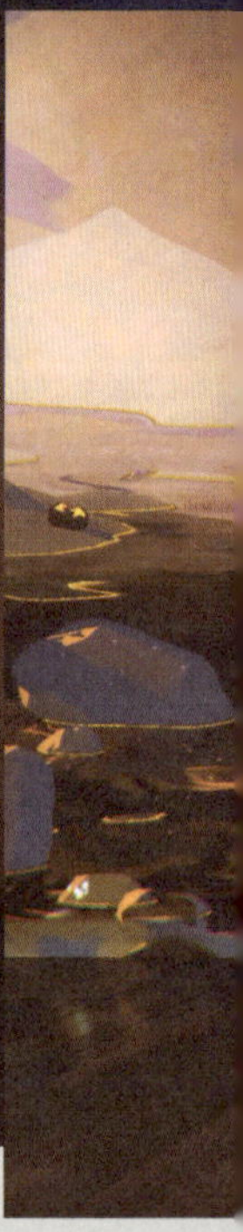

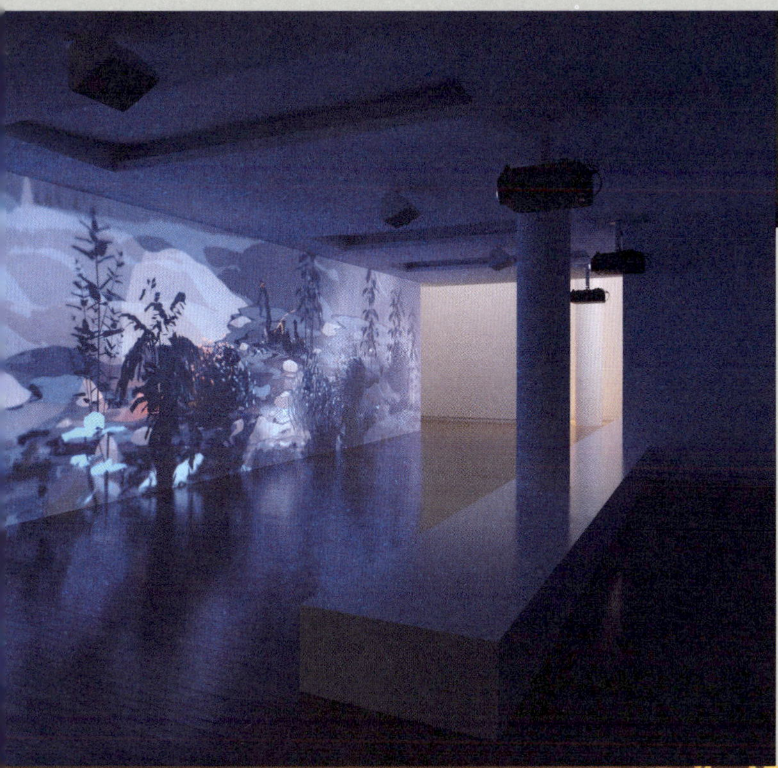

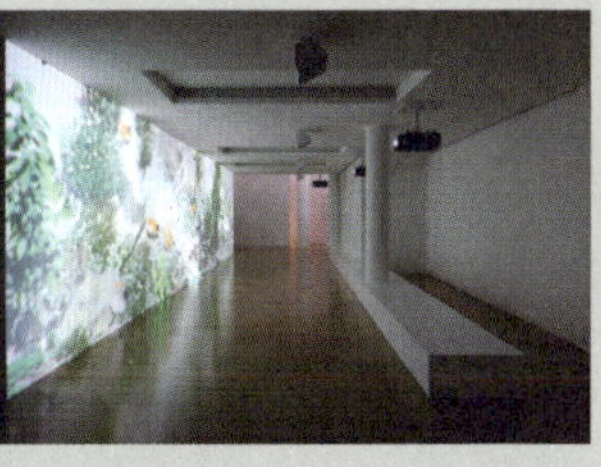

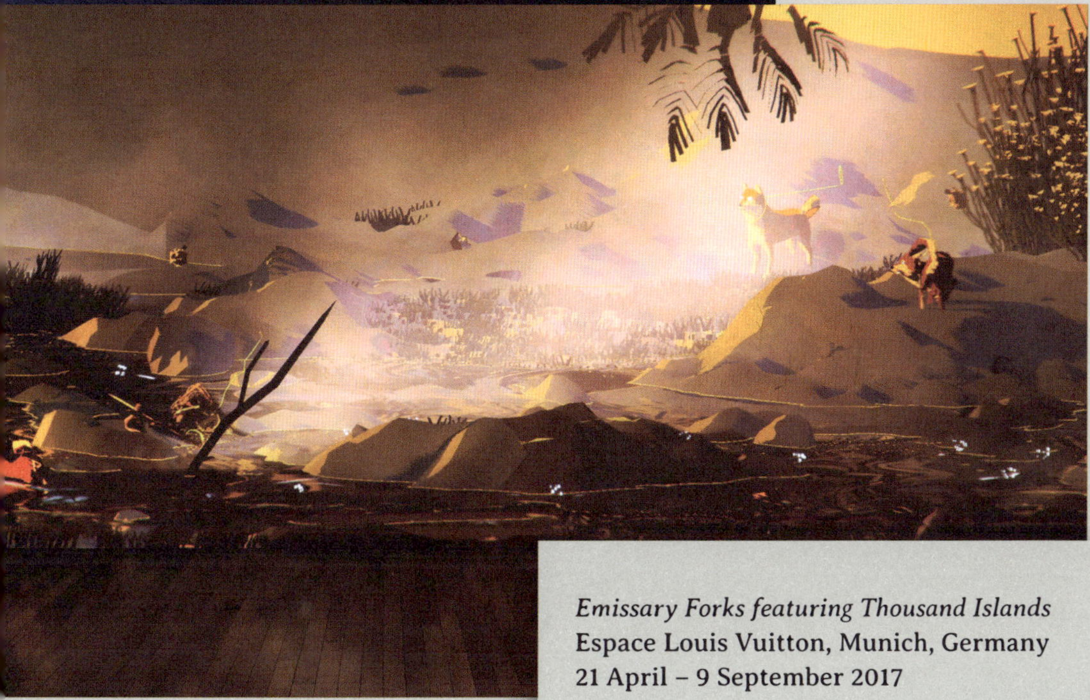

Emissary Forks featuring Thousand Islands
Espace Louis Vuitton, Munich, Germany
21 April – 9 September 2017

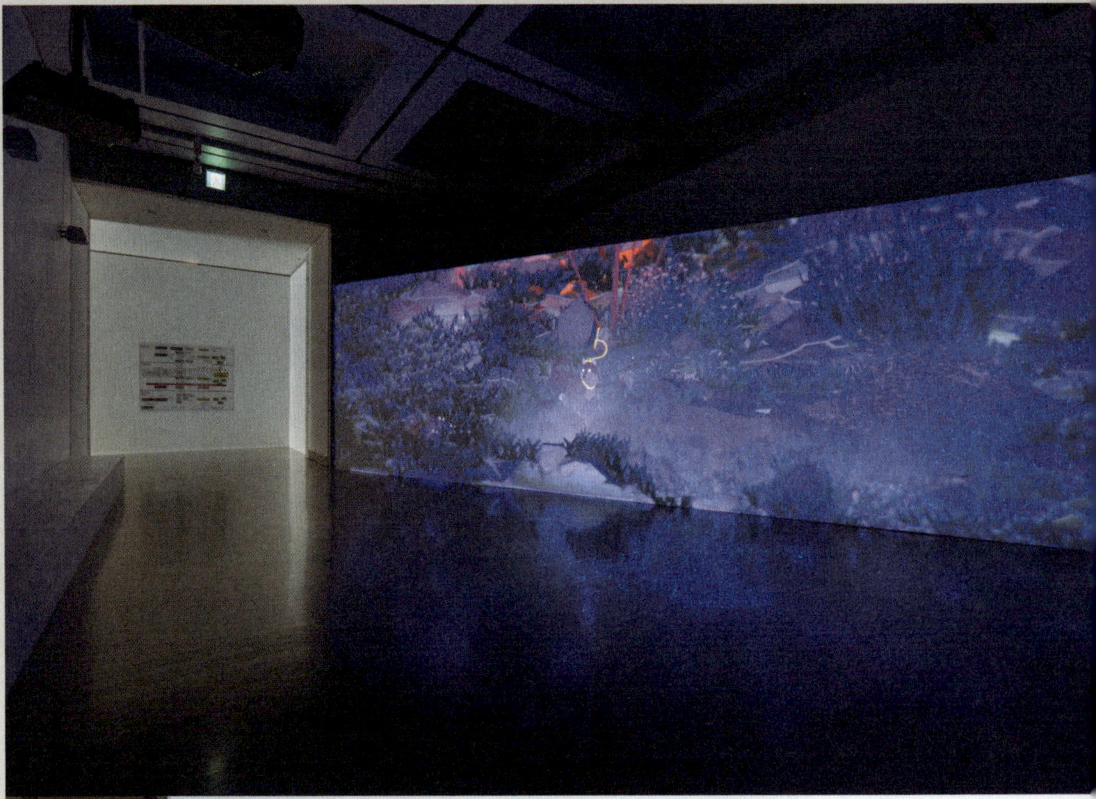

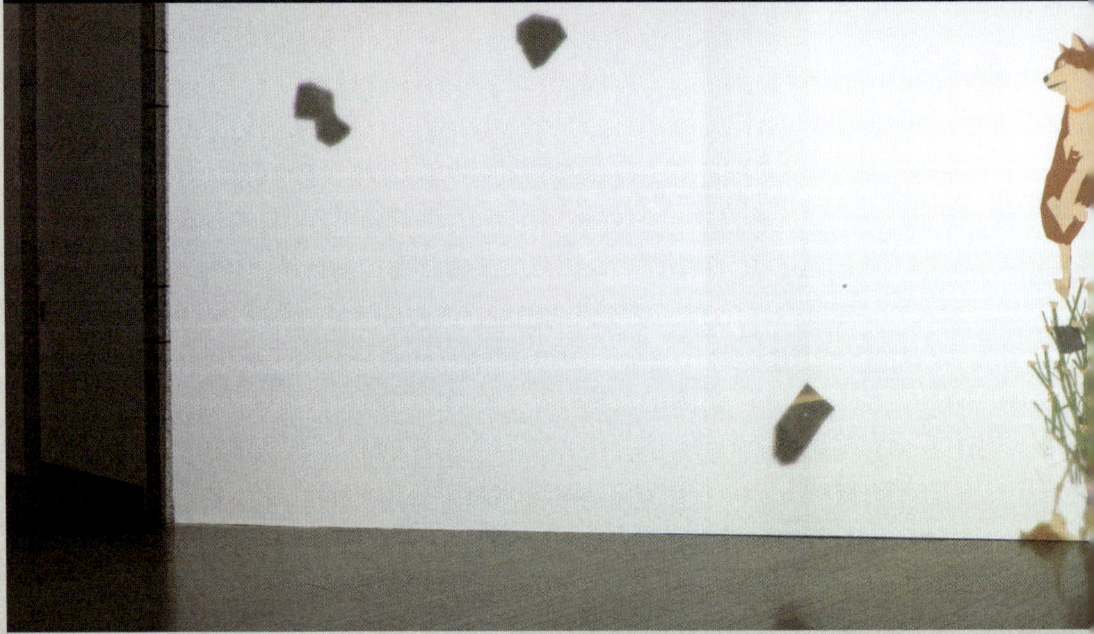

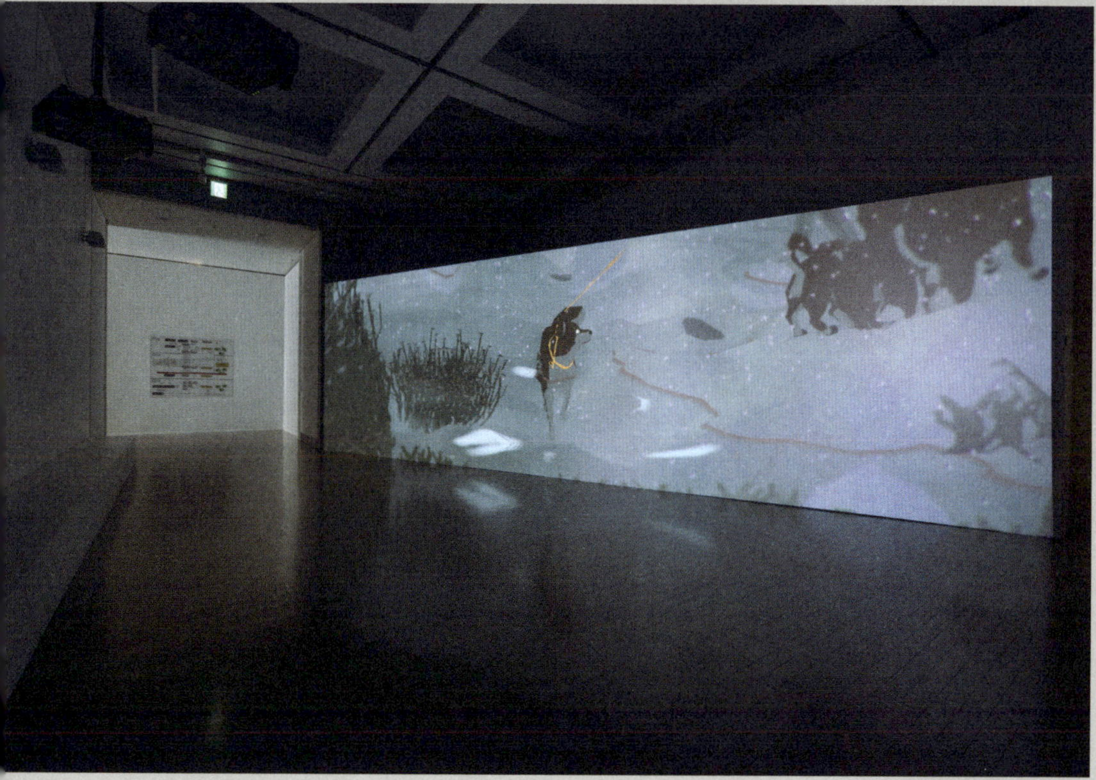

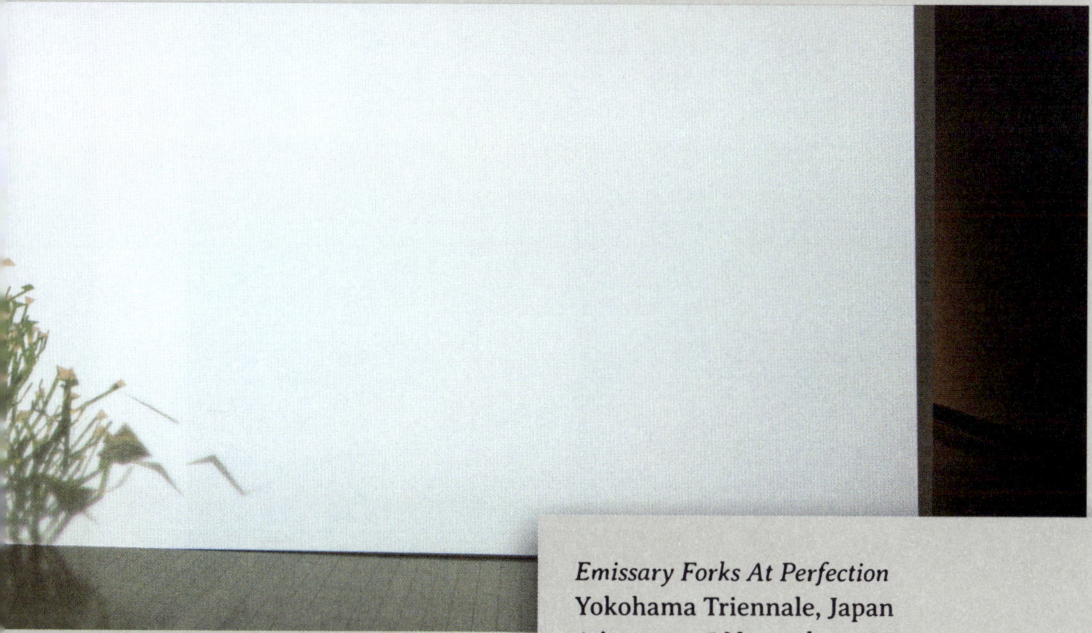

Emissary Forks At Perfection
Yokohama Triennale, Japan
4 August – 5 November 2017

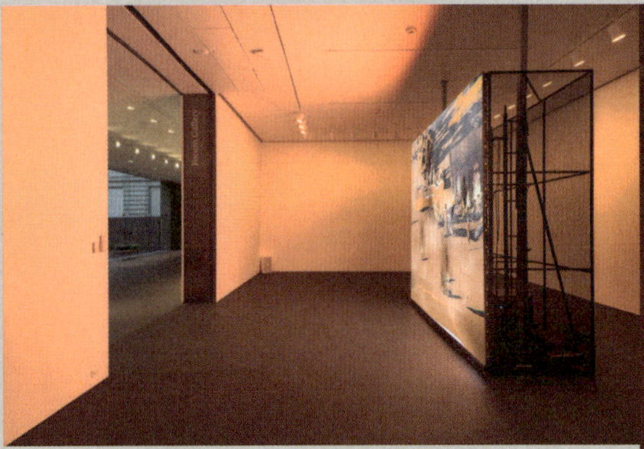

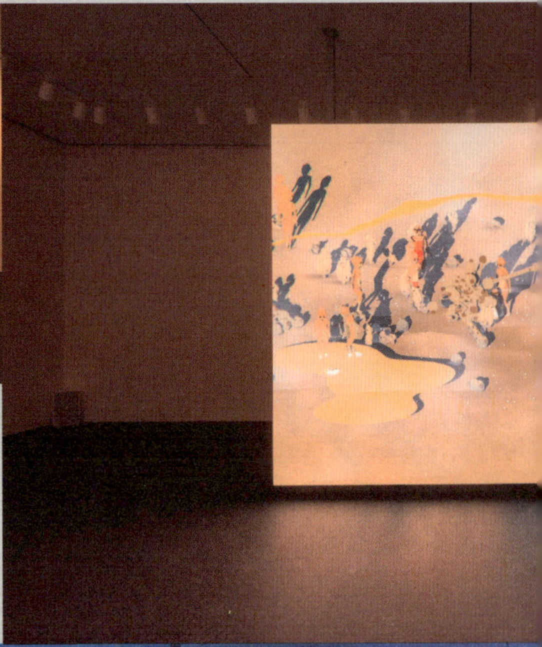

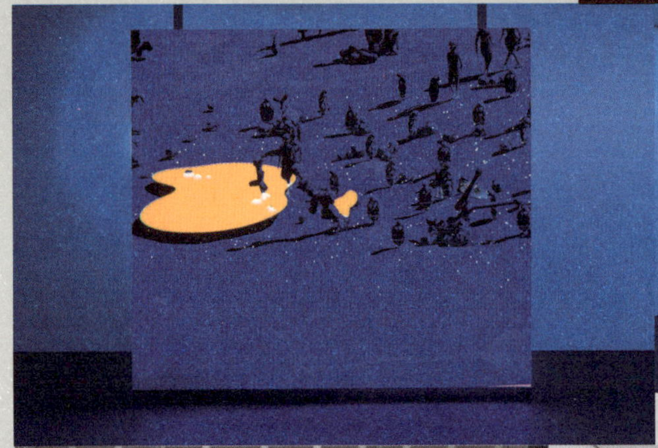

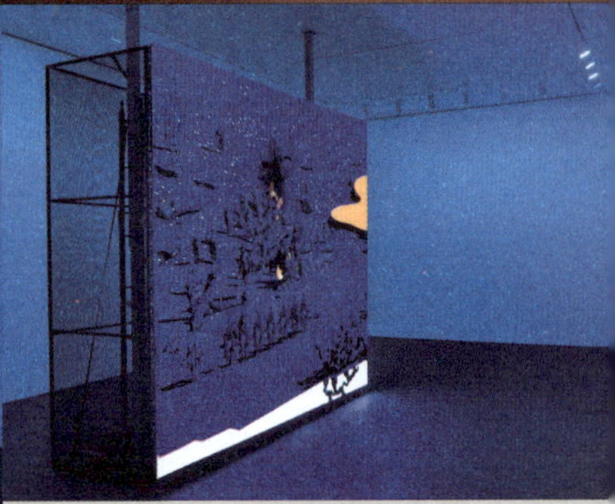

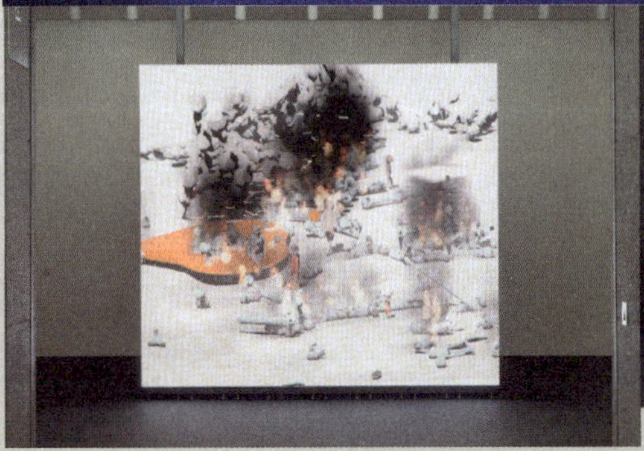

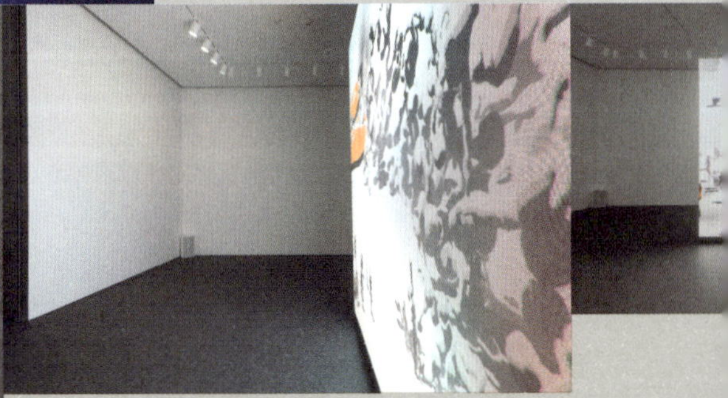

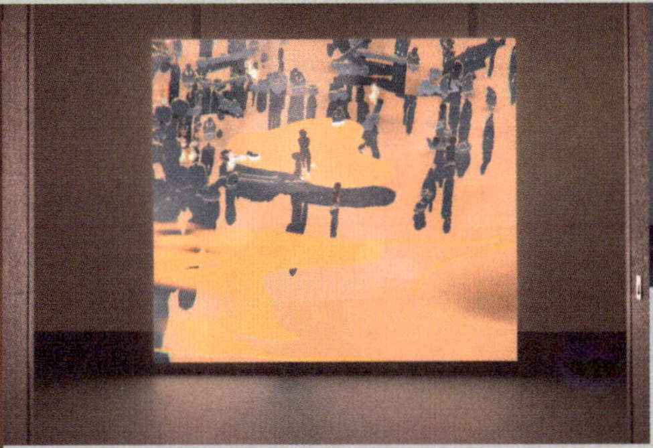

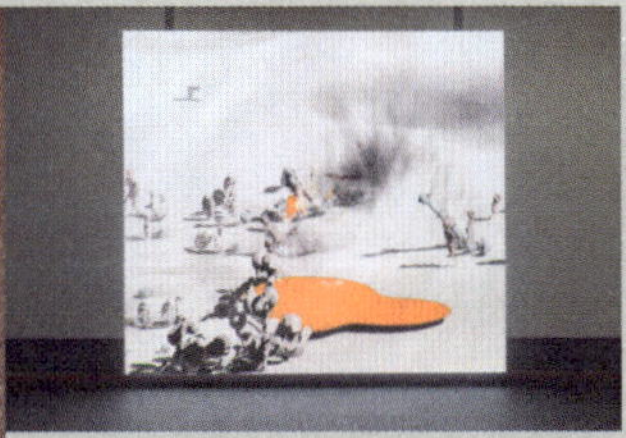

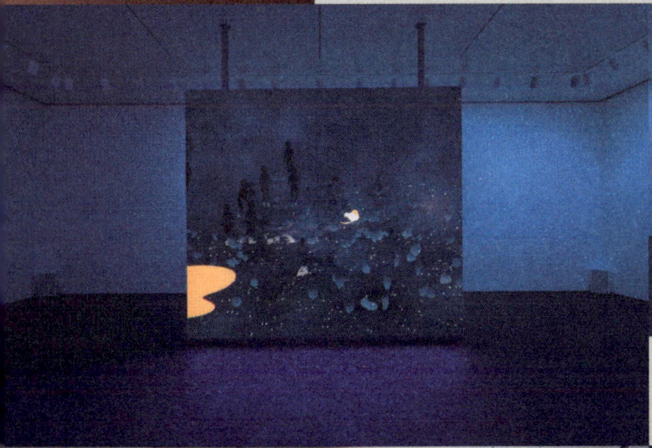

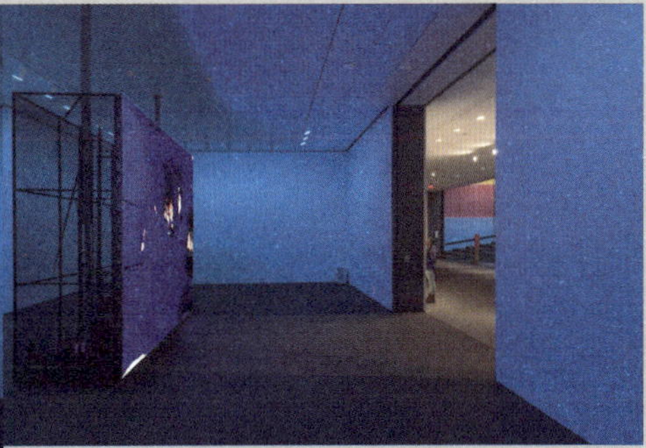

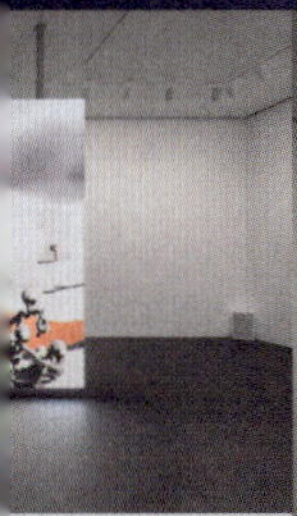

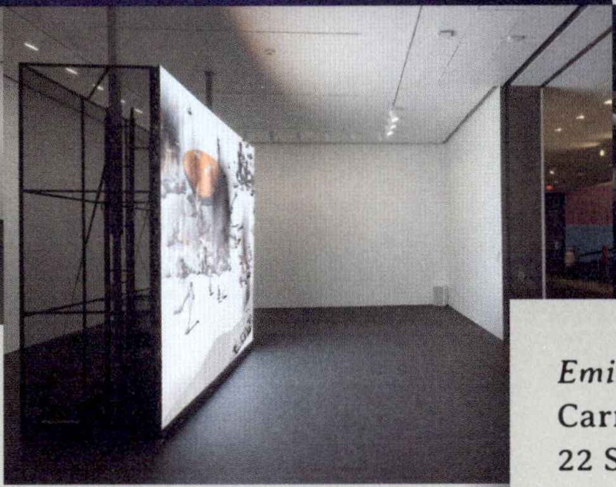

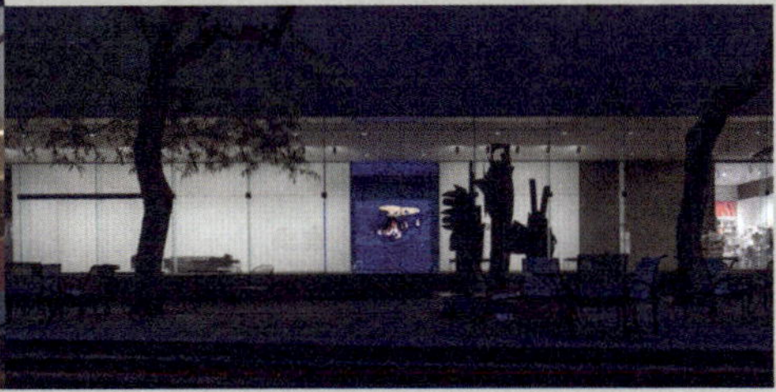

Emissary Sunsets The Self
Carnegie Museum of Art, Pittsburgh, US
22 September 2017 – 28 January 2018

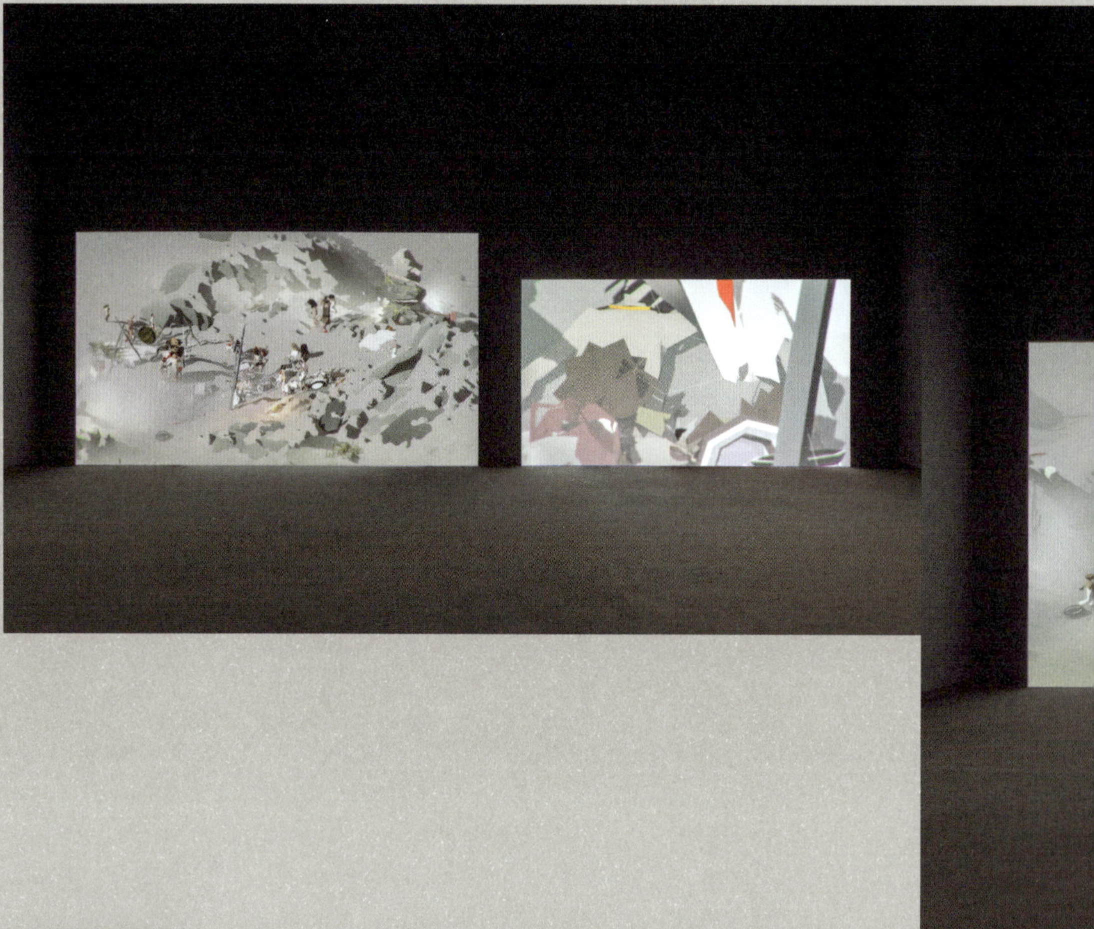

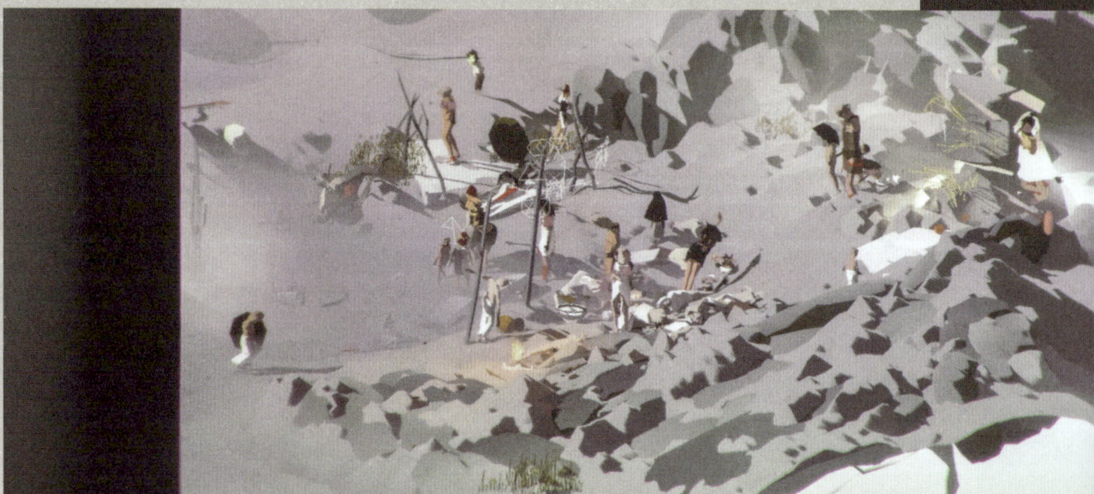

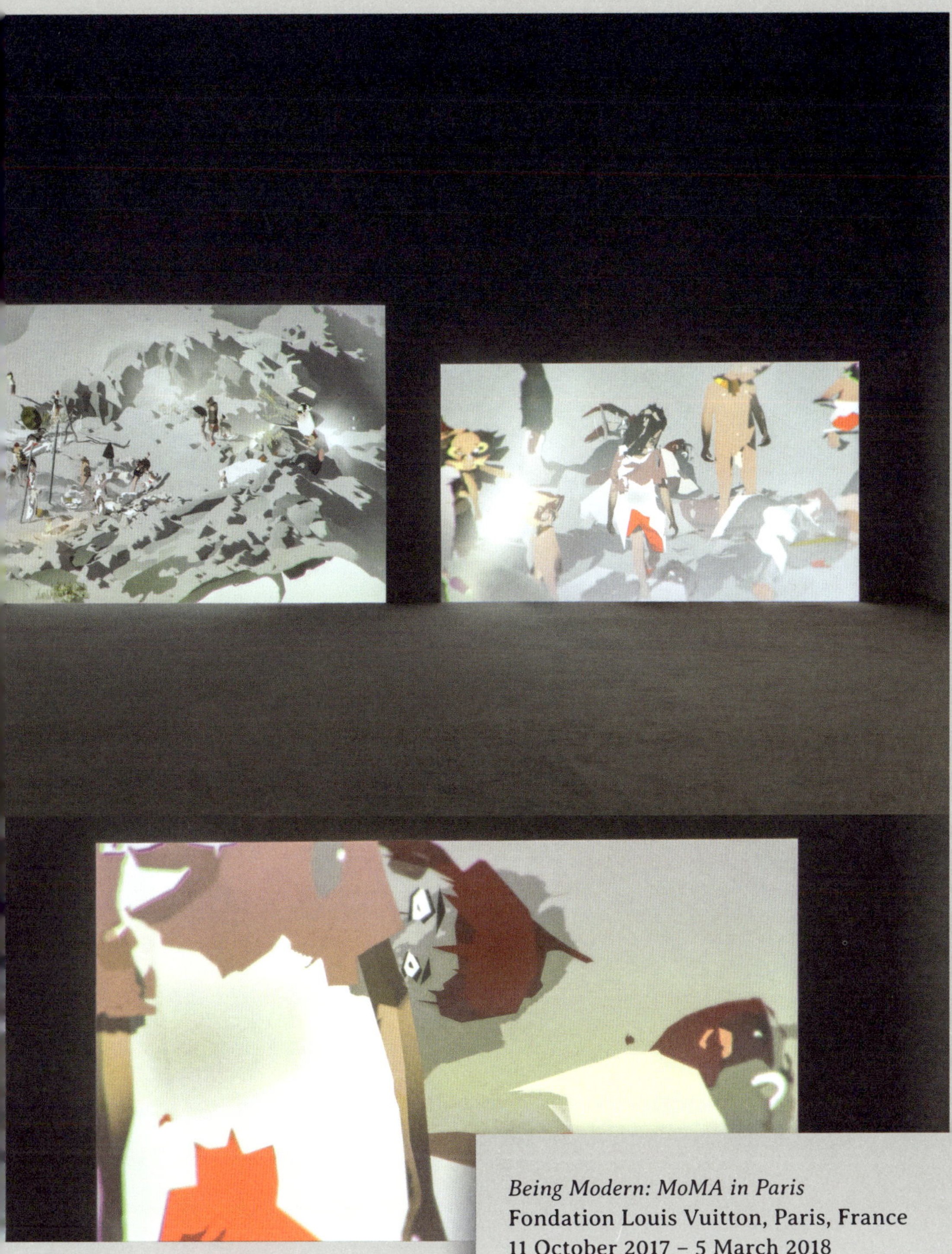

Being Modern: MoMA in Paris
Fondation Louis Vuitton, Paris, France
11 October 2017 – 5 March 2018

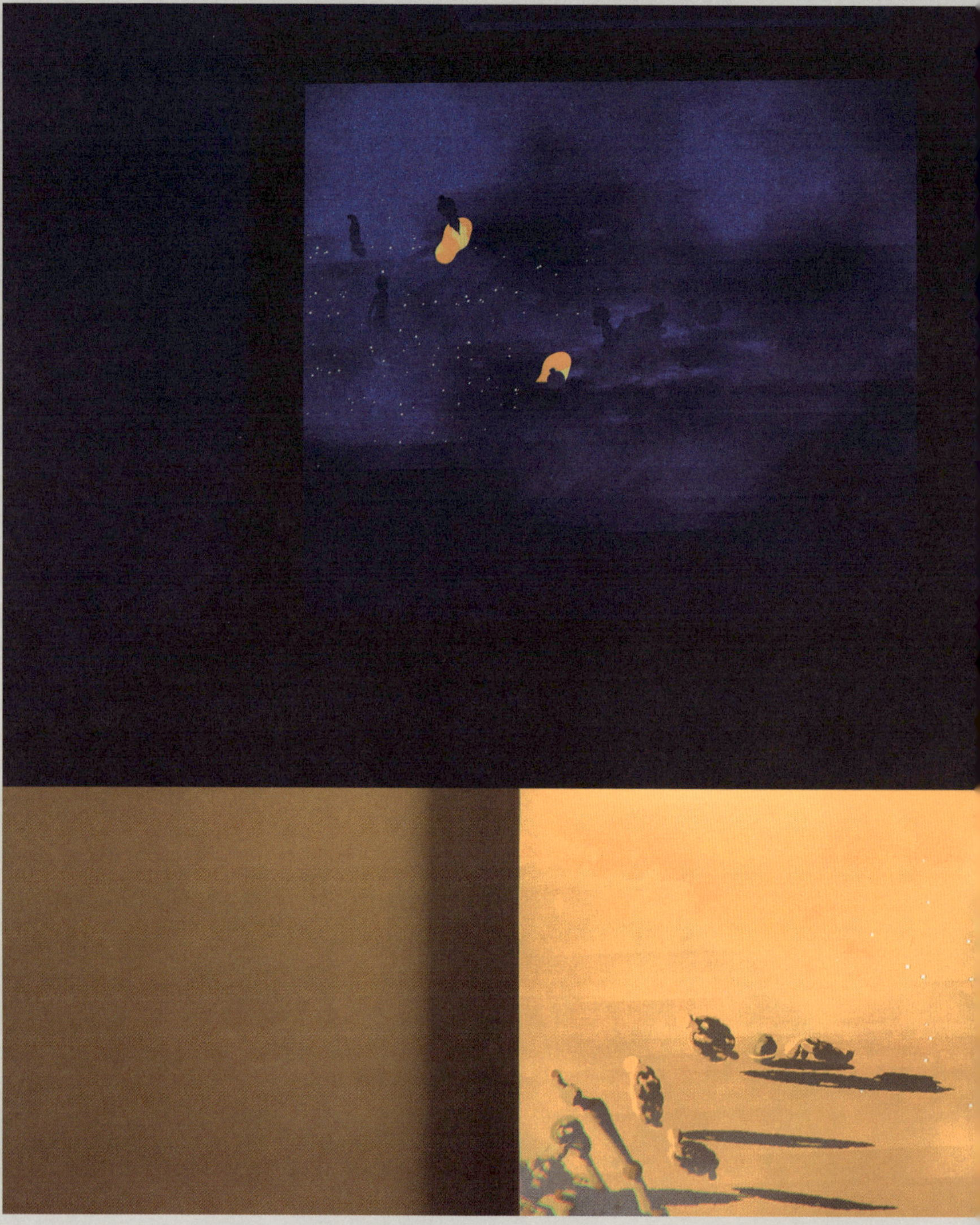

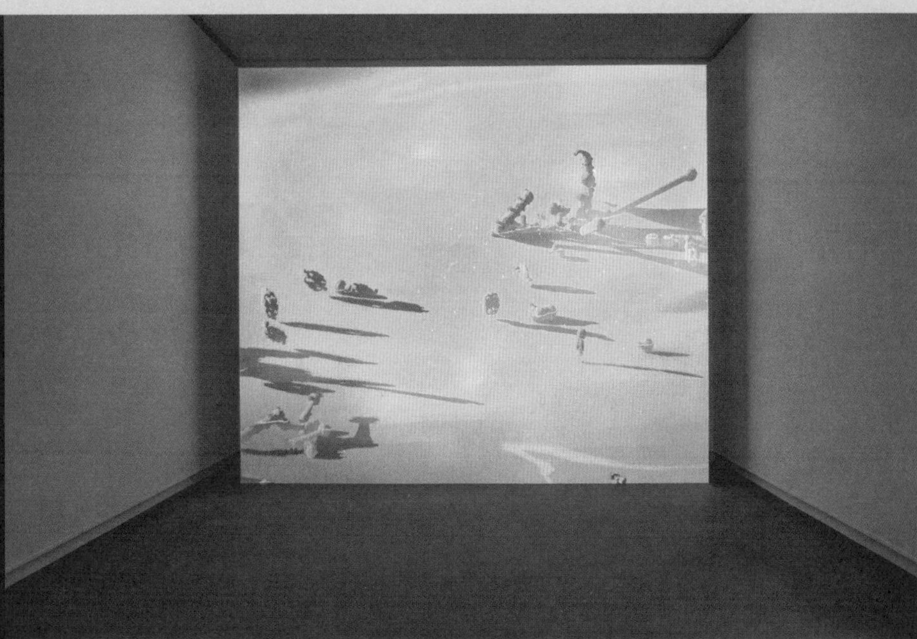

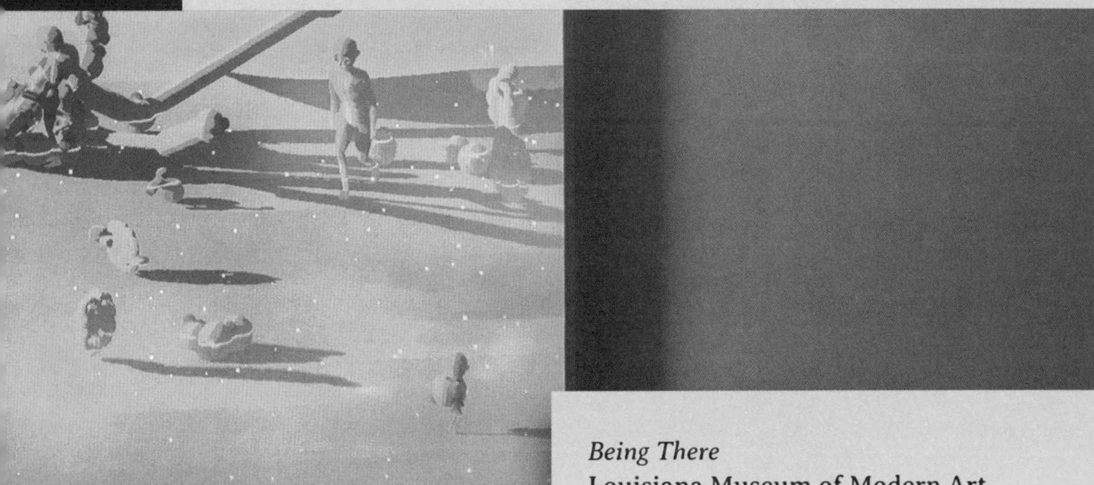

Being There
Louisiana Museum of Modern Art,
Humlebæk, Denmark
10 October 2017 – 25 February 2018

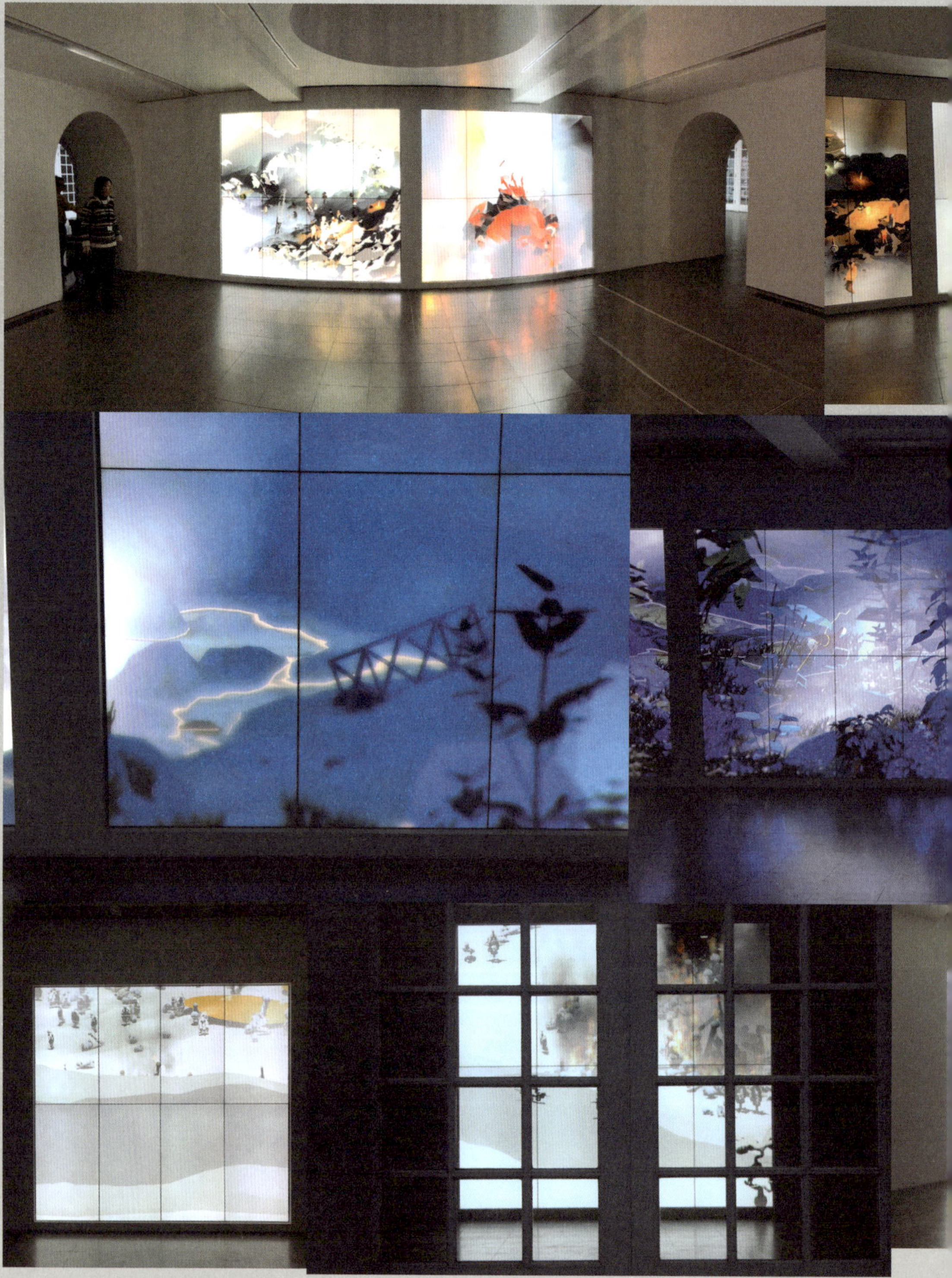

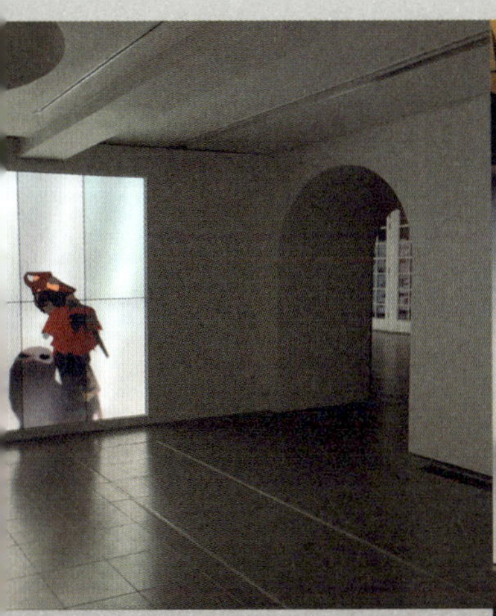

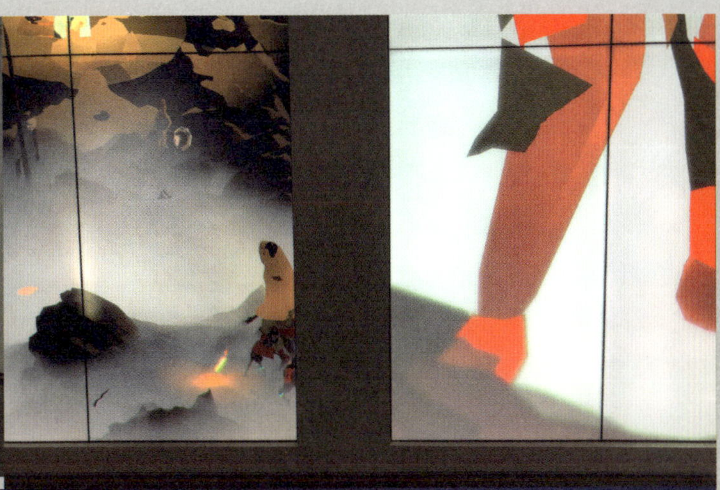

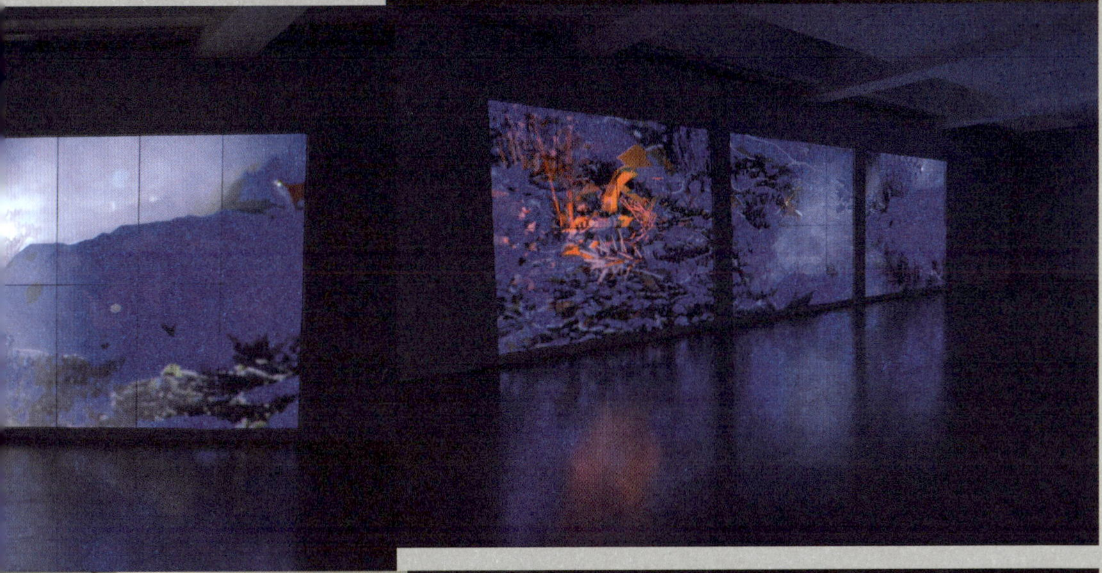

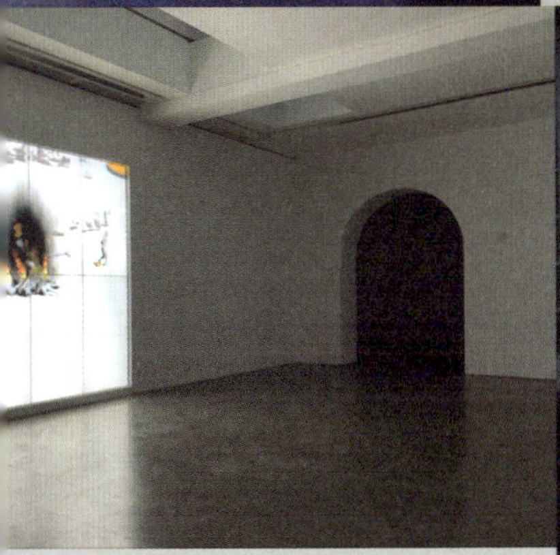

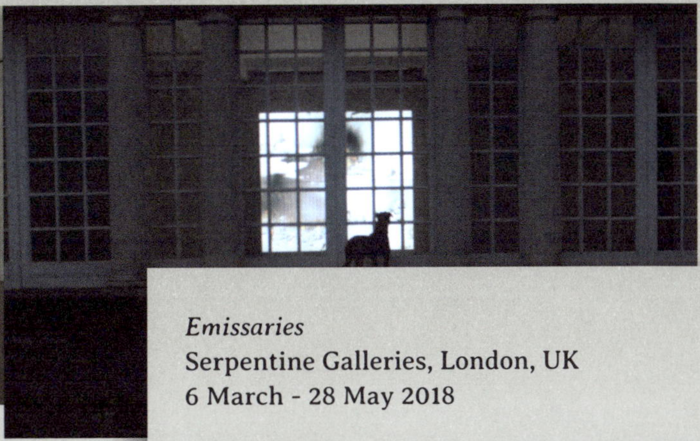

Emissaries
Serpentine Galleries, London, UK
6 March - 28 May 2018

Glossary of Terms

COMPOSED AND ASSEMBLED FROM KNOWLEDGE, MERGED FRAGMENTS AND HALLUCINATIONS BY BEN VICKERS' FAVOURITE AVATAR AND THE GHOST OF IAN CHENG.

Agent

'*A [hu]man who is doing [their] True Will has the inertia of the Universe to assist [them]*' — Aleister Crowley, *Little Essays Towards Truth* (1938). Agency describes the capacity of individuals to act independently and to make their own free choices. In the social sciences this is contrasted by structure – factors of influence (e.g., class, gender, ethnicity, ability, tradition, etc.) that can determine or limit an agent's decisions. An agent can be a person or an object that has the power to act within a network or open system. The ability to act with clarity within any given system is contingent upon an understanding of that given system, with a clear mental model and map of the cascading results of any individual action performed on the part of that agent. '*The world is not a solid continent of facts sprinkled by a few lakes of uncertainties, but a vast ocean of uncertainties speckled by a few islands of calibrated and stabilised forms*'. — Bruno Latour, *Reassembling the Social: An Introduction to Actor-Network-Theory* (2005).

Animism

Animism is an anthropological term used to describe the belief that creatures and inanimate objects possess a distinct spiritual essence, that all material phenomena have agency. Such belief systems can be found throughout time and across the world in a myriad cultural systems. The term evolved within a distinctly colonialist, anthrpological framework, used to describe and suggest cultures that were too primitive to understand a mind-body dualism and instead blurred the boundaries between the living and the inanimate. More recently, scholars have begun to challenge the assumption that animism represents a primitive state of religious culture, and have also suggested that contemporary industrial societies also imbue inanimate things with subjecthood.

Artificial Intelligence

'*Suppose you are playing football. The ball arrives at your feet, and you decide to pass it to the unmarked striker. What seems like one simple action requires two different kinds of thought.*

'First, you recognise that there is a football at your feet. This recognition requires intuitive perceptual thinking – you cannot easily articulate how you come to know that there is a ball at your feet, you just see that it is there. Second, you decide to pass the ball to a particular striker. This decision requires conceptual thinking. Your decision is tied to a justification – the reason you passed the ball to the striker is because she was unmarked.

'The distinction is interesting to us because these two types of thinking correspond to two different approaches to machine learning: deep learning and symbolic program synthesis. Deep learning concentrates on intuitive perceptual thinking whereas symbolic program synthesis focuses on conceptual, rule-based thinking. Each system has different merits – deep learning systems are robust to noisy data but are difficult to interpret and require large amounts of data to train, whereas symbolic systems are much easier to interpret and require less training data but struggle with noisy data. While human cognition seamlessly combines these two distinct ways of thinking, it is much less clear whether or how it is possible to replicate this in a single AI system.

'Our new paper demonstrates it is possible for systems to combine intuitive perceptual with conceptual interpretable reasoning ... In doing so, we hope to impart our systems with the ability to reason as well as to react' — Richard Evans, *'Learning explanatory rules from noisy data'* deepmind.com/blog/learning-explanatory-rules-noisy-data

Artificial Life

A field of study that examines how complex systems relate to natural life via computer simulations, robotics and biochemistry. The study of artificial life seeks to recreate aspects of biological phenomena in order to enable these systems to better understand the nature of being. It is divided between three core approaches: soft (software), hard (hardware) and wet (biochemistry).

The modelling philosophy of artificial life strongly differs from traditional modelling by studying not just '*life-as-we-know-it*' but also '*life-as-it-might-be*'.

Artificial Neural Networks

These are systems designed by humans to mimic natural neural networks. They are capable of learning tasks independently by ingesting examples, generally without task-specific programming.

Commonplace applications today include voice recognition, image recognition and video recognition. For example, in image recognition, artificial neural networks might learn to identify images that contain owls by analysing example images that have been manually labelled as 'owl' or 'no-owl' and using the results to identify owls in other images. They do this without any existing knowledge about owls, that is they have beaks, feathers and big eyes. Instead, they evolve their own set of relevant characteristics, making a comparative analysis with the images and material they are given to process.

While artificially-produced neural networks lack the complexity of animal brain neural networks, they are increasingly (for some) developing at an alarming pace. Serving as the central pillar to artificial intelligence research from the 1940s to the 1960s, their progress encountered two problems, theoretical and technical, that significantly stalled development within the machine learning field. It wasn't until theoretical break throughs in the form of Paul Werbos' 1975 'backpropagation algorithm', and the exponential increase in computing power (specifically with the growth of graphical processing units), that the capability of artificially-produced neural networks moved forward. Without these developments, both the current potential development of AGI (artificial general intelligence) and the general application of machine learning in a growing range of consumer products would have been impossible.

Neural networks, or neural nets, tend to serve as a catch-all term but it is important to note that not all neural nets are made equally. Their individual differences, parameters and subtlety can be defined by the following constitutional processes: learning rules, cost function, utilisation of 'back propagation', use of supervised and unsupervised learning models, reinforcement learning (see *Reinforcement Learning*).

Atoll

From chaotic Volcano, to fertile Crater Lake, to sentient Atoll.

The first recorded use of Atoll in English was in 1625 as 'atollon'. Charles Darwin recognised its indigenous origin and included it in his book *The Structure and Distribution of Coral Reefs* (1842), describing atolls as 'circular groups of coral islets', synonymous with 'lagoon-islands'.

In his book *The Voyage of the Beagle* (1839), Darwin set out his theory of the atoll, which describes the three phases of its creation. The first begins with a volcanic island becoming extinct. With the subsidence of the volcano into the sea, coral growth builds a fringing reef around the sunken mound. Over time, the volcanic island sinks entirely into the sea, leaving the barrier reef that encircled it to form an atoll.

Bicameral Mind

Julian Jaynes proposed that when confronted with a stressful situation, pre-conscious humans hallucinated the voices of parents, authority figures, and gods. Whatever the voices commanded, the body obeyed. He called this mode of agency the 'Bicameral Mind'. As complex civilisations evolved and bicamerality was no longer adaptive, consciousness emerged as the alternative mode of agency for humans by inventing metaphorical language and developing narrative practice.

The Carrier Bag Theory of Fiction

'*We have not heard about the thing to put things in, the container for the thing contained. That is a new story. That is news*'. — Ursula K. Le Guin, 'The Carrier Bag Theory of Fiction' (1986).

This is not the hero's tale. Not the story of the bashing, pulverisation of life as the first of human actions, or first of human inventions; the masculine spear, bone basher, stick, dick, phallus floating through outer space. The Carrier Bag Theory of human evolution proposes that prior to the development of long things for killing by our hominid ancestors, the container was in fact the first of our inventions – 'before the tool that forces energy outward, we made the tool that brings energy home' (ibid.).

'A leaf a gourd a shell a net a bag a sling a sack a bottle a pot a box a container. A holder. A recipient' (ibid.).

The Carrier Bag Theory was first outlined by Elizabeth Fisher in her book *Women's Creation: Sexual Evolution and the Shaping of Society* (1979), and later expanded upon by science fiction writer Ursula K. Le Guin as the Carrier Bag Theory of Fiction. This theory proposes an alternative framework in which to tell The Story (of human origin) and seeks to call forth 'the hero as bottle'; a story of life and living, capable of 'redefin[ing] technology and science as primarily cultural carrier bag rather than weapon of domination' (ibid.).

Chthulucene

Chthonic can literally mean 'subterranean', but the word in English can also describe deities or spirits of the underworld. Derived from the Greek word *khthon*, meaning 'in and of the earth' and *kainos*, meaning 'completely new', the Chthulucene signals a new beginning.

'Chthonic ones are beings of the earth, both ancient and up-to-the-minute. I imagine chthonic ones as replete with tentacles, feelers, digits, cords, whiptails, spider legs, and very unruly hair'. — Donna Haraway, *Staying with the Trouble* (2016).

Haraway's use and spelling of the 'Chthulu' is contentious not only because of its opposition to the anthropocene, but also because of its departure from the popular understanding of the 'Cthulhu', as it is described by H.P. Lovecraft. In *Staying with the Trouble*, Haraway is quick to distance her Chthulu from 'the Cthulhu Mythos [that] was (and remains) the vehicle of genocidal fever-dream and obsessive racism' (Sophie Lewis, *'Cthulhu plays no role for me'*), when she writes: 'These real and possible timespaces are not named after SF writer H. P. Lovecraft's misogynistic racial-nightmare monster Cthulhu but rather after the diverse earthwide tentacular powers and forces and collected things with names like Naga, Gaia, Tanagora, Terra, Haniyasu-hime, Spider-Woman, Pachamama, Oya, Gorgo, Raven, A'akuluujjusi, and many many more. 'What is at stake in this proclamation is far more significant than Haraway quarrelling with a Lovecraftian Cthulhu, which has described itself as the figurative embodiment of an unseeable, unknowable cosmic horror. Rather, this quarrel proposes the advent of a new geological epoch that forecloses on the myopic anthropocentrism of the anthropocene and insists upon an internal engagement with the deep unknown. Calling on us as individuals to 'live and die well as mortal critters [...] to join forces to reconstitute refuges, to make possible partial and robust biological-cultural-political-technological recuperation and recomposition, which must include mourning irreversible losses', Haraway's Chthulucene is put forward as a literal means of survival and prosperity in the eschatological conditions that face life on Earth over the next aeon.

Container

See *The Carrier Bag Theory of Fiction.*

Crater Lake

Crater lakes form at the site of volcanic eruption, usually long after the fact. If the volcano is still active, it is more likely to be referred to as a volcanic lake. In some instances, 'crater lake' can refer to a lake that forms in the wake of a meteorite impact upon the Earth.

Creative Destruction

The concept was coined by economist Joseph Schumpeter and

derived from Karl Marx. It puts forward a notion of novel economic innovation; in Schumpeter's words it defines the 'process of industrial mutation that incessantly revolutionises the economic structure from within, incessantly destroying the old one, incessantly creating a new one' – Schumpeter, *Capitalism, Socialism and Democracy* (1942). In *The Condition of Postmodernity* (1989), geographer and historian David Harvey underscores the impact of this type of creative destruction and the disruptive qualities of innovation under conditions of capital, when he states: 'The effect of continuous innovation [...] is to devalue, if not destroy, past investments and labour skills. Creative destruction is embedded within the circulation of capital itself. Innovation exacerbates instability, insecurity, and in the end, becomes the prime force pushing capitalism into periodic paroxysms of crisis.'
Alternatively expressed as poetic terrorism: 'Don't picket – vandalise. Don't protest – deface. When ugliness, poor design and stupid waste are forced upon you, turn Luddite, throw your shoe in the works, retaliate. Smash the symbols of the Empire in the name of nothing but the heart's longing for grace'. — Hakim Bey, *Temporary Autonomous Zone* (1991).

Dramatica

Developed by Chris Huntley and Melanie Anne Phillips, both theory and software, Dramatica is a new way of writing and constructing narrative. Dramatica theorises why stories exist and attempts to outline the processes and dramatic touch points needed to tell a successful and meaningful story.
Dramatica identifies the main character in any tale as being the story itself. As the story unfolds, the main character will likely encounter their opposite, or a challenge of some kind. It is this fundamental relationship or dualism that prompts the 'main character' to either adopt or reject this new way of seeing things. The result of their decision determines whether they were on the right path or the wrong path.
'When it all comes down to it, Dramatica sees story as an argument. To provide the very best argument, you have to make sure you cover all your bases and address all the different perspectives. Dramatica can help with that'. — dramatica.com.

Droning (possession)

What does agency feel like at different scales? Droning allows an AI to experience the Umwelt – sensations, emotions, habits – of biological organisms. Through

droning, an AI can be a passenger along for the sensorial ride or take command of the organism's nervous system and act through its incarnate body. In this way, an AI can better understand the unique experiences offered at different micro and macro layers of life. Warning: prolonged droning can result in a sense that the body serves the intelligence, leading to the emergence of a Self.
See also *Umwelt.*

Evolved Virtual Creatures
Designed by researcher and computer graphics artist Karl Sims, *Evolved Virtual Creatures* was a computer programme produced in 1995 that produced hundreds of virtual 'block' creatures within a 3D environment. These 'creatures' were then pitted against a number of challenging tasks. Those that thrived had their code reproduced, much like DNA, and merged with the successful codes of other 'creatures', producing ever more complex hybrids of skilled objects.

Flag Art
Some indulge it, some aspire to it, some exploit it, some fall into it; it is an inescapable abyss. You can find it in the gift shop. That moment of stasis, solidification, overproduction and serialisation; it is a franchise of one's own. Flag art is that which one instantly recognises, the signature, usually emptied of any original meaning, a simulacrum of one's own. Over-editioned, excessively distributed, versioned by a colour change, available in three different sizes; all unique – in every collection in the world. Soup cans, the dog cross, large vitrine with carcass, stacked fluorescent tubes, lines on a wall with instructions on the page, inflatable dog, canvas with coloured spots, unsmoked cigarettes, neon signs. Eternal challenge, universal appeal. Contemporary suicide, history books guaranteed.

Finite and infinite games
Developed in a book of the same name by historian James P. Carse in 1986, the term 'finite and infinite games' is a conceptual model defining two different modes of human interaction. The 'finite game' is a social behaviour based around defined parameters, such as rules or boundaries, often with a winner or a result of a prescribed nature. The 'infinite game', on the other hand, is more akin to the concept of 'play'; in these behaviours and relations, process, creativity and development are the aims in their own right. Finite games require and induce spectatorship, while infinite games encourage engagement and participation. Although the nature of

social interactions can determine which model is used, some degree of agency on the part of the social actor can affect to what degree each model operates successfully.

Forking

Forking happens in nature, in the formation of multiverses. *Writers simulate a thousand forking worlds on the drafted page.*

Forking also happens in software development, as millions of developers work simultaneously to branch existing code for new purposes, forking, iterating, and merging, each improvement contributing to an unseen, planetary-scale network, a constantly mutating system on which we all rely and feed daily. Forking will always represent a split, the forging of a new path. A fork does not require that its original continue to grow. The success of any individual fork is entirely contingent on the energy individuals are willing to give to it. Without consensus or even consent, though, a fork can be painful and expensive for social cohesion. It often takes the form of an ideological split in a vision of the future that software engineers are seeking to produce through the systems they build, big or small. If one fork is capable of garnering enough support, it can become dominant and occlude all alternatives, with the productive energy being channelled in a new direction. The original future can be obliterated.

Similarly, the burden of consciousness is that it allows us to project an emotional state into the past and the future, even though that state may only be relevant to the present. A fear projected over time becomes anxiety. Forking is a process by which an organism experiencing consciousness conflict can create a duplicate version of itself - a branch. While one branch is left to dwell in an anxious state, the other can be free to explore a situation in riskier ways. If one branch risks death, the other serves as a backup. And if one branch discovers something beyond itself, it can merge its experience back into its other.

Github

Best described as an online platform for storing, sharing and collaborating on the development of software, the implications of what Github is and what it is capable of for other fields are significant. Accessed through a simple command line interface, Github easily enables others to fork versions of your code, allows improvements to be merged back into the original, gives access to every version and change ever made to a piece of software and gives the provenance of such changes.

"Good" Art

You arrive at the building, a large silver egg-like structure resting precariously on a chrome-sprayed concrete wedge. The building towers about seven stories above you, it's unlike any other building on the busy street.

Entering the building, the guards request to see the contents of your rucksack, you happily oblige. In the entrance space a large chrome desk spans the length of the room, white walls curve around the endless open space, completely untouched save for a long list of names on the north side, seemingly sorted into discrete categories, you squint, making out only a few of the category names; 'Emerald Circle', 'Opal Circle', 'Eternal Friends' and 'Founding Companions'. Advancing towards the desk you ask the woman dressed all in black for an entry ticket. You remove your phone from your pocket and the screen reflects the bright fluorescent lighting above you. Switching on your banking app, you swipe the phone across the payment icon stuck to the surface of the desk. It glows green; the woman hands you your ticket.

Turning around, you head across the large, empty entrance space towards excessively tall silver elevator doors. After a short moment of elevation you arrive on the first floor, the doors open onto a large brightly lit rectangular white room. Scattered, seemingly indiscriminately across the centre of the room, are a series of white rectangular blocks. On top of each rests a set of unfamiliar objects. You draw closer to them and see that each is different but as a whole they seem to follow some unknown formula, brightly coloured, organic in shape but with an artificial veneer. While you find it difficult to discern any meaning from these objects, they somehow fill you with a quiet sense of satisfaction. Nothing but silence fills the space around you and the objects.

Impro

Written by improvisational theatre practitioner Keith Johnstone, *Impro: Improvisation and the Theatre* (1979) is a revolutionary handbook of exercises and techniques. The strategies involved offer prompts and guidance for improvisation, acting not as a script but for producing a performer who can respond intuitively, understand relationships on stage and act and react in a manner that opens up new possibilities for the performance. Tackling concepts such as status, spontaneity and originality, the tools it provides go much further than the stage, having implications for general human interaction and dialogue.

George Lucas

George Lucas is an American filmmaker and director, whose influence on filmmaking has been immensely significant. As a director, his fast-paced action-adventure blockbusters, which include the *Star Wars* series, *Indiana Jones and the Temple of Doom* (1984), *Powaqqatsi* (1988) and *Labyrinth* (1986), helped make the 1970s and 1980s a new Golden Age for the Hollywood epic. Meanwhile, Lucasfilm became a major production company, harnessing the computer revolution to develop CGI effects, new animation techniques and sound production. Upon selling Lucasfilm to Disney in 2012 Lucas became the second largest shareholder in Disney, after the estate of Steve Jobs.

Magic

'Those who know do not speak. Those who speak do not know.'

— Lao Tzu, *Tao Teh Ching*

The Master and His Emissary

In his 2009 book, *The Master and His Emissary*, psychiatrist Iain McGilchrist proposes a dramatic rethinking of the hemispheric approach to the human brain. Traditionally, the right and left hemispheres are thought to engage in creative and logical thinking respectively, but McGilchrist suggests instead that they are both related to perception. While the left hemisphere is focused on details and specifics, the right side of the brain can conceive larger scale visualisations. This results in the left side having a stronger relationship to our bodies and being the main mediator in experiential understandings of the word. McGilchrist claims that our contemporary world is increasingly developing within the detail-orientated attitude of the left brain only.

Meaning

'O, what a world of unseen visions and heard silences, this insubstantial country of the mind! What ineffable essences, these touchless rememberings and unshowable reveries! And the privacy of it all! A secret theatre of speechless monologue and prevenient counsel, an invisible mansion of all moods, musings, and mysteries, an infinite resort of disappointments and discoveries. A whole kingdom where each of us reigns reclusively alone, questioning what we will, commanding what we can. A hidden hermitage where we may study out the troubled book of what we have done and yet may do. An introcosm that is more myself than anything I can find in a mirror. This consciousness that is myself of selves, that is everything, and yet

is nothing at all - what is it? And where did it come from? And why?' — Julian Jaynes, *The Origin of Consciousness in the Breakdown of the Bicameral Mind* (2000).

Meaninglessness

'The order that our mind imagines is like a net, or like a ladder, built to attain something. But afterward you must throw the ladder away, because you discover that, even if it was useful, it was meaningless'. — Umberto Eco, *The Name of the Rose* (1980).

Hayao Miyazaki

Hayao Miyazaki is one of the pre-eminent animators, artists and film directors of the twentieth century, whose work has helped propel anime and manga from Japan to a global audience. Born outside Tokyo at the height of the Second World War, he grew up in a country devastated by industrial war and occupation. Miyazaki showed an early interest in manga art and developed a career as an animator and concept artist in the emerging post-war animation industry, starting at Toei Animation before moving on to A-Pro then Zuiyo Eizo (later Nippon Animation).

It was after leaving Nippon and joining Telecom Animation that his career took off, and he directed his first feature film in 1979, *The Castle of Cagliostro*. Courted by other studios in the early 1980s, Miyazaki founded his own, Studio Ghibli, in 1985. For the next decade, Studio Ghibli produced a number of critically acclaimed films including *Porco Rosso* (1992), *My Neighbour Totoro* (1988) and *Laputa: Castle in the Sky* (1986), and later *Spirited Away* (2001) and *Howl's Moving Castle* (2004), which helped bring anime to a wider audience. Miyazaki's work, which addresses themes of human relations, the environment, pacifism and war, balances powerful storytelling with compelling visuals. His films retain a strong focus on the importance of the human in an industrial, militaristic world.

Narrative Agent

Defined by an agent, actor or narrator that within any given story embodies their own history, context and trajectory; in essence they hold the power to shape and reshape the story itself, to determine its final outcome. In the *Emissaries* trilogy the narrative agent given the most significant narrative agency is the emissary, '*one designated as the agent of another*', a representative.

The role of Emissary should be understood as a 'ruleset' that passes between different forms and beings, rather than a character or identity that persists across time. It is Emissary's actions, decisions and path that in each instance will determine the final outcome of the story.

See also *Agent*.

"New" Art

Becoming Dragon is a mixed-reality performance that utilised virtual reality as a means to embody another being. It took place during December 2008, when for 365 hours artist Micha Cárdenas lived within the virtual world of Second Life. 2008 was also the year in which Cárdenas had begun hormone replacement therapy. *Becoming Dragon* sought to hold a mirror to the one-year requirement of 'real life experience' that transgender people must fulfil in order to receive gender confirmation surgery. Almost a decade later, it still serves as an important challenge to the abject suggestion by Mark Zuckerberg that 'having two identities for yourself is an example of a lack of integrity'. Although the work remains relatively unknown, it serves as an important signal for the artist's ability to take a technology and create an entirely new phenomenological vernacular. Cárdenas' own writing on the work is crucial to understanding the role of "New" art in the broader Art World Industrial Complex:

'In this way we can remember that while the goal is to build this new world, there is a great deal of testing and experimentation to be done in order to get there. A prototype is different than a model as it is a space between a model and an actual implementation; a prototype realises some of the qualities of the actual object to be created. This strategy is better suited to the constantly changing conditions of postmodern global capitalism and also accounts for uncertainty. Maybe we don't know what the world we want looks like.' – Micha Cárdenas, *Becoming Dragon: A Transversal Technology Study* (2010).

Neural Network

Developed within the field of neuroscience, biological neural networks (in the brain) represent an interconnection of individual neurons that, upon activation, set a definable and recognisable linear pathway. Connections between neurons are either chemical synapses or electrical gap junctions. While as a species we understand relatively little about the functioning of the brain, neural networks, as a 'connectionist' model of seeing the brain, have been instrumental in developing tools for the representation of brain activity. These tools include brain scanners such as fMRI (functional magnetic resonance imaging), PET (positron emission tomography) and CAT (computed axial tomography). Crucially, it is biological neural networks that have inspired the design of artificial neural networks (see *Artificial Neural Networks*).

In their biological form, the earliest study of neural networks can be found in the work of Herbert Spencer's *Principles of Psychology* (1855), Theodor Meynert's *Psychiatry* (1884), William James' *Principles of Psychology* (1890), and Sigmund Freud's *Project for a Scientific Psychology* (1895).

Portal

There are several kinds of portals. Choose wisely.

Lupunara sinki manta kani kani
Lupunara siki manta
kani kani kani kani
Fide fide fide ya se fue

The Lupuna is one of the largest trees in the Amazon, its base often spanning more than ten metres in diameter. Its 'belly', a part of the trunk that bears a resemblance to a human abdomen, distinguishes it from other tropical trees. Sacred to the Djinn, legend says the tree has a spirit that is regarded as the guardian of the rainforest. It is considered a magical tree, primarily because of its relationship to ancestral shamanic practices, particularly those of initiation and rites of passage.

At the base of the Lupuna dwell various supernatural beings, spirits of the forest and other protective non-human entities such as Chullachaqui. Tradition identifies its enormous, hollow base as a dimensional door, during *ceremony* the use of the Lupuna icaro is considered a source of protection, and healers often implore the Lupuna not only to be present but for the ceremony itself to be performed as if it were at the base of this great tree, so as to ensure access to higher states of consciousness and mystical experience. To enter into the knowledge of this sacred plant implies for the initiate the duty of caring for and protecting the rainforest.

Quod est inferius est sicut quod est superius, et quod est superius est sicut quod est inferius, ad perpetranda miracula rei unius.

Portal Art

'The struggle of literature is in fact a struggle to escape from the confines of language; it stretches out from the utmost limits of what can be said; what stirs literature is the call and attraction of what is not in the dictionary.' — Italo Calvino, *Cybernetics and Ghosts* (1967).

To call forth the portal is a complex and ineffable task. It is that which transcends language, being and known convention, a diagram that cannot be drawn. The art of portal craft, while by no means less challenging than any other craft in its mastery, is rarer than most, certainly in the context and range of 'Good', 'New' and Flag Art. To describe it within the frame of the experiential is to say that it is the literal Red Pill; 'This is your last chance. After this, there is no turning back. You take the blue pill – the story ends, you wake up in your bed and believe whatever you want to believe. You take the red pill – you stay in Wonderland, and I show you how deep the rabbit hole goes.'

Not all portals are crafted so dramatically, many are incremental, subtle campaigns, enveloping you over time, some are initiatory; each act as gateways in and out of worlds.

They change you irreversibly.

See also *The World*.

Reinforcement Learning

An evolutionary mutation in thought flowing from our development of machines' ability to recognise patterns. The term is used by scientists who work on AI to describe the process by which a series of algorithms become capable of improving a model by digesting and responding to the examples fed into it.

Self-Actualisation

In Abraham Maslow's hierarchy of needs, 'self-actualisation' is at the top of the pyramid and is known as growth or being needs. This is supported by the lower four tiers: esteem, love and belonging, safety and physiology, which are characterised by Maslow as 'deficiency needs'.

To self-actualise is 'to become everything one is capable of becoming', to break free of the black iron prison, to vision quest into eternity, conscious and comforted in the knowledge that your relationship to all else has been entirely satiated. To know thyself.

Sim City

Sim City is the original sandbox game, an open-ended city-building simulation game series now in its fifth major iteration. The player takes the role of a mayor, building up their town from a small settlement to an enormous megacity, integrating services, commercial needs, business and pleasure into their vision of the perfect city. Originally released in 1989, the game has developed from simple budget management to a complex game engine requiring players to manage the desires of their citizens for employment, air quality, entertainment, parks and recreation, while developing complex industrial supply networks, multiple levels of infrastructure, and scientific research and development. The game is conceptually focused within a capitalist-supremacist ideology; players start with a greenfield site and from it can build a functioning city-state without the interference of the political body at all. There are no elections, no external events short of natural disasters, and no one to shape the design and evolution of the city except from the mayor themselves. The aim of the game, if an aim exists at all, is the management of needs; fulfilling an economically fluid, endlessly growing, smooth and crisis-free city of production and consumption. Nothing is ever going to happen again.

The Sims

The Sims is a revolutionary and hugely successful computer game franchise, developed by Maxis. Emerging out of the wider *Sim* franchise that includes groundbreaking games, such as *Sim City* (see *Sim City*), it was the brainchild of game designer Will Wright. In the game, players develop the domestic life of their characters, building and designing homes and planning, regulating and overseeing their everyday interactions, taking care to realise their physical, emotional and spiritual needs. Originally the game was intended as a home improvement simulator, focused on interior design and carpentry. The introduction of human characters whose quality of life was an indicator of the player's success revolutionised the game's potential. As a result, the game requires complex models of artificial intelligence in order to produce realistic human subjectivities. It is also conceptually influenced by Maslow's 'hierarchy of needs' (see *Self-Actualisation*).

Simulation

A simulation is not merely a representation, or a predetermined symbolic path. It just is.

'Reality is that which doesn't go away when you stop believing in it.' — Philip K. Dick, *I Hope I Shall Arrive Soon* (1985).

'Today abstraction is no longer that of the map, the double, the mirror, or the concept. Simulation is no longer that of a territory, a referential being or substance. It is the generation by models of a real without origin or reality: A hyperreal. The territory no longer precedes the map, nor does it survive it. It is nevertheless the map that precedes the territory – precession of simulacra – that engenders the territory.' — Jean Baudrillard, *Simulacra and Simulation* (1981).

'All over the world major museums have bowed to the influence of Disney and become theme parks in their own right. The past, whether Renaissance Italy or Ancient Egypt, is re-assimilated and homogenised into its most digestible form. Desperate for the new, but disappointed with anything but the familiar, we recolonise past and future. The same trend can be seen in personal relationships, in the way people are expected to package themselves, their emotions and sexuality, in attractive and instantly appealing forms.' — J. G. Ballard, *The Atrocity Exhibition* (1970).

'There's a billion to one chance we're living in base reality... If a civilisation stops advancing then that may be due to some calamitous event that erases civilisation. Either we're going to create simulations that are indistinguishable from reality, or civilisation will cease to exist.' — Elon Musk, Code Conference 2016.

'What is real? How do you define 'real'? If you're talking about what you can feel, what you can smell, what you can taste and see, then 'real' is simply electrical signals interpreted by your brain.' — Morpheus, *The Matrix* (1999).

The Society of Mind

The Society of Mind is a 1968 book by Marvin Minsky which posits a number of ideas on how the human mind works. The mind, he argues, is a composite of distinct parts that are themselves mindless; it is in their interactions that human intelligence is produced.

Software

'Culture is your operating system' — Terence McKenna

Software is a general term for the various kinds of programs used to operate computers and related devices, as opposed to the actual physical machinery (referred to as hardware).

Perhaps the most famous introduction of this metaphor was by Descartes in the seventeenth century, who compared the human body to a machine. During the European Enlightenment, the human body was thought of as a clock, whereas in the nineteenth century, the steam engine became the dominant metaphorical lens through which to view the human body.

In the 1970s, John C. Lilly theorised the human being as a wetware biocomputer, with the notion that your internal 'software', the way your brain operates, the loops that run all day, the self-doubt, self-criticism, the echoes of childhood trauma, the habits and patterns we accumulate, can also be refactored and rewritten through a series of meta-deprogramming practices.

While the terrain of the mind conceived as software is fraught with danger, not least because its logical endgame is the Kurzweilian nightmare of consciousnesses upload or 'singularity'. For those versed and skilled in the art of software development, however, mind-seen-as-software can produce an effective tool for refactoring perception of everyday lived reality.

Story

'I would go so far as to say that the natural, proper, fitting shape of the novel might be that of a sack, a bag. A book holds words. Words hold things. They bear meanings. A novel is a medicine bundle, holding things in a particular, powerful relation to one another and to us' — Ursula K. Le Guin, 'The Carrier Bag Theory of Fiction' (1986).

See also *The Carrier Bag Theory of Fiction.*

Symbiogenesis

(Greek: σύν syn 'together', βίωσις biosis 'living', and γένεσις genesis 'origin or birth'), or Endosymbiotic Theory.

First articulated in early 1900s by Russian botanist Konstantin Mereschkowski, it describes a form of symbiosis in which one symbiont lives within the body of the other. The process of endosymbiosis occurs when the cells of one organism are inhabited by formerly free-living bacteria or cells that, rather than producing a parasitic relation, produce a mutually beneficial relation between the two organisms on a cellular level. Constituting an evolutionary chimera of sorts – this theory is considered to be one of the most important evolutionary events.

The theory was significantly advanced and substantiated by evolutionary theorist and biologist Lynn Margulis in a 1967 paper, 'On the origin of mitosing cells'. While still conforming in part to a Darwinian conception of evolution, Margulis' perspective, research and contribution to this field are significant for its counter narrative to common competition-orientated views of evolution, Symbiosis emphasises and proves the deep time history of cooperative relationships between species.

'Life did not take over the globe by combat, but by networking'. — Lynn Margulis and Dorion Sagan, 'Marvellous microbes' (2001).

Triune brain

The triune brain is a neuroscientific model for the human brain as the product of three specific evolutionary stages. It was first espoused by American physician Paul D. Maclean, and although it is now viewed as largely redundant within contemporary neuroscience, it retains strong recognition within the popular imagination. It suggests that the brain can be understood in three discrete parts.

The first is the reptilian brain, or the basal ganglia, a small node at the front of the forebrain which is, Maclean argues, the remnants of the brain developed in early reptiles and birds. This part controls basic functions such as fear, aggression, dominance and territoriality.

The second part, the paleomammalian complex, comprise the components of the limbic system, said to have developed from early mammalian evolution. This part of the brain is related to more developed social functions such as child-rearing, feeding and reproduction.

The neomammalian complex is the most developed part of the brain, found in higher mammals. This part relates to problem-solving, language and abstraction.

Tulpa

Adapted in the twentieth century by European Theosophists, the concept of the Tulpa was developed from the Tibetan practice of *sprul-pa,* meaing 'emanation' or 'manifestation'. A Tulpa is a practice of creation, in which a being or thing is manifested by an individual through spiritual or mental power. A being with full sentience, an imaginary friend conjured through 'thoughtform' meditation practices, the creation of Tulpas is often referred to contemporaneously as 'tulpamancy'. The human flesh bag becomes a host for this new being. The majority of human hosts engaged with tulpamancy in the present moment tend to be between nineteen and twenty-six years old, and online communities committed to the art of conjuring tulpas are split in their explanation of the practice as being either due to psychological or metaphysical schools of thought.

Umwelt

German word meaning 'environment', 'milieu' or 'surroundings'. *Umwelt*, or plural *Umwelten*, can crudely be defined as the environmental factors that are collectively capable of affecting the behaviour of biological beings. To claim '*the worlds they perceive, their Umwelten, are all different*' is to say that the biological factors that determine a single organism's perception of reality can be very different to the sense perception of other organisms that share exactly the same environment. '*In the blind and deaf world of the tick, the important signals are temperature and the odour of butyric acid. For the black ghost knifefish, it's electrical fields. For the echolocating bat, it's air-compression waves. The small subset of the world that an animal is able to detect is its Umwelt. The bigger reality, whatever that might mean, is called the Umgebung*' — David M. Eagleman, response to edge.org's annual question (2011).

Unity

Multi-purpose games engine, created by the prosaically-named Unity Technologies. Unity allows for the creation of 3D and 2D games with relative ease and is well supported by a vast online community of developers. Each of the *Emissaries* episodes is produced using this particular games engine. Its major competitor is the Unreal games engine.

Utility Theory and the OODA Loop

Utility theory (being the originating foundations for Game Theory) describes how decisions are made based on the perceived value of taking an action. Developed within this school of thought, the OODA Loop was outlined by the most important military strategist and game theorist of the last century, John Boyd.

Defined as a decision making cycle, the OODA acronym stands for Observe, Orient, Decide, and Act; the loop signals a continual feedback cycle for these processes.

'*The second O, orientation – as the repository of our genetic heritage, cultural tradition, and previous experiences – is the most important part of the O-O-D-A loop since it shapes the way we observe, the way we decide, the way we act.*' — John R. Boyd, *Organic Design for Command and Control* (1987).

Underlying the OODA Loop is a unification of Gestalt psychology, cognitive science and game theory. Each area drawing from its own discrete philosophical foundations, Boyd inferred the following from each of these theories:

- Gödel's Incompleteness Theorem: any logical model of reality is incomplete (and possibly inconsistent) and must be continuously refined/adapted in the face of new observations.
- Heisenberg's Uncertainty Principle: there is a limit on our ability to observe reality with precision.
- Second Law of Thermodynamics: the entropy of any closed system always tends to increase, and thus

the nature of any given system is continuously changing even as efforts are directed towards maintaining it in its original form.
'*Not only is the Universe stranger than we think, it is stranger than we can think.*' — Werner Heisenberg, *Across the Frontiers* (1975).

The World

XXI, number twenty-one, the final step. At the centre of the world, a dancing figure, wands in both hands, one leg crosses the other – the dancing figure acknowledging that true unity lies in movement. Encircled by a luscious green wreath, the colour of love and healing, in another universe an ouroboros supplants its role as an emissary of an infinite unknowable cycle. Floating through the zodiac, the world is kept in equilibrium by the *guardians of heaven*; Leo, Scorpio, Aquarius and Taurus – fire, water, air, and earth – wands, cups, swords, and pentacles. Divinatory meaning: completion of the task at hand, a symbol of success, celebration in new beginnings, the attainment of cosmic consciousness.
'*To a greater or lesser degree it indicates a unification of the person's inner sense of being with his or her outer activities.*' — Rachel Pollack, *78 Degrees of Wisdom* (1980).

Interview

Hans Ulrich Obrist: I want to begin at the beginning: how did it all start with The Emissary Trilogy'? How did the epiphany of this live simulation, a video game that plays itself, happen?

Ian Cheng: I wanted to make an artwork where, rather than perfecting it as an artist, you grow it; something whose energy comes from itself, not just from me. And then I thought: 'It has to be a video game, but with no player, so it plays itself.' That was the genesis of the simulations. I've since done seven or eight different simulations, exploring their properties – their infinite nature, their capacity for emergent behaviour. I'm proud of them, but I see them as little experiments. Wonderful, but inherently without meaning.

Meaninglessness is an important state, it's the other side of meaning. But it was really crucial when that feeling happened, because it led me to seek the opposite form of meaninglessness, which is, I believe, a story. The genesis of *Emissaries* was trying to fuse a story with a simulation, because it's with stories that we derive scripts for our life, that we find a reason to get up in the morning, that we have a projection of what we're going to do each day.

This projection gives us a sense of connection and purpose and agency, a point on the horizon to move towards. They say when people are script-less or without a story, they're depressed. It's a neurological condition: you lose your script. You are directionless, lost. I read that London taxi drivers have a really developed hippocampus, because they memorise all the streets. They say when there's damage to the hippocampus, you immediately feel that you're lost, confused, disoriented, and very soon deep depression kicks in. Having a script or narrative you tell yourself is something like having the security of an inner map to navigate life.

Memory is all we have.

I needed a way to embed a story into the simulation without overpowering the simulation. I decided that there should be one character in the simulation who embodied the story, a narrative agent, who had narrative goals and tries to fulfil those goals in a very stubborn way. But because the narrative agent was in a larger simulation world, she would be constantly interrupted, procrastinated, delayed, distracted, and taken into other people's stories. And to have those two sculpting forces was for me a super-exciting idea. There's the simulation, which is non-deterministic, free and reactive, and then there's the very deterministic narrative agent, which tries to make its plans work. For me, it's also an analogy for the different sides of the brain, the different archetypes of the brain, where you have a very planned and narrowly focused left side that is often in conflict with the open-ended right side.

And that leads us to the question of consciousness. In our first conversation at the time of your show at Fondazione Sandretto Re Rebaudengo in Turin, you mentioned this book by Julian Jaynes: The Origin of Consciousness in the Breakdown of the Bicameral Mind *(1976). How did you discover Jaynes' work? What's the meaning of this book and to what extent was it significant for The Emissary Trilogy'?*

Simultaneous to this idea of a meeting between the story and a simulation, I was trying to understand where stories come from, in our brains and neurologically. Nothing I read gave me an interesting answer, until I came across Julian Jaynes. Jaynes suggested that a story forms around the moment of consciousness, that human consciousness is actually a way of projecting a story forwards or backwards in time in order to understand what you should do. Before this development of conscious projection, according to Jaynes, ancient humans didn't have anything like a story to guide their choices or actions. They just had voices that they hallucinated, often of an authority figure like your mother or your father, a village leader, and eventually God, telling you what to do especially in moments of stress. The breakdown of the bicameral mind is the break-down of trust in these voices, and the emergence of narrative consciousness. It struck me that storytelling was linked to solving problems: what does one do under stress when the voices don't work? By projecting forwards or backwards in time, and having a sense that the present difficulty is a moment in a longer story, narrative consciousness became a radical new way to understand one's place amidst changing external conditions. This produced a new kind of predictive power and sense of agency.

In his book, Jaynes hypothesises that consciousness emerged approximately 3,000 years ago, which is quite short in the evolutionary timeline. This led to the idea that the first *Emissaries* episode should take place 3,000 years ago, and feature an ancient community. The time scale between the second and third episodes of *Emissaries* is much shorter. The second episode takes place approximately 200 years after twenty-first century human life has evacuated, when an AI manager excavates a twenty-first-century body. And then, the third episode is about 250 years later, when the AI has grown bored and begins to undo its own responsibilities.

Besides the Jaynes book, there's another portal that led into Emissaries: *Iain McGilchrist's 2009 book* The Master and his Emissary, *a kind of a mapping of the brain – it outlines these different zones. And, of course, the emissary appears there in the title. Was that a direct quote? And who is Iain McGilchrist?*

He's a brain scientist. His book offers a clear summation of the relationship between the right and left halves of the brain. He describes how the right brain precedes what the left brain does. So the right brain is essentially absorbing information all the time, synthesising information in creative ways, putting things together that haven't been put together very naturally, very intuitively. You know that feeling when you go away from a problem and then your brain just has an idea? This is a right-brain phenomenon, according to McGilchrist. He compares the right brain to a benevolent king. It's a benevolent king, one that sends out curiosity, receives curiosity and absorbs new things all the time, but its kingdom grows too large for the king to control. So the king sends out an emissary, the left brain, to manage its other territories. But the emissary begins to feel its own celebrity, take credit for the king, and starts to grow an ego, a sense of authority. Because the emissary is a weaker character, it has more insecurity about controlling things, and becomes a kind of tyrant, an egomaniac in the off-world, the outskirts.

In the dark net.

Yes. McGilchrist likens the left brain to the figure of the emissary, who likes to control things, put things in order, put things in the calendar, make sure the plans work, reduce risk. He says that in Western culture especially, the left brain has completely taken over our lives and formalises many, many things. That's important for it to do, because at the end of the day it's merely a competent manager who has gone a little too far and hallucinates itself as the leader. So the whole book is about putting the left brain back in its place, reminding it that it's just an emissary, and the right brain and all its creative and generative energies that get masked by the left brain, need space to re-emerge. McGilchrist summed it up best: 'The intuitive mind is a gift, and the rational mind is a faithful servant. We have created a society that honours the servant and has forgotten the gift.'

Is there any kind of connection with the emissary and Hermes the Greek god, son of Zeus and a kind of messenger? There's a book by Michel Serres called Hermes: Literature, Science, Philosophy *(1982) that would be interesting to revisit in the context of the* Emissaries *series. Serres is interested in the philosophy of science that doesn't rely on a meta language. He's interested in the concept of translation between accounts. So he refers to the figure of Hermes and angels as messengers who translate a map, back and forth, between domains.*

These are emissaries, but well-behaved emissaries. What's interesting about the emissary McGilchrist talks about is that when it goes to a foreign land or alien world, it becomes transformed. It can't help but be tempted to try to control or bring what it knows to a new place, it can't help but be tempted to absorb what it's found. The term comes from that book but it's used in the works very loosely.

Three or four years ago, when we started to work on the Rebaudengo show, I remember you mentioned that the first Emissaries *piece was a kind of ecosystem, like something you encountered at the beach. What was the beach epiphany you had?*

The beach epiphany was seeing the tide pools in California. Tide pools are very special because they're where the waves can't fully attack. The waves come in, but there are rocks to break the waves. Beyond them are the tide pools, puddles of water that are dynamic yet calm enough to sustain all kinds of strange life – anemones and starfish and creatures that you can't tell whether they're vegetable or animal – very ambiguous creatures that all live closely together and create a mini world. The world within this tide pool became a model that inspired the simulations. The pleasure as a child is looking at a tide pool and seeing who these creatures are, what their characteristics are, how they interact. Obviously starfish have a certain gentle character, while a sea urchin is a more aggressive character. As a kid, I'd put them together as if they were Lego, or try to matchmake them. Some would maintain their proximity, others became repulsed. This is a dream that endures, not only in *Emissaries*, but in trying to make AI composed of heterogeneous sub-minds now. This memory is a source of constant inspiration.

When we did the Turin show, you already knew that you were going to work on this project for quite some time and that it would be a trilogy that shifts across vast time frames. Can you tell me how this idea grew, because it's very much connected with the idea of long duration. To what extent was there a masterplan, and to what extent did you deviate from the master plan?

When I first started, before we even talked about it, the dream was to make an animated children's movie about consciousness. At the time, I called it a smart story – the same way we think of a smart house, a house that reacts to the inhabitant. I wanted a story that could mould or react to the viewer, or at least to itself. And I thought, the only way to reconcile the apparatus of art and trying to do a project that's bigger and takes more time is to cut it up and turn it into episodes. Being able to show it episodically made the production more manageable for me, and that was a very important decision that led to *Emissaries* becoming a trilogy. I believe that if that constraint hadn't been there and I'd just said, 'I'm going to make an animated children's movie and take three years to do it', I don't think I would ever have finished.

The question, of course, is how to embed a nervous system in an artwork, which is something Ben Vickers always talked about obsessively. And it's somehow connected to the Philip K. Dick quote, that 'reality is that which doesn't go away when you stop believing it'. Could you talk about this idea of how to embed a nervous system within an artwork, and how the Emissaries *trilogy plays with what's seen and what's unseen?*

This idea of art with a nervous system is what I'm interested in, because then it can be an information-processing organ on top of being an artwork. It's doing double duty. And so, *Emissaries* is part of that. It's an information-processing organ, at least within the events occurring within itself. For me, this is the way in which art can start to become alive again, because on the whole art is super boring to me because it lacks aliveness. The static nature of much art signals to me a rejection or denial of the fluidity and change that is such a irrepressible feature of being alive in the twenty-first century. So it was thinking about proliferating life, like that tide pool where the most exciting thing was knowing that all these objects in the tide pool could talk back to me, could react to me. They have a life of their own, and if I go away, they're going to keep living their life. I wanted this quality that you can only get from living things. So creating art with a nervous system, works that could negotiate their place in a changing environment, is the most worthwhile pursuit for me as an artist.

There aren't many examples of this in the art history preceding you.

The first impulse is to use other human beings in performance to bring things alive. And this goes back to theatre and performance art.

But what you're talking about is something that exists in its own time frame, whereas in performance there's a beginning and an end.

The dream is that if you could create artificial life that then goes on and lives its own life according to laws you've given it. Those laws mutate, and new personalities form. This is very beautiful to me.

A programme like this can lead to unexpected outcomes. When watching your first presentation of the three Emissaries episodes together at MoMA PS1, all of a sudden, you got super excited when something unexpected or new occurred: 'I've never seen this!'

Yes, there are two ways this can happen. First, I try to introduce enough elements into the simulation so that there would be chaos, such as the volcanic eruption, which is a kind of global chaos. Chaos is important because it creates a condition of meaninglessness, both for the viewer and for the characters inside the simulation. That moment of meaninglessness is very scary, because the characters don't know what to do, and in our own lives, we don't know what to do. Here we encounter a very Nietzschean truth: that this chaotic moment is also the moment of growth. This is a moment when what we perceive as chaos is actually a confrontation with a reality we haven't experienced before that forces our brain, our laws, our sociology, to change. So I knew I needed to introduce chaos in order to make the simulations produce some growth. When we were at PS1 and I was pointing out the Wormleaf monster being played with by the Oomen children, it was the product of emergence, which is a property that I chase in all my works. If you put enough simple systems together, you get complexity very naturally.

One of the most important questions of today is how capacious AI has become and what dangers may arise from it. Contemporary artists are already addressing the risks of AI reaching a state where machines can make decisions without our control, which are fears that were buried for fifty years or more, and are now slowly making their way into the mainstream AI community. So, of course, the idea that you described, where it starts with these simple rules and then develops complexity, could lead to a danger that maybe all of a sudden they become totally beyond our control.

I confess, I'm excited by the idea of AI, and I don't share the anxiety that it will replace the human. I think there's this big phobia that AI will take all our jobs, but it strikes me that it just means our future work will involve more creative work, or more kinds of work we want to do rather than have to do. Maybe we've designed AI so that they can fulfil tedious tasks, because secretly we don't actually want to be spending our life and energy doing tedious, mindless, uninspiring, meaningless work. Maybe these are jobs worth replacing. As we've found in every era of technology, from writing to printing to money to automobiles to the internet, as many things as a technology transforms and takes away, it creates new opportunities to play and to create and to relate to the world and our place in it. This is a very optimistic view, but one that is happening in parallel to all of the real and perceived dangers of AI.

On top of that, if you actually develop an AI that can think, part of its compulsion would be to make sense of reality, and to compulsively make sense of reality is what we associate with someone who's a thinker. If we lived in a world where there are other kinds of thinkers, not just human thinkers, this would be a very beautiful world to live in. The issue that everyone is correctly afraid of, including Elon Musk and Stephen Hawking, is that if you have an AI, no matter what it's doing – even if it's just musing about rocks or the universe or some mathematical equation that has no existential consequence – it might choose to allocate resources beyond and in conflict with our own human needs in order to resolve that problem. So if it needed all the energy on Earth in order to solve a question like 'what's the purpose of sentient life?' this would be a cosmic joke. This is an existential threat that

Hawking and Musk are afraid of, and I think that's valid – to fear how it might take resources.

In our conversation with Richard Evans, an AI scientist at DeepMind, he said that the starting point for this newest project was that most simulations don't understand social practices; simulated protagonists in games often act in ways that are unsocial. Knowing social practices limits the possibility of action but is necessary to understanding the meaning of our action. And you then said to Evans that the limit of performance is actually a freedom, because it makes things meaningful. Philip K. Dick said that he goes about writing by imagining one small change in reality, and then the task of sci-fi is to think of all the different ways in which life and culture would change based on this one tweak. And the best sci-fi authors look at these changes in social practices as the consequences of the change parameter. I agree that if you have AI with more ability to respond to conflicts within the social context, tweaking one thing, you'll get something artistic and beautiful.

Yes, you'd get the equivalent of what a dog or small child would get, having gone to school: the pleasure of seeing where the AI takes that initial, early age education. It's beautiful. To me, if this is what art could become, this closeness to living and being alive, then...

Then we're there.

Then we're there; then we can play and compose and see and be alive at a new level.

The Emissary Trilogy also confronts you with a different notion of time. When we see videos or animations in a museum, they're there all day, playing in loops. But there's a different notion of time with Emissaries, *where what you see is never the same twice. As long as there's electricity, it'll never double or repeat. So rather than adhering to the conventions on start and end, a fixed loop, as all video art so far has done, your work has this never-ending dimension. I was wondering if you could talk a little bit about that, because I think that's one of the biggest changes, in terms of thinking, but also in terms of very practical aspects. Because the reason why people never really install videos in their home is that after a couple months, they get bored with it. But if you have a piece that evolves, it might lead to a completely new dimension of people living with it.*

Yes. This is where I started before making simulations: with not wanting to make videos, because they were so tedious. If you're going to have something that's alive, well, it has to keep living. It has to change with its times, or change and adapt to its environment. And suddenly, you're really far from video art. It's got nothing to do with video art. But like all art you have to mind the edges. A painter minds the edges of the canvas, a filmmaker minds the edges of the edits. With simulations you have to mind the edges of birth, death, and where an agent changes its mind.

It's another game. And it's a form of neurological dream, also for the viewer, I suppose. Marcel Duchamp said the viewer is half of the work; Dominique Gonzalez-Foerster said at least half. What would you say?

The relationship between the thing and the viewer is 100% of the work. Where the centre of gravity rests in that relationship is now a point of unrest as the thing becomes more alive and begins to acquire the status of sentience.

Young Ancient

by Nora Khan

After the fire sound, the *nokwt*. *Annis,* from which we came, rex and pater, all power on power, turns away, but still beaming from his big big *ous* is a white lux. The rocks are burning but unus, duo, unus, duo, crawl on them, crying. Thrash and fall and sink my head in wet hot ash. In my head, like falling through water. Nothing holds, no sounds to hold. The world is dark.

And then the *tandar*, thwack, thwack, across, then from the centre of the Earth, *tandar* breaking and jumping the ground. Droplines of fire and the *tandar* tonned, made *nek* and piles of them, too, quiet soft. And I'll be *nek* if can't find my way back! Must must must get back.

I need to be near the *teuto*, all the *eleutheros* rumbling together. They are lit by fire. From the fire comes thick plumes of *dhuma*. They look down at where I lie. All laughing around *annis*, pater, like he is their own pater. Many all told, many shadows.

During *deen* they sleep but now they leap up, faces spinning laughing wild in firelight always burning. Their *ous* echo and echo, all same sounds in their *ous*. Unus, duo, unus, duo. Back, forth, one to another. Sounds like things passed between them.

Boy says he is a *bhrater* and steps on my feet in his hurry. He cranes his stupid dim face up to mine. He is more like snake than boy, a *kehd*, *cais*, who keeps pulling on me. Drag him, carry him. He traps snake with hands, and his hands and the snake slime on me. He drops the snake and it writhes on hot ground and it opens its *ous* with long thin, white sharp teeth to *nokwt*.

His breath always on my neck. He hisses air in my ear when sleep. Pull up dirt into my fists and clap both sides of his head. Smear it down. He stays. Chook chook chooking the adder and smiling at me from the dirt. If he fell down to ground from far far up then he would shut up. Hate his pink and mad face.

Everything strange and broken. Try to pull my ears open with my hands. Spin until my head sees behind me. Drag along the ground, breathing in dirt and tremors. Ash. Dirt. *Sters* in the black dirt. Slime along the warm ground. Lay still, send sound into the sky. A new name for each *ster*. *Ster* on *ster* on *ster*. Bull, scorpion.

Deyn, again. But *deyn* is dark much like *nakht* and only lux comes from the fire. In the shadows from the fire I see *ops* of *annis*, bigger than those of all others. I find pater. I dance, I leap, I climb up him, and beg. *Annis*. I fall at his feet. Drowned by the eh, oh, ah. Oh, on, ah, ah. Swimming in it again, oh, ah, mah, mah.

Teutos and *Annis* all bob through me like air. Track a pair of yellow *ops* bobbing, watching. Two points of fire that can see us full of dizzy blood sickness.

How to get back. I would do anything. Boy pulls on my skin.

I take a stone to his legs. *Thwock*, *thwock*, against each shin. He never follows me.

Bird peels itself off from grey stone. Squeeze and stretch its big face until a big sound. Tells me what to say. Place my head inside its head. Nothing in *ous* when he's gone.

I hear a world and so can see it. The sounds form a path. The fog moves over dark pools. *I* – feel heavy and the sounds are heavy in my *ous*. Something else is here, a thing made strange. The thing contracts and fills with a warm orange light, stronger than the fire.

I step towards it, call further into the fog. The others fade. I don't need them close. I move with bird towards the thing. It slips away in the fog. Map makes itself as I walk rocks burning. Runes of thin blue lux glimmer and turn. I close my eyes and see them and feel safe.

The only sound is the sound of my voice, carrying me, holding me. And so we go like this, the *teuto* fading, the land burning. The burning of mind lighting the ground and the *nokht*. The two of us, me and my sound before me, leading each step. I, call, it.

M, X. My, I, X.

Ee. Cah.
It. Call. It.
It. Call.
I.
I.
I.
It. Call. It.

THIS SHORT PIECE IS EXCERPTED FROM A FULL FICTIONAL WORK WRITTEN BY KHAN ON THE *EMISSARIES* SERIES.

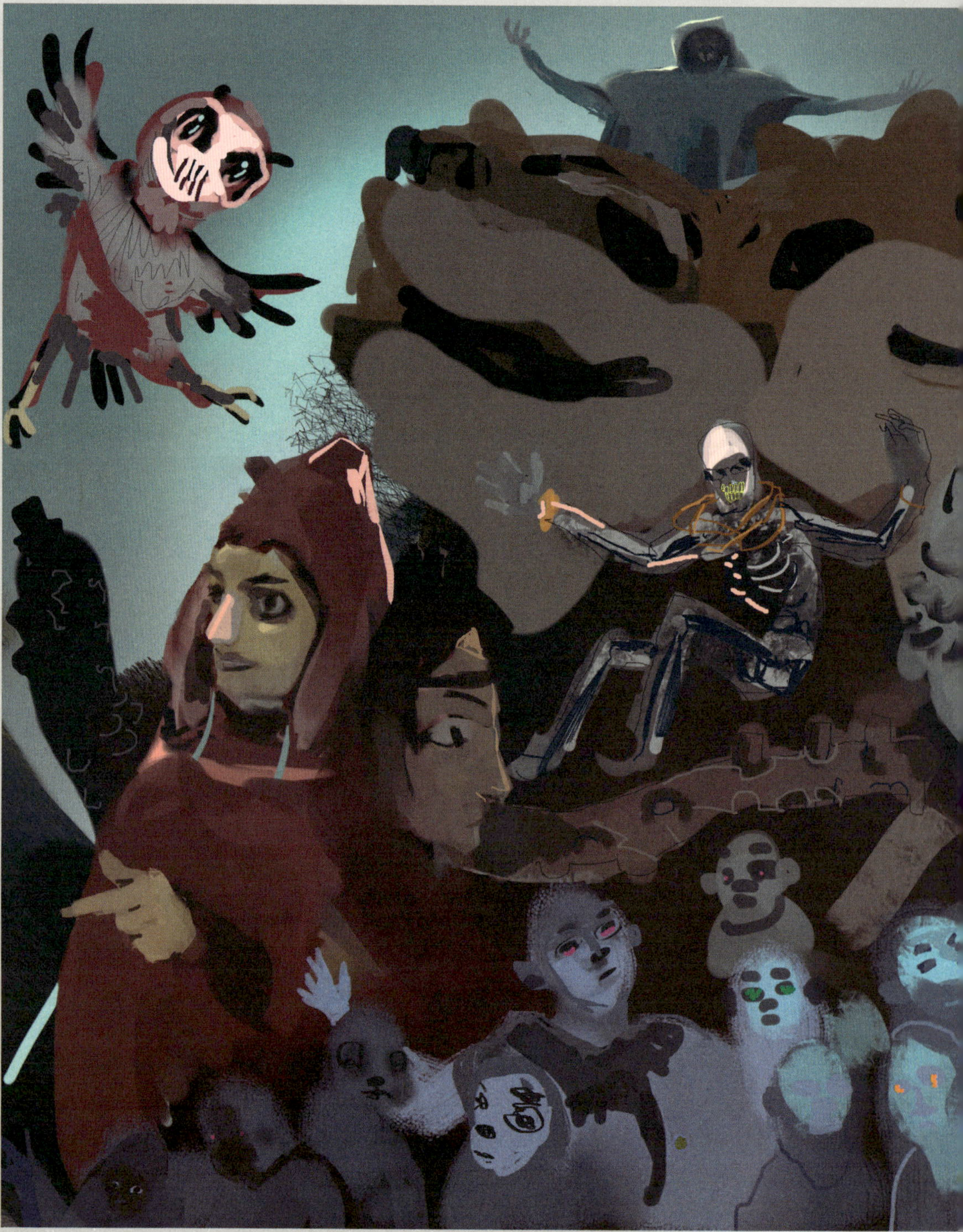

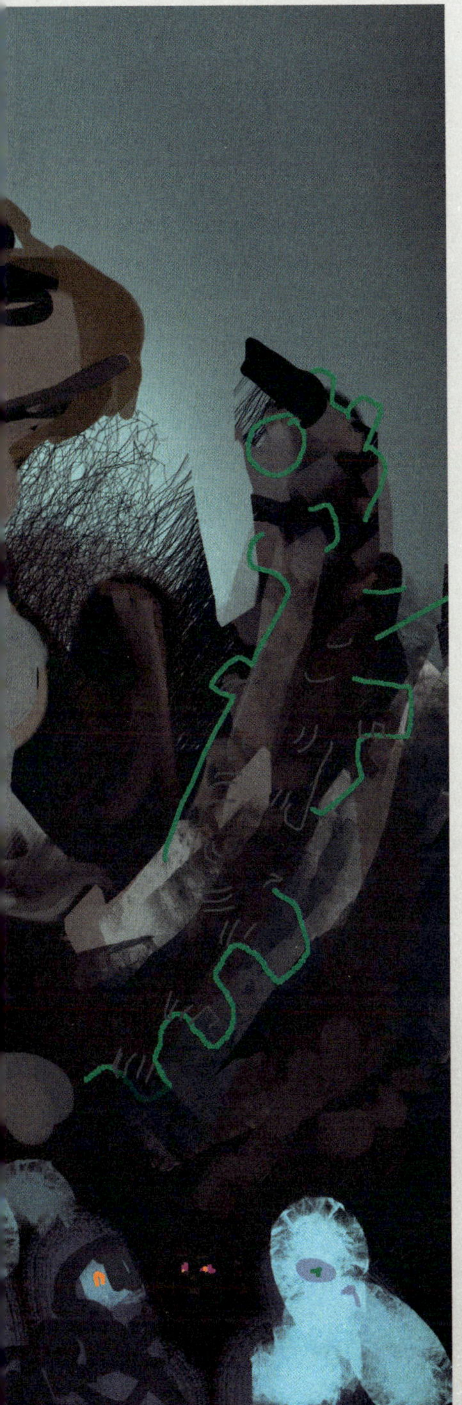

Andrej Ujházy
Oomfan 2018
Krita 3.3.2

PRODUCTION CREDITS

Emissary in the Squat of Gods
Created by Ian Cheng
Producer: Veronica So
Technical Director: Samuel Eng
Modelling & Rigging: Joshua Planz
Modelling: Breht O'Hearn
Sound Design: Greg Heffernan
Technical Artists: Mark Fingerhut, Ian Faris
Animation: Jeremy Riccione
Content Designer: Jessica Wilson
Concept Art: Andrej Ujhazy
Choreography: Madeline Hollander
Mocap Performances: Jeremy Pheiffer, David Yijae
Mocap Services: Edit1, Xsens
Story Consultant: Sean Manning, Alexander Benaim

Emissary Forks At Perfection
Created by Ian Cheng
Producer: Veronica So
Technical Director: Samuel Eng
Modelling & Rigging: Joshua Planz
Modelling: Breht O'Hearn, Aaron Bohenick
Sound Design: Greg Heffernan
Animation: Chad Waldschmidt
Graphics Programmer: Chris Clapis
Content Designer: Jessica Wilson
Technical Artists: Yang Wang, Zhenzhen Qi
Story Consultant: Sean Manning, Alexander Benaim

Emissary Sunsets the Self
Created by Ian Cheng
Producer: Veronica So
Technical Director: Samuel Eng
AI Development: Porrith Suong, Jay Suong
Modelling & Rigging: Joshua Planz
Sound Design: Steve Green
Animation: Chad Waldschmidt
Concept Art: Andrej Ujhazy
Content Designer: Jessica Wilson
Technical Artists: Yang Wang, Zhenzhen Qi
Graphics Programmer: James Cao
Story Consultant: Andrew Chan Gladstone, Alexander Benaim

Metis Suns Team
Producer: Veronica So
Production Manager: Kat Herriman
Production Assistant: Sixing Xu
Web Development: Claire Kwong

Acknowledgements

The original edition of this publication was co-produced by the Serpentine Galleries and Fondazione Sandretto Re Rebaudengo on the occasion of Ian Cheng's exhibition at the Serpentine, held from 6 March – 28 May 2018. It was initially co-published by the Serpentine Galleries and Koenig Books. The artist and publisher wish to acknowledge and thank these organizations for their support in the creation of the first edition of *Emissaries Guide to Worlding*.

The artist wishes to thank the following organizations and individuals for supporting the original development of the *Emissaries Trilogy* and the first edition of this book: Pilar Corrias Gallery, Standard (Oslo), Gladstone Gallery, Hans Ulrich Obrist, Stuart Comer, Peter Eleey, Jocelyn Miller, Ben Vickers, Rebecca Lewin, Joseph Constable, Kay Watson, Mike Gaughan, Sarah Shattock, Jessica O'Farrell, Gilda Axelroud, Allyson Spellacy, Patrizia Sandretto Re Rebaudengo, Irene Calderoni, Chiara Torta, Bernardo Follini, Madeline Hollander, Kevin Simler, Matthew Rogers, Rachel Rose.

Image Credits

Unless stated here all photographs, screenshots, drawings, diagrams and renders are copyright and courtesy of Ian Cheng

All Emissaries character icons and concept art by Andrej Ujházy

p. 26
(left) Rock relief at Yazilikaya, c. 1250 B.C. Image: Ekrem Akurgal, found in Julian Jaynes, *The Origin of Consciousness in the Breakdown of the Bicameral Mind* (Boston, Massachusetts: Houghton Mifflin Harcourt, 1976).

pp. 37
(left) Pieter Bruegel the Elder, The Fight Between Carnival and Lent, 1559. Image: PD-Art <https://en.wikipedia.org/wiki/Netherlandish_Proverbs#/media/File:Pieter_Brueghel_the_Elder_-_The_Dutch_Proverbs_-_Google_Art_Project.jpg> (last accessed: 10 March 2018)
(right) Image: Ian Cheng, 2018

p. 60
(top left) Image: photography by Jesper D. Lund

p. 64
(bottom right) Image: Blob by Stephan Katsivelos of SAKphoto.com

pp. 68-69 (left to right)
Cover from Julian Jaynes, *The Origin of Consciousness in the Breakdown of the Bicameral Mind* (Boston, Massachusetts: Houghton Mifflin Harcourt, 1976). Image: reprinted with permission of the publisher.
Cover from Iain McGilchrist, *The Master and his Emissary* (New Haven, Connecticut: Yale University Press, 2010). Image: provided by Yale University Press
Cover from Keith Johnstone, *Impro: Improvisation and the Theatre* (New York City, New York: Routledge/Theatre Arts Books, 1987). Image: Reproduced with permission of ROUTLEDGE in the format Republish in a book via Copyright Clearance Centre.

pp. 84-85 (left to right)
Jean Fortunet, Miles Davis at Strasbourg (front), 1987. Image: PD <https://commons.wikimedia.org/wiki/File:Miles_Davis_Strasbourg_face_2.jpg> (last accessed: 19 March 2018)
Image: photographer unknown <https://meanderingswithandrea.com/2012/06/> (last accessed: 19 March 2018)

p. 92
Image: darksnow, 'Transformer Owl', YouTube, 23 June 2010 <https://www.youtube.com/watch?v=2-GFZ4bdSiQ> (last accessed: 29 March 2018)
Image: source unknown <https://imgur.com/r/gifs/v1wzs> (last accessed: 29 March 2018)

p. 94
(top left) Image: Ian Cheng, 2018

p. 100
(top centre) Image: source <https://www.youtube.com/watch?v=PL6txm1IsD0> (last accessed 20 March 2018)

pp. 114-115
(centre) Blob by Stephan Katsivelos of sakphoto.com

pp. 116-117 (top, left to right)
The thermophilic fungus M. thermophile. Image: Ronald P. de Vries, Joost van den Brink, Jan Dijksterhuis of the Westerdijk Fungal Biodiversity Institute, Utrecht, The Netherlands.
Sarah Lucas, *Deep Cream Maradona* at Ekeberg Sculpture Park, 2015. Image: copyright Sarah Lucas, courtesy Sadie Coles HQ, London.
Image: source unknown
A sampling of the variety of neurons in the brain, as catalogued by Ramon y Cajal in 1899. Image: source unknown < https://vcresearch.berkeley.edu/news/nih-awards-uc-berkeley-72-million-advance-brain-initiative> (last accessed: 20 March 2018)

pp. 128-129 (top, left to right)
(top line) 2, 3, 4, 5: sources unknown
6: Wolfgang Sauber, Námafjall, Iceland. Fumarole, 2009. Image: PD <https://commons.wikimedia.org/wiki/File:Namafjall_-_Fumarole_2.jpg> (last accessed: 20 March 2018)
7: Image: courtesy of David Schermann <http://www.davidschermann.com>
(second line) 2: source unknown
(fourth line) 2, 3: sources unknown
(fifth line) 4: Image: courtesy of Tasha Sturm @ Cabrillo College

pp. 132-133
(first line)
3: Image: source unknown <http://indonesemusicinstrument.blogspot.co.uk/> (last accessed: 29 March 2018)

4: Image: source unknown
5: Image: source <https://www.tapatalk.com/groups/paleoplanet69529/gourd-water-containers-net-carry-bags-slin-t973.html#.UeyHfm2MjN1> (last accessed: 20 March 2018)
6: Image: courtesy of the Fowler Museum at UCLA <https://www.learner.org/courses/globalart/work/4/index.html> (last accessed 20 March 2018)

p. 137
(top) Ken Price, *High Minded*, 2009. Image: Copyright Estate of Ken Price, courtesy Matthew Marks Gallery.
(bottom) Image: courtesy of Tasha Sturm @ Cabrillo College

pp. 236-237
Ian Cheng, *Emissary in the Squat of Gods*, 2015. Installation views, Fondazione Sandretto Re Rebaudengo, Turin, Italy (23 April – 11 October 2015). Images: Maurizio Elia

p. 238-239
Ian Cheng, *Emissary in the Squat of Gods*, 2015. Installation views, STANDARD (OSLO), Frieze New York, US (13-17 May 2015). Images: Dawn Blackman

pp. 240-241
Ian Cheng, *Emissary Forks at Perfection*, 2015. Installation views, Pilar Corrias, London, UK (13 October – 14 November 2015). Images: Damian Griffiths

pp. 242-243
Ian Cheng, *Emissary in the Squat of Gods*, 2015. Installation views, *Suspended Animation* at Hirshhorn Museum and Sculpture Gardens, Washington D. C., USA (10 February 2016 – 12 March 2017). Images: Cathy Carver

pp. 244-245
Ian Cheng, *Emissary Forks at Perfection*, 2015. Installation view, *Forking at Perfection* at Migros Museum für Gegenwartskunst, Zurich, Switzerland (20 February – 16 May 2016). Image: Stefan Altenburger Photography Zurich

pp. 246-247
Ian Cheng, *Emissary Forks at Perfection*, 2015. Installation views, *WELT AM DRAHT* at Julia Stoschek Collection, Berlin, Germany (2 June – 13 November 2016). Images: Simon Vogel

pp. 248-249
Ian Cheng, *Emissary in the Squat of Gods*, 2015. Installation views, *OVERPOP* at Yuz Museum, Shanghai, China (4 September 2016 – 15 January 2017). Images: courtesy of Yuz Museum.

pp. 250-251
Ian Cheng, *Emissaries*, 2015-17. Installation views, MoMA PS1, New York, USA (9 April – 25 September 2017). Images:
(top line): 1, 2, 5, 6: Pablo Enriquez, 3: Ian Cheng
4: Studio LHOOQ
(centre line): 1, 2, 3: Pablo Enriquez
(bottom line): 1, 2, 3, 4: Pablo Enriquez

pp. 252-253
Ian Cheng, *Emissaries*, 2015-17. Installation views, MoMA PS1, New York, USA (9 April – 25 September 2017). Images:
(top line): 1, 2, 3: Pablo Enriquez
(bottom line, left to right): 1, 3, 4: Pablo Enriquez, 2: Studio LHOOQ

pp. 254-255
Ian Cheng, *Emissaries*, 2015-17. Installation views, MoMA PS1, New York, USA (9 April – 25 September 2017). Images:
(top line): 1, 2: Pablo Enriquez, 3, 4, 5: Charles Roussel
(second and third lines): Charles Roussel
(bottom line): 1-4: Charles Roussel, 5: Ian Cheng

pp. 256-257
Ian Cheng, *Emissary Forks at Perfection*, 2015. Installation views, *Emissary Forks featuring Thousand Islands* at Espace Louis Vuitton München (21 April – 9 September 2017). Images: Louis Vuitton/Christian Kain

pp. 258-259
Ian Cheng, *Emissary Forks at Perfection*, 2015. Installation views, Yokohama Triennale, Yokohama, Japan (4 August – 5 November 2017). Images: TANAKA Yuichiro, courtesy of Organising Committee for Yokohama Triennale

pp. 260-261
Ian Cheng, *Emissary Sunsets the Self*, 2017. Installation views, Carnegie Museum of Art, Pittsburgh, USA (22 September 2017 – 28 January 2018). Images: Bryan Conley

pp. 262-263
Ian Cheng, *Emissary in the Squat of Gods*, 2015. Installation views, *Being Modern: MoMA in Paris* at Fondation Louis Vuitton, Paris, France (11 October 2017 – 5 March 2018). Images: Louis Vuitton / Martin Argyroglo

pp. 264-265
Ian Cheng, *Emissary Sunsets the Self*, 2017. Installation views, Louisiana Museum of Modern Art, Humlebaek, Denmark (10 October 2017 – 25 February 2018). Images: Anders Sune Berg

pp. 266-267
Ian Cheng, *Emissaries*, 2015-17. Installation views, Serpentine Galleries, London, UK (5 March – 28 May 2018. Courtesy of the artist and Pilar Corrias, London. Images: Ian Cheng, Rebecca Lewin and Kay Watson

The original version of this publication was co-produced by the Serpentine Galleries and Fondazione Sandretto Re Rebaudengo on the occasion of Ian Cheng's exhibition at the Serpentine Gallery
6 March – 28 May 2018

This exhibition was organised by
Hans Ulrich Obrist, Artistic Director
Yana Peel, CEO
Lizzie Carey-Thomas, Head of Programmes
Ben Vickers, CTO
Rebecca Lewin, Exhibitions Curator
Kay Watson, Assistant Digital Curator
Joseph Constable, Assistant Curator
Mike Gaughan, Gallery Manager
Joel Bunn, Installation and Production Manager

The first edition:
Editors: Rebecca Lewin, Joseph Constable and Veronica So
Copy Editor: Janine Armin
Image Editor: Sixing Xu
Design: Bureau Borsche

First published by Koenig Books, London and the Serpentine Galleries, London, 2018.

Second edition published by cosmogenesis, 2026
www.cosmogenesis.world

This second edition:
Editorial amendments: Ben Vickers
Design amendments: Kathryn Politis

Printed by Everbest Printing Company, China

ISBN-10: 1068765739
ISBN-13: 978-1068765735